The Center for South and Southeast Asia Studies of the University of California is the coordinating center for research, teaching programs, and special projects relating to the South and Southeast Asia areas on the nine campuses of the University. The Center is the largest such research and teaching organization in the United States, with more than 150 related faculty representing all disciplines within the social sciences, languages, and humanities.

The Center publishes a Monograph Series, an Occasional Papers Series, and sponsors a series of books published by the University of California Press. Manuscripts for these publications have been selected with the highest standards of academic excellence, with emphasis on those studies and literary works that are pioneers in their fields, and that provide fresh insights into the life and culture of the great civilizations of South and Southeast Asia.

RECENT PUBLICATIONS OF THE CENTER FOR SOUTH AND SOUTHEAST ASIA STUDIES:

Kenneth E. Bryant
Poems to the Child-God: Structures and Strategies in the Poetry of Surdas

Frank F. Conlon
A Caste in a Changing World: The Chitrapur Saraswat Brahmans

Padmanabh Jaini
The Jaina Path of Purification

Karen B. Leonard
Social History of an Indian Caste: The Kayasths of Hyderabad

M. N. Srinivas
The Remembered Village

Land, Landlords, and the British Raj

This volume is sponsored by the
CENTER FOR SOUTH AND SOUTHEAST ASIA STUDIES,
University of California, Berkeley

Land, Landlords,

The Maharaja of Balrampur, wealthiest landholder in Oudh, surrounded by his courtiers. (Reproduced by courtesy of the Director of the India Office Library and Records.)

Thomas R. Metcalf

and the British Raj

Northern India in the Nineteenth Century

University of California Press | *Berkeley • Los Angeles • London*

University of California Press
Berkeley and Los Angeles, California
University of California Press, Ltd.
London, England
Copyright © 1979 by
The Regents of the University of California
ISBN 0-520-03575-5
Library of Congress Catalog Card Number: 77-08574
Printed in the United States of America

1 2 3 4 5 6 7 8 9

Contents

Illustrations, Charts, Tables, and Maps

Illustrations

Charts

Tables

Maps

Abbreviations

B.I.A.	British Indian Association
B.R.	Board of Revenue
C.C.	Chief Commissioner
C.O.A.	Commissioner's Office, Agra
C.O.F.	Commissioner's Office, Faizabad
D.G.	*District Gazetteer*
F.C.	Foreign Consultations
IESHR	*Indian Economic & Social History Review*
IOL	India Office Library
NAI	National Archives of India
P.P.	*British Parliamentary Papers* (Commons)
Progs.	Proceedings
Sec.	Secretary (to)
S.C.	Secret Consultations
S.R.	*Settlement Report*
S.V.N.	*Selections from the Vernacular Newspapers of the N.W.P. & O.*
UPSA	Uttar Pradesh State Archives

Preface

THIS VOLUME is a study of the interplay of state and local power in rural India during the nineteenth century. Central to this undertaking is an assessment of the phenomenon of British colonialism, and of the changes British rule brought to the structure and functioning of rural society. In the past most writers, English and nationalist alike, commonly argued that colonial rule, with its alien property laws and forced sales of land, wrought a devastating upheaval in the Indian countryside. By contrast, other scholars have more recently insisted that the British presence affected rural society but little. Traditional power relationships at the local level, they claim, continued basically unaltered throughout the nineteenth century; such limited change as did take place was the product of economic or demographic, not institutional, variables. In this volume I will endeavor, if not wholly to resolve this controversy, at least to deepen our understanding of the nature and extent of social change in rural India.

The central figures in this study are those, known as *zamindars* and *taluqdars*, who by their control of land dominated rural society. The volume focuses in particular upon the great estate holders called taluqdars, for these men played a critical role throughout much of northern India as intermediaries, or brokers of power, between state and village. The first two chapters, after an examination of the basic structure of rural society, present an account of the taluqdars' origin and position on the land in the later days of Muslim rule. In subsequent chapters I have endeavored to trace their fate and fortune as British subjects. The taluqdars' relations with the British, with each other, and with those beneath them, are examined in turn, and the changes British rule brought to their position assessed. The concluding chapters analyze the taluqdars' distinctive style of life, and ask what values and principles moved these wealthy landlords in their day-to-day behavior.

The petty landholders and coparcenary communities who held single villages, though always men of consequence in the countryside, figure less prominently in these pages. I have sought to make clear their position within society, and to indicate generally their changing fortunes under British rule. I examine in particular their response to the novel award of unfettered proprietary rights in the soil, and their persisting struggles with their taluqdari overlords. But evidence for the behavior of these men is scarce, and its full assessment would in any case require a different focus upon land management at the level of the locality or village. Similarly, although I have tried to take account of economic developments, and to keep them in view through-out, a full discussion of prices, productivity, cropping patterns, and the like would be a massive undertaking, and one beyond the scope of this volume.

To give coherence to this study I have chosen to examine one major region of India, the present state of Uttar Pradesh, in the central Ganges valley. As the most populous state in the country, and one of the richest in agricultural potential, the U.P. offers an exceptionally fine arena in which to study the British colonial system in operation. Indeed the study of its colonial past may help us understand why this area is so backward in the present day. During the nineteenth century the U.P. comprised two distinct provinces, Agra, or as it was known from 1835 to 1902 and will be called consistently in this volume the North-Western Provinces, and the twelve central districts of Oudh. The two came under British rule fifty years apart, in 1801–1803 and 1856; and were placed under systems of revenue administration informed by markedly different principles. Hence a side-by-side study of the early years of British rule in the two provinces, so similarly situated at the outset, offers a rare opportunity for close comparative analysis.*

I do not carry the discussion of the North-Western Provinces much beyond 1870, nor that of Oudh beyond 1900. In both provinces the land settlements of the first decades of British rule laid down a framework for agrarian rela-tions which persisted with but little alteration until well into the twentieth century, and brought with it a remarkably stable social order. Great changes, of course, took place with the coming of nationalism to rural India after 1920. Though this volume may shed some light on why nationalism in the U.P. took the form it did, that is a separate subject which demands study on its own terms.

To avoid confusion in terminology I have confined the term *zamindar*, which can denote any landholder, so far as possible to the petty village pro-prietor, whether holding singly or as a cosharer with other members of the dominant village lineage. The term *taluqdar* is used to refer to a rent-receiving intermediary holding several villages. In Oudh after 1860 it denotes those great landlords specifically awarded the title by the British. Other tech-nical terms are defined when first used, and in the glossary. Specifically Western tenurial terms (e.g., landlord, proprietor, owner) are used inter-changeably with their more general equivalents, such as landholder, when discussing the land system under the British. For ease of reading I have avoided diacritical marks, and Indian terms that recur frequently are not italicized after their first appearance. The spelling of Indian words conforms to the most recent usage except where earlier forms are more appropriate and comprehensible. "Benares," for instance, is preferred to the Sanskritized "Varanasi," and the British Indian "Oudh" to the more correct "Awadh."

---

*The eastern, or Benares, region of the N.W.P., annexed earlier and placed under the Bengal Permanent Settlement, is largely excluded from consideration, as are the peripheral hilly areas of Bundelkhand and Kumaon.

I am indebted to the American Institute of Indian Studies, the Office of Education Fulbright-Hays program, and the Committee on Research and the Center for South and Southeast Asia Studies of the University of California, Berkeley, for supporting my research on this subject. Their grants enabled me to spend over two years in India, and to employ research assistants both in India and in this country. Susan Neild, Michael Metelits, and above all Sandria Freitag, by their ready help over several years have made this volume more comprehensive and more accurate than it would otherwise have been; Moazzam Siddiqi gave me invaluable assistance in translating taluqdari estate records and other difficult Urdu material; while Pamela Price provided a number of useful theoretical insights from the South Indian perspective. David and Cathy Ludden drew the maps with painstaking care. Warren Fusfeld prepared the glossary and helped standardize spellings and footnote citations.

The staffs of several archives have been most helpful in making their holdings available to me. Much of the research was carried out at the U.P. State Archives, Allahabad, under the charge of G. N. Salatore and K. P. Srivastava. Their cooperation was an essential ingredient in the success of this project. In Lucknow the staffs of the Secretariat Record Room and Library were unfailingly cordial, and made my stay there always enjoyable. The National Archives in Delhi and the India Office Library in London remained always welcoming homes away from home. Both supplied me with extensive microfilms of rare documents and publications so that I could carry on my work on my return to Berkeley. The Nehru Memorial Museum and Library likewise made its microfilming facilities available to me, as well as allowing me to consult its uncataloged collection of papers of the taluqdars' association. I am indebted especially to Miss D. Keswani at the National Archives and Mr. V. C. Joshi at the Nehru Museum.

In Lucknow many taluqdars put up patiently with my requests to discuss the working of the old land system and to visit their estates in search of old records. Audhesh Pratap Singh took me in hand in Faizabad; Anand Singh gave me a fascinating tour of Mankapur; the Raja of Bhinga introduced me to the Colvin School; while the Raja of Pratabgarh, Ajit Pratap Singh, gave me access to the records of both his and the Balrampur estate. In Pratabgarh itself Abhay Pratap Singh was always a most courteous host. I owe a special debt to Maharajkumar Amir Haidar Khan of Mahmudabad. He took a sustained and enthusiastic interest in my work; made available a manuscript history of his family, which he helped me translate and interpret; and he took me twice, under difficult circumstances, to Mahmudabad. Without his help my view of taluqdari life and culture would have been much more incomplete than it is.

I am grateful to a number of friends and colleagues who have read portions of the manuscript in draft, and given me their comments. Among them I must mention John Richards, Richard Barnett, Peter Reeves, Burton Stein,

Part One | Before the British

One | *The Structuring of Rural Society*

ALTHOUGH the settlement of the middle Ganges valley can be traced back many centuries, to the Aryan invasions and the mythic kingdom of Ram, the creation of rural society as we know it was a long-drawn-out process. The basic elements of the village system seem to have been established, and the various cultivating castes—Ahirs, Kurmis, and the like—marked off from each other in the years after the fall of the Gupta dynasty in the sixth century A.D. During the subsequent centuries cultivation slowly extended across the fertile plain, and the one-time tribesmen settled as *raiyats* to till their fields. But though these resident cultivators, with their artisan and untouchable dependents, generated the wealth that sustained society, they did not control its disposition. They were but observers of the struggle that raged over their heads between imperial dynasties and local power-holders as each sought to increase its hold over the grain, and men, of the countryside.

This enduring contest was given a new, and lasting, form by the Muslim invasion of northern India in the twelfth century. Muhammad Ghor's victory over the illustrious Prithviraj before Delhi in 1193 not only established Muslim rule in India, it also set in motion a process of migration which

Map 1. The North-Western Provinces and Oudh by Districts.

slowly spread a new dominant elite across the villages of the central plain.
While some remained, reduced to cultivators, many bands of defeated war-
riors fled down the Ganges and southward to the inaccessible highlands of
Rajasthan, Malwa, and Bundelkhand. In their wake, as Muslim authority
was consolidated in the early thirteenth century, came other dispossessed and
disinherited members of the Hindu ruling class, or *kshatriya varna*, for the
most part Rajput in caste status.[1] During the subsequent three centuries
these exiles and their descendants, together with adventurers from throughout northern and central India, brought under their control vast tracts of
land from the lower Doab across Oudh to the Benares region. This dominance has endured, in varied shape, to the present day, and forms the subject
of our study.

1. The term "Rajput" means prince, or son of a king, and is used here to denote not an endo-
gamous caste group (*jati*) but the members of a dispersed caste category united by a claim to a
common attributional rank and a common life style defined as Rajput.

This introductory chapter will examine briefly the early organization of Rajput society, focused about the institution of the clan, or extended patrilineal descent group, and explore the relationship between these invaders and those other conquerors, the Muslim rulers of Delhi, who for so long controlled the state authority above them.[2] Change at the center—the exploits of kings and the alternation of dynasties—is conspicuous, and has caught the attention of most historians. But developments within rural society are equally significant, and perhaps of more lasting consequence.

The Pattern of Settlement: Colonies and Conquests

Except in the remote and heavily forested country along the Himalayan foothills the early Rajput settlers did not find the land wholly uninhabited. At best the area chosen for settlement might be thinly populated by a people easily dispersed. Such was the experience of the Dikhits of Unao, who when they entered the district in the early thirteenth century encountered no effective resistance. Udebhan, their chief, "founded a village on the banks of the Sai river, in uncultivated land, and called it Neotinee, from the new 'tin' grass which flourished there, and was cleared away preparatory to cultivation." From this center Dikhit power spread rapidly to encompass the whole district, which was known as Dikhtheana until the time of the Mughals.[3]

In populated areas the contest for supremacy commonly involved not pitched battles with the indigenous rulers (about whom very little is known) but a drawn-out process of infiltration and subversion by small bands of invaders. Several of the largest Rajput clans in eastern Oudh, for instance, trace their ancestry back to one man, Barriar Singh, who migrated to Sultanpur, probably in the late thirteenth century, from the previously established Chauhan settlement at Mainpuri in the middle Doab. From his four sons come the Rajkumar, Bachgoti, Rajwar, and Hasanpur (Khanzada) clans, who made good claims to substantial lands in Faizabad, Sultanpur, and Pratabgarh districts during the fourteenth century.[4] Rajput tradition sometimes even represents the clan founder gaining power by guile instead of military prowess. He is portrayed as taking service with an aboriginal chief,

2. The term "clan" was initially applied to Rajput kin groups by the British, who saw in them a resemblance to the society of early eighteenth-century Scotland. The term is here used loosely as a convenient label to denote those who claim a common descent and share a common name. It should be borne in mind, however, that only the local lineage segments of a dispersed clan, buttressed by government recognition, ever acted corporatively as kin units. For a discussion of Rajput clan organization, though within the framework of a not wholly satisfactory cyclic theory of lineage development, see Richard G. Fox, *Kin Clan Raja and Rule* (Berkeley, 1972), esp. chs. ii and iii. For an account of similar clan organization among the Jats of the Upper Doab see M. C. Pradhan, *The Political System of the Jats of Northern India* (Bombay, 1966).
3. C. A. Elliott, *The Chronicles of Oonao* (Allahabad, 1862), pp. 34–37.
4. For the territories controlled by these four lineages, see the maps in Fox, *Kin Clan Raja and Rule*, pp. 29 and 72. For the early history of the Chauhans see H. M. Elliott, *Memoirs on the History, Folklore, and Distribution of Races of the North Western Provinces of India* (London, 1869), 1:63–67.

or giving him his daughter in marriage; slowly gathering around him his kinsmen and other followers; until at last, perhaps on the occasion of a feast when his opponent would be off guard, he would suddenly throw off his dependence, murder his employer, and make himself the master of the estate. The Kalhans of Gonda and the Sombansis of Pratabgarh both claim to have achieved their initial footing in this fashion.[5] Such stories, too, on occasion unquestionably obscure wholly indigenous origins, for it was not uncommon for a newly powerful chief of low caste to lay claim to the prestigious Rajput status, which denoted martial valor as much as descent, and then, with the help of well-paid bards and Brahmins to fabricate an appropriate genealogy.[6]

The process of subjugation owed much also to Muslim support. From the outset, despite their mutual hostility, Muslim and Rajput worked easily together. Given land on distant frontiers, Rajput adventurers could extend the authority of the state, while at the same time they gained legitimacy for their own conquests. Bariar Sah, the youngest son of a Janwar chieftain of Gujerat, as a youth joined the army of Firoz Shah Tughlaq as a cavalry commander. In 1374, after an imperial march through the area, the Sultan charged the young Rajput with restoring order in eastern Bahraich, a task accomplished with such success that Bariar Sah was rewarded with the control of the whole tract he had subdued. From their center at Ikauna the family spread throughout much of Bahraich and neighboring Gonda, and in time produced the powerful Janwar houses of Balrampur, Pyagpur, and Gangwal.[7] The Sombansi chief Lakhan Sen, before challenging the Bhar raja of Aror in Pratabgarh, likewise took care to arm himself with a grant of the *pargana* (revenue subdivision) from Delhi and a contingent of imperial troops.[8] The Rajputs were usually the greatest beneficiaries of such collaboration. In Mainpuri the sixteenth-century Chauhan chieftain Jagat Man, when he was awarded a number of villages held by indigenous Chirars who had long defied the imperial government, did not simply assert his authority over them, but, joined by Kayastha allies from nearby Bhongaon, massacred them all—men, women and children—and settled his own dependents in their place. Soon afterwards, reflecting his enhanced position, Jagat Man assumed the title of raja, never before borne by his family, and founded a

5. B. N. Tholal, *History of the Sombansi Raj and Estate of Pertabgarh in Oudh* (Kanpur, 1897), pp. 6-11, (hereafter *Sombansi Raj*); *Gazetteer of the Province of Oudh* (Lucknow, 1877), 1:539-41, (hereafter *Oudh Gazetteer*); and W. Oldham, *Historical and Statistical Memoir of the Ghazepoor District* (Allahabad, 1870), Part I, p. 47.

6. Among the clans generally regarded as of local origin are the Kanhpuria, Bandhalgoti, Gaur, and Bisen. See W. C. Benett, *A Report on the Family History of the Chief Clans of the Roy Bareilly District* (Lucknow, 1895), pp. 17-20, (hereafter *Chief Clans*); and his "Introduction" to the *Oudh Gazetteer*, 1:xxxvi-xxxvii. For a general discussion of "Rajputization" see Surajit Sinha, "State Formation and Rajput Tribal Myth in Central India," *Man in India* 42 1962): 35-80.

7. H. R. Nevill, *Bahraich District Gazetteer* (Allahabad, 1903), pp. 122-23 and 128-29.

8. Tholal, *Sombansi Raj*, pp. 9-10.

new capital at Mainpuri. Under the walls of this fort sprang up the town that was later to give the district its name.[9]

Even with the indigenous tribes subdued, however, the early Rajput settlers still had to contend with neighboring clans and with new bands of invaders seeking land and power. Sometimes the earlier colonists were able to push aside or subordinate latecomers, as in Etawah where from the thirteenth century onward the Sengar and Chauhan Rajputs divided "all real power" in the district between them.[10] But ouster was a frequent occurrence. During the sixteenth century both the Dikhits of Unao and the Kalhans in Gonda were unseated from their positions of dominance. In the seventeenth, the Sultanpur Rajkumars moved across the Gumti into the Aldemau pargana, where they prospered at the expense of their predecessors until they had made themselves the predominant landholders of the area.[11] Such upheavals did not necessarily involve armed combat between clans. Dikhit power was broken by an unwise defiance of the Emperor Akbar, while the fall of the Kalhans was precipitated by the death of the unpopular Achal Narain Singh, and sealed by a devastating flood. In the chaos that followed, the subordinate local clans made good their independence; one, the Bisens of Digsar, ultimately carved out a domain that encompassed a thousand square miles in the center of the district.[12]

The Rajputs were not the only invaders seeking land and power in the Gangetic plain. Muslims came as settlers as well as conquerors from the earliest days of Muslim rule onward. They commonly settled initially in the garrison towns, and then moved out into the rural areas as they received grants of land from the Muslim rulers. The Mahmudabad family, ultimately Oudh's largest Muslim landholders, *qazis* (judges) under the early Delhi Sultans, got their footing in the countryside when one Sheikh Nathan, sent by Muhammed bin Tughlaq to campaign against the Bhars, was rewarded for his success with a large estate in Bara Banki. The Jarwal Sayyids, residents of the small town of Bado Sarai, became landholders about the same time when the Sultan, full of remorse over the unjust execution of one brother gave the other a large revenue-free grant, of which half, however, had first to be wrested from the Bhars.[13]

Other Muslims, in later years, also turned imperial service to good advantage. Most striking perhaps was the enterprise of the Nanpara family, which

9. E. T. Atkinson, ed., *Statistical,Descriptive, and Historical Account of the North-Western Provinces of India*, Vol. 4 (Allahabad, 1876), 1:551–52, (hereafter *Statistical Account*); and E. R. Neave, *Mainpuri District Gazetteer* (Allahabad, 1910), pp. 92–93. The founder of the Pratapnir Chauhan family of Etawah, Sumer Sah, likewise first marched into the district with a commission from the Sultanate to subdue its indigenous Meos. *Statistical Account*, 4:1:302.

10. *Ibid.*, pp. 368–69.

11. *Oudh Gazetteer*, 1:27–30.

12. *Ibid.*, pp. 540–42 and 556–57.

13. H. R. Nevill, *Sitapur District Gazetteer* (Allahabad, 1905), pp. 62–63; and Nevill, *Bahraich D.G.*, p. 121. See also the very similar history of the Qidwai Sheikhs in H. R. Nevill, *Bara Banki District Gazetteer* (Allahabad, 1904), p. 100.

put together its extensive estate from a nucleus of five villages awarded the Pathan keeper of the Bahraich fort for the pay of his troops by Shah Jahan.[14] But even with the favor of the state Muslim landholdings, after centuries of Muslim rule, rarely amounted to more than one-quarter of the land in any district. For the most part Muslim lands were concentrated in the west, near Delhi, and in the environs of the various provincial capitals, such as Lucknow, where the authority of the state provided a protective umbrella. In Oudh only Lucknow and the adjacent district of Bara Banki had as much as one-third of their land in Muslim hands at the time of the British annexation. Elsewhere, as in Pratabgarh, with the land controlled by entrenched Rajput clans, Muslim settlement was confined to the immediate vicinity of the seat of royal government at Manikpur.[15]

The later years of Mughal rule saw a final wave of invasion, confined again to the west. Afghan Rohillas, taking advantage of the Mughal weakness in the eighteenth century, subjugated the extensive area afterwards known as Rohilkhand, while bands of Jats, torn loose during the seventeenth-century Jat rebellion, moved from Rajasthan and Agra across the Jumna into the middle Doab, where they rapidly expanded their holdings. In Aligarh, led by the enterprising descendants of one Makhan, who established himself near Mursan around 1600, the Jats had by the early years of British rule made good a claim to one-quarter of the district's land.[16]

Few of these conquests, whether Jat or Muslim, or of one Rajput clan by another, ever wholly uprooted the vanquished from the soil. Most commonly, as the victors wished only to control the disposition of the produce, the former inhabitants were left in possession of their lands, but reduced in wealth and importance. Hence in those districts subject to repeated invasion members of different clans usually lived intermingled, but stratified vertically, with the most recent group of conquerors at the top and the oldest hardly distinguishable from common cultivators. In Faizabad the invasions of the Rajkumars from the south, and later of the Palwars in the east, together with the early nineteenth-century rise of the Mehdona Brahmin family in the center of the district, left the populous and long-established clans, the Bais, Bisen, and Chauhan, holding as proprietors very few of the villages in which they resided. The outcome was a struggle for dominance

14. Nevill, *Bahraich D.G.*, p. 130. See also the accounts of the founding of Pyagpur (*ibid.*, p. 131), and of Saadatnagar (*Sitapur D.G.*, p. 66), among others. The tiny holdings of the Hindu Kayasthas originated in much the same way, as administrative grants in return for service, often as pargana *qanungos*.

15. H. R. Nevill, *Partabgarh District Gazetteer* (Allahabad, 1904), pp. 72–73. Muslims held 900 out of 2,000 villages in Bara Banki and 555 out of 1,416 in Lucknow. The cities of the province, even such small towns as Sandila, Bilgram, and Malihabad, were always disproportionately Muslim in population and contained such influential urban landholders as the Sheikhzadas of Lucknow. See H. R. Nevill, *Lucknow District Gazetteer* (Allahabad, 1904), pp. 66, 142–47, 236–38.

16. Irfan Habib, *The Agrarian System of Mughal India* (Bombay, 1963), pp. 339–41; and W. H. Smith, *Final Report on the Revision of Settlement in the District of Aligarh* (Allahabad, 1882), pp. 25, 66, (hereafter *Aligarh S.R.*). For an account of the history of the Mursan family see below ch. 3.

marked by continuing rent disputes and, under the British, a frequent recourse to subproprietary revenue settlements.[17] Much the same was true of
Aligarh, where the eighteenth-century Jat conquests displaced the old Rajput
chieftains, depressed the village holders, and so bred an antagonism which
persisted well into British times.[18] Where one clan by contrast maintained its
dominant position undisturbed from an early date the settlement pattern
took on a very different shape. In Pratabgarh, for instance, the original
Rajput settlers formed such compact and stable kin groupings that their
landholdings, and to some extent the lineage populations as well, were
sharply demarcated from one another. Of the district's parganas one, Patti,
was dominated by Bachgotis, who owned 700 of its 800 villages, including all
those held by large proprietors, and contributed the bulk of the Rajput cultivators. Sombansis predominated in neighboring Pratabgarh and Kanhpurias
in Ateha, while Bisens were the leading landholders, and most numerous
Rajput tenantry, in Bihar, Dhingwas, and portions of Manikpur and
Rampur.[19] While these kinship ties did not ensure a harmonious social
order, they did often mute conflict, and, as we shall see, secure favorable rent
rates for the Rajput tenantry.

The Organization of Rural Society: Rajas, Zamindars, and Villagers

The Rajput lineages who settled in rural U.P. embodied their dominance
in sturdy mud forts placed in the center of their domains. Surrounded by
moats and thick bamboo hedges, these forts formed the residence of the lineage chiefs, their immediate kinsmen and dependents, and the militia whose
job it was to overawe the surrounding villagers. The upper ranks of this
militia were usually horsemen drawn from the members of the lineage, while
the foot troopers were low-caste retainers, supplemented, on the occasion of
fights with neighboring clans or government troops, by local villagers
impressed into service. In addition to its role as a clan center, the fort often
took on as well what Fox has called a "rurban" character in which agricultural pursuits were supplemented by craft production, the holding of markets, and ceremonial and religious observances. The lesser members of the
lineage, cadet families and distant relatives, unless they broke away to found
new centers of their own, lived dispersed in the countryside amongst the ordinary artisan and cultivating castes in wholly agricultural villages.[20]

17. *Oudh Gazetteer*, 1:434 and 461-65. See also Fox, *Kin Clan Raja and Rule*, pp. 88-90.
For the conflict over subproprietary rights see below chs. 2 and 9.
18. For Jat-Rajput strife in Aligarh during the Mutiny see below ch. 6.
19. J. Sanders, *Final Settlement Report of Pratabgarh District* (Allahabad, 1898), pp. 23,
51-52, (hereafter *Pratabgarh S.R.*); and Nevill, *Partabgarh D.G.*, pp. 68-69 and 78. For a
similar distribution of clans in Ballia, see Fox, *Kin Clan Raja and Rule*, map on p. 18.
20. See Richard G. Fox, "Rurban Settlements and Rajput 'Clans' in Northern India," in
Richard G. Fox, ed., *Urban India: Society, Space and Image* (Durham, N.C., 1970), pp.
167-85; and Kashi N. Singh, "The Territorial Base of Medieval Town and Village Settlement in
Eastern Uttar Pradesh, India," *Annals of the Association of American Geographers* 58 (1968):
203-20. For the Rajput militia see Habib, *Agrarian System*, pp. 163-68.

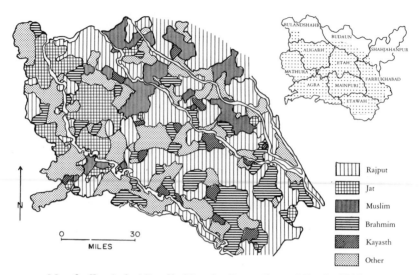

Map 2. Zamindari Landholding by Caste, Central Doab, 1844.

These settled Rajputs were known collectively as *zamindars*, or landhold-ers, and effectively controlled, as quasi-proprietors, the land under their sway.[21] The zamindar cultivated some land directly as *sir*, or home farm, with hired labor. The remainder was distributed to resident cultivators who normally possessed an inalienable and hereditary right of occupancy in their family plots. The zamindar regulated the settlement of newcomers in the village, distributed land for cultivation, and took in return as his *haq* (right) a share of the surplus produce. This share, normally some 10 percent of the land revenue assessed on the peasant's land, was either collected by the zamindar as a separate impost on the cultivator or awarded to him as a re-mission, called *malikana* (proprietor's dues), from the total revenue paid to the state. Ordinarily, too, the zamindar was appointed *malguzar*, or revenue payer, for the lands comprising his zamindari. By itself, this position brought the holder little material benefit. He had the difficult task of negotiating with the *muqaddam* (headman) of each village to collect the revenue, and he had then to deposit the state share with the local authorities. In return he got only a small *nankar*, or service allowance. Yet the post of malguzar was highly coveted, for it gave the zamindar enhanced power, and so enabled him to encroach upon the shares of others. In addition to their share of the land revenue, zamindars were entitled to certain petty perquisites including taxes on trade and forest products, as well as customary presents from their culti-vators at the time of marriage, death, and the like.

21. The following two paragraphs are based on Habib, *Agrarian System*, ch. v; and Asiya Siddiqi, *Agrarian Change in a Northern Indian State* (Oxford, 1973), ch. ii. Intermixed with the zamindari holdings were *raiyati*, or peasant-held, villages in which no superior rights existed. It is difficult to ascertain just how extensive such lands were, but they do not appear to have been anywhere predominant.

Although salable, zamindari rights normally descended by hereditary succession within the same family, and were partitioned among the heirs according to the principle of equal division among brothers. As a result after several generations an individual zamindar might possess no more than a fractional part (*patti*) of a village, with the other portions held by his near relatives. For the most part in such cases the shares were not physically marked out on the ground, *sir* land usually excepted. Rather the land was held jointly by the village cosharers, under the *bhaiacharya* or *pattidari* tenure, and the income only distributed. But the zamindari remained always divisible; hence it could easily break down into its constituent elements, with each *pattidar* left to manage his own fragment separately, perhaps even to subside into the common body of cultivators.

Fragmentation of his holding was by no means the only danger the village zamindar had to face. Equally threatening was a process of centralization which brought him ever more tightly under the control of his own lineage elite, the so-called intermediary zamindars, who resided in the clan fort.[22] Though recognized as superior in rank and ritual status, and the acknowledged leaders of the clan militia, these chieftains do not appear initially to have exercised any direct control over the lands of their lesser kinsmen. But the early Muslim state, lacking an effective bureaucratic apparatus of its own in the countryside, often turned to those men to collect the land revenue due from the entire clan territory. Indeed the government seems frequently to have framed the boundaries of its lowest administrative units, the pargana and *tappa*, to coincide with the Rajput kin divisions, and thus facilitate this delegation of authority. The lineage chiefs, with their control over the clan militia, were held responsible as well for the maintenance of law and order in the pargana. By aligning themselves with the state in this fashion the clan leaders not only gained the perquisites of office, including *inam* (revenue-free) land and a commission of some 5 percent on collections, but substantially enhanced their power at the expense of those beneath them. Much as state commissions had quickened the pace of Rajput colonization in the early days, so too, later on, did appointment as malguzar or *chaudhari* (chief revenue collector) spur the lineage elite to move against their village kinsmen. Their consistent objective was to strip these lesser holders of their zamindari rights, and so to reduce them to the status, if not of ordinary cultivators, then of privileged tenants with little say in the management of their villages. When estates were put together by conquest, and contained villages of different castes and clans, the process of dispossession was pursued, as we have seen, with even greater vigor.

This struggle for dominance between primary and intermediary zamindars

22. For the term "intermediary" as opposed to "primary" or village-level zamindar, see S. Nurul Hasan, "Zamindars Under the Mughals," in R. E. Frykenberg, ed., *Land Control and Social Structure in Indian History* (Madison, 1969), pp. 17-31, esp. pp. 24-27. For a general theoretical account of this internal lineage conflict, see Fox, *Kin Clan Raja and Rule*, esp. pp. 47-49, 75-77, and 90-97.

will loom large in the subsequent pages. Here we need only say that the contest was never wholly one-sided, nor irreversible. The village zamindars
rarely gave up their rights without a struggle, and while the state often drove
them into the arms of their superiors, it was at times their ally as well. A
weak state might look to the rural magnates for its revenue, or to tax-farmers
from whom the larger landholders could alone protect the smaller. A powerful state by contrast sought invariably to bypass these chieftains. Anxious to
increase his revenue and his hold over the countryside, a strong ruler would
not tolerate the defiance of these overmighty subjects, who withheld the
state's dues as they squeezed those beneath them. The beneficiaries, in
British as in Mughal times, when powerful bureaucratic states were established in northern India, were the village zamindars, entrusted with the
collection of the revenue from the village lands either as a group or through a
headman.[23]

Out of the interplay between state and clan there frequently emerged the
figure of the hereditary raja. Such a chieftain, at the head of the lineage, was
by no means an invariable element of the Rajput polity. Some clans remained
always fragmented and leaderless. Others flourished with authority diffused
among a larger elite of chaudharis and headmen. But where rajas did grow
up they gave Rajput power a solid and lasting base, and helped sustain as
well the values and culture of Hindu society in the face of the overwhelming
Muslim presence. By Mughal times these principalities formed the predominant feature of the political landscape throughout much of the province.

The consolidation of authority into the hands of an autocratic raja was not
an easy task.[24] The lesser members of the lineage, like the state, realized only
too well that the raja wielded his power at their expense. Neither simple
headship of a clan therefore, nor exercise of zamindari rights over a group of
villages, made possible a claim to the title. Success required as well some external stimulus or incentive which would persuade the lesser kinsmen to subordinate their interests to those of their chief. Most commonly this was
military. Where a Rajput clan was placed over a large and restive subject
population, or was constantly faced with the threat of attack from its neighbors, obedience to a single leader was almost a prerequisite of survival; and
this habit of obedience could easily grow into a permanent relationship of
subordination. Conquest too, when it involved the subjugation of powerful
rivals, required discipline, which could be turned to lasting advantage.
Victory in battle brought the lineage chieftain not only enhanced prestige,
which he could use to validate his claim to be a raja, but wealth and property
which he could appropriate for himself and his family, and so widen the dis-

23. Although the muqaddam was frequently the head of the cultivating raiyats, at times,
especially when the zamindari lineage was widely dispersed and close to the soil, the post might
be held by a member of the proprietary body. See Habib, *Agrarian System*, pp. 129–34; and
Siddiqi, *Agrarian Change*, pp. 26–29. For the enhancement of the position of the muqaddam
under early British rule see below ch. 3.

24. For an informed discussion of this question see Fox, *Kin Clan Raja and Rule*, pp. 75–87.
See also *Oudh Gazetteer*, 2:41–43 and 223–25.

tance separating him from his clan followers. The raja, once in power, continued in peacetime to control the local militia, and he served as well as final arbiter of most disputes arising within his domain. The receipt of tribute, and the award of honors at regular *durbars*, where the raja sat enthroned on the *gaddi*, sealed afresh the tie between ruler and subject. Continuity was secured for the *raj* by the adoption of primogeniture in inheritance. Never a feature of ordinary zamindari landholding, indivisibility was associated always with these Rajput principalities, except where portions were assigned to cadet families for their maintenance. In this respect they resembled sovereign states, and were of course the stronger for it.[25]

At no time, however, was the raja ever wholly independent. Above him always stood the imperial Muslim government. Sometimes the government helped intending, or even sitting, rajas to consolidate their power, when it appointed them to collect its revenues or subdue rebellious tracts. But if it lent the raja its authority it exacted in return a recognition of its own supremacy. Although the balance of power between Hindu raja and Muslim governor fluctuated over time, as we shall see, they remained bound together in a single political system. Perhaps the most striking manifestation of this tie was the role the Muslim ruler played as the fount of honor. Occasionally a chieftain, successful in battle, would assume the title of raja himself, with no sanction other than his own armed might, and perhaps the concurrence of his kinsmen. Such was the case with Jagat Man of Mainpuri after his victory over the Chirars, and of Udebhan, the founder of the Dikhit raj in Unao as well. But for the most part, at least from the sixteenth century, the imperial government's monopoly of the symbols of legitimacy was never questioned. No new title, nor succession to an old one, was recognized as valid without a distinct award by the emperor or his representative.[26] The investiture ceremony, at least in later years, took the form of a gathering of the raja's kinsmen and the leading chiefs of the neighborhood, who by their presence attested to his legitimacy; and it had as its central feature the placing of the *tilak* (a mark of paint) as the royal insignia on the new raja's forehead.[27]

When provincial regimes, such as Jaunpur or Oudh, made good their independence, they took upon themselves the right of conferring titles without reference to Delhi. Many Oudh rajas owe their titles to the Lucknow Nawabs, who sought in this way to conciliate, or reward, these powerful rural chieftains.[28] But by far the most striking delegation of this royal authority was

25. For the distinctive character of the raja see W. C. Benett, *The Final Settlement Report on the Gonda District* (Allahabad, 1878), pp. 37–43, 52–53, (hereafter *Gonda S.R.*); and Benett, *Chief Clans*, pp. 60–63. Partition did occasionally take place on the initiative of an incumbent raja, or as a result of family feuds.

26. For the use of force to secure compliance with this procedure see Benett, *Chief Clans*, pp. 41–42. It is not clear how far this practice existed under the Delhi Sultans.

27. Elliott, *Chronicles of Oonao*, pp. 39–40. The new raja had of course to meet all costs of the ceremony, including lavish feasting and presents to participants.

28. For an early instance, by Shuja-ud-daula in 1765, see *ibid.*, p. 76. Among the prominent rajas ennobled by the Oudh government in the nineteenth century were Mahmudabad, Jahangirabad, and Mehdona.

that to the Bachgoti raja of Hasanpur, who was empowered by the sixteenth-century Sur ruler Sher Shah, to invest with the tilak all the rajas of south-eastern Oudh. The award may have been prompted by the family's almost contemporaneous conversion to Islam, but it did not lessen the respect in which the Khanzadas (as they were known) were held by their Rajput neighbors. One clan alone, that of the Bais, seems to have held out against this subordination, and defiantly arranged its own succession, the younger brother placing the tilak on the forehead of the elder.[29]

Although the Muslim rulers of northern India by their award of honors gave a symbolic sanction to the authority of the Hindu raja, the power these chieftains wielded was double-edged. It could as easily be turned against the state as used on its behalf to control the countryside. Hence Muslim emperors and sultans sought consistently to prevent the rise of such men, and the consolidation of authority in their hands. The center of Muslim power, in the area of the present U.P., lay always toward the west of the province. The upper Doab districts, within easy striking distance of the royal capitals at Delhi and Agra, formed part of the heartland of empire, while the highway to the east, dotted with garrison towns, marched across Rohilkhand and the Hardoi district of Oudh. Scattered through the western countryside, too, were small Muslim urban centers, or *qasbas*, seats of markets and of local gentry. In the face of such an entrenched Muslim presence the Rajputs of the area could gain but little footing. Potential rajas were defeated, compact lineages broken up, and all driven back together to the soil. In both Hardoi and neighboring Sitapur, for instance, though Rajputs always remained dominant as zamindars, the different clans never made good claims to distinct territories, nor united under their own rajas.[30] In the eastern districts, by contrast, where the Muslim authorities were isolated in a Hindu sea, they could but look on as the Rajput chieftains put together their clan-based principalities. By the end of the Muslim era there were as many hereditary Hindu rajas in the three southeastern Oudh districts of Rae Bareli, Sultanpur, and Pratabgarh as in the remaining nine districts together.

The power of the Muslim state, however, was by no means fixed or unchanging. When the government was in the hands of a weak monarch, or distracted by war or succession, central control could slacken even over the Doab itself. Occasionally too, as with the Sharqi dynasty of Jaunpur, a strong state could grow up in the east, and coerce the Rajputs of the area into an unaccustomed subjugation. Twice the Jaunpur armies forced the chieftain of the powerful Bais clan to flee into exile in Mainpuri.[31] For the most part, even in the east, the Rajput principalities were consolidated during periods of

29. *Ibid.*, pp. 69-70; and H. M. Elliott, *Memoirs*, 1:48. The accounts of these events are unfortunately somewhat confused and inconsistent. See *Oudh Gazetteer*, 1:466, 3:229-31 and 465-66.
30. H. R. Nevill, *Hardoi District Gazetteer* (Naini Tal, 1904), pp. 73-74, 128-29; and Nevill, *Sitapur D.G.*, pp. 62, 122-23.
31. Benett, *Chief Clans*, pp. 12-14.

imperial decay, when the restraints of government were temporarily relaxed. During the years of vigorous Mughal rule by contrast, from 1556 to 1707, the Rajput clans everywhere, even in remote Gonda, were pushed down, and their pretensions to political power drastically curtailed. Indeed deprived of external enemies to unite them the clans turned their energies in upon themselves. The younger branches of many of the ruling houses then cast off their allegiance to the head of the clan, and set up independent lineages of their own, which conceded only a ceremonial precedence to the elder line. The famous Balrampur house, by British times the premier estate in Oudh, originated in this way about 1600 when a younger son of the Janwar raja of Ikauna separated from his brother to settle in the neighboring district of Gonda.[32]

As the fall of Jaunpur to the distant and relatively weak Lodi state had opened the way to a resurgence of Bais power under the famous Tilokchand, who spread his hegemony over the whole of eastern Oudh, so too did the death of Aurangzeb touch off a new burst of Rajput expansion, as the long suppressed chieftains everywhere reasserted their independence. Almost all withheld the revenue due the Mughal treasury, while the more venturesome among them set out to put together new rajadoms or enlarge old ones. By 1720 the Kanhpuria raja of Tiloi, Mohan Singh, had spread his authority over fourteen parganas in southeastern Oudh, while across the Ganges in Fatehpur the Khichar family under Bhagwant Rai had built up a state of almost equal size.[33]

The Muslim conquest, then, brought lasting changes to the organization of rural society in northern India. The continuing wave of Rajput migration touched off by the Ghorid invasion, though usually of very small bodies of men, by Mughal times had spread across the plains a new elite comprised largely of the proliferating lineages of these early settlers, but including as well upstart indigenous peoples who had successfully adapted to a Rajput style of life, together with scattered Jats and Muslims in the west. As zamindars these men controlled the bulk of the land. But even the Rajputs among them were by no means a homogeneous group. Divided on the ground into mutually hostile clans, they were commonly stratified internally as well, with a chieftain or raja and his immediate family superimposed upon the ordinary village-dwelling zamindars. The Muslim state, though it might play upon these divisions, never had, as a premodern polity, the resources wholly to eradicate these competitors for power. Frequently in fact it had to seek the help of the Rajput chieftains to maintain order and collect its revenues. The result was a layering of authority, and of rights over land, in which state, raja, and village zamindar each struggled to increase his share.

To some extent this political order, using the terminology of Stein (derived

32. *Ibid.*, pp. 59–60; and *Oudh Gazetteer*, 1:216–17.
33. Benett, *Chief Clans*, pp. 43–44. For a list of Rajput principalities formed in successive periods of Muslim decline see *Oudh Gazetteer*, 2:42.

from Southall), can be called a "segmentary state," in which power was decentralized and structured pyramidally, with the lesser units duplicating on a smaller scale all the functions of the greater, and the center giving a coherence to the whole by its exercise of a predominantly ritual sovereignty.[34] In the northern Muslim empires, however, the central authority seems always to have been able to enforce substantially greater transfers of resources to itself than was the case in the southern polities described by Stein; while by the time of the Mughal Empire the state had grown so strong—with orders flowing from the imperial capital, and revenue to it—that the political system more nearly approximated the hierarchical or bureaucratic model. Yet the Mughals but rarely tried to deal directly with the cultivating raiyats over the heads of the local lineages. Nor did even the coming of the British, with their intrusive bureaucracy, at once put an end to the power of these entrenched landholding elites. The triangular encounter between state, raja, and zamindar remained, from Mughal times on into the twentieth century, the central theme of much of the rural history of the Gangetic plain.

34. See Burton Stein, "The Segmentary State in South Indian History," in Richard G. Fox, ed., *Realm and Region in Traditional India* (Delhi, 1977), pp. 3-51, esp. pp. 9-11 and 43-45.

| *Two* | *Oudh Under the Nawabs* |

I N 1722 THE Mughal Emperor Muhammad Shah appointed as Governor of Oudh an ambitious young man of Persian descent, Saadat Khan Burhan ul-mulk who had risen in the imperial service by adroit manipulation of factional rivalries in the Delhi court. His appointment to Oudh, following two years' service as Governor of Agra, seemed in no way unusual. Yet, within a few years, defying his nominal superior, Saadat Khan had laid the foundations of a dynasty that was to rule Oudh for 130 years, and to leave a lasting imprint on the structure of rural society.

The Mughal *suba* (province) of Oudh or Awadh comprised five *sarkars* (districts). Of these four—Faizabad, Lucknow, Bahraich, and Khairabad—comprehended roughly the area of the twelve districts of the later British Indian province of Oudh. (The fifth sarkar, Gorakhpur, annexed in 1801, was administered as part of the North-Western Provinces.[1]) The grouping

1. Some portions of the later British Indian province were not included in its Mughal namesake. These areas, then part of the Allahabad suba, comprised the eastern and southern portions of the present districts of Faizabad, Sultanpur, and Rae Bareli, and the whole of Pratabgarh. The Allahabad suba was placed under the charge of the Oudh Nawab in 1748. Rohilkhand to the west was added to his domains after the Rohilla War of 1774. Both these additions, which doubled the total area of the state, were ceded to the British (except for the areas specified above), together with Gorakhpur, in 1801.

17

together of these five districts in one province was for the Mughals purely a matter of administrative convenience. Apart from geographical contiguity, and a certain isolation from the main channels of riverine trade, which flowed along the Ganges and Jumna to the south and west, the Oudh districts had little to mark them off from their neighbors of the Agra, Allahabad, or Delhi subas. The Awadhi dialect gave the common people of the province a shared tongue and a literature that included some of northern India's greatest epic poetry.[2] Yet Awadhi was spoken across the Ganges in Allahabad, while Oudh's Hindu devotionalism, which focused upon Ram's birthplace at Ajodhya, differed little if at all from that of Mathura or Benares. The distinctive character of the province was in large measure a product of its eighteenth- and nineteenth-century historical development.

As a Mughal province Oudh had been administered according to the standardized procedures of that empire. Its governors, members of the imperial corps of *mansabdars*, were strictly supervised by the center, and shifted at frequent intervals. Their exploits as individuals left no mark in local tradition.[3] The transformation of this province into an independent state, albeit one still acknowledging the titular supremacy of the emperor, dramatically altered its character. Above all the existence of a hereditary ruling family, with a court and a capital, gave the province a coherence and a sense of common destiny. It was no longer an arbitrary collection of districts, united only by their participation in a larger whole, but a center of political power and a focus of cultural aspiration. Where such states emerged, in Hyderabad and Bengal as well as Oudh, the collapse of Mughal central authority did not at once lead to anarchy. Power was instead dispersed from the imperial to the regional level, and there concentrated afresh. The rulers of these new states could each, within his own domain, enforce law and order as Aurangzeb's weak successors could not over a far-flung empire.

The Rajput chieftains of Oudh for the most part submitted quietly to their new overlord. In the northern districts alone, where the traditions of independence were deeply rooted, did Saadat Khan encounter sustained resistance. There the Balrampur raja agreed to pay revenue only after he had been defeated in two pitched battles, while his neighbor the Bisen raja of Gonda overpowered the first Nawabi force sent against him and killed its commander.[4] This ready submission was won, however, as much by conciliation as by force of arms. The head only of a small regional state, Saadat Khan possessed but limited resources, and there was no one to whom he could turn for assistance. He was thus obliged, unlike his Mughal predecessors, to treat leniently with the Rajput chieftains. The powerful northern

---

2. G. A. Grierson, *Linguistic Survey of India* (Delhi, 1968 reprint), 6:9–11. For the distinctive geographical features of the Doab, and its commercial activity, see below ch. 3.

3. Elliott, *Chronicles of Oonao*, p. 123.

4. For Saadat Khan's subjugation of the Oudh chiefs see A. L. Srivastava, *The First Two Nawabs of Oudh* (Lucknow, 1933), pp. 35–43. In the central plains only the Kanhpuria raja Mohan Singh fought vigorously against Saadat Khan, and he was killed on the field of battle.

rajas gained the most. The Gonda raja, his territories made into a separate jurisdiction, exercised unhindered the full powers of government, while, together with his neighbors of Balrampur and Tulsipur, he was made to pay only a lump sum into the Nawab's treasury. But even the chiefs nearer Lucknow and Faizabad were confirmed in their holdings and entrusted with the collection of the government revenue, often over extensive pargana-sized tracts.[5]

Emboldened by this recognition of their authority, the chieftains in subsequent years withheld the revenue due to the Nawab whenever they thought they could get away with it. As a result Saadat Khan was forced to devote much of his energies not to routine administration but to coercive military campaigns against recalcitrant chieftains. Some of these rebellions assumed formidable dimensions. In 1737, for instance, while the Nawab was occupied with the defense of Delhi from the Marathas, the Tiloi raja led an insurrection in Rae Bareli and Sultanpur which was put down only after a long investiture of the fort of Tiloi. Two years later many chieftains took advantage of the opportunity offered by the death of Saadat Khan to throw off once again their allegiance to the Nawabi government. Saadat Khan's successor, Abulmansur Khan Safdar Jang, was thus obliged, like his uncle, to initiate his rule by a military progress through his dominions and the investiture of numerous Rajput forts. In each instance these tests of strength ended with Rajput acknowledgement of Safdar Jang's supremacy, and Nawabi recognition of the defeated chieftain's right to collect the government revenue in the territory he controlled.[6]

Despite this persisting strife Rajput and Nawab were still bound together in a mutual dependence. The Rajput chieftains, much as they might fight for greater freedom, had never the resources to defy the Nawab for long, nor could they ever surmount the rivalries of kin and clan which kept them apart. The Nawab, on his part, as we have seen, while he could defeat any chief, or group of chiefs, in battle, could not do without them in the government of the province. He simply had not the military force to collect the revenue directly from the village zamindars over any substantial part of his territories. Much of the enduring resilience of the Oudh political system under the early Nawabs derived from each side's recognition of these constraints. Both Rajput and Nawab seem, too, to have accepted as valid the distinctive eighteenth-century conception of political order in which widely diffused local power was given form and legitimacy by the superior Muslim authorities. As the Nawabs, while acting independently, always sought legitimation for their position from the Mughal Emperor, whose deputy in theory they remained, so too did the major rajas of Oudh acknowledge the superior authority of the

5. Raja Udayapratapa Sinh, *History of the Bhinga Raj Family* (Calcutta, 1906), p. 23; *Oudh Gazetteer*, 1:543; and Benett, *Chief Clans*, pp. 64–65.

6. Srivastava, *First Two Nawabs*, pp. 93–95. See also the account of the Rajput rising during the short-lived Pathan invasion of Oudh in 1750–1751. *Ibid.*, pp. 166, 174; and Nevill, *Bara Banki D.G.*, pp. 161–62.

Chart 1. The Nawabs of Oudh

Saadat Khan Burhan ul-mulk	1722–1739
Safdar Jang	1739–1754
Shuja-ud-daula	1754–1775
Asaf-ud-daula	1775–1797
Wazir Ali	1797–1798
Saadat Ali Khan	1798–1814
Ghazi-ud-din Haidar[a]	1814–1827
Nasir-ud-din Haidar	1827–1837
Muhammad Ali Shah	1837–1842
Amjad Ali Shah	1842–1847
Wajid Ali Shah	1847–1856

[a]Ghazi-ud-din assumed the title of king in 1819. The term however never gained popular currency, and is not used here. See Elliott, *Chronicles of Oonao*, p. 122.

Nawab, whose sanction alone gave their rulership its legitimacy. The Rajput chieftains, in other words, while ever ready to seek better terms from their Muslim overlord, had no enduring vision of themselves other than as zamindars. They might, when the power of the state was in abeyance, as from 1707 to 1722 or, as we shall see, in 1857–1858, make a bid for independence. But, reconciled to subordination, they remained ready always, whether under Nawabi or British rule, to take up that role again. To this legacy of the Mughal Empire, which brought order to so much of the subcontinent for so long, eighteenth-century India owed a great deal of its continuing stability.[7]

The Coming of the British

The Battle of Baksar, on October 23, 1764, brought a new military power, that of Great Britain, at a bound into the heart of northern India. Established in Bengal and Bihar since Clive's momentous encounter at Plassey, the British did not long rest content with the veiled predominance they had there secured. In 1763, outraged at the independent behavior of their puppet Nawab Mir Qasim, the ambitious servants of the East India Company in Calcutta drove him from office. Mir Qasim then sought refuge with the Nawab of Oudh, Shuja-ud-daula, with whose help, and that of the Mughal Emperor Shah Alam he challenged the British at Baksar in Bihar. The battle was fiercely contested, but the outcome was never in doubt. Abandoned by his allies, Shuja-ud-daula, after a bitter last-ditch resistance, fled for his life to Farrukhabad, leaving his territories in the hands of the British. The British now at last openly acknowledged their predominant position in Bengal and

7. For a general theoretical account see Bernard S. Cohn, "Political Systems in Eighteenth Century India: the Banaras Region," *Journal of the American Oriental Society* 82 (1962):312–20. For a similar attitude among zamindars in the south see J. F. Richards, *Mughal Administration in Golconda* (Oxford, 1975), pp. 133–34, 252.

Bihar by accepting from the Emperor the *diwani* (revenue administration) of the province. But they had no desire to extend their frontier so far up the Ganges as to include the extensive territories of the Nawab of Oudh. So by the Treaty of Allahabad of August 1765 Shuja-ud-daula was restored to his former dominions, with the exception of two districts which were handed over to the Mughal Emperor for his maintenance. The Nawab agreed to pay a war indemnity of fifty lakhs of rupees, and the Company in return agreed to furnish troops to the Nawab if needed for the defense of his frontiers.[8]

The Allahabad treaty was in form an agreement between equals. Apart from duty-free trading rights the British gained no special privileges for themselves. Yet the position of the Oudh Nawabs had been irreversibly transformed by the events of Baksar and the succeeding months. No longer could they pretend to be an independent power. Oudh was now no more than a "buffer" state, kept up for the purposes of British Indian foreign policy, and inextricably trapped in a relationship that was soon to sap its strength and self-confidence. Nor did the consequences take long to unfold.[9] In 1773, as part of a bargain that gave him the use of British troops for an attack on neighboring Rohilkhand, Shuja agreed to support in his territory a permanent garrison of East India Company troops, and to accept at his court a British political officer, or Resident. These two provisions, though not very onerous at the time, were to be his, and his successors', undoing. Within two years the British had begun increasing the subsidy demanded for the support of their troops in Oudh, and soon after they added to their number as well. The Resident meanwhile had become the focus for disaffected elements at the Nawab's court and a channel for British intervention in the internal affairs of the country. By the 1790s, with the subsidy payments, now grown to over fifty lakhs of rupees a year, hopelessly in arrears, the Nawab was nearly bankrupt and his government demoralized.

The British determined upon a decisive intervention in the hope of retrieving the situation. The first step was taken by Sir John Shore. As Governor-General in 1797 he overturned the succession of the Nawab Asaf-ud-daula's chosen heir Wazir Ali on the grounds of his illegitimacy and hostility to the British government, and placed on the *masnad* (throne) instead the deceased Nawab's brother Saadat Ali Khan. Shore then exacted from the new Nawab a treaty under which the Company took responsibility for the entire defense of Oudh in return for an increased annual subsidy of seventy-six lakhs, or over seven and a half million rupees, together with the cession of the fort of

8. For the terms of the treaty see A. L. Srivastava, *Shuja-ud-daula* (Calcutta, 1939), 2:14–16. After Baksar, as in similar periods of upheaval before, the Oudh chiefs at once threw off their allegiance to the Nawab. A few months later, in early 1765, when the British temporarily occupied Oudh, they submitted readily to the new conquerors. *Ibid.*, 1:235–36, 247–51.

9. For a general account of these developments see C. Colin Davies, *Warren Hastings and Oudh* (Oxford, 1939); Purnendu Basu, *Oudh and the East India Company, 1785–1801* (Lucknow, 1943); and R. B. Barnett, "Regional Politics in a Mughal Successor State: Nawabi Awadh, 1720–85" (Ph.D. diss., University of California, Berkeley, 1975).

Allahabad. Shore's successor, the imperious and imperially minded Lord Wellesley, not content with this arrangement, after bullying and threatening the Nawab for some two years, in 1801 imposed upon him yet another treaty. Under it the Nawab's own military establishment, some 80,000 in number, was almost wholly disbanded, and half his territory permanently ceded to the British for the maintenance of a substantially increased Company force in Oudh. The Nawab further promised to establish within his remaining territories "a system of administration (to be carried into effect by his own officers) . . . conducive to the prosperity of his subjects," and to act at all times in conformity with the advice of the Resident. This treaty—a definitive settlement at last—remained the basis of Britain's relations with Oudh until annexation in 1856. The Nawab was henceforth spared the burden of subsidy payments, but at the cost of half his revenue and all his independence. From a "buffer" state Oudh had now become a passive instrument of British supremacy in India.[10]

This transformation of the Nawab's relations with the outside world precipitated equally tumultuous and far-reaching, if less well-known, changes in the internal organization of the country. Above all it destroyed the balanced system in which the mutual weakness of Nawab and Rajput chieftain had secured a substantial degree of social stability. The continual drain of the subsidy, and after 1801 the loss of half his accustomed revenue, left the Nawab in desperate financial straits. The problem was made worse by a shift among the Nawabs from Asaf-ud-daula onwards from a martial to a settled pattern of life, for which the British alliance was at least partially responsible. The elaboration of luxury which this brought about—the splendid magnificence of the court, the lavish patronage of the arts, and the construction of such imposing monuments as the Great Imambara—further drained the treasury without adding materially to the sources of revenue.[11] As a way out of this embarrassment the Nawabs turned to enhancement of the land revenue. Standing in the way were the large Rajput chieftains. So the Lucknow government set out to displace them and collect directly from the village zamindars.

The first step in this direction was taken in the 1750s with the reduction of the great Pratabgarh Raj. After two successive rajas had been slain in battle with the Nawab, Safdar Jang brought the pargana under direct state administration for several years, and then parceled it out among the lesser Sombansi chieftains and zamindars. The old lineage fort of Qila Pratabgarh was garrisoned with Nawabi troops, while the town and several adjacent

10. P. E. Roberts, *India Under Wellesley* (London, 1929), ch. xi. The ceded territories included Rohilkhand, the Ganges-Jumna Doab below Agra, and the districts of Azamgarh, Gorakhpur, and Basti on the east. Benares had already been taken in 1775. See map 3.

11. For a contemporary account of the splendor of Asaf-ud-daula's court see Abu Talib, *History of Asaf-ud-daula* (Allahabad, 1885), pp. 37–39 and 91–94. Much revenue was also intercepted by Shuja's widow, the Bahu Begam, who retained control of Shuja's treasure together with extensive rent-free *jagir* lands.

villages were settled with its Muslim *qanungo* (pargana accountant).[12] Some forty years later Asaf-ud-daula moved against the virtually independent Gonda Raj. Its ruler, defeated, was driven into the hills and the minor heir taken captive to Lucknow. Although the title was not extinguished the old principality was effectively broken up. Its lands, assigned to the Bahu Begam (Shuja-ud-daula's widow), were for the first time brought under the jurisdiction of the Nawab's officials, with the revenue assessed directly on the village zamindars.[13]

By the time of Saadat Ali Khan the displacement of the old rajas had become a guiding feature of Nawabi revenue policy. A vigorous and effective ruler despite the constraints of the 1801 treaty, Saadat Ali thoroughly reorganized the revenue administration. He revalued and separately assessed the lands of each village, did away with the inams so lavishly bestowed by his easygoing predecessor, and deprived the old chieftains, so far as possible, of their nankar allowances as well as their privileged position as intermediaries. Efficiency and fairness were secured by a constant vigilance on the part of the Nawab, aided by a network of informers in every district who reported directly to him. The success of this policy can be seen in the full treasury Saadat Ali left to his successor and the plaudits he won from the British.[14]

Much of this success was, however, the product of exceptional and short-lived circumstances, above all the immense energy of Saadat Ali Khan himself. Nor was the new policy, even during Saadat Ali's lifetime, as fully implemented or as successful as often appeared on the surface. Almost always the old chiefs and rajas stubbornly resisted reduction to the level of their own subordinate zamindars, and rarely were they severed for long from all connection with their former holdings. The Nawab had many advantages in the struggle, not the least of which was the aid of British troops, whose superior firepower and discipline invariably swept all before it. But the rajas had local connections and influence, and the Nawab soon found it very difficult to collect the revenue without their assistance. Even quite small chieftains could not be wholly pushed aside. In Rae Bareli, for instance, Din Shah of Gaura commanded a fort with two guns and a hundred matchlockmen, and could call upon a local militia force of some two thousand men. When his fort was burned by the Nawab's troops he at once had it rebuilt. When neighboring zamindars agreed to pay revenue, he had their crops destroyed. When caught himself and shut up in the Dalmau fort, he soon escaped to the jungles. But as an outlaw he was even more troublesome than before, and so he was brought back by the bribe of a village rent-free. To this he soon added eleven more. After he had been slain in a rash challenge to the local *tahsildar*, his

12. Tholal, *Sombansi Raj*, pp. 27–31, 36–37; and Nevill, *Partabgarh D.G.*, pp. 84–85.

13. Benett, *Gonda S.R.*, pp. 22–23; and H. R. Nevill, *Gonda District Gazetteer* (Naini Tal, 1905), pp. 148–51, 154. The power of the Utraula raja was broken at about the same time.

14. Saadat Ali had allegedly amassed a surplus of fourteen crores of rupees by his death in 1814. See Kamal-ud-din Haidar, *Tawarikh-i-Awadh* (Lucknow, 1896) (Urdu), 1:186–87; and *Oudh Gazetteer*, 1:lii.

brother and nephew continued the same policy so that by 1810 they held the
revenue rights for twenty-nine villages. Of these twenty-one belonged to other
zamindars, who, reported the tahsildar, "still attend my *kachcheri* (court) in
person, although I am obliged to let their villages remain in the Gaura
engagement."[15]

Yet estates put together in this fashion, in the face of continued government harrassment, were not the same as before. Less extensive than the old
raj domains, which survived only in the remote north, they were for the most
part fortuitous collections of villages wrested from the Nawab's revenue
officers a few at a time, and lumped together arbitrarily in a single revenue
engagement. The dispossessed raja of Gonda, allowed to return home with
thirty-two villages allotted for his support, over time pieced together from the
villages of his old raj the extensive Bishambarpur estate, comprising by
annexation some 250 square miles, or one-tenth of the total area of the district. But this was still less than half the territory controlled by his powerful
predecessors.[16] In Pratabgarh, though the bulk of the old raj holdings remained in Sombansi hands, they were now held in separate small pieces by a
number of only distantly related kinsmen, each of whom put together his own
estate village by village as his enterprise won from the Nawab the right to collect the revenue from it. The two largest of these, each with over sixty villages
by 1850, were Bahlolpur, initially awarded an illegitimate son of the slain
raja Prithipat for his maintenance in 1798, and Taroul, founded about the
same time by the able Abhiman Singh.[17]

These agglomerations of villages were called *taluqas* (literally, dependence
upon or connection with someone as revenue payer), and their holders were
known as *taluqdars*. Despite the change in nomenclature the break with the
past was not dramatic. The same men, and the same families, still held much
of the same land as in the days before the upheaval of the late eighteenth
century. Yet the new term denoted a new style of landholding, based more
upon the amassing of revenue collecting rights over individual villages and
less upon the corporate ties of kin and clan. Under the rule of the weak
Nawabs who succeeded Saadat Ali Khan this tenure was to spread across the
face of the country until it had become the predominant pattern of landholding.

The Contract System and the Mushroom Taluqdar

Although based upon Mughal practice, from which it was descended
directly and uninterruptedly, the Nawabi revenue system by the time of
Saadat Ali Khan diverged in many important respects from its imperial predecessor. The four Mughal sarkars left to the Nawab after 1801 had been
broken into smaller units called *chaklas*, roughly equivalent in size to British

15. Benett, *Chief Clans*, pp. 66–68. See also pp. 49–52.
16. *Oudh Gazetteer*, 1:xlv–xlvi and 564.
17. Tholal, *Sombansi Raj*, pp. 37–44; and Nevill, *Partabgarh D.G.*, pp. 85–90.

Indian districts, and were placed under the charge of *chakladars*, who were responsible for the collection of revenue and the maintenance of law and order. The chaklas, some twelve in number, were then incorporated in the four *nizamats* of Khairabad, Gonda-Bahraich, Faizabad-Sultanpur, and Baiswara. The *nazim*, much like an English divisional commissioner, exercised a general supervision over the government and deployed the military force, which often included artillery and English-officered sepoys, posted in his jurisdiction. Beneath these new administrative units were the old parganas. These, kept up unchanged, remained under the charge of chaudharis or tahsildars, who, together with the qanungo, levied the actual assessment on the villages and collected the revenue from them.[18]

By far the most momentous administrative innovation of the late eighteenth century, however, was the use of the *ijara* (contract) system of revenue collection. Under it the posts of nazim and chakladar were let at auction or awarded directly to individuals who, in return for the appointment, agreed to pay a fixed sum for a certain term of years into the Nawab's treasury. The contractor bore the expenses of collection, and appointed the collecting staff. Any amount collected beyond the stipulated sum went into the contractor's pocket. The initial attraction of the scheme was its convenience. For Saadat Ali, who used it widely, the farming of the revenue provided a secure income at a minimum cost. So long as its agents were carefully selected and tightly supervised, it was clearly well contrived to meet the needs of a regional kingdom with only limited administrative resources. But under Saadat Ali's inept successors the contract system quickly became an instrument of extortion, as the contractors, unchecked so long as they fulfilled their contracts, set out to amass personal fortunes. From the early years of Ghazi-ud-din Haidar's reign (1814–1827) the British thundered against the iniquities of the contract system. Yet under the circumstances of the time the alternatives were not necessarily any freer from abuse.[19]

Most attractive was the *huzur tahsil* system, under which the revenue management was entrusted to the head of the proprietary body of each village. Freed of all interference by the district authorities, the village chief stood security himself for the amount agreed upon, and paid it directly into the treasury at Lucknow. But it was administratively cumbersome for the central government to deal individually with thousands of villages, nor were zamindars of sufficient "wealth and respectability" always forthcoming.

18. The boundaries of the chaklas and nizamats varied over time, and have never been precisely plotted. The chaklas nearest Lucknow or on the distant northern frontier were often placed directly under the central government, with the posts of nazim and chakladar combined. See Elliott, *Chronicles of Oonao*, pp. 131–32; E. Thornton, *Gazetteer of Territories Under the East India Company* (London, 1854), 4:38–39; and P. D. Reeves, ed., *Sleeman in Oudh* (Cambridge, 1971), pp. 300–03.

19. For general discussion of these various arrangements see Jagdish Raj, "The Revenue System of the Nawabs of Oudh," *Journal of the Economic and Social History of the Orient* 2 (1959):92–104; and G. D. Bhatnagar, "Revenue Administration of Wajid Ali Shah," *Journal of the U.P. Historical Society* 4 (1956):43–52.

Huzur tahsil lands normally contributed no more than about 10 percent of the total revenue of the Oudh state.[20] There remained the *amani*, or trust, system of revenue management. Under it the government appointed a nazim or chakladar to a district without binding him to pay over any fixed amount. He was instead to remit whatever sum he could collect. The collector was paid a fixed salary, and in addition was allowed to retain a certain percentage of the collections for his expenses. The revenue demand was settled annually on each village in negotiations between the chakladar, the pargana staff, and the village zamindars.

In part no doubt because they saw in the amani chakladar a figure akin to their own district collector, the British for over thirty years, until the 1840s, remained ardent partisans of the amani system. They kept careful track of the districts under this form of revenue management, and continually urged the Nawab to extend it more widely. With this demand was often coupled a request that the Nawab institute a fixed assessment for a period of at least five years.[21] On several occasions, and with varying degrees of enthusiasm, the Oudh government bowed before the storm, and introduced the amani system throughout the greater part of the country. In every instance the attempt was abandoned as a failure within a very few years. Even the vigorous efforts on its behalf made by the Nawab Muhammad Ali Shah during the five years of his reign (1837–1842) brought the new system no closer to success. Indeed by the time the Governor-General, Lord Hardinge, while visiting Lucknow in 1847, lectured the Nawab once again on the advantages of amani collection the British officers in Oudh were already reporting that the contract system was less oppressive and should not be disturbed.[22]

The failure of the amani experiment cannot obviously be attributed either to lack of enthusiasm on the part of the British or to lack of willingness on the part of the supine Nawab. The cause must be sought elsewhere, above all in the administrative incapacity of the Lucknow government. As the contractors were unchecked, so too were the nazims and chakladars of the amani districts. And the extortion in consequence was no less. Indeed it might even be greater. Although the amani *amil* (collector) was not bound to pay the government a fixed sum and could therefore claim remission in the event of crop failure or other natural catastrophe, he was in fact usually expected to hand over a standard amount settled in advance if he wished to retain his post. Indeed the ability to claim remission enabled the official in an amani district to defraud both government and peasant, for he could by "timely

20. Resident Lucknow to Sec. Govt. India 15 July 1841, NAI Foreign Consultations (hereafter F.C.) 20 September 1841, No. 40; and R. Montgomery, "A General Report on the Administration of Oudh for 1859," NAI Foreign Miscellaneous File (hereafter For. Miss. File) No. 382, pp. 24–25. For the exceptional use of huzur tahsil by the large landholders see below p. 42.
21. See, for instance, Resident Lucknow to Sec. Govt. India 13 June 1832, For. Miss. File No. 184, pp. 830–36; and Resident Lucknow to Sec. Govt. India 24 November 1848, F.C. 30 December 1848, No. 99–104.
22. John Low, Resident from 1831 to 1842, was one of the first to become disillusioned. See Resident Lucknow to Sec. Govt. India 15 July 1841, F.C. 20 September 1841, No. 40.

donations" to the appropriate secretariat officials in Lucknow obtain a reduction of the assessment and pocket the difference.

The contractor by contrast, though sometimes subjected to the rigors of an auction system that drove him to extortion to make good his bond, had a substantial incentive to conciliate the landholders, for he could make no profit from the proceeds of a desolate land. Where he was allowed to hold a district for several years in succession, self-interest itself prompted him to encourage agricultural prosperity. Mian Almas Ali, the first great contractor, who held districts yielding one-third the revenue of Oudh for forty years, left the country so peaceful and productive that the days of his rule in Asaf-ud-daula's time were later looked back upon as a "golden age."[23] Even in the 1830s, when the rains failed, the farmers of the districts along the Ganges advanced funds to the villagers for digging wells and building tanks. By mid-century, however, with contracts transferred at frequent intervals, and their award enmeshed in court politics, the distinctive advantages of the contract system had nearly disappeared.[24]

The revenue contractors were not by and large men of established family either in the countryside or at the Nawab's court. They sprang rather from the ranks of the lowly but ambitious who were drawn to Lucknow by the prospects of wealth in one of the last remaining native principalities. Almas Ali, the son of a Jat cultivator, was a eunuch who formed part of the dowry of one of Asaf-ud-daula's wives. Perhaps the greatest, and certainly the most famous of these men, Darshan Singh, came from a Brahmin family of petty zamindars, migrants to Oudh from Bihar. Darshan's elder brother Bakhtawar Singh, a trooper in the Bengal Cavalry stationed at Lucknow, caught the eye of Saadat Ali Khan, who brought him from the Company's service into his own. As Bakhtawar rose in the Nawab's favor so too did his younger brothers. Darshan, the ablest, secured first the post of chakladar in 1822 and then five years later that of nazim over extensive territories in eastern Oudh.[25] As nazim, he prosecuted the Nawab's interests with vigor, on one occasion even chasing a refractory raja of Balrampur over the border into Nepal. This episode won him the ill will of the British government, which

23. W. H. Sleeman, *A Journey Through the Kingdom of Oude in 1849-50* (London, 1858), 1:320-22; and Elliott, *Chronicles of Oonao*, pp. 124-25. Much the same was true of Hakim Mehndi, contractor of Muhamdi from 1804 to 1818.

24. For the actual working of both contract and amani systems of collection at midcentury see Resident Lucknow to Sec. Govt. India 21 March 1848, F.C. 31 March 1848, No. 40; Resident to Sec. Govt. India 24 September 1849, F.C. 17 November 1849, No. 225; Resident to Sec. Govt. India 16 February 1852, F.C. 27 February 1852, No. 180; and Sleeman, *Journey*, 1:200-02. For a detailed account of one district, Sultanpur, see letter from Captain A. Orr 9 January 1855, *British Parliamentary Papers* (*Commons*) (hereafter *P.P.*) 1856, 45:409-18.

25. Sleeman, *Journey*, 1:150-51; and Benett, *Gonda S.R.*, pp. 31-33. Darshan was in turn nazim of Sultanpur, Salone, and Gonda-Bahraich, and contracted for revenues averaging over fifty lakhs of rupees a year. After his death in 1844 his brother Inchha Singh, and his sons Raghubar Dyal and Man Singh, were nazims in the same area. For Man Singh see P. Carnegy, "Pargana Pachhimrath" (1868), in his *A Historical Sketch of Fyzabad Tehsil* (Lucknow, 1896), Part II, pp. 13-14, (hereafter *Fyzabad Tehsil*).

secured his temporary banishment, but the inability of his successors to collect the revenue soon brought about his release and restoration to power. Even the British officials in Oudh admitted that although Darshan Singh was unscrupulous he "allowed no one to be tyrannical but himself." The common people of Sultanpur, Colonel Low insisted in 1841, "were far more happy and far less molested" under Darshan than under the amani nazims, and the revenue was paid more regularly into the Nawab's treasury.[26]

But if Darshan served the Nawab's interests well, he also looked after his own. The family's fortunes were laid by Bakhtawar Singh when he obtained from Saadat Ali Khan the estate of Shahganj in Faizabad district. Saadat Ali's successor Ghazi-ud-din Haidar bestowed upon him the title of raja, subsequently granted in perpetuity by Muhammad Ali Shah, who also remitted the revenue demand on forty-two of the estate's villages. As Bakhtawar resided most of the year at the court in Lucknow, retaining as his permanent seat the family's ancestral village near Baksar, Shahganj was taken over by his brother Darshan. On the site he built a commodious fort with a double rampart of *kachcha* (mud) walls three miles in circumference and surmounted by fourteen guns. Inside were two squares of *pakka* (masonry) houses, some in the European style, decorated with ornamental sculptures brought from the ruins of Faizabad or crafted of Mirzapur stone. These buildings, which together with the fortifications cost ten lakhs of rupees, earned the praise of one European observer as "the handsomest structures now [in the 1830s] under erection in Oudh outside Lucknow."[27]

With this stronghold as his base Darshan set out from the 1820s onward to expand his family's holdings. The method he used was that of turning to his own advantage the powers he possessed as nazim. As Sleeman described it:

He [Darshan] imposed upon the lands he coveted, rates which he knew they could never pay; took all the property of the proprietors for rent, or for the wages of the mounted and foot soldiers, whom he placed over them, or quartered upon their villages, to enforce his demands; seized any neighboring banker or capitalist whom he could lay hold of, and by confinement and harsh treatment, made him stand security for the suffering proprietors, for sums they never owed; and when these proprietors were made to appear to be irretrievably involved in debt to the State and to individuals, and had no hope of release from prison by any other means, they consented to sign the *bynamahs*, or sale deeds for lands, which their families had possessed for centuries.[28]

Protest was rarely of much avail, for Darshan commanded influence at court in the person of his brother Bakhtawar, together with a body of the Nawab's troops, and armed retainers of his own. As a result, by 1850 the Shahganj or

26. Resident Lucknow to Sec. Govt. India 15 July 1841, F.C. 20 September 1841, No. 40. See also letter of Capt. A. Orr 9 January 1855, *P.P.* 1856, 45:417–18.

27. D. Butter, *Outline of the Topography and Statistics of the Southern Districts of Oudh* (Calcutta, 1839), pp. 136–37, (hereafter *Southern Disricts*); and Sleeman, *Journey*, 1:149. For the award of honors see P. Carnegy, *Fyzabad Tehsil*, Part II, pp. 9–11.

28. Sleeman, *Journey*, 1:152–53.

Mehdona estate, as it became known, spread across the whole of western Faizabad and into Gonda, and paid a revenue of almost two lakhs of rupees on a rent roll of perhaps twice that amount.[29]

Not all revenue contractors built up estates in this fashion. Agha Ali, nazim of Sultanpur for most of the decade from 1847 to 1856, preferred cash to land. Nor was revenue contracting the only route from obscurity to landed wealth. The Brahmin Pande family of Gonda amassed their initial fortune as bankers for the rajas of Gonda, to whom they advanced money for the payment of the government revenue and from whom they obtained the nucleus of their later estate. In the 1840s and 1850s the enterprising brothers Ram Datt Ram and Krishn Datt Ram rapidly expanded the family's holdings by standing security with the nazim for the principal landholders of the district. The local zamindars were relieved in this way to be free of the pressure of the nazim, but when they defaulted their lands were made over to their guarantor on the condition of his making good the government demand upon it. By the mid-1850s the Pande estates of Singha Chanda and Akbarpur comprised some 350 square miles assessed at a revenue of two lakhs of rupees.[30] In similar fashion the Khatri family of Mauranwan in Unao, from bankers to the raos of Daundia Khera and treasurer to the nazim of Baiswara had become by the 1820s substantial landholders in their own right, with an estate assessed at a lakh of rupees.[31]

These upstart or "mushroom" taluqdars (as they were sometimes called) testify to the opportunity for rapid social mobility under the later Oudh Nawabs. By working with the state, which could not secure its revenue without the help of outside contractors and financiers, but at the same time taking advantage of its growing weakness, a skillful individual could within a few years put together an estate of exceptional size. Yet the number of such outsiders, catapulted overnight to landed prominence, was never very great. The taluqdari ranks on annexation included but a handful of Brahmins and Khatris, while the total lands held by self-made entrepreneurs amounted to no more than 15 percent of the area of any district, and reached that figure only in Faizabad and Gonda.[32]

Far more important in shaping Oudh rural society was the simultaneous growth in the holdings of the old landed families. Now free of the constraints

29. Sleeman, *Journey*, 1:153. The bulk of the estate was located in the parganas of Pachhimrath and Haveli Oudh. In 1856 the Mehdona assessment was Rs. 1,91,174 after deduction of Rs. 66,053 nankar allowance. Carnegy, *Fyzabad Tehsil*, Part II, p. 17.

30. For the rise of the Pandes see Benett, *Gonda S.R.*, pp. 24-25; Nevill, *Gonda D.G.*, pp. 99-101; and Sleeman, *Journey*, 1:129-35.

31. Elliott, *Chronicles of Oonao*, pp. 135-39.

32. See Benett, *Gonda S.R.*, pp. 57-58 for that district. The Bahraich total was only 7 percent. See *Oudh Gazetteer*, 1:180. For the figures of Brahmin, Khatri, and Kayastha landholdings in the British period, which however overstate the Nawabi totals because of post-Mutiny awards to loyalist members of these castes and their later purchases, see Tables in Appendix 1 below.

imposed by Saadat Ali, these Rajput and Muslim taluqdars rapidly extended the areas under their control. Sometimes this took the form of the establishment of new taluqas by aspiring cadet lineages, as among the Sombansis of Pratabgarh, but most commonly it involved simple lateral expansion at the expense of weaker neighbors. It owed much in either case not only to armed might but to the contract system of revenue collection. Anxious to cut down on administrative costs, which ate into their profits, the revenue contractors much preferred to collect from a few large landholders rather than a horde of petty zamindars. Hence they readily let the estates of defaulters to neighboring taluqdars who pledged themselves to liquidate the balance due and pay promptly in the future.[33] Indeed they were prepared even to collude with local landholders to bring about this result. As Sleeman recounted of the Mahmudabad estate:

Mithun Sing, of an ancient Rajpoot family, held the estate of Semree, which . . . consisted of twelve fine villages, paid to the Government 4000 rupees a year, and yielded him a rent roll of 20,000. Nawab Allee [the raja of Mahmudabad] coveted very much this estate, which bordered his own. Three years ago he instigated the Nazim to demand an increase of 5000 rupees a year from the estate; and at the same time he invited Mithun Sing to his house, and persuaded him to resist the demand to the last. He took to the jungles, and in the contest between him and the Nazim all the crops of the season were destroyed, and all the cultivators driven from the lands. When the season of tillage returned in June, and Mithun Sing had been reduced to the last stage of poverty, Nawab Allee consented to become the mediator, got a lease from the Chuckladar for Mithun Sing at 4500 rupees a year, and stood surety for the punctual payment of the demand. Poor Mithun Sing could pay nothing, and Nawab Allee got possession of the estate in liquidation of the balance due to him; and assigned to Mithun Sing five hundred pucka-beegas of land for his subsistence.[34]

Even when the interests of taluqdar and nazim clashed, and the defiant landholder, unwilling to pay the revenue demanded, was driven into the jungle, he was usually soon restored to his estate at a reduced assessment, while the nazim moved on to deal with other recalcitrant landholders. The taluqdar's gain was not, however, confined to the immediate reduction of his assessment. Unable to collect the full revenue demand from the large landholders, the nazims and chakladars tried to make up the deficiency by piling it on the small zamindars and village coparceners. Driven to the edge of bankruptcy by the increased pressure thus put upon them, these latter in many cases soon found themselves handed over as defaulters to the nearest taluqdar, who then obtained a reduction of the high demand by force or bribery.

33. Sleeman, *Journey*, 1:55–56; and Elliott, *Chronicles of Oonao*, p. 134.
34. Sleeman, *Journey*, 2:223–24. The Mahmudabad archives contain several such mortgage deeds (*tamassuk*), including one executed by Ratan Singh of Bajhera in 1853 for lands with an unpaid balance of Rs. 3,000 on an estate then assessed at Rs. 17,300. For Bajhera, which survived Mahmudabad's encroachments though very much reduced in size, see Nevill, *Sitapur D.G.*, p. 86.

Table 1. Villages Held by Taluqdars on Annexation, 1856

District	Villages Taluqdari	Total	District	Villages Taluqdari	Total
Lucknow	575	1,570	Gonda	3,483	4,129
Unao	368	1,236	Bahraich	3,761	3,949
Rae Bareli	1,052	1,551	Mahumdi	1,759	3,130½
Faizabad	3,116	4,215	Hardoi	464	1,427
Sultanpur	2,133	3,351½	Daryabad	1,087	2,506
Pratabgarh	3,032	3,633	Sitapur	2,692	4,422

Grand total — Taluqdari 23,522
                  Total   35,174

Source: Spec. Commr. Revenue to Sec. Govt. India 24 June 1859 in *Papers Relating to Land Tenures and Revenue Settlement in Oude* (Calcutta, 1865), Appendices "A" and "B," pp. 53, 79.

To avoid this fate the villagers might come to terms with a neighboring taluqdar to act as their protector, or even form a nominal taluqa themselves under the headship of one of their number. In Unao, for instance, one Kalandar Singh collected together all the members of the Parihar brotherhood who were of common descent, "and persuaded them to mass their divided holdings nominally into one large estate, of which his nephew Golab Singh should be the representative Talookdar, so that while in reality each small shareholder retained possession of his own share, they should present the appearance of a powerful and united Talooka" which the Nawab's chakladars would be afraid to touch. Such arrangements were, however, of limited utility. The protecting taluqdar might easily swallow up his protégés, or the nominal holder set out to make himself a taluqdar "in deed as well as in name."[35]

In the absence of reliable statistics it is difficult to trace in detail the stages by which taluqdari dominion was extended over rural Oudh during the years following the death of Saadat Ali Khan. The process was, however, both rapid and visible. Sleeman reported in 1850 that the value of the *khalisa*, or directly assessed smallholders' lands, in Bahraich district alone had declined from Rs. 7,25,000 to Rs. 69,000 since 1807. Patrick Orr, speaking of the Bahraich pargana five years later, asserted that all but 20 or 25 of its 650 khalisa villages had "been given to the Pyagpore, Churdah, and Bourhee Rajahs . . . ; and all over Oudh it is the same case."[36] By annexation some 300 taluqdars controlled two-thirds of the villages of Oudh. (See Table 1.)

35. Elliott, *Chronicles of Oonao*, pp. 59–61.
36. Sleeman, *Journey*, 1:49; and letter of Capt. P. Orr 5 January 1855, *P.P.* 1856, 45:408. For a further account of the growth of taluqdari tenures in Bahraich, with slightly different figures, see *Oudh Gazetteer*, 1:129–32, 203. For Kheri see Sleeman, *Journey*, 2:116.

Taluqdars, Nawabs, and Villagers

Once securely established in the possession of their estates, the taluqdars set out to maximize their control over the resources of the area. This at once involved them in conflict both with the Nawabs above them, and the subordinate village holders beneath. From the one they sought to withhold revenue; the other they sought to displace from their privileged position as intermediaries. In both arenas they achieved a substantial degree of success.

In the nineteenth as well as in the eighteenth century the landholders paid revenue only after a show of armed resistance. Their most important assets in the prosecution of these contests were their mud forts and bands of armed retainers. Darshan's fort at Shahganj was by no means exceptional in size or armament. Every landholder of consequence throughout the country built himself a fortified residence proportioned in size and sturdiness to his means. When the British annexed Oudh in 1856 they counted 623 forts, of which 351 were in a state of good repair.[37] Rarely were these forts impregnable or meant to withstand a long seige. Indeed their most effective defensive weaponry was not the cannon mounted on their walls, but the extensive growths of jungle that surrounded them. The jungle made it difficult for a small force to mount a tight blockade or to starve out the inhabitants of a fort, and it impeded the march of a powerful army so that the defenders could slip away. Further large patches of jungle, strategically located throughout the country, often in areas cut up by ravines or along the banks of rivers, provided safe retreats from which fugitive landholders could raid and plunder into the cultivated area until they were restored to their own estates.[38]

As the area held under taluqdari tenure, and by individual taluqdars, grew in extent, so too did the ability of the landholders to resist the government. Each accession of territory made available to the taluqdar more resources, and enabled him to keep more men under arms. Hence he could put up a stronger show of resistance at the time of the annual visit of the chakladar, and so gain a lower assessment. This in turn made possible a yet stronger resistance the following year. Moreover neighboring taluqdars often assisted each other. When the raja of Ikauna defied the nazim in 1839, gathered in his fort at the start of the battle were "500 servants of the talookdar of Piagpore; 500 from the talookdar of Bakha, 300 men from Hursurrun Sing Talookdar of Gungowal, 700 servants of Munoowur Khan Talookdar of Nanparah, 400 servants of the Talookdars of Churda and 600 servants of the Talookdars of Puskah and Kummrar and other zemindars of Chaidwarrah."[39]

---

37. Sec. C.C. Oudh to Sec. Govt. India 3 September 1856, F.C. 31 October 1856, No. 136-52. Sleeman in 1850 had estimated the total number of mud forts at 250, mounting 500 guns, and containing an average of 400 armed men each. *Journey,* 2:210.

38. Sleeman estimated the extent of these jungles at 886 square miles outside the Terai forest. For a complete listing, and an account of how they functioned as retreats, see *Journey,* 2:279-86. This material is reprinted in Reeves, ed., *Sleeman in Oudh*, Appendix I, pp. 292-99. See also Butter, *Southern Districts*, pp. 8-9.

39. "Items of Intelligence from Oudh . . . dated 31 December 1839," F.C. 3 August 1840,

The Nawabs by contrast were rarely able to utilize effectively even those forces which they did possess. Under the treaty of 1801 the Nawab's army was vastly reduced in size, and Company's forces substituted instead. After the days of Saadat Ali Khan, however, the Company became increasingly reluctant to let its troops be used by the Lucknow authorities. Corps commanders and Residents alike recoiled from the harsh methods employed by the Oudh government to extract revenue from recalcitrant landholders, and so scrutinized requests for assistance with a cold and unsympathetic eye. In each case the justice of the claim had to be fully proven before the troops were released.[40] The process of inquisition was as distasteful to the Nawab's ministers as the results of Company intervention were disappointing to the British. Hence the Nawabs during the 1820s surreptitiously increased the size of their own army to some 60,000 men, while the British a few years later withdrew most of their forces from the province and concentrated the rest at Lucknow. By the 1840s the only British military presence in the countryside were four regiments of Auxiliary Force, locally raised but British officered, and a small contingent of Oudh Frontier Police charged with the apprehension of fugitives from British territory and the suppression of *thagi* and *dacoitie*.[41]

The troops raised by the Nawabs suffered from the same absence of discipline that afflicted the revenue administration. An "ill-paid rabble," so Butter called them, with no cantonments, drill, or uniform, the 45,000 men at the disposal of the local chakladars spent much of their time simply foraging for supplies in the countryside. Indeed this plunder of thatch, timber, and grain was frequently regularized by the *qabz* system of revenue collection, in which the local officials, given no money to pay the troops, assigned a regiment a portion of the district with an assessment equal to its expenses, and told them to collect their own pay.[42] The British-officered Auxiliary Corps were alone effective fighting units, and hence in great demand. Auctioned off to the highest bidder, they might cost the successful nazim or chakladar up to Rs. 10,000 for a few months' use.[43] These were, however, but an attenuated remnant of the force Saadat Ali could command, and did little more than evoke the memory of the days when the power of the Company

No. 62-71. See also "State of the Country from Personal Observation Elaka of Byswara," in Acting Resident Lucknow to Sec. Govt. India 28 March 1840, *ibid.* Taluqdars could of course by the provision of suitable rewards sometimes be induced to join forces with the Nawab in the coercion of other landholders.

40. See, for instance, Resident Lucknow to Sec. Govt. India 9 November 1831, For. Miss. File No. 236, pp. 565-66.

41. For a history of the Oudh military see Sleeman, *Journey*, 2:190-200; and Safi Ahmad, *Two Kings of Awadh* (Aligarh, 1971), pp. 183-86. *Thagi* was ritual murder, and *dacoitie* armed robbery.

42. Butter, *Southern Districts*, pp. 102-04. For the qabz system see "A General Report on the Administration of Oudh," For. Miss. File No. 382, pp. 31-32, 39-42.

43. Resident Lucknow to Sec. Govt. India 24 September 1849, F.C. 17 November 1849, No. 225; and Sleeman, *Journey*, 1:195, 201. See by contrast his account of the regular Oudh force, *ibid.*, pp. 198-99.

stood behind the Nawab's revenue collectors. Without British aid, and lacking an effective army of their own, the Oudh Nawabs had no alternative but to deal with the taluqdars and other large zamindars wherever they existed. Occasionally a strong nazim might refuse to recognize the forced sales of villages by which taluqdari aggrandizement so often took place, or force a recalcitrant landholder to pay a punitive assessment.[44] But for the most part taluqdars had no difficulty winning recognition of their position, and on increasingly favorable terms.

Meanwhile on their estates the taluqdars had begun afresh the task of subduing the subordinate village proprietors. The relations between the two, never amicable, were in no way improved by the upheaval of the late eighteenth century. Briefly given independent status, the zamindari communities then found themselves incorporated into the new taluqas. These, as arbitrary collections of villages, contained far fewer subordinate holders than before with whom the taluqdari chief had previous ties of kinship or affection. Even those estates held by old rajas now almost invariably combined in a haphazard way old villages and new, those held by kinsmen and by strangers. On "mushroom" properties ties that might mute antagonism were, of course, conspicuous by their absence. As a result when pressed for revenue—or indeed simply to build up their own resources—the taluqdars turned without hesitation upon the privileged holders beneath them. The most enterprising estate-builders were usually also the most unscrupulous in asserting their authority over their new subjects. Loni Singh of Mitauli, who increased his rent role from forty to one hundred and fifty thousand rupees a year, sometimes, Sleeman reported, "attacked, plundered, and murdered" the old proprietors, and thus "established such a dread among them that he now [in 1850] manages them with little difficulty."[45] On Darshan Singh's Mehdona property Butter noted as early as 1839 that "the rack-rent system of the brothers is rapidly verging to a raiyatwari settlement; the situations of the zamindars being made so uncomfortable that instead of bringing up their sons to succeed themselves in the management of their farms, they are obliged to send them into the Company's and other military services: in many places the rate of assessment has been raised, from one to three rupees, within the past six years."[46] But the newer taluqdars were not always the most grasping. In Gonda the old rajas, as they put together the Bishambarpur estate, methodically crushed the zamindari communities, even of their own Bisen clan, confining them at favorable rates to the lands in their own cultivating occupancy. Their Pande neighbors by contrast, though up-

44. In Gonda, for instance, officials not of Darshan Singh's family for a long time ignored the sales of villages to that family, and collected the revenue themselves from the villages so transferred. Benett, *Gonda S.R.*, p. 32.

45. Sleeman, *Journey*, 2:121. For the growth of the Mitauli estate see *ibid.*, pp. 89–96; and Nevill, *Kheri District Gazetteer* (Allahabad, 1905), pp. 145, 148–49.

46. Butter, *Southern Districts*, p. 138. But the contest was not ended. For the intense, continuing strife on the Mehdona estate after annexation see below ch. 9.

start landholders, were well regarded throughout the district, and treated with leniency their new exproprietary tenants.[47]

The Pandes, like other landholders, were restrained from too great a severity by the need to staff their militia forces. Substantial numbers of men were kept under arms in this way. The major landholders of Rae Bareli in 1840 each had in their service at least 400 to 500 men, while several, including the Nain taluqdars and the rajas of Shankarpur and Khajurgaon, employed from 3,000 to 5,000.[48] Some of these retainers were low-caste Pasis, or *chaukidars* (watchmen), armed only with bow and arrow, who served at nominal pay for the sake of plunder. Others, in estates bordering the Terai, were sturdy hillmen or Paharis. But for the most part the taluqdars were dependent upon their tenantry and kinsmen, armed usually with matchlocks.[49] For the village zamindars this opportunity for service, and the remuneration it brought, did much to check the decline in their position. They were, as we shall see, by no means wholly at the mercy of the taluqdar even when the British took over Oudh in 1856.

If the zamindars suffered from the growth of the taluqdari tenure, the cultivating raiyats benefitted. Far from posing a threat to the supremacy of the great landholder, they were the base upon which his power rested. They added to the total available resources of the estates and were cherished accordingly. This was true even for the most grasping "mushroom" taluqdars. Sleeman on his tour through Oudh was profoundly impressed by the "contented and prosperous" state of the cultivators on the lands held by Bakhtawar and Darshan Singh. Despite the fraud and violence by which they acquired their lands, he said, the brothers "keep their faith with the cultivators, effectually protect them from thieves, robbers, the violence of their neighbors, and, above all, from the ravages of the King's troops; and they encourage the settlement of the better or more skillful and industrious classes of cultivators in their villages, such as Kachies, Koormies, and Lodhies." The merchants and artisans of Shahganj were at the same time "better protected than in any other town in Oudh."[50] Loni Singh too, no matter how harshly he treated his Rajput tenants, gave the "peaceful" Kurmis "all the aid they require."[51]

The incentives held out to settlers included not only protection from the chakladar, but substantial material benefits. Darshan Singh's family sometimes advanced a new cultivator as much as twenty-five rupees for a pair of bullocks, thirty-six rupees for subsistence until his first crops ripened, and

47. *Oudh Gazetteer*, 1:563–65; and Sleeman, *Journey*, 1:129–30.
48. Butter, *Southern Districts*, pp. 51, 111–12; and Sleeman, *Journey*, 1:246.
49. Sleeman, *Journey*, 1:333–34: and Residency Intelligence Report of 29 November 1832, For. Miss. File No. 185, pp. 941–42. For the employment of Paharis in Tulsipur see Memorandum of Lt. G. E. Hollings 14 July 1841, F.C. 20 September 1841, No. 41.
50. Sleeman, *Journey*, 1:150, 162.
51. *Ibid.*, 2:88. See also his account of the Bahraich taluqdars, 1:56; the Kheri landholders, 2:116; and the Mahmudabad estate, 2:223.

another thirty for building a house or sinking a well. The money would be paid back, often without interest, over a period of years. Alternatively the Mehdona taluqdars would prepare a well, and plant a grove of mango trees, on a small patch of land which would then be made over to "a gardener (*kachhi*) or other good cultivator to be tilled for his own profit." The grove and well would give the cultivator a bond to hold him to the village, so that the estate as a whole would prosper. The Mehdona lands, as Sleeman crossed them, were "like a rich garden."[52]

The cultivators on the taluqdari estates could not of course entirely escape the turmoil that raged around them. Occasionally they were pressed into temporary service as porters or *lathiwallas* (clubmen). Often too they were subjected to extra exactions beyond the normal rental demand in order to finance bands of retainers or the building of fortifications.[53] When the taluqdar was obliged to flee to the jungle, in order to sustain himself there he might make a summary levy from the raiyats, and then leave them to face the chakladar, who on arrival would endeavor to collect more revenue from them; or he might insist that his cultivators leave their fields untended, or even desert their homes and villages, in order to deprive the government authorities of any revenue until they restored the estate to its rightful holder. In either case, whether squeezed or uprooted, the peasantry bore the brunt of the struggle.[54] In quieter times, however, and when their taluqdari masters were strong, the cultivators usually fared the best, and paid the least, as tenants of the large landholders.[55]

Decadence, Decay, and Anarchy

Ever since the days of the Nawabs themselves the conditions of life in Nawabi Oudh have been painted in the most bleak and dismal terms. It has been a historical commonplace that the country was scandalously misgoverned—the court a sink of iniquity, the ruler indolent, and his agents vicious and oppressive. Indeed it was on these grounds that Lord Dalhousie recommended, and the Court of Directors sanctioned, the annexation of Oudh in February 1856. This decision was backed up by the submission to Parliament of a fat Blue Book of documents and dispatches, including reports from two distinguished Residents at the court of Lucknow, John Low and James Outram.[56] Yet it is by no means certain, even from the documents presented

52. *Ibid.*, 1:162-64, 170-71.
53. See, for instance, Residency Intelligence Report of 16 October 1832, For. Miss. File No. 185, pp. 634-39; and letter of Capt. Banbury 1 January 1855, *P.P.* 1856, 45:405.
54. Butter, *Southern Districts*, pp. 52, 101. See also Resident Lucknow to Sec. Govt. India 6 April 1850, F.C. 23 May 1850, No. 161 (para. 3); and Sleeman, *Journey*, 1:253. Sleeman attributed some of the exceptional fertility of the soil in Oudh to these periods of fallow, when the land was given over to cattle grazing and the dung left to enrich the soil.
55. See, for instance, Butter's account of Tiloi. *Southern Districts*, p. 110.
56. Outram Minute of 15 March 1855, *P.P.* 1856, 45:353-88; and Low Minutes of 28 March, 21 July, and 18 August 1855, *ibid.*, pp. 488, 538-40, and 561-69. For Sleeman's views see *Journey*, 1:xxi-xxii, lx-lxix.

in this volume, that Oudh had slid into anarchy, much less that its cultural and social life were decadent. Much depends on what one regards as "anarchy" and where one seeks "authority." Certainly there was ample disorder in rural Oudh. The continuing open clashes which marked the contest for mastery in the countryside are themselves sufficient evidence of that. In addition bands of dacoits, frequently headed by dispossessed or disgruntled landholders, infested the jungle and unpatrolled border areas. From there they descended to prey upon the roads and isolated villages, often in collusion with neighboring landholders who offered them protection and profited from their activities. Sleeman in his diary detailed eloquently and at length the depradations of these roving bands, who infuriated the British especially by their habit of raiding into British territory, and then taking refuge across the border in Oudh.[57]

In the midst of this chaos the Lucknow court stood aloof, preoccupied, and increasingly helpless. The paralysis stemmed in part from the vast gulf that separated Lucknow from the countryside. It was not simply a matter of the difference between urban and rural concerns, or the natural antagonism of taxpayer and tax collector, although these were present as well. More importantly, the Lucknow court and the rural chieftains were moved by strikingly different patterns of culture and behavior. With the decline of Delhi, Lucknow, as the remaining Islamic capital in northern India, became the center of a rich and sophisticated culture. Poets and musicians flocked there to find sustenance in the patronage of cultivated rulers; new styles of polished Urdu verse, and of dramatic composition, grew up to appreciative audiences; while the refinement of taste in architecture, dress, and even language achieved a luxuriance that won for it the condemnation of contemporary Englishmen.[58] Despite its Islamic character, this Lucknawi culture was not marked by any antagonism toward Hinduism. The Nawabs participated in the great Hindu festivals, on occasion even supporting the construction of temples, and freely employed Hindus as senior officials and bankers. The Oudh *diwan*, or revenue minister, for over forty years, from 1815 to 1856, was drawn from the members of one Hindu family. These Hindus in turn joined in the Muharram celebrations and the cultivation of Urdu literature. The communal riots that shook Lucknow were those of Shia and Sunni, not Hindu and Muslim.[59]

57. Sleeman, *Journey,* 1:176, 306; and 2:40-41, 135-36, 218-19, 247-49, 251-78. For border raiding see Magistrate Allahabad to Resident Lucknow 24 March 1855, and Magistrate Azamgarh to Resident Lucknow 2 June 1855, F.C. 28 December 1855, No. 331-34.

58. On Lucknawi culture see Abdul Halim Sharar, *Lucknow: The Last Phase of an Oriental Culture* (London, 1975); and Safi Ahmad, *Two Kings of Awadh*, chs. x-xii.

59. Safi Ahmad, *Two Kings*, pp. 130-35. For a list of the Nawab's ministers in the 1850s see G. D. Bhatnagar, *Awadh Under Wajid Ali Shah* (Varanasi, 1968), ch. xi; and Finanl. Commr. to Sec. C.C. Oudh 5 April 1856, F.C. 24 April 1857, No. 178. The one exceptional communal outburst was an 1855 clash at Ajodhya, triggered by a Muslim claim that a mosque lay buried in the precincts of the Hanuman Temple. Both Hindu and Muslim opinion throughout Oudh remained inflamed for some months until the Nawab, whose complicity in the affair is not clear, finally dispersed the dissident Muslim forces. For a narrative account see Bhatnagar, ch. ix.

The hold of this culture, however, did not extend much beyond the environs of the capital, nor include many Hindus other than the Kayastha and Khatri families tied to the court. In the countryside, outside the qasba towns and the estates of Muslim landholders, traditional Hindu values held uncontested sway. Taluqdars might learn the Persian script, but they cared little for the literature the script opened up to them. They studied instead the Hindu classics, the Sanskrit language (usually taught by a pandit allowed rent-free lands for his maintenance), and sometimes astrology as well. Above all else in a life oriented about war and the chase landholders strove to become proficient in the martial arts of combat and survival.[60]

Nor were the distinctions between city and country at all softened by social intercourse. Apart from those few exceptional landholders who came up through the court, like the Mehdona family, taluqdars and courtiers never intermarried, and rarely even laid eyes on one another.[61] The city aristocracy —the officials, the members of the royal family, the relatives and favorites of former sovereigns and their descendants—ventured into the country only occasionally on sporting excursions to the Terai forest. Even on those journeys they lived an isolated existence in large encampments surrounded by armed guards. Alone they would "none of them be safe a single night beyond the Capital or Cantonments," for they would at once "be plundered and destroyed by the landholders."[62] The taluqdars, as fearful for their safety, went into Lucknow rarely and hesitantly. Some, like the raja of Tiloi, a friend of Wajid Ali Shah, might make an "annual and politic" visit to the seat of government, but most entrusted their affairs to *vakils* or agents and only visited the capital to complain about the exactions of local officials. Even then there was no certainty of satisfaction. Hanwant Singh of Kalakankar confided to Sleeman that he had twice gone to Lucknow in search of justice; but though he had some good friends at court, among them Raja Bakhtawar Singh, "he was obliged to return without finding access to the sovereign or his minister, or anyone in authority over the viceroy."[63]

The British in Lucknow, caught up in the prejudices of those about them, shared in large part this "absence of all sympathy" with the landed classes. No Resident before Sleeman had ever traveled extensively in the rural areas, and so the Residency staff readily fell in with the Lucknow view that the taluqdars were predatory robber barons, boorish and uncultured. For the

60. See Butter, *Southern Districts*, p. 114; Tholal, *Sombansi Raj*, pp. 23, 52; and Kunj Behari Seth, *The Seths of Biswan* (Lucknow, 1906), pp. 8 and *passim*. Information on taluqdari upbringing in the Nawabi period is very scanty.

61. Darshan Singh gave two daughters to Ghazi-ud-din Haidar but the older families married into other Rajput families of equal or higher caste standing, often outside Oudh. The taluqdars of southeastern Oudh, for instance, sought alliances with the Central Indian rajas of Baghelkhand and Sagar. Butter, *Southern Districts*, p. 136; and Sleeman, *Journey*, 1:237–38.

62. Resident Lucknow to Sec. Govt. India 23 February 1849, F.C. 21 April 1849, No. 108–09. See also Safi Ahmad, *Two Kings*, pp. 102–04, 116–19; and W. D. Knighton, *The Private Life of an Eastern King* (London, 1855), ch. iv.

63. Butter, *Southern Districts*, p. 113; and Sleeman, *Journey*, 1:232.

British, as for the urban elite, the focus of interest was the court—its personalities, its intrigues, and its policies. Events in the hinterland were simply ignored.[64] More than simple prejudice, however, was involved; for the British, coming as they did from a society where government was visible and effective, continually looked toward, and sought to sustain, its counterpart in India. Because the Lucknow court was the recognized governmental authority in Oudh, the British continued to fix their attention upon it long after its vitality as an institution had disappeared. This preoccupation with the capital city effectively disabled the British from appreciating the significance of events in the countryside. Indeed their obsession with the efficacy of administrative tinkering kept them from seeing why the Nawab's government had itself become so demoralized.

During the last quarter of the eighteenth century, as we have seen, the intrusion of British power into northern India upset the traditional balance of indigenous authority and reduced the Nawabs of Oudh to the status of dependent clients. At first this loss of power was obscured by the availability of British troops, which enabled Shuja-ud-daula to mount the Rohilla War and Saadat Ali to move against the Rajput chieftains. After 1815, however, and more decisively with the withdrawal of British troops from the countryside in the 1830s, the debilitating effects of the British alliance became apparent. Throughout this period the British claimed to follow a policy of non-intervention in the internal affairs of princely states. To a certain extent in Oudh they did so. They neither schooled the Nawabs in European principles of government, nor aided them in their attempts to rule in the old way. Yet at the same time the British lectured the Oudh rulers on the need for administrative reform, above all pressing doggedly and persistently for the use of the amani, or trust, system of revenue collection. In doing so the British betrayed once again not only their abhorrence of extortion but their dislike of unsystematic and disorderly procedures. As the dissident F. J. Shore pointed out, the cannonading of taluqdari forts was not necessarily a vicious or extortionate way of collecting revenue. It simply did not meet British standards of orderliness and regularity.[65]

Such pressures, however, put the Nawab in an intolerable position. With the subsidiary alliance drawn tightly about him, he could not ignore the British and act as before. But he had neither the training nor the military force to act upon the injunctions of his European advisers. So the Nawabs

64. Although full of the details of petty bickering at the court, and of the difficulties of revenue collection, the Residency records contain little, and that usually imprecise and superficial, on the various landholding families, and on the way they put together their estates and conducted their affairs. Contemporary Indian chroniclers paid even less attention to rural society. See, for instance, the courtly focus of Abu Talib, *History of Asaf-ud-daula*.

65. F. J. Shore, *Notes on Indian Affairs* (London, 1838), 1:155–56, and 2:265–67. Shore further insisted that the collection of the revenue with an armed force, by revealing the weakness of the Oudh government, meant that the people were more lightly taxed than in the British territories where an overwhelming military force was always available but never deployed.

who succeeded Saadat Ali Khan, one after the other, increasingly abandoned the attempt to govern and retired into the *zanana*, where they amused themselves with wine, women, and poetry. The sensuous life of the "Orchid House" might not attract the Victorian Englishman, but it did not reflect sheer perversity or weakness of character on the part of the Nawabs. Indolence was rather the only appropriate response to the situation in which the princes of Oudh were placed: in which they could not be overthrown but could not act effectively in either the old way or the new.[66]

The ineffectuality of the Lucknow court, scandalous though it might have been, did not plunge the kingdom of Oudh wholly into anarchy. Beneath the turbulence and confusion can be found new centers of order. Of these the most important were the taluqdari estates. Far from simply collecting rent the taluqdars administered justice and enforced law and order on their properties. The fullest account is perhaps Butter's description of the Tiloi estate in Rae Bareli:

Even in the country immediately surrounding the Tiloin estates, private robbery is unknown, except as a consequence of boundary disputes, which generally terminate in a battle, followed by the plundering and burning of the village of the defeated party, who then complain to the chakledar, but without ever receiving redress. When similar disputes occur within the Tiloin boundary, they are instantly put down by the rajas, and speedy justice afforded. The rajas also investigate all criminal cases occurring within their estates, and send the parties, when convicted, to Lak'hnau for punishment. When they find or anticipate any difficulty in apprehending criminals, they apply to the darbar for assistance, which is given to them, through the chakledar. Civil suits also are investigated, and adjudicated in a summary manner, by the rajas, the just claimant being informed, that his demand shall be satisfied out of the defendant's first crop, should any surplus remain after payment of the revenue; but that, should this surplus prove insufficient to discharge the debt, no further judicial process shall take place in that suit.[67]

Nor was the situation any different on the Mehdona estate despite its "mushroom" character. Before the estate was put together, Sleeman reported, there used to be "fearful contests" between the small proprietors of the military classes over boundaries and rights to water for irrigation. "Now no such dispute leads to any serious conflict." They are all settled at once by arbitrators, guided in their decisions by the accounts of the *patwaris* and *qanungos*, and backed up by the power of the landlords, who are "able to enforce whatever decision is pronounced." Theft and robbery are unknown, and the peasantry "seem to live without fear."[68]

As the Nawabs sank into lethargy, then, the effective locus of power in the countryside shifted downward from the regional to the local level, and was

---

66. For contemporary sympathetic views of the Nawab's plight see Shore, *Notes on Indian Affairs*, 2:275–76; and Henry Lawrence, *Essays on the Indian Army and Oude* (Serampore, 1859), pp. 289–90.

67. Butter, *Southern Districts*, pp. 112–13.

68. Sleeman, *Journey*, 1:164–65. The rajas of Balrampur and Tulsipur also appointed arbitrators to settle disputes over boundaries and grazing rights. Benett, *Gonda S.R.*, p. 40.

there diffused among a number of centers. The process was not unlike that which had taken place a century before when imperial authority gave way to that of the various successor states. As the Nawabs of Oudh in the eighteenth century took over many of the functions of the Mughal Empire, while retaining the forms of subservience, so too in the nineteenth, the taluqdars, while never defying their nominal superior, expanded their authority into the room left vacant by the Nawab. Nor did it make much difference to the working of this incipient political system whether the taluqdars were ancient or upstart, Rajput or Brahmin. All were bound by the same constraints and so adapted, with the passage of time, to the same role. What counted was not origin but ability.[69]

The analogy with the eighteenth century should not be pushed too far, however, for the powers of the Nawab in the mid-nineteenth century, when annexation cut short the growth of the new system, were still far more extensive than those of his Mughal predecessor a hundred years before. To the very end the Nawab commanded sufficient force to ensure the respect and subordination of all but a handful of the landholders of Oudh. The taluqdars might intercept a good deal of the government revenue, but they were never wholly secure in its possession, nor were their mud forts, the symbols of their independence, ever impregnable bastions. Indeed, with the rajas of Tiloi, they sometimes sought the help of the local officials not only in the apprehension of criminals but in collecting rent from their own subordinate zamindars. The Nawab's government furthermore exercised considerable uncontested judicial authority. Not only did the nazims and lesser district officers administer justice, both criminal and civil, as part of their overall authority within their separate jurisdictions, but appeals lay in most cases, from the taluqdars' as well as the nazims' courts, to the High Court in Lucknow. Criminals were also commonly sent to Lucknow for punishment.[70]

Annexation too halted the spread of the new system before it encompassed the whole of Oudh. To some extent the taluqdari estates can be regarded as "oases," albeit rapidly growing ones, amidst the surrounding chaos. Indeed the very growth of the taluqdari domains increased the severity of the exactions of the local officials and roving dacoit bands, who found the area in which they could operate unhindered ever more constricted. Nor did the taluqdars' estates always escape the disorder around them. The extortionate activities of the more ruthless contractors, in particular, involved large and small landholders alike in a common ruin. Raghubar Dyal Singh, one of the sons of Darshan Singh, during his tenure as nazim in 1846–1847 reduced many of the estates of Gonda and Bahraich to a condition of almost complete devastation, from which, particularly in Bahraich, they did not recover until

69. For some comments on this process see Benett, *Chief Clans*, pp. 69–70; and Fox, *Kin Clan Raja and Rule*, pp. 111–13.
70. On the Oudh judiciary see "General Report on the Administration of Oudh for 1859," For. Miss. File No. 382, pp. 35–37; and Bhatnagar, *Awadh Under Wajid Ali Shah*, ch. xiii.

well into the British era.[71] Elsewhere the more enterprising taluqdars usually managed to avert such a fate either by outright resistance or by having their estates placed under huzur tahsil whereby they paid their revenue directly into the Lucknow treasury instead of through the local nazim.[72]

The last forty years of Nawabi rule in Oudh thus witnessed the slow but steady enfeeblement, to the point of ineffectuality, of the Lucknow government, and a corresponding rise in the numbers and position of the large landholders. The growing strength of these men, as Sleeman pointed out in 1849, "has led to disorder, and disorder has added to their strength." But, he continued, "had they not been so strong and the Government so weak the country would not have been so well tilled and peopled as it is, nor would it enjoy the same gradation of rank among the landed interest."[73] In the process, not only was Oudh preserved from the worst excesses of anarchy, but the landholding elite was itself substantially altered in character. Above all the taluqdari tenure, with estates wrested a few villages at a time from the Nawab's revenue officials, brought together in a common enterprise the old rajas, the more enterprising of their kinsmen and neighbors, and a few of the courtiers and financiers who had turned the weakness of the Lucknow government to their own advantage.

The taluqdars' lands were not spread evenly across the face of Oudh. The total amount they held, as well as the size of individual estates and the composition of the landholding community itself, varied substantially from place to place. One can mark out several regional clusterings. In the west and center of the province, near Lucknow, with the power of the Nawabs close at hand, taluqdari estates were fewer and smaller than elsewhere, and held more frequently by Muslims, who benefitted from court favor.[74] In the southeastern districts, from Rae Bareli to Faizabad, where Rajput power had long been consolidated in the hands of clan-based rajas, the same pattern of dominance persisted under the new taluqdari tenure. Apart from the exceptional Mehdona Brahmin family, almost all taluqdars were long-settled Rajputs; the bulk of the land was in their hands; and many estates were of a substantial, though not immense size, of from 20 to 100 villages. To the northwest, in Kheri and Sitapur, taluqdari lands again predominated, and

71. Sleeman, *Journey*, 1:70-97.
72. The Balrampur, Tulsipur, Mehdona, and Baiswara taluqdars all used huzur tahsil at times to escape the exactions of the nazim. See Sleeman, *Journey*, 1:37, 143, 245-46; and letter of Capt. A. Orr 9 January 1855, *P.P.* 1856, 45:417.
73. Resident Lucknow to Sec. Govt. India 23 February 1849, F.C. 21 April 1849, No. 108-09.
74. Taluqdars held only 29 percent of Unao, 32 percent of Hardoi, and 36 percent of Lucknow in 1856, while Muslim taluqdars were disproportionately predominant (except for Unao) in all these districts, together with adjacent Sitapur and Bara Banki. For a detailed list of taluqdari holdings by caste and community for each district see Appendix 1 below. It must be borne in mind that these figures relate to the period 1875-1905, after a quarter century and more of British rule, and are not therefore wholly reliable as a guide to the years before 1856. For the alterations in landholding as a result of confiscation of rebel property after the Mutiny see below Table 19.

most taluqdars were Rajput, though with a sizable contingent of Muslims. But the absence of established rajadoms, and the intermixture of clans, opened the way during the Nawabi years to a great scramble for land, with the result that many of the taluqdari families had but recently come to prominence.[75] Most distinctive were the estates of the far north. Here, along the frontier "marches" of Gonda and Bahraich, protected by their remoteness from Lucknow, and the rivers and jungles of the Terai, the old chieftains kept up a virtually independent position. The rajas of Balrampur and Tulsipur, though beaten in many battles, were never unseated, nor did they ever allow the Nawab's revenue officials to establish themselves in their domains. They continued to pay only a lump sum tribute to Lucknow.[76]

Despite this heterogeneity the Oudh landholders, whether as rajas or as taluqdars, remained throughout the years of Nawabi rule essentially rulers of men. They valued their estates, that is, primarily as sources of wealth which could be converted into political and military power. With the coming first of annexation in 1856, and then of the sepoy revolt a year later, they had an opportunity to test their strength against a new opponent.

75. See Nevill, *Kheri D.G.*, pp. 81–82, 148–50; and Nevill, *Sitapur D.G.*, pp. 54–55, 62.

76. *Oudh Gazetteer*, 1:125–26, 133, 543; and 3:499. On Tulsipur's defiance see letter of Lt. Sinclair 12 December 1854, *P.P.* 1856, 45:420. Neighboring Nanpara, Bhinga, and Baundi were only slightly less independent. Southern Bahraich and Gonda shared in the development of the ordinary taluqdari tenure.

Part Two | The North-Western Provinces

Three | *The Shaping of an Agrarian Policy*

I n 1801 the Nawab of Oudh was forced to cede to the British half his territories. These lands—the districts of Bareilly, Moradabad, Farrukhabad, Etawah, Kanpur, Allahabad, and Gorakhpur—surrounded the Nawab's domains like a crescent on three sides. Their cession extended British rule at a bound into the heart of the upper Ganges plain. Two years later the remaining districts of the Ganges-Jumna Doab, together with the adjacent districts of Agra and Delhi, were conquered from Daulat Rao Sindia by Lord Lake. The same year Bundelkhand was ceded to the British by the Peshwa. Within three years the British thus came to control a vast territory extending from the Himalayan foothills to the Central Indian plateau and encompassing most of the heartland of traditional Hindustan.[1]

As might be expected this far-flung tract was a land of great geographic and social diversity. The eastern districts, with their dominant Rajput elites and rich well-watered agriculture, had much in common with the adjacent districts left with the Oudh Nawab. In the west, however, and especially

1. The districts later established by the British differed substantially from those existing at the time of conquest. For the stages of territorial expansion see Map 3, and Dharma Bhanu, *History and Administration of the North-Western Provinces 1803–1858* (Agra, 1957), ch. iii.

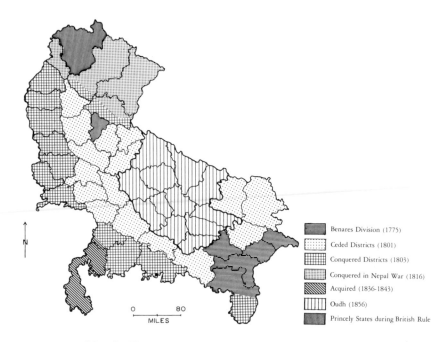

Benares Division (1775)
Ceded Districts (1801)
Conquered Districts (1803)
Conquered in Nepal War (1816)
Acquired (1836-1843)
Oudh (1856)
Princely States during British Rule

0   80
MILES

Map 3. The N.W.P.&O., Dates of British Acquisition.

across a broad band of territory stretching from Bundelkhand through Agra and Delhi north along the Jumna, the pattern of landholding took on a somewhat different shape. An area of scanty and uncertain rainfall, subject to frequent drought and famine, the Upper Doab was marked by low agricultural yields and a low population density. Hence there was little opportunity for the growth of a class of zamindars supported by rental income. The soil simply did not supply sufficient produce to sustain them. The village proprietors were thus of necessity also its cultivators; some, for the most part tightly knit Jat kin groups, even shared out the lands equally among themselves in the bhaiacharya tenure. These coparcenary communities, with their absence of social and economic stratification, closely approximated the "village republics" celebrated by Sir Charles Metcalfe.[2]

The Doab districts at the same time benefitted from their position astride the two great commercial arteries of pre-railroad northern India, the Ganges and Jumna rivers, which flowed past Delhi and Agra, Kanpur and Allahabad, to Benares, Patna, and the sea. Though riverine commerce had never been wholly extinguished even in the dark days of midcentury, the British conquest of Bengal, and the extension upriver of the East India

2. See Eric Stokes, "Agrarian Society and the Pax Britannica in Northern India in the Early Nineteenth Century," *Modern Asian Studies* 9 (1975); esp. pp. 515-27. For the structure of village society in the Delhi Territory see Percival Spear, *Twilight of the Mughuls* (Cambridge, 1951), ch. vi.

Company's commercial activities touched off from the 1760s onward a major trade expansion. As the British sought commodities for the European and Far Eastern markets, old industries revived and new ones sprang up. Hand-loomed cotton piece goods, the traditional luxury export of Hindustan, together with sugar and opium poppy, formed initially the major items of trade. Locally manufactured piece goods worth four lakhs were exported from Benares alone in 1787, while a further nine lakhs, imported from the western provinces, were shipped through the city downriver to Bengal and Bihar.[3] In the 1790s, with a greater participation in the trade of private European merchants and planters, the boom widened and deepened. By 1795 piece goods worth nearly thirty lakhs were being exported from the areas then under the Oudh Nawab's control.[4] During the same years, spurred by a rapidly rising European demand, indigo cultivation spread from Bengal across the middle Doab, into Oudh, and as far upriver as Agra and Aligarh. In the last years of the decade some four million pounds annually, the bulk of it from the Doab tracts north and west of Benares, were being shipped from Calcutta to London.[5]

After the turn of the century and the cession of Gorakhpur, the Doab, and Rohilkhand, the East India Company set out energetically to develop the commercial potential of its new territories. With one commodity they were unsuccessful. Hit by Manchester competition abroad, and the decay of the old Muslim gentry who had provided much of the local demand, the trade in silk and cotton piece goods steadily declined. Yet the loss was made good by a continued growth in the demand for indigo, together with an expansion of the trade in raw cotton. Long imported from Bundelkhand and the Deccan to supply local weavers, cotton drawn by the overseas market now began to be widely cultivated in the Upper Doab as well. After the end of the Napoleonic wars, with the reestablishment of peace in Europe and India, boom times set in for both commodities. During the 1820s, fueled by a spectacular rise in prices, indigo production especially rose dramatically throughout the Doab districts.[6] Nor was this commercial agriculture solely a product of European enterprise. Begam Samru, on her *jagir* at Sardhana near Meerut, by a combination of high assessments, compulsion, and credit advances, secured on her lands a "preponderant" cultivation of "the more profitable products," above all sugarcane and cotton, which found a "ready sale" at a number of nearby marts.[7]

3. For the Benares trade see Kamala Prasad Mishra, *Banaras in Transition, 1738-1795* (Delhi, 1975), ch. v, esp. pp. 136-39, 149, 156-59.
4. P. J. Marshall, "Economic and Political Expansion: the Case of Oudh," *Modern Asian Studies* 9 (1975):473-76.
5. *Ibid.*, pp. 476-77. During the 1790s under the protection of the Maratha general deBoigne six European planters set up indigo factories in Aligarh alone. H. R. Nevill, *Aligarh District Gazetteer* (Lucknow, 1926), p. 39.
6. For indigo and cotton cultivation see Siddiqi, *Agrarian Change*, pp. 140-55.
7. Meerut Settlement Report of 16 March 1840, in *Reports on the Revenue Settlements of the North-Western Provinces* (Benares, 1862), 1:228, 230.

This commercial expansion brought with it a growth of new urban centers. Many—Bareilly, Hathras, Farrukhabad, among others—owed their foundation to the zamindars and lineage chieftains who had prospered at the expense of the Mughals, and grew on the patronage these new magnates supplied. Other older cities, such as Agra, Allahabad, and Benares, gained a new prominence from their position as wholesale markets and shipping centers for the new produce. Most spectacular perhaps was the rise of Mirzapur, on the Ganges where the Bundelkhand and Doab trade routes met. A tiny "palace mart" of the local raja, the town had by 1815 become the center of the cotton trade for the whole of Upper India.[8]

The districts left after 1801 with the Nawab of Oudh, isolated from the flow of riverine trade except along the side of the Ganges, did not by and large participate in this growth of commerce. Only one town in Oudh, Tanda, a center of handloom textile production, owed its prosperity wholly to manufacturing.[9] Lucknow, as the thriving capital of one of northern India's last remaining native principalities, was a mart for vast quantities of grain from the surrounding countryside, and it sustained an array of fine luxury crafts, from embroidered cotton goods to pottery and jewelry. Yet with Faizabad, the province's only other city, which it succeeded as capital, Lucknow was far more a center of consumption than of an export trade.[10] Oudh's position off the major commercial arteries was, however, by no means wholly disadvantageous. Its moderate regular rainfall and fertile soils secured for it instead a stable agrarian economy based on food grain production, and a reputation as the "Garden of India."[11] In the western Doab, by contrast, the uncertainties of climate were compounded by fluctuations of trade. Held hostage by the demand for indigo and cotton, whose prices were determined in unpredictable distant markets, the commercial prosperity of the early nineteenth century remained always fragile and narrow based. By the 1820s but a small shift in the structure of prices was required to turn boom to bust, and so precipitate a ruinous agrarian crisis.

Despite their extensive involvement in its commerce, when the British took charge of the Doab, they did not find a ready acquiescence in their rule. They had, therefore, before they could develop a settled revenue policy, to assert their mastery over the countryside. This was not to be a task easily or quickly accomplished. The half-century preceding the British conquest had been an

8. See C. A. Bayly, "Town Building in North India, 1790-1830," *Modern Asian Studies* 9 (1975):483-96. For the regional distribution of commercial production, which brought with it a considerable monetization of the economy and the growth of an extensive trade in grain as commercial producers purchased their foodstuffs in the market, see Siddiqi, *Agrarian Change*, pp. 158-67.

9. For Tanda see *Oudh Gazetteer*, 3:490-93. Private European merchants controlled much of the Tanda trade from the 1780s onward.

10. See *Oudh Gazetteer*, 2:332, 387-92. For a comprehensive account of Lucknow crafts see W. Hoey, *A Monograph on Trade and Manufactures in Northern India* (Lucknow, 1880).

11. The average annual rainfall was 40 inches. See *Oudh Gazetteer*, 1:i-xii; and H. C. Irwin, *The Garden of India* (London, 1880). Grain comprised the bulk of Oudh's exports.

era of exceptional disorder and confusion in the central and northern Doab. Those districts which had been subject to the Nawabs of Oudh were located at the furthest extremities of that kingdom, and had but recently come under its jurisdiction, and thus were none too easy to keep in order. Elsewhere the collapse of Mughal authority had left the countryside at the mercy of a procession of invaders—Afghan, Maratha, and Jat—who marched and countermarched across the land. In this setting of political instability the local chieftains everywhere threw up fortifications, enlisted men-at-arms, and measured their swords against all comers. The result was not total anarchy, for each chieftain, anxious to increase his revenue, encouraged trade, and even agriculture, in the area he controlled. Yet the political order was somewhat different from that in the central districts of Oudh. There emergent taluqdars consolidated enduring principalities within a hierarchically structured political system. In the Doab, by contrast, the constant upheaval and military campaigning made difficult the construction of lasting rulerships, while at the same time it encouraged, where indeed it did not force, all powerholders from lineage chiefs to village zamindars to adopt a defiant independence.

Hardened by this eighteenth-century disorder, the Doab landholders did not relish the sudden imposition upon them of British rule. Matters were made worse by the Governor-General Lord Wellesley's decision, immediately upon taking over the government, to abolish the transit duties which the landholders had levied on all goods passing through their estates. Thus when revenue was demanded in 1802 the more powerful chieftains refused to pay and shut themselves up in their forts. Prominent among them was Raja Bhagwant Singh, with 20,000 men and two mud forts at Sasni and Bijaigarh in Aligarh. The Sasni fort held out for two months, and then was taken only with "some difficulty and disproportionate loss" when the Commander in Chief Lord Lake arrived to lead the attack in person.[12]

The initial reduction of their forts did not put an end to the discontent of these "refractory" landholders. For some years the building of small forts continued to be the "daily occupation" of many of them, while some gave shelter to roving gangs of dacoits who raided far down the Doab. At the same time they made it a point of honor never to pay the revenue until the last possible moment to which they could delay it.[13] Yet these chieftains were not treated at all harshly by the new government. Thakur Daya Ram, the most powerful of the Aligarh chiefs, was confirmed in possession of the Hathras taluqa on a fixed life-time assessment of Rs. 93,620. He was awarded two further taluqas (Gubrari and Simardhari) rent-free in jagir, and his entire estate was exempted from the operation of the British police system. He was,

12. J. R. Hutchinson, *Allygurh Statistics: Being a Report on the General Administration of that District from 1803 to the Present Time* (Roorkee, 1856), p. 6. For a general account of the extended military operations against the Aligarh chiefs see Nevill, *Aligarh D.G.*, pp. 174–81.

13. Hutchinson, *Allygurh Statistics*, p. 16; and Atkinson, *Statistical Account*, 2:400–01, 410. Gangs were established on the estates of Hira Singh of Awa Missa, Bhagwant Singh of Mursan, Daya Ram of Hathras, and Himmat Singh of Etah.

the settlement officer commented later, "practically independent, paying his revenue like a tribute."[14] Bhagwant Singh held the Mursan taluqa on very similar terms. Such concessions were not of course simply a product of British benevolence. They reflected rather the inability of the new regime to maintain order or collect the revenue without the help of these men.

Daya Ram was, however, still not reconciled to British rule, nor were the British at all happy with his continued quasi-independent status. At length in 1816, when Pindari raids and an impending conflict with the Marathas began to unsettle the Doab districts, the British decided to reduce both Daya Ram and Bhagwant Singh to the level of ordinary subjects. An "overwhelming" force including the largest park of artillery so far employed against any fortified place in India was brought together before Hathras in February 1817; on the first of March after an all-night fusillade Daya Ram slipped away and the rest of the garrison surrendered. Bhagwant Singh soon afterwards agreed to dismantle his fort without a contest. Thus some fifteen years after its conquest British rule was finally consolidated in Aligarh district. Indeed, the Deputy Collector reported in 1835, "whenever the inhabitants of the Pergunnah refer to the commencement of our dominion, they always allude to the subsequent period of Thakoor Dya Ram's expulsion."[15]

The Early Revenue Experiments

As annexation did not at once bring with it effective control of the countryside, so too was the collection of revenue for many years a haphazard process. The new rulers at the outset possessed neither the detailed knowledge nor the reliable staff they needed to assess and collect the revenue in an orderly fashion, while their uncertain hold over the land further enforced upon them policies of short-term expediency. As a result, the first three decades of British rule in the Doab and Rohilkhand were an era of experimentation, at times of almost disastrous trial and error, in the collection of the land revenue.

The British carried with them to the newly conquered territories of northern India the preconceptions derived from their quarter century's experience of Bengal. They set out to find large zamindars of the sort they were accustomed to, and they expected to form a settlement with these men in which the award of proprietary rights would soon be followed by a perpetual assessment of the land revenue. "In all possible cases," Henry Wellesley instructed his subordinates in 1802, "the settlement is to be made with the zamindars if not men of notorious character or otherwise disqualified, provided that they offer a fair and equitable jumma [jama]." Only

---

14. Smith, *Aligarh S.R.*, p. 16.
15. Report on the Settlement of Pargana Hathras by J. Thornton 10 May 1836, UPSA B.R. Progs. 27 September 1836, No. 16. Bhagwant Singh was restored to his estate, while Daya Ram, stripped of his property, was awarded a pension of Rs. 1,000 per month for himself and Rs. 750 for his dependents.

where the zamindars or "other actual proprietors" declined to enter engagements for their estates, or where there were no proprietors, was a village settlement to be made, "giving the preference to the mokuddums, perdhauns, or any respectable Ryotts of the village."[16]

Unfortunately, however, the pattern of landholding in the Doab differed markedly from that in Bengal. While in Bengal at the time of the British occupation some fifteen zamindars, their estates for the most part put together by conquest and official favor under Murshid Quli Khan (1707–1737), controlled some 60 percent of the land, in the Doab large landholdings were few in number, and confined for the most part to a handful of districts. Over substantial areas of the province, especially toward the west, the structure of the village communities, and the lack of sufficient resources to sustain a rentier class, effectively barred such a consolidation of holdings. The hammering of constant warfare over half a century too, with its continual dislocation and disruption, brought about much the same result. Where landholders did put together sizable estates, or taluqas, they owed much of their success, as in Oudh, to the favor of government authorities above them, anxious to share the burdens, and the risks, of revenue collection.

The growth of the Mursan and Hathras taluqas in Aligarh provide a classic instance of this process of estate building. Daya Ram and Bhagwant Singh, Tenwa Jats, were both descendants of one Makhan, who settled near Mursan about 1600. During the subsequent half-century, partly by a timely marriage alliance with its previous Jat inhabitants and partly by bringing new land under cultivation, this family acquired possession of the tract known as tappa Jawar. Its chieftain in 1658, Nandram, by an early submission to the emperor Aurangzeb in the Mughal war of succession obtained the revenue management of Jawar and nearby Tochigarh, and soon after the control of the police as well, with the title of *faujdar*. After Nandram's death in 1695 his sons divided their holdings and established separate houses. Nandram's grandson Khushal Singh won the favor of Nawab Saadat Khan, who gave him revenue rights over the core of what was to become the Mursan estate. Khushal's son Phup Singh substantially enlarged the estate by obtaining from the local *amils* leases for those villages which had fallen partially out of cultivation or from which the revenue was collected with difficulty. By the time Bhagwant Singh succeeded his father in 1798 the estate, now formed into a separate pargana, had reached its full extent of 300 villages. Meanwhile another of Nandram's grandsons, Baran Singh, was putting together the extensive Hathras taluqa, the centerpiece of which he obtained in 1752 when he induced the amil of the district to transfer the revenue management of Hathras town and its surrounding villages from its Porach Rajput holder to himself. A few years later in 1760, when Raja Surajmal of Bharatpur vanquished the Rajput chief of Mendu, he secured that tract as well.

16. Proclamation of 14 July 1802, IOL Home Miscellaneous 582:2464.

Daya Ram, Baran Singh's grandson, in the years after 1775 completed the process of expansion by expelling various other descendants of Nandram from their estates.[17]

The process of taluqdari aggrandizement was, however, cut short by the British annexation. In 1801 taluqdars controlled no more and perhaps rather less than 20 percent of the land in the newly acquired provinces.[18] This figure contrasts sharply with the total of 66 percent in the hands of the Oudh taluqdars some fifty years later, in 1856, when that province was finally brought under British rule. The relative scarcity of large landholders in the Doab and Rohilkhand meant that the British had in the long run no option but to deal directly with the village-level zamindars and coparcenary communities. Their land policy was, however, only slowly shaped to this end. Initially, where large taluqdars did not exist, the British, anxious to secure a regular payment of the revenue demand, turned to the farmers who had held revenue contracts during the days of Nawabi or Maratha rule. These men had the considerable advantage of being on the scene, well connected, and able to put up the securities that the government required. In Rohilkhand forty-two lakhs of rupees out of a total demand of forty-six lakhs at the first settlement were in the hands of revenue farmers, while in Etawah district the entire revenue demand for 1802 was divided among seventeen farmers.[19] Similarly in Aligarh both the initial summary settlement and the first triennial settlement (of 1806) were formed primarily with revenue farmers. Among their number were not only professional farmers but prominent local chieftains, such as Daya Ram and Bhagwant Singh, as well as other "men of family" in the district, all awarded extensive farms outside their taluqdari holdings. The Aligarh Collector in 1806 readily admitted that these farmers rarely had any "proprietary right" in the lands for which they contracted, but he saw no alternative to farming arrangements if he was to maintain order and get in the revenue.[20]

Slowly, as the British consolidated their power and gained a more intimate knowledge of local tenures, the revenue farmers were set aside in favor of occupying zamindars both large and small. In Moradabad, which had seen two-thirds of its revenue farmed at the cession, and almost as much as late as

17. For the rise of the Mursan and Hathras families see Hutchinson, *Allygurh Statistics*, pp. 236–39; Atkinson, *Statistical Account*, 2:427–30, 435–36; and Table 3. The 300 original Mursan villages were reduced by consolidation to a total of 225. For a similar process of taluqdari expansion in Gorakhpur see Siddiqi, *Agrarian Change*, pp. 41–48.

18. There is no comprehensive list of taluqdari lands in the N.W.P. They were most numerous in Aligarh, Mainpuri, Allahabad, and Gorakhpur districts. For some indication of the scale of holdings, and their geographical spread, see Tables 4 and 5, of lands *taken from* taluqdars during the 1834–44 settlement.

19. Imtiaz Husain, *Land Revenue Policy in North India, 1801–33* (Calcutta, 1967), pp. 35–36.

20. Hutchinson, *Allygurh Statistics*, pp. 32–33; and *Aligarh S.R.*, pp. 57–59. In 1806 a total of 827 persons engaged for the entire revenue of Aligarh district.

1808, the area of land let out to farmers had by 1815 shrunk by half to one-third of the total. In Bareilly the number of persons engaging as proprietors rose from 461 at the first settlement to 2,733 twelve years later.[21] In Aligarh also from 1808 onward the farming leases of the early settlements were terminated, and the Jat chieftains confined to their ancestral estates, many of which of course had themselves originated only a few decades earlier as revenue collecting rights.

Even when the farmer was ousted British revenue policy, as enshrined in the Bengal Regulations, still insisted that each holding be held in full proprietary title by a single owner. The greatest beneficiary of this decision was the village headman, or muqaddam. From the outset many villages had been let in farm to muqaddams, often from the refusal of the resident zamindars to accept engagements for their holdings. As disillusionment with the large "speculative" contractors grew in the years after 1808 the British revenue authorities turned increasingly to muqaddami farmers. In Bareilly during the five-year settlement ending in 1817-1818 they may have engaged for as much as 20 percent of the land revenue.[22] Hence the search for a single owner commonly ended with the award of title over the village lands to its muqaddam. As chief raiyat or head of the local zamindari body he clearly stood in a favorable position to secure the status of malguzar, or revenue engager. But no more than the speculating contractor did the muqaddam have any legitimate claim to be regarded as the owner of the village lands. He was at best the first among equals in a community of cosharers.[23]

Almost everywhere these early settlements were based upon an exaggerated notion of the resources available to government, and the assessments were sharply enhanced at frequent intervals. The Aligarh demand, for instance, set at Rs. 19,29,978 in 1804-1805, had risen to Rs. 33,14,022 by 1815-1816, or 71 percent in the first twelve years of British rule; and a further enhancement of 25 percent took place in the subsequent period up to 1833.[24] For the Ceded and Conquered Provinces as a whole (exclusive of Delhi) the land revenue demand rose from Rs. 1,88,12,617 in 1803-1804 to Rs. 2,97,30,997 in 1817-1818, or more than 50 percent within fourteen years.[25] These extraordinarily severe assessments were a product in part of the ignorance of the new British Collectors, who were confronted with revenue records of doubtful accuracy and a subordinate native staff who revealed nothing to their nominal superiors. At the same time, however, the British clearly wished to make

21. L. Brennan, "Social Change in Rohilkhand 1801-33: the Formation of a Zamindar Class," *IESHR* 7 (1970):447-48.
22. *Ibid.*, pp. 45-57.
23. On the position of the muqaddam see Siddiqi, *Agrarian Change*, pp. 26-31.
24. *Aligarh S.R.*, p. 54.
25. Holt Mackenzie Minute of 1 July 1819, *Selections from the Revenue Records of the North-West Provinces 1818-1820* (Calcutta, 1866), pp. 156-57, (hereafter *Rev. Select. 1818-20*).

their new acquisitions pay, and they were anxious to see the revenue rapidly raised to a level sufficient to permit the conclusion of a permanent settlement on the Bengal pattern.[26]

Whatever the reasons for their existence, assessments pitched so steeply simply could not be met. From 1803 onward arrears mounted up rapidly, and nowhere more quickly than on the holdings of the impoverished muqaddams and village zamindars. Although extensive remissions were authorized, particularly following the drought year of 1803–1804, the government soon turned to the forced sale of land to recover the arrears. During a single four-year period from 1810 to 1814, 228 villages with an aggregate *jama* of Rs. 2,53,942 were put up to sale in Aligarh alone.[27] Many sales too, it rapidly became apparent, were marked by fraud, and benefitted only the government officials and bankers who conducted them. These men took advantage of their inside knowledge to buy at depressed prices the most valuable of the properties legitimately brought to sale, and at the same time they contrived to bring about further sales by manipulating the records to show arrears where none were due, or to show a defaulting farmer as the possessor of a salable title. In Kanpur, for instance, Nazir Ali, diwan of the Collector's office, bought eighty-one estates with an assessed revenue of Rs. 1,21,000 for a total sum of Rs. 79,968, while in Allahabad Devikanundan Singh, employed as an amil and revenue surety during the first years of British rule, managed to expand one paternal estate with a jama of Rs. 800 into a property assessed at two lakhs of rupees and comprising one-tenth of the land area of the district.[28]

The enormity of this upheaval, described both at the time and by later historians as "a very extensive and melancholy revolution" in the property rights of the province, precipitated a rancorous controversy within the government, and led in 1821 to the appointment of a special investigative commission.[29] Yet this "revolution" was more apparent than real. Widespread fraud took place only in the three districts of Gorakhpur, Allahabad, and Kanpur, to which alone the jurisdiction of the special commission extended. Elsewhere throughout the Doab and Rohilkhand comparatively little land found its way into the hands of subordinate government servants. Indeed a great many of

26. The plan for permanent settlement was ultimately quashed by the Home Government, reluctant to lose the future revenue such a course would entail in a country still relatively undeveloped. For full discussion of the proposed permanent settlement see Husain, *Land Revenue Policy*, ch. ii.

27. Hutchinson, *Allygurh Statistics*, p. 39.

28. F. N. Wright, *Cawnpore Settlement Report* (Allahabad, 1878), pp. 32–33; Judge Allahabad to Sec. Govt. 1 September 1814, *Selections from Revenue Records North-West Provinces* (Allahabad, 1873), pp. 22–28; and Special Commission Report of 27 April 1822, *ibid.*, pp. 104–17.

29. See, e.g., Mackenzie Minute of 1 July 1819, *Rev. Select. 1818–20*, p. 98; Sulekh C. Gupta, *Agrarian Relations and Early British Rule in India* (Bombay, 1963), p. 118; and Bhanu, *History and Administration*, p. 48. For the official controversy and appointment of the Special Commission see *Selections from Revenue Records* (1873), Part I.

the estates advertised for sale never left the hands of their original holders. So imperfectly developed was the land market that few buyers turned out at most auctions, with the result that the government was obliged to buy up the property at a nominal price. The situation in Aligarh may well have been typical of most of the upper Doab. There:

few estates were purchased and the remainder were resettled in many cases with the original zamindars at reduced jummas. In other cases, where they were temporarily resettled with farmers, they were subsequently restored to the real proprietors on their paying up the balances for which they had been sold. In fact the zamindars seem to have regarded the sale regulation as a kind of Insolvent Act, which released them from their embarrassments, and gave them a fresh lease of their villages on more favorable terms.[30]

In Kanpur and Allahabad the activities of the Special Commission worked in the same direction. By 1828, 96 estates with a jama of Rs. 2,86,826 had been restored to their former owners in Allahabad, while in Kanpur, where a total of 405 auction sales had taken place, 243 were complained against and 185 reversed.[31] Holt Mackenzie, reviewing the sales throughout the province, admitted so early as 1819 that their outcome on the whole provided the "gratifying spectacle of a very extensive restoration of the village proprietors to the independent management of their lands."[32]

As a result, when the work of settlement revision began in earnest in 1833, the land was everywhere still held largely by the same classes as at the time of annexation. In Aligarh, for instance, despite the sale of numerous individual villages throughout the district, "nothing approaching a general change of ownership" had taken place in any pargana.[33] Even in Kanpur district where the early sales were the most severe, the number of villages in the hands of descendants of the founding families, which had already at the time of the cession sunk to 84 percent of the total, had by 1840 declined only a further 24 percent to 60 percent of the total.[34] Extensive social upheaval was to be the product only of the years after 1835, when the new settlements by fixing the rights of all those on the land gave it a value it had never had before. A land market required purchasers as well as sellers, a cognizable title as well as control over the soil. These the proceedings of Bird and Thomason alone brought to rural North India.

30. Hutchinson, *Allygurh Statistics*, p. 39. Of the 228 villages brought to sale in 1810–14, 142 were purchased by the government for Rs. 5 each, and the total sale proceeds amounted to only Rs. 13,232.
31. R. Montgomery, *Statistical Report on the District of Cawnpoor* (Calcutta, 1849), p. 36; and Husain, *Land Revenue Policy*, pp. 55–57. The Special Commission made no attempt to provide redress for complainants in Gorakhpur. In 1829 it was disbanded, and its powers transferred to the new divisional commissioners appointed throughout the province to supervise the work of the district collectors.
32. Mackenzie Minute of 1 July 1819, *Rev. Select. 1818–20*, p. 98.
33. *Aligarh S.R.*, pp. 62–63.
34. *Cawnpore S.R.*, pp. 36–37.

Toward Village Settlement

In 1819, as Secretary to Government in the Territorial Department, Holt Mackenzie drafted a lengthy and detailed Minute on the tenures of northern India. On this foundation was to be built over the subsequent decade and a half a lasting structure of revenue administration for the entire region from Allahabad to the Punjab. Acknowledging that the government still after almost twenty years knew little of conditions in the countryside, Mackenzie advocated, as a starting point for all else, a minute local inquiry into the rights, interests, and privileges of all the classes connected with the soil. This should include, he urged, not only a survey of the land area of each village, and of the individual holdings within it, but the collection of data on such subjects as soil conditions, cropping patterns, livestock, marketing facilities, and caste customs as well. Such information would make possible a land tax based firmly upon ascertained assets, and at the same time apportioned fairly among the various holders of landed rights.[35]

Mackenzie went on, however, anticipating the results of the inquiry, to assert that the village coparcenary bodies were the "sole owners of the land," and as such entitled to a full proprietary title. Where the members of the community held their lands jointly, in pattidari or bhaiacharya tenure, title should be vested in the village body as a whole, and one or two representatives charged with paying the government revenue demand. Taluqdars by contrast were mere middlemen, creatures of the native governments who had handed over to them the right to collect their revenue. Mackenzie was too observant a man not to recognize that such rights were commonly inherited, and that they conveyed if not full ownership of the soil then an accepted right of revenue management. Yet he refused to acknowledge the implications of this admission. He maintained that as taluqdari tenures were the creation of government, what one ruler had created "another might not unnaturally be entitled to destroy." He further argued rather disingenuously that "as far as the tenure was official it could not . . . consistently with the Mahomedan code . . . be considered as strictly hereditary, although in practice almost all the offices connected with the collection of the land revenue and the record of landed property appear to have been continued from father to son."[36] This antagonism toward taluqdars did not originate with Mackenzie. Lord Hastings, the Governor-General, had argued in 1815 that the taluqdar, never a proprietor, had "only a more permanent sort of lease or contract than a common farmer."[37] But Mackenzie was the first to assert boldly that the continued existence of the taluqdars as a class served the interests neither of the state nor of the agricultural community. No longer, he insisted, should the government compromise its authority or the rights of the village proprietors

35. Mackenzie Minute of 1 July 1819, *Rev. Select. 1818-20*, pp. 73, and *passim*.
36. *Ibid.*, pp. 89-92, 149-50.
37. Hastings Minute of 21 September 1815, *ibid.*, p. 334.

"in deference to the supposed influence and ill-subjugated strength" of these men.[38]

Regulation VII of 1822 gave the force of law to most of Mackenzie's recommendations, and set on foot an inquiry unprecedented in the history of rural India. The regulation did, however, permit the officers of government, where such dual "properties" existed, to form the settlement with either the taluqdar or the subordinate village community. In such cases the obligations of both parties, including the rental payments of the subordinate holders, were to be specified in the revenue engagements taken from them. Nor were proprietors alone to be given a secure position on the land. Cultivating raiyats too, so long as they were permanent residents of the village, were entitled to have their rents ascertained and recorded, with the rates established at settlement "maintained during the term of such settlement as an essential part of the assessment."[39]

Unfortunately, however, almost none of these good intentions was ever carried out, for the inquiry soon foundered under its own weight. Too much information was required from too few revenue officers, who in turn were dependent upon too many ill-trained native subordinates. By 1831, nine years after the enactment of Regulation VII, only some 3,600 villages in the entire province had been resettled under its provisions, and of these the settlements of only 69 had been confirmed by the government.[40] The Collectors in the field estimated at the time that forty to fifty years or more would be required to complete the work, while Lord William Bentinck, as Governor-General, looking back on the project in 1835, calculated that it would have taken five times the revenue staff available to see the job through on the scale envisaged by Mackenzie. In the 1820s the British government was simply incapable of carrying out in rural India the kind of detailed statistical inquiry that Mackenzie's Minute and the Regulation of 1822 prescribed.[41]

Apart from its glacial pace, the 1822 settlement was also bedevilled by overassessment. Pressed from above by demands for increased revenue, the settlement officers could not resist the temptation to screw the assessment up to the highest possible figure. In Aligarh, for instance, out of thirty-seven villages in four parganas settled under Regulation VII, thirty-five required reduction of revenue a decade later to the extent of Rs. 6,440 on a jama of Rs. 47,533. Yet this high assessment was not so much the product of a rigid adherence to the principles of "scientific" inquiry as of a complete abandonment of these principles in favor of idiosyncratic estimates. In the Aligarh

38. Mackenzie Minute of 1 July 1819, *ibid.*, pp. 100, 133.
39. Resolution of 1 August 1822, *Selections from Revenue Records North-West Provinces, 1822-1833* (Allahabad, 1873), pp. 20-21, 26, 31, (hereafter *Rev. Select. 1822-33*). For a full account of the Regulation VII settlements see Husain, *Land Revenue Policy*, ch. iv; and Siddiqi, *Agrarian Change*, ch. iii.
40. Bentinck Minute of 20 January 1831, *Rev. Select. 1822-33*, p. 365.
41. For the staffing difficulties that hampered the settlement see John Roselli, "Theory and

villages, when the settlement officer was not satisfied with the jama that his papers suggested as appropriate, he simply appointed "native assessors for the express purpose of raising the estimate of assets."[42] Robert Glyn in Meerut, instead of undertaking a minute investigation of the various sources of income, calculated the gross produce by a rough accounting of the quantity and character of culturable land and by a comparison with the former assessment. Having done this, he then arbitrarily distributed the demand over the various villages so as to make up an account the amount of which would agree with the predetermined total.[43] In such conditions measurement and survey were reduced to little more than a facade behind which "guess and estimate" methods, with their uncertain results, continued to flourish.

The effects of overassessment were exacerbated after 1828 by a severe agrarian depression. Precipitated by a sudden collapse in the indigo market and a decline in raw cotton exports from northern India, the depression took the shape of a shortage of currency and a consequent fall in prices. The agricultural community was exceptionally hard hit. Many, driven to produce crops for export by the pressure of the assessment and the need for ready cash, found themselves overnight with neither markets nor food, while the general fall in prices substantially increased the burden of the assessment for all landholders, who were obliged to pay a fixed revenue demand in cash. One writer has estimated the increase in the real value of the jama from this cause over the period 1828–1833 at some 22 percent.[44] As a result arrears everywhere mounted up, land was thrown out of cultivation, and buyers often could not be found. John Thornton as settlement officer in Aligarh in 1834 saw clearly that the arrears which confronted him were "in almost every case attributable to the assets sinking below the jumma in consequence of the decrease of cultivation."[45] So great was the distress that although the government continued to press for the collection of the full revenue demand, it nevertheless found it necessary over the course of the decade 1822–1833 to relinquish outstanding revenue balances amounting to Rs. 27,02,561.[46]

By 1830 the Bengal government had begun casting about for some way to speed up the pace of settlement. The moving force behind the revision of procedure was the Governor-General, Lord William Bentinck, who remained on tour in the north for three years, from 1830 to 1833, until he had finally

Practice in North India: The Background to the Land 'Settlement' of 1833," *IESHR* 8 (1971):146–51.

42. Hutchinson, *Allygurh Statistics*, pp. 41–42.

43. Husain, *Land Revenue Policy*, p. 165. For further instances see Rosselli, "Theory and Practice," pp. 141–45.

44. Siddiqi, *Agrarian Change*, p. 173. For a general account of the commercial depression see her ch. v.

45. Mursan Settlement Report of 20 December 1834 in Hutchinson, *Allygurh Statistics*, p. 267. See also Stirling's Report of 19 May 1832, *ibid.*, pp. 42–43; and Husain, *Land Revenue Policy*, pp. 179–87.

46. Husain, *Land Revenue Policy*, p. 177. Over one-third of the total sum remitted came from cotton-producing Bundelkhand, the most severely depressed region in the province.

mastered its agrarian system. Bentinck had no doubt as to what was required:

> . . . no time should be further lost in the pursuit of imaginary perfection in the security of the rights of the people and of the just claims of government through forms and surveys that your servants are utterly unable to execute, but we should immediately proceed to ascertain, as best we can, by the simplest plan . . . the real resources of each village, and to give a long lease upon a moderate rent.[47]

With Mackenzie, Bentinck agreed that the taluqdari tenure was "adventitious and artificial," and its holders originally "neither more nor less than contractors with Government for its revenue." But he refused to go on, as Mackenzie had done, to argue for the wholesale eradication of such tenures on grounds of abstract social utility. Some taluqdars, he said, had by royal grant or the tacit consent of the villagers "unquestionably" come to hold their estates in "proprietary" tenure; and these tenures were as deserving of preservation as any other. Nor did the lack of documentary proof necessarily tell against the taluqdar's title, for "circumstantial and traditionary evidence . . . , actual possession, and prescriptive usage" had also to be taken into account. Where proprietary right could not be proven, and the taluqdar was in consequence excluded from management, he should still be awarded a percentage on the revenue and any residuary rights protected.[48]

As it was essential to discriminate carefully between those taluqdars who had, and those who did not have, proprietary rights, so too, Bentinck argued, must the government differentiate between raiyats entitled to fixed rents and those who should be left to fend for themselves. Regulation VII, under Mackenzie's influence, had awarded a fixed rent to all resident cultivators. In the debates of the early 1830s, after Mackenzie had left India, Robert Merttins Bird, as member of the Sadr Board of Revenue on Deputation, took up the advocacy of the raiyat's cause. Convinced that no right of property had ever existed between the monarch and the cultivator, Bird found his ideal in Madras, where Sir Thomas Munro's raiyatwari settlement alone preserved, in his view, the "pure original system of Indian revenue administration." Taluqdars and zamindars were alike no more than intermediaries, dependent for their privileges upon the favor of government. Though this "host of unproductives" could not perhaps be wholly dispossessed, still the government's responsibility was to the raiyat, who was entitled, on the basis of "uninterrupted prescriptive usage," to an authoritatively fixed rent.[49] Bentinck, though anxious to see the raiyats secured in the possession of their fields, refused to go so far. Arguing in 1832 that there was no reason

47. Bentinck to Ravenshaw 11 December 1832, cited in John Rosselli, *Lord William Bentinck* (Berkeley, 1974), p. 258. For a full account of the policy discussions of these years see Husain, *Land Revenue Policy*, ch. v.

48. Bentinck Minute of 26 September 1832, *Rev. Select. 1822–33*, pp. 390–96.

49. R. M. Bird Minute of 25 September 1832, *ibid.*, pp. 419–43, esp. pp. 419–23, 432–33, 441–43.

why the state "should interfere to regulate the wages of agricultural more than that of any other description of labour," he proposed that only those who had held at the same money rent for a consecutive period of twelve years had a right to be protected against enhancement. The following year, fearful that such a rule might involve the creation of rights for some at the expense of others, Bentinck decided to confine the award of fixed rents to those whose right was acknowledged by the proprietor or could be established in court.[50]

How far did any of this accord with the cultivator's actual position on the soil? Though the evidence is ambiguous and conflicting, *khudkasht* (resident) raiyats were usually settled in their holdings and assigned fields for cultivation, which they were not allowed to sell or transfer, by their zamindari overlords. They consequently had no right to occupy land against the will of their superior, much less to pay a fixed or any particular rent. Individual cultivators nevertheless frequently held their lands, often with rents unchanged, for prolonged periods of time, and even passed them on to their heirs. In so doing they acquired by usage a claim to continue such cultivation; or as one settlement officer put it, a "social tie on a zamindar which approximates to a right."[51] Such claims never took on a legal form, however, for in the absence of a rental market and of competition for land, there was no reason for them to do so. Only with the coming of the British, and the definition of property rights in land, did it become necessary to specify what rights the raiyats, now reduced to tenants, possessed, or rather ought to possess. Inevitably, this enterprise took the form of arbitrary rules whose effect was to carve out for certain classes of people certain exemptions from the working of the market forces the British had themselves set in motion. The debate concerned only the groups of people to be favored, and the benefits to be conferred. It was not possible to recover, or preserve, the old ties of raiyat and zamindar.[52]

With regard to the mode of assessment, the Revenue Board proposed, and Bentinck readily agreed to abandon the detailed field-by-field procedure of Regulation VII, formally known as detail-to-aggregate, in favor of its opposite—working down from the top, from aggregate to detail. This meant that the settlement officer would no longer attempt the arduous task of calculating an assessment for each field based on its potential net produce but would rather assess an entire *mahal* (revenue paying unit) at one time on his ascertainment of the aggregate cultivated area and his "general acquain-

50. Bentinck Minute of 20 January 1832, *ibid.*, p. 375; and Sec. G.-G. to Sec. Bd. Rev. 21 May 1833, *ibid.*, pp. 478-79.

51. J. T. Reade, "Minute on the Rights and Conditions of the Ryots of Chukleh Azimgurh," 1 September 1822, cited in Siddiqi, *Agrarian Change*, pp. 35-37. Nonresident (*paikasht*) raiyats, who cultivated land on annual leases, had no recognized rights in the soil, and were excluded from British tenancy legislation.

52. For discussion of the creation, and subsequent restriction, of a rental market see Walter C. Neale, *Economic Change in Rural India* (New Haven, 1962), esp. pp. 34-36, 64-72, and 82-87. For similar developments in Oudh from the 1860s see below ch. 8.

tance" with its peculiar characteristics. The state of irrigation, actual rents paid, the past fiscal history of the village, and its present general state of prosperity would all be taken into consideration, but there would be no "interminable investigation into produce, price, and minute classifications of soil." The assessment would be preceded by, and built upon, a professional survey and measurement of all the village lands, together with the compilation of a permanent record of rights. But once this had been done the settlement operations could proceed expeditiously, and revision on the expiry of the initial term (now set at fifteen to twenty years) would be a relatively easy process. The fairness of the demand could be tested in any individual instance by comparing it with genuine patwari records where they existed or with the data gathered by government officers in the adjudication of rent cases. When the jama was once fixed for a mahal or village, the members of the cosharing body were to be left to distribute it amongst themselves without further interference by the Collector.[53]

The new assessment procedure, on one level, simply involved the abandonment of the attempt to achieve the impossible. In effect it regularized and codified the rough-and-ready methods men like Glyn in Meerut had already adopted in an effort to expedite the process of settlement under Regulation VII. At the same time the new procedure clearly marked a step away from the attempt to apply a theoretical view of rent to Indian land tenures. Not only was the Collector now openly encouraged to exercise his individual discretion in arriving at assessments, but with the net produce of each field not calculated and the actual rents of the cultivating raiyats not fixed, a considerable portion of the profits of cultivation was bound to remain in the hands of the intermediary tenure holders. Under these circumstances, as Bentinck cogently observed, the government revenue demand inevitably became a "tax" on the rental profits these "proprietors" had amassed rather than being a portion of the "rent" defined in Ricardian terms. Nor did this prospect trouble him. Indeed in order to secure adequate remuneration to the holders of such property Bentinck ruled that the state should take only two-thirds of the total outturn of the soil (after the expenses of cultivation and the wages of labor had been deducted) instead of the full rental value to which Ricardian theory entitled it and the 80 to 90 percent it had claimed under Regulation VII.[54]

Ideology and Reform

For years it has been a commonplace of Indian historical writing that the British rulers of India during the 1820s and 1830s were moved by a powerful impulse to reshape the society of that backward land in accordance with the

53. Sec. Bd. Rev. to Sec. G.-G. 25 May 1831, *Rev. Select. 1822-33*, pp. 275-78; and Bentinck Minute of 26 September 1832, *ibid.*, pp. 402, 411-16.
54. Bentinck Minute of 26 September 1832, *ibid.*, pp. 389-91.

abstract theories of early nineteenth-century political economy. This view found its classic expression in Eric Stokes's influential volume, *The English Utilitarians and India*, published in 1959, which argues that Benthamite utilitarianism, and above all Ricardo's theory of rent, exercised a "powerful influence," largely through the work of James Mill as Examiner at the East India House, in shaping the settlement arrangements throughout northern India and Bombay.[55] Later writers, however, have increasingly questioned both the importance of utilitarian theory in shaping revenue policy and the extent to which abstract considerations of any sort made their presence felt in the actual working out of settlements on the ground. Far more consequential, it has been argued, were such factors as the strength of the various powerholders in the countryside, the government's financial requirements, the reliability of the subordinate staff, and the great price deflation of the late 1820s.[56]

No useful purpose surely would be served by opening up all these controversies afresh. It might, however, be convenient to look briefly at the three men most intimately connected with the settlement of the North-Western Provinces—Holt Mackenzie, William Bentinck, and R. M. Bird—to see how far they were moved by a commitment to agrarian reform. For Mackenzie there can be no doubt as to the intensity of his attachment to the Ricardian theory of rent. In his Memorandum of July 1819 he had insisted, echoing Ricardo, that the state had the right to take the full economic rent of the land, calculated according to the net produce principle; and he incorporated much of this doctrine in Regulation VII of 1822.[57] The demand that the government fix the rent paid by each raiyat, with its implication that the settlement holder would not be allowed to make of his holding a valuable private property, was a logical corollary of Ricardo's principles, and one that Mackenzie tenaciously defended. So too was his attack upon aristocratic privilege. James Mill had himself in his *History of British India* vigorously denounced the Bengal zamindars as parasitic rent receivers, unworthy of consideration by the British government; and he returned to the charge in his testimony before a House of Commons committee in 1831, when he argued that taluqdars and zamindars contributed nothing to agricultural improvement but simply lived off the rent fund which rightly belongs to govern-

55. Eric Stokes, *The English Utilitarians and India* (Oxford, 1959), esp. pp. 109-10, 114-15, and 132-33.

56. See, e.g., Husain, *Land Revenue Policy*, pp. 151-62, 237-40, 251-53; Asiya Siddiqi, "Agrarian Depression in Uttar Pradesh in 1828-33," *IESHR* 6 (1969):165-78; Rosselli, "Theory and Practice," esp. pp. 138-39, 145, 163; and Rosselli, *Bentinck*, pp. 252-65.

57. *Rev. Select. 1818-20*, p. 85. For discussion of the Ricardian influence on Mackenzie see Stokes, *English Utilitarians*, pp. 94-99; and Husain, *Land Revenue Policy*, pp. 153-55. The "rent," or "net produce," in Ricardo's view was the surplus above the costs of cultivation which fell to the landholder as an unearned increment merely by virtue of his possessing land of a better than marginal quality.

ment.[58] In urging that these classes be pushed aside Mackenzie simply reiterated the view of the master.

Yet Mackenzie did not go the whole way with James Mill. He was prepared to leave some rent in private hands where the right to appropriate it had been given the sanction of tradition. In particular he was willing to continue the practice of alienating one-tenth of the rent fund to the revenue-engager as an incentive to the improvement of agriculture.[59] Nor did he share Mill's enthusiasm for raiyatwari settlement. While agreeing with Mill that the cultivator represented the best hope for "improved husbandry" in Indian agriculture, Mackenzie refused to bypass the village community in order to secure this objective. Nor was he anxious to see these cosharing bodies broken up. The rights of each individual cosharer were to be ascertained and recorded, and he was to be permitted upon petition to enter into a separate revenue engagement with the government; but Collectors should give this process of separation no encouragement. Mackenzie seems to have realized that these communities could not endure forever under British rule—"we can scarcely touch without danger of destroying"—but he did not wish to see dissolution come about prematurely.[60] In all of this can be found more than a touch of the paternalist's solicitude for ancient rights and customs, together with an administrator's pragmatic desire to avoid disruptive social upheavals. Mackenzie wanted above all to create a revenue system that would work, that would enable the government to collect its dues fairly and expeditiously. To this end he directed the bulk of his energies.

But what then of the taluqdars? Surely they too, as revenue-collecting intermediaries of long standing, had rights that deserved protection. Yet neither Mackenzie nor R. M. Bird were prepared to award them more than a pension, and that grudgingly bestowed. No doubt Ricardian rent theory, and the vision of an egalitarian society that it enshrined, helped drive them to this unyielding position. But here the political and administrative arguments reinforced rather than cut across the dictates of utilitarian theory. The British experience with taluqdars in the Ceded and Conquered Provinces had never been very satisfactory. Refractory and obstructive, these men had not taken easily to the yoke of British law and order, nor had they shown any marked interest in agrarian improvement. Many of the taluqdars had as well, like the Aligarh Jats, risen to prominence only during the disorder of the eighteenth century, and had gained much of their initial footing as revenue contractors for government. As the distinction between revenue

58. James Mill, *History of British India* (London, 1820), 5:416; and Evidence to House of Commons Committee 2 August 1831, *P.P.* 1831, 5:292, and 4 August 1831, *ibid.*, p. 309.
59. Minute of 1 July 1819, *Rev. Select. 1818-20*, pp. 82-84. Mackenzie wished also to base a large part of the assessment on past collections rather than calculations of net produce. *Ibid.*, pp. 75, 79, and *passim*.
60. *Ibid.*, pp. 130, 150.

farming and independent management involved little more than the passage of time and an uninterrupted tenure, together with a vigorous intimidation of the subordinate holders, the British found it easy to tar the one with the brush of the other, and so ensure that even the taluqdars' legitimate claims received scant consideration.

In revising Mackenzie's settlement scheme Bentinck used a good deal of the language of Ricardian rent theory, and he shared many of the prejudices of his adviser R. M. Bird. He even argued on behalf of one of the basic tenets of Ricardian doctrine, the principle that "lands equally productive should be equally taxed, whatever they are made to produce." The productive power of the soil, that is to say, should be assessed rather than the actual crops grown at any one time, with the aim of encouraging the cultivation of more valuable commodities.[61] An integral part of the "net produce" theory of taxation, this scheme was dependent for its success upon detailed field-by-field assessment and the fixing of raiyat rentals. Otherwise its purpose could easily be defeated by the landlord after settlement simply varying the rental according to the crop. Yet Bentinck, as we have seen, explicitly rejected both detail-to-aggregate assessment and any intervention on behalf of the raiyat. For him soil assessment was presumably in large part simply a way to encourage a more productive agriculture. In any case he made no attempt to bring its principles into force in the 1833 settlement.[62]

Despite his familiarity with rent theory Bentinck was clearly moved far more by a pragmatic concern for existing rights than by any enthusiasm for reform. In his view all rights in land, even those of the taluqdars, ought whatever their origin to be maintained, and those who held them made secure in their possession.[63] So far as abstract principles entered into his calculations Bentinck looked to the encouragement of capitalist enterprise. In a manner reminiscent of Adam Smith, if not Lord Cornwallis, he argued that whatever surplus the land could produce ought not to be frittered away among a multitude of needy cultivators, but should rather be concentrated in the hands of the zamindars, for "after all may not this be considered as the capital by which improvement is to be accomplished?"[64] Bentinck's proceedings throughout—from his abandonment of the net produce principle and the attempt to fix raiyat rentals to his relinquishment of a larger proportion of the gross rental—all were directed to this central objective: to give a secure proprietary title and adequate financial resources to those substantial landholders who could be expected to give a lead in the improvement of agriculture.

Like Holt Mackenzie, R. M. Bird frequently used utilitarian theory to

61. For Bentinck's use of "rent" terminology see his Minute of 20 January 1832, *Rev. Select. 1822-33*, p. 370; and Minute of 26 September 1832, *ibid.*, p. 389. For soil assessment see G.-G. to Bd. Rev. 7 April 1831, *ibid.*, pp. 263-64.

62. For the fate of soil assessment see Husain, *Land Revenue Policy*, pp. 217-20.

63. Bentinck Minute of 26 September 1832, *Rev. Select. 1822-33*, pp. 392, 416.

64. G.-G. to Bd. Rev. 7 April 1831, *ibid.*, p. 261.

bulwark his arguments. Defending his advocacy of the fixing of rents, he pleaded that "it was nothing but a desire for the welfare of the people which led me to press it on various occasions. I thought it conducive to the 'greatest happiness principle.'"[65] The business of settlement making in the Ceded and Conquered Provinces, he insisted, where many vested rights cumbered the soil, was "unavoidably a synthetic process," in which government must proceed upward from the tiller of the soil and fix its final assessment on the basis of a detail-to-aggregate procedure.[66] Similarly his denunciation of intermediary rent-receivers was fully in keeping with utilitarian prejudice. Yet on balance Bird appears somewhat less theoretical in his approach to Indian land questions than either James Mill or Mackenzie. The net produce principle, for instance, figures much less prominently in his writings, and then too primarily as an object of skepticism. While it was doubtless wise and right, he said, to try to ascertain the "net rent" payable on each field, such an undertaking, for which there was no precedent in India, could only be a "bootless and hopeless task." He preferred instead to see the money rents actually paid over a series of years made the basis for the fixation of the demand.[67] Bird seems to have been fired above all by a straightforward desire to protect "the weak against the strong." To this end he was bent not only by utilitarian ideology but by the paternalist tradition of Sir Thomas Munro which insisted that the raiyat was the most appropriate object of British solicitude.[68]

The "Revised" Settlement

The discussion of land policy in the North-Western Provinces was brought to an end with the enactment of Regulation IX of 1833, which codified Bentinck's final views on the questions under dispute, and established the legal framework for the ensuing settlement. The long delayed work of revision was entrusted to R. M. Bird and taken up at once. Even with the new and simplified assessment procedures the work dragged on for over a decade. But by the time Bird retired in 1842 the land system of the North-Western Provinces had taken the basic shape it was to retain until the end of British rule.

Despite the enactment of Regulation IX Bentinck's views were not always or everywhere carried into effect during the settlement operations that followed. Part of the problem arose from the inherent difficulties the British faced in carrying through any policy in a land they did not wholly understand with servants who were not wholly reliable. Nor were the policy directives laid down by Bentinck always faithfully adhered to by his successors. Some of these difficulties will be examined in detail in subsequent chapters. For the

---

65. Undated memorandum cited in Husain, *Land Revenue Policy*, p. 200.
66. Minute of 25 September 1832, *Rev. Select. 1822–33*, pp. 419–20.
67. *Ibid.*, pp. 425–26. He was also, like Mackenzie, anxious to avoid the dissolution of the cosharing village community. *Ibid.*, pp. 443–44.
68. *Ibid.*, p. 431. For his praise of Munro see *ibid.*, p. 419.

present it is perhaps sufficient to notice that even Bentinck's own appointee to the charge of the settlement, R. M. Bird, did not attempt to carry all of his superior's views wholeheartedly into practice. Rather he revived much of the earlier program of agrarian reform, and so gave the settlement of the North-Western Provinces a distinctive imprint of his own.

As chief settlement officer Bird did not challenge the basic principles of Regulation IX. He took up and even refined the aggregate-to-detail mode of procedure that the Regulation prescribed, and he willingly permitted the intermediary settlement holders to intercept a portion of the net rent. But, as we have seen, Bird did not share Bentinck's concern to sustain a substantial landholding class, nor the latter's solicitude for the rights of taluqdars. Driven on by the vision, which radical and paternalist shared, of an egalitarian society, Bird turned the settlement machinery instead to the purposes of an attack on class privilege. The taluqdars, who had survived the paper upheavals of the 1820s largely untouched, their leases extended five years at a time, were finally dispossessed and broken after 1835. This process will be examined in detail in the following chapter. But the taluqdars were not the only privileged class to suffer at Bird's hands. Even more harshly treated were the *lakhirajdars*, or *muafidars*, the holders of revenue-free grants.

The award of land free of revenue for religious or charitable purposes, or to reward deserving individuals for their services to the state, was a time-honored Indian custom, followed as readily by the Mughal Emperors and their eighteenth-century successors as by those who had gone before. By the time of the British conquest revenue-free tenures had proliferated to such an extent that they encompassed up to one-sixth the total number of villages in some districts.[69] So early as 1803, two years after the cession, the new rulers, convinced that a good many lakhiraj tenures were held under fabricated titles, ordered the registration of all such holdings, and announced their intention of resuming those of recent or uncertain origin. Little progress was, however, made until 1828 when a special tribunal was set up to adjudicate such cases. The work was then prosecuted with vigor as part of the general revision of settlement. By 1840 the government had resumed over 1,750,000 acres of land assessed with a revenue demand of some twenty-three lakhs of rupees.[70]

Newly victorious conquerors in India had of course never felt themselves under any obligation to uphold the grants of their predecessors, especially where such grants were in return for services no longer rendered; and so earlier regimes, like the British, had from time to time set out to recover some of the lost revenue. But the British were perhaps less scrupulous than those who had gone before, and less haphazard in seeking out tenures for

69. Husain, *Land Revenue Policy*, p. 176.
70. Statement of Sec. Bd. Rev. of 15 May 1840, UPSA B.R. Progs. 15 May 1840, No. 3. See Table 2. A further 360,000 acres were reclaimed after 1840. No detailed breakdown by district is available for these later resumptions.

destruction. The rules for adjudication of lakhiraj cases promulgated in 1825 and 1828, in addition to placing the burden of proof on the claimant, ordered that only grants made by "royal authorities" (such as the Mughal Emperors and the Nawabs of Oudh) would be considered as conveying a valid claim to exemption, and then only if they had been distinctly declared as hereditary. The mere fact of one or two successions having taken place would not constitute proof of hereditary title. The rules further directed that all land that had not been registered under the original orders of 1803 was to be summarily resumed, and released only if the holder could show sufficient cause.

The ruthless character of these proceedings, and the highly authoritarian view of the rights of the state with which they were intertwined, reflected above all the determination of the British to make their Indian possessions pay. Bird, who believed that not even former royal grants should have been spared, argued that the British government "from its nature and position" was of necessity "an expensive Government to India," and one that therefore "must for a long time press on the resources of India." The British, in other words, simply could not afford the luxury of maintaining revenue-free grants. But behind this argument lurked Bird's intense hostility toward leisured aristocratic elites. "If we are to search for the most libertine and disaffected and useless race whom the British Government holds in control it would be found among those who are the principal holders of the Maafee tenures in upper India." It was inequitable and unjust, Bird insisted, to secure benefits to these men—"the favorites of the favorites of Mushroom Nawabs, the dependents of Amils, the spawn of the followers of a host of ephemeral potentates"—at the expense of the ordinary cultivators and hardworking village zamindars. Nor was it sufficient simply to bring these grantees' lands under assessment at the regular rates. As these men had for the most part, in Bird's view, no rights over the soil apart from their position as revenue intermediaries, resumption of their muafi or lakhiraj holdings inevitably brought with it their complete ouster. The settlement was then awarded to the village communities as the "real proprietors and immemorial possessors." The former lakhirajdar got nothing but a subsistence allowance of no more than half the assessed revenue for one life.[71]

Not all officials applauded the stringency of these resumption proceedings. Lord Auckland as Governor-General in 1838, after pointing out that the sudden disturbance, however justifiable, of rights long enjoyed could not but be accompanied by a "loss of confidence and affection," urged Bird to relax the letter of the law wherever possible so as to avoid an "unduly vexatious" scrutiny. In particular he suggested leniency in resuming tiny parcels of land and in interpreting the rule that the grantee must prove the hereditary nature of his tenure. Where grants had already been resumed, he pleaded for the prompt payment of a liberal stipend to those in distress, and a stop put to the

71. Bird Minute of 31 January 1840, B.R. Progs. 31 January 1840, No. 21.

practice of indiscriminately making over all holdings to the local villagers without first investigating whether they might form "distinct properties in the hands of the maafeedars."[72] Auckland's complaints were echoed five years later by H. H. Thomas, a special commissioner in Agra, who condemned bitterly the "sweeping and arbitrary measures" of the revenue authorities, which, he said, "loudly called for correction."[73] Yet very little remedial action took place. Not even Auckland's "relaxation" of the resumption laws made much difference. Though this measure roused the muafidars to flood the offices of government with petitions, many were women secluded in *parda* or men so impoverished they were unable to prosecute their claims, while others so long delayed submitting their appeals that the statute of limitations had run out.[74]

As Bird set out during the revised settlement to break the hold of the privileged classes on the land, so too did he endeavor to secure as best he could the position of the resident cultivating raiyat. Although his cherished scheme for the government fixation of rents was repudiated by Bentinck, nevertheless as the settlement proceeded Bird, together with the officers working under him, managed to secure widespread acceptance for a principle equally arbitrary, but of another sort; that twelve years' continuous occupancy gave the cultivator a prescriptive right to remain on the land. The "Directions for Settlement Officers," first published in 1844, gave a cautious but authoritative sanction to this practice by stating that: "Those, who have for a number of years occupied the same field at the same or at equitable rates, are held to possess the right of continued occupancy, whilst those, whose tenure is not similarly defined, are considered tenants at will."[75] By 1856 the existence of cultivating rights of occupancy had become so generally acknowledged that the Board of Revenue laid it down as a matter of course that immunity from summary ejectment consisted "simply in independent occupancy for twelve

---

72. Sec. Govt. N.W.P. to Sec. Bd. Rev. 9 March 1838, NAI Rev. Dept. Consultations April 1839, No. 50. Auckland at that time held the government of the N.W.P. under his direct charge.

73. Add. Spec. Commr. Agra to Sec. Govt. N.W.P. 25 March 1843, B.R. Progs. 28 April 1843, No. 16.

74. *Ibid.* In response to Thomas's letter the government ordered that all petitions of appeal which could not be taken up under the rules then in force, but which might be favorably considered under the "*present intentions* of government," be forwarded to the Divisional Commissioners (ital. in original), Sec. Govt. N.W.P. to District Judges 13 April 1843, *ibid.*, No. 17. In 1844 the government also acknowledged that, while there was a "presumption" in favor of the existence of "proprietors with whom the settlement should be made" on the estates of ex-muafidars still "it may be otherwise"; and so settlement officers were ordered to investigate all cases on their merits. "Directions for Settlement Officers," reprinted in *Directions for Revenue Officers in the North-Western Provinces* (Calcutta, 1858), pp. 59-60. By that time, however, most of the settlements had already been concluded.

75. "Directions for Settlement Officers," pp. 64-65. The first explicit reference to a twelve-year rule for the award of occupancy rights occurs in James Thomason's Azamgarh Settlement Report (1837), *Selections from the Records of the Government of the North-Western Provinces*, Part 14 (Agra, 1854), p. 149, (hereafter *Sels. Recs. Govt. N.W.P.*). For a general account of the origin and growth of the twelve-year occupancy rule see Note of 29 May 1863 by W. Muir, Senior Member Board of Revenue, in N.W.P. Rev. Progs. 9 September 1865, No. 19.

Table 2. Resumption of Revenue-Free Land, to 1840

Division	District	Quantity of land resumed (acres)	Jama (rupees)
Delhi	Panipat	13,354	19,681
	Haryana	8,905	2,828
	Delhi	14,263	10,918
	Rohtak	12,277	11,891
	Gurgaon	15,507	26,317
Total		64,306	71,635
Meerut	Saharanpur	1,74,033	1,95,737
	Muzaffarnagar	45,948	53,126
	Meerut	40,858	54,263
	Bulandshahr	80,130	79,294
	Aligarh	29,703	68,377
Total		3,70,672	4,50,797
Rohilkhand	Bijnour	91,702	1,77,671
	Moradabad	43,614	41,640
	Budaon	82,561	81,700
	Pilibhit	8,267	11,107
	Bareilly	32,218	43,291
	Shahjahanpur	22,879	24,531
Total		2,81,241	3,79,940
Agra	Mathura	88,708	1,60,780
	Agra	90,278	1,63,628
	Farrukhabad	27,490	37,411
	Mainpuri	6,157	10,132
	Etawah	10,332	23,247
Total		2,22,965	3,95,198
Allahabad	Kanpur	[Collector's returns not completed]	
	Fatehpur	20,464	49,881
	Hamirpur	26,438	56,180
	Banda	17,468	20,288
	Allahabad	60,088	1,19,547
Total		1,24,458	2,45,896
Benares	Gorakhpur	2,63,643	1,70,542
	Azamgarh	1,07,215	1,61,939
	Jaunpur	21,333	62,686
	Mirzapur	72,200	54,150
	Benares	28,457	28,000
	Ghazipur	2,03,117	2,93,117
Total		6,95,965	7,70,434
Grand total[a]		17,59,607	23,21,953

a. The total jama computed by Divisions (Rs. 23,13,900) does not agree with the grand total. The inconsistency is in the original manuscript. See Sec. Bd. Rev. Statement 15 May 1840, B.R. Progs. 15 May 1840, No. 3.

years," and looked ahead to the growth of a transferable title on the part of the cultivators.[76] The protection thus afforded fell well short, of course, of an authoritatively fixed rent, but it left the raiyat no longer wholly at the mercy of custom and the courts.

In 1859 the twelve-year occupancy rule was incorporated in the famous Act X, which for the first time gave it legal standing. The Act further strengthened the position of the occupancy tenant by securing to him—what so far had been more talked about than implemented—a right to pay rent at a "fair and equitable rate" liable to enhancement only if the rate was below the prevailing rental of the area, or if the value of the land and its produce had increased other than by the efforts of the cultivator.[77] Bird's concern for the well-being of the raiyat had thus by midcentury found its way onto the statute book, where it remained at the heart of all later tenancy legislation in the province.

The Regulation IX assessment procedures also came increasingly under scrutiny as the settlement progressed. From the outset Bird, although supporting the detail-to-aggregate mode of procedure, had argued for the use of cash rents actually paid, rather than some abstract "net produce," as the basis for determining the level of assessment. Bentinck, rejecting this suggestion, had, as we have seen, turned instead to assessments based upon general estimates of productivity for entire mahals. While no doubt a great improvement over the arbitrary and erratic methods used before 1822, this aggregate-to-detail procedure had in practice severe shortcomings of its own. Above all it still left, as we shall see in a subsequent chapter, altogether too much room for a heavy assessment, with the pernicious social consequences that brought in its wake. Nor, despite its reputation for "scientific" precision, was the 1833 settlement everywhere built upon the detailed field surveys and accurate records of rights the law prescribed. The official revenue manual of the province itself acknowledged in 1848 that the record formed at the time of settlement was "often erroneous and imperfect." No blame was attributed to anyone. But the system then "was new, and imperfectly organized; the persons selected for its performance were not always the best qualified; and the work was necessarily performed with far more rapidity than was compatible with accuracy."[78]

As time went on, and agriculture became increasingly commercialized,

76. Sec. Bd. Rev. to Sec. Govt. N.W.P. 11 July 1856, Abstract B.R. Progs. 11 July 1856, No. 246.

77. The "Directions for Settlement Officers" had authorized the settlement officer, while fixing the demand at the time of settlement, to "fix the rates payable by the cultivators to the proprietors." But there was to be no prohibition upon the proprietors "raising their terms upon the cultivators in such amount as may be equitable during the period of the settlement" (*Directions for Revenue Officers*, pp. 66–67). How far rents actually were fixed, or their "equitableness" determined, is not clear from the available evidence. Where rents had been fixed, Act X made their enhancement easier, for now revenue officers, and not just the courts, were empowered to award an increase when a case could be made out on grounds of equity.

78. "Directions for Collectors" (1848) reprinted in *Directions for Revenue Officers*, p. 266.

cash rents spread ever more widely across the countryside. Hence when the Regulation IX settlements began to come up for revision in the 1850s on the expiry of their initial thirty-year terms, Bird's proposal that the assessment be based on actual cash rents at last came into its own. With the "more certain information" as to the assets of an estate which cash rents provided, a closer approach to scientific precision was now for the first time possible in assessment. Under the Saharanpur rules of 1855, therefore, the government formally abandoned the aggregate-to-detail procedure in favor of the separate assessment of each individual village on the basis of its prevailing rent-rates. But this new procedure carried with it, as the government was fully aware, the potentiality of even more severe overassessment, for two-thirds of the "*real* average assets" was a heavier rate than could be borne over a long course of years by the average village proprietor. So the new rules reduced the state demand to 50 percent of the average net assets.[79] The last remnants of utilitarian theory, if not of actual overassessment, thus disappeared from the land system of the North-Western Provinces. The shaping of an agrarian policy was complete.

79. For the Saharanpur rules see Sec. Bd. Rev. to Commr. Meerut 16 January 1855, B.R. Progs. 16 January 1855, No. 39 (ital. in original). For a general account of the changes in assessment procedure see W. H. Moreland, *The Revenue Administration of the United Provinces* (Allahabad, 1911), pp. 41–43. For the problems encountered in using actual rentals for assessment purposes see Elizabeth Whitcombe, *Agrarian Conditions in Northern India* (Berkeley, 1972), pp. 122–32; and below ch. 8. The Court of Directors in 1837 had extended the term of the settlements from twenty to thirty years.

Four | *The Fall of the Taluqdars*

T OWARD THE large landholders, or taluqdars, the attitude of R. M. Bird and his disciples was, as we have seen, one of undisguised hostility. Whether moved by an idealized vision of the Indian village community, or Ricardian schemes for agrarian reform, or even simply a desire to increase the government's revenue, these men, placed in charge of the settlement under Regulation IX of 1833, wasted no time in moving against their landed adversaries. Yet the dispossession of the taluqdars was not to be easily or quickly accomplished, nor was it to be done without controversy. Moreover, even when the settlement was completed, and the reformers' victory confirmed, the taluqdars still remained a force to be reckoned with on the rural scene. So it is worth examining the process of dispossession with some care, and with particular attention to the social context in which events took place.

Mursan: The Policy Enunciated

In December 1833 John Thornton arrived in Aligarh as settlement officer with instructions to complete the revised land revenue settlement of the district. Among the first areas to come under his scrutiny was the pargana of Mursan, together with its neighbor Hathras. Both tracts were held by Tenwa

Map 4. Aligarh District.

Jat taluqdars, descendants of the enterprising Nandram who had won from the Emperor Aurangzeb the revenue management of tappas Jawar and Tochigarh. Jawar, the site of the initial Tenwa Jat settlement in the area, was by the late seventeenth century subdivided into a half dozen clusters of villages, each inhabited by Jat zamindars who traced their origin to the common ancestor who had founded the parent village. These clusters in the course of time became known as taluqas and were parceled out after Nandram's death among his sons and grandsons. Nandram's acquisition of revenue-collecting rights provided the family with a springboard for further expansion. Indeed even before Aurangzeb's award Nandram had taken advantage of the confusion of the 1658 war of succession to incorporate several non-Jat villages into Jawar tappa. With the legitimation of the state revenue authority, and the secure footing of their zamindari possession in Jawar, Nandram's descendants in the eighteenth century, as we have seen, were able to bring under their control the entire parganas of Mursan and Hathras. So strongly based was their position that even occasional reversals of fortune did not threaten it. When Phup Singh was expelled from Mursan by Surajmal of Bharatpur in 1757, he simply retired to Sasni, some twelve miles away, where he built a "celebrated fortress" from which he returned to Mursan in 1761. Driven away a second time by Najaf Khan, and kept out of possession for almost twenty years, he was yet able within a few years of his return in 1785 to recover all his lost territories.[1]

1. Atkinson, *Statistical Account*, 2:1:427–30; and H. R. Nevill, *Aligarh D.G.*, pp. 93–94, 286–87. See also pp. 53–54 above.

At the time of the British conquest Mursan and Hathras estates thus comprised areas of ancestral Jat settlement together with those wrested forcibly from other holders. Much of Hathras, its lands conquered from such men as the Porach taluqdar Rattan Singh, was of the latter sort, and left Daya Ram master of its settled Rajput villagers. In Mursan by contrast, though much of the estate, including Mursan town itself, fell outside Nandram's original grant, the raja (as he was now known) was of the same caste and clan with many of the village occupants, and stood over them as lineage chieftain as well as revenue-paying intermediary.[2] After the upheaval that saw the defiance and expulsion of Daya Ram in 1816 the Hathras estate was broken up into several smaller taluqas. The five Jawar estates Daya Ram had swallowed in the later eighteenth century were restored to their former chieftains, Daya Ram's distant relatives, while the remainder of the property was handed over to members of the elder line whom Daya Ram had superseded. The discontinuity between villager and taluqdar throughout all except the Jawar holdings remained unaltered.[3]

In 1824, following the death of Raja Bhagwant Singh of Mursan, the British first began to move against the Aligarh taluqdars. Over the protests of the district Collector, who urged that Bhagwant's son Tikam Singh be awarded a lifetime assessment similar to the one his father had enjoyed, the Board of Revenue ruled that the revenue demand should be settled directly upon the village zamindars, and left open to revision after five years. The raja retained the title of *sadr malguzar*, or principal revenue engager, but his power of interference was confined to the collection of the sum fixed upon each village and its payment into the government treasury. He was permitted to retain 15 percent of the revenue as a maintenance allowance, plus a further Rs. 644 a month to meet the expenses of collection.[4] This arrangement, however, soon proved unworkable. Not only had the question of proprietary title been left purposely vague, but the assessment pressed unequally upon the various villages of the estate. As a result arrears mounted up, and the raja, forced to make good the difference, suffered heavy losses, nearly a lakh of rupees in five years, which a summary revision in 1829 did not materially lessen.[5] Thornton thus arrived confronted with problems of both assessment and tenure.

In his final report Thornton admitted that he began his work prejudiced in

2. Smith, *Aligarh S.R.*, p. 27. For details see Table 3.
3. Atkinson, *Statistical Account*, 2:433. Of the original 313 villages of the Hathras estate, 89 were included in the five Jawar taluqas of Simardhari, Barha, Gubrari, Karil, and Karas. A further 96 villages were given to the son and grandson of Daya Ram's elder brother Nawal Singh as taluqas Mendu and Shahzadpur. These totals were later reduced by consolidation to 41 (Jawar) and 52 (Mendu and Shahzadpur).
4. Colltr. Aligarh to Sec. Bd. Rev. 31 July 1824, UPSA B.R. Progs. 19 August 1824, No. 4; and Sec. Bd. Rev. to Sec. Govt. 19 August 1824, *ibid.*, No. 5. The Collector had, however, recommended that the fixed assessment be raised from Bhagwant's Rs. 80,000 to Rs. 1,50,000 annually.
5. Atkinson, *Statistical Account*, 2:437; and Hutchinson, *Allygurh Statistics*, pp. 241-42.

favor of the settled village zamindars "as having the first and most un-doubted claim to be admitted to engagements on fair and equitable terms." Wherever he found in possession descendants of the original settlers, who had held their village uninterruptedly since before it came under the taluq-dar's authority and had not by their own act forfeited their position, Thorn-ton awarded them the right to engage for the revenue. Such was the case in two-thirds of Mursan and nearly all of Hathras. The Mursan raja's claim that the original zamindari lineages had everywhere died out, leaving the current holders mere cultivators planted by his predecessors, Thornton disputed by examining the pattern of village settlement. In each village he found the zamindars for the most part of the same caste, descended from a common ancestor, and in possession of plots that had remained distinct from the remote past. In many cases, he said, describing his work in nearby Hasayan, "I could trace that gradual spread of cultivation from a central point and consequent formation of new villages as offshoots from the one first established, which affords such undeniable proof of the rights of those who in times past thus appropriated and parcelled out the soil." Moreover, he asserted, the right of these men to manage the village lands had been recognized by the different eighteenth-century rulers of the Doab, who had had them recorded in the qanungos' papers as zamindars or muqaddams.[6]

   In one-third of Mursan, however, and in smaller tracts elsewhere, Thorn-ton discovered that the original zamindari stock had become "extinct." These areas he awarded in full proprietorship to the taluqdar. Just how this "extinction" was brought about, and in which areas it took place, are not en-tirely clear. In Jawar certainly, and in that "large part" of Mursan where the local communities were Tenwa Jats, of the same original stock as the taluq-dars themselves, there existed "in every village" the descendants of those who first settled there and for whom the villages were named. In Mendu and Shahzadpur too, taluqas formed out of Daya Ram's estate, the grantees, per-haps because of the recency of their tenure, had made "no attempt" to set aside the subordinate holders, with the result that the village occupants there were recorded under Thornton's settlement as the "hereditary owners."[7] In Kanka and Kajraut by contrast, together with the neighboring Moheriya taluqa of Mursan, the "ancient zamindars," Janghara Rajputs, had been almost wholly dispossessed. In part this outcome was the result of some un-known "calamity" associated with the invasion of the Jat Raja Surajmal and the great famine of 1783, but those Rajput zamindars who escaped its effects

   6. Hutchinson, *Allygurh Statistics*, pp. 243–44; and Thornton Settlement Report of Taluqa Hasayan 20 December 1836, B.R. Progs. 9 May 1837, No. 25.
   7. Thornton Settlement Report of Pargana Hathras 10 May 1836, B.R. Progs. 27 September 1836, No. 16; and Assessment Statement for Jawar Taluqas, *ibid.*, No. 20. In Jawar, however, "the structure of the village communities had in many cases been entirely broken up, and required renewal from their foundation," by the adjudication of disputes among shareholders and the adjustment of debts, before the settlement could be concluded. In Jawar also *sir* land amounting to 6 percent of the total acreage was left with the former taluqdars.

Table 3. The Consolidation of the Mursan Estate

Taluqa	Number of: Villages	Acres	Original Zamindari holders	Date of acquisition	Villages settled with muqaddams
			(Acquired by Khosal Singh by Favor of Saadat Khan)		
Ahri	4	1,270	Tenwa Jats	1731	4
Baramai	6	1,748	Bhumronea Jats	1733	5
Dayalpur	5[a]	2,303	Tenwa Jats	1731	5
Gopi	7	2,012	Tenwa Jats	1731	6
Mursan Khas	9[a]	1,443	Brahmins, Khoken Jats, and Tenwa Jats (site of Makhan's original settlement)	1732	9
Puteni	12	1,921	Dhatra Jats	1732	7
			(Acquired by Raja Phup Singh)		
Arr. Lashkarpur	11	5,212	Soreit Jats	1767	11
Bisana	15	3,703	Gahlot Rajputs	1753	13
Chotwa	6	1,226	Tenwa Jats	1767[b]	5
Kotha	17	4,150	Porach Rajputs (6 villages), Pahtowat Jats (11 villages)	1750	16
Moheriya	45	26,035	Janghara (17 v.), Bhat (22 v.), and Porach Rajputs (6 v).	1760s	12
Patta	4	1,732	Dhatra Jats (3 v.), and Brahmin purohit (1 v.). Subsequently Tenwa Jats acquired share by marriage.	1767[b]	4
Rohi	2	1,710	Gahlot Rajputs. Subsequently 3 Brahmin families acquired shares; estate divided by mutual consent.	1750s	2

				1760s[b]	2
Tuksan	13	4,337	Original Porach holders dis-possessed. Only the 2 Brahmin muqaddams remained.		
			(Acquired by Raja Bhagwant Singh)		
Dunaitia	16	3,299	Pachi Jats, with their Brahmin purohits (15 v.), and Tenwa Jats (1 v.)	1796	16[c]
Madan	5	1,723	Dingraha Jats	1795	5[c]
Sonk	13	3,195	Jats	1795	13[c]
Miscellaneous	20	8,704	Various	Varied	12

[a] A further 13 villages, not included in the above totals, were held revenue-free (*muafi*) by the rani and other members of the taluqdar's family. Two villages were given over for the support of temples in Brindaban.

[b] The villages of these taluqas, held by Nandram's son Bhoj Singh, were transferred after his death to Phup Singh in return for the payment of debts.

[c] The zamindars of three villages in Dunaitia, three in Madan, and one in Sonk at the time of settlement were induced by the raja in return for a consideration to relinquish their claims in his favor. As a result a total of 140 villages were actually settled with the village muqaddams under the Thornton settlement, and 70 remained with the raja.

Source: This information is taken from the tabular statements appended to Thornton's Mursan Settlement Report of 20 December 1834, IOL N.W.P. Rev. Progs. October 1837, No. 113. (This material is not printed, with the rest of the report, in Hutchinson, *Aligurh Statistics*.)

were then "expelled" by the taluqdars. Most commonly this involved loss of managerial rights and a reduction to the status of an ordinary cultivator, but "in some instances many years had elapsed since they [the former zamindars] had even ceased to reside in the villages for which they sued."[8]

Thornton speculated that "the extent to which the original communities have been annihilated is proportioned to the smallness of the Talookdar's estate. Whenever the latter is of small size, the interest of the Talookdar clashes more immediately with that of all others who put forward a claim to the occupancy of the soil. So that . . . the weaker party if hopeless of protection is forced to yield, and their [the zamindars] entire expulsion is effected."[9] But the process surely had much to do as well with the nature of the ties between taluqdar and village holder. Where the two enjoyed no shared heritage of caste or kinship, the likelihood of struggle, and of eviction, was, in Aligarh as in Oudh, undoubtedly greater. Almost certainly the opposition of Jat taluqdar and Rajput villager exacerbated the conflict in Kanka and Kajraut. In Somna, where the settled Chauhan Rajputs came under the authority of a Jadon taluqdar in the late eighteenth century, the three sons of the original holder after 1825 secured "the entire deprivation and expulsion" from the estate of all those who had once possessed zamindari rights.[10] Here too the difference in clan affiliation no doubt gave an edge to the persisting antagonism of superior and subordinate landholder. By the 1820s the growing British intention to define and settle landed rights may also have added an element of urgency to the process of dispossession as the taluqdar came to realize that only an uncontested zamindari title could secure his future position.[11]

Despite his award of revenue rights in Mursan to the village zamindars, Thornton wished to see the raja continued as sadr malguzar for the entire estate. This he felt was due the raja in view of his long continued tenure as taluqdar, and carried with it the right not only to collect the revenue on behalf of the government but to eject defaulters and assume the management of their villages. To forestall extortion Thornton placed the tahsildar who supervised the collections under the joint control of the taluqdar and the district Collector.[12] This arrangement had, however, but a short life, for no sooner had it come into operation than Tikam Singh petitioned to be freed of its obligations, while the already hesitant Thornton saw in the raja's refusal

8. Thornton Settlement Report of 18 October 1836, B.R. Progs. 9 May 1837, No. 30. In Hasayan also, Thornton was unable to restore the original zamindars in 26 of its 43 villages "in consequence of their long and entire dispossession" (Settlement Report of 20 December 1836, *ibid.*, No. 25).

9. Kanka and Kajraut Settlement Report of 18 October 1836, *ibid.*, No. 30.

10. Thornton Settlement Report of 12 September 1837, B.R. Progs. 24 September 1839, No. 2.

11. For further discussion see ch. 1; and Stokes, "Agrarian Society and the Pax Britannica," *Modern Asian Studies* 9 (1975):509–13.

12. Hutchinson, *Allygurh Statistics*, pp. 250–51, 267.

to cooperate ample evidence of his intention to bring the independent villages of the estate to ruin. As a result the raja in September 1835 was relieved from all responsibility for the collection of the revenue, and the village zamindars were instructed to pay their dues directly to the government tahsildar at Hathras. The raja's malikana, or maintenance allowance, was then paid over to him in cash by the tahsildar.[13]

The Commissioner of Agra, T. J. Turner, who had taken the initiative in overturning Thornton's scheme, insisted that direct collection from the village communities would not "in the slightest degree" infringe the rights of the taluqdar. Indeed, he said, the raja would have "no just cause of dissatisfaction" for the payment of his malikana allowance would be "equally certain and unattended with the expense of realizing both his own and the Government's dues."[14] Yet the new collection procedure soon precipitated a dramatic change in the position of the raja. As it was obviously inappropriate to make a man responsible for arrears, or the beneficiary of default, on the part of tenure holders over whose revenue payments he had no control whatsoever, when the new settlement was confirmed Tikam Singh was stripped of the title of sadr malguzar for the two-thirds of his estate awarded to the village occupants. At the same time his allowance, being no longer even partly a return for services rendered, was converted to a resumable grant, awarded the raja for one lifetime only "in conformity with the liberal plan of the British Government not to resume even an usurped right without some compensation."[15]

Mainpuri: The Policy Established

The precedents set in Mursan were soon followed elsewhere. In the Shiurajpur estate of Kanpur district the right to engage for the revenue had already in 1819 been awarded to the muqaddams in all but six villages, but the district officers of the time had looked upon the raja, because of his ancient lineage and possession of zamindari *sanads* (grants) dating back to Akbar's time, as holding the ultimate right of proprietorship. A special survey undertaken in 1840 by H. Rose, the settlement officer, brought the pargana fully into line with Mursan. The village communities were vested with proprietary title as well as malguzari management, while the raja's sanads were read as giving him no more than a money assignment from the revenue in return for services rendered. Rose grudgingly conceded, however, that it would be unwise suddenly to withdraw perquisites so long acknowledged, even if initially usurped; and so he recommended that the Shiurajpur

13. Depty. Colltr. Aligarh to Commr. Agra 16 February and 5 April 1835, B.R. Progs. 14 July 1835, Nos. 25, 31; and Sec. Govt. Agra to Sec. Bd. Rev. 4 September 1835, IOL Agra Rev. Progs. September 1835, No. 13.

14. Commr. Agra to Depty. Colltr. Aligarh 2 April 1835, UPSA B.R. Progs. 14 July 1835, No. 30; and Commr. Agra to Sec. Bd. Rev. 28 May 1835, *ibid.*, No. 24.

15. Sec. Bd. Rev. to Sec. Govt. Agra 14 July 1835, *ibid.*, No. 34.

taluqdar, like his counterparts in Mursan and Hathras, be granted a cash allowance for his lifetime.[16] In Etah, seat of a Chauhan raj for centuries, the settlement officer G. F. Edmonstone, conscious of the family's "antiquity and rank" and its "unswerving loyalty" to the British government, recommended that the raja be continued in possession of his taluqa. The Board of Revenue under R. M. Bird would, however, have none of it. They directed the Commissioner to have the estate resettled so far as possible with the village communities, with the result that the taluqdar lost 119 of the 139 villages of the estate.[17]

By far the most controversial taluqdari settlement, however, was that of the estate of the raja of Mainpuri. A Chauhan Rajput family settled in the district since the time of the Delhi Sultans, the Mainpuri rajas had over the centuries carved out for themselves an estate, known as taluqa Manchanna, which comprised in 1840 some 158 villages assessed with a jama of just over one lakh of rupees. Throughout much of the central portion of the estate, in parganas Mainpuri and Bhongaon, the land was held by Chauhan zamindars who looked up to the raja as the head of the clan. Edmonstone as settlement officer had initially thought to secure the rights of the village holders by sub-settlement under the raja, as he had proposed in Etah, but the Board of Revenue ordered him here as well to carry out the settlement according to "the established principle and method," while Edmonstone himself came to the same conclusion during his tour of the estate. That experience convinced him that "proprietary communities" existed throughout the estate, that they had resided in their respective villages for centuries, and that they had either been entrusted by the raja with the management of the cultivation or been given an annual money compensation in recognition of that right. Indeed "in some cases the tenure of these unfortunate people has been so completely recognized, and so stable, that the lands are divided into thokes and puttees [shares] paying separately their respective portion of the jumma by mutual agreement, in the manner of a perfect byachara estate." The raja by contrast, despite his own lengthy possession and admitted power to regulate the tenure of these subordinate holders, had no claim to be recognized as the "rightful proprietor" of the estate. Edmonstone accordingly recommended that some 110 villages, or two-thirds of the estate, be settled with the occupying *muqaddam biswadars* as the village holders were now termed. These beneficiaries included both Chauhans, who gained 29 of the estate's 46 villages in pargana Mainpuri, as well as Brahmins, Bais Rajputs, and even Kachhis and Chamars in the recently conquered Laygaon taluqa.[18]

16. Settle. Offr. Cawnpore to Commr. Allahabad 22 August 1840, IOL N.W.P. Rev. Progs. 31 December 1842, No. 337. See also Montgomery, *Statistical Report*, pp. 75–78. Shiurajpur estate comprised a total of 106 villages with a jama of Rs. 50,001.

17. Edmonstone Settlement Report of 5 September 1839, UPSA B.R. Progs. 3 September 1841, No. 5; and Commr. Agra to Sec. Bd. Rev. 26 March 1841, B.R. Progs. 14 May 1841, No. 45.

18. Settle. Offr. Mainpuri to Commr. Agra 18 April 1840, B.R. Progs. 15 May 1840, No. 25; Sec. Bd. Rev. to Commr. Agra 28 April 1840, *ibid.*, No. 23; Edmonstone Settlement Report of

Before Edmonstone's proposals could reach the Board of Revenue, where they would be assured of a favorable reception, they had to pass through the office of the Commissioner of the Agra Division. Similarly, before the board's orders could take effect, they had to be approved by the Lieutenant Governor. Both these officials came out strongly in opposition to Edmonstone's arrangements, and thus precipitated what ultimately became the last great debate over settlement policy in the North-Western Provinces. The Commissioner, R. M. Hamilton, denying that "the rule followed in Talooka Moorsaun" was necessarily binding everywhere, pointed to the assistance rendered by the rajas of Mainpuri in the days when the Marathas were a menace to the Doab and urged that the government had still some obligations to that "remnant of rank" which the British system had not yet swept away. Nor, he maintained, was the alleged incapacity of the present raja any ground for depriving the family forever of their importance. After all the British revenue system had itself not infrequently been marked by exaction and unjust proceedings. He concluded by suggesting that at the very least the taluqdari allowance should be declared the right of the rajas of Mainpuri in perpetuity, not merely a resumable life interest.[19]

Countering the Commissioner's arguments, the Board of Revenue went laboriously over the whole ground traversed years before in the discussions over Mursan. Indeed the passage of time had, if anything, driven them to a more extreme position, for they now asserted that the taluqdar was only a superior holder created by patent, "appointed in former times by Government at its pleasure, holding his office *durante bene placito* and consequently removable at will." They larded their letter to the government with sarcastic remarks at the Commissioner's expense, and totally repudiated his comparison of British and taluqdari revenue administration. They even suggested pointedly that the interests of the raja's family would be better served by a life than by a hereditary allowance, for a spendthrift holder would then be unable to mortgage it to the impoverishment of his successors.[20]

But the last word lay with the Lieutenant Governor. A conservative of the old Bengal school, sympathetic to rank and tradition, T. C. Robertson was appalled by the wholesale destruction of the aristocracy in the North-Western Provinces. In April 1842 while reviewing the progress of the settlement operations to that date he had vigorously protested the "levelling character" of the new policy. It was, he said, "a fearful experiment" to try to govern without the aid of any intermediate agency of indigenous growth.[21] Three months later, following a series of bitter exchanges with the Board of Revenue, he

15 November 1840, B.R. Progs. 3 September 1841, No. 19; and M. A. McConaghey, *Report on Settlement of Mainpuri District* (Allahabad, 1875), pp. 131, 216, 294, and *passim*, (hereafter *Mainpuri S.R.*). There is no indication of the fate of the zamindari communities in the villages settled with the raja, which included 17 villages in pargana Mainpuri and 7 in Laygaon, of a total of some 51.

19. Commr. Agra to Sec. Bd. Rev. 30 April 1841, B.R. Progs. 3 September 1841, No. 18.
20. Sec. Bd. Rev. to Sec. Govt. N.W.P. 3 September 1841, *ibid.*, No. 39.
21. Minute of 15 April 1842, *P.P.* 1852–53, 75:125.

overturned the settlement of Manchanna. In language much like Hamilton's he spoke of the long possession and the presumption thus arising in the raja's favor, the acknowledged services rendered by his predecessors and the impolicy "of appearing forgetful in our prosperity of obligations incurred in a season of difficulty," and lastly of the necessity for some clear proof of misconduct on the part of the raja before pronouncing a sentence of "perpetual degradation" on his family. In the absence of any convincing evidence of mismanagement Robertson saw no reason why the arbitrary rule of Mursan should outweigh the rights derived from length of possession and loyal service, and so he ordered revenue engagements to be taken from the raja for the entire taluqa.[22]

Robertson's decision did not, however, by any means still the controversy. There was first of all the matter of the expenses of collection which would now have to be borne by the taluqdar. To ease the burden Robertson suggested that the raja be given an allowance of 3 percent on the government revenue. The board protested that since the raja was still to retain the 18 percent taluqdari allowance, given in large part as compensation for exclusion from management, it was hardly appropriate to restore him to management and then given him a further allowance for the expenses occasioned by the restoration. If the raja wished to possess the "dignity and consideration," and the rights over the holdings of defaulting undertenants, which taluqdari management would bring him, then he should be prepared to bear the expenses of management out of his own pocket. Robertson bowed to the logic of this argument, and withdrew his proposal.[23]

Meanwhile the village communities, uncertain as to their eventual fate and reluctant to pay at the considerably enhanced rates of the new assessment, had begun withholding payment of the revenue demand. By April 1843 the 110 biswadari villages of the estate were in arrears to the extent of Rs. 40,168 on the previous two years' accounts. In July despite vigorous attempts at collection and the remission by the government of some Rs. 8,500 on the grounds of overassessment, Rs. 23,676 still remained outstanding.[24] When the raja was offered the estate, he was told that he would be responsible for the realization of these balances, and that he could not alter the demand on individual villages so as to make up the deficiencies of one from the surplus of another. Under these conditions he refused to have anything to do with the

22. Sec. Govt. N.W.P. to Sec. Bd. Rev. 24 May 1842, B.R. Progs. 14 June 1841, No. 1; and Sec. Govt. N.W.P. to Sec. Bd. Rev. 29 July 1842, B.R. Progs. 23 August 1842, No. 1. For the board's counter-arguments see Sec. Bd. Rev. to Sec. Govt. N.W.P. 1 April 1842, B.R. Progs. 1 April 1842, No. 2; and Sec. Bd. Rev. to Sec. Govt. N.W.P. 14 June 1842, B.R. Progs. 14 June 1842, No. 2.

23. Sec. Govt. N.W.P. to Sec. Bd. Rev. 23 September 1842, B.R.Progs. 28 October 1842, No. 1; Sec. Bd. Rev. to Sec. Govt. N.W.P. 28 October 1842, ibid., No. 2; and Sec. Govt. N.W.P. to Sec. Bd. Rev. 30 November 1842, B.R. Progs. 3 January 1843, No. 1.

24. Colltr. Mainpuri to Commr. Agra 28 March 1843, B.R. Progs. 21 November 1843, No. 19; Commr. Agra to Colltr. Mainpuri 4 April 1843, ibid., No. 20A; and Commr. Agra to Sec. Bd. Rev. 31 July 1843, ibid., No. 16.

management. Protesting that he could barely pay the old assessment much less an enhanced sum levied from defiant village communities, he insisted that the estate be handed over to him free from balance and that he be empowered to vary the demand on individual villages as he saw fit.[25] As the government would not accede to these demands, especially the latter which called into question the basic equity of Edmonstone's assessments, the Mainpuri settlement arrangements remained at a standstill throughout the year 1843.

In January 1844 Robertson's successor as Lieutenant Governor, James Thomason, at last put an end to the uncertainty. Arguing that it was neither just nor fair to abandon in some few cases the precedents of Mursan and Shiurajpur, and thereby place the parties concerned in a very different position from that which prevailed on neighboring and similar estates, Thomason ruled that the settlement of Manchanna must follow "the established course of proceeding."[26] This decision did not of course go against Thomason's own inclinations. Like R. M. Bird, Thomason was convinced that "inferior proprietary right" was widespread throughout the taluqdari estates of the province, and that it deserved the support and encouragement of the government. He was largely responsible for seeing through to completion in 1849 the village settlement begun by Bird under Regulation IX of 1833. Yet Thomason was by no means as doctrinaire in his views. He recognized that the inferior proprietors were often unable to stand alone when deprived of the support of the taluqdar; and he was willing, at least in theory, to see the taluqdar awarded the revenue engagement where the superior and inferior holders were of the same family or tribe and mutually anxious to maintain their connection.[27]

With Thomason's decision on Manchanna the protracted official controversy over settlement policy in the North-Western Provinces was finally brought to an end. There remained only a few sputtering embers of discontent among those who refused to be reconciled. Of these perhaps the most influential, and certainly the most outspoken, was H. S. Boulderson, Junior Member of the Board of Revenue. No sooner had the Manchanna award been handed down than Boulderson launched into a series of impassioned attacks upon the principles of the new settlement. He insisted that the biswadars in Manchanna as elsewhere had got wrongful possession of the estates of the taluqdar, that the settlement officers had been "drilled" by

---

25. Sec. Bd. Rev. to Commr. Agra 3 January 1843, B.R. Progs. 3 January 1843, No. 2; Raja Ganga Singh to Colltr. Mainpuri 5 February 1843, B.R. Progs. 7 March 1843, No. 45; and Colltr. Mainpuri to Commr. Agra 9 February 1843, *ibid.*, No. 41.

26. Sec. Govt. N.W.P. to Sec. Bd. Rev. 17 January 1844, B.R. Progs. 9 April 1844, No. 1. See also Lt. Gov. N.W.P. to Governor-General-in-Council (hereafter G.-G.-in-C.) 31 January 1844, NAI Home Rev. Dept. Progs. 15 April 1848, No. 10. Both documents are printed in *Thomason's Despatches* (Calcutta, 1858), 1:16–33.

27. See his "Directions for Settlement Officers" (1844), in *Directions for Revenue Officers*, pp. 54–59.

their superiors to secure this result, and that their so-called investigations were based upon preconceived judgments which rendered the results worthless.[28] Thomason, exasperated by the "pertinacity and violence" of Boulderson's forays, solicited permission from the Government of India to add a third member to the two-man Board of Revenue so that his antagonist could be reduced to a minority. Calcutta refused this request—indeed one member of the Governor-General's Council even supported Boulderson—but the excitement died away with the final confirmation of the settlement.[29]

Challenge in the Courts

Stymied in their efforts to secure a favorable outcome by administrative action, the taluqdars of the North-Western Provinces soon turned to the courts. The first to do so was the man who had first felt the pressure of the new settlement, Raja Tikam Singh of Mursan. In 1837 he brought suit against the muqaddams of Nugla Mani, taluqa Tuksan, for possession of the zamindari right of the village. Why the raja singled out this village is not clear. Perhaps because Nugla was one of only two of the twelve Tuksan villages not awarded to him at settlement, or perhaps its Brahmin muqaddams, out of possession for some years in the late eighteenth century, were at odds with the other village zamindars, some of whom testified in the raja's favor. In any case, after a long series of pleadings, the Principal Sadr Amin of Aligarh in May 1839 ruled in the raja's favor, and ordered him reinstated in the management of the village. Nor was the judge content simply to decide on the facts of the case. He ruled more generally that "the title biswadar appertains to zemindars . . . and zemindars have in all cases the power to change moquddums because moquddums are appointed by the zemindars for managing the village concerns and under the British Government no rights have been conferred upon them."[30]

This decision stunned the revenue authorities. Caught unawares, they set out at once to have it reversed in a higher court. The Collector was in the meantime ordered not to make any change in the settlement record. Unfortunately for the government, the aggrieved muqaddams Goverdhan and Nathram, although induced to present a petition of appeal, took no further notice of their case. The appeal was therefore struck off the file in December 1840, leaving the government with no option but to execute the decree in favor of Raja Tikam Singh.[31] Before doing so, however, the Board of Reve-

---

28. Minute by Boulderson of 2 April 1844, NAI Home Rev. Dept. Progs. 15 April 1848, No. 51. See also Boulderson Note of 7 September 1844, B.R. Progs. 20 September 1844, No. 82.

29. Minute by Thomason of 17 April 1844, NAI Home Rev. Dept. Progs. 4 May 1844, No. 11–18; and Sec. Govt. India to Sec. Govt. N.W.P. 4 May 1844, *ibid.* Boulderson's supporter in Calcutta was T.H. Maddock.

30. Copy of Decree of Principal Sadr Amin of 1 May 1839, B.R. Progs. 9 June 1844, No. 13.

31. Commr. Meerut to Sec. Bd. Rev. 7 June 1839, B.R. Progs. 21 June 1839, No. 24; Sec. Bd. Rev. to Commr. Meerut 12 July 1839, B.R. Progs. 12 July 1839, No. 1; and Colltr. Aligarh to Commr. Meerut 3 May 1841, B.R. Progs. 18 May 1841, No. 149.

nue, as a punishment of sorts, cut off his taluqdari allowance, and insisted that he pay the full revenue demand of Rs. 762 levied on Nugla Mani rather than the Rs. 595 paid by the muqaddams.[32] The raja for some time refused to accept the settlement on these terms, but he ultimately acquiesced and his name was entered on the proprietary register in 1842.[33]

With one case successfully behind him, Tikam Singh at once moved on to challenge the settlement of the other villages of his former estate. Following the precedent of Nugla Mani, however, he carefully refrained from involving the government as a defendant or bringing a general suit for the whole estate, preferring instead to move quietly against individual muqaddams. By June 1844 he had won possession of four villages, including Nugla Mani, and had gained favorable decrees in six more cases.[34] In September 1846 he instituted fifty-seven further suits, in which he obtained favorable decisions in the Sadr Amin's court in all but five.[35]

The British had by this time become genuinely alarmed. From the outset the Board of Revenue had seen in the Nugla Mani decision a dangerous precedent, potentially subversive of the whole North-Western Provinces settlement. As the number of judicial decrees mounted up, the government took an increasingly active part in the preparation and conduct of the muqaddams' cases. The government *vakil* (pleader) had participated in the pleading even of the original Nugla Mani case. After its disastrous outcome the government instructed the muqaddami litigants as to the precise line of defense they should adopt, and required them to submit their pleadings for inspection and revision before they filed them in court. The government vakil was again placed at their service, and in addition a special officer, J. R. Hutchinson, was deputed to supervise the conduct of the suits. Beyond this the government offered financial assistance in the form of advances to meet court costs to those who were too impoverished to defend themselves. Between 1846 and 1851 some Rs. 6,286 were disbursed to the defendants in the suits brought in Aligarh by the taluqdars of Mursan and Gubrari.[36]

In 1839, when the initial Nugla Mani decision was announced, the Board of Revenue had considered ordering the Collector not to execute any decrees in favor of Tikam Singh until he had brought a successful action directly

32. Sec. Bd. Rev. to Commr. Meerut 19 November 1841, B.R. Progs. 19 November 1841, No. 20; and Sec. Bd. Rev. to Sec. Govt. N.W.P. 12 April 1842, B.R. Progs. 12 April 1842, No. 11.

33. Commr. Meerut to Sec. Bd. Rev. 8 March 1842, B.R. Progs. 24 June 1842, No. 42; Petition of Raja to Lt. Gov. enclosed in Sec. Govt. N.W.P. to Sec. Bd. Rev. 19 March 1842, B.R. Progs. 12 April 1842, No. 10; and Colltr. Aligarh to Commr. Meerut 2 December 1842, B.R. Progs. 27 December 1842, No. 103.

34. Colltr. Aligarh to Commr. Meerut 29 June 1844, B.R. Progs. 30 July 1844, No. 15-16. These ten villages were scattered across the estate, in six of its eighteen component taluqas. Suits for a further eight villages had been dismissed by the court.

35. Depty. Colltr. Aligarh to Commr. Meerut 24 February 1851, B.R. Progs. 21 March 1851, No. 26.

36. Hutchinson, *Allygurh Statistics*, p. 140.

against the government for the entire estate. Such a proceeding would of course have pitted the revenue and judicial branches of the British government directly against each other, and so had to be abandoned. Yet to work through the individual village muqaddams was a very tiresome and exasperating business. From the beginning many of these men, like the muqaddams of Nugla Mani, intimidated by the wealth and rank of their antagonist, despaired of a favorable outcome, and so did little to defend themselves. In 1844 the defendants refused to appeal in five of the six cases initially decreed in favor of Tikam Singh, while two years later the Collector reported that the "biswadars of three villages have declared that from their poverty, their debts, and other demands on them they are unable to defend their suits in the civil courts."[37] Nor were the villagers fully alive to the advantages of government assistance. When offered the services of the government vakil they would often all choose different private pleaders instead.[38]

Vexing, too, was the problem of distributing and securing the funds made available for advances. To cover itself against loss the government required those taking advances to put up a security of an equivalent amount. As the impoverished biswadars generally had no valuables apart from their land, they developed a system of mutual security, in which the biswadars of one village would stand security for those of a second, while the biswadars of the second were the securities for those of the first. This arrangement worked adequately so long as the taluqdar did not bring suit simultaneously against both sets of biswadars, but once they had been dispossessed the security vanished overnight. Still, so anxious was the government to see these cases through to a successful conclusion, that it gave its blessing to this system, and even on occasion advanced funds without any security whatsoever.[39] The working of the system of advances can perhaps best be appreciated by examining one case in detail.

On December 17, 1846 an advance of Rs. 42 was made to the villagers of Amrah, pargana Mursan, to enable them to defend a suit brought against them by Tikam Singh in the Sadr Amin's court. This advance, secured by the biswadars of Nugla Surkorea, was expended as follows:

	Rupees/Annas
Registry of bond and security	4 - 0
Vakil's fee	18 - 8
Stamp papers for replies	3 - 0

37. Colltr. Aligarh to Commr. Meerut 2 November 1846, B.R. Progs. 20 November 1846, No. 5.

38. In at least one instance this was due to lack of confidence in the government vakil. The Collector of Aligarh reported in May 1848 that "Sahib Roy the Government Vakeel does not stand very high in the opinion of the Native community, and that unless forced to employ him very few of the biswadars are likely to do so" (Colltr. Aligarh to Commr. Meerut 23 May 1848, B.R. Progs. 20 June 1848, No. 12).

39. Colltr. Aligarh to Commr. Meerut 9 January 1847, B.R. Progs. 22 January 1847, No. 66; and Sec. Bd. Rev. to Commr. Meerut 22 January 1847, ibid., No. 67.

Copies from Collector's office	11 - 0
Talabana and subsistence while in attendance at court	5 - 7
Total	Rs. 41 - 15

The case, decreed against the villagers by the Sadr Amin, was then appealed to the Zila Judge in Aligarh. For the expenses of this appeal the biswadars of Amrah in July 1848 received a further Rs. 75. This money was given without security because, as the Collector later explained, "on the then hopeless state of affairs no one would become their security, and I believe it would have been contrary to the wishes of Government to have been deterred by their poverty from giving them the opportunity of appealing." This money was spent on the following:

	Rupees/Annas
Stamp paper for petition of appeal	32 - 0
Stamp paper for *wakalatnama*, etc.	2 - 0
Vakils' fees	18 - 8
Copies for Collector's office	20 - 0
Talabana, etc.	2 - 8
Total	Rs. 75 - 0

Subsequently yet another advance of Rs. 27 was awarded without security to the Amrah biswadars for appeal charges in the Sadr Diwani Adalat at Agra. In this court, the highest in the province, they at last won a favorable decision. But the costs decreed to them by the court amounted to only Rs. 73, "from which sum they paid in refund of the loan Rs. 64, and retained the balance; their village having been in the meantime farmed to Raja Teekum Singh it was impossible to realize from them the rest of the advance." Indeed, as the Collector pointed out in soliciting a remission of the sum due, the unsecured advances not only in this but in many other villages could only be realized by the enforced sale of the village—a proceeding which would have defeated the whole purpose of contesting the taluqdari suits.[40] Ultimately in April 1851 the government approved the remission of Rs. 529 in outstanding balances due from the muqaddams on Tikam Singh's estates.[41]

At no time was Tikam Singh successful in all the suits he instituted even before the local Sadr Amin, and in the appeal courts he rarely made good his claim to be restored to zamindari management. Much of this ill fortune was doubtless due to the increasing effectiveness of the arguments the government put forward on the biswadars' behalf. From the outset they had denied that the civil courts could upset settlement arrangements legally constituted

40. Colltr. Aligarh to Commr. Meerut 14 July 1851, B.R. Progs. 26 August 1851, No. 82; Colltr. Aligarh to Commr. Meerut 1 August 1851, *ibid.*, No. 84; and Colltr. Aligarh to Commr. Meerut 13 December 1851, B.R. Progs. 30 December 1851, No. 15.
41. Sec. Govt. N.W.P. to Sec. Bd. Rev. 2 April 1851, B.R. Progs. 8 April 1851, No. 41.

under Regulation IX of 1833. In cases where the village muqaddams and the taluqdar both claimed hereditary rights in the soil, they argued, the settlement officer possessed full power to investigate and determine the extent of these claims, and his proceedings were subject only to confirmation by the government. As long as the lawful interests of both parties were secured, the choice of the party who should be admitted to engage was left by law to the revenue authorities alone; any interference by the courts would be "wholly subversive of the paramount authority of Government." Nor did the mere fact of former settlements having been made with an individual, or his having enjoyed some title such as zamindar, confer by itself any presumptive right to engage for the revenue under the revised settlement. The terms "zamindar" and "muqaddam" were subject to a variety of usages, and could not be permitted to fetter the discretion of the settlement officer. All that the civil courts were empowered to do, the government insisted, was to determine whether in the village under dispute there really existed a party besides the recorded taluqdar or malguzar possessing a hereditary and transferable right in the soil. Once this fact was admitted, the jurisdiction of the court had reached its limit.[42]

To drive home its point, the government induced the Sadr Diwani Adalat in January 1845 to issue a Circular Order to all civil judges in the province. In this circular the court pointed out that the existence of subordinate tenures coexistent with those of the taluqdar had been "distinctly recognized" by Regulation VII of 1822, which also reserved to the administrative authorities the power of determining which party should be admitted to engage for the revenue. The court warned its subordinate judges that the recognition of a taluqdar's former zamindari management would be by no means conclusive against the existence of other subordinate properties, "and could not of itself be held to justify the entire exclusion of the parties possessing such properties from proprietary occupancy of the soil, and the enjoyment of the rights thereupon contingent." While admitting that each suit in court "is of course a suit *de novo* and to be tried on its own merits," they also instructed the lower court judges to give "due advertence" to the facts elicited by the settlement officer, which of course in nearly every instance supported the position of the government.[43]

Thomason, the Lieutenant Governor, exulted in the appearance of this circular, which, he crowed, "directly condemned" the "erroneous principles maintained by some of the inferior Civil Courts." And he looked forward to a "more reasonable and consistent" practice in the courts once a few cases had been appealed to the Sadr Diwani and there "decided on right principles."[44]

42. Sec. Bd. Rev. to Commr. Meerut 30 July 1844, B.R. Progs. 30 July 1844, No. 20; and Revenue Dept. Note on Talukdari and Mokudumi Tenures of 24 August 1844, B.R. Progs. 18 March 1845, No. 49.

43. Register Sadr Diwani Adalat to all Civil Judges in N.W.P. 31 January 1845, B.R. Progs. 11 April 1845, No. 10.

44. Sec. Govt. N.W.P. to Sec. Bd. Rev. 7 March 1845, B.R. Progs. 18 March 1848, No. 48.

The high court was not, however, wholly an instrument of the government's will. When Thomason in 1846 urged the court to take into account not only the vernacular proceedings of the settlement officer in the particular case and the documents brought forward by the parties concerned, but to examine also the English correspondence that lay behind and influenced the decisions of the revenue officers, the court defiantly refused. It was not their duty, they insisted, to advocate the interests of either party or to seek out evidence; their function was simply to receive whatever evidence the parties might produce and to judge accordingly.[45]

Despite this setback Thomason was not long to be denied the "more reasonable and consistent" judicial practice that he sought. Tikam Singh's suits had already been followed by a spate of suits brought by the taluqdars of neighboring districts, all of whom were anxious to mitigate the harsh fate meted out to them at settlement. In almost every instance the taluqdars elsewhere, as in Aligarh, were successful in the court of the local Sadr Amin, only to have their claim thrown out on appeal. The reversal was not, however, always easy to secure, even after the issuance of the court's circular of January 1845.

In 1844 Raja Ganga Singh of Mainpuri brought suit for the village of Syedpur Baghoni. The Principal Sadr Amin awarded him the village the following spring on the ground that the muqaddams had claimed the entire property rather than a biswadari right, and that too without producing any documentary evidence in support of their assertions. The Zila Judge on appeal, to the government's surprise, confirmed the Sadr Amin's decree. This prompted the Sadr court to order the case tried afresh from the start. But the Sadr Amin was no more accommodating on the second hearing than he had been before, so the revenue authorities redoubled their efforts to secure a favorable outcome in the Judge's court. Despite the Sadr court's reluctance to sanction their use, the Collector supplied the Judge on his own initiative with English records supporting the muqaddams' position. These showed that in 1802 the ancestors of the present muqaddams had been recorded as *maliks* of Syedpur Baghoni, and that they had consented to the award of taluqdari rights to Ganga Singh's father. With the support of this evidence the new Zila Judge, Mr. Unwin, at last reversed the Sadr Amin's decree.[46] As the Board of Revenue cogently remarked in summarizing the case, the village zamindars obtained their "just decree" only because of the "accidental change of the Officer appointed to hold the Office of Judge, and the disregard by him of that order of the Sudder Court which prohibits the

45. Sec. Govt. N.W.P. to Register Sadr Diwani Adalat 21 August 1846, B.R. Progs. 27 November 1846, No. 4; Register Sadr Diwani Adalat to Sec. Govt. N.W.P. 7 October 1846, *ibid.*, No. 7; and Register Sadr Diwani Adalat to Sec. Govt. N.W.P. 7 June 1847, B.R. Progs. 27 July 1847, No. 12.

46. Commr. Agra to Colltr. Mainpuri 24 April 1845, B.R. Progs. 27 May 1845, No. 50; Colltr. Mainpuri to Commr. Agra 26 November 1845, B.R. Progs. 6 February 1846, No. 26; and Colltr. Mainpuri to Commr. Agra 9 July 1847, B.R. Progs. 23 July 1847, No. 61.

inferior courts from . . . referring to official and other documents and evidence not recited by either of the parties."[47]

The rani of Powayn in Shahjahanpur district, who at settlement had been stripped of 121 of the 247 villages in her taluqa, in 1846 instituted suits for the recovery of 21 of these villages. She readily obtained decrees in 13 of these cases before the Sadr Amin, who ruled in her favor on the ground that she had previously been recorded as sole zamindar. Complaining that the Sadr Amin had "entirely neglected" the instructions given by the court of Sadr Diwani for the decision of such cases, the Rohilkhand Commissioner urged that a covenanted European officer be appointed to collect evidence on behalf of the muqaddams, and that the judge before whom the appeal came should be a man "prepared to admit the existence of such rights in the talooqa generally, and to accept slight evidence as proof in individual cases."[48] The Board of Revenue, equally exasperated, suggested that it might be best to avoid the ordinary courts altogether and to bring such cases before a special tribunal "composed of persons who understand land tenures and who shall not be prohibited from seeking out the facts by any rules of practice or technical formalities."[49]

An independent-minded judiciary was not, however, the only obstacle to a successful resolution of these cases. As in the early days of the Mursan litigation so too were the Powayn muqaddams reluctant to prosecute appeals against their wealthy superior. Some were intimidated, a few bought off, and others so indifferent or despairing that the Collector could only "with difficulty secure the attendance of the mukuddums even at the Sudder Station [Shahjahanpur]. Those sent to Bareilly [to the Appeal Court] went absolutely by compulsion."[50] As a result appeals were instituted in only eight of the thirteen cases in which the rani had won decrees. These eight were, however, all decided in the muqaddams' favor by the Zila Judge, and his decision on further appeal was reaffirmed by the Sadr Diwani Adalat in January 1849. As both parties had already agreed to accept the decisions reached in these eight cases as binding precedents, no further suits were instituted, and the muqaddams consequently remained in possession of almost everything they had gained at settlement.

By 1850, then, the struggle in the courts had reached its end. Throughout the province the taluqdars were forced to admit defeat, with only a few scattered villages here and there to show for the time and money they had invested in litigation. More striking than their ultimate defeat, however, was the closeness of the result. In courtroom and countryside alike the taluqdars had come tantalizingly near to undoing what the executive government had

47. Sec. Bd. Rev. to Sec. Govt. N.W.P. 23 July 1847, B.R. Progs. 23 July 1847, No. 62.
48. Commr. Rohilkhand to Sec. Bd. Rev. 3 July 1847, B.R. Progs. 16 July 1847, No. 1.
49. Sec. Bd. Rev. to Sec. Govt. N.W.P. 16 July 1847, *ibid.*, No. 5.
50. Colltr. Shahjahanpur to Commr. Rohilkhand 5 August 1847, B.R. Progs. 28 September 1847, No. 70. See also Commr. Rohilkhand to Sec. Bd. Rev. 13 July 1847, B.R. Progs. 23 July 1847, No. 48.

decided upon as a final resolution of the land question. They owed much, of course, to the lower-level judiciary. Recruited by patronage from groups traditionally learned in the law, these men remained bound by ties of class and interest to the landed elite. So too did the local vakils, even those in the muqaddams' employ, whom the government often suspected of collusion with their clients' adversaries.[51] Nor did these men, unfamiliar with the English language, have an occasion to appreciate the new revenue policy, or to grasp its subtleties. One reason indeed why the Sadr court opposed the production of English settlement records in the lower courts was the inability of the *munsifs* and sadr amins to read them.[52] The district and high court judges were as Englishmen more aware of the objectives of government, and in the end more amenable to pressure to conform to established policy. But as judges they were inevitably affected by the conservative sentiments and reverence for established property rights of the English judiciary of the time. They may also have been to some extent officials of an older generation imbued with the aristocratic sympathies of the Bengal Regulations. In any case advocacy of long-neglected rights formed no part of their conception of their duty.

One important outcome of the taluqdar challenge to the settlement was that it forced the government to examine and defend its actions. In this case, as so often happens, the very vigor of the attack helped bring into the open many of the tacit assumptions upon which a generally accepted policy was based. As the controversy progressed it became increasingly clear that for those who worked with Bird and Thomason no lapse of time could tell against the rights of the village zamindars. A Revenue Department Note of 1844 put the matter forcefully:

Again, the rights of the village communities have never been so completely in abeyance as that their recognition should be barred by the statute of limitations. They may, or may not, have held a theeka [lease] under the Talookdar. Where this has occurred it was a distinct revival of their original claim and tenure. But even where this has not been the case, it has hardly ever happened that they have been reduced to the mere rank of common ryots. Whatever privileges they may have enjoyed above such ryots may be considered as indications of their original condition, and as keeping alive their claim to be restored to that condition.[53]

Thomason himself at the same time acknowledged that the decision to settle with the village occupants was in the initial instance an act not of justice, but of expediency. "The rights of both parties, of the Talookdars and of

51. For an instance see Colltr. Mainpuri to Commr. Agra 26 November 1845, B.R. Progs. 6 February 1846, No. 26. In Aligarh the government vakil petitioned to be allowed to take up taluqdari cases as well as those of the biswadars. Petition of Sahib Roy to Colltr. Aligarh 1 May 1848, B.R. Progs. 20 June 1848, No. 12.

52. Register Sadr Diwani Adalat to Sec. Govt. N.W.P. 7 June 1847, B.R. Progs. 27 July 1847, No. 12.

53. Note on Talukdari and Mokudumi Tenures of 24 August 1844, B.R. Progs. 18 March 1845, No. 49.

the Biswadars, were held to be fully compensated; and whether the one or the other were permitted to engage direct with the Government, the Law contained provisions for securing the rights of both."[54] Subsettlement under the taluqdar, as Thornton had first proposed in Mursan, would, in other words, have fully secured the rights of the village zamindars. The reduction of the taluqdar to a pensionary of government was not a necessary part of an equitable settlement of the North-Western Provinces. That step was rather the product of that antagonism to landed elites which saw in them only parasitic usurpers who had laid hold of the rights of the villagers and the revenues of the government.

Malikana: A Rearguard Struggle

As compensation for the loss of their biswadari villages the taluqdars were from the outset regarded as entitled to a cash allowance, or malikana. In the initial settlement of Mursan this took the form of a payment to the raja from the government treasury of 18 percent of the assumed gross rental of each biswadari village in the estate. (The villagers retained 20 percent and the government took the remaining 62 percent.) While approving this award, which brought Tikam Singh an annual income of Rs. 26,492, the government stated, however, that it was a "grant of favor," not a claim of right, and that its continuance was open to reconsideration on the death of the raja.[55] The same general principles, though without the explicit reservation of the right to reduce the allowance on the first holder's death, were followed out in the subsequent settlements of Shiurajpur, Powayn, and elsewhere. By 1844 some three lakhs of rupees had been awarded as malikana to the taluqdars of the North-Western Provinces.[56]

In January 1844, while giving final approval to the exclusion from settlement of the raja of Mainpuri, Thomason went on to lay down definitive rules for the award of malikana. He fixed the ordinary taluqdari allowance at 22½ percent of the government revenue demand upon the biswadars, but then proceeded to distribute the total into two distinct portions. One was a fixed minimum of 10 percent claimable under all circumstances. This sum, which Thomason regarded as a just and equitable compensation for the taluqdar's loss of management, was to be the indefeasible right of the grantee and his heirs for all time. The remainder was given "as of grace" during the holder's lifetime, and was open to revision upon his death or upon the resettlement of the estate.[57]

On November 16, 1847 Raja Ganga Singh of Mainpuri died, leaving

54. Thomason to G.-G. 31 January 1844, NAI Home Rev. Dept. Progs. 15 April 1848, No. 10.
55. Sec. Bd. Rev. to Sec. Govt. Agra 14 July 1835, B.R. Progs. 14 July 1835, No. 34; and Sec. Govt. Agra to Sec. Bd. Rev. 4 September 1835, B.R. Progs. 25 September 1835, No. 18.
56. See Tables 4 and 5.
57. Sec. Govt. N.W.P. to Sec. Bd. Rev. 17 January 1844, *Thomason's Despatches*, 1:30-31.

Table 4. Taluqdari Holdings Settled with Village Biswadars[a]

District	Jama (rupees)	Number of villages	Taluqdari allowances (rupees)
Saharanpur	3,610	6	360
Muzaffarnagar	955	1½	164
Moradabad	3,805	7	380
Bareilly	7,001	80	1,260
Shahjahanpur	99,084	121	25,696
Aligarh	2,86,538	220	64,262
Mathura	26,341	54	7,853
Agra	34,616	41	10,920
Farrukhabad	60,568	53	4,417
Mainpuri	1,59,278	265	46,810
Etawah	38,262	65	9,996
Kanpur	50,001	99	8,819
Allahabad	2,69,578	401	48,525
Gorakhpur	3,88,939	3,247	75,295
Total	14,40,847	4,660	3,04,759

Source: Enclosure to Sec. Bd. Rev. to Sec. Govt. N.W.P. 25 October 1844, B.R. Progs. 25 October 1844, No. 65.

[a]For a slightly different set of figures, omitting Gorakhpur altogether but including estates assessed at Rs. 1,13,466 in Ghazipur, see Sec. Bd. Rev. to Sec. Govt. N.W.P. 9 November 1849, B.R. Progs. 9 November 1849, No. 75. There is no way of reconciling these discrepancies other than by divergent definitions of who was to be accounted a taluqdar. The Gorakhpur and Ghazipur figures may be inflated by the inclusion of petty zamindars to whom payments were made on their exclusion from settlement.

behind as his heir a brother Nirpat Singh and fourteen other relatives dependent upon him for their maintenance. Under the rules laid down by Thomason the Mainpuri malikana allowance of Rs. 22,573 was now liable to be reduced to Rs. 9,944, or 10 percent of the biswadari jama. Ganga Singh had further enjoyed a special nankar allowance of Rs. 7,500 originally awarded to his father for aid in repelling Holkar's invasion of the Doab in 1817. This, too, lapsed upon his death. The potential net loss to the Mainpuri raj therefore amounted to some Rs. 20,000, which was roughly half the total income enjoyed by Ganga Singh at the time of his death. To soften the blow to this "once powerful" and "very ancient" family the Agra Commissioner recommended that both allowances be continued to Nirpat Singh at the full rate. In this he was supported by the Collector of Mainpuri, who listed in detail the raja's expenses, amounting to some Rs. 14,084 on domestic establishment and maintenance allowances alone.[58] The Board of Revenue concurred. They

58. Offg. Commr. Agra to Sec. Bd. Rev. 27 December 1848, B.R. Progs. 26 January 1849, No. 90; and Colltr. Mainpuri to Commr. Agra 14 July 1848, *ibid.*, No. 104. See also Colltr. Mainpuri to Commr. Agra 10 April 1850, B.R. Progs. 3 May 1850, No. 29.

Table 5. Taluqdari Holdings—Detail of Selected Estates[a]

District	Taluqa	Villages settled with Biswadars	Villages settled with Taluqdar (where available)
Saharanpur	Jaberbari	15	20
Moradabad	Bahari	7	2
Bareilly	Bilhairi	80	—
Shahjahanpur	Powayn	121	111
Aligarh	Mursan	96	69
	Shahzadpur	20	0
	Mendu	31	0
	Kanka and Kajraut	4	54
	Hasayan	17	26
	Chakathal	17	—
Mathura	Sonk, Dunaitia, Lashkarpur (Mursan)	40	7
Agra	Jharki	20	21
Farrukhabad	Lukatpur	41	—
	Tirua	11	—
Mainpuri	Manchanna	110	43
	Etah	119	20
Etawah	Chakarnagar	25	2
	Ruru	29	—
Kanpur	Shiurajpur	99	6
Allahabad	Burrakhar	30	—
	Chaurassi	104	—
	Daya	87	59
	Kharar	46	—
	Khurka	56	—
	Manda	78	—

[a]This table includes only estates that lost villages during revision of settlement between 1834 and 1844. A few taluqas, including Awa Missa and Bara, were settled after 1844.

regarded the haq taluqdari as a right vested in the raja's family which could not be altered during the term of settlement, while the nankar allowance, they urged, should be continued as a mark of appreciation of the family's loyalty and "useful services," particularly the example set by the late raja in having "reared a daughter whom the custom and prejudice of the clan would have doomed to death at birth."[59]

Thomason as Lieutenant Governor preferred instead to ease the raja's admitted difficulties by awarding him a special life pension of Rs. 10,000 in addition to the reduced malikana of Rs. 9,944. In this way he pointed out the

59. Sec. Bd. Rev. to Sec. Govt. N.W.P. 2 June 1848, B.R. Progs. 2 June 1848, No. 7; Sec. Bd. Rev. to Sec. Govt. N.W.P. 26 January 1849, B.R. Progs. 26 January 1849, No. 110; and Sec. Bd. Rev. to Sec. Govt. N.W.P. 3 May 1850, B.R. Progs. 3 May 1850, No. 30.

government would at the same time "be the gainer" by more than Rs. 10,000.[60] The Government of India approved Thomason's scheme, but unfortunately one year later in 1851 Nirpat Singh died, so the whole matter had to be opened up once again. The discussion on this occasion was brief, for it was obvious that the estate's financial situation had in no way improved. Indeed Nirpat's son Tej Singh had inherited debts of some Rs. 71,700. Hence the Board of Revenue and the Lieutenant Governor joined in recommending, and the Government of India approved, the continuance of the special grant to Tej Singh for five years at Rs. 10,000 and for the remainder of his life at Rs. 5,000.[61]

Support for this special grant, however, did not in any way alter Thomason's fierce opposition to the perpetuation of taluqdari malikana on the lavish scale of 22½ percent of the government revenue. From the outset, not only in Mainpuri but throughout the province, he had almost always ordered a reduction of the allowance to 10 percent when the incumbent taluqdar died.[62] In each case the reduction was carried out over the vigorous protests of the Board of Revenue, who insisted time and again that the government had no authority to interfere with the rate of taluqdari allowance fixed at settlement, any more than with the jama itself.[63] When the rani of Powayn died, and the allowance to her successor was cut by Rs. 7,183, the Divisional Commissioner protested as well.[64] Ignoring these objections, Thomason in a general Minute of October 24, 1851 went on to rule that the taluqdari allowance must in every case be reduced to 10 percent at the earliest possible opportunity, normally the death of the first incumbent. Neither justice nor expediency, he insisted, required the sacrifice of the revenue, which he estimated at Rs. 85,000 annually, involved in leniency toward the taluqdars.[65]

When the documents connected with the settlement were sent home for approval, the Court of Directors at once took exception to Thomason's ruling. Though as reluctant as the Lieutenant Governor to lose the additional revenue, they agreed with the Board of Revenue that the public faith was pledged to the taluqdars. Except where the terms of confirmation, as in Mursan, specified reduction on the demise of the first incumbent, they

60. Sec. Govt. N.W.P. to Sec. Govt. India 31 May 1850, B.R. Progs. 12 July 1850, No. 103.
61. Sec. Govt. N.W.P. to Sec. Govt. India 3 October 1851, B.R. Progs. 13 January 1852, No. 118; Sec. Govt. N.W.P. to Sec. Govt. India 25 November 1851, *ibid.*, No. 120; and Sec. Govt. India to Sec. Govt. N.W.P. 5 December 1851, *ibid.*, No. 121.
62. For his justification of his action in taluqa Jharki (Agra), see Sec. Govt. N.W.P. to Sec. Bd. Rev. 21 May 1850, in *Thomason's Despatches*, 2:89-93. He claimed there that since the overall settlement arrangements of Jharki were modeled on those of Mursan, the taluqdari allowdance was subject to the same restrictions.
63. See Sec. Bd. Rev. to Sec. Govt. N.W.P. 26 March 1850 and 4 June 1850, NAI Home Rev. Dept. Progs. 12 December 1851, No. 15, for taluqa Jharki; and Sec. Bd. Rev. to Sec. Govt. N.W.P. 4 January 1850, B.R. Progs. 4 January 1850, No. 7, for taluqa Daya in Allahabad.
64. Commr. Rohilkhand to Sec. Bd. Rev. 1 May 1851, B.R. Progs. 20 May 1851, No. 22. See also Sec. Govt. N.W.P. to Sec. Bd. Rev. 18 June 1851, B.R. Progs. 27 June 1851, No. 98.
65. "Minute on Talookdaree Allowances," in *Thomason's Despatches*, 2:199-202.

stated, the entire arrangements must be considered to have been concluded for the full term of the settlement. No doubt, as Thomason had argued in several cases, the Mursan arrangement had been intended as a general precedent, but it had not been expressly so declared until the orders of January 1844, by which time the bulk of the settlements had been completed. Hence the taluqdars were entitled to their full 22½ percent for the thirty years of the settlement. Where allowances had already been improperly reduced, the government was to refund the difference.[66]

Over the course of the next few years some Rs. 64,000 were refunded to various taluqdars, most notably those of Powayn in Shahjahanpur (Rs. 24,907), Daya in Allahabad (Rs. 22,232), and Jharki in Agra (Rs. 9,132). The raja of Mainpuri on this occasion received Rs. 5,769 and his allowance was restored to its former level of Rs. 22,502 per annum.[67] Twenty years later when the settlement expired the government as a further act of grace to this still heavily burdened family extended the taluqdari allowance of the then raja Ram Partab Singh at its previous amount for his lifetime. Elsewhere the settlement revision of the 1870s saw the final reduction of the taluqdari allowance to 10 percent.[68]

The struggle over malikana, then, followed much the same course as the battle in the courts. Often already reduced to "straitened circumstances" as a result of their exclusion from settlement, the taluqdars were quick to protest the further fall in their incomes brought about by Thomason's policy. They found champions among the district officials, many of whom were sympathetic witnesses of their plight, and on the Board of Revenue, troubled by the legal aspects of Thomason's rulings. They gained a measure of relief too when the Directors of the East India Company took up their case and stayed Thomason's reductions for a full thirty years. The immediate returns were somewhat greater than in the legal battles, for cash payments were handed out each year the malikana was kept at its old level. But the stakes were much less. After all who could compare a petty squabble over allowances with an endeavor to overturn the entire settlement by judicial decree!

66. Revenue Dispatch from Court of Directors of 2 August 1853, B.R. Progs. 9 December 1853, No. 4-5.

67. Refunds were also made to taluqdars in Mathura (Rs. 1,002) and Etawah (Rs. 253). In the other districts of the Rohilkhand, Agra, and Allahabad Divisions no alterations had been made in taluqdari allowances since settlement. In the districts of the Meerut Division reductions had been expressly provided for in the original agreements. See Sec. Bd. Rev. to Sec. Govt. N.W.P. 17 November 1854, Abstract B.R. Progs. 17 November 1854, No. 19; Commr. Agra to Sec. Bd. Rev. 2 January 1855, B.R. Progs. 30 January 1855, No. 104; Commr. Rohilkhand to Sec. Bd. Rev. 25 January 1855, and reply of 2 March 1855, B.R. Progs. 2 March 1855, No. 14-15; and Commr. Agra to Sec. Bd. Rev. 14 April 1855, and reply of 24 April 1855, B.R. Progs. 24 April 1855, No. 32-33. With the restoration of the full malikana the Mainpuri raja's special pension was terminated.

68. Sec. Govt. N.W.P. to Sec. Bd. Rev. 8 August 1873, N.W.P. Rev. Progs. October 1873, No. 31. Another important, though seemingly unlikely, exception was the Mursan estate. There, despite the explicit provision for reduction on his death, Tikam Singh won a perpetual reprieve for himself and his heirs as a reward for loyalty during the 1857 revolt. See *Aligarh S.R.*, pp. 115-16; and p. 142 below.

Perhaps the most striking feature of the contest was the uncompromisingly hostile position adopted by the Lieutenant Governor. Opposed to settlement with the taluqdars (in practice if not always in theory), Thomason was equally opposed to endowing them lavishly as pensionaries of the government. He could, of course, be compassionate in individual cases of hardship. But, unlike the Board of Revenue, he refused to let moral or legal scruples stand in the way of reclaiming from the hands of an indolent class revenue he thought rightly belonged to the government. Thomason's orders were nevertheless never repudiated by his superiors, nor cancelled by his successors. All agreed that a higher rate of allowance served one purpose only—that of easing the taluqdars down gently from their former preeminence—and that in time it would come to an end.

The Persistence of Taluqdari Power

By the 1850s the taluqdars of the North-Western Provinces, stripped of most of their former sources of income, had to content themselves with the few villages they owned outright as zamindars, and with their beleaguered malikana allowances. But their hold over their former tenants had by no means wholly disappeared, nor their ability to dominate rural society. It was not by accident that village biswadars in places as distant as Mursan and Mainpuri time and again backed off from challenging their erstwhile superior in court. Even though they had the inducement of defending their newly won titles, and were assured of support by the revenue authorities, they did not relish an encounter with a man who, even in his straitened circumstances, was still far richer and controlled more resources than themselves. Each case decided in the taluqdar's favor, and indeed the mere bringing of a suit, even if later thrown out, was a forcible reassertion of the taluqdar's preeminence in society, and served notice on those beneath him that he remained a man to be reckoned with. The taluqdar often retained as well the loyalty of the subordinate tahsil and pargana staff, including even the village patwaris, many of whom owed their initial appointments to him. No matter how much they appreciated the award of proprietary title—and they rarely declined engagements for their villages—the biswadari holders had little stomach, when challenged outright, for a fight with the taluqdar.

The taluqdar did not have to resort always to crude or heavy-handed means to secure his predominance. In Shiurajpur the raja at the time of settlement held some seventy-nine old decrees for arrears of rent against his former tenants. These decrees he had not so far executed in large part because the defaulters then possessed nothing liable to seizure except their personal property, and the returns from the sale of such goods hardly justified the expense and bother. As biswadars under the revised settlement, however, they held their lands in full proprietorship. Hence "various parties, and the Rajah himself, who hold these decrees, pray for the sale of the newly acquired rights in satisfaction of their old claims, and a large portion of the property is thus in danger of changing hands."[69] The Lieutenant Governor, T. C. Robertson, stayed these sales for some months, but neither he nor the Board of Revenue, bound by Victorian notions of *laissez-faire*, could discover any "effectual remedy" for the impending upheaval. Indeed the board coldly reported that sale of land for debt was a widespread phenomenon and that even newly recognized biswadari proprietors had no right to expect the board to rescue them from their own prodigality and mismanagement. Ultimately the raja brought to sale, and purchased himself, the rights of the shareholders in nine villages, while in thirty-seven others the rights and interests of the proprietors were sold to outsiders, mainly persons residing in the pargana unconnected with the raja.[70]

Shiurajpur was no doubt a somewhat exceptional case, for few taluqdars were likely to have substantial numbers of old decrees with which they could threaten the newly installed biswadars. More useful as a way of asserting his position was the preferential right accorded the taluqdar of taking over biswadari villages sold up, or about to be sold up, for arrears of government revenue. In February 1842 Robertson noted that, rather than "suffer them at once to pass to a stranger," it would only be fair to give Raja Tikam Singh the option "of obtaining the villages, the management of which he had lost by the settlement proceedings, on their falling into balance"; and he proceeded to authorize the Board of Revenue to transfer such villages to their former holder on a farming lease of up to fifteen years on payment of the arrears due.[71] Two years later Thomason as Lieutenant Governor went on further to rule that when no farmer or purchaser could be found at the initial auction sale, and the government had therefore to purchase the property itself, the taluqdar should be given the first opportunity to buy it after the holding had been resettled and its assessment reduced.[72]

There is no comprehensive list of the villages redeemed in this fashion. But the widespread overassessment of the new settlement and the inexperience of the new biswadars in revenue management, when combined with continued commercial depression and the failure of the rains on several occasions between 1837 and 1841, brought about considerable revenue defalcation during the early 1840s, of which the taluqdars were not slow to take advantage. Raja Tikam Singh, for instance, reclaimed not only several isolated villages in Aligarh but the taluqas of Sonk and Arr. Lashkarpur in Mathura,

69. District Judge to Sec. Bd. Rev. 22 April 1842, cited in Montgomery, *Statistical Report*, pp. 78–79.

70. Sec. Bd. Rev. to Sec. Govt. N.W.P. 6 December 1842, and Sec. Govt. N.W.P. to Sec. Bd. Rev. 31 December 1842 and 21 September 1843, *ibid.*, p. 79. In the bulk of his cases the raja either compounded with the muqaddams for payment, or realized the amount by the sale of their effects.

71. Sec. Govt. N.W.P. to Sec. Bd. Rev. 10 February 1842, B.R. Progs. 15 February 1842, No. 136.

72. Sec. Govt. N.W.P. to Sec. Bd. Rev. 17 January 1844, NAI Home Rev. Dept. Progs. 15 April 1848, No. 34.

comprising twenty-three villages which were made over to him in farm "in consequence of the misconduct of the Mokudums and their inability to manage their estates."[73] The raja of Mainpuri benefitted as well. Zorawar, biswadar of mouza Partabpur, obtained the settlement of his village in 1841 at a jama of Rs. 442. As the assessment was too heavy for the village in the deteriorated condition to which it had been reduced by the 1838 famine, with over twice as much waste as cultivated land, Partabpur was put up for sale the following year and purchased by the government, who leased it out to a farmer at a reduced jama of Rs. 300. When the farmer also proved unable to meet the revenue demand, the village was held *kham* for two years and then leased to the raja in 1845 on a progressive jama rising from Rs. 160 to Rs. 343 over the course of five years. The nearby village of Nugla Kheria, originally settled with the muqaddams Lallju and Gowrie, was farmed for arrears in 1843. The farmer proved to be a cultivator more influential than the muqaddams, who were unable to cope with him. The farm was revoked, the jama reduced, yet Lallju and Gowrie still refused to engage, so in June 1845 the Officiating Collector "finding the village going to ruin under Kham holding leased it to the Rajah on reduced Juma."[74]

But such gains were not always long lasting. In Mainpuri, despite an impassioned appeal on the raja's behalf by the Collector, the Board of Revenue, as hostile to the taluqdars as ever, overturned the leases of Partabpur and Nugla Kheria, and ordered the muqaddam biswadars readmitted. They further directed, disregarding Thomason's orders of January 1844, that "whenever the assessment has been reduced the mauza should always be offered to the biswadars before the Rajah can be allowed to engage."[75] Elsewhere, too, the board did its best to keep the taluqdars from retrieving their position. In 1840 the biswadars of Unnhi Garhi, formerly part of the Mursan taluqa, fell into arrears. The village was purchased by the government in the absence of bidders and then leased to a farmer for fifteen years at a slightly reduced jama. Raja Tikam Singh complained that his rights had been ignored, and his malikana improperly reduced, by this transaction. The Board of Revenue complacently told the Lieutenant Governor that the raja was "clearly at liberty" under the recent orders of the government to assume the management of any biswadari estate that fell into arrears, and that if he neglected to do so, and thereby let the property fall into other hands, "he must stand the consequences, and put up with the loss which may ensue." Robertson in reply caustically noted that when the village was first put up for

73. Sec. Bd. Rev. to Sec. Govt. N.W.P. 25 October 1844, B.R. Progs. 25 October 1844, No. 65. For the general problem of arrears and sales see ch. 5 below.

74. Colltr. Mainpuri to Commr. Agra 21 August 1845, B.R. Progs. 24 October 1845, No. 38; and Colltr. Mainpuri to Commr. Agra 4 February 1846, B.R. Progs. 24 March 1846, No. 10.

75. Sec. Bd. Rev. to Commr. Agra 30 December 1845, B.R. Progs. 30 December 1845, No. 12; and Sec. Bd. Rev. to Commr. Agra 24 March 1846, B.R. Progs. 24 March 1846, No. 11. The Agra Commissioner agreed with the board. See Commr. Agra to Sec. Bd. Rev. 2 March 1846, B.R. Progs. 24 March 1846, No. 6.

sale the board had not inquired whether the raja wished to resume the management, nor had they ever evinced any desire to carry out any measures designed to "conciliate or allay his not unnatural opposition" to the new settlement.[76]

Nor did this hostility die out with the conclusion of the settlement. Apart from their legal scruples with regard to malikana the board remained determined throughout the subsequent decades to confine the power of the taluqdars within the narrowest possible bounds. When the revised settlement expired in 1870 at the end of its thirty-year term, the then raja of Mainpuri, Ram Partab Singh, put forward a claim to engage anew for the biswadari villages of his ancestral estate. The claim was thrown out at once as untenable wherever the biswadars had maintained themselves in possession, but exceptions to the general rule might be made, the Agra Commissioner and the Board of Revenue agreed, "wherever the biswadars have mismanaged their estates, or the management has been transferred to other parties, or has passed into the hands of the talookdar."[77] The settlement officer accordingly proposed to settle with the raja some fourteen villages of which he had already taken over the management as mortgagee or farmer. In over half of these, he reported, "the obstinate and continued recusancy" of the biswadars had led to the transfer of management. When faced with the confirmation of these settlements, however, the Board of Revenue hurriedly drew back. Roundly denouncing the settlement officer's plan to give money payments as compensation to the excluded biswadars, they ordered revenue engagements taken instead from the old holders. At the same time, revoking their earlier instructions, they ruled that where the raja was already in possession of biswadari rights by purchase or mortgage, nothing less than a joint settlement with them would protect the interests of the inferior holders.[78]

Much of the board's hostility to the taluqdars had from the outset rested upon the presumed "incompetence" of these men as estate managers. Time and again, with the settlement officers under them, they had flayed these chieftains for their indolence, irresponsibility, and extortion. Thornton in Mursan and Edmonstone in Mainpuri had both singled out for special condemnation their lax control over their agents in the countryside. These subordinate agents, so Thornton charged, never entrusted with long-term leases which would encourage them to improve cultivation, devoted themselves instead to defrauding their master and oppressing the tenantry, and were left in power even after their shortcomings had been pointed out. Tikam Singh further, Thornton insisted, had "no method for regulating his accounts, and

76. Sec. Bd. Rev. to Sec. Govt. N.W.P. 7 March 1843, B.R. Progs. 7 March 1843, No. 4; and Sec. Govt. N.W.P. to Sec. Bd. Rev. 3 April 1843, B.R. Progs. 11 April 1843, No. 69.

77. Commr. Agra to Sec. Bd. Rev. 22 April 1870, N.W.P. Rev. Progs. October 1873, No. 20; and Sec. Bd. Rev. to Commr. Agra 18 May 1870, ibid., No. 23.

78. Settle. Offr. Mainpuri to Commr. Agra 31 March 1873, ibid., No. 36; Commr. Agra to Sec. Bd. Rev. 22 April 1873, ibid., No. 35; Sec. Bd. Rev. to Commr. Agra 14 July 1873, ibid., No. 37; and Sec. Bd. Rev. to Sec. Govt. N.W.P. 14 July 1873, ibid., No. 16.

indeed appears ignorant of the manner in which his large income is expended." But what disturbed the British the most about the taluqdars' management was their persisting endeavor to subjugate the village zamindars. Complaints about "undue exaction" and "flagrant acts of injustice" in the end usually focused upon the practice, as Thornton tellingly put it, of collecting rent from the "common asamies" rather than the "regular Malgoozars."[79] What the revised settlement sought to achieve was not simply more orderly procedures in the countryside, nor even an increased revenue for the state, but an end to this pressure upon the landholding communities at the village level.

With the resources of a powerful bureaucratic state behind them, the British achieved a substantial measure of success in this endeavor. The taluqdars' fall in status over the course of a few short years was, as we have seen, dramatic and precipitous. But the outcome was not everywhere the same, nor was it wholly the product of British initiative. Much depended upon how the taluqdar had consolidated his position in the countryside before the settlement commenced. Where, as in Jawar, or the Bara taluqa of Allahabad, the conquering taluqdar had by the early eighteenth century supplanted the old zamindars by his own dependents, these men were themselves a century and a half later often well placed to make good their own claims to engage for the revenue. The lineage tie remained but the taluqdar's control of the land had vanished.[80] Similarly where the conquest had been so recent or the village zamindars so entrenched that displacement was not possible, as in most of Hathras, the taluqdar lost almost everything at settlement. But where a vigorous campaign of reduction and expulsion of the subordinate holders had taken place, the taluqdar could salvage a good deal even from the Thomason settlement.

The taluqdar's ability to maintain his position under the new order was ultimately determined by his own relative strength as compared with that of the subordinate village holders. Sometimes, in alliance with local officials, the latter, even if they commanded few resources, could be too much for him. In the Laygaon taluqa of Mainpuri the patwari Shiblal Kaith, dismissed by the raja two years before settlement, joined with the villagers to secure for them proprietary title to nineteen villages. When the Collector visited Laygaon he found "this Shiblol the most influential person there, the Mocuddim Biswahdars in no respect differing from ordinary cultivators and

79. Depty. Colltr. Aligarh to Commr. Agra 23 and 24 April 1834, B.R. Progs. 13 May 1834, No. 29–30; Depty. Colltr. Aligarh to Commr. Agra 26 September 1834, B.R. Progs. 14 July 1835, No. 27; "Moorsaun Settlement Report," in Hutchinson, *Allygurh Statistics*, pp. 264–65; and Edmonstone Settlement Report of Manchanna, B.R. Progs. 3 September 1841, No. 19.

80. In Bara only 9 of the taluqa's 243 villages were awarded to descendants of the original Rajput zamindars. 92 villages were settled on the basis of long-continued occupancy with those holding by virtue of feudal service grants from the taluqdar, blood relationship with him, or allocation of the land by him; 20 were awarded to the taluqdar; and the remainder farmed. R. Temple, "Report on the Moquddumee Biswahdaree Settlement of Pergunnah Barrah, Zillah Allahabad," 9 December 1850, *Sels. Recs. Govt. N.W.P.*, Part 27 (1856):399–413.

generally referring me to him for information as to the amount of their Jumma."[81] Had Shiblal remained in the raja's employ the outcome might well have been different.

For the most part the village muqaddams were most likely to stand up to the taluqdar, or so it would seem, where they were well-to-do, controlling productive lands amidst a proprietary body not too numerous and not pressed too close to the soil. Where profits existed those who enjoyed them, formerly targets for "extinction" by ambitious taluqdars, now might well more readily challenge the taluqdar in court, and more successfully fend off his attempts to regain control of their land. Where the taluqdar by contrast retained as proprietor substantial tracts of productive land, or could even without revenue-collecting rights exploit ties of deference and lineage binding him to those beneath him, he could the more easily retain his former dominance. As we shall see in examining the revolt of 1857 the taluqdars remained a force of consequence in rural society. Yet the work of the generation of officials who served under Bird and Thomason was still profound, and lasting in its impact. By the mid-nineteenth century the face of society in the Doab, once hardly distinguishable from that in Oudh, bore little resemblance to that of its neighbor across the Ganges.

81. Colltr. Mainpuri to Commr. Agra 4 February 1846, B.R. Progs. 24 March 1846, No. 10. The raja was left with seven villages.

Five | *Debt, Default, and Dispossession*

THE AWARD OF proprietary title over their lands did not by any means usher in for the village communities a golden age of prosperity. Even though the burden of supporting the taluqdar had been lifted from them, and the officers responsible for the new settlement ceaselessly proclaimed its fairness, the condition of these village bodies did not at once markedly improve. Indeed throughout the 1830s, and into the years of midcentury, the combination of commercial depression and continued harsh assessments drove them increasingly into debt, and into arrears on their revenue payments. At the same time the settlement brought with it a new and more precise definition of all landed rights. The result was a dramatic and altogether unforeseen rise in the enforced transfer of property through the agency of the civil courts. The beneficiaries of the new settlement were to be its victims as well. In this chapter we will try to gauge the extent and character of such transfer in the North-Western Provinces in the years from 1835 to the Mutiny, and assess the effects of enforced sale upon the organization of rural society.[1]

1. In addition to the sales enforced by government order there were numerous private sales of land. Though some were the product of desperation, to raise capital for the payment of the revenue or to meet the demands of creditors, others were transactions incidental to the normal running of an estate and not necessarily a mark of impoverishment.

105

Assessment, Depression, and Sales: Aligarh

The first few years after settlement were exceptionally trying, and nowhere more so than in Aligarh. Even before Thornton arrived agriculture in the district was deeply distressed. The Collector in 1833, in an almost biblical style, lamented "the indifferent and small produce of last year's crops, the destruction of locusts, two successive bad seasons, the want of capital, the contraction of currency, the failure of Bhorahs, the ruin of indigo manufacturers, and the want of effective demand for the produce of their estates," which had reduced the village proprietors to despair, and to default.[2] Above all the collapse of the indigo trade hit Aligarh with great force. During the speculative boom of the 1820s the large Agency Houses of Calcutta, operating out of Farrukhabad, had recklessly pushed advances upon the village malguzars to induce them to grow indigo as a cash crop for export. Many villagers, caught up in the excitement, accepted the money, only to find themselves destitute, with no means of repayment and no market for their produce, when the bubble burst. In Mursan and Hathras alone by 1839 the recorded agricultural debt was twelve lakhs of rupees, of which nine were owed to the four bankrupt indigo factories at Jawar, Hathras, Mendu, and Sasni. Sold along with the factories at very low prices to local bankers, and for years forgotten, these unrecovered balances took on a fresh value with the conclusion, ironically, of the Thornton settlement, for the debtors' lands, pledged as security, had now a new worth. It was a misfortune, the district officer again lamented, that the settlement "has made these claims in a great measure good which before the people had any transferable property were not considered worth one anna in the rupee."[3]

The load of revenue debt, which had accumulated more slowly over the years, was the product of consistently heavy assessments. Thornton in his initial tour of the district had found the village communities already mired in debt. Time and again he reported instances "in which the juma was in the first place considerably too heavy; and in which the Malgoozars seem to have lost all hope of improving their condition, or of bearing up against the burden imposed upon them. . . . They are now deeply in debt, and utterly incapable of making any arrangements for defraying their arrears."[4] One of the worst hit was the small taluqa of Arr. Lashkarpur, in a "progressive state of decay" for years from a jama it was "altogether unequal to discharge." In 1830 Tikam Singh, still responsible for the payment of the revenue despite a settlement with the village muqaddams, desperate for funds sent in his "own

2. Colltr. Aligarh to Commr. Agra 13 September 1833, B.R. Progs. 20 September 1833, No. 24.

3. Settle. Offr. Aligarh to Commr. Meerut 22 October 1839, B.R. Progs. 19 November 1839, No. 16. See also Sec. Bd. Rev. to Sec. Govt. N.W.P. 10 November 1840, B.R. Progs. 10 November 1840, No. 12; and R. M. Bird, "Report on the Settlement of the N.W.P.," 21 January 1842, *P.P.* 1852-53, 25:148-49.

4. Depty. Colltr. Aligarh to Commr. Agra 26 September 1834, B.R. Progs. 14 July 1835, No. 27.

Agents to collect the rents from each separate assamee as well as from the seer land of the members of the village communities," who were thus left with "nothing but the name" of malguzar. These agents then proceeded to seize and sell the cultivators' plough oxen, where necessary, to make good "the arrears which the failure of their crops had occasioned." By the time Thornton arrived on the scene four years later 58 cultivators had fled the estate, some to Agra and Mathura; 6,664 *bighas*, or one-third of the culti-vated land, had fallen out of cultivation; and the estate was in arrears on the government revenue demand by nearly Rs. 10,000.[5] Nor were affairs in much better shape in Mursan itself. There Thornton found that "many of the village moqudums were unable to engage on the terms which I proposed, and that it was not sufficient to offer a remission for the first year, because having become involved in debt during their former struggles, they had not the power of advancing the necessary funds for renewing the cultivation of the villages. I have exerted myself to send for the asamies who have absconded, but have invariably found them destitute of everything but a grass cutter's knife."[6]

Thornton reduced the Mursan assessment by 13 percent, from Rs. 1,66,874 to Rs. 1,52,053. That of neighboring Hathras he lowered by 10 per-cent, to Rs. 2,62,186. Thornton's superiors, who approved these assess-ments, praised them as "fair and equitable."[7] Yet the condition of the village bodies did not improve. Part of the problem was the continued grip, for the first few years after settlement, of commercial depression, together with a run of bad seasons in which drought and famine followed one another in swift succession. As a result tillage fell off still further, and fresh arrears mounted up, while the government did little to alleviate the distress. Indeed in Mursan the relief effort ran afoul of the "incapacity" of the tahsildar, swayed by the "evil influence" of the local qanungo.[8] Yet even without fresh disasters the assessment itself remained too high. Thornton's reductions, W. H. Smith pointed out from the vantage point of the subsequent settle-ment, had been made from the assessments of the 1820s. But these were based not only on the exaggerated expectations of the indigo years but on the heavy exactions and sometimes paper demands of the old taluqdars and former Jat rulers. Hence they were not fit, even when reduced 10 percent, to form the basis for revenue collections over a long term.[9]

For some years the villagers' difficult position remained obscured by the ease with which they could obtain credit. As one of the foremost marts of

5. *Ibid.* See also Depty. Colltr. Aligarh to Commr. Agra 24 April 1834, B.R. Progs. 13 May 1834, No. 30. The Board of Revenue authorized a full remission of these arrears in October 1834.

6. Depty. Colltr. Aligarh to Commr. Agra 23 April 1834, B.R. Progs. 13 May 1834, No. 29.

7. Hutchinson, *Allygurh Statistics*, pp. 139, 145. Balances of Rs. 35,000 were at the same time written off as irrecoverable.

8. Settle. Offr. Aligarh to Commr. Meerut 22 October 1839, B.R. Progs. 19 November 1839, No. 16.

9. Smith, *Aligarh S.R.*, p. 91. For the assessments of the 1820s see above ch. 3.

northern India, Hathras town was home to a large banking and commercial population, who sought avenues of investment for their surplus capital in the neighboring countryside. As Thornton wrote of the pargana in 1836, "The unprecedented amount of debt here [which he then estimated at two lakhs exclusive of the old indigo balances] could never have been incurred but for the great number of native Sahookars resident in the Gunge of Hattrass, and generally throughout the pergunnah." He speculated further that "these individuals would appear to have found difficulty in the investment of their capital if I may judge from the avidity with which they have advanced it for the discharge of the Government revenue even when the individuals so borrowing were known to be overwhelmed with debt to other people. If this readiness to advance money had not existed among the capitalists, the balance book of the Government . . . would have shewn a very different result."[10]

The drought of 1838, by making repayment difficult and discouraging fresh loans, precipitated at last an open crisis for the embarrassed village malguzars. Their creditors did not seek foreclosure and sale of their properties for they were too depreciated to bring much of a return. Besides, the muqaddams of some villages had gained a reputation as being "intractable and troublesome," so that no one cared to tangle with them. The Hathras *banias* (moneylenders) were content with matters as they stood, with a "sufficient hold on many Estates, as to reap most, if not all, the profits and frequently of late part of the Revenue" as the harassed malguzars used the money due the government to purchase a temporary respite from their creditors' demands.[11] An insistence upon enforced sale had to await the coming of better times.

The villagers' plight was made worse during the first years of the settlement by their inexperience as revenue managers. Uncertain of their responsibilities, they often found themselves at the mercy of the local patwari, who controlled the records and frequently colluded with the tahsildar to have himself rather than the recognized malguzars made the channel of revenue payment. Sometimes too, for a consideration, the patwari aided creditors in their efforts to get hold of the village proceeds, or even advanced funds himself to the local malguzars. In Arr. Lashkarpur, where the muqaddams had been charged with the management of their villages since the late 1820s, and had fallen deeply in debt to the patwari Sita Ram, they protested, when confronted with a list of arrears, that they had paid the revenue, but that the

10. Hathras Settlement Report of 10 May 1836, B.R. Progs. 27 September 1836, No. 16. A year later he commented upon "the great abundance of native moneylenders . . . found everywhere in this district," and the advantage that provided for the improvement of cultivation and the security of the revenue. Settle. Offr. Aligarh to Commr. Meerut 12 September 1837, B.R. Progs. 24 September 1839, No. 2.

11. Depty. Colltr. Alligarh to Commr. Meerut 2 September 1840, B.R. Progs. 16 October 1840, No. 21.

patwari had instead credited the money to their private accounts with him, and so unwittingly driven them to default.[12]

As the arrears mounted up, to some Rs. 36,000 in Hathras and Mursan alone for the two years 1837 and 1838, the district officials began casting about for some way to meet the crisis. In October 1839 W. B. Wright, the Aligarh settlement officer, proposed that half the amount due, or Rs. 18,419, be remitted, where poverty made realization impossible. But he urged that the remainder be recovered by sale of the encumbered properties. Such a course was necessary, he said, "because I see no probability of the Malgoozaree being satisfactorily conducted by the present people, many of whom have decrees of the Civil Court hanging over them to an amount which there is not the slightest probability of being liquidated; others are unfitted by incapacity from continuing in the management and besides those who have absconded some few are known bad characters who have no fair plea for withholding the Government demand." Even if the truculence of the zamindars kept bidders from coming forward, he insisted, these estates should still "for the sake of example" be put to the hammer and then taken in by the government.[13] The Board of Revenue, less sanguine as to the benefits of sale, ordered that such drastic measures should not ordinarily be resorted to except where the proprietors had "contumaciously resisted the local authorities" or had "made away with the proceeds from which the revenue should have been defrayed." Those incapacitated by debt alone should only be deprived of management, and their estates farmed, for a term of years.[14] By the beginning of 1841 remissions of Rs. 22,461 had been sanctioned, and nine villages sold, in Mursan and Hathras. Two further villages had been let in farm.[15]

This bout of sales was soon followed by another, this time in pargana Tappal in the extreme northwest of the district. A land of tightly knit Jat communities, who owned 67 of the pargana's 86 villages and cultivated the bulk of the land themselves as *sir*, Tappal was held in jagir, until her death in 1836, by Begam Samru of Sardhana. The Begam's assessments, though pitched high and never altered, were rarely realized in full. Remission was frequently granted, and malguzars were never evicted from their holdings. Indeed outsiders feared to enter "so close a borough" as the Jat lands of

12. Settle. Offr. Aligarh to Commr. Meerut 31 January 1840, B.R. Progs. 14 April 1840, No. 23; and Arr. Lashkarpur Taluqa Statistics appended to Mursan Settlement Report of 20 December 1834, N.W.P. Rev. Progs. October 1837, No. 113.

13. Settle. Offr. Aligarh to Commr. Meerut 22 October 1839, B.R. Progs. 19 November 1839, No. 16.

14. Sec. Bd. Rev. to Commr. Meerut 19 November 1839, *ibid.*, No. 19; and Sec. Bd. Rev. to Commr. Meerut 14 April 1840, B.R. Progs. 14 April 1840, No. 24.

15. Sec. Bd. Rev. to Commr. Meerut 12 January 1841, B.R. Progs. 13 January 1841, No. 17; and Sec. Bd. Rev. to Sec. Govt. N.W.P. 7 December 1841, B.R. Progs. 7 December 1841, No. 1. Over the period from 1839 to 1852 estates assessed at Rs. 22,685 in Hathras, and Rs. 7,272 in Mursan, were sold for arrears of revenue. Hutchinson, *Allygurh Statistics*, p. 286.

Tappal. As a result defiance of the revenue authorities was common practice, and the habit persisted into the days of British administration.

From 1836 onward the British set out to collect at the Begam's paper rates, a demand made more onerous by the commercial depression of the time and one which, when Thornton came to revise it, he found absorbed often the full rental value of the land. The pargana's soils were at the same time of inferior quality, but little irrigated and dependent for their fertility in large part on the annual flooding of the Jumna. Yet the Jat communities of the pargana, reluctant to part with lands they themselves cultivated, contrived as best they could to meet the government's demands. In the process they fell ever more deeply into debt. In the Begam's time, though the villagers were almost always "entirely dependent" on moneylending Bohras to secure their crops, the overall load of debt was light and took the form largely of advances for seed repaid at harvest. Under the British, pressed for funds, the village communities found themselves increasingly at the mercy of their creditors. These monied men, as in Arr. Lashkarpur but unlike the more commercial Hathras, were commonly the local patwaris, who thus gained a double hold over the village and its hard-pressed managers.[16]

The landholders' situation was made more difficult by the principle of joint responsibility for the revenue, making them liable as a body for the default of any of their number, which the British enforced upon the cosharers of pattidari villages. A reflection of its poverty and its extended Jat proprietary communities, Tappal pargana encompassed within its 86 villages a total of 750 distinct pattis, or individual shares, with some villages split into as many as 30 to 40 minute fragments. With so many shareholders in each village, some few were almost invariably in arrears; yet the solvent members, unused to such responsibility and often strapped for funds themselves, were reluctant to bail out their brethren. Indeed the knowledge that the shares of all might be sold for the default of a few induced the solvent pattidars to withhold their own revenue payments. If they must necessarily be involved in a common ruin, they reasoned, why should they keep their own accounts paid up; and so the arrears mounted.[17]

The final blow came with the failure of the rains, and the inundation of the Jumna, during the two successive years of 1843 and 1844. These bad seasons made it at once impossible for the impoverished landholders to pay back their advances, while the moneylenders as quickly withheld further assistance. So early as July 1843 the Collector reported that as "the proprietors are not generally in good circumstances, and are consequently unable to lay out any funds for the digging of wells and as the cultivation is entirely depen-

16. Tappal Settlement Report of 31 January 1837, B.R. Progs. 2 May 1837, No. 30; and Colltr. Aligarh to Commr. Meerut 28 February 1846, B.R. Progs. 26 June 1846, No. 52.

17. Colltr. Aligarh to Commr. Meerut 13 June 1844, B.R. Progs. 16 May 1845, No. 15; and Colltr. Aligarh to Commr. Meerut 28 February 1846 (see n. 16 above). For further discussion of sales of undivided pattis see below pp. 119-20.

dent upon rain, the continuance of bad seasons has nearly ruined them."[18]
Sales began that year with three estates and five pattis, assessed at a jama of
Rs. 3,225, put to the hammer. The following year a total of 66 sales involving
22 villages took place. Overall during the first decade of the regular settlement, up to 1847–1848, 33,657 acres, or more than one-third of the entire
pargana, were either sold or farmed for arrears of revenue in Tappal.[19]

Unlike the earlier sales in Hathras and Mursan, the Board of Revenue
made no attempt to halt these enforced transfers. In December 1845 the
Lieutenant Governor ordered a special inquiry into this sudden upsurge of
sales, but the outcome was a blanket exoneration of the Collector's action,
and indeed of Thornton's assessment, in which no blame was imputed to
anyone. Much of the problem, so the Collector argued, arose from the difficulty of finding farmers for the lands of defaulting villages. "I sent for all the
large and influential landholders of the surrounding pergunnahs and some
from Bolundshuhur district," he reported, "but all my efforts to induce them
to take the villages in farm were of no avail. The continuance of bad seasons
and the difficulties they knew they would experience in managing the villages
whilst the old proprietors held any interest in the villages deterred them from
coming forward, whilst the depressed state of the cultivation would render a
large outlay necessary beyond the payment of the balances, before they could
expect to realize even the Government juma." Where farmers were procured
they were obliged to pay only the subsequent assessments, not the old
balances.[20]

Nor was sale always easy to arrange, for the Jat proprietors of the pargana,
impoverished and usually "in some way connected" by descent, refused to
purchase each other's villages. Yet the local officials remained determined to
oust these indebted and "refractory" holders in favor of more "opulent" or
enterprising newcomers. Hence even when bidders did not come forward,
and the government had itself to take over the property with the balances
unrealized, they still persevered. Of the 66 sales that took place in Tappal
during 1844 the government found itself the owner of the property in 48.
Once their holdings were in the government's hands, so the Collector
reasoned, the former proprietors would either leave the village, or, reduced
to the status of mere cultivators, be in no position to interfere with the measures farmers or purchasers might adopt for the improvement of the village.
Sometimes the government went on itself physically to displace the old
owners. In Narwari the "whole Mewatee proprietary," who had gained a

18. Report on the Revenue Administration of Aligarh District for 1842-1843, of 6 July 1843,
B.R. Progs. 20 September 1844, No. 16.
19. Sec. Govt. N.W.P. to Sec. Bd. Rev. 27 December 1845, B.R. Progs. 13 January 1846,
No. 11; and Atkinson, *Statistical Account*, 2:609. The total jama of the land sold was Rs.
25,567, and the balances Rs. 28,561, over the period up to 1852. Hutchinson, *Allygurh
Statistics*, p. 286.
20. Colltr. Aligarh to Commr. Meerut 23 March 1846, B.R. Progs. 26 June 1846, No. 55;
and Sec. Bd. Rev. to Sec. Govt. N.W.P. 26 June 1846, *ibid.*, No. 59.

reputation as "the terror of the surrounding countryside," were swept away, and Jats related to the Jat families of the pargana installed in their stead. "The village is now one of the most flourishing in the district and yields a profit of more than three times the jumma."[21] While the Tappal Jats might be unwilling to take advantage of each other's weakness, they had no hesitation in profiting at the expense of outsiders, and so further entrenching themselves in power in the countryside.

Assessment and Sales: An Overview

The harsh assessments and extensive sales in Aligarh were by no means unique. Farther down the Doab in Mainpuri conditions were remarkably similar, and sales during the early years of the revised settlement even more widespread. As in Aligarh much of the distress stemmed initially from the drought and famine of 1837–1838, which hit Mainpuri severely, leaving fields untilled and villages deserted everywhere. Some of this loss was made good in the subsequent year, but the run of unfavorable seasons persisted into the early 1840s, and so prevented any effective recovery. Indeed further land sometimes fell out of cultivation after 1838 from the continuing effects of depopulation and loss of cattle. The settlement officer G. F. Edmonstone, engaged at the time in the work of revision, made little allowance for these setbacks. Though some temporary measures of relief were granted on the occasion of the drought, land "lately abandoned" and land prepared but not sown at the time of the survey in the summer of 1838 were included in the cultivated area liable to assessment, and then assessed at full rates. The resulting revenue demand, though increased but Rs. 43,000 over its predecessor, pressed heavily upon the village communities from the start. When further deterioration followed, rather than the improvement Edmonstone had so confidently expected, default, and with it enforced sale, were the inevitable outcome. In 1841 alone lands assessed at Rs. 54,000 were sold for arrears in Mainpuri district.[22]

One of the worst hit areas was taluqa Manchanna, already buffeted by the storms of the settlement controversy. There the uncertainty of tenure during the early 1840s encouraged many village communities to withhold payment, while for others the burden of the raja's malikana, which had to be paid in addition to the revenue, cut sharply into their profits, and helped drive them over the brink into default. Beyond this over much of the estate the demand was "based upon realizations made in better times by the Rajah, much above the result of rates, who always took what he could get from the industrious communities of Lodhies, Brahmins and (sometimes) Aheers, while he let off

21. Colltr. Aligarh to Commr. Meerut 28 February 1846, *ibid.*, No. 52. For further discussion of the outcome of the Tappal sales see below pp. 131–33.

22. *Mainpuri S.R.*, pp. 45–46. In Kanpur in similar fashion land thrown out of cultivation due to famine, and land only partially irrigated, was assessed at full rates. Montgomery, *Statistical Report*, p. 16.

the Chowhan Thakoors (his own tribe) sometimes on easier terms either from favor or difficulty of coercion." Nor were the biswadari villages alone in arrears. Those left with the raja as zamindar suffered as well. Though not charged with malikana, they were, in the Mainpuri Collector's view, poorly managed by the raja's agents and often of "a very inferior nature." Indeed he speculated that the "wretched condition" of these villages at the time of settlement may have accounted for the relative paucity of claims in them and, where claims were made, for refusal of the village communities to engage on Edmonstone's terms, thus facilitating their consequent award to the raja.[23]

By the end of 1844, despite the remission during 1843 of Rs. 8,573, taluqa Manchanna was in arrears on the government revenue of the preceding three years to the extent of Rs. 43,893. To avert sale the government granted a complete remission of the balances due, together with a permanent lowering of the assessed demand. Initially Rs. 25,862 in 1844–1845, this reduction, from an original assessment of Rs. 98,742, was to be decreased by stages until the jama stood at Rs. 87,300, where it would remain until the end of the settlement. Over the district as a whole the revenue demand was at the same time reduced by two lakhs of rupees, to Rs. 10,45,000, a sum that rose gradually to Rs. 11,40,000 in 1851.[24] But there was a special urgency to avoid sales in Manchanna. H. Unwin, the Collector, in proposing the Manchanna remissions, had recommended as well that some especially turbulent village communities be sold out, not so much to recover the balances as to secure the payment of the revenue and the prosperity of the villages in the future. His superiors, however, flatly prohibited any such sales. As the Agra Commissioner caustically remarked, "If we sell the estate we do not get rid of the difficulty, for nobody will buy an estate full of Chowhans, and if Government buy, they have exactly the same difficulties to deal with as before, namely, a village populated by 'ignorant poor reckless Thakoors disputing among themselves and obstinately withholding the Government' *rent* as they before withheld revenue."[25]

Generally, throughout the North-Western Provinces, sales for arrears during the early years of the new settlement were confined to the Doab districts from Aligarh to Allahabad and the adjacent Bundelkhand districts of Hamirpur and Banda. Rohilkhand was nearly exempt from sale, as were the eastern districts (Benares alone excepted) and those to the northwest of the province bordering on the Punjab. (See Tables 6 and 7.) It is not possible to account precisely for this pattern of sale without examining each instance in

23. Colltr. Mainpuri to Commr. Agra 10 October 1844, B.R. Progs. 6 May 1845, No. 2. As a whole, however, the Manchanna lands were of superior quality. See below p. 145.

24. Sec. Govt. N.W.P. to Sec. Bd. Rev. 14 June 1845, B.R. Progs. 27 June 1845, No. 1. A similar reduction of Rs. 32,326 was also sanctioned for Kanpur district. Montgomery, *Statistical Report*, p. 16.

25. Commr. Agra to Sec. Bd. Rev. 31 December 1844, B.R. Progs. 6 May 1845, No. 1 (italics in original). The subordinate quotation is from Unwin's initial report.

Table 6. Sales for Arrears of Revenue, N.W.P., 1838–1859[a]

Year	Number of estates and pattis sold	Jama (rupees)	Balance due (rupees)
1838 (July-Dec. only)	—	1,22,782	1,42,138
1839	206½	1,86,143	1,24,917
1840	148	1,39,712	95,385
1841	179	1,74,879	1,77,170
1842	167	1,55,630	1,29,396
1843	186	1,36,940	92,081
1844	190	1,35,382	1,13,530
1845	92	66,720	41,809
1846	110	89,976	78,322
1847	63	50,480	24,249
1848	64	55,854	25,005
1849	—	not available	—
1850	66	74,232	37,426
1851	94	77,887	38,545
1852	115	1,04,408	46,934
1853	88	43,709	27,427
1854	—	not available	—
1855	22	18,680	12,233
1856 & 1857	—	not available	—
1858	12	15,098	11,677
1859	35	68,556	70,357

[a]Information for 1838 through 1841 taken from quarterly returns of sales and purchasers submitted to Board of Revenue; from 1842 onward from annual Statements of Estates Sold for Recovery of Arrears of Revenue under Acts XII of 1841 and I of 1845, in the Proceedings of the Board of Revenue.

detail. Yet the most severely affected districts do share to a substantial extent an involvement in the commercial agriculture of the 1820s and 1830s, with the higher assessments such agriculture brought, and they were all hard hit by the depression that followed. All, most strikingly, in an era when commercial cropping was wholly dependent upon river transport, bordered either the Ganges or the Jumna, the major arteries of northern India. Indigo, focused upon the great mart at Farrukhabad, was a central Doab crop *par excellence*. Cotton, funneled through the markets of Mirzapur and Benares, was grown primarily in Bundelkhand and in the Jumna parganas of Allahabad, Fatehpur, and Kanpur. Rohilkhand, by contrast, was largely a grain-producing region, as were the remote northerly Doab districts toward Saharanpur, while the eastern Azamgarh possessed a varied commercial agriculture with opium, sugarcane, and indigo.[26]

26. For a fuller analysis, taking a more precise account of regional variations, see Siddiqi, *Agrarian Change*, ch. v, esp. pp. 158–67.

Table 7. Sales for Arrears of Revenue, N.W.P., by District
(rupees)

Division	District	Assessed jama			Total
		1838–1842	*1843–1847*	*1848,1850–1853*	
Delhi	Delhi	15,162	700	0	15,862
	Gurgaon	12,147	6,783	0	18,930
	Rohtak	1,715	0	489	2,204
	Haryana	0	1,300	550	1,850
	Bhuttiana	0	1,000	5,775	6,775
	Panipat	1,148	0	613	1,761
Meerut	Saharanpur	2,687	0	0	2,687
	Muzaffarnagar	2,943	0	0	2,943
	Meerut	905	843	0	1,748
	Bulandshahr	2,655	818	0	3,473
	Aligarh	44,553	33,060	2,300	79,913
Rohilkhand	Bijnour	369	5,967	7,184	13,520
	Moradabad	750	395	2,472	3,617
	Budaon	6,488	2,571	1,600	10,659
	Bareilly	6,157	4,337	2,664	13,158
	Shahjahanpur	8,998	2,400	1,359	12,757
	Pilibhit	2,752	0	0	2,752
Agra	Mathura	52,361	61,867	1,525	1,15,753
	Agra	34,656	55,702	2,480	92,838
	Mainpuri	69,387	74,065	690	1,44,142
	Farrukhabad	41,768	45,068	237	87,073
	Etawah	1,82,438	4,341	0	1,86,779
Allahabad	Kanpur	38,877	5,605	0	44,482
	Fatehpur	65,938	4,535	2,084	72,557
	Allahabad	89,955	29,079	27,076	1,46,110
	Kalpi	2,500	10,864	0	13,364
	Hamirpur	32,102	1,257	36,489	69,848
	Banda	18,872	82,253	2,32,764	3,33,889
Benares	Gorakhpur	84	2,210	1,098	3,392
	Azamgarh	393	2,390	0	2,783
	Jaunpur	3,386	14,361	3,874	21,621
	Mirzapur	5,551	4,341	687	10,579
	Benares	19,080	17,032	6,972	43,084
	Ghazipur	13,268	4,343	1,652	19,263

Hence when the depression hit, its impact was regionally highly differentiated. The settlement officer in Bulandshahr in 1834 congratulated himself on the still "flourishing" state of the district. Indigo, he wrote, "has never been an article of large speculation here except in isolated spots so that the district has been little affected by the late fluctuations of the markets; the cultivation of cotton in like manner has never been carried to an extreme, and sugar is very little grown." Nor did the contraction of the currency cause much dislocation, for "nearly all the transactions between the cultivator and his landlord are carried on in kind. The landlord easily obtains from the neighboring large markets money to pay his revenue in payment for his grain, and the cultivator's few wants are in like manner supplied by the sale of the surplus of his share of the produce above what he requires for his consumption."[27] Azamgarh, together with much of the east, adapted to the collapse of its old export commodities by shifting to production of the newly profitable sugarcane. The agriculture of this region thus remained commercial; but, a rich and well-watered land, it was able by diversification to escape the worst effects of the depression, while it had not to contend with the drought that drove landholders in the west over the brink into default.[28]

In Aligarh, and throughout the Agra Division, where rainfall was scanty and alternative cash crops did not exist, the double blow of depression and drought was all too often overwhelming. Nor did the distress come to an end quickly. Only in the mid-1840s, as trade recovered and regular rainfall enabled the losses of cattle and seed to be made good, did the middle Doab districts pull out of their depressed state, and sales for arrears fall off to the levels elsewhere.[29] By far the worst hit area, and the only one where sales for arrears continued into the 1850s, was cotton-producing Bundelkhand. Assessed at a high rate in 1815 when the cotton market promised well, and subsequently farmed to speculators, this region, always one of uncertain rainfall, was utterly devastated by the collapse of its trade and the onset of famine in the 1830s. Hence its recovery, which involved the repopulating of entire villages, was extremely prolonged.[30]

Sales for Arrears: Controversy and Policy

When confronted with the prospect of a sale for arrears, the British revenue officials had always to choose between two competing policy objectives. Was it best, in the interests of a settled rural order, to keep in possession traditional village holders, and hence to avoid sale? Or was it desirable, in the interests of agrarian improvement, to get rid of refractory and deeply indebted proprietary bodies? At one level all the officers of government were in agreement: the sale process, as the Board of Revenue put it in 1839, "is not the proper mode of enforcing payment of revenue in Upper India." That much everyone had learned from the upheavals of the first decades of British

27. Assist. Settle. Offr. Bulandshahr to Commr. Meerut 19 June 1834, IOL Elliot Mss. Eur. D. 310.

28. See J. Thomason, "Report on the Settlement of Chuklah Azimgurh," 16 December 1837, *Sels. Recs. Govt. N.W.P.*, Part 14 (1854):128-32. I am endebted to C. A. Bayly for some useful insights into the relations between cropping patterns, depression, and land sales. For some indication of the later spread of sugarcane as a cash crop see Saiyid Muhammad Hadi, *The Sugar Industry of the U.P. of Agra and Oudh* (Allahabad, 1902), pp. 108-09.

29. The Mainpuri settlement officer dated the "great depression" in that district as lasting from 1837 to 1844, and the period of recovery from 1845 to 1850. *Mainpuri S.R.*, p. 46.

30. See Siddiqi, *Agrarian Change*, pp. 154-57; and "Report on the Settlement of Bandah, 23 October 1848," in *Thomason's Despatches*, 1:452-61.

rule. The reasons were, however, almost wholly economic and political, rather than humanitarian:

The fact is there is yet little amassed capital in these provinces, and there is less temptation to employ what exists in the purchase of a property swarming with a high spirited and warlike population banded together by the closest ties; supported by the sympathy of the whole surrounding country, generally of the same stock, always having one common interest in the exclusion of strangers, and all sworn to maintain war to the knife against the interloper. A system of periodical sale of such properties, if regularly enforced, would but have the effect of rendering land altogether unsaleable, and exciting a spirit of disaffection throughout the country.[31]

All agreed too that the most appropriate measure to recover arrears was to let the encumbered property for a term of years to a farmer, and then at its conclusion to reinstate the original holder. In this way social upheaval would be avoided and the government's revenue simultaneously secured. Immediate recourse to sale was, in the board's view, justifiable only in the case of nonresident proprietors who neglected their holdings and took no interest in cultivation. Such persons were "a hindrance to the agricultural prosperity of their properties," and of course politically impotent in the countryside as well, and so could be set aside at once. Otherwise, the board insisted, sale was permissible only when the less severe means of recovering the arrear had been tried and found wanting. Nor did they anticipate much likelihood of sale even then except in two sorts of cases. One was where the proprietors had through "debts or extravagance" let their lands fall into the hands of creditors who collected what they could and paid no revenue. In such a situation prompt sale could alone secure the public treasury from continuing loss. The other was where the property was held by a community of "wasteful habits and bad character" who defied the government and drove away prospective farmers. Here sale was necessary to enforce the lesson that "law and rule" could not be flouted.[32] These general principles met with the approval of the government, and were codified, together with certain procedural rules, in Act XII of 1841, which also required the Board of Revenue to review individually all applications for sale.

But what if no one came forward with a farming offer on a defaulting property? Should the arrears then be remitted, or the holding put up for sale? Who again was to determine whether a given proprietary body was of sufficiently "bad character" or "wasteful habits" as to have forfeited all claim to indulgence? At this point the board's general guidelines broke down, leaving each individual case to be examined on its own merits. By no means was there always full agreement as to the course that should be followed. When Thornton in 1839 proposed a light assessment for the "indolent and improvident" Chauhans of taluqa Morthal, already badly hit by distress

31. Sec. Bd. Rev. to Sec. G.-G. 7 June 1839, N.W.P. Rev. Progs. 12 August 1840, No. 93.
32. Sec. Bd. Rev. to Sec. Govt. N.W.P. 3 December 1841, B.R. Progs. 3 December 1841, No. 6.

and auction sales, the Board of Revenue fiercely proclaimed that "it is contrary to the duty of a good Government to encourage by indulgence men of ascertained and notoriously indolent and extravagant habits." While accepting the proposed assessment, they said they would "enforce the punctual realization of the revenue fixed by the immediate application of all legal modes of duress" and that they would feel no regret "should these villages be eventually alienated and fall into the hands of those who will render them profitable to themselves and to the country."[33] Most commonly, however, when faced with actual arrears, the district Collector was the one who advocated a ready resort to sale. Closer to the rural scene than the board, he had to wrestle daily with the problem of getting in the revenue, and his reputation was the one that suffered in the case of shortfall. Such clearly were the motives that lay behind Wright's enthusiasm for sale in Mursan and Hathras, and Unwin's in Manchanna.[34]

Anxious to preserve settled zamindari families, and little concerned about the fate of newcomers, James Thomason as Lieutenant Governor in 1846 broadened the guidelines permitting prompt sale to include not only estates in the hands of nonresidents but those previously acquired by sale at public auction, as well as those of "irremediably ruined" defaulters.[35] Concerned to find out how many properties were thus made liable to immediate sale, the Board of Revenue asked the district officers to compile lists of estates purchased at public sales, together with those "notoriously profitable when held by non-resident or non-cultivating proprietors."[36] The lists, which included 1,225 estates assessed at nearly ten lakhs for Benares Division alone, came in accompanied by strong objections to ready sale as a principle of revenue management on any occasion. Particularly strong was the outcry against treating the auction purchaser differently from the hereditary owner. It is of much importance, the Meerut Commissioner insisted, "that all should be treated with even-handed impartiality, with a view to encourage the investment of money in landed property." Indeed, so the Etawah Collector argued, as the auction sale had removed the defaulter who was deserving of punishment his successor was if anything entitled to be dealt with leniently.[37] Bowing to this unanimous opposition from below, in which it now itself shared, the government in 1854 cancelled the Thomason guidelines. Henceforth all cases of default were to be scrutinized on their own merits,

33. Taluqa Morthal Settlement Report of 30 November 1838, B.R. Progs. 24 September 1839, No. 61; and Sec. Bd. Rev. to Sec. G.-G. 24 September 1839, ibid., No. 12.

34. For a similar instance in Agra see "Orders Regarding Mouza Olinda Zillah Agra," of 23 November 1844, in Thomason's Despatches, 1:150–53.

35. Directions for Revenue Officers, p. 213.

36. Board's Circular of 30 July 1847, B.R. Progs. 30 July 1847, No. 48.

37. Commr. Benares to Sec. Bd. Rev. 25 October 1852, B.R. Progs. 19 November 1852, No. 54; Commr. Meerut to Sec. Bd. Rev. 8 October 1853, B.R. Progs. 10 January 1854, No. 67; and Commr. Agra to Sec. Bd. Rev. 26 May 1853, ibid., No. 69.

with none singled out for exceptional treatment by virtue of being in some special category.[38]

One especially vexing problem of revenue management was that of default among the shareholders of undivided pattidari estates. According to the regulations governing the revised settlement although each individual patti or share was separately defined and assessed, the cosharers were liable as a group for the default of any of their number. This joint responsibility was confirmed by Act I of 1841, yet the act at the same time gave the government the option of proceeding directly against the persons or property of individual members of the community. Under cover of this provision it became increasingly common during the next few years to bring to sale the property of the individual defaulter alone. This practice reached its height in the Tappal sales of 1844, when sixty-two undivided pattis were sold for arrears without enforcing any penalties on the other shareholders. During the inquiries that followed the government reaffirmed once again the principle of joint responsibility. There remained, however, the question of whether and how far the option allowed by Act I of 1841 should be exercised. The Board of Revenue, sympathizing with the plight of the solvent shareholder who saw no justice in his being forced to make good the arrears due from someone else, in June 1846 urged that the government abstain from enforcing the principle of general responsibility "whenever there is reason to believe that the solvent shareholders are too poor to pay what is due . . . or are ignorant of the responsibility they have incurred."[39]

Thomason, the Lieutenant Governor, in reply deplored the board's willingness to brush aside so readily the principle of joint responsibility. This was, he argued, "an original and well recognized principle in all Village Communities," the "very bond which had held them together for so many years in so extraordinary a manner," and one of which the village proprietors were little likely to be in ignorance. He admitted that there were occasions when individual pattis rather than entire estates should suffer the penalties of default, most notably when sale of the whole property would injure the resources of the country or deter others from exertion. And he agreed that "every effort" should be made to realize the balance from the individual before proceeding against the community as a whole. But it was nevertheless essential to make the community feel "the strength of the bond which unites them, and the necessity of common exertion for the safety of the whole." Even poverty and ignorance, he insisted, might themselves be sufficient reason for holding the entire community responsible, as a warning and a spur to enterprise for others.[40]

38. Sec. Govt. N.W.P. to Sec. Bd. Rev. 8 February 1854, B.R. Progs. 14 March 1854, No. 31.

39. Sec. Bd. Rev. to Sec. Govt. N.W.P. 26 June 1846, B.R. Progs. 26 June 1846, No. 59.

40. Sec. Govt. N.W.P. to Sec. Bd. Rev. 27 July 1846, B.R. Progs. 11 December 1846, No.

Thomason's views prevailed with the Court of Directors, and were embodied in his authoritative "Directions for Collectors." Not everyone at once fell into line. In August 1848 the members of the Board of Revenue, led by the outspoken H. S. Boulderson, were still protesting the enforcement of joint responsibility, especially in cases where the initial balances were incurred by a stranger over whom the other shareholders had no effective control.[41] Ultimately, however, it was not so much the board as the village proprietors themselves who undid the principle of joint responsibility. The settlement regulations made provision not only for cooperative enterprise but, on petition, for the complete division of pattidari estates, and the registration of each portion as a distinct revenue-paying mahal. Increasingly common by midcentury, as outsiders purchased portions of villages and dissident shareholders sought to get out from under their obligations to their brethren, this separation of interests at once put an end to all responsibility on the part of the former pattidars for the revenue of land controlled by others.[42]

This controversy over the sale of undivided pattis was part of, and reflected, a persisting conflict between Thomason's conservative paternalism and the more rigorous *laissez-faire* individualism of the Board of Revenue. Much less extensively argued, though of far greater consequence for rural society, was whether the pitch of the assessment and the method of revenue collection forced on arrears and sales. Few revenue officials at the time were prepared openly to acknowledge the existence of any connection between their assessments and forced sale. At the outset, while framing the rules for sale, the Board of Revenue had confidently proclaimed that "the moderation of the present settlement places it within the power of every malgoozar to pay punctually and well." Rarely was this tone of self-congratulation abandoned. Even in the midst of the sales in Mainpuri the board referred to it as "though an unevenly not an overassessed district."[43] Yet critics were not altogether lacking. The dissident F. J. Shore for one, in his *Notes on Indian Affairs*, passionately argued that a Collector "is in various ways made to feel that his reputation and prospects depend upon his realizing a large revenue; and that a recommendation for a reduction in the amount of the assessment is only considered in the light of a register of his own inefficiency." A man has only to tax the people of his district at a higher rate than his predecessor, Shore claimed, "and his name is established."[44] The accuracy of such sweeping

15; Sec. Govt. N.W.P. to Sec. Bd. Rev. 8 February 1847, B.R. Progs. 19 February 1847, No. 63; and *Directions for Revenue Officers*, pp. 194–98.

41. Note by H.S. Boulderson of 19 January 1848, B.R. Progs. 15 August 1848, No. 125; and Minute by F. H. Robinson of 15 August 1848, *ibid.*, No. 126.

42. *Directions for Revenue Officers*, pp. 238–46. For an illustration of this process in operation see Charles Raikes, *Notes on the North-Western Provinces of India* (London, 1852), pp. 93–107.

43. Sec. Bd. Rev. to Sec. Govt. N.W.P. 3 December 1841, B.R. Progs. 3 December 1841, No. 6; and Sec. Bd. Rev. to Sec. Govt. N.W.P. 3 December 1841, *ibid.*, No. 2.

44. Shore, *Notes on Indian Affairs*, 1:171–72.

charges cannot of course easily be established, but they are not entirely at odds with the evidence of the way the assessments were framed, nor with the retrospective accounts of later settlement officers.

One indicator of possible overassessment which attracted considerable attention was the price fetched by estates sold for arrears of revenue at government auctions. Invariably this was below the price of land sold by order of the civil court, and far below that of land sold privately. The Commissioner of Rohilkhand in 1849 supplied the figures shown in Table 8 for the preceding three years' sales in his division.[45] The Commissioner attributed the "remarkable" lowness of the arrear sale prices to the "comparatively highly assessed and deteriorated" condition of the estates sold, though they could of course also have contained much marginal, hence undesirable, land. Yet the issue did not rest. Indeed the year before, the Senior Member of the Board of Revenue had spoken in much the same terms. The "very small number of years' purchase of the Government juma" of estates sold for arrears, he said, "sufficiently indicates that these lots even though they may be from other causes partially deteriorated, are suffering generally from overassessment, particularly when it is also considered that a sale for arrears of revenue affords the most secure title."[46] In Mainpuri as well, looking back on this period from the 1870s, the author of the first district gazetteer noted that "the price of land at public sales was abnormally low." This he attributed "principally to the fact that most of the sales were on account of arrears of revenue where the estates were either overassessed or the landlords were contumacious and too powerful for outsiders to come in and bid up to the full value."[47]

The widespread arrears of the early 1840s were linked not just to the level of the revenue demand but to the way in which it was collected. Up to 1840 the revenue installments (*qists*) were numerous, eight or ten in a year, and so timed that the demand preceded the cutting of the crop. To secure payment the government often put a lien (*shahna*) on the standing crops for the amount of revenue due, which then was made good at harvest time. Under the revised system of collection the qists were reduced to four, and so spaced that the crops could be cut and sold before the government demand was due. No longer could the government intercept the proceeds of the harvest before they reached the landholder's hands, but the latter gained the substantial benefit that he had no longer to take out from a local capitalist the expensive *badhni* loan he had formerly required to meet the early payment date.[48]

45. Commr. Rohilkhand to Sec. Bd. Rev. 11 October 1849, B.R. Progs. 6 November 1849, No. 1.
46. Sec. Bd. Rev. to Sec. Govt. N.W.P. 15 August 1848, B.R. Progs. 15 August 1848, No. 1. The Junior Member felt that it was premature to give an opinion one way or the other on the question.
47. Atkinson, *Statistical Account*, 4:605. See also *Mainpuri S.R.*, p. 51.
48. For an account of the old system of revenue collection see Siddiqi, *Agrarian Change*, pp. 122–33. It was not always possible, even after the change of *qists*, to market the produce before

Table 8. Sales of Land, Rohilkhand

	1846-1847		1847-1848		1848-1849	
	Price per acre (rupees)	Proportion of price to jama	Price per acre (rupees)	Proportion of price to jama	Price per acre (rupees)	Proportion of price to jama
Sale for arrears	1-14-11	1.03	1-1-10	0.76	2-10-5	1.26
Sale by decree of court	4-12-6	2.73	3-10-5	2.27	2-7-2	1.62
Private sale	5-8-2	5.69	6-6-9	4.63	6-13-4	4.21

Despite this lightening of the burden upon the landholder H. S. Boulderson on the Board of Revenue saw in the new mode of collection a cause of the increased arrears and sales which marked the years following its imposition. Men "notoriously childish and improvident," the village proprietors were, in his view, wholly unable to resist the temptation of "spending the produce which forms the source of payment of their obligations long before ever the demand was to be made upon them." It would require, he insisted, at least a generation and "a change of almost all the proprietors of the country" before these men could be broken to the new style of payment.[49] Thomason, the Lieutenant Governor, acknowledged that the new system of collection might have contributed to the frequency of sales for arrears, but he refused to accept Boulderson's pessimistic appraisal of the character of the people. In classic Victorian fashion he urged that "the measures of the Government ought to be made to favor the industry of the thrifty, rather than to save the unthrifty from the effects of their unthriftiness," and he insisted that the new mode of collection had already added to the prosperity of many "industrious persons." It was a further "triumph" of the new revenue system that in place of such "severe" practices as personal constraint and the employment of shahnas it had given the government a lien upon the landed property of the defaulter, which was, if used with discretion, the "very best means of obtaining payment of the demand." The temporary increase in sales notwithstanding, the system of revenue collection remained "sound in principle."[50]

Debt and Coercive Transfer

Over time, as the most inequitable assessments were reduced, the most impoverished and recalcitrant landholders sold out, and the effects of the depression dissipated, sales for arrears of revenue became less frequent.

the revenue was due, nor of course could the landholder then get the best price for it. See Whitcombe, *Agrarian Conditions*, pp. 155-56.

49. Minute by H. S. Boulderson of 27 January 1844, B.R. Progs. 18 June 1844, No. 56. T. J. Turner, the other member of the board, denied that the recent sales had any connection with the mode of revenue collection. Minute of 7 June 1844, *ibid.*, No. 57.

50. Sec. Govt. N.W.P. to Sec. Bd. Rev. 31 August 1844, B.R. Progs. 27 September 1844, No. 13. See also Thomason to G.-G. 15 June 1844, in *Thomason's Despatches*, 1:126-36.

Government sale policy worked toward the same objective. By the mid-1850s sale was sanctioned only in cases of extreme contumacy or misappropriation of assets. But enforced land transfer in no way came to an end, for sales by order of the civil courts made good most of the deficiency.

Recourse to enforced sale as a way of recovering funds advanced to insolvent landholders first became practicable with the demarcation and registration of individual holdings which accompanied the revised settlement of the 1830s. Prior to that time there was no authoritative record of the lands held by an individual, nor was his title legally cognizable in the courts. The new settlement, however, gave the landholder an exclusive and transferable title conveying unrestricted rights of ownership. He had thus for the first time a valuable property, one that could be mortgaged in return for cash but at the same time transferred by the civil court to a creditor on the occasion of default. Moneylending had to be sure always been a prominent feature of the rural scene, for zamindars and cultivators alike were dependent upon credit not only for the purchase of luxury goods but for funds to obtain seed and cattle and often to meet the government revenue demand as well. Nor were all moneylenders of one sort, the mythical bania of nineteenth-century caricature. Those who lent funds included almost all those who possessed surplus capital. They comprehended not only professional bankers, from the prosperous *sahukars* of Hathras to petty village *mahajans*, but wealthy agriculturists as well, village muqaddams and patwaris, *thikadars* (rent contractors) of local landlords, and even taluqdars, who by the provision of credit gained a further hold over those beneath them. But before the 1830s creditors had been restrained in their activities by the lack of any substantial security. The debtor's person and movables, even his crops, provided little to proceed against, while the indigenous judicial institutions offered the creditor little assistance. The moneylender's nineteenth-century rise was built upon the greater creditworthiness of the zamindar, together with the willingness of the British courts to decree him the property of his debtors on the production of a valid mortgage bond.[51]

The introduction of the new mortgageable tenure coincided with both the series of bad years that began with the famine of 1837 and the unequal assessments that so often disfigured the early working of the revised settlement. The distress this occasioned, as we have seen, drove many landholders to the moneylender. Some, anxious to avert a sale for arrears, used the funds to pay off the government, while others simply sought the means of subsistence. In either case loans contracted out of such desperation, and which generated so few new assets, could not easily be cleared off, but rather mounted up to ever higher sums. At the same time the coming into force of the new settlement gave a new value to old debts. In Hathras, the Agra Commissioner pointed out in 1835, bonds for debts bearing interest at up to 44

51. For a general discussion of credit and debt, though with data drawn mainly from the 1860s, see Whitcombe, *Agrarian Conditions*, ch. iv.

Table 9. Land Sold by Decree of the Civil Courts, N.W.P., 1840-1854

Year	Number of sales	Acres	Jama (rupees)	Amount paid (rupees)
1840	1,256	—	—	6,94,937
1841	1,671	—	—	6,92,046
1842	2,266	—	—	8,33,398
1842-1843	1,889	—	—	8,18,369
1843-1844	2,070	—	—	8,00,018
1844-1845	2,398	—	—	10,32,770
1845-1846	1,999	2,70,486	2,64,300	9,26,651
1846-1847	—	1,61,552	1,95,223	5,46,734
1847-1848	—	1,07,261	1,18,501	4,40,921
1848-1849	—	1,27,576	1,30,919	3,73,704
1849-1850	—	1,07,324	1,27,173	4,31,264
1850-1851	—	1,23,343	1,41,805	4,92,861
1851-1852	—	97,769	1,15,347	5,41,925
1852-1853	—	1,14,592	1,20,141	5,01,886
1853-1854	—	1,20,818	1,31,818	5,36,770

percent annually and "involving . . . nearly the whole of the malgoozars of the pergunnah are in abeyance ready to be sued on the expected recognition of the rights of these men as zemindars on the approaching settlement." Nor did a lowering of the assessment necessarily improve the landholder's situation, for the "increase of profit" only excited the creditors "to bring forward and press their claims," leaving "the malgoozars as hopeless as before of even distant extrication."[52]

Sales in execution of court decrees began immediately after the inauguration of the settlement, and rose rapidly until by the early 1840s they were averaging some two thousand cases a year. Many of these early sales took place in those districts not affected by drought or depression, and whose lands consequently had not lost their value. In Azamgarh the number of sales rose from 45 in 1837 to some 200 five years later. Sales in neighboring Gorakhpur jumped from 6 to 186 between 1837 and 1840, and, at from 400 to 600 annually, were the most numerous of any district in the entire N.W.P. between 1843 and 1847. (See Tables 9 and 10.)[53] By 1843 the Board of Revenue had become thoroughly alarmed by the rapid rise in sales for debt. They bemoaned "the entire prostration of the indigent but powerful debtor

52. Commr. Agra to Sec. Bd. Rev. 14 January 1835, B.R. Progs. 27 January 1835, No. 36. See also Hathras Settlement Report of 10 May 1836, B.R. Progs. 27 September 1836, No. 16.
53. For sales before 1843 see Sec. Bd. Rev. to Sec. Govt. N.W.P. 31 January 1843, B.R. Progs. 31 January 1843, No. 7; and "Statement of Sales for 1840-43," B.R. Progs. 1 April 1845, No. 40. For subsequent years see the annual Revenue Administration Reports of the Board of Revenue. Districts outside the east with high levels of sales in the early 1840s included the hard-hit Aligarh, Agra, and Fatehpur, together with Saharanpur and Bareilly. These averaged from 100 to 200 sales per year.

Table 10. Land Sold by Decree of Court, N.W.P., by
District, 1845–1846 to 1853–1854

Division	District	Acres	Jama (rupees)
Delhi (all districts)		28,623	21,374
Meerut	Dehra Dun	3,733	454
	Saharanpur	59,545	50,287
	Muzaffarnagar	22,594	31,442
	Meerut	5,526	9,365
	Bulandshahr	21,802	24,629
	Aligarh	31,807	74,404
Kumaon	(both districts)	743	576
Rohilkhand	Bijnour	30,978	50,215
	Moradabad	38,897	42,075
	Budaon	58,935	43,787
	Bareilly	32,413	29,293
	Shahjahanpur	15,814	12,780
Agra	Mathura	10,325	27,586
	Agra	34,269	64,520
	Farrukhabad	12,315	19,378
	Mainpuri	29,436	44,500
	Etawah	19,491	33,807
Allahabad	Kanpur	86,748	1,21,859
	Fatehpur	16,358	22,150
	Allahabad	1,12,967	1,58,966
	Kalpi (to 1848)	7,705	5,181
	Hamirpur	56,125	33,660
	Banda	35,842	33,123
Benares	Gorakhpur	1,99,297	83,874
	Azamgarh	27,495	26,086
	Jaunpur	65,116	78,730
	Mirzapur	40,858	34,874
	Benares	24,694	44,813
	Ghazipur	92,263	1,02,394

Source: Data taken from "Statements of Select Public and Private Sales of Land" in annual *Revenue Administration Reports* of N.W.P. Sadr Board of Revenue.

before the weak but wealthy creditor" which the British system had brought about, and they feared that this "frequent result of our system" might be seen as an ingenious device "for breaking the power of all those who from hereditary wealth or influence might endanger our supremacy." A year later the Commissioner of Agra went on to lay at the door of the courts responsibility for "the constant formation of successive bands of robbers which give us so much trouble." Yet neither had any remedy for this "evil," which, despite its ominous political implications, they regarded as an inseparable part of India's transition from a "state of semi-barbarism" to the rule of law. The Board of Revenue recommended only that the sale laws be carried into effect fairly and openly. All sales, they said, should be conducted with suffi- cient advance notice and publicity to avoid *ex parte* or collusive decrees, and the district Collector, not a Judge, should be charged with executing the decrees.[54]

In the absence of any effective check, sales for debt continued at a high level even after the end of the immediate economic crisis. Although the num- ber of such sales declined after 1845, they leveled off at a figure substantially above that for arrears of revenue. In the years just before the Mutiny estates assessed at over one lakh of rupees changed hands annually by decree of court, while sales for arrears rarely exceeded one half lakh of assessed jama and were often much less than that amount. The fall in sales for debt was arrested not only by the continued contraction of new indebtedness but by the slow recovery of the old. In the depressed districts of the Doab, as we have seen, not all creditors were anxious in the years just after settlement to foreclose and take possession of their debtors' property. They preferred instead to control the profits of the estates, leaving title and a mounting backlog of interest payments in the hands of the hapless village owners. Only after the depression had lifted, and the value of the land had risen, from the mid-1840s onward, did they press their claims and bring the estates to sale, "that they might buy them in themselves and obtain a valuable investment for their money."[55]

As prosperity returned, and the grain trade revived, agricultural land along the channels of commerce throughout the province gained an en- hanced value. In the east, as well as in the riverine areas of the Doab, a revitalized commercial agriculture by midcentury made the heavy Thomason assessments easier to bear, and so reduced sales for arrears. Yet at the same time an increased value for land meant that it could be mortgaged for larger sums of money, and so tempted the landholder to increase his borrowing. But rural debt, so much of it incurred for economically nonproductive expen- diture, all too often brought in its wake default, and then sale. In the years before the Mutiny the districts with the highest rates of sale for debt lay in the richer eastern region of the province, above all in the environs of the great urban centers of Kanpur and Allahabad, where newly amassed capital sought a remunerative outlet in the purchase of land. In those areas by con- trast where commercial opportunity remained limited and the proprietors, pressed close upon the soil, had little margin for rental profit, as in Bundel- khand and Delhi, and portions of the northern Doab, enforced land sale through the courts was a much less frequent occurrence.[56]

54. Sec. Bd. Rev. to Sec. Govt. N.W.P. 31 January 1843, (see n. 53 above); and Agra Divi- sional Revenue Administration Report for 1843–44, of 12 December 1844, B.R. Progs. 16 May 1845, No. 30.
55. Atkinson, *Statistical Account*, 4:606.
56. Further study of the economic and tenurial situation of individual estates would be

The continuing high level of sales provoked in the mid-1850s a full-scale inquiry into the frequency and causes of land transfer in the North-Western Provinces. Anxious to exculpate themselves, the Collectors invariably denied that "undue pressure of the assessment" was at all involved. The bulk of the debt they ascribed to extravagant expenditure on the part of the landholders, who wasted their substance on jewelry and lavish weddings. (The British were of course always unable to appreciate the utility of such expenditure in enhancing the status and position of Indian landholders.) The remainder of the debt was put down to poverty and the recurrence of poor seasons which forced the agriculturists to the moneylender for seed, grain, and cattle. With but two exceptions none of the officials consulted brought forward any proposals for legislation. Most saw in the increased thrift brought about by education the only "effectual" remedy for debt, while some even looked upon the enforced transfer of land as a beneficial process which got land out of the hands of impoverished petty zamindars and into the possession of "enterprising capitalists" who could improve it.[57] Most outspoken perhaps was John Strachey, Collector of Moradabad, who argued that the "ancient village institutions of the country" were doomed to decay "with the establishment of good government and the progress of civilization." One of the greatest advantages indeed "which the proceedings connected with the last settlement conferred upon these provinces was this possibility, before almost unknown, of disposing freely of land like any other property."[58] The Victorian commitment to *laissez-faire* of necessity made the bania not the villain but the savior of Indian agriculture.

The Social Effects of Sale

To trace out the extent of land sold by coercive processes, and the ways in which it was brought to sale, although essential, is but a first step in understanding the effect of such transfers on rural society. We must ask as well which groups were losing, and which gaining land. As only title was transferred, not cultivating occupancy, how did the auction purchaser enforce his authority over the subordinate tenants and others on the soil? What happened to the dispossessed former zamindars? What difference overall did it make to the working of rural society that so much land changed hands through the British revenue and judicial machinery?

For decades it has been accepted as a commonplace that these transfers amounted almost to an agrarian revolution. Indeed the social dislocation they brought about has often, as we shall see in the following chapter, been described as a major cause of the uprising in the countryside during 1857. Throughout the last half of the nineteenth century too, the British viewed the

required to substantiate, or alter, this analysis. So far no work has been done on the patterns of sale at the local level.

57. For the reports of the district officers see "Frequency of Transfer of Proprietary Title," *Sels. Recs. Govt. N.W.P.* (Agra, 1856) 4:183–233.

58. Colltr. Moradabad to Commr. Rohilkhand 16 July 1855, *ibid.*, p. 213.

Table 11. Occupations of Purchasers of Land Sold for
Arrears, N.W.P., 1838–1842

Profession		Jama (rupees)	Percent
Zamindar or malguzar		1,43,392	23
Banker, etc.[a]		71,448	11
Service		26,554	4
Cultivator		10,177	2
Religion[b]		8,434	1
Other[c]		9,860	2
Mixed			
zamindar and banker	5,786		
zamindar and service	90,694		
service and banker	3,001	99,481	16
Government		2,44,118	39
Unknown		10,540	2
Total		6,24,004	100

[a]The professions included in this category are banker, *sahukar*, *shroff*, *mahajan*, trader, merchandizing, moneydealer, cloth merchant, indigo merchant, and Bohra.
[b]This group includes Brahmin, Chaube, Pirzada, and Qazi where no secular occupation is given.
[c]This group includes sugar manufacturer, chaudhari, military, noble, and vakil.

continued enforced sale of land as a dangerous potential source of unrest, particularly in such sensitive areas as the Punjab, where transfer outside certain named agricultural castes was prohibited in 1900.[59] Recent scholarship, however, has cast doubt, if not on the extent, then on the significance of enforced land transfer. After an examination of the Benares region Bernard S. Cohn argued that "the majority of individuals, families, and lineages who 'lost' land between 1795 and 1885 retained their positions, economically, politically, and socially *within* the local areas in which they had held rights as zamindars." In part this was because the entrenched former zamindars by their control over the subordinate cultivators were able to prevent the auction purchasers from raising rents or displacing them from their rich *sir* (home farm) lands. But there was as well, in an era of rising agricultural prices and expanded cash cropping, "enough enhanced value in agriculture for the former zamindars to profit along with the auction purchasers." As a result they did not suffer from their formal dispossession.[60]

A few facts are incontrovertible. One is that the very substantial amount of

59. For a summary of British views see my "The British and the Moneylender in Nineteenth Century India," *Journal of Modern History* 24 (1962):390–97.
60. Bernard S. Cohn, "Structural Change in Indian Rural Society, 1596–1885," in R. E. Frykenberg, ed., *Land Control and Social Structure*, pp. 89–114, esp. pp. 96–99, 112–13.

Table 12. Landholding by Caste, Kanpur, 1801–1850

Caste	Villages held at cession	Villages held in 1850	Increase	Decrease
Rajput	992	839	—	153
Brahmin	335	522	187	—
Kayastha	219	189	—	30
Muslim	191	325	134	—
Kurmi	144	159	15	—

transfer that took place in the North-Western Provinces was everywhere accompanied by the rise to power of new landholding groups. Cohn supplies data on 183 auction sales in Benares between 1795 and 1850. In these approximately 41 percent of the land transferred went to families whose principal occupation was recorded as moneylending, service, or law rather than zamindari management. Viewed in caste terms the result was the same. Rajputs, traditional controllers of land in the pre-British period, were the losers in 40 percent of these transfers, while the main beneficiaries were Kayasthas and Banias, groups who had not previously had much connection with the land.[61] The figures of land sold for arrears of revenue throughout the province between July 1838 and January 1842 support the same general conclusion. Of sales involving land assessed overall at Rs. 6,24,004, villages with a jama of Rs. 1,43,392, or 37 percent of the total (exclusive of that bought by the government), were purchased by men whose occupation was recorded as zamindar or malguzar. Commercial men and those in government or private service, together with those who combined both occupations, bought land assessed at just over one lakh, or 27 percent of the total.[62] (See Table 11.)

Nor do the district figures, despite the inevitable local peculiarities, differ much in character. In Kanpur, for instance, the first half-century of British rule saw shifts in landholding for the five principal caste groupings shown in Table 12.[63] Invariably the most prominent losers were the Rajputs, while those who gained were the Brahmins and the various commercial castes. Overall, during the thirty years of the revised settlement, groups not ordinarily connected with the land increased their holdings from a total of 10 to some 27 percent of the revenue-paying area.[64]

61. *Ibid.*, pp. 71–76.
62. Data are taken from the "Quarterly Statements of Sales for Arrears" in the Board of Revenue proceedings between 22 February 1839, No. 44, and 1 July 1842, No. 71. Detailed citations are available with the author.
63. Montgomery, *Statistical Report*, p. 38. The Brahmin purchasers included "some of the most successful mercantile speculators in the district"; the Muslim beneficiaries had profited by the public sales in the early years of British rule. For similar data for Mainpuri see *Mainpuri S.R.*, p. 52.
64. *Papers on Agricultural Indebtedness* (Simla, 1898), 1:40–41. For transfers in Aligarh during these years see below ch. 6.

But the dispossessed landholders were by no means always willing to oblige the auction purchaser by at once handing over the profits of the estate. Indeed their hostility and "refractoriness" manifested themselves well before the fall of the hammer. In cases of arrears of revenue the government, as we have seen, almost always tried to let the defaulting property out on farm before resorting to sale. Often, however, as in Tappal, no one could be found who was willing to brave the wrath of the entrenched proprietors. Similarly in pargana Hathras the Collector complained of village Bussoli that "the customary proclamations have been issued and farming offers invited from the sharers and the public at large, but owing to the notorious character of the village community no one has ventured to come forward."[65] Nor did sale necessarily solve the problem. Five of the eight properties brought to sale in Tappal in 1842–1843, and forty-eight of the sixty-six sold the subsequent year (the bulk of them shares in undivided estates), were purchased by the government for want of bidders. Even after taking title the government could only procure farming offers for these properties by abandoning the attempt to collect the balances for which they had been sold, and in five they were forced to resort to the expensive expedient of *kham* (direct) management.

In Mainpuri, with its "prevalence of large cultivating Thakoor communities," the difficulties were if anything greater. The Collector in 1845 cited as a "case similar to many others in the district" the village of Lyampur Bhatpura, the property of a body of "idle, poor and contumacious" Chauhan Rajputs. Although the assessment had been reduced at settlement from Rs. 526 to Rs. 365, and remissions of Rs. 792 awarded for the years of drought, "the revenue was never paid afterwards." When sold for balances, the village was purchased by the government for one rupee. "No farmer could be found, and it has been held kham since the sale, yearly falling into worse condition."[66] By 1847 the Agra Commissioner, despairing of "getting people to either buy or take in farm" such villages, reported that "we are driven to bring our demand as nearly as possible to the ripening of the crops," by for instance increasing the May *qistbandi* (collection) at the expense of the June. In no other way, he said, could the government get round "the comparative weakness in that district of our lien on the soil."[67]

Some indication of the overall extent of the problem can be gathered from the figures cited in Table 11, which show 39 percent of the land sold for arrears between 1838 and 1842 purchased by government. The results were no different in subsequent years (see Table 13). Not all government purchases were of course due to the "refractory nature of the inhabitants." Much land was so overassessed or so depreciated that buyers could not be found on that account. But the difficulties of control added substantially to those of the

65. Settle. Offr. Aligarh to Commr. Meerut 4 April 1840, B.R. Progs. 28 July 1840, No. 67.
66. Colltr. Mainpuri to Commr. Agra 25 April 1845, B.R. Progs. 26 June 1846, No. 55.
67. Commr. Agra to Sec. Bd. Rev. 11 February 1847, B.R. Progs. 26 February 1847, No. 34.

Table 13. Land Sold for Arrears and Purchased
by Government, N.W.P., 1842–1848

Year	Jama of land sold for arrears (rupees)	Jama of land purchased by Government (rupees)
1842	1,55,630	98,289
1843	1,36,940	95,070
1844	1,35,382	63,360
1845	66,720	35,248
1846	89,976	46,601
1847	50,480	18,510
1848	55,854	18,227

harvest and the season in keeping potential buyers away from the government auctions.

Much of the land purchased by the government ultimately found its way, surprisingly, back into the hands of the original owners. In some instances the initial sales were themselves clearly contrived. Defending his enhanced assessment of pargana Sukait in Mainpuri despite the "numerous Government purchases" that had taken place there, Edmonstone pointed out that the old zamindars, when offered the opportunity of being readmitted as farmers, were willing "not only to engage for their respective estates at the new juma, but at the same time to liquidate the arrear for which they were sold, as the price of their restoration." As a result "their possession was not even disturbed." So little indeed did such sales mean to the community at large that the zamindars of one village "actually mortgaged one thoke [share] of the estate long after all their rights of transfer had been annihilated by the sale." Why then were the villages brought to sale in the first place? Because the zamindars realized that they could by "designed defalcation" both retain possession and at the same time deprive their creditors of their lien on the property, for land could not be brought to sale in execution of decrees of court unless held in full proprietorship. As farmers the old holders were safe from disturbance.[68]

On occasion too the old owners regained possession by a form of subterfuge in which a reluctant government was forced to acquiesce. In 1848, four years after the auction sales had taken place, the government was still the owner of thirty-nine pattis in Tappal. Anxious to disentangle itself from the

68. Settlement Report of 5 September 1839, B.R. Progs. 3 September 1841, No. 5. Much the same result was sometimes brought about by collusive private sales, in which land was nominally transferred to a friend or relative to evade sale in execution of a decree of court. See Colltr. Bijnour to Commr. Rohilkhand 10 March 1855, *Sels. Recs. Govt. N.W.P.* (1856) 4:211; and Colltr. Jaunpur to Commr. Benares 10 October 1854, *ibid.*, p. 228.

"embarrassing position" of being a joint sharer in these estates, it decided to sell the properties for the "bare amount" of the original sale balance to the farmers who had subsequently taken them on contract. Inquiry soon revealed, however, that the farmers were in most instances relatives and connections of the old proprietors, or members of the same extended lineages, who were willing to "sacrifice a great deal ere they allowed a stranger to enter." Rightly suspecting collusion, the Board of Revenue insisted that the Collector obtain from every purchaser before the award of title a "distinct certificate" stating that he was acting only on his own behalf. Otherwise "a bad example will be held up, that men may retain balances, and then after sale, may get the property back, on a promise to pay by installments, which promise is likely to be kept as ill as the previous engagements."[69] Despite these precautions nearly all the Tappal villages ultimately found their way back to their original owners or their close relations. At the expiry of the settlement Jat families still held all but three of the pargana's sixty-nine original Jat villages.[70]

The figures for Mainpuri, although not conclusive, provide some indication of the overall extent of restoration. From 1845 to 1851 some thirty estates were purchased by the government at sales for arrears of revenue. Of these, seventeen were restored to the original proprietors. In six instances restoration was justified on the ground that overassessment was the cause of the balance and consequent sale.[71] Over the whole period from 1840 to 1857 a total of 87,646 acres of cultivated land changed hands by forced sales of all kinds in the district. Of this, 19,355, or just short of one-quarter of the total, found its way back to the original owners.[72] It is impossible to apportion this land between that sold initially for arrears of revenue and that transferred by decree of court. Nor can one discover which passed through private hands, instead of being taken in by the government, before restoration. Speaking generally of the entire province, however, the Board of Revenue in 1854 noted that almost all instances of the permanent reinstatement of former proprietors were those in which the government itself purchased the property and then readmitted the former owners "either after revision of the contract, or remission of burdens, or restoration by the aid of its capital without interest of property deteriorated by calamity of season."[73]

69. Commr. Meerut to Sec. Bd. Rev. 14 February 1848, B.R. Progs. 31 March 1848, No. 110; and Sec. Bd. Rev. to Commr. Meerut 31 March 1848, *ibid.*, No. 114.

70. Atkinson, *Statistical Account*, 2:609.

71. These figures are drawn from an inspection of the Mainpuri District Index to the Board of Revenue proceedings. As a result they do not necessarily include all cases of sale or restoration that may have taken place during the years concerned.

72. Atkinson, *Statistical Account*, 4:602; and *Mainpuri S.R.*, p. 49.

73. Sec. Bd. Rev. to Sec. Govt. N.W.P. 10 January 1854, B.R. Progs. 10 January 1854, No. 72. Some land seems also to have been retransferred by prearrangement with the creditor on repayment of the debt for which the property had been originally sold. See Colltr. Aligarh to Commr. Meerut 20 April 1855, *Sels. Recs. Govt. N.W.P.* (1856) 4:198; and Commr. Benares to Sec. Bd. Rev. 8 December 1854, *ibid.*, p. 226.

Restoration was thus in large measure a product of lack of bidders at the initial sales, combined with a desire on the government's part to see justice done to those who had been the victims of overassessment or seasonal misfortune. When the Mainpuri Collector asked what steps he should take to dispose of the village of Lyampur Bhatpura, so long in government hands, the Board of Revenue promptly replied that so long as the former zamindars were willing to engage and were not "greatly in the wrong" in provoking the original sale, they should, "in this case as in others" where a reduction of jama was allowed, be given the option to reengage before the village was offered in farm to a stranger.[74] In Tappal restoration was clearly facilitated by the poverty of the soil and the tenacity of the people. Had the Jat communities been less tightly knit, and the pargana's soils more productive, and hence a more valuable investment, much more of the land would doubtless have found new owners. Both the extent of the original sales and the extent of their undoing were part of the same phenomenon.

Restoration of the old proprietors was not practicable, so the Board of Revenue argued, once they had lost their hold on the tenantry and the respect of the neighborhood, either by removal elsewhere or by subsidence into the ranks of ordinary cultivators.[75] But was the contrary also true? Was transfer to a new purchaser equally "hopeless" when those ties remained intact? There can be no doubt, as Bernard Cohn argues, that an auction purchaser was at a disadvantage in consolidating his hold over his property when confronted by powerful and well-connected ex-zamindars. At times the struggle for supremacy could be violent, even bloody. Reporting a case of murder in Mathura, the Agra Commissioner noted that the deed arose from a sale by decree. If, he said, in all cases of enforced sale, the Collector were to settle the terms on which ousted proprietors should hold their lands "many violent crimes would be prevented."[76]

Despite the opposition he encountered, an auction purchaser, if determined, was almost always able to make good his claim to the profits of his new estate. The process might of course take considerable time. It sometimes benefitted from government assistance, as in the Tappal village of Narwari where the Mewati proprietors were physically expelled in favor of a body of well-connected local Jats. Sometimes too it involved the displacement of the

74. Sec. Bd. Rev. to Commr. Agra 13 June 1845, B.R. Progs. 13 June 1845, No. 89. By the time of sale the jama had been further reduced to Rs. 277. For further instances of restoration after purchase by the government on account of overassessment see Colltr. Allahabad to Commr. Allahabad 23 June 1860, N.W.P. Rev. Progs. 8 September 1860, No. 92, discussing settlement revision in pargana Khairagarh.

75. Sec. Bd. Rev. to Sec. Govt. N.W.P. 10 January 1854, B.R. Progs. 10 January 1854, No. 72.

76. Commr. Agra to Sec. Govt. N.W.P. 18 July 1849, B.R. Progs. 17 August 1849, No. 151. The government in reply ordered purchasers to record the rents to be paid by those deprived of ownership by decree of court and to submit disputes to the Collector. (Sec. Govt. N.W.P. to Commr. Agra 9 August 1849, *ibid.*, No. 152.) For instances of violence and intimidation directed against auction purchasers see Cohn, "Structural Change," pp. 107-11.

initial purchaser by a more stout-hearted successor. When the Muslim proprietors of village Athsaini in Meerut fell into debt and were sold out at auction, the estate "was purchased by Ramchurn Doss, sahookar, who was unable to control these quarrelsome people. They almost drove him out, and he was glad to dispose of the estate for the recorded sum of Rs. 30,000 to Gholam Allie Khan. . . . The present purchaser, being a man of some energy and determination, finds good profit in the land, having ejected many of the old cultivators on account of non-payment, and introduced a body of more tractable and industrious Jat asamees."[77] Even Cohn, despite his insistence on the ability of the old zamindars to hold off purchasers, admits that events on the Ghazipur estate of Saidpur Bhitri "exemplify a widespread process." There "in the face of sustained and strong opposition from the former zamindars," the auction purchaser, Shivnarayan Singh, after some two decades of effort was able to increase by two and one-half times the amount of rent collected from the tenants of the estate, thus gaining for himself a profit of Rs. 1,75,000.[78] Persistence, combined with an ability to play upon factional disputes within the zamindari lineage, or the introduction of new dependent cultivators, usually brought success.[79]

There remains the question whether the former zamindars, once they had admitted defeat, were materially worse off than before the sale. From the point of view of the low-caste cultivators within the village the old zamindar still remained an important personage whom they dared not affront. For them, living even with dispossessed Rajputs was like "living under a thorn bush."[80] But on the larger political stage, and in the view of the other Rajputs of the neighborhood, the zamindar almost certainly suffered a tremendous fall in prestige with the loss of his property. As a mere tenant, even at favorable rates, he counted for little with the British administration; he may well have had more difficulty marrying off his daughters, as evidenced by the high rate of Rajput female infanticide through the first half of the nineteenth century; and he was usually hard pressed to keep up the style of life he had formerly enjoyed.

The introduction of cash crops such as sugarcane, together with a rise in agricultural prices in the years after 1800, no doubt provided, as Cohn argues, enough "enhanced value" in agriculture for some ex-zamindars, especially those who grew the valuable new crops on their lightly rented *sir* lands, to profit along with the auction purchasers. But during the first half of the nineteenth century the cultivation of the new crops was far more common

77. Colltr. Meerut to Commr. Meerut 2 December 1854, *Sels. Recs. Govt. N.W.P.* (1856) 4:195.

78. Cohn, "Structural Change," pp. 94, 109.

79. When the zamindars were too powerful or defiant to be effectively subjugated by an outsider the most common result was a lack of bidders at the original sale rather than expulsion of a purchaser. The original owners were then frequently restored, as we have seen, after purchase of the property by the government.

80. Cohn, "Structural Change," p. 112.

in the Benares region, from which Cohn draws his evidence, than in the areas farther west, where agriculture remained less commercialized and the cultivation of the principal cash crop, indigo, fell off dramatically after the crash of 1829. During the long years of depression and drought that followed there was scant profit to be had in agriculture in the Doab for anyone. Benares, moreover, enjoyed a permanent land revenue settlement on the Bengal pattern. The profits the new crops and higher prices brought thus remained in the hands of the agricultural classes. In the rest of the North-Western Provinces by contrast assessments were revised at regular intervals, and, as we have seen, they were usually pitched at the highest level the land could bear. There was therefore little scope for accumulation, and whatever could be squeezed from the land after the government had taken its share, and the costs of cultivation met, most probably went into the owner's pocket. While the displaced zamindar in Benares may sometimes have successfully maintained his position within his locality, few of his counterparts in the Doab or Rohilkhand could hope to preserve so much. For them *izzat* (status) and income fell together.

Those, then, who see in the enforced land sales of the first half of the nineteenth century the source of a far-reaching agrarian upheaval are substantially wide of the mark. By themselves the sale figures give an unduly colored picture of what was happening in the countryside, as do the exaggerated accounts of those British officers who saw only what came before them in the courts. Old families were not everywhere and invariably ousted, nor were the dispossessed always reduced to penury. Traditional social ties, and traditional forms of power within the village, could not at once be set aside by a sale for arrears or debt. Yet one can hardly say that "nothing happened." At least through the vast region stretching from Aligarh to Allahabad lasting social changes did accompany the forced sales which overassessment, depression, and debt brought about. Many old landholding families were permanently severed from all connection with their ancestral estates, especially during the years after the 1837 famine, while others were much reduced in status and influence. In their place, and sometimes beside them, rose up new landholding groups—often absentee, city-based, of commercial or service castes—yet increasingly adept at exploiting the resources of their new properties. As with the decline of the taluqdars, so too with the enforced sale of land, the British revenue and judicial system in the days of Bird and Thomason left a powerful imprint on the structure of rural society.

Six | *The Revolt in the Countryside*

O N MAY 10, 1857, after several months of increasing excitement, the Indian troops of the Bengal Army stationed in Meerut rose in mutiny, murdered their officers, and then fled to Delhi where the old Mughal Emperor Bahadur Shah sat enthroned in impotent splendor. The next day the sepoys proclaimed the restoration of the Empire. During the subsequent six weeks, as native troops throughout northern India joined the revolt, British authority vanished over large tracts of the country. Outlying and isolated posts, where reliable troops could not be found, were rapidly abandoned until by the end of June only the beleaguered cities of Agra and Lucknow, Allahabad and Benares kept alive the ideal of British dominion in the Gangetic plain. Elsewhere mutineers and rebels were free to march and countermarch at will.

When confronted with the breakdown of British administration, taluqdars and village zamindars alike had to decide whether to throw in their lot with the rebels or remain adherents of the British cause. Either course was fraught with both dangers and opportunities. Should the British return they were bound to punish those who had aided the rebels or taken the law into their own hands, and to reward those who had stayed faithful. Yet it often appeared, especially during the summer of 1857, that British rule was gone forever, in which case prudence dictated support for the victorious rebel armies. Nor did a landholder's decision as to his course of action depend solely upon such calculations. Much turned as well upon the nature of his own discontents and grievances. Did he see in the anarchy about him an opportunity to right the wrongs done to him by the British government, and perhaps to prosecute long dormant quarrels? Or was the occasion one that evoked a sense of gratitude for benefits conferred in the past? As blanket explanations, by failing to take into account the complexity of individual motives, do not always fit the facts, it is perhaps best to begin by examining in detail the course of events in one or two districts.

The Mutiny: Aligarh and Mainpuri

News of the outbreak at Meerut reached Aligarh on May 12.[1] A week later the local garrison rose, and the European residents of the station fled in disarray to Agra. Reluctant to abandon the district altogether, the Collector, Mr. Watson, gathered a force of about forty European and Eurasian volunteers and reoccupied Aligarh town on May 29. During the first two weeks of June Watson's volunteer force "continued at Allyghur and its neighborhood, making demonstrations continually in different directions with a view of preserving some semblance of order and keeping open the communications between Agra and Merutt." About the middle of the month this force, somewhat reduced in numbers, retired to a ruined indigo factory seven miles outside the town. On July 1, after repulsing an attack by a party of 500 to 1,000 Mewatis and Muslims from the city, Watson withdrew to the safety of Agra.

As the area under British control shrank ambitious local chieftains at once set out to turn British misfortune to their own advantage. Perhaps the first to do so was Rao Bhopal Singh, head of the Chauhans of Khair. Immediately after Watson's initial departure from Aligarh on May 20 Bhopal Singh marched on the town of Khair with a large following, deposed the tahsildar and took possession of the tahsil building. His victory was, however, short-lived, for Watson's first move after the reoccupation of the district was to mount a surprise attack on Khair. He found Bhopal Singh with but a few attendants and had him summarily hung. But Watson with only his small force of volunteers was no more able to hold the town than Bhopal Singh had been. In mid-June the Chauhans of the pargana, "intent on revenge," called in the Jats to their help, attacked Khair, plundered and destroyed nearly all the government buildings, as well as the houses of the banias and mahajans,

1. This account is based on W. J. Bramley, Colltr. Aligarh, to A. Cocks, Special Commr., 4 May 1858, B.R. Records Aligarh, File 3; and W. J. Bramley, "Collector's Narrative of Events Connected with the Mutiny in Aligarh District," of 17 November 1858, UPSA, C.O.A. Dept. 17, File No. 41/1858. Portions of the latter account are printed in S.A.A. Rizvi, *Freedom Struggle in Uttar Pradesh* (Lucknow, 1960), 5:656-60 and 865-68.

and after a brief siege of the tahsil office forced the tahsildar and the remaining officials to retire in the night. A similar series of events took place in Iglas where "a large body of Jats" marched on the tahsil buildings.

Once the British had vacated the district, the inhabitants of Aligarh were of necessity thrown back upon their own resources. During the first half of July in the city of Koil a *panchayat* of local notables vied for power with Muhammad Ghaus Khan, a zamindar of Sikandra Rao, supported by Nasim-ullah, a vakil of the Judge's court, and other prominent Muslims. Ultimately Muhammad Ghaus Khan went off to Bulandshahr to get sanction for his position from Nawab Walidad Khan of Malagarh, who had been appointed *subadar* of the district by the Mughal Emperor at the outbreak of the rebellion. Armed with a sanad naming him *naib subadar* (deputy governor), Ghaus Khan returned to Aligarh and was then allowed to assume control of the city. He appointed Nasim-ullah as his deputy, and enrolled in his service a large number of men, including many of the police *chaprassis* and jail guard. Ghaus Khan had, however, little authority beyond the limits of the town, and collected no land revenue.

On August 20, barely a month after Ghaus Khan had set up his rebel government in Koil, a British force under Major Montgomery set out from Agra to reoccupy the district. They marched first to Hathras, where they received a warm welcome from the Jat Thakur Gobind Singh and the wealthy bankers of the town. Together with his neighbor Tikam Singh of Mursan and Chaube Ghansham Das, the blind ex-tahsildar, Gobind Singh had maintained order in the town, and secured it from plunder, during the critical month and a half that followed Watson's final departure from the district. When Montgomery moved on from Hathras toward Koil, Gobind Singh joined the column and assisted in the defeat of Ghaus Khan just outside the city. As British strength was insufficient to provide a garrison, Major Montgomery placed Gobind Singh in charge of Koil and authorized him to raise a body of men for its defense. Montgomery withdrew to Hathras on September 2.

Three weeks later on September 25, before Gobind Singh had made much headway in consolidating his power, he was surprised by a body of "Mahomedan rabble" under Nasim-ullah and forced to abandon Koil with considerable loss of life and property. On the very next day Major Montgomery's force, which had so far remained at Hathras, finding itself threatened by a large force of rebels in retreat from Delhi via Mathura, fell back on Agra. Aligarh district was thus for the third time in as many months abandoned to its fate. On this occasion, however, the British returned quickly and in strength. On October 10 a force of 150 Europeans with two guns reoccupied the city of Koil, and then cleared and garrisoned the old fort of Aligarh, two miles away. Secure behind its bastions, this force, augmented by 100 Sikhs, soon pacified the entire district. Police were posted to the various tahsil and *thana* points, and supported by levies of horse and foot raised in the district.

The city of Koil was entrusted once again to Gobind Singh, who during the six months or more that he remained in charge kept his followers ready to perform all police duties, including even the escort of treasure to Agra and Bulandshahr. From November onward, although the district was occasionally harried by flying parties of rebels from outside, both the urban and the rural population remained quiet, and the collection of revenue proceeded steadily. Six months after it had begun the revolt in Aligarh was over.

One hundred and fifty miles down the Doab in Mainpuri the district Magistrate John Power, on receipt of the news of the rising at Meerut, at once set out to enlist volunteers to help protect the station.[2] As the raja of Mainpuri Tej Singh was in Naini Tal, Power turned to the raja's cousin Rao Bhawani Singh, who put together a small force of horse and foot from amongst his Chauhan clansmen. Ten days later, on May 22, the Mainpuri sepoys rose in mutiny, took one Lieutenant De Kantzow prisoner, and marched round to the kachcheri and treasury. Power with six other Europeans was about to rush to De Kantzow's aid when Bhawani Singh appeared and convinced him that it would be foolhardy to face the mutineers with his tiny band. Bhawani Singh gave the Europeans shelter in the raja's fort, while he went himself to parley with the rebels. When they attempted in turn to threaten him, Bhawani Singh quietly told the sepoys that he could not hurt men for whose safety he had taken responsibility, and that if they persisted he had "ten or twelve thousand men of his own kindred" ready on all occasions to die with them. Thus rebuffed the sepoys released De Kantzow, and after looting the Quarterguard they marched off to Etah.[3]

Once the sepoys had left, Power conveyed the government treasure to the raja's fort, and then returned to the kachcheri, which he fortified and garrisoned. During the next few days the beleaguered officials raised a small force of irregular cavalry and two hundred matchlockmen, in part through the assistance of Bhawani Singh. For the next several weeks, while Power and his subordinates remained shut up in the kachcheri, this force reconnoitered in the countryside and occasionally punished a refractory village. But British authority was fast ebbing away. By mid-June all the thanadars and tahsildars had left their posts, and the tahsil buildings in Bhongaon had been sacked.

About this time Raja Tej Singh returned to Mainpuri and entered upon a series of inconclusive negotiations with Power and his staff. The raja's intentions at this stage are by no means clear. He is reported as having told Power

2. This account is based on Power's narrative in Atkinson, *Statistical Account*, 4:634–40; a letter of William Martin, Head Clerk Mainpuri, of 21 May 1858 in *Freedom Struggle*, 5:636–41; H. J. McGlow, Magistrate Clerk, n.d., "Account of the Outbreak at Mainpuri," *ibid.*, pp. 642–47; and Madhu Sudan, Writer, n.d., "Account of the Outbreak at Mainpuri," *ibid.*, pp. 647–51.

3. The details of Bhawani Singh's conversation with the sepoys are taken from Madhu Sudan's "Account" (p. 648). The other narratives state only that Bhawani Singh went alone to the rebels and induced them to retire.

shortly after his arrival that he would do his best to help keep order in the town.[4] Yet Power later insisted that Tej Singh had throughout treacherously plotted against the British in nightly meetings at the fort and had sent emissaries in all directions to draw some mutineer force to Mainpuri.[5] In any case the raja did not break off ties with the British until June 29, when a large rebel force of some 1,500 men from Jhansi with two guns was seen approaching the city. Pressed to stand firm against these rebels Tej Singh equivocated. According to one account he told Power that he personally was ready to assist, but that he could not trust his companions.[6]

Power at once decided that the time had come to leave Mainpuri. After consigning the government treasure to the joint care of the raja and Bhawani Singh, the garrison marched for Agra. The next day the mutineers entered the city and looted whatever they could lay hands upon. The raja then took charge of the district administration. He appointed thanadars and tahsildars to restore order and collect revenue and recruited most of the district police into his service. Now firmly committed to the rebel cause, Tej Singh devoted the remainder of the summer to a vigorous assertion of his authority throughout the district. On one occasion, for instance, he marched with a large number of his kinsmen to the village of Bharaul in pargana Shikohabad to punish its Ahir zamindars, who had refused to submit to him. Several were killed, and after putting the rest to flight he plundered the village and fired many of its dwellings. He also repelled at Bewar a proposed invasion of the district by the Nawab of Farrukhabad.

On October 19 a British force under Brigadier Hope Grant occupied the city of Mainpuri without opposition, Raja Tej Singh having already fled. Rao Bhawani Singh remained behind, and handed over to the British some two lakhs worth of the treasure that had been entrusted to his care in June. Hope Grant invested him with the powers of a nazim, and then moved on with his force toward Kanpur. Left by himself, however, Bhawani Singh was unable to sustain his position. He soon had to surrender the reins of administration once again to his rebel cousin Tej Singh, who remained in undisturbed possession of the district for a further two months. On December 27 a British force some 2,000 strong from Delhi reached Mainpuri. This time, supported by a large body of men and six guns, Tej Singh elected to stand and fight. Decisively worsted in the encounter, his guns captured and 250 of his followers killed, the raja fled toward Lucknow with only sixteen attendants. Mainpuri was restored to British control.

Despite his defeat Tej Singh remained for some months a force to contend with. Even as a fugitive his influence over his clan was considerable, and the district as a result only slowly settled down. Disturbances were reported so

4. *Ibid.*, p. 649.
5. Atkinson, *Statistical Account*, 4:638.
6. Madhu Sudan's "Account," p. 650. McGlow reports that the raja talked with Major Raikes, but he knew nothing of the substance of their conversation. *Ibid.*, p. 646.

late as March 1858, and in mid-April Tej Singh with 250 cavalrymen made a dash across the district in the hope of finding sanctuary in Rewah State. Two months later, however, on June 11, promised his life and a confinement free from humiliation, Tej Singh surrendered to A. O. Hume, the Collector of Etawah. He was then sent to Benares, where he was provided with a house and a pension of Rs. 250 a month provided he lived quietly and did not interfere in the affairs of Mainpuri.[7]

The British celebrated their victory by a widespread confiscation and redistribution of land. In Aligarh district ninety-three mahals with a jama of Rs. 43,181 and an estimated value of over two and a quarter lakhs of rupees were taken up, together with various houses, gardens, and shops valued at an additional Rs. 35,145. Apart from one large parcel belonging to a resident of Bulandshahr who had fought and died at Delhi, all this land was taken from Aligarh residents who had participated in one phase or another of the rebellion in the district. Rao Bhopal Singh was stripped of land assessed at Rs. 1,363 for his attack on Khair; Ghaus Khan and his associates lost land assessed at over Rs. 3,000, plus shops in Koil worth Rs. 2,560; the petty Muslim zamindars of Koil and its neighborhood who joined with Nasim-ullah in the surprise attack of September 1857 lost land with a jama of Rs. 5,398, and shops valued at Rs. 12,295; Mangal and Mahtab Singh, Rajput zamindars of Akrabad, who after the plunder of the tahsil treasury by sepoys permitted further plunder and the destruction of the office records by their own people, were stripped of land assessed at Rs. 4,067; the Muslims of Atrauli, who rose and murdered the tahsildar in September 1857, lost land assessed at Rs. 1,600 but including muafi holdings worth over Rs. 10,000. The remainder of the land confiscated was taken from various petty Rajput and Jat zamindars throughout the district.[8] In Mainpuri by contrast, although the total amount of land confiscated was about the same, one person alone, Raja Tej Singh, bore the brunt of the burden. Some sixty villages assessed at Rs. 35,646, out of a district total of ninety-five with a jama of Rs. 42,961, were taken from him, and he was stripped of his title and malikana allowance as well.[9]

Almost all of this land was at once given out to those who had helped the British during the uprising. Tej Singh's holdings, together with the title of raja of Mainpuri, were awarded to his loyalist cousin, Bhawani Singh. The

7. "Narrative of Proceedings of the Lt. Gov. N.W.P. in the Foreign Department for the 2nd Quarter of 1859," cited in *Freedom Struggle*, p. 857.

8. Statement by Colltr. Aligarh of 18 November 1859 combined with earlier statement of 30 September 1859, C.O.A. Dept. 12, File 6/1859.

9. Sec. Bd. Rev. to Sec. Govt. N.W.P. 29 May 1862 and enclosures, N.W.P. Rev. Progs. 14 June 1862, No. 74–77. The raja's malikana allowance amounted to Rs. 22,502 on 124 biswadari villages. An earlier statement gives an assessed jama for Tej Singh's holdings of Rs. 40,350, and for the confiscated land in the district as a whole of Rs. 47,041. Colltr. Mainpuri to Commr. Agra 10 December 1858, B.R. Records Mainpuri, File 2. The higher figures include mortgaged and temporarily held land later restored to its original holders.

remaining Mainpuri villages were distributed among eleven petty zamindars including the loyal Ahirs of Bharaul, who received a village assessed at Rs. 737.[10] In Aligarh the largest grants were given to Gobind Singh and Tikam Singh. Gobind Singh, who entered the Mutiny with nothing more than his ancestral house at Brindaban and a pension of Rs. 750 a month, came away exceptionally well endowed. He was awarded confiscated land in and around the city of Koil, which he had so staunchly defended, assessed at Rs. 4,042. In addition he received the title of raja, an annual pension from the Aligarh Treasury of Rs. 9,000, a cash grant of Rs. 50,000 to make good the losses he had suffered during the uprising, some rent-free land in Tochigarh, the parent village of the Jat family, and *nuzul* (government owned) shops and gardens in Hathras town formerly owned by his father with an annual rental income of Rs. 2,700.[11] Nor was this all. Grants outside Aligarh were made to him of lands assessed at Rs. 9,498 in Mathura district and Rs. 6,055 in Bulandshahr district. His total annual income thus amounted to some Rs. 40,000.[12] Though not so richly, Tikam Singh was still well rewarded. He obtained land assessed at Rs. 9,400 taken from several rebel Jat zamindars, a remission of the revenue demand, amounting to Rs. 6,550, for two generations on five villages already in his possession, exemption in perpetuity from the reduction of his malikana allowance to 10 percent laid down in the Thomason settlement, and reimbursement of Rs. 12,000 for the pay of men employed to keep order and seek out rebels on his estate.[13]

Of the remaining twenty grantees in Aligarh several were Gobind Singh's relatives and followers. His nephew Randhir Singh, who remained at Gobind's side throughout, received land assessed at Rs. 2,799; another nephew, Kesri Singh, got a village assessed at Rs. 768; while Karrack Singh, a distant relative and *risaldar* in the seventy-man Jat Horse put together by Gobind Singh during the reconquest of the district, received a confiscated village with a jama of Rs. 748. Small grants of land were also made to Shib Singh, a Jat zamindar of Pisawa who brought his followers into Gobind Singh's camp, and to Bakhshi Nand Kishore, an old Brahmin servant of Gobind Singh in Hathras. The rest of the confiscated land in Aligarh was awarded to a number of loyalist Jat and Rajput zamindars, to bankers in Sikandra Rao and Hathras, and to several petty government servants and militiamen.[14]

10. Sec. Bd. Rev. to Sec. Govt. N.W.P. 29 May 1862, N.W.P. Rev. Progs. 14 June 1862, No. 74-77.

11. Colltr. Aligarh to A. Cocks 4 May 1858, and Sec. Govt. N.W.P. to Cocks 7 June 1858, B.R. Records Aligarh, File 3. For the award of the title see Sec. Govt. N.W.P. to Sec. Govt. India 7 June 1858, and Sec. Govt. India to Sec. Govt. N.W.P. 20 June 1858, *Mutiny Reward Statements of the North-Western Provinces*, 1:7.

12. For a list of all Gobind Singh's holdings see Colltr. Aligarh to Commr. Meerut 17 October 1861, B.R. Records Aligarh, File 11.

13. Commr. Meerut to Sec. Govt. N.W.P. 25 July 1859, and Sec. Govt. N.W.P. to Commr. Meerut 27 September 1859, C.O.A. Dept. 12, File No. 26/1859. A few years later he was further rewarded with the decoration of the Star of India (C.S.I.).

14. "Register of Confiscated Estates," enclosed in Commr. Meerut to Sec. Bd. Rev. 2 April 1862, C.O.A. Dept. 12, File No. 6/1869.

The Taluqdars and the Revolt

One of the most striking features of the Mutiny in both Aligarh and Mainpuri was the way those great taluqdars "who had lost out under our rule" turned out to be "our firmest friends in the time of trouble and need." Thakur Gobind Singh was the son of the famous Daya Ram of Hathras, whose fort had been stormed in 1817 and whose lands had subsequently been confiscated in their entirety. Raja Tikam Singh, the son of Daya Ram's Jat kinsman Bhagwant Singh, was, as we have seen, the first taluqdar to run afoul of the reform-minded settlement officers of the Thomason era, who first took away two-thirds of his estate and then stymied his efforts to regain it through the courts. Yet both men were conspicuously loyal throughout 1857. In awarding him the title of raja, the government said of Gobind Singh that "his services have not been surpassed by those of any other subject in these Provinces," while W. H. Smith later remarked that "without the aid of these two men Hathras would have been plundered and our footing in the district for the time at least have been lost."[15] Nor was the situation much different in Mainpuri. There Raja Tej Singh, who owed his title to the British, joined the revolt, while the disappointed claimant Bhawani Singh threw in his lot with the government.

The British openly admitted at the time that they had not expected Tikam and Gobind Singh to be friendly, nor Tej Singh to be hostile.[16] Later historians have been little more successful in incorporating such seemingly paradoxical behavior into their theories of the Mutiny. It is therefore necessary to look at the matter again, and from a fresh perspective. That Gobind and Tikam Singh, like almost all taluqdars in the North-Western Provinces, had grievances arising from their treatment at settlement is, of course, an obvious fact. But this was by no means a measure of the full impact of the British system upon them. As important was the overall economic situation in which they found themselves. Enhanced productivity on a smaller portion could, for instance, make good much of the loss of income from the whole, while diversification into other activities might reduce dependence on land altogether and so render its loss of less consequence. Similarly a loss of some land might not be felt as a severe deprivation if others nearby were suffering greater hardships.

The parganas of Hathras and Mursan were renowned by the early settlement officers as by far the most fertile portion of Aligarh district. By midcentury, although there was a nearer approach to equality in the various subdivisions, Hathras still reigned supreme, with Mursan only a short way behind.

15. Sec. Govt. N.W.P. to Sec. Govt. India 7 June 1858, *Mutiny Reward Statements*, 1:7; and *Aligarh S.R.*, p. 19.

16. Bramley, the Aligarh Collector, after describing Gobind Singh's family history, commented that "with such antecedents it would perhaps have been no matter of surprise if Thakoor Gobind Singh had on the occurrence of the Mutiny like others in his situation taken part against the Government" (Colltr. Aligarh to A. Cocks 4 May 1858, B.R. Records Aligarh, File 3). For Mainpuri see Neave, *Mainpuri D.G.*, p. 174.

"In natural capabilities," the settlement officer reported in 1875, "Hathras is unequalled in the district." At that time in Hathras 95 percent, and in Mursan 96 percent, of the culturable land was under the plow, and of this cultivation almost all—some 93 percent in the tahsil as a whole—was irrigated.[17] Nor can this be attributed to the Ganges canal, opened just before the Mutiny, for 82 percent of the cultivated area was already irrigated by wells at the time of Thornton's settlement, while the canal distributaries touched only a corner of Hathras and bypassed Mursan altogether.

This fertile well-watered soil provided the base for a rich commercial agriculture. Indigo, the beneficiary of the great boom of the 1820s, did not wholly disappear from the district after the crash. Although the ruined European planters never returned, as the depression lifted the trade slowly revived under Indian management. By the early 1870s Aligarh possessed 171 factories producing 3,626 maunds of marketable indigo annually.[18] Even more widespread was the cultivation of cotton. By 1870 it covered 13.6 percent of the cultivated area in the district as a whole and 15 percent in Hathras tahsil. With the increase in area under commercial crops went a rise in the prices such produce commanded. The price of indigo rose 25 percent over the period of the revised settlement from 1837 to 1873, while cotton went up almost 50 percent in value over the twenty years from 1844 to 1863.[19]

It is impossible to calculate precisely how far the returns from these commercial crops made good the losses suffered by the taluqdars at settlement. Almost certainly they did not fully compensate a man such as Tikam Singh for the loss of two-thirds of his estate. Still the growing profitability of cotton and indigo, together with the high productivity of the soil in Hathras and Mursan even when put down to food grains, doubtless cushioned the blow. Indeed, as the Aligarh settlement officer remarked in the 1870s, on the whole the Thornton settlement "has been favourable to the prosperity and maintenance of the high position of the talukdars; and where it has appeared to fail, its failure is not due to the nature of the policy itself but to the minute subdivision of property consequent on the laws of Hindu inheritance or to the fatal extravagance of the original talukdar." Tikam Singh not only emerged unscathed from the enforced sales of the 1840s, but prospered sufficiently to buy in the biswadari rights of four villages and so convert his hold over them to full ownership.[20] A man who had so successfully adapted himself to the new conditions of landholding had every incentive to remain loyal.

17. *Aligarh S.R.*, p. 90; and Atkinson, *Statistical Account*, 2:373-74, 562, and 564-65.
18. Atkinson, *Statistical Account*, 2:472-73. Indigo then extended over 29,000 of the 433,516 acres put down to *kharif* crops in the district. In 1839-40 it had covered 14,935 acres.
19. *Aligarh S.R.*, pp. 102-03. The bulk of the rise in prices, however, took place in the years after the Mutiny.
20. *Ibid.*, p. 118. On the basis of this evidence Eric Stokes claims that the magnate class in Aligarh, led by Tikam Singh, "forged ahead," along with the moneylending and trading classes, in amassing wealth. Eric Stokes, "Traditional Elites in the Great Rebellion of 1857," in Edmund Leach and S.N. Mukherjee, eds., *Elites in South Asia* (Cambridge, 1970), p. 21. It is, I believe, more accurate to say that men such as Tikam Singh at best held their own, or in W. H.

Thakur Gobind Singh's behavior is more puzzling, for he did not share directly in the prosperity of the pargana after his father's dispossession in 1817. One can only speculate as to the motives for his loyalty in 1857. He may simply have been carried along on the loyalist current of his neighbor taluqdars. No doubt he sympathized as well with the wealthy Hindu bankers of Hathras town who handled the sale of cotton from the area and looked to him for protection from the plunderers in the rebel camp. He may also have seen that the British were likely to emerge victorious, in which case conspicuous loyalty was the best if not the only way to recover something of his former wealth and property. Beyond this there was, as we shall see presently, a fierce Jat-Rajput rivalry in Aligarh district, in which Gobind Singh doubtless shared, and which drove many influential Jats to the British side.

In Mainpuri Edmonstone's settlement placed the then Raja Ganga Singh in a position almost identical with that of Tikam Singh, bereft of two-thirds of his estate. Even more galling perhaps was the indecisiveness of British policy which led him to expect for well over a year that he would in the end regain everything. Yet taluqa Manchanna was, like Mursan, an exceptionally well-watered and fertile tract, "as favorably circumstanced with regard to agricultural population, lines of communication, markets and streams, as any pargannah in the district."[21] So it is impossible to predict how Ganga Singh would have behaved in 1857. As it was, however, he died suddenly in November 1847, leaving behind neither male issue nor a will. The ensuing succession dispute distracted the family for the entire subsequent decade, and almost certainly played a decisive role in determining the course of events during the outbreak.

On the death of Ganga Singh three members of the family at once put forward claims to succeed to the estate: Rani Ghylwar, widow of Lal Chattar Singh, deceased son of the raja; Rao Bhawani Singh, the eldest son of Ganga Singh's deceased brother Zalim Singh; and Rana Nirpat Singh, the only surviving brother of the late raja. The rani based her claim upon a family custom that permitted a deceased raja's widow to nominate and adopt a successor from among the male children of the family. Bhawani Singh contended that both the raja and his deceased son Chattar Singh had verbally nominated him as heir before they died, and pointed out that he had

---

Smith's words "remained unaffected," by the "revolution in proprietary titles" that followed upon the Thornton settlement. Nor did all taluqdars prosper. The Mendu, Hasayan, and Simardhari taluqdars were wholly dispossessed, while others lost portions of their estates. *Aligarh S.R.*, pp. 92, and 118–19.

21. Edmonstone Settlement Report of 15 November 1840, B.R. Progs. 3 September 1841, No. 19; and Atkinson, *Statistical Account*, 4:592, 673. Though the villages awarded the raja may have been the least attractive of the old taluqa (see above p. 113), there is no evidence to support Stokes's claim that the Mainpuri raja's estates were situated in the portion of the district "least given to cash-crop farming, with lower transfer and lower revenue rates" (Stokes, "Traditional Elites," p. 32). See, e.g., the pargana-wise transfer data in Atkinson, *Statistical Account*, 4:603. After the Mutiny too the new raja prospered and purchased additional villages. (See below p. 162.)

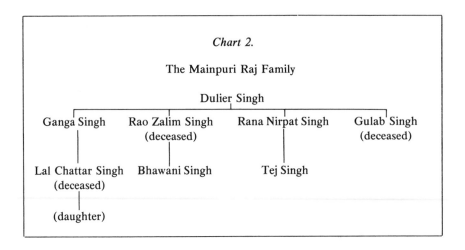

Chart 2.

The Mainpuri Raj Family

Dulier Singh

Ganga Singh   Rao Zalim Singh   Rana Nirpat Singh   Gulab Singh
                  (deceased)   (deceased)

Lal Chattar Singh   Bhawani Singh   Tej Singh
  (deceased)

  (daughter)

in consequence performed the funeral ceremonies over the dead body of
Ganga Singh. He further asserted that according to family custom the gaddi
of Mainpuri went to the descendants of an elder brother in preference to a
younger brother. Nirpat Singh, on the other hand, insisted that he was the
nearest male heir, and as such entitled to succeed.[22] (See Chart 2.)

Confronted with these conflicting claims, and the intense antagonisms
within the family which they provoked, the British were at a loss as to how
best to proceed. They first tried to resolve the matter by soliciting opinions
from the pandit of the Sadr Diwani Adalat at Agra, and from neighboring
rajas of the same Rajput clan. This, however, only made matters worse, for
the pandit supported Nirpat Singh, on the basis of provisions of classical
Hindu law which gave precedence to the claim of a brother over that of a
nephew, while the neighboring rajas declared that family custom gave the
widow the right to adopt an heir. The local authorities next turned to arbitration. After securing the approval of Nirpat and Bhawani Singh, and the
rani's *mukhtar*, the Agra Commissioner appointed a board consisting of the
Collector of Etawah and the Indian Deputy Collectors of Etawah and Mainpuri. Before the case was submitted to the arbitrators, however, the rani dis-
avowed her mukhtar's signature, and so the scheme fell through. As the
Revenue Board later speculated, the rani's decision might have been
motivated by a reluctance to have "a purely Hindoo succession" decided by a
board consisting of "two Moosulmans and one Christian."[23] Ultimately, in

22. Offg. Commr. Agra to Colltr. Mainpuri 18 February 1848, B.R. Progs. 26 January 1849,
No. 93; and Rani's Petition to the Board of Revenue 8 January 1849, *ibid.*, No. 106.
23. Offg. Commr. Agra to Sec. Bd. Rev. 27 December 1848, *ibid.*, No. 90; Colltr. Mainpuri
to Commr. Agra 30 June 1848, *ibid.*, No. 102; and Sec. Bd. Rev. to Sec. Govt. N.W.P. 26
January 1849, *ibid.*, No. 110.

February 1849, the government invested Charles Raikes, the Mainpuri Collector, with special powers to settle the dispute.

Raikes at once set aside the rani's claim. Despite the numerous letters on her behalf submitted by various local rajas, many of them solicited by the rani herself, he ruled that the family custom permitting a rani to succeed applied only to the deceased raja's own wife, not to that of a son. Bhawani Singh's story of a verbal deathbed bequest Raikes regarded as "incredible," and the performance of the funeral rites as giving no preferential right to the deceased's property. The heart of the matter was whether "in this particular case family usages should prevail over and supersede the ordinary laws of Hindoo inheritance which are opposed to the claim of Bhowany Singh." Here, finding local tradition an inconclusive guide, the Collector considered "the clear exposition of the Hindoo law and usage" furnished by the pandit to be "decisive," and so ruled in favor of Nirpat Singh.[24] The Board of Revenue protested this disregard of family custom, and the abrupt dismissal of the rani's claim, but the Lieutenant Governor upheld Raikes.[25] Nirpat Singh was installed as raja of Mainpuri on November 29, 1849.

A year and a half later, in May 1851, Nirpat died, and was at once succeeded by his seventeen-year-old son Tej Singh. Still aggrieved at his exclusion from the gaddi, Rao Bhawani Singh saw in the death of his uncle an excellent occasion to renew his claim. He brought suit in the court of the Judge of Mainpuri, H. Unwin, from whom he won a favorable decision. Unwin regarded ordinary Hindu law as inapplicable to an undivided raj property, and so set aside as "a mere element of perplexity" the sadr pandit's statement. He turned instead to family custom. Unable to find any controlling precedent in the history of the Mainpuri family itself, Unwin scoured the annals of the Chauhan families of the middle Doab, and even solicited opinions from some of the premier chieftains of Rajasthan. "Of opinions, especially such as are entitled to respect," he concluded, "there is a preponderance in the plaintiff's favor." Beyond this, Unwin insisted, "sound inference from the principle of primogeniture" would itself give the succession to the elder line of descent in preference to the younger in the absence of an explicit rule to the contrary.[26]

Infuriated at this reversal of his decision, Raikes, still Collector of Mainpuri, lashed out bitterly at his judicial colleague. "From such a chaos as these Rajpoot legends supply . . . it seems hopeless to educe order or . . . illustrate the subject in dispute. Yet from these jarring and discordant elements . . .

24. Colltr. Mainpuri to Commr. Agra 30 May 1849, B.R. Progs. 6 November 1849, No. 23; and Colltr. Mainpuri to Commr. Agra 27 December 1852, B.R. Progs. 18 February 1853, No. 10.
25. Sec. Bd. Rev. to Sec. Govt. N.W.P. 6 November 1849, B.R. Progs. 6 November 1849, No. 27; and Sec. Govt. N.W.P. to Sec. Bd. Rev. 29 November 1849, B.R. Progs. 11 December 1849, No. 50.
26. "Judicial Decision by H. Unwin," enclosure in Colltr. Mainpuri to Commr. Agra 27 December 1852, B.R. Progs. 18 February 1853, No. 11.

Mr. Unwin thinks he has collected light enough to guide him to a decision and to set aside the clear and undoubted verdict of the common law of the country and people." Raikes insisted, as before, that the question was not one between an elder and a younger line, but between a nephew and a brother; and that in such a case, failing a "clear and undisputed" custom to the contrary, "we must turn to the law of the people as expounded by the highest indigenous legal authority, and supported by the entire Hindoo code."[27]

The Agra Commissioner and the Board of Revenue agreed that Unwin's decision must be overturned. A Plaint of Appeal drawn up by the government vakil Babu Ram Narain was quickly approved by the board, which also authorized him to conduct the suit on behalf of Tej Singh in the Sadr Diwani Adalat.[28] The appeal was argued to a successful conclusion in Agra, but Bhawani Singh, undaunted, carried a further appeal to the Privy Council in London. His suit was pending before the council, the highest judicial body in the British Empire, when the Mutiny broke out in May 1857.

His bid to succeed to the estate twice turned aside, and with only an uncertain prospect of success at the hands of the Privy Council, Bhawani Singh had little cause to side with the British in the time of disorder. His initial friendliness to the beleaguered garrison can be regarded as a simple act of mercy. Few zamindars during the Mutiny murdered, or refused to shelter, small bands of helpless Europeans. Decency alone demanded at least this much. But once the unwelcome guests had been sent on their way, those so inclined had no hesitation in joining the revolt. Bhawani Singh's behavior, however, was decisively affected by the fact that he was not the raja. Immediately upon his return from Naini Tal, Tej Singh took up the initiative in dealing with the British. At the outset, while negotiating with Power during June, he was obviously playing for time. He wanted no doubt to keep open his lines of communication to both sides for as long as possible. By the end of the month he had decided to throw in his lot with the mutineers. From that time onward until his surrender ten months later he remained a devoted adherent of the rebel cause.

Why did Tej Singh turn against those who had placed him, and his father, on the gaddi of Mainpuri? In the absence of family papers we cannot, of course, give a certain answer. Tej Singh did, however, have grievances against the British, as well as cause for gratitude. His father Nirpat Singh, on succeeding to the estate, was awarded, as we have seen, malikana allowances some Rs. 10,000 less than those enjoyed by Ganga Singh. When Tej Singh himself came to the gaddi he was threatened with a further loss of Rs. 5,000 of annual income after five years. Although these reductions were reversed by the Court of Directors in 1853, and the malikana ordered restored to its

27. Colltr. Mainpuri to Commr. Agra 27 December 1852, *ibid.*, No. 10.
28. Commr. Agra to Sec. Bd. Rev. 31 January 1853, *ibid.*, No. 9; and Sec. Bd. Rev. to Commr. Agra 18 February 1853, *ibid.*, No. 15.

former level, a sense of grievance surely remained, and as surely fed upon the avowed determination of the government to reimpose these reductions at the earliest opportunity. This attack upon his malikana dues no doubt rankled the more because of the severity of the settlement, which had left Tej Singh so dependent upon these regular cash payments.[29]

Once his cousin had joined the rebels, Bhawani Singh as promptly took up the British cause. Whatever his grievances against the British, he recognized at once that loyalty alone could secure a reversal of the unfavorable decree handed down by the sadr court at Agra. The family struggle for control of the Mainpuri raj was thus at a stroke transferred from the courts to the field of battle. One can indeed regard the Mutiny in Mainpuri as a testing ground on which this decade-long dispute between the two branches of Ganga Singh's family could at last be decided. British victory made possible its final resolution in favor of Bhawani Singh, much as a rebel triumph would forever have affirmed Tej Singh's supremacy. In Bhawani Singh's case at least Mutiny loyalty was in no way a product of gratitude or sympathy for the British government. It was rather a calculating maneuver for immediate personal advantage. As such it succeeded completely.

The Thomason settlement cannot therefore be regarded as decisive in determining the behavior of the taluqdars of the North-Western Provinces during the upheaval of 1857. To be sure almost all the large landholders were hurt, many of them severely, by the settlement proceedings of the 1830s and 1840s. No doubt some were propelled into rebellion by a sense of resentment stemming from those years. But too many taluqdars remained loyal, and the motives even of those who rebelled are too mixed, to enable us to lay the blame for the rising solely at Thomason's doorstep. As important as the fact of dispossession was the ability of the taluqdar to adapt to the new institutional conditions in which he found himself. Those, like the raja of Mursan, who retained after the settlement a substantial block of land in an area of advanced commercial agriculture, and who could transform themselves into what Eric Stokes calls "an enterprising magnate element," were likely to remain loyal. Those, on the other hand, who, declining and aggrieved, lacked such opportunity, and clung to their old way of life, were more easily tempted to give vent to their resentment in revolt.[30]

29. For the controversy over malikana allowances see ch. 4 above. For a similar argument see Neave, *Mainpuri D.G.*, p. 174. Neave further notes that the raja "seems to have been a dissipated and incapable youth" and that he was worked on by "interested evil counsellors." Among them may have been Bhawani Singh himself. It is possible that Bhawani, shrewdly pursuing his own advantage, played a double game, first inciting the hapless Tej Singh to revolt, and then coming forward himself as a staunch loyalist. The evidence is however inconclusive, and the government in the end took no action against its new raja other than to deny him a promised *khillat* of investiture worth Rs. 5,000. See Magistrate Mainpuri to Sec. Govt. N.W.P. 22 September 1859, N.W.P. Polit. Progs. September 1859, No. 218; and Sec. Govt. N.W.P. to Sec. Govt. India 27 September 1859, *ibid.*, No. 219.

30. Stokes, "Traditional Elites," esp. pp. 29 and 31–32. Stokes argues that Tikam Singh not only benefitted from the advanced state of agriculture in Mursan but was allowed to continue the

Nor can we brush aside as irrelevant such matters as caste rivalries and personal antagonisms. These too, whether between Jat and Rajput or hostile members of the same family, helped shape behavior in the critical days of 1857, and so must be taken into account. No more than the Thomason settlement was the British presence itself invariably decisive. For many the Mutiny was little more than a convenient arena in which preexistent disputes of all kinds could be fought out afresh.

Land Transfer and the Revolt

It has long been a commonplace of Indian historical writing that the enforced sale of land for debt and for arrears of revenue played an important role in rousing the petty landholding classes of the North-Western Provinces to revolt in 1857. Invariably the moneylender, or bania, who benefitted the most from this "agrarian revolution," is cast as the villain of the piece. In the view of S. B. Chaudhuri, for instance, the courts, by offering facilities to "the most oppressive moneylenders" for the recovery of ordinary debts by the sale of land, "produced the greatest resentment amongst the agricultural population and a dangerous dislocation of social structure." The protection afforded these commercial men in the purchase of land was, he insists, the "sole reason" why in 1857 "the peasants and other inferior classes of wage earners . . . were so vindictive and uncompromisingly hostile against the English."[31]

Certainly the British officers of the time were in no doubt as to the central role of the British sale laws, in unwitting alliance with the bania, in provoking rural unrest. No men, Dundas Robertson of Saharanpur pointed out, "have acted with so vindictive a hatred against us as the smaller class of landholders whom the bunyas had dispossessed through the medium of our courts."[32] Thornhill in Mathura, and Edwards in Budaon, echoed the same point of view. "To the large number of these sales during the past twelve or fifteen years, and the operation of our revenue system, which has had the result of destroying the gentry of the country," Edwards wrote, "I attribute solely the disorganization of this and the neighboring districts in these provinces."[33]

---

direct collection of his malikana dues from the villagers. A privilege denied the rajas of Mainpuri, this helps account, in Stokes's view, for Tikam Singh's greater prosperity and consequent loyalty. Although proposed by Thornton in his report, this special arrangement was not sanctioned by government or brought into effect (see above pp. 80-81). Stokes also accepts much of the contemporary British characterization of the Mainpuri rajas as "devoid" of aptitude, if not "weak and dissolute." Yet Tikam Singh's management of his estates was bitterly assailed as well by Thornton and the Board of Revenue. All British assessments of taluqdari character and ability must be received with considerable skepticism.

31. S. B. Chaudhuri, *Theories of the Indian Mutiny* (Calcutta, 1965), pp. 135-36. See also his *Civil Rebellion in the Indian Mutinies* (Calcutta, 1957), p. 21. For a similar interpretation see my *The Aftermath of Revolt: India 1857-1870* (Princeton, 1964), pp. 63-65 and 209-10.

32. H. Dundas Robertson, *District Duties During the Revolt in the North-West Provinces of India in 1857* (London, 1859), pp. 135-37.

33. William Edwards, *Personal Adventures During the Indian Rebellion* (London, 1858), pp. 12-13.

In recent years, however, historians engaged in detailed studies of the rebellion in individual districts have cast doubt upon the validity of this hypothesis. In Rohilkhand, E. I. Brodkin insists, "the 'turbulent agrarian upheaval' arising from a pre-Mutiny 'wholesale agrarian revolution' is entirely illusory," while Eric Stokes, after discussing the character of the Mutiny in Saharanpur and Muzaffarnagar, concludes that in the mechanism of rebellion the moneylender was "but the fly on the wheel." The principal elements of revolt, he insists, came from "castes and areas where the mahajan [moneylender] hold was lightest and the land revenue heaviest." Whether among the backward Pundir Rajputs and Batar Gujars of Saharanpur district, or the advanced cash-crop Jat farmers of western Meerut and northeastern Mathura, it was the "heavy differential revenue assessment" laid upon them, and not the loss of their land, that drove the tightly knit village proprietary bodies into revolt. In fastening upon the mahajan, Stokes argues, the British were "consciously or unconsciously seeking a scapegoat."[34]

Space does not permit any such detailed investigation here, but it might be useful to examine briefly the course of events in Aligarh to see what light they throw on this matter. Aligarh district, as we have seen, suffered heavily from overassessment and enforced land sale during the two decades that preceded the Mutiny. Some 115,000 acres, or just under 10 percent of the total area of the district, was transferred by revenue process between 1839 and 1858, while another 565,000 acres changed hands either privately or by forced sale in satisfaction of decrees of the civil courts.[35] (See Table 14.) The district was also the scene of sustained and widespread rural unrest during 1857. To what extent was support for the revolt a result of the loss of land?

In the process of sale the old landed castes suffered most severely. Looking back over the entire thirty years of the settlement, W. H. Smith reported that "in Atrauli, Jats and Rajputs together have lost more than half their former possessions; in Morthal the Chauhans have yielded to the Nau-muslim Bargujars . . . ; in Khair, Jats, Nau-muslims and Chauhans have all suffered in various degrees; in Tappal the Chauhans have been almost obliterated from the list of zamindars; in Hathras and Mursan few of the old clans of Rajputs survive, and even in Sikandra Rao and Akrabad there have been great changes of ownership." The Jats of Iglas too, despite a "tough resistance," were slowly losing ground. Nor do the caste figures give a full picture of the changes that took place, for much land, especially among the cultivating Jat communities, was purchased by a member of the same caste as the

34. E. I. Brodkin, "Proprietary Mutations and the Mutiny in Rohilkhand," *Journal of Asian Studies* 28 (1969):667–83; and Eric Stokes, "Rural Revolt in the Great Rebellion of 1857 in India: A Study of the Saharanpur and Muzaffarnagar Districts," *Historical Journal* 12 (1969): 606–27, esp. pp. 618–22. Brodkin argues that the Mutiny in Rohilkhand was accomplished by Muslim Rohillas, who had not lost land, but were moved by a sense of grievance arising from their loss of political control following the Rohilla War of 1774.

35. *Aligarh S.R.*, p. 65. It should be noted that "these figures represent the total area transferred, and therefore wherever a village has been two or three times, or even more often still alienated, its area has been calculated as many times." The small number of transfers by revenue process in Koil and Atrauli tahsils were excluded from the totals reported.

Table 14. Land Transfer in Aligarh District, 1839–1868
(acres)

Period	Transfer by revenue process	Transfer by other modes	Total
1839–1848	95,285	316,809	412,094
1849–1858	19,779	248,823	268,602
1859–1868	19,488	305,085	324,573
Total	134,552	870,717	1,005,269

old proprietor, so that while one individual suffered the caste statistics remained unchanged. Perhaps the most striking instance of such a transfer, however, was the taluqa of Hasayan, sold by its distressed Porach Rajput owner to the prosperous Jadon Rajput Raja of Awa.[36] Overall during the course of the settlement the old proprietors lost possession of from 50 to 60 percent of the lands they had held in 1840. In Mursan only 32 percent, and in Hathras 39 percent, of the land was still in the hands of its original holders.[37] (See Table 15.)

Jat and Rajput alike therefore had ample cause for rebellion in 1857. On occasion this unity of interest took shape in concerted action. The attack on Khair, after Rao Bhopal Singh had been deposed in June, found Rajput and Jat leagued together, and the houses of the banias as well as the government offices marked out for destruction.[38] Often, however, their interests diverged. By and large the Rajputs seem to have been more deeply involved in the rebellion, and more bitterly hostile. Even in Khair it was they who led, while the Jats followed. No doubt their substantially greater loss of land helped exacerbate their sense of disaffection. But it was by no means their only grievance.

Before the "unsettled times" of the eighteenth century Rajput taluqdars had held sway over most of Aligarh district. Akrabad and Sikandra Rao were controlled by the Pundir clan, Khair and Chandaus by Chauhans, and Hathras by the Porach Rajputs.[39] The Chauhans of Khair were an exceptionally distinguished family, whose head enjoyed the title of Rao and the revenue management of the pargana. The Porach Rajputs, as "lords of the Hathras pargana," held the forts and taluqas of Hathras, Mendu, and

36. *Ibid.*, p. 67. The Awa family also purchased the Rajput-held taluqa of Dariapur and half that of Gambhira. Raja Pirthi Singh had the reputation of being a "grasping and severe landlord." *Ibid.*, p. 25.

37. *Ibid.*, pp. 65, 92. The caste-wise statement of landholding is on p. 66. See also Atkinson, *Statistical Account*, 2:560–61, 590.

38. For the attack on Khair see Bramley's account of 17 November 1858 in *Freedom Struggle*, 5:658–59; and pp. 137–38 above.

39. This account is drawn primarily from *Aligarh S.R.*, pp. 23–27 and 31–32. See also Atkinson, *Statistical Account*, 2:442–48.

Table 15. Land Holdings of Major Castes, Aligarh
(acres)

Caste	Area held 1839	Area held 1868	Loss	Gain
Rajput	466,921	346,648	120,273	—
Jat	303,055	284,328	18,727	—
Pathan	125,261	156,148	—	30,887
Brahmin	111,047	113,576	—	2,529
Nau-muslim	47,822	72,218	—	24,396
Kayastha	30,927	38,381	—	7,454
Bania	21,699	115,450	—	93,751

Dariapur, and had been preeminent in that portion of the district from the time of the Emperor Alla-ud-din Ghori. None of these families, however, could withstand the onslaught of the Jat and Maratha invaders during the last half of the eighteenth century. The taluqdar of Hathras was expelled by the Jat Thakur Baran Singh in 1752, and the Mendu chief was ousted by Suraj Mal of Bharatpur eight years later. During the days of Maratha rule General Perron unseated the Rajput chieftains in Khair and Chandaus, and awarded the management of the taluqas to his lieutenants. The Jat Mukhram Singh got the lease of Chandaus, while the Chauhan holdings in Khair were divided between the Muslim Dunde Khan and the Jadon Thakur Jai Ram Singh. The Pundir villages in Sikandra Rao were in similar fashion made over to the Jat Raja Bhagwant Singh of Mursan.

The British, when they took over the district, restored the Pundirs to their holdings in Sikandra Rao, confined Mukhram to a portion of his estate known as taluqa Pisawa, and dispossessed Dunde Khan entirely in favor of the petty village zamindars. Yet the change of regime benefitted the Rajputs surprisingly little. The Jat taluqdars retained the bulk of their conquests, including the whole of Hathras, while the small holders in Khair were mostly Jat by caste as well. As the Rajput clans were by no means forcibly uprooted from their old settlements, but simply reduced in wealth and consequence, the process of dispossession left them aggrieved and discontented, bitterly at odds with their Jat neighbors. So intense was the spirit of rivalry, especially along the western side of the district where the Jat settlements were concentrated, that the two castes "seldom reside in the same village, and if let alone would at once fly at each other's throats."[40]

In 1857, the Rajputs, still nursing their grievances, saw in the upheaval a convenient opportunity to avenge themselves against their Jat rivals. As Atkinson recounted, "The old Rajput and Jat feuds broke out with their accustomed fury during the Mutiny. In the western portions of the district, and especially towards Sadabad and Muttra, internal struggles raged until

40. *Ibid.*, 2:396. See also *Aligarh S.R.*, p. 35.

the fall of Delhi."[41] When the Rajputs joined the revolt, their Jat antagonists commonly remained loyal. In no other way could they hope to preserve their dominant position. In Pisawa, as in Hathras, where the Jats owed much of their predominance to British support, "the more influential" among them did good service during the revolt. Shib Singh of Pisawa, for instance, was commended for "having shown his loyal feeling very decidedly." Many of Gobind Singh's best men, the Magistrate reported, were Shib Singh's followers.[42] Nor is it easy to attribute Gobind Singh's own loyalty to motives other than those of caste rivalry.

The uprising in Khair was almost certainly a product of this Rajput sense of grievance. The Chauhans of Khair had suffered severely from overassessment and land sale, losing some 30 percent of their holdings in the pargana, but their chieftain Rao Bhopal Singh, descendant of the Pirthi Singh who had been dispossessed by Perron, was driven above all "by the vain hope of recovering the former influence of the tribe" when he led the attack on the Khair tahsil offices.[43] The Jats of the neighborhood, however, were not beneficiaries of British rule, with newly built-up estates and interests to defend. They were rather petty zamindars, long resident in the pargana, who had suffered like the Rajputs, if not as severely, from the pressure of a heavy revenue assessment. Hence they were willing to put aside their rivalry and join Bhopal Singh in revolt.

Where Rajputs instead of Jats were the new men who had prospered under British rule, then they remained loyal despite the example of rebellion set by their caste fellows elsewhere. The Pundirs of Sikandra Rao, for instance, had been restored to their holdings by the British in 1805. Although one branch of the family, that of Bijaigarh, dissipated most of its inheritance during the subsequent fifty years, the Thakurs of Nayi, "careful and prosperous managers," substantially increased the size and value of their holdings. By 1857 Kundan Singh of Nayi had become "a man of great influence" among the Pundirs of the pargana. This influence he turned to the service of the British. At the end of August 1857 he was made nazim of the pargana, and with a body of 1,500 of his own followers reinstated the tahsildar in Sikandra Rao and maintained him in that position until authority was thoroughly reestablished.[44] In similar fashion the Jadon Rajputs of Somna in Khair, who had won the management of the taluqa from the Chauhans in the time of General Perron, consolidated and expanded their authority under the British. "These men are now considerable landholders; but their property, though some of it was acquired by their ancestors, has been all obtained from the surrounding Chohan Rajpoots, most of it during our rule. Consequently they lost it all at

41. Atkinson, *Statistical Account*, 2:503.
42. Bramley to Cocks 4 May 1858, B.R. Records Aligarh, File 3. Shib Singh was awarded confiscated land with a value of Rs. 4,400. See also *Aligarh S.R.*, p. 24.
43. *Ibid.*, p. 31. Rajput holdings in Khair tahsil fell from 96,943 acres in 1840 to 68,190 in 1870. *Ibid.*, p. 66.
44. *Ibid.*, pp. 24–25.

the first outbreak and had good reason to be loyal." They were rewarded with confiscated property assessed at Rs. 2,333 for their assistance in supplying intelligence about rebel movements to the Special Commissioner Mr. A. Cocks.[45]

Nor were the Jats always followers in rebellion. Along the western side of Aligarh, and in the adjacent parganas of Mathura from Noh Jhil to Sadabad along the Jumna, the Jat communities rose up without any outside leadership as soon as the hand of the British government was withdrawn. At Iglas "a large body of Jats of that Pergunnah," under the guidance of one "Amani Jat ex-pattidar of Gahon . . . who had then come to the surface and dubbed himself Raja," boldly attacked a strong British-officered force guarding the tahsil buildings. Their reckless charge halted by a sudden shower of rain, which rendered their matchlocks useless, the Jats were driven back and scattered by Major Burlton's mounted *sowars.*[46] The same body of Jats took a large share also in the attack on Khair, and "attacked, plundered and burnt" many villages throughout the surrounding area. For their part in the rebellion the Jats of Iglas lost three of their "largest and most notorious villages" assessed at Rs. 9,400.[47]

Iglas was the heart of the Jat tract of Aligarh district. Jats comprised one-quarter of the total population of the tahsil, and held three-quarters of the land. Although they had lost a good deal of land—some 9,500 acres out of a total of 110,000 during the thirty years of the settlement—their dominant position was in no way challenged, nor were their losses anywhere near as severe as those of other communities. Their most burning grievance, as Eric Stokes no doubt correctly suggests, was the severity and unequal incidence of the revenue demand. This alone seems to have prompted these tightly knit bhaiacharya communities to rebel.[48]

Where Jats took the lead in revolt, the Rajputs often remained loyal. When rebellious Jats threatened Sadabad, across the district border in Mathura, the townspeople appealed for help to one Sawant Singh of Bisana in pargana Hathras, who was known as "a leader of the Rajpoots in those parts." Sawant Singh, "mindful of the Jat and Rajpoot feuds, responded, and came to Saidabad with a large body of men, and fought the Jats for several days, eventually without success. The Jats in revenge attacked his village in force, burnt it and killed several of his men."[49] On this occasion roles were reversed, but the basic pattern of caste rivalry remained the same.

45. Bramley to Cocks 4 May 1858, B.R. Records Aligarh, File 3; and *Aligarh S.R.*, p. 23.

46. See Bramley's account of 17 November 1858 in *Freedom Struggle*, 5:660; and Report by Magistrate of Aligarh on the Jat Zamindars of Tahsil Iglas, n.d., *ibid.*, pp. 663–64.

47. See statement of lands confiscated in Aligarh 18 November 1859, C.O.A. Dept. 12, File 6/1869.

48. Stokes, "Traditional Elites," pp. 23–24. For an account of similar Jat risings in Mathura district see *ibid.*, pp. 25–27.

49. Bramley to Cocks 4 May 1858, B.R. Records Aligarh, File 3. Sawant Singh was given a village in Mursan assessed at Rs. 535 as a reward for his loyalty.

A similar pattern of rivalry can be detected in some parts of Mainpuri district. There, once Raja Tej Singh had led the Chauhans into revolt, their traditional Ahir antagonists had a strong incentive to remain loyal. In Shikohabad the Ahirs, "formerly the most insubordinate subjects of the Government," successfully repulsed Tej Singh when he attempted to take the pargana, while to the north in Kuraoli the Isan Ahirs defeated the rebel raja and took two of his guns. For this act two of their leaders received the reward of a village in Kanpur district. In the latter case, however, economic as well as caste motives were unquestionably at work, for the Isan Ahirs are described as "good cultivators and successful zamindars" who were adding to their holdings.[50] In Mustafabad, by contrast, sides were reversed. There the Ahir leaders Ram Ratan and Bhagwan Singh "kept the whole Pergunnah in a state of rebellion," while many of the local Chauhans, led by the head of the Uresar family Kunwar Gajadhar Singh, "did good service" during the Mutiny. Again it is not perhaps altogether by chance that these loyal Chauhans, "more provident," had "succeeded in retaining their ancestral property intact."[51]

Yet neither caste antagonism nor Rajput disaffection, nor even the pressure of the revenue assessment, can by themselves fully account for the course of events during 1857. Hathras tahsil in Aligarh was, for instance, like Iglas an area of heavy Jat settlement, where the burdens of the revenue demand had been made heavier still by the widespread levy of malikana for displaced taluqdars. At the same time the Rajput proprietors had suffered fearfully, first from the conquests of the Jat *thakurs* in the eighteenth century and then from the workings of the British revenue system. During the thirty years of the revised settlement (1839–1868) the Rajput brotherhoods of Hathras lost over half their lands—some 35,284 out of 69,550 acres—and saw almost as much land pass into the hands of the banias.[52] Yet neither Rajput nor Jat joined the revolt. Here the powerful example set by the big taluqdars seems to have been decisive. Once such men as Tikam Singh and Gobind Singh had thrown in their lot with the British, the lesser proprietors and village communities had no option but to go along. For even an aggrieved Rajput to have defied the wealthy Tikam Singh, or Gobind Singh's seventy-man Jat Horse, would have been foolhardy. For a Jat clansman of the Mursan raja to have challenged his chief would have been unthinkable. Hence the tahsil remained quiet throughout. Indeed Tikam Singh also helped the British pacify the neighboring, and heavily Jat, pargana of Mahaban in Mathura district, where he held the small taluqas of Sonk and Arr. Lashkarpur. Given charge of the pargana as nazim, Tikam Singh "did his best" to keep the rebellious Jat peasantry in order.[53]

50. Neave, *Mainpuri D.G.*, pp. 169, 225, 258–59; and *Mainpuri S.R.*, p. 113.
51. Memo by H. Chase, Jt. Magistrate Mainpuri, 27 May 1859, C.O.A. Rev. Dept. File 67/I of 1859; and *Mainpuri S.R.*, p. 235.
52. See figures in *Aligarh S.R.*, p. 66.
53. Colltr. Mathura to Commr. Agra 15 April 1859, C.O.A. Dept. No. 12, File 26/1859.

Much of the pattern of rebellion was thus determined by the presence or absence of a thriving magnate element heavily committed by interest to British rule. Where such a class existed, whether comprised of Jats or Rajputs, new men or old, they were able almost invariably to smother the sparks of revolt in the countryside as far as their influence reached. Absentee bania landlords could not of course fulfill this role. They were invariably swept away, and the districts in which they predominated, such as Kanpur and Banda, carried into the rebel camp. Nor could the holders of tiny estates, with limited resources and influence, do much to stem the tide of disaffection around them. But elsewhere magnate power and influence were usually strong enough to carry the superior peasant castes with them. Such influence was not of course always enlisted on the British side. As powerful landholders could hold down peasant unrest and even collect land revenue for the beleaguered British government, so too could they carry into rebellion districts much less severely hit than Aligarh by the dislocations of British rule. Such clearly was the case in Mainpuri. There, the *Gazetteer* writer reports, "there seems to have been little or no real disaffection in the district or city"; had it not been for the constant passage through the district of large bodies of mutineers and the defection of the raja of Mainpuri, the head of the great Chauhan tribe, "the district would very probably have remained loyal."[54]

In the absence of such structures of leadership the impetus for revolt of necessity came from the village zamindari communities. These petty landholders were moved, from district to district and caste to caste, by a host of grievances, and turned the opportunities of 1857 to account in a variety of ways. At the heart of much of their discontent was an imperial government that sought a maximum revenue from the soil at the same time as it sought to remold rural society around the principles of private property and *laissez-faire*. For many landholders, as we have seen, this was a fatal combination. Yet it is too easy to lay the blame for the upheaval of 1857 simply upon the enforced sale of land, and the consequent rise of the moneylender. The bania was to be sure never a popular figure in the countryside, and where he had recently gained control of land he was often the target for vilification and even violence during 1857. But resentment at his new predominance was rarely the sole, or even the primary, cause of rural rebellion. Behind it lay the deeper dislocations brought about by an obtrusive and expensive bureaucracy, together with the temptations of unexpected anarchy. The pitch and incidence of the assessment, for instance, doubtless drove into the rebel camp some who had lost little land, while many saw in the collapse of authority an occasion to settle old scores or seek new advantage against old

54. Neave, *Mainpuri D.G.*, p. 169. The losses suffered by the dominant agricultural castes were much less severe in Mainpuri than in Aligarh. Between 1840 and 1870 Rajput holdings fell only from 48 percent of the total villages to 44; while Brahmins rose from 14 to 18 percent and banias from 1½ to 3½ percent. *Mainpuri S.R.*, p. 51. See also Stokes, "Traditional Elites," pp. 28–29, 32; and his "Traditional Resistance Movements and Afro-Asian Nationalism: The Context of the 1857 Mutiny in India," *Past and Present* No. 48 (August 1970):110, 116–17.

rivals. The pattern of land tenure and community organization also made a difference. Where the land, as among the Jats of the Upper Doab, was held by tightly knit clan groups in bhaiacharya tenure, a shared sense of grievance could easily emerge, and then take shape in armed revolt. Those less well organized, or less homogeneous as village cosharing bodies, might well suffer passively greater losses of land. The institutional innovations of the Thomason era did much to provoke agrarian unrest. Yet they were but a single strand in the complex web of motive that led some of the village zamindars of northern India to rebel and others to remain loyal in the tumultuous summer of 1857.[55]

After the Mutiny

By the end of 1858 the revolt in the North-Western Provinces had been thoroughly crushed. The British now had before them, where their hands were not tied by the past, an unparalleled opportunity to reconstruct agrarian relations on a sounder footing. Their first move, naturally enough, was to confiscate all property in the hands of those whom they regarded as rebels, and to award it to those who had remained faithful during the time of trouble. Some extent of the upheaval this involved can be gathered from incomplete figures which show land assessed at Rs. 16,90,461 in twenty-three districts confiscated for rebellion, and Rs. 9,18,295 given out in reward.[56]

The government next turned its hand to conciliation of the landlord community. They were regarded, correctly, as having been on the whole favorably disposed to the British cause, and hence deserving of better treatment than they had previously received. The British furthermore saw that even those landlords who had joined the rebel side, such as Raja Tej Singh of

55. For a discussion of the limitations of the concepts of loyalty and rebellion in 1857 see E. I. Brodkin, "The Struggle for Succession: Rebels and Loyalists in the Indian Mutiny of 1857," *Modern Asian Studies* 6 (1972):277-90.

56. See Table 16. Data are taken from the "Register of Confiscated Estates" compiled after the Mutiny for each district, and preserved in various N.W.P. Revenue Proceedings between 1861 and 1867. No information is available for the Kumaon, Dehra Dun, Saharanpur, Bijnour, Bareilly, Pilibhit, Kanpur, and Jhansi districts. Land not distributed in reward was either sold at auction, released to the former owner, made over to decreeholders or mortgagors, or retained as government property. On average between 10 and 15 percent of the confiscated property was released. In Budaon, Moradabad, Banda, and Gorakhpur, however, the total was close to 25 percent. Earlier divisional figures give the following totals of land confiscated:

Division	Assessment
Meerut	Rs. 4,34,852
Agra	2,97,911
Rohilkhand	5,28,331
Allahabad	4,52,128
Benares	1,99,370
Jabalpur	32,693
Jhansi	2,60,989
Total	Rs. 22,07,954

NAI, F.C. 30 December 1859 (Supplement), No. 579-89.

Table 16. Land Confiscated and Given in Reward, N.W.P.

District	Mahals confiscated	Jama (rupees)	Mahals in reward	Jama (rupees)
Muzaffarnagar	250	48,212	47	21,470
Meerut	339	1,89,344	86	64,537
Aligarh	93	43,181	56	38,451
Bulandshahr	463	1,89,917	195	99,181
Mathura	37	36,589	31	31,964
Agra	80	70,281	61	55,472
Etah	163	39,509	87	32,134
Mainpuri	95	42,961	80	41,661
Etawah	85	53,659	66	49,310
Farrukhabad	356	41,183	65	24,670
Shahjahanpur	541	79,213	214	50,617
Moradabad	920	1,21,135	190	68,326
Budaon	530	43,138	106	18,018
Fatehpur	161	48,804	59	24,688
Allahabad	359	1,03,864	223	76,076
Hamirpur	42	41,166	8	6,713
Banda	199	2,34,711	26	21,921
Gorakhpur	2,051	1,81,413	1,044	1,17,268
Azamgarh	131	20,672	129	20,452
Jaunpur	123	58,161	113	54,879
Mirzapur	1	81	0	0
Benares	4	1,168	0	0
Ghazipur	1	587	1	587

Mainpuri, could command the loyalty of many of the subordinate zamindars and peasantry. It was not possible, of course, after the passage of so many years, to put back together the old taluqdari estates. But the properties taken from the rebel taluqdars were not broken up and distributed among the resident villagers. Rather they were kept intact, or even consolidated, and awarded to large landholders who would, it was hoped, throw their influence into the scale on the British side in any future disturbance.

The most tangible mark of this new policy was the decision to award magisterial powers to selected large landowners. Impressed like the Viceroy Lord Canning with the success of the scheme then being introduced in Oudh, G. F. Edmonstone, the Lieutenant Governor, in 1861 ordered its extension to the North-Western Provinces. Since these territories had come under British rule, he said, "no power has been conceded to the Native Aristocracy, or, in other words, to the Chiefs and representatives of the people." The tendency of the British system had been rather "to obliterate all distinctions, and reduce all to one common level." The time had now come, he insisted, to initiate a more generous policy, and to call into the service of government "the large influence, both local and personal" which these men possessed.[57]

Unfortunately, however, in large part because of the policy of sale and dispossession which had been pursued for so long, it was difficult to find suitable candidates. Many of the old aristocracy had been replaced by "mahajuns and other monied individuals who reside in large towns and not in their estates, in which they had little or no influence." Others were often so burdened with debt, or held such small and fragmented properties, that they were regarded as unqualified to act as honorary magistrates. The Allahabad Commissioner recommended only six men for his entire division, and few district officers put forward more than one or two names.[58] In the end fifty-seven men, including thirteen European planters, were invested with the power of deciding petty criminal cases within the pargana of their residence.[59]

Despite the high expectations with which it was launched, and the enthusiastic reports submitted from time to time by the Lieutenant Governor, the system of honorary magistrates never achieved much success. Persisting hostility among the district officers and on the Board of Revenue kept the small initial number of magistrates from being appreciably increased, while the landowners themselves found little satisfaction in doing the government's work. In 1899, after almost forty years of operation, the provincial government admitted that the "principle of investing important landlords with the power of exercising magisterial functions when sitting singly has not been recognized in the North-Western Provinces to the same extent as in Oudh," and they asked the district officers to submit recommendations for further magisterial appointments.[60] As before, however, little came of this request. The Commissioner of Gorakhpur, a landlord enthusiast who had served in Oudh, and who bitterly condemned the government for its reluctance to call to its aid the "great power" of the gentry, came up with only two names. In Allahabad Division, with a total of three sitting landlord magistrates (including one European planter), the Commissioner had no new appointments to suggest. In Bulandshahr district, where three of the four incumbent magistrates had been debarred from using their powers because of "oppressive treatment of their tenantry," one additional nominee, Munshi Ahmad Husain of Chaprawat, was put forward, but he was later rejected by the government on the ground that he lived too close to Bulandshahr city. Nor

57. Circular No. 106 of 19 January 1861, N.W.P. General Progs. 2 March 1861, No. 20. See also Edmonstone to Canning 15 July 1860, Canning Papers, Harewood, Leeds. For the working of the Oudh scheme see below, ch. 10.

58. Commr. Allahabad to Sec. Govt. N.W.P. 28 March 1861, N.W.P. General Progs. 24 May 1862, No. 189. For the reports of the district officers see *ibid.*, No. 170-99.

59. For the list of those nominated for investment see Sec. Govt. N.W.P. to Sec. Govt. India 14 October 1861, N.W.P. General Progs. 21 December 1861, No. 85. The government also sanctioned the award of revenue powers but did not confer them at this time.

60. Sec. Govt. N.W.P.&O. to Commrs. 10 June 1899, N.W.P.&O. Judl.-Crim. Progs., November 1899, No. 22.

was the situation at all different in Benares, Rohilkhand, or the middle Doab, where the district officers raised all the objections heard forty years before, and together came up with the name of only one landholder, Lal Ishri Prasad Narain Singh in Mainpuri, whom they thought fit to be added to the roster of honorary magistrates.[61]

But landlord well-being was by no means wholly dependent on administrative favor. Those who had survived the blows of the Thomason settlement, and had played their cards shrewdly during the Mutiny, found themselves well placed to take advantage of the increasing prosperity of agriculture, and the growing population pressure, of the decades after 1860. In Mainpuri the thirteen years after the Mutiny saw "communications opened in every direction, irrigation extended, and the competition for land increased so as to more nearly approach its true value." By 1870 the average price of land on the open market had doubled, to Rs. 13-4-8 from its pre-Mutiny average of 6-12-4 per acre.[62] In Aligarh likewise an unprecedented "reign of high prices" set in after the Mutiny. Over the course of the decade 1858–1868 the prices of the four major food grains rose some 49 percent above the average of the preceding nineteen years. Nor was this rise simply an acceleration of a long-term secular trend, for food-grain prices in the decade just before the Mutiny had fallen some 11 to 30 percent beneath those of the decade 1838–1847, and were marginally lower than even those of the years 1828–1837. Cotton prices rose even more dramatically, from an average of Rs. 7-9-5 in the sixteen years before the Mutiny to Rs. 14-5-0 in the sixteen after. Land values too moved steadily upward. From an average of Rs. 5-2-8 during the early 1840s, and Rs. 8-9-5 a decade later, the price of land sold or mortgaged privately reached Rs. 11-11-1 per acre, or an increase of 126 percent, by 1868.[63] Nor was the rise in value confined to the Doab. The Rohilkhand Commissioner, so early as 1855, reported that investments in land were "eagerly sought," and that it was "a rare case for estates to fall into the hands of Government for want of purchasers."[64]

Under such conditions, even with the enhanced revenue assessments high prices naturally brought in their wake, land ownership became ever more profitable. It is impossible to tell precisely who were the greatest beneficiaries. Almost certainly it was not the petty village communities. No doubt, wrote the Aligarh settlement officer, "there are instances where villages or

61. For the reports of the Divisional Commissioners see *ibid.*, No. 23–32. The two appointments in Gorakhpur and the one in Mainpuri were approved in a Notification of 16 September 1899, *ibid.*, No. 36. The Chaprawat appointment was refused sanction in Sec. Govt. N.W.P. to Commr. Meerut 19 September 1899, *ibid.*, No. 38.
62. Atkinson, *Statistical Account*, 4:605. The figures given are combined averages for the two periods 1840-57 and 1858-70. Over the same period the average price of wheat rose 55 percent. *Ibid.*, pp. 621–22.
63. *Aligarh S.R.*, pp. 100–04.
64. Commr. Rohilkhand to Sec. Bd. Rev. 6 August 1855, *Sels. Recs. Govt. N.W.P.* (1856) 4:209.

portions of villages have been purchased by cultivating families, but they are not many, and land is too rapidly increasing in value to allow these classes a chance of acquiring much more than they already possess."[65] They had in fact already lost much of what they had gained from the settlement proceedings of the 1830s and 1840s. While Tikam Singh was buying villages, his former tenants, together with the other biswadari holders in Aligarh were being sold out. Of the 218 villages in the district which Thornton had awarded to the village proprietary bodies, 79 had by 1870 passed entirely out of the hands of their former occupants, another 120 had been alienated in part, and only 19, paying some 6 percent of the original revenue demand, remained intact in the possession of their initial owners.[66]

By 1870 the worst of the damage had been done. Those villagers who had managed to survive the assessments that had overwhelmed their neighbors were now tough and resilient, "in a more prosperous condition than they were," and well placed to benefit from high prices and rising rents. The settlement revision of the 1870s at the same time brought down the level of the demand on biswadari villages from 80 to 55 percent of the net assets, and so, even when it involved a slight absolute enhancement, considerably eased the burden on the smallholder.[67]

But the petty village proprietor was still in no position to compete with the large zamindar or taluqdar. The latter alone was free from the compulsions of subsistence agriculture, and the dependency that invariably accompanied it. He too by primogeniture or simple foresight could more easily get round the laws of inheritance that constantly fragmented and subdivided property rights. Hence the enterprise and adaptability which had stood so many large landholders in good stead in the face of the initial Thomason settlement brought ample prosperity afterwards. In 1871 the Mainpuri raja's Bhongaon villages, as compared with those of his former tenants, "seemed the most comfortable; many in a high state of prosperity."[68] His purchases too offset the losses of the other Rajput landholders, and so enabled the caste as a whole to hold its own in the pargana.[69] In 1903, looking back on the previous thirty years in Aligarh, the settlement officer W. J. Burkitt remarked that "the large landholders in this district have, as a rule, done well." Only the Purid Thakurs of Sikandra Rao, he said, were heavily indebted, and that was due to their own incompetence. The other major families, Jat, Rajput, and Muslim alike, were, like the Afghans of Datauli, "sound business men," steadily "increasing their possessions."[70]

65. *Aligarh S.R.*, p. 128.
66. *Ibid.*, p. 119.
67. *Ibid.*, pp. 68, 117, 120. On Tikam Singh's estates the village zamindars had to pay an additional 10½ percent of their net assets because of the decision to reward the raja for his Mutiny loyalty with an enhanced malikana allowance.
68. Rent Rate Report of Pargana Bhongaon, 7 June 1871, C.O.A. Rev. Dept. File 361/8 of 1872.
69. Atkinson, *Statistical Account*, 4:607.
70. W. J. D. Burkitt, *Aligarh Settlement Report* (Allahabad, 1903), pp. 5-7.

The gains of these rich zamindars were of necessity made at the expense of the smaller and poorer landholders. The most severely hurt seem to have been the holders of middling sized properties, men such as the old Sayyid gentry of the upper Doab, too poor to succeed in commercial agriculture but too proud to work the soil themselves, and whose meagre rental income would not sustain them. They were hard hit too by the growth after 1859 of occupancy tenure, which secured much of the benefit of rising prices to those whose rents were fixed. By 1900 the Aligarh cultivators, "comfortably off," held occupancy rights to over half their lands.[71] As a result over the years intermediate-sized holdings were, as Eric Stokes described it, slowly "squeezed out of existence," leaving little between the large estate owner and the cultivating proprietor.[72]

These continuing sales of land did not, however, bring with them an agrarian upheaval at all comparable to that which followed the Thomason settlement thirty years earlier. Brahmins and Banias continued to gain land at the expense of the old Rajput and Jat holders. In Aligarh during the thirty years from 1870 to 1900 the two former castes increased their holdings by some 58,340 acres, while the Rajputs lost 74,640 acres and the Jats 10,356.[73] But this was a substantially reduced rate of transfer over that which had gone before, and involved much less disturbance of the pattern of landholding as it had existed at the outset of the settlement. Already well entrenched, the commercial castes simply extended their reach somewhat further. Nor were any great new estates put together during the later decades of the century. The old properties, though sometimes burdened with a heavy load of debt and litigation, still managed to survive intact.[74] Only zamindari abolition in 1952 put an end to their dominance of the rural scene.

The years after the Mutiny, then, marked out an era of relative stability in landholding. Change there was in plenty. Higher prices, the spread of railways and irrigation canals, and the increasing commercialization of the rural economy brought with them a host of changes, as yet little understood, in cropping patterns, labor mobility, income distribution, and the like.[75] But in the structure of land control the decisive break had taken place earlier, in the 1830s and 1840s, and was the product of institutional not economic change.

71. *Ibid.*, pp. 8-9. The settlement officer estimated that nonoccupancy rentals were 31 percent higher than those paid by occupancy tenants.

72. Eric Stokes, "The Structure of Landholding in Uttar Pradesh, 1860-1948," *IESHR* 12 (1975):113-32, esp. pp. 116-20.

73. Burkitt, *Aligarh S.R.*, p. 7.

74. The U.P. government reported in 1919 that about half the landed proprietors in the province were indebted, and one-sixth were heavily encumbered. Sec. Bd. Rev. to Sec. Govt. U.P. 6 August 1919, U.P. Rev. Dept. Confidential File No. 578/1918. See also Stokes, "The Structure of Landholding," pp. 121-23.

75. For a preliminary account see the chapters on northern India in Dharma Kumar, ed., *Cambridge Economic History of India* (forthcoming), Vol. 2.

Part Three | Oudh

Seven | *Annexation and Revolt:*

The Consolidation of British Authority in Oudh

Wajid Ali built the Kaiser Bagh, but did not enjoy it.[1]

1.

On all sides turrets of gold and in the middle a throne was placed.
An English force came and settled and assumed the authority.
What a Kaiser Bagh Wajid Ali built, but did not enjoy it.

2.

Noble and peasant all wept together, and all the world wept and wailed.
Alas! The chief has bidden adieu to his country and gone abroad.
What a Kaiser Bagh Wajid Ali built, but did not enjoy it.

3.

Clothed in red, the king put on the guise of a mendicant.
Clothed in red, his followers put on the guise of mendicants.
O, my Lord built the Kaiser Bagh, but did not enjoy it.

O N FEBRUARY 7, 1856, the Governor-General Lord Dalhousie annexed the Kingdom of Oudh to British India. The reigning monarch Wajid Ali Shah, given an opportunity to hand over the administration of his kingdom while remaining its nominal sovereign, refused, and so was sent into exile in Calcutta as a pensionary of the East India Company. British troops occupied the province, and a regular administration was quickly set up in the Nawab's capital of Lucknow. But the peaceful transfer of power was to be illusory. Within eighteen months the province was aflame with rebellion. Though triggered by the sepoy mutiny, the revolt in Oudh soon took on the shape of a popular uprising in which all classes of the population participated. Reconquest was a difficult and time-consuming affair, completed only at the end of 1858, and successful then only because the major opposition force, the taluqdars, was won over by a timely gesture of conciliation. This chapter will examine the process of consolidation of British rule in Oudh during these first fateful years after annexation. Central to its concerns

1. "Wajid Ali Shah and the Kaiser Bagh—A Lament," a folk song, including both text and translation, in William Crooke, "Songs About the King of Oudh," *The Indian Antiquary* 40 (February 1911):62–63.

throughout will be the complex interaction of British and taluqdari power which culminated not only in the final fixing of the British yoke upon the province but in the restoration of the recently ousted taluqdars to dominance in the countryside. At the end we must ask what "restoration" meant and what the British hoped to achieve by it.

The 1856 Settlement

No sooner had Oudh been brought under British control than the new government carried out a three-year summary settlement of the land revenue. The month of April was set aside for a preliminary investigation of tenures and assets, and the new arrangements came into force on May 10. Not much of course could be learned about the state of rural society during such a cursory inquiry, but that mattered little, for the government had already, before the province was annexed, made up its mind as to the appropriate course to follow. In his preliminary instructions to the new Chief Commissioner, Lord Dalhousie had stated as a fact that the "tenures in land, the distinctive characteristics of proprietary village communities and the usages of the agricultural classes" in Oudh were "identical" with those in the neighboring North-Western Provinces. Hence there was "hardly any room" for difference of opinion. The "system of village settlements in the North-Western Provinces as described in the *Directions for Revenue Officers . . .* should unquestionably be adopted." The officers of government, that is, were to deal with the "village zemindars, or with the proprietary coparcenaries, which are believed to exist in Oude, and not to suffer the interposition of middle men, as talookdars, farmers of the revenue and such like." The claims of these men were to be held over for consideration at the time of the regular settlement.[2]

These instructions were not uncongenial to the officers placed in charge of the new province. Almost all had come to their appointments in Oudh from the North-Western Provinces or Punjab, and had been trained under Thomason or his disciple John Lawrence.[3] They naturally brought with them the enthusiasms of their mentors. These sentiments were reinforced by the persisting British view of the Oudh taluqdars as a rapacious set of robber barons who had under the Nawabs too long been allowed free rein. To curb the depredations of these men provided in fact much of the justification for the annexation of the province. Martin Gubbins, the Financial Commissioner, set the tone in his initial settlement circular. The settlement, he said, was to be made with the "actual proprietors," who should on no account be

2. Sec. Govt. India to Sec. C.C. Oudh 4 February 1856, *P.P.* 1856, 45:606, 608, 610.
3. Of 45 British officers in civil employment in Oudh in 1856, 20 were from the "convenanted" civil service, 18 from the Indian Army, and 6 from the Oudh Local Service. Of the civil servants, 13 had previously served in the N.W.P. and 6 in the Punjab. NAI F.C. 6 June 1856, No. 189-241. See also Jagdish Raj, *The Mutiny and British Land Policy in North India 1856-68* (Bombay, 1965), p. 15.

confounded with the "malgoozars of whatever description who have been paying the Government demand." Even claims to malikana put forward by ousted taluqdars were to be scrutinized rigorously. Where the taluqdar's possession was a product of violence or fraud, and of recent origin, he was to get nothing. Where, on the other hand, he had acquired a "prescriptive right" to the malguzari engagement by virtue of the long dispossession of the village holders, "malikana shall be guaranteed to him and his heirs for the term of the revised settlement."[4] A temporary allowance of 10 percent on the government revenue, in other words, was for Gubbins, and his superior Sir James Outram, adequate compensation for the loss of the most ancient revenue collecting rights.[5]

Meanwhile the taluqdars were being asked to pay to the new government the final installments due on their contracts with the Nawab for the agricultural year 1855–1856. In accordance with their usual custom many of the taluqdars withheld payment in the hopes of getting better terms. Under the British regime, however, this was a fatal error. The raja of Tulsipur in Gonda district, long in the habit of defying the Nawab's officers, refused to pay either the March or April 1856 installment. He had under arms some two thousand men, and so had rarely paid much to the Nawab.[6] But at the time of annexation the young raja, exhausted from armed conflict with his father's manager, had already spent much of the estate income, and was besides in arrears over a lakh of rupees in the pay of his soldiery. Prudence and necessity together counseled defiance. The British waited patiently until the end of May. Then the Commissioner, Charles Wingfield, marched with a force of cavalry to the raja's fort at Tulsipur, occupied it without opposition, and surprised the raja in his hiding place nearby. The raja was taken as a prisoner to Lucknow and his estate settled with the subordinate proprietors and contractors who had held under him.[7] Raja Man Singh, the holder of the famous "mushroom" taluqa of Shahganj in Faizabad district, likewise shut himself up in his fort, and refused to pay revenue balances amounting to Rs. 40,000. A troop of cavalry was sent belatedly to seize him in July, but the raja escaped to flee as a fugitive through the countryside. In his absence the estate was seized and the entire property, apart from six villages, settled with the

4. Finanl. Commr. to C.C. Oudh 31 March 1856, UPSA Oudh Abstract Rev. Dept. Progs. 4 April 1856. The Financial Commissioner in Oudh exercised powers equivalent to those of the Sadr Board of Revenue in the N.W.P.

5. In reviewing Gubbins's proposed circular Outram cut down the length of the term for which malikana could be guaranteed to that of the summary settlement. He further ruled that such claims should "always be admitted with much caution," and that the allowance should never exceed 10 percent. C.C. Oudh to Finanl. Commr. 4 April 1856 and 22 April 1856. *Ibid.*

6. For the raja's behavior during the Nawabi see above ch. 2, note 76.

7. For the Tulsipur affair see Commr. Bahraich to Finanl. Commr. 21 April 1856, F.C. 20 June 1856, No. 441–48; Sec. C.C. Oudh to Sec. Govt. India 29 May 1856, F.C. 27 June 1856, No. 185–86; Sec. C.C. Oudh to Sec. Govt. India 21 June 1856, F.C. 15 August 1856, No. 63–69; and Sec. C.C. Oudh to Sec. Govt. India 2 July 1856, *ibid.*

local coparcenary communities. Once apprehended, Man Singh was confined to a house within his fort at Faizabad, where he remained peaceably until the outbreak of the Mutiny.[8]

Exasperated by this recalcitrance, the Chief Commissioner authorized the district officials, where a taluqdar had collected the revenue but willfully withheld payment, not only to strip him of all control over his villages but to deny him malikana as well. Yet not all default could fairly be laid at the door of the taluqdar. Many were simply unable to collect their dues from the village holders, who saw only too well how uncertain the taluqdar's tenure was under the new government. Nor could the harried taluqdar temporarily make good the default by borrowing from the local banker, for the mahajan knew as well as the villager which way the wind was blowing. The only remedy Gubbins could suggest for this costly *impasse*, in cases where the feeling between the taluqdar and the villagers was "sufficiently bitter to endanger the peace," was to set the taluqdar aside at once in favor of his antagonists.[9]

Altogether during the course of the summary settlement the taluqdars lost some 9,900 of the 23,500 villages they had held at annexation. Their losses were heaviest in Gonda and Faizabad districts, where they were stripped of up to two-thirds of their former holdings. In some other districts by contrast they lost as few as 200 villages. (See Table 17.) In view of the government's avowed hostility toward them it is perhaps surprising that the taluqdars retained so many villages as they did. Most likely, they were simply too firmly rooted, and the villagers' rights too indistinct, to permit everywhere their being ousted from power. Certainly Dalhousie's successor as Governor-General, Lord Canning, and Sir Henry Lawrence, who took over as Chief Commissioner of Oudh in March 1857, both regarded Gubbins's treatment of the taluqdars as needlessly and unjustifiably harsh. Lawrence in particular spoke heatedly of Gubbins's "strong views about breaking up estates and destroying the aristocracy," and went on to say that "A dead level seems to be the ideal of many civil officers, both military and civilian."[10] The same hostile evaluation of Gubbins's proceedings was echoed by the British in Oudh in later years after the policy of 1856 had been reversed. Major L. Barrow, who was in charge of the resettlement of Oudh after the Mutiny, described his predecessor's work in these terms:

8. Commr. Faizabad to Sec. C.C. Oudh 15 July 1856, Oudh Abstract Rev. Progs. 28 July 1856, No. 21; Sec. C.C. to Commr. Faizabad 28 July 1856, *ibid.*, No. 22.; C.C. Oudh to Finanl. Commr. 2 August 1856, Oudh Abstract Rev. Progs. 2 August 1856, No. 114; and Finanl. Commr. to C.C. Oudh 24 December 1856, Oudh Abstract Rev. Progs. 13 January 1857, No. 16.

9. Finanl. Commr. to C.C. Oudh 13 April 1856, Oudh Abstract Rev. Progs. 14 April 1856 (unnumbered); C.C. Oudh to Finanl. Commr. 14 April 1856, *ibid.*; Finanl. Commr. to C.C. Oudh 14 April 1856, Oudh Abstract Rev. Progs. 15 April 1856 (unnumbered); and C.C. Oudh to Finanl. Commr. 15 April 1856, *ibid.* For a detailed account of taluqdar-zamindar strife in Faizabad after the Mutiny see below ch. 9.

10. Henry Lawrence to James Bernard 7 April 1857, in Sir H. B. Edwardes and H. Merivale, *Life of Sir Henry Lawrence* (London, 1872), 2:300–01. See also Canning to Henry Lawrence 27 April 1857 in Canning Papers.

Table 17. Changes in Landholding, Oudh, 1856

Division	District	Number of villages composing Taluqs under Nawab's Government	Number of villages settled with taluqdars in 1856		Number of villages settled with others in 1856	
			Villages	Jama (rupees)	Villages	Jama (rupees)
Lucknow	Lucknow	575	407	1,68,479	168	96,384
	Rae Bareli	1,052	553	3,02,593	502	3,83,443
	Unao	368	164	1,32,229	233	1,98,135
Total		1,995	1,124	6,03,301	903	6,77,962
Faizabad	Faizabad	3,116	687	1,47,839	2,380	6,78,452
	Sultanpur	2,133	1,240	3,42,899	891	2,86,423
	Pratabgarh	3,032	1,648	3,54,412	1,384	4,07,785
Total		8,281	3,575	8,45,150	4,655	13,72,660
Bahraich	Gonda	3,483	1,377	3,58,412	2,104	5,14,418
	Bahraich	3,761	2,769	3,97,604	976	2,00,144
	Mahumdi	1,759	1,468	2,89,735	249	56,446
Total		9,003	5,614	10,45,751	3,329	7,71,008
Khairabad	Hardoi	464	271	1,72,408	195	1,46,252
	Daryabad	1,087	760	2,83,740	327	1,29,217
	Sitapur	2,692	2,296	5,58,169	494	1,11,220
Total		4,243	3,327	10,14,317	1,016	3,86,689
Grand Total		23,522	13,640	35,08,519	9,903	32,08,319

Village Zumeendars did not [at first] come forward in large numbers, they either did not realize the intention to deal with them, or the Talooqdars still had power to keep them back. But when they once found that they might recover long dormant rights, they came forward in thousands. And appeals were so numerous that District officers were allowed and exhorted to reverse their own settlements which had first been with the Talooqdar in favor of the Zumeendar. The contention was fierce, and the struggle ended in the dispossession of a large portion, sometimes all of their estates, to the Talooqdars.[11]

Even more widely felt than the new settlement arrangements were the heavy assessments imposed by the British regime. The local officers were told initially to base their assessments upon the revenue collected by the Oudh government during the preceding five years. But these figures often could not be procured, for they were usually computed by taluqa rather than by village, and when available they were not always reliable. Attempts to check the accuracy and appropriateness of these Nawabi figures by calculating the zamindar's *nikasi* (total net assets) ran afoul of the shortness of time allowed for the summary settlement. In Kakori, Lucknow district, the settlement officer made no regular estimate of the rental, "but fixed the jumma at what he considered just and assumed the rental to be the double of it."[12] The Nawabs of Oudh had of course never collected revenue at the half-assets rate the British had themselves just adopted, but had rather screwed as much out of the villages as they could get away with, and piled their demands upon the weaker and more vulnerable smallholders to make up for the losses they suffered at the hands of recalcitrant taluqdars. Past collections therefore, especially those from the "ordinary village zumeendar neither possessed of influence or interest," as the British came to realize by the end of the year, provided no guide to equitable assessment. From January 1857 onward Gubbins set in motion downward revisions of the assessment by up to 20 or 25 percent.[13]

With the summary settlement underway the British turned their attention to the reduction of the taluqdars' forts, and the disbandment of their armed retainers. As in the North-Western Provinces so too in Oudh the British were determined from the outset to monopolize the military force of the state and to retain in their own hands the power to enforce law and order. The

11. L. Barrow, "Memo on Former Administration in Oudh," 3 June 1858, UPSA B.R. Oudh General File 305. Barrow had been settlement officer in Salone district during 1856. For a similar view see W. C. Benett, "Introduction," *Oudh Gazetteer*, 1:lv. Jagdish Raj unduly minimizes the extent of the upheaval by accepting as the total number of villages in the province a figure that relates only to the total number of villages held by taluqdars on annexation. He thus is erroneously led to state that the taluqdars "retained more than half the province in their possession" in 1856. Raj, *Mutiny and British Policy*, pp. 18–19. For the correct position see Table 17.

12. Memo by M. Gubbins on Pargana Kakori of 29 December 1856, B.R. Oudh General File 66, Part I.

13. *Ibid.* See also his memoranda of 1 and 7 January 1857 surveying the assessments of other parganas in Lucknow and Purwa districts, Oudh General File 66, Part I; and Barrow's "Memo on the Former Administration in Oudh," (see n. 11 above).

taluqdars' six hundred forts, half in a tumble-down state, were mostly constructed of mud, and some were little more than fortified houses.[14] Even the strongest, as the Judicial Commissioner M. C. Ommanney admitted, were unlikely to prove formidable to the forces of the British government. Still as they kept up "the remembrance of the lawless times" when the taluqdars exercised military power, and might "encourage the disaffected," they deserved to be leveled. Accordingly in September 1856 the Chief Commissioner ordered all forts, together with their ordnance and ammunition, surrendered to the government within one month.[15] At the same time the taluqdars were directed to disband the armed levies with which they had so often contested for mastery with the Nawab's revenue collectors.

Little was done, however, to see these measures carried through to a successful conclusion. Although after their initial defiance the taluqdars had quietly watched while their estates were being taken away, the British had none too many troops available in Oudh and no wish needlessly to antagonize these still powerful landholders. Hence, no military forces were dispatched to search for armaments or to level taluqdari fortifications. Similarly only one body of retainers was forcibly disarmed, that of the recalcitrant raja of Tulsipur. In this case the government's hand was forced by the raja's inability to control his men, a "rabble military force" who had taken to plundering villages in order to recover the arrears of pay due to them. When the Tulsipur raja was taken prisoner these retainers were rounded up, given small gratuities, and dismissed.[16] The prospect of more such discontented men loosed suddenly upon the countryside may well have helped deter the government from proceeding more rapidly with its avowed policy of general disarmament.[17]

By the time of the Mutiny outbreak therefore, the settlement of Oudh was far from completed. In many districts the reductions in assessment ordered by Gubbins had not been carried into effect, while in some the extent of relief had not finally been determined. No progress at all had been made toward preparing a basic record of rights or determining the shares of the coparceners in any of the newly independent villages. The taluqdars had been antagonized both by the settlement operations and by the seizure of their fortifications, which portended a dramatic reduction in their status, but

14. For the taluqdars' forts see above ch. 2.
15. Judl. Commr. to Sec. C.C. Oudh 18 August 1856, F.C. 31 October 1856, No. 136-52; and Sec. C.C. Oudh to Sec. Govt. India 3 September 1856, *ibid.*
16. Commr. Bahraich to Finanl. Commr. 21 April 1856, F.C. 20 June 1856, No. 441-48; and Sec. C.C. Oudh to Sec. Govt. India 2 July 1856, F.C. 15 August 1856, No. 63-68. Some taluqdars may have discharged their retainers themselves so as to do away with the "clamorous demands" for pay of these men, for whom there was now no longer any real use. See Finanl. Commr. to C.C. Oudh 16 September 1856 and C.C.'s reply of 24 September, Oudh Abstract Rev. Progs. 24 September 1856, No. 23.
17. For speculation along these lines, and a general account of the progress of disarmament during 1856, see Lord Stanley's Dispatch of 13 October 1858, in McLeod Innes, *Lucknow & Oude in the Mutiny* (London, 1895), pp. 325-26.

neither measure had been pushed through to its logical conclusion. The taluqdars still held over half their lands, while most of their forts remained intact with the cannon concealed or buried. One raja, that of Ikauna, in Bahraich, had even openly moved his artillery across the border into Nepal. So the British found themselves in early 1857, as their own military strength began to evaporate, confronted with a restive yet still powerful group of landholders in their newest province.

The Taluqdars and the Mutiny

The sepoys at Lucknow, following the example set by their colleagues in Meerut three weeks before, rose in mutiny on May 30, 1857. The outstation garrisons broke into revolt immediately thereafter. By mid-June the civil government had collapsed throughout the province. The taluqdars used the ensuing anarchy to take possession at once of the villages they had lost during 1856. They did not however, despite this initial repudiation of the British system, immediately go into active opposition. Some few, among them the raja of Mahmudabad, Nawab Ali Khan, who encouraged the Sitapur mutineers to march on the besieged Residency at Lucknow, threw in their lot with the rebels at the outset. But most temporized throughout the summer and often gave succor to fugitive Englishmen. Even Man Singh, who had no reason to be grateful to the British and had been placed in confinement as a "dangerous" character at the initial outbreak in May, carefully kept open his lines of communication with the government. In early June, when the Faizabad sepoys rose, released from confinement, he took into his fort at Shahganj the women, children, and civil officers of the British garrison, some twenty-nine in all. He then provided them with boats and sent them safely down the Ghagra to Dinapur.[18]

The failure of General Havelock to reach Lucknow with a relief force in August finally convinced the bulk of the taluqdars that the British cause was hopeless, and so prompted them to join the rebellion. By the end of the year all the principal landholders, with the exception only of the raja of Balrampur and a handful of others, were openly hostile. Most, at one time or another, took an active part in the siege of the Residency. Man Singh was among those who contested the advance of Havelock and Outram in September, and he manned a battery at the Baillie Guard for a further two months. As the taluqdars' grievances were fresher, and rankled more deeply, than those of almost any other class of British subjects, their hostility surprised no one. But universality of opposition should by no means be taken to imply unanimity of motive. Too often the British at the time ascribed the hostility of the taluqdars to simple repugnance with the 1856 land settlement. As the

18. Memorandum by J. Reid, late Depty. Commr. Faizabad, n.d., NAI Secret Consultations (hereafter S.C.) 28 May 1858, No. 419; and Sec. C.C. to Sec. G.-G. 13 December 1858, B.R. Oudh General File 574. For a general account of taluqdari behavior during June see C.C. Oudh to Sec. Govt. India 27 June 1857, S.C. 25 September 1857, No. 639.

Deputy Commissioner of Faizabad wrote from his refuge at Dinapur on June 29, 1857, "By my last accounts from Oudh there was fearful anarchy and bloodshed. Our settlement operations created such a social revolution that this was to be expected."[19] The behavior of the taluqdars during 1857 cannot unfortunately be explained so easily. Motives are rarely obvious, and in this case, as in most others, can only be discerned by examining individuals within their particular social contexts.

Some of the most inveterately hostile of the taluqdars were men who had lost no land, or very little, during the summary settlement. The rajas of Bhinga and Charda, in Bahraich district, lost no villages; the raja of Gonda lost 30 villages out of 400, but had his assessment lowered by some Rs. 10,000; while the raja of Nanpara and Ashraf Bakhsh Khan, the chief of Burhapara in Gonda, were restored to their estates by the British. Yet all these men, together with the Raikwar chieftains of Bahraich and the raja of Ikauna, were bitter opponents of the British and conducted a last-ditch resistance in Bahraich until December 1858. For many British officers it was a "matter for surprise" that taluqdars so well treated should have been ungrateful enough to rebel. Lord Canning and Charles Wingfield, the Bahraich Commissioner at the time of the outbreak, attributed the behavior of these men simply to reluctance to give up the arbitrary powers they had hitherto exercised over those about them. They hated British rule, as Wingfield put it, "because it reduced them to a level with the meanest before the law . . . because it compelled them to disband their armies, pay their revenue regularly, and not oppress their ryots."[20]

No doubt there is much truth in this. The taluqdars of the remote Bahraich and Gonda districts, cut off from the seat of government at Lucknow by the Ghagra River, had long been in the habit of defying the Nawab's officials, and (apart from the brief interval of Raghubhar Dyal's *nizamat*) had successfully kept up almost regal pretensions.[21] But what then of the raja of Balrampur, whose estates were located in the very heart of this tract, who had never submitted to the Nawabs, and who had besides lost 144 villages during 1856; but who nevertheless staunchly supported the British throughout the revolt? Some part of the explanation may be found in the workings of clan rivalry. The head of the Raikwar clan in Bahraich, the raja of Baundi, had been excluded from settlement for all 305 of his villages in 1856 for failure to pay the initial *rabi qists*. He naturally joined the rebellion at the first opportunity, and brought with him his kinsmen, the taluqdars of

19. Depty. Commr. Faizabad to Sec. Govt. India 29 June 1857, S.C. 25 September 1857, No. 517.

20. Sec. Govt. India to C.C. Oudh 31 March 1858, in Rizvi, *Freedom Struggle*, 2:337-38; *Oudh Gazetteer*, 1:135 and 546-47; Commr. Gorakhpur to Sec. Govt. India 6 February 1858, in Canning Papers, Miscellaneous File 273; and Wingfield Memorandum of 17 May 1858 on the Mutiny in Bahraich, B.R. Oudh General File 1037.

21. See above ch. 2.

Rahwa, Chahlari, and Bhitauli. The rani of Tulsipur, stepping into her im-
prisoned husband's shoes, also supported the rebel cause from the outset and
called up her levies from among the subordinate zamindars. The Balrampur
raja, a member of the Janwar clan of Rajputs, had long been at odds with his
neighbors of Tulsipur. For centuries the Balrampur family had laid claim to
the lordship of the then forested Tulsipur pargana; around 1800, when the
Tulsipur raj was established by a Chauhan chieftain fleeing from the new
Gurkha rulers of Nepal, this claim was commuted to an annual money
payment of Rs. 1,500. Despite its small size this sum often remained unpaid,
and provided the pretext for several armed encounters between the two rajas
during the later days of Nawabi rule. The last ended with the defeat of
Tulsipur and the award to Digvijai Singh, the Balrampur ruler, of several
forest villages. Hence when Digvijai at the outbreak of the Mutiny gave
shelter to Charles Wingfield and the British garrison at Bahraich, his old
enemies, with the support of the rebel government at Lucknow, eagerly
turned upon him. His estates were ordered divided among Tulsipur, Ikauna,
and Utraula, and a nazim was sent to enforce the order. Digvijai managed to
hold out until the British could reach him, even though, as Wingfield
noticed, "Of his own men there are not 3,000 on whom he could rely; the
sympathies of the rest and of all about him are with the rebels."[22]

Once his rivals had committed themselves to the rebel side, and mobilized
their clansmen against him, the Balrampur raja obviously had no alternative
but to turn to the British. To have joined the rebellion would have been to
place himself at the mercy of those who had little incentive to treat fairly with
him. At the same time, although many taluqdars sheltered fugitive Englishmen and then turned against the government they represented, Digvijai
Singh seems clearly to have had exceptionally close and friendly ties with the
British officers in Oudh. The first taluqdar of the Bahraich Division to offer
his allegiance to the new government in February 1856, he was always on
good terms with the Commissioner Charles Wingfield.[23] As a result of this
association he may well have realized that the British had come to stay, and
that to defy them, or to attempt to oust them, would be foolhardy.

Not only clans, but families as well, used the occasion of the Mutiny to
fight out afresh ancient rivalries. The Taroul estate in Pratabgarh district,
put together by the Sombansi chieftain Babu Abhiman Singh at the turn of
the nineteenth century, was soon after his death wrested away from his easygoing son Bhairon Bakhsh Singh by his brother's son Gulab Singh. Enterprising and influential, Gulab quickly won the favor of the Oudh government
and the respect of the neighboring taluqdars. Although Gulab by generous
treatment won over most of his uncle's family, several of the younger generation remained unreconciled. When one young man was killed, allegedly at

22. Wingfield Memo of 17 May 1858 (see n. 20 above). For the history of Balrampur, and its
rivalry with Tulsipur, see *Oudh Gazetteer*, 1:217–19; and Benett, *Gonda S.R.*, pp. 28–29.
23. See Thakur Baldeo Singh, "Life of Digvijai Singh" (Balrampur MSS, c. 1930), pp.
196–97; and Sayyid Aqa Hasan Rizvi, *Ahsan-ut-Tawarikh* (Lucknow, 1863–65), 2:202–10.

the instigation of the Taroul taluqdar, a blood feud sprang up between the two families. The aggrieved leader, Ajit Singh, brother of the murdered man, had for many years to bide his time, and was only occasionally able to force some of the villagers to pay him their rent. In the annexation he saw an opportunity at last to dislodge his hated rival, and so brought suit in the British settlement court for possession of the estate. Before the case could be decided the Mutiny broke out. But that upheaval presented Ajit with yet another chance to regain his ancestral property.

Even though he had lost at settlement only four of the ninety villages in the estate, Gulab Singh threw in his lot with the rebels from the outset. In early June, when the women and children of the Sultanpur garrison, some forty-four in all, sought shelter at Taroul, Gulab Singh turned them from his door, and let his followers plunder them. The fugitives then "stopped in the noon-day sun to drink and rest, and were being surrounded by people with sinister intentions, when their deplorable condition was made known to Ajeet Singh, whose village was not far distant. He immediately went out with 20 or 30 of his armed retainers, and with some difficulty induced the fugitives to accompany him home; he kept them there and fed them for several days . . . ; and eventually, having collected 200 or 300 armed men, he saw them safe into the fort at Allahabad." Gulab, enraged, at once drove Ajit out of the district, and then proceeded on behalf of the rebel government to take pos-session of the adjacent Jhusi and Soraon parganas of Allahabad district. Himself now a fugitive, Ajit joined the British Field Force at Jaunpur, where he put his local knowledge at the service of the Intelligence Department. He marched alongside the British troops in the reconquest of Oudh and was present at the fall of Lucknow. After the final defeat of Gulab Singh, Ajit Singh was awarded the estate of Taroul, which he had so long coveted.[24]

Rather like Rao Bhawani Singh in Mainpuri, Ajit Singh clearly saw that loyalty to the British, once his powerful antagonist had committed himself to the rebel side, could be turned to advantage in his family dispute. Ajit was to be sure a more enthusiastic British partisan than his Mainpuri counterpart. He had after all not had to face the repeated rebuffs in court to which Bhawani Singh had been subjected. But his behavior during 1857 was still in no way an expression of gratitude for the blessings of British rule, any more than Gulab's hostility was a product of the loss of four villages in the 1856 settlement. For these men, as for many families elsewhere, the Mutiny was simply an arena in which old rivalries could be fought out anew.[25] Sometimes

24. Depty. Commr. Salone to Commr. Faizabad 15 September 1858, UPSA B.R. Pratab-garh File 62. This letter is printed in Tholal, *Sombansi Raj*, pp. 64–68. For the history of the Taroul taluqa see *ibid.*, pp. 43–47 and 52–54. There is no evidence as to why Bhairon Bakhsh's four sons, who had lost as much as Ajit and whose hereditary claims to the estate were even stronger, joined Gulab Singh in rebellion. Because of this their claims were set aside in the redis-tribution of land after the Mutiny.

25. For further instances of family feuds determining behavior during the Mutiny see the accounts of the Dikhit raja of Parenda, and the Sengar Rajputs of Kantha in Elliott, *Chronicles of Oonao*, pp. 42, 47, 50–51.

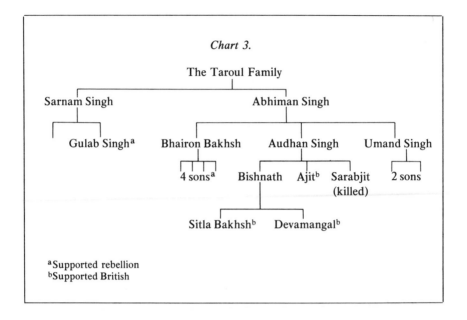

Chart 3.

The Taroul Family

Sarnam Singh — Abhiman Singh

Gulab Singh[a]   Bhairon Bakhsh   Audhan Singh   Umand Singh

4 sons[a]   Bishnath   Ajit[b]   Sarabjit (killed)   2 sons

Sitla Bakhsh[b]   Devamangal[b]

[a]Supported rebellion
[b]Supported British

indeed the splitting of a family into loyal and rebel factions did not even require a preexisting feud. It could instead be a consciously calculated maneuver. Among the Bais of Faizabad district, one British officer reported in the 1860s, as it was common in Mughal times to have one son converted to Islam so that they "might have a near and certain friend privileged with the entree of the Musalman Courts," so too did these taluqdars show "similar caution at a more modern date by sending one relative to the British force, and another to the rebels, to make sure of safety . . . whichever side might win."[26]

Despite this atmosphere of calculation some of the most prominent among the Oudh taluqdars distinguished themselves by their devotion to the ousted Lucknow court. For such men the political objectives of the revolt clearly mattered. The most famous among their number was the Bais chieftain Beni Madho Bakhsh of Shankarpur in Rae Bareli district. Despite a ready submission to British rule in 1856, Beni Madho lost 119 of the 223 villages in his estate during the summary settlement. At the outbreak of the Mutiny he mobilized his followers, some 12,000 strong, and placed them under the command of the rebel authorities in Lucknow. As the Shankarpur fort was one of the strongest in the province, and lay athwart the roads to southern Oudh, the British were anxious to win him over. Even when promised restoration of his estates, however, he did not submit. He owed allegiance, he said,

26. Carnegy, *Fyzabad Tehsil*, Part II ("Pargana Mangalsi"), p. 35. The original report was written by J. Woodburn, Settlement Officer, in 1868.

not to the British government, but to the royal dynasty of Oudh. "Now if I were to swerve from his [Birjis Qadar's] directions I shall be faithless, and in my disposition there is no grain of faithlessness toward anyone." After putting up a stout resistance to the British advance throughout 1858, he ultimately fled with the Begam to the jungles of Nepal.[27] The raja of Gonda had even less cause for hostility toward the British as he had been confirmed in possession of almost all his estate. But he too refused all offers to submit, claiming that once he had accepted service with the Begam he could never acquiesce in the rule of her enemies.[28]

Even those who tendered their allegiance in the end were often powerfully attracted to the cause of the Oudh dynasty. Raja Hanwant Singh of Kalakankar, one of the oldest and most powerful landholders in Oudh, after resisting payment of the initial British revenue demand in 1856, had taken from him 161 villages comprising two-thirds of his estate. At the outbreak of the revolt he took the Salone garrison into his fort at Dharupur, in Pratabgarh district, and after two weeks conducted them safely into Allahabad. During the height of the disturbances he fought against the British in southern Oudh, but he never took his forces into Lucknow, and he ceased fighting immediately after the fall of that city. His taking up arms, Major Barrow speculated, could be "attributed more to the great pressure around him than to

Raja Hanwant Singh in 1880.

27. See Beni Madho letter of 21 April 1858 to Nawab Munawar-ud-daula, Major Barrow's reply to Beni Madho of 22 April 1858, and Barrow's Memorandum of 10 November 1858 on the conduct of Beni Madho, B.R. Rae Bareli File 819. For short accounts see Chaudhuri, *Civil Rebellion in the Indian Mutinies*, pp. 118–19; and S.N. Sen, *Eighteen Fifty-Seven* (Delhi, 1957), pp. 360–62.

28. *Oudh Gazetteer*, 1:565. The rani of Tulsipur, together with several of the other northern chieftains, also refused to submit, and so joined the band of fugitives in Nepal.

any hopes he had of ultimate success."[29] Indeed he was perfectly ready, as he told P. Carnegy, the Deputy Commissioner, in a secret midnight interview in September 1858, "to declare openly for us," and even "to fight on our side," whenever a British force appeared to protect him. Yet he went on at once to say that "he hoped we would never tax his loyalty to his King by asking him to fight against *him*, for that would be ingratitude, as bad as our Sepoys were guilty of." There was, he insisted, "still a very strong feeling that Oude was unjustly annexed, and everyone wishes to see the King restored, if not to the throne, at least to the country."[30]

Raja Man Singh of Mehdona by contrast gave no thought to anyone's interest but his own. The holder of one of the largest taluqas in Oudh, he was vigorously wooed by both sides from the outset. But, anxious to come out on the winning side, he carefully avoided committing himself prematurely to either. Even while his forces were deployed in front of the beleaguered Residency in September 1857, he kept up an inconclusive correspondence with the British. Later in the year, after he had withdrawn from Lucknow, this "wily diplomatist," as Barrow described him, continued shrewdly playing off one side against the other. He tendered his allegiance to the British after the final fall of Lucknow in March 1858, when victory was certain, and he then remained staunch even when a rebel force besieged him in his fort of Shahganj for over a month. Not a man to hold back out of sentiment, Man Singh waited only to see which way the wind was blowing. Had the rebel side been victorious he would as promptly have put forward claims to the restoration of his estate based on his participation in the siege of the Residency.[31]

Few taluqdars appear to have joined the revolt with much enthusiasm. Their initial throwing off of the British yoke was clearly an instinctive, even habitual, response to the weakening of central authority. As they had in the years after Aurangzeb's death, and later when the power of the Nawabs seemed threatened, so too in 1857 they simply took advantage of the fortuitous sepoy mutiny to make a bid for independence. In itself it involved no particular antagonism toward their new rulers, whose coming the previous year they had not strongly contested. Almost invariably during the course of the revolt the taluqdars followed rather than led the sepoys and the ex-royal court of Oudh into active hostilities against the British. In part indeed their

29. Memo by L. Barrow of 25 October 1858, B.R. Oudh General File 1037. Barrow attributed Hanwant Singh's reluctance to support the rebel cause wholeheartedly in part to his "near relationship" to the raja of Rewah, who remained a loyalist throughout.

30. Memo by P. Carnegy of 21 September 1858, B.R. Pratabgarh File 385, Part I. Hanwant Singh also felt a strong sense of loyalty to his "great friend" Beni Madho, and so refused to take any Shankarpur villages when offered them as a reward for his service in sheltering British fugitives. He ultimately accepted instead three villages in Bahraich. Memo by L. Barrow of 3 May 1859, B.R. Rae Bareli File 820.

31. For an account of Man Singh's behavior during the Mutiny see Sec. C.C. Oudh to Sec. G.-G. 13 December 1858, B.R. Oudh General File 574. A selection from Man Singh's correspondence with the British can be found in Rizvi, *Freedom Struggle*, 2:219–32.

participation may have been prompted by pressure from below, for the sepoys, the bulk of them Oudh residents, had close ties of caste and kinship with the most influential among the taluqdars' tenantry, the underproprietary village zamindars. Once committed to the rebel cause, however, the taluqdars had little incentive to deal with the British. Remembering their treatment in 1856, they had no expectation of receiving favorable terms. Their resistance was further stiffened by Lord Canning's Proclamation of March 1858, which ordered confiscated all the land in Oudh as punishment for the rebellion of its people. Although this proclamation was never implemented—indeed the local authorities in Oudh protested strongly against its issuance—it nevertheless added fuel to the fire of taluqdari discontent. The bulk of the taluqdars thus remained in arms into the summer months of 1858, while those few, like Man Singh, who had earlier professed their allegiance, carefully avoided appearing in person in the British camp. Before agreeing to submit they required some visible assurance of favorable treatment under the new regime, as well as a guarantee of protection against the marauding bands of sepoys who still roamed the countryside. The former they obtained from May 1858 onward, when Major L. Barrow, appointed Special Commissioner of Revenue for this purpose, opened negotiations with the taluqdars for their submission. By October, when a large British force under the Commander in Chief Lord Clyde took the field in Oudh for the final campaign of the Mutiny, two-thirds of the taluqdars had already come in, yielding one at a time to the "fair arguments and political treatment" Barrow offered them. "The main argument was the settlement as proprietor of his estate with each talookdar as he presented himself. . . . As one came in, another saw the treatment he received; so gradually was confidence restored."[32]

Only those who remained hostile to the bitter end had their estates confiscated. The rest, even those who, like the raja of Mahmudabad, had been "notorious rebels" from the outset, were given back their old lands so long as they ultimately tendered their allegiance.[33] Offers were even made as late as November 1858 to Beni Madho and the raja of Gonda, promising the return of their estates if they would come in.[34] Altogether, land assessed at some nine and a half lakhs was confiscated for rebellion in Oudh. The bulk of this

32. For the pacification of Oudh see Barrow's letter of 3 January 1866, written when he was Commr. Lucknow, to Sec. C.C. Oudh, NAI For. Rev. A, June 1867, No. 30. For a general account see Metcalf, *Aftermath of Revolt*, pp. 71–72, 138–43.

33. For the negotiations with Mahmudabad see J. R. Reid to Barrow 11 April 1858, B.R. Oudh General File 396; and Barrow to Banda Ali Khan, brother-in-law of the Mahmudabad raja Nawab Ali Khan, 21 May 1858, B.R. Sitapur File 546. Reid opposed the restoration of the Mahmudabad estate to the raja.

34. See, for instance, L. Barrow to Beni Madho 30 November 1858, B.R. Rae Bareli File 819. Hanwant Singh of Kalakankar, who Montgomery called "our most active agent in persuading the rebel leaders to lay down their arms," took this offer to Beni Madho. See Sec. C.C. Oudh to Sec. Govt. India 31 December 1858, B.R. Oudh General File 574.

land was taken from some fifteen prominent taluqdars, and over half of it was located in the Bahraich Division. It was given out, in large part, to land-holders who had actively supported the British cause, either by taking arms against the rebels or by giving succor to European fugitives during the desperate days after the initial outbreak. Among the major beneficiaries were Digvijai Singh of Balrampur, Raja Man Singh of Mehdona, and the Sikh raja of the Punjab state of Kapurthala. Small parcels were also given to deserving native soldiers, private European settlers (most of whom soon sold their property to neighboring taluqdars), and even one Bengali babu, Dakhinaranjan Mukherjee, who was awarded a portion of Beni Madho's Shankarpur estate. (See Tables 18 and 19.)[35]

A New Land Policy

Throughout Oudh the sepoy rising was followed by a prompt repudiation of the 1856 settlement. The taluqdars everywhere took possession of the villages they had lost the year before, while the village zamindars whom the British had then befriended trooped in to offer their allegiance to their former masters. One district officer, given shelter by the taluqdar Hanwant Singh, saw his courtyard crowded with these men less than a week after the dissolution of government in the district. A few days later, from the safety of Allahabad, he reported disconsolately that "They [the taluqdars] have most of them resumed the villages they had at annexation. The villagers except in rare instances don't seem to have made a struggle even against it. They certainly gave us no assistance."[36] Later in the year when the taluqdars took up arms against the British, the villagers contributed substantial numbers of men to the rebel forces. There was "hardly a village in Bainswara," according to Barrow, that did not furnish its quota for the huge force of some 12,000 men brought together by Beni Madho.[37] The Shankarpur raja's militia, though large, was by no means exceptional. The raja of Amethi had some 10,000 soldiers with 26 guns in his fort of Ramnagar, Man Singh led a force of 5,000 foot and 50 mounted *sowars*, while a number of other leading taluqdars gathered together from 2,000 to 3,000 armed followers. Altogether the British estimated the taluqdari forces at some 32,000 in December 1857, and at 58,600 nine months later.[38] Nor were these men, and the funds needed

35. For the European grantees see Sec. Govt. India to C.C. Oudh 31 October 1859, C.O.F. Bundle No. 113, File 57, and Nevill, *Kheri D.G.*, pp. 98-99; for Dakhinaranjan see below pp. 334-35. The latter was "specially deputed" to Oudh for the purpose of "influencing the influential chiefs of this province." Sec. C.C. Oudh to Sec. Govt. India 2 February 1871, NAI For. Pol. A May 1871, No. 83.

36. Depty. Commr. Salone to Sec. Govt. India 28 June 1857, NAI S.C. 25 September 1857, No. 509.

37. Memo by L. Barrow, Spec. Commr. Rev., of 9 April 1859, B.R. Rae Bareli File 819.

38. For estimates of taluqdari strength see Chaudhuri, *Civil Rebellion in the Indian Mutinies*, pp. 130-31. P. Carnegy, Depty. Commr. Salone, in a memo of 21 September 1858, listed the number of foot and mounted soldiers under each major taluqdar, together with the size and armament of his fortifications. B.R. Oudh General File 395. It is not clear just who

Table 18. Land Confiscated for
Rebellion in Oudh[a]

Division	Assessment (rupees)
Lucknow	2,38,222
Faizabad	65,687
Khairabad	62,692
Bahraich	5,80,232
Total	9,46,833

[a]For the basic list of confiscated lands see Major L. Barrow, Spec. Commr. Rev., to Sec. C.C. Oudh 24 June 1859 in *Papers Relating to Land Tenures and Revenue Settlement in Oude* (Calcutta, 1865), Appendix "D," pp. 57-78. The original manuscript is in B.R. Oudh General File 574; further detail can be found in the divisional and district reports included in Oudh General Files 396 and 2030. A further Rs. 57,229 of land was later confiscated for concealment of arms.

to support them, always collected by coercion. The villagers in many instances paid their revenue to the rebel authorities before it was due, or the crops ripe. On Beni Madho's estate, Charles Wingfield noticed, the village zamindars "warmly sympathized" with the rebel taluqdar, and "paid him not from fear but from attachment."[39]

This ready acquiescence in the reassertion of taluqdari authority puzzled and angered the British. They had expected that the village holders, for whose benefit the new government had incurred the wrath of the most powerful men in the province, would come to its assistance in its time of trouble. Yet, wrote Barrow in October 1858, "our gradual resumption of districts has not even yet brought to our assistance those village communities, nor have they except in rare instances demanded restitution of those rights we had conferred on them prior to the outbreak. The assumption is, they are content with their inferior position."[40] Canning, writing at the same time, made the same point even more forcefully:

made up these militia. Presumably it was the same groups as in Nawabi times, with the increase in numbers accounted for by the short-term enrollment of *lathi*-bearing village zamindars.

39. Commr. Lucknow to Sec. C.C. Oudh 17 June 1859; and Sec. C.C. Oudh to Commr. Lucknow 22 June 1859, B.R. Oudh General File 2058. Collectors were permitted, in cases where zamindars had paid revenue to the rebel authorities before it was due, to collect the same installment a second time.

40. Memo by L. Barrow of 25 October 1858, B.R. Oudh General File 1037.

Table 19. Major Taluqdari Estates Confiscated for Rebellion

District	Estate	Jama (rupees)	Rebel owner	New owner(s)[a]
Unao	Fatehpur	20,384	Jassa Singh	Raja Kashi Prasad (Rs. 14,405)
Rae Bareli	Shankarpur	1,45,007	Beni Madho	Sikh sirdars (Rs. 28,636) Raja Digvijai Singh of Murarmau (Rs. 21,568) Dakhinaranjan Mukherjee (Rs. 5,000)
	Daundia Khera	11,817	Babu Ram Bakhsh	Raja Digvijai Singh of Murarmau (Rs. 8,234)
Pratabgarh	Mustafabad	19,079	Ram Ghulam Singh	Raja Jagpal Singh of Tiloi
	Taroul	14,699	Gulab Singh	Ajit Singh
Sitapur	Maholi	28,254	Lone Singh of Mitauli	Mirza Abbas Baig of Baragaon (Rs. 5,000) Jawahar Singh of Basaidih (Rs. 3,000) Seth Murli Manohar of Muizuddinpur (Rs. 2,000)
Bara Banki	Bhitauli	9,970	Raja Gur Bakhsh Singh	Raja Sir Randhir Singh of Kapurthala (Punjab)
Hardoi	Ruia	17,387	Nirpat Singh	Chaudhuri Hashmat Ali of Kakrali (Rs. 8,287) Barat Singh of Atwa (Rs. 8,049)
Gonda	Tulsipur	1,69,379	Dignarain Singh	Maharaja Digvijai Singh of Balrampur
	Bishambarpur	94,635	Raja Devi Bakhsh Singh of Gonda	Raja Man Singh of Mehdona
Bahraich	Baundi	47,037	Raja Hardatt Singh	Raja Sir Randhir Singh
	Ikauna	96,892	Raja Udit Prakash Singh	Raja Sir Randhir Singh (Rs. 81,892) Maharaja of Balrampur (Rs. 15,000)

Table 19. Continued.

Bahraich	Charda	45,441	Raja Jodh Singh	Maharaja of Balrampur (Rs. 25,369) Nawab Ali Raza Khan of Nawabganj-Aliabad (Rs. 15,061)
	Banki[b]	61,235	Dignarain Singh of Tulsipur	Maharaja of Balrampur
Kheri	Mitauli	51,373	Raja Lone Singh	Capt. A.P. Orr, Capt. W.M. Hearsey, Mr. G. Schilling, *et al.*

[a]Numbers in parentheses represent the jama of grants of less than an entire estate. Confiscations and awards of small size, or to petty and unimportant taluqdars, have been omitted.
[b]Banki pargana was ceded to Nepal in 1860.

Our endeavour to better, as we thought, the village occupants in Oudh has not been appreciated by them. . . . They acted in fact as though they regarded the arrangements made at settlement as valid, and to be maintained, just so long as the British rule lasted and no longer, and as though they wished the talookdar to re-assert his former rights and resume his ancient position over them at the first opportunity. Their conduct amounts almost to the admission that their own rights, whatever these may be, are subordinate to those of the talookdar; that they do not value the recognition of those rights by the ruling authority; and that the Talookdaree system is the ancient, indigenous, and cherished system of the country."[41]

Out of this disillusionment came a new land policy, that of settlement with the taluqdars.[42]

Political expediency as well drove the British toward a lenient treatment of the taluqdars. As the British military position improved during 1858, the government could no doubt have determined to treat with these men only as rebels, and so to root them out of the soil. The taluqdars by their behavior had given the British ample justification for such a policy, and indeed Canning's Confiscation Proclamation of March 1858 was a bow in that direction. But to have carried through such a wholesale confiscation would have much prolonged the military operations in Oudh, and left a substantial legacy of bitterness. So the local British authorities, led by the Chief Commissioner Sir Robert Montgomery, impatient for results, decided instead to pacify the province by winning over these rebellious landholders, and then turning to the purposes of order the uncontested influence they possessed in the countryside. Whenever a taluqdar came in to tender his allegiance, he

41. Sec. Govt. India to Sec. C.C. Oudh 6 October 1858, NAI F.C. 5 November 1858, No. 193.
42. For the origin and development of this policy see Metcalf, *Aftermath of Revolt*, pp. 134–50.

was required as a proof of his loyalty to "establish such posts as may be requisite for maintaining the peace." He was not expected "actually . . . to fight for us," but he was asked to place police outposts in advance of the line of British control, to secure lines of communication, and to rally the populace behind the British cause.[43] The Oudh taluqdars submitted, as Barrow cogently pointed out later, not as "a beaten foe claiming mercy at our hands, but men yielding to a *political invitation*." And such an invitation could be effective, in the absence of military force, only if it carried with it the promise of a "most unreserved settlement."[44]

The taluqdars therefore got back after the Mutiny all that they had lost in 1856. But their position under the British "restoration" was to be markedly different from what it had been under the later Nawabs. The taluqdars had now, what they had never found in the Lucknow court, a powerful patron and protector. From the outset the British were determined that the taluqdars' title to their newly restored estates should be secure. So early as January 1859 Montgomery had ruled that the settlement then in progress, although only a summary proceeding, would be "final," and that appeals by disappointed claimants would not be heard. Landholders, he said, "are to be encouraged to feel that what they receive now they will retain forever."[45] This declaration was followed later in the year by the award of *sanads* (patents) to all the principal taluqdars. These documents, distributed at a grand durbar in Lucknow presided over by the Viceroy Lord Canning, confirmed the holders in the full proprietary possession of their estates provided only that they paid their revenue, remained loyal to the British government, encouraged agricultural prosperity, and preserved the rights of those beneath them on the land. By this act all claims to land in taluqdari possession, no matter how that land had originally been acquired, were forever debarred.[46]

Yet, even while restoring the taluqdars to a position of unquestioned supremacy in rural society, the British were at the same time determined that these landholders would never again be able to mount an attack on their own supremacy. The very use of the taluqdars to restore order during 1858 was tied to their ultimate disarmament. As Barrow said of Hanwant Singh of Kalakankar, "I would make him responsible for the peace in his part of Oudh, and then disarm him with the rest."[47] As British authority was extended throughout the province, therefore, the taluqdars were required to disband their followers, surrender their cannon, and dismantle their forts. Attempts to evade these orders were severely punished. The raja of Bhinga tried to conceal several cannon, and promptly found one-half of his estate,

43. Memo by L. Barrow of 2 November 1858, B.R. Oudh General File 396.
44. Commr. Lucknow to Sec. C.C. Oudh 3 January 1866, NAI For. Rev. A, June 1867, No. 30 (italics in the original).
45. Circular No. 31 of 28 January 1859, F.C. 30 December 1859 (Supplement), No. 504.
46. For the text of the sanad see *P.P.* 1861, 46:429.
47. Memo by L. Barrow of 29 September 1858, B.R. Pratabgarh File 385, Part I.

some 138 villages assessed at Rs. 15,400, confiscated. Several smaller taluq-dars, among them the raja of Kurri Sidauli in Rae Bareli, who tried the same game, met the same fate. In all, land assessed at Rs. 57,229 was confiscated for retention and concealment of arms.[48]

The thoroughness of this disarmament, so different from that of 1856, effectively deprived the taluqdar of the political and military power he had formerly exercised. Remnants of his old position persisted, as we shall see later. But for the most part the taluqdar under the British was fitted for a new role in society—that of landlord. Such a transformation was an integral, even necessary, part of the British reconquest of Oudh. Unlike the Nawabs the British were unwilling to tolerate the existence of centers of power outside themselves; fresh from their victories over the rebels they were, again unlike the hapless Nawabs, able to enforce this view upon those about them. Hence a British-officered army and police force supplanted the taluqdars' armed bands, while the landholders' jurisdiction gave way to a civil administration whose officers collected revenue and meted out punishments according to the laws of British India. At the same time the transformation of the taluqdar from "robber baron" to peaceable landlord accorded perfectly with British notions of how society ought to be organized. For the mid-Victorian English-man, if not for the radical Benthamite, a landed aristocracy was the most appropriate capstone to the social edifice. Standing at the head of society, sustained by the deference of those below yet posing no challenge to the government, a class of landed gentry gave leadership, cohesiveness, and stability to the social order in a way no other group could duplicate.[49]

Yet the landlord class the British created in Oudh were as different from their presumed English counterparts as they were from their Nawabi prede-cessors. In part this was a product of their origin in administrative fiat. Unlike the English gentry, whose position in society was a product of slow organic growth, and who retained a sizable measure of autonomy, the taluq-dar-landlords after 1858 owed their prominence to the fact that a group of alien conquerors had decided as a matter of political expediency to rescue them from certain defeat, and prop them up anew. The artificiality of their position can most readily be appreciated by examining the way in which the British set out to decide who was, and who was not, a taluqdar.

In the days of the Nawabs the term "taluqdar" was applied indiscrim-inately and rather loosely to those who had succeeded in the struggle for power in the countryside, and so could claim the right to engage for the revenue of an agglomeration of villages. The British decision after the

48. Spec. Commr. Rev. to Sec. C.C. Oudh 24 June 1859, *Papers Relating to Land Tenures . . . in Oude*, p. 48; Nevill, *Bahraich D.G.*, p. 144; and H. R. Nevill, *Rae Bareli District Gazetteer* (Allahabad, 1905), p. 79.
49. For a brief note on the appeal of aristocracy to the English in India see Metcalf, *After-math of Revolt*, pp. 169–71.

Mutiny to give the taluqdars a special and privileged status meant that the term had now to be defined more precisely. Initially, in 1860, Charles Wingfield, the Chief Commissioner, told his subordinates, engaged in compiling a list of the taluqdars in their districts, that the term should be understood as meaning "an opulent landholder," and went on to add that "I should not consider any man who paid less than Rs. 5,000 as revenue as an opulent landholder."[50] But no sooner had the rule been laid down than it was subjected to qualification. Wingfield ruled, first of all, that no one who was not a "sole proprietor" should be awarded a sanad. Among those disqualified for this reason were such wealthy landholders as Jagannath Bakhsh and Basant Singh, who together held an estate assessed at Rs. 32,000 in Pratabgarh district. They were refused taluqdari status, despite the fact they had been addressed as taluqdars by the Nawab's government, because they were only two out of a large brotherhood who jointly held the Nain estate, and they were not "sole owners" of even their own share.[51]

At the same time a few landholders were awarded taluqdari status despite revenue assessments below the Rs. 5,000 minimum. In such cases, the decision was usually justified on the ground that the applicant was a man of high social standing, often the head of a clan, and was the owner of an estate that had descended undivided in his family for several generations. As Wingfield noted in approving the application of Karamat Husain of Kataria, whose assessment was only Rs. 2,763, "it seems clear that Nubbee Bux [Karamat's uncle, the previous holder] was always regarded and treated as a Talooqdar. The estate is a small one, but . . . it is sufficiently extensive to have gained for the owner the estimation and treatment of a Talooqdar both with his neighbours and the Government officials [of the old regime]."[52] In similar fashion Mehpal Singh of Umri, chief of the Bilkaria Rajputs, was given a taluqdari sanad despite a jama of Rs. 3,600 because he held the hereditary title of raja and the rule of primogeniture had prevailed for many generations on his estate.[53]

Sometimes, too, exceptions were the result of accident or inadvertence. Jagmohan Singh, one of four sharers in the undivided taluqa of Dariapur in Pratabgarh, told a charming story of how he got his sanad:

50. Sec. C.C. Oudh to Commr. Lucknow 24 April 1860, Wingfield to Barrow 26 June 1860 (demi-official), and Sec. C.C. Oudh to Commr. Lucknow 2 July 1860, B.R. Oudh General File 1964.
51. Commr. Rae Bareli to Finanl. Commr. 20 January 1870, B.R. Oudh General File 4, Part II. See also the comments of W.A. Forbes, n.d., on another Nain applicant: "The petitioners are *two putteedars*. Their property is simply a *zemindari*, and they are merely offshoots of the *Nain* family. They have no title whatever to the privileges of Talookdars. If they are Talookdars so are *all* the Nain men." *Ibid.*
52. Sec. C.C. to Settle. Commr. 3 February 1864, B.R. Faizabad File 634.
53. Sec. C.C. Oudh to Sec. Govt. India 19 April 1876, B.R. Oudh General File 4, Part II. The decision in this case was so long delayed because Mehpal Singh's title had been challenged in court by some of his relatives.

I was at Putty [Patti] when I heard that the Tehseeldar had ordered all the Talooqdars to present themselves at Lucknow. Accordingly I went there also. At Lucknow Baboo Ajeet Singh [of Taroul] and myself went to pay our respects to Mr. Tucker [Commr. Baiswara]. I told him that I had not received my Sunnud, and asked him to get it for me. He gave me a note and ordered me to go and present it to the Secretary Sahib. I went there and sent in the Chit by a Chuprassee. . . . The next morning I attended again at the Secretary Sahib's house with a number of other Talookdars. We all received orders to go to Moonshee Madho Pershaud Serishtadar, and get our names registered. We accordingly did so and the day after that I received my Sunnud. I did not go to the Governor General's Durbar but the Lord Sahib was encamped at Lucknow when I got my Sunnud. Neither Mr. Hogg [Depty. Commr.] nor the Tehseeldar of Puttee [Patti] gave me any direct orders to go to Lucknow. I simply went because I heard that all the Talookdars had been ordered to attend.[54]

The process of definition was brought to an end with the enactment of Act I of 1869. Under the provisions of that act the district officers were called upon to submit lists of all those whom they believed entitled to be called taluqdars. These lists were then scrutinized by Barrow, now Financial Commissioner, with the assistance of Maharaja Man Singh, and a final authoritative list drawn up for the entire province. Much of the work was done by Man Singh, who, Barrow reported in June 1869, "has been in almost daily attendance on me for the last two months, has personally investigated a large number of claims, and has drawn up a brief account of every Taluka of importance."[55] The list contained the names of some 276 individuals, including of course all those who had previously been awarded sanads, and was officially promulgated in the *Gazette of India* on July 31, 1869.[56] Thereafter a taluqdar was a person whose name appeared on this list, or an heir of such a person; and no one else. The society of taluqdars thus became close and exclusive. No amount of opulence could henceforth gain a newcomer admission, nor would penury lead to a member's removal. So long as a taluqdar held any land whatsoever, even a small fraction of his original estate, he was entitled to all the perquisites of the position. In 1883 one exasperated district officer, pointing to the taluqas of Asrenda, then held by six pattidars paying a total revenue of Rs. 2,883, and Jajamou, whose holder "now possessed no estate only a few bighas of sir land," sought permission to remove the names of such "petty" holders from the taluqdar list. He was told sternly

54. Offg. Depty. Commr. Pratabgarh to Commr. Baiswara 11 April 1861, B.R. Pratabgarh File 588. Once awarded, the sanad could not be rescinded. It was however redrafted to include all four cosharers and given over into the possession of Bhagwant Singh, the head of the family. See Sec. C.C. to Commr. Baiswara 14 May 1861. *Ibid.*
55. Sec. C.C. to Finanl. Commr. 19 January 1869, and Finanl. Commr. to Sec. C.C. 23 June 1869, B.R. Oudh General File 2336.
56. The original list is printed in Chhail Bihari Lal, *The Taluqdari Law of Oudh*, 2nd ed. (Allahabad, 1921), pp. 565–74. The names of three additional taluqdars were added during the 1870s. Revised lists were printed and distributed by the government or the taluqdars' association at regular intervals up to 1964.

that no tampering with the lists, or the definition of a taluqdar, would be permitted. The names must stay.[57]

In this fashion, within little more than ten years, the British changed almost beyond recognition the meaning of the term "taluqdar." What had been used in a vague and general way to designate those who controlled substantial amounts of land had now acquired a precise legal meaning. It denoted those of the defeated rebels of Oudh whom the British for reasons of imperial policy had pardoned and admitted as an act of administrative favor to the privileges of a special position on the land. To be sure, most of the new British taluqdars were the same men who had held the title in the later days of Nawabi rule, and claims to taluqdari status were in large part decided in accordance with previous Nawabi usage. Those whose preeminent position in the old order was unquestioned or who could produce evidence that they had been addressed as taluqdars by the Nawab's officers usually had little difficulty in gaining recognition under the new regime. But the British did give the lands and title of taluqdar to favorites of their own choosing, including, as we have seen, Sikhs, Europeans, and a Bengali babu. What is more important they did not hesitate to ride roughshod over Nawabi practice where it suited their purposes. The five-thousand-rupee limit, for instance, was highly arbitrary, and often enforced with a harsh rigidity. One taluqdari claimant in Faizabad district was turned away with a jama of Rs. 4,988.[58] The existence of this cut-off line no doubt reflected the British determination to insure that the taluqdars would remain a wealthy landed elite. As Barrow himself pointed out, in justifying the rejection of 108 applicants, "no useful purpose can be served by conferring a special distinction on any but those who are able to maintain it."[59] Yet the use of such an arbitrary criterion surely reflects as well the British passion for orderliness and tidiness. They could neither comprehend nor tolerate the haphazardness, one might even say the flexible accommodation to individual circumstance, which marked the old usage.

There was similarly no precedent in Nawabi practice for the refusal of taluqdari status to cosharers in jointly held properties, or for the preferential treatment accorded those whose estates descended by primogeniture. It had never been, despite Wingfield's confident assertion to the contrary, "one of the main characteristics of a talooqa that it descends undivided."[60] Yet the British were convinced that a landlord community could flourish, in Oudh as in England, only by adhering to the laws of property which had brought the

57. Depty. Commr. Unao to Commr. Lucknow 23 August 1883, B.R. Oudh General File 985. When a taluqdar lost all his land he retained the title for his lifetime, but it was not passed on to his heirs.
58. Petition of Balkishen and Lachman Parshad of Rajapur, pargana Tanda, of 3 June 1869; and Notes by Barrow of 15 June and 4 July 1869, B.R. Faizabad File 167.
59. Finanl. Commr. to Sec. C.C. 23 June 1869, B.R. Oudh General File 2336.
60. Sec. C.C. to Settle. Commr. 3 February 1864, B.R. Faizabad File 634.

English gentry to its position of preeminence.[61] Numbered and labeled, the taluqdars were thus cut loose from their old moorings, and expected to sail by a set of strange new bearings. In this enterprise there was not much reason to anticipate success.

From Policy to Ideology

The new status the taluqdar found marked out for him under the British was not solely the product of his conqueror's aristocratic prejudice or sense of orderliness. Behind this effort of definition lay as well a distinctive ideology, which much as it sought outwardly to reshape the taluqdars on an English pattern, in fact widened the distance separating them from their presumed English counterparts, and exacerbated the artificiality of their position in Indian society. Canning set the tone for this new attitude in October 1858, when he referred to the taluqdars as the "ancient, indigenous, and cherished" leaders of rural society.[62] The history of Oudh was thus rewritten at a stroke. No longer upstart robber barons or parasitic exploiters, the taluqdars had overnight become not only respectable, but men of ancient lineage, presiding over a deferential society. To some extent this new view of the character of Oudh society was forced upon the British by their policy of conciliation. Canning had almost of necessity to rehabilitate the taluqdars in order to restore them to their estates. But these ideas rapidly took on an independent existence, until within a few years the "Oudh Policy" (as it came to be known) formed a pervasive intellectual environment which helped shape all the activities of the British in Oudh.

The first detailed statement of the goals and assumptions of this "Oudh Policy" was the work of W. C. Benett. An Indian Civil Service (ICS) officer with a historical and philosophical cast of mind who had served in Oudh since the Mutiny, Benett in the 1870s wrote the history of two Oudh districts (Rae Bareli and Gonda) and the authoritative "Introduction" to the *Oudh Gazetteer*.[63] At the center of his argument lay a view of Hindu society as stable and unaltering, "equally incapable of development and impervious to decay." The most powerful element of stability in that system was the institution of caste. This divided men among a number of "natural orders" and prevented any upward movement to a higher rank through the sanction of ritual pollution. Thus secured from "the convulsions with which individual ambition might threaten it," society was further stabilized by the isolation of the various castes from each other, which made change from within "almost an impossibility." At the same time the pride of race "which is common to all

61. For further discussion of the British attempt to enforce special laws of inheritance upon the taluqdars see below ch. 8.
62. Sec. Govt. India to Sec. C.C. Oudh 6 October 1858, F.C. 5 November 1858, No. 193.
63. The district histories are the *Chief Clans of Roy Bareilly* (1870) and the *Gonda S.R.* (1878). The *Gazetteer* was published in 1877.

humanity" combined with the belief in caste to "resist all influence from without."[64]

At the head of this caste order were the Brahmins, who were invested with a reverence inconceivable in the West, but who in return renounced actual rulership in favor of the "Chattris" (or *kshatriya*). This latter class, the acknowledged repository of political authority, was "as indispensable as the Brahmin priest," and its might and magnificence were "gloried in by the people as the visible manifestation of their national prosperity."[65] Such was the strength of the system that even five hundred years of foreign rule, by Sultan and Mughal alike, had hardly affected its working. "Thousands might be slain and tens of thousands led into captivity, but the Brahman still controlled the family life of the people; their Chattri lord collected them for battle and disposed of their disputes in a court governed by rules which appealed to their sense of justice, and the cultivator continued to till his fields. . . ."[66]

The Nawabi era, Benett admitted, had seen the transformation of the raja into a taluqdar. But he insisted that despite this the position of the "Chattri" ruler had remained, up to annexation, essentially that of a national king. However small his territories might have been, he still received as of right the share of the cultivators' produce which formed the principal source of revenue; assessed and collected all the minor taxes within his domain; called out at his discretion the militia of his territory; and apportioned the waste lands to tenants for cultivation. Even after the upheaval of annexation and rebellion, he maintained, the taluqdars still retained their hold upon the affection of the people in a way no rulers of a foreign race and religion could ever emulate.[67]

This view of Indian society as stable and deferential, though seemingly the product simply of a conservative political philosophy, diverged in fact as much from Burke as from Bentham. The slow processes of accretion and adaptation by which the organic body politic of classic conservatism adjusts itself to changing circumstances find little place in Benett's thought. Hindu society is seen instead as static and unchanging, held firmly in place by the rigid sanctions of caste. Those changes which Benett could not ignore, such as the conversion of the raja into a taluqdar and the rise of new power holders, he deprecated as superficial or transitory. The auction taluqas, he conjectured, had it not been for annexation, must "eventually have returned to the old chieftainships" from whose territories they had originally emerged.[68] Indeed the major elements of Oudh society—the laborer, the village communities, the great landowners—were all of them ready "when left to their own unchecked action" to resume their ancient places in an immemorial structure.[69] This neoconservative traditionalism (as we might

64. *Oudh Gazetter*, 1:xxv–xxvii. 65. *Ibid.*, p. xliv.
66. *Ibid.*, p. xxxviii. 67. *Ibid.*, p. xliv.
68. *Ibid.*, p. xlvi. 69. *Ibid.*, p. liv.

perhaps call it) had its source in the varied intellectual currents which together underpinned later nineteenth-century imperialism: that authoritarian paternalism which insisted fiercely upon British supremacy, the pseudoscientific ethnography that ascribed ineradicable differences to the various races of mankind, and the idealist philosophy that sought immutable essences and moral imperatives beneath the flux of everyday life.[70]

Of greater importance here, however, than the parentage of Benett's views are their implications. He himself derived certain policy directives from them. Harking back to the ideals which he saw motivating the first two Nawabs in the eighteenth century, Benett argued that "happiness is best secured by . . . a strong central government, which preserves while it keeps in subjection all the elements of a native society."[71] Of these elements by far the most consequential were the great chieftains now become taluqdars. Rather than unsettling these men, as was done in the initial 1856 settlement, Benett urged the British government, while maintaining at all times its own supremacy, to uphold the living authority of this traditional ruling elite beneath them. Their prosperity was essential to the prosperity of the British Raj.

Once extended beyond these generalities, however, Benett's theory involved a considerable effort of self-delusion, for much of it flew in the face of facts. Indeed Benett was himself not always consistent. In *The Chief Clans of Roy Bareilly*, his first published work, far from opposing the "traditional" to the "auction" taluqdar, Benett insisted that the new men who came to power on the land during the later years of Nawabi rule were rapidly and fully integrated into the landed aristocracy. This he attributed to the continuing vitality of the old Hindu clan organization. The clans were, in his view, the vehicle for a rising spirit of national opposition on the part of the people of Oudh to "their Muhammadan conquerors," and one into which all that was "most vigorous" in the previous regime could easily be recruited.[72] Benett further admitted, not least in the very organization of this work, which provided a detailed account of the continuous rise and fall of landed families in the district before the coming of the British, that traditional society was remarkably open and "elastic," and that annexation alone had "frozen the waves."[73] In the *Gazetteer*, with its overwhelming emphasis upon the static quality of the Hindu social order, Benett backed away from these views, or at any rate from their implications. They were after all hardly compatible with an ideology of "traditionalism."[74]

70. For general discussion of the intellectual climate of the British in India during the later nineteenth century see Metcalf, *Aftermath of Revolt*, ch. viii; and Francis Hutchins, *The Illusion of Permanence* (Princeton, 1967). Benett was particularly hostile to utilitarianism, which he called "the grovelling Scotch philosophy of the last century" and in opposition to which he wrote in retirement a volume called *Justice and Happiness* (Oxford, 1911). See his letters to Harcourt Butler of 13 October 1910 and 14 May 1911 in Butler Papers IOL MSS Eur. F. 116/30.

71. *Oudh Gazetteer*, 1:xlii.

72. *Chief Clans*, pp. 69–71.

73. *Ibid., passim*, esp. pp. 54, 74.

74. In the 1895 reprint of the *Chief Clans* Benett noted that "the views expressed in this

Benett's difficulties did not end here, however. He could not deny that British rule had already had a devastating effect upon Oudh rural society. "The mistake which vitiates almost all our political theories in India," he wrote in the *Chief Clans*, "is that we are the successors of the Mussalman Emperors. . . . The vital fact is that we have, or at any rate think we have succeeded, where the Muhammadans in their strongest days never attained complete success, in taking the places of the local princes, and in substituting our own for native law and organization. The Commissioner has supplanted not so much the Nazim [the Nawab's deputy] as the Raja [the local chieftain]."[75] Even in the *Gazetteer* Benett had to admit that one of the "general tendencies" of British rule was to hasten the "disintegration" of the old structure of society.[76] Yet how was this "solvent" quality of the new regime to be reconciled with its "preservationist" professions? Here was the basic contradiction at the heart of the "Oudh Policy," and it was one that was never truly faced. Despite Benett's praise of Saadat Khan the British never for a moment entertained the notion of stepping into the shoes of an eighteenth-century Nawab. No one, not even Benett, was willing to give substantial executive and judicial powers to the taluqdars, or to permit the recruitment of private militia forces. He would concede no more than that the taluqdars be fitted for posts in the British administration.[77] Yet without real power, held firmly in their own hands, the taluqdars were incapable of fulfilling their "traditional" role in society. Their position could at best be an attenuated one, wholly dependent on the whims and vagaries of their British rulers. The self-confident "Oudh men" refused, however, to see any inconsistency between their principles and their practice. So proud indeed were they of their handiwork that the young Harcourt Butler, before he rose to become their most distinguished twentieth-century spokesman, was drawn to remark of Benett that "like most of the Oudh men he thinks there is no place like Oudh, no officer like a man who has served in Oudh, and no officer who has served in Oudh like himself."[78]

The principles of the "Oudh Policy" did not escape altogether unchallenged. From the outset there had been much grumbling and covert opposition to the taluqdari settlement among the lower district officers in Oudh.[79] Although vigorously suppressed by the senior officials in Lucknow and Calcutta, this dissenting strand of opinion remained alive and vocal throughout the later nineteenth century. The first fully argued critique of the new settle-

---

report have been amplified and corrected in subsequent publications, such as the Gonda settlement report and the Oudh Gazetteer" (p. 75).

75. *Chief Clans*, pp. 74–75.

76. *Oudh Gazetteer*, 1:lxiv. He also recognized that the introduction of English law had led to the chieftains being "entirely superseded in one of their main functions, that of independent arbiter" (p. lxv).

77. *Ibid.*, p. lxvi.

78. Butler to his mother, 5 December 1893, in Butler Papers IOL MSS Eur. F. 116/5.

79. See Metcalf, *Aftermath of Revolt*, pp. 152–53.

ment, and of the assumptions that lay behind it, was the work of C. W. McMinn, a warm-hearted but high-spirited young ICS officer who was assigned in the early 1870s to write a draft "Introduction" to the forthcoming *Oudh Gazetteer*. McMinn turned the essay, a long rambling exposition of the state of Oudh at the time, into a ringing denunciation of contemporary British policy toward the province.

He opened his attack by charging that under the conditions of British rule the taluqdars served no useful function either politically or economically. The kshatriya raja, he argued, whatever kingly role he may once have played, "is no longer the national champion; he has in Oudh neither a cause nor a weapon, for the whole country has been disarmed. The Kshatris have lost prestige largely, power entirely, and the people no longer feel the need of them."[80] They could no doubt be rehabilitated and restored to the position of true feudal lords, but—and here McMinn exposed the basic fallacy of the "Oudh Policy"—this would require such measures as the reduction of the English army in Oudh to a guard of honor for the Chief Commissioner, and the award to every taluqdar of a permanent settlement and magisterial powers.[81]

Nor was the political demise of the taluqdars at all compensated by economic advantage. Again and again throughout the essay McMinn insisted that the taluqdars could not manage their estates efficiently, that they had no idea of agricultural improvement, and that they now all too often regarded their tenants as fit subjects for exploitation.[82] Part of the problem was the enormous size of estates in Oudh. But the basic difficulty arose from the fact that the old raja had been turned into a landlord, with no longer any opportunity of keeping up the "nobler part" of his role and with no restraints upon the use (or abuse) of his power over the land. His power, McMinn insisted, was as great as ever, in some ways "more absolute," but now, constricted to these narrower channels, it had "meaner developments," and brought him the dread not the deference of those living under him.[83]

The coming of British rule had not therefore, apart from a few specially favored groups, materially benefitted the people of Oudh. Worst off of all were the cultivating masses, whose condition was one of "considerable suffering." Their misery was not of course wholly the result of the taluqdari settlement. An increasing population and a heavy burden of debt took their toll, as did the annual export of revenue and grain out of the province, the favorable treatment accorded creditors in the courts, and the loss of employment opportunities for artisans and soldiers. But there was not much hope of

80. C. W. McMinn, "Introduction to the Oudh Gazetteer," (proof copy in the India Office Library), n.d., ca. 1873, p. 71.
81. *Ibid.*, p. 204. McMinn was not particularly hostile to the taluqdars. He believed that if they were vested with real power the majority of them would as hereditary rulers, "probably govern very fairly."
82. See esp. pp. 109, 199, 211, 364.
83. *Ibid.*, pp. 120–21.

relief so long as the British continued to uphold an "unsound and uneconomical" tenure of land.[84]

McMinn's essay was, naturally enough, refused publication by the Oudh government under Sir George Couper, which replaced it with Benett's shorter, more graceful, and altogether "sounder" work already discussed. This encounter with the official "Oudh Policy" left McMinn an embittered and discontented man for the rest of his life. While compiling the *Gazetteer* he had already won the enmity of the Oudh administration by a series of critical articles in the press. After the *Gazetteer* episode he was transferred to Agra and denied the promotion to independent charge of a district to which he was entitled. He nevertheless soon ran afoul of authority once again when he criticized the administration of famine relief in his district, and sought the direct intervention of the Governor-General instead of going through the usual official channels. This display of insubordination (even though inquiry substantiated many of his charges) brought down upon him yet another transfer, this time to the Central Provinces, where he remained for the rest of his career. Thirty years later in retirement he still felt deeply the injustices done to him because, as he put it, of his "strong sympathy with the people of India."[85]

Despite the treatment of McMinn the standard of dissent did not fall altogether to the ground. In 1880, in a volume entitled *The Garden of India*, H. C. Irwin, himself an ICS officer in Oudh, gently but with biting satire tore apart the foundations on which the "Oudh Policy" had been constructed. Above all he insisted, in opposition to the Benett of the *Gazetteer*, "feudal sentiment" was on the wane. Already there was little difference between the ancient chieftain and the "mushroom" taluqdar. "In no very long time" the relations between the taluqdar and his tenants would depend almost entirely on the way in which each individual landholder chose to exercise "the great power" he possessed over those beneath him.[86] Irwin dismissed as nonsense the notion that the villagers' support of the revolt during 1857 involved any preference on their part for the taluqdari system of land tenure. "The utmost inference," he said, "that can logically be deduced from their conduct is that their dislike of the great landholders who had oppressed them was not, in

84. *Ibid.*, pp. 181, 197–201, 226.
85. C. W. McMinn, *Famine Truths, Half Truths, Untruths* (Calcutta, 1902), pp. 46, 48. For an account of his chequered early career, and evidence of the local government's hostility toward him, see Sec. Govt. N.W.P.&O. to Sec. Govt. India 27 July 1878, N.W.P.&O. Rev. Progs. August 1878, No. 43. Couper felt that McMinn was "unfit" to be a member of the civil service and should, if not dismissed, be sent to some remote place like Assam or Burma. The Viceroy, while critical of McMinn's behavior, saw in the practical "defects" that marred the relief administration and in the "unconfiding way" McMinn had been treated by his superiors some palliation of his conduct. Sec. Govt. India to Sec. Govt. N.W.P.&O. 31 December 1878, N.W.P.&O. Rev. Progs. January 1879, No. 129; and Sec. Govt. India to Sec. Govt. N.W.P.&O. 28 April 1879, N.W.P.&O. Rev. Progs. June 1879, No. 58.
86. H. C. Irwin, *The Garden of India; or Chapters on Oudh History and Affairs*, pp. 9–10. See also p. 13.

some instances, strong enough to prevent their taking part with them . . . fighting what they believed to be the battle of their own religion, against an alien and newly imposed power."[87] In consigning the people of Oudh once again to the "prison of feudalism," but now furnished with none of the "sentiments and customs" that could alone make feudalism tolerable, Canning had thrown over the principles upon which British rule in India was based. "The policy of conciliating the strong by allowing them to lord it over the weak may be safe, but it is not noble. If we are not here to uphold the cause of the poor and of him that hath no helper, we have no right to be here at all."[88]

At the end of the century a new champion of the "Oudh Policy" arose in the person of Harcourt Butler. Initially skeptical, as we have seen, Butler soon swung round to support of the taluqdars and friendship both with them and with their old patron Benett. So early as March 1894 he said of Benett's *Gazetteer* "Introduction" that it "gives the best general idea of Oudh that I know."[89] Two years later, on the occasion of Benett's retirement, which he described as a "provincial calamity," Butler said of his writings on Oudh history that they are "by themselves a liberal education and should be bound about the neck of every new Oudh official."[90] So it is no wonder that in his own writings, most prominently in two pamphlets on "Oudh Policy" published in 1896 and 1906, Butler elaborated and extended Benett's arguments. Butler insisted first of all, like Benett, that the Brahmin priest and the "Chattri Raja," joined in an "indissoluble alliance," together upheld the traditional Hindu social order.[91] But he went on at once vehemently to deny that the transformation of the raja into a taluqdar had in any way caused him to "forfeit his old world claim and grasp upon the reverence of Hindus." Clearly stung by the criticisms of McMinn and Irwin, Butler argued that the taluqdar's preeminent position in society did not derive simply from his exercise of kingly powers, but was inextricably bound up with his status as a kshatriya within the caste system. No matter whether he discharged a particular kingly function or not, the taluqdar/raja remained always the "visible and outward embodiment of Hindu secular power." He thus retained, even under British rule, his hold on the people.[92] Indeed his political influence itself, though temporarily "latent," was not extinguished. "There can be no doubt," Butler wrote in an early draft of his 1896 pamphlet, "that in the

87. *Ibid.*, pp. 184-86.
88. *Ibid.*, pp. 188-89, 194-95.
89. Butler to his family 14 March 1894, Butler Papers IOL MSS Eur. F. 116/5.
90. Spencer Harcourt Butler, *Oudh Policy Considered Historically and With Reference to the Present Political Situation* (Allahabad, 1896), "Preface" (p. i).
91. *Ibid.*, pp. 6-7. See also S. H. Butler, *Oudh Policy: the Policy of Sympathy* (Lucknow, 1906), p. 33.
92. Butler, *Oudh Policy* (1896), ch. iii, esp. pp. 27, 30-32. In 1906 Butler called the "continued influence of the raja" the "keystone of the Oudh political and social structure, and the source of its unrivalled stability" (p. 36).

event . . . of any serious political disturbance, the Raja would resume his position of politico-social supremacy, and the clansmen would fall naturally into the various positions of politico-social subjection." For political purposes, he concluded, "the Taluqdars are Oudh."[93]

Butler's defense of the "Oudh Policy" was prompted in large part by the unsettled political situation at the turn of the century. The cow protection movement which spread across North India in the early 1890s he saw as a portent of a revived Brahmanical Hinduism, which could easily, especially in the orthodox eastern districts, spill over into "serious disorders." To isolate and suppress such disturbances required a "solid buffer of loyalty" nearby. This Oudh, and the taluqdars, could alone supply. To ensure their support, Butler urged the government to treat the taluqdars liberally, and above all to assess their estates lightly during the settlement revision which was then in progress.[94] An even greater threat to tranquility, in Butler's view, came from nationalism, and from British willingness to conciliate it by constitutional reform. In 1896 he had written that a "contented body of taluqdars will greatly ease the tensions of premature reform." And he went on to call for measures that would preserve and enhance the taluqdars' influence in the local political arena. As counsellors and right-hand men of the district authorities, vested with substantial judicial powers, they would, he said, "accomplish their proper and original purpose in the economy of the Province."[95] A decade later, with the Morley-Minto reforms in prospect, taluqdari participation in the political process had become an even more compelling objective. In his 1906 pamphlet Butler insisted that the rural masses were incapable of politics, and that the taluqdars, as the "natural leaders of the people," therefore afforded "the only possible foundation for the devolution of political power." They had now to take their place not only at the Collector's side but in the Legislative Councils as well.[96]

Not everyone of course, even among his contemporaries, shared Butler's enthusiasm for the taluqdars. Antony MacDonnell, the Lieutenant Governor, shown an early draft of Butler's first pamphlet, dismissed it as "immature and exaggerated." Next to Butler's assertion that "Ten landlords may meet in a room at Lucknow, and in ten minutes ten parganas may be in flames" he penciled the single word "prodigious!"[97] But Butler's views were sufficiently powerful to carry him rapidly up the Indian official hierarchy. A junior settlement officer when he wrote his first tract on "Oudh Policy," he was soon promoted to the important post of Secretary to the Board of Reve-

93. S. H. Butler, "Note on the Political Aspect of the Oudh Settlements," n.d., ca. 1895, N.W.P.&O. Rev. Dept. File No. 158B. See also Butler, *Oudh Policy* (1896), pp. 55–56.
94. Butler, *Oudh Policy* (1896), pp. 3–4, 61–64, 68–69. For discussion of the settlement revision of the 1890s see below ch. 8.
95. *Ibid.*, pp. 70–71. See also Butler's "Note on . . . the Oudh Settlements," (see n. 93 above).
96. Butler, *Oudh Policy* (1906), p. 40.
97. Note by A. P. MacDonnell of 3 February 1896, N.W.P.&O. Rev. Dept. File No. 158B.

nue. From there he rose to the charge of the sensitive district of Lucknow, and finally, after service in Calcutta and Burma, to the Lieutenant Governorship of the province. Nor were the reasons for his rapid ascent at all obscure to his fellow officers:

> And I tickled the tail of the Taluqdar,
> I tickled his tail so successfully
> That now I am Sir Harcourt and the next L.G.[98]

With Butler then, the "Oudh Policy" reached the full extent of its power and influence. But it remained as remote as ever from the actual state of affairs in Oudh. Indeed in Butler's hands sentimentalized myth increasingly took the place of whatever analytic cogency the "Oudh Policy" had originally contained. The raja may be "over-bearing, often cruel," Butler wrote in 1907, "but his people live at his gate, where his horses and cattle and elephants are stalled, and there is a strong bond of common humanity between them. It is the old idea 'You shall be my people and I will be your God.' Their lives are dull; their outlook is tinged with the deepest pessimism; when the day's work is over they long to huddle together under the blanket of common humanity. This feeling comes to all. . . . It is in the eastern air."[99] Oudh in short was a "traditional" society where nothing ever changed and the people lived in perfect harmony with each other. The sharpening of class antagonisms, and the attenuation of the taluqdar's claims upon the loyalty of his tenantry, were simply willed out of existence.

98. Anonymous verse cited in Philip Woodruff, *The Men Who Ruled India: The Guardians* (London, 1954), p. 289.
99. Harcourt Butler to Dunlop Smith 1 December 1907, in Martin Gilbert, *Servant of India* (London, 1966), p. 97. I am indebted to P. D. Reeves for this reference.

Eight | *The Framework of Rule:*
Laws, Taxes, and the Land

T

HE STRUCTURE of governance in Oudh, though built around the taluqdari settlement, was not shaped by that act alone. It was informed as well, for Oudh was a province of British India, by the goals of the policy-makers at the center, and it reflected in its working the conflicts of personality and principle found elsewhere from Calcutta to Lahore. During the decades after the Mutiny, with reforming enthusiasm at a discount, the British focused their efforts in rural India on the collection of revenue, the maintenance of law and order, and the dampening down of social conflict within established patterns of agrarian relations.[1] To be sure, the outcome of this intervention in society did not always conform to the expectations of the government, nor did the British ever put a halt to those processes of change, economic and social alike, which their very coming had precipitated. Yet it is with the framework of law, and of revenue policy, which gave shape to so much else, that we must begin.

1. For general accounts of policy and attitudes toward rule in the post-Mutiny years see my *Aftermath of Revolt*; S. Gopal, *British Policy in India, 1858-1905* (Cambridge, 1965); and Hutchins, *The Illusion of Permanence*. For a study focused upon the interaction of status and personality in the ICS see Bradford Spangenberg, *British Bureaucracy in India* (Delhi, 1976). Public works were alone prosecuted with vigor. For an account of the working of the government in the countryside, based mainly on data from the N.W.P., see Whitcombe, *Agrarian Conditions*.

Settlement and Assessment

The first settlement of Oudh under the new taluqdari arrangements was, like that of 1856, a three-year summary assessment. Taken in hand in November 1858, as soon as the province had been reconquered, it was completed, under Major Barrow's direction, by the following spring. The speed was in large part a product of the government's determination "to *settle* the country" politically. This objective clearly required keeping to a minimum the disturbance that settlement proceedings necessarily entailed. A rapid pace was further ensured by the decision, taken so early as May 1858, to base the new assessments on the jama fixed in the previous summary settlement. Barrow was aware that the settlement bore "somewhat heavily on the people," and that substantial reductions had been ordered just before the revolt.[2] But little was in fact done to secure relief. In most cases the settlement officers, driven by the need for speed, mechanically applied the 1856 figures, and checked them only against the collections of the three preceding years, on which of course the 1856 assessment had itself largely been based. The result was an assessment only slightly less heavy than its predecessor. The total reduction amounted to Rs. 68,685 on an assessment of over a crore of rupees; and of this sum some Rs. 58,000 were on account of estates settled at half-rates with the Maharaja of Kapurthala as a reward for his services during the Mutiny. (See Table 20.)

The regular settlement, begun in 1860, proved to be a time-consuming affair. Although the award of sanads to the taluqdars had by that time foreclosed any possibility of change in the basic pattern of landholding, there still remained an enormous mass of claims to shares, villages, and underproprietary rights of all kinds which had to be sorted out before a definitive record of rights could be drawn up.[3] In determining the level of assessment, moreover, the government now threw over the summary procedures used in 1856 and 1858–1859 in favor of the principles recently adopted in the North-Western Provinces and embodied in the Saharanpur rules of 1855. At the heart of these rules was the insistence that actual cash rents be taken as the basis for the calculation of the rent-rates from which the government demand at half-assets was then deduced. In practice, however, "actual" rents often proved elusive or unsatisfactory. The figures of rentals recorded in the patwari's books, in particular, were almost wholly unreliable, for, as several officers complained, "the putwarees wrote just as the zemindars wished them to." Lacking any alternative measure of rental assets, the assessing officers as a result inevitably turned to the calculation of assumed rentals based largely upon soils. This process, as well as the reconciling of the assumed with the

2. Barrow Memo of 1 May 1858, and Circular of 5 October 1858 to all Divisional Commrs. UPSA B.R. Oudh General File 66, Part I.
3. For discussion of underproprietary rights see below ch. 9.

Table 20. Assessment by District, Oudh, 1855–1859

Division	District	Number of villages	Recorded jama under Nawabs (rupees)	Jama in 1856 (rupees)	Summary settlement demand (rupees)
Lucknow	Lucknow	1,570	11,41,149	9,03,569	9,00,255
	Rae Bareli	1,551	10,42,319	8,53,659	8,42,690
	Unao	1,236	12,03,916	10,26,872	10,34,989
Total		4,357	33,87,384	27,84,100	27,77,934
Faizabad	Faizabad	4,215	11,85,889	11,26,284	11,33,778
	Sultanpur	3,351½	13,17,600	8,44,554	8,32,037
	Pratabgarh	3,633	11,20,574	8,70,250	8,47,692
Total		11,199½	36,24,063	28,41,088	28,13,507
Bahraich	Gonda	4,129	12,74,777	9,18,873	9,29,885
	Kheri	3,130½	5,53,144	6,09,969	5,73,306
	Bahraich	3,949	6,71,080	4,46,888	4,55,035
Total		11,208½	24,99,001	19,75,730	19,58,226
Khairabad	Hardoi	1,427	13,84,339	10,57,380	10,36,329
	Daryabad (Bara Banki)	2,560	11,85,906	8,61,770	8,61,474
	Sitapur	4,422	12,02,344	9,69,686	9,73,520
Total		8,409	37,72,589	28,88,836	28,71,323
Grand Total		35,174	1,32,83,037	1,04,89,754	1,04,20,990

Source: Spec. Commr. Rev. to Sec. C.C. Oudh 24 June 1859. *Papers Relating to Land Tenures . . . in Oude,* p. 46; and Appendices "A" and "B" (pp. 53–55).

recorded rentals, left much scope for arbitrariness and with it for assessments based upon little more than estimates.[4] In the end the settlement took eighteen years to complete, and brought about an enhancement of the total revenue demand on Oudh by some 38 percent, to Rs. 1,42,69,796. (See Table 21.)

How heavily these new assessments pressed upon the landholders can be judged only in individual instances. In many areas the reclamation of wasteland and the extension of cultivation in the years following annexation had substantially increased the landholder's income, and so justified an

4. For the Saharanpur rules see above pp. 72–73. For discussion of the difficulties encountered in the attempt to use actual rentals see Moreland, *Revenue Administration of the United Provinces,* pp. 44–46; and Whitcombe, *Agrarian Conditions,* pp. 124–29. For dissatisfaction with the patwari's records see P. Carnegy to Barrow 7 January 1859, B.R. Rae Bareli File 62; Carnegy's annual settlement report for Faizabad, 7 May 1864, B.R. Faizabad File 11, Part I; and Whitcombe, *Agrarian Conditions,* pp. 252–60. The patwari in Oudh was wholly the landlord's servant. For discussion of his position, see below ch. 10.

Table 21. Assessment by District, Oudh, 1859-1900[a]

District	Summary settlement (rupees)	First regular settlement (rupees)	Enhancement (Percentage)	Second regular settlement (rupees)	Enhancement (Percentage)
Lucknow	6,86,986	8,02,657	17	9,86,569	23[b]
Rae Bareli	9,47,917	12,39,189	31[b]	16,07,628	30[b]
Unao	11,76,185	12,87,271	9	15,45,303	20
Faizabad	8,70,188	11,68,462	34	14,61,922	25
Sultanpur	9,03,013	12,37,677	37	14,86,353	20[b]
Pratabgarh	7,30,534	9,85,619	35	13,46,522	36
Gonda	9,62,401	15,26,487	60	17,70,189	15
Kheri	4,91,922	8,02,411	63[b]	10,28,510	28[b]
Bahraich	5,79,706	10,91,656	72	11,29,595	13[b]
Hardoi	10,16,712	13,30,139	31	15,53,027	17[b]
Bara Banki	11,93,834	15,84,534	33	20,76,921	30
Sitapur	9,39,897	13,03,694	38	16,15,760	24[b]
Total	1,04,99,295	1,42,69,796	38	1,76,08,299	23

[a]The figures used here are taken from the district gazetteers. A slightly different set of figures which cannot be reconciled with those in the gazetteers is found in *Memorandum upon Current Land Settlements in the Temporarily Settled Parts of British India* (Calcutta, 1880), pp. 153-73.
[b]For this district a percentage of enhancement is given in the text of the district gazetteer which differs from that calculated here using the figures of total revenue demand. There is no apparent way of reconciling these differences.

enhanced demand. Elsewhere the demand was clearly pitched too high, and enforced with too little concern for the difficulties of payment. In the Khandasa pargana of Faizabad, for instance, pressed for time, the settlement officer, J. Woodburn, did "little more than compare the general features of the neighboring villages, and check the entries of the amins [clerks]: consequently in assessing, the basis of the assessment was a comparison of one village with another." On this shaky foundation Woodburn raised the demand some 70 percent, to Rs. 86,438, and then ordered it brought into force in full at once. He did not wait to obtain sanction from his superior officers, nor did he permit progressive enhancements or any other device that might cushion the blow and give the landholders time to adjust their rents upward. Faced with this sudden and staggering increase, the landholding community for a long time steadfastly refused to sign the *qabuliyats* which would signify their acceptance of the new demand. Matters were made worse by the fact that the bad seasons of 1870 and 1871, "two of the worst years on record," followed directly after the inauguration of the new settlement.[5]

5. H. F. House, Assessment Report of Pargana Khandasa of 22 September 1896, N.W.P.&O. Rev. Progs. July 1897, No. 28; and A. F. Millett, *Fyzabad Settlement Report* (Allahabad, 1880), pp. 473-76.

Nor was Khandasa at all exceptional. The same excessive zeal moved many of the Oudh settlement officers. In the Dharmanpur pargana of Bahraich, H. S. Boys brought into force, "either immediately before, or simultaneously with, the occurrence of bad seasons," an assessment of Rs. 33,380, or nearly three times the summary jama.[6] In Kheri, C. W. McMinn and J. C. Williams enhanced the revenue by 140 percent, in part by such devices as anticipating the rapid extension of irrigation and the clearance and cultivation of extensive tracts of wasteland. They also valued the crops not by the prices the cultivator might hope to obtain but in accordance with the much higher retail prices in distant markets. Their offered qabuliyats were as a result "everywhere refused" so that "it became impossible to collect the revenue."[7]

Arrears in consequence mounted up rapidly. In Faizabad district, where even the summary demand had been realized with difficulty, balances during the first years of the new settlement sometimes reached over a lakh of rupees, while Kheri and Hardoi lagged only a little behind. For the province as a whole the annual balances of unpaid revenue by 1872 had climbed to the record figure of Rs. 6,52,218 (see Table 22). Even those who, like the taluqdars, for the most part met the demand did so only with "extreme difficulty" and in almost every case by means of loans raised "at perfectly ruinous interest."[8]

As the distress brought on by the settlement became increasingly visible, the government moved slowly to provide relief. From 1870 onwards uncollected balances were freely remitted throughout the province, while several especially hard-hit areas were awarded permanent reductions in their assessments.[9] The Khandasa assessment, limited in 1870 to a maximum increase in the first ten years of 50 percent over the summary demand, was a few years later, as part of a revision of much of the Faizabad settlement, in which recorded rent rolls were given greater weight than before, reduced permanently by 6.8 percent.[10] The Dharmanpur assessment, found to be "unworkable" after only two years in operation, was canceled and a fresh settlement made from the rent rolls. At Rs. 22,375 this halved Boys's initial enhancement.[11] In Kheri almost the entire district was resettled, and the rise in the

6. P. Harrison, Assessment Report of Pargana Dharmanpur of 3 August 1899, N.W.P.&O. Rev. Progs. December 1899, No. 9; and *Oudh Revenue Administration Report for 1872-73* (Lucknow, 1874), Part I, p. 24.

7. *Oudh Rev. Admin. Report for 1872-73*, Part I, p. 8; and Nevill, *Kheri D.G.*, pp. 111-14.

8. *Oudh Revenue Administration Report for 1871-72* (Lucknow, 1873), Part I, p. 13. See also pp. 10-12, and *Oudh Revenue Administration Report for 1867-68* (Lucknow, 1869), Part I, pp. 7-10.

9. In 1873, for instance, one-quarter of the revenue demand was remitted for the entire district of Faizabad. For a general discussion of relief measures see *Oudh Rev. Admin. Report for 1872-73*, Part I, pp. 13-27.

10. Millett, *Fyzabad S.R.*, pp. 477-79; and *Oudh Revenue Administration Report for 1869-70* (Lucknow, 1871), Part II, p. 26. During the course of this revision the district assessment as a whole was reduced 6.1 percent. *Fyzabad S.R.*, p. 481.

11. P. Harrison, Assessment Report of Pargana Dharmanpur of 3 August 1899, N.W.P.&O. Rev. Progs. December 1899, No. 9.

Table 22. Annual Revenue Balances[a]
(rupees)

Year	Faizabad district	Oudh total
1864–1865	35,915	87,390
1865–1866	3,300	32,044
1866 (5 months)	94,159	2,62,838
1866–1867	78,678	1,71,736
1867–1868	2,54,362	5,87,893
1868–1869	65,845	3,54,202
1869–1870	2,833	1,45,375
1870–1871	18,707	2,91,499
1871–1872	99,903	5,61,068
1872–1873	1,75,202	6,52,218

[a]These figures are taken from the annual provincial revenue administration reports. The five-month entry for 1866 is the result of a change in the dates of the official revenue year, which from 1866 onward began on October 1 rather than May 1.

demand brought down from 140 to 73 percent above the summary settlement jama.[12] In Hardoi, where the initial increase had been 41 percent, about half the villages were resettled on the basis of actual assets, and the total revenue reduced by 7 percent.[13]

Despite these sometimes substantial reductions few officers were prepared to find much fault with the settlement. Before 1870, when leniency could have prevented much hardship, the settlement officers invariably insisted that their assessments were moderate, and even disregarded a warning, conveyed in the 1868 annual report, against too hasty an introduction of the revised settlements.[14] In the end it took a visit to Lucknow from the Viceroy in 1873 to get the process of revision generally underway. Yet even then almost no one, including the Chief Commissioner, was willing seriously to call into question the pitch, as distinct from the mode of imposition, of the assessments.[15] As a result the settlement underwent no major alteration during the 1870s. There was, for instance, in Faizabad no systematic overhaul of the field records, while the revision itself was confined to those villages where special complaints had been registered.[16] Nor were those assessments that were revised downward necessarily made much lighter. In Khandasa, even

12. Nevill, *Kheri D.G.*, pp. 114–15.
13. Nevill, *Hardoi D.G.*, pp. 104–05.
14. *Oudh Revenue Administration Report for 1868*–69 (Lucknow, 1870), Part I, p. 10. See also *Oudh Revenue Administration Report for 1866–67* (Lucknow, 1868), Part I, p. 9; *Oudh Rev. Admin. Report for 1867–68*, Part I, pp. 11–12; and Millett, *Fyzabad S.R.*, pp. 338–39.
15. See *Oudh Rev. Admin. Report for 1871–72*, Part I, pp. 19–21; *Oudh Rev. Admin. Report for 1872–73*, Part I, pp. 18–19; and Millett, *Fyzabad S.R.*, pp. 340–41.
16. Millett, *Fyzabad S.R.*, pp. 364–66.

with the initial increase cut to 50 percent, "the greatest difficulty was experienced in collecting the demand, and for some years the Peshkar of the tahsil had to be almost permanently located in this Pargana."[17] In the Mangalsi pargana, although the revisional operations extended to every village but twelve and reduced the demand by 10.6 percent, still, wrote H. F. House in 1896, "there can be no doubt that this pargana was heavily assessed." There has, he said, "always been some difficulty in realising the demand," while "nearly everywhere there is the same tale of indebtedness, with its concomitant rackrenting."[18] In Dharmanpur, too, the settlement officer reported at the end of the century that progress had been much retarded by the "comparative severity" of even the reduced assessment of 1876.[19] Surely there is not much room for doubt but that the zeal which drove forward the "crack collectors" of Thomason's day in the North-Western Provinces was still alive in Oudh in the decades after the Mutiny.[20]

The revenue burden in Oudh was, moreover, rendered more onerous by the government's refusal during the settlement operations to take into account either the widespread extent of subordinate tenures under the taluqdars or the practice of awarding preferential rates to clansmen and high-caste tenants. Together these privileged holders intercepted a good deal of the rental income which otherwise might have gone to the superior landlord. Yet the government, not wishing to see its own revenue curtailed, from the outset ignored all such arrangements in calculating its rent-rates. So early as 1861 the Chief Commissioner stated flatly that the government would take "half the legitimate rental" no matter what the superior holder might receive.[21] The taluqdars as a result found themselves under substantial pressure to raise the rents of their privileged tenants to the level paid by ordinary cultivators (and to raise the rents of the latter as well, where the rent rolls had not formed the basis of the assessment, to twice the government demand). This subjected the relations of the taluqdars with their subordinate holders, already under strain as a result of the imposition of British law and order, as we shall see later, to further severe stress.[22]

Quite substantial sums of money were often at stake. Raja Hanwant Singh of Kalakankar, whom Barrow called "a good specimen of the real Oudh Talookdar," had let out all or part of some 200 of his 300 villages, with a loss of income totalling Rs. 64,000, to "his relatives, his retainers, the old proprietors of the villages, Shunkullupdars, Mafeedars, and others who have

17. *Ibid.*, p. 477. See also H. F. House, Assessment Report of Pargana Khandasa of 22 September 1896, N.W.P.&O. Rev. Progs. July 1897, No. 28. At the end of the ten years the new revised jama, still some 59 percent above that of the summary settlement, went into effect.

18. Mangalsi Assessment Report of 28 September 1896, N.W.P.&O. Rev. Progs. July 1897, No. 24.

19. P. Harrison, Assessment Report of Pargana Dharmanpur of 3 August 1899, N.W.P.&O. Rev. Progs. December 1899, No. 9.

20. See above, pp. 120–21.

21. Sec. C.C. Oudh to all Commrs. 7 October 1861, B.R. Oudh General File 1492.

22. See below, ch. 9.

enjoyed a favorable position under him."[23] Despite the coming of British rule, Hanwant Singh wished to uphold these allowances, for they enhanced the status of his family and put the recipients under obligation to him. In the face of a revenue demand raised at the revised settlement from Rs. 71,984 to Rs. 1,00,537, and with the estate already heavily in debt, this could not easily be done. Barrow consequently recommended, not a lowering of the assessment, which he regarded as fair, but a progressive jama in which Rs. 15,000 of the increased demand would be spread over a period of 15 years.[24] More commonly, requests for a lightening of the revenue burden on such grounds met with an even colder response. When Rustam Sahai of Dera petitioned in 1859 for a reduction of his assessment because he was "embarrassed having to provide for so many old retainers," the Deputy Commissioner replied curtly that "he cannot eat his cake and have it too. He has alienated a good deal of his land in jageer and sunkulp for value received. . . . I do not believe Government receives from Deera more than its proper share of profits." The Chief Commissioner concurred. The government revenue, he said, could not be allowed to suffer simply because a landed family chose to "dissipate their means." The taluqdar always had open to him in such cases the remedy of imposing rent at the regular rates.[25]

Where land was held at favorable rates as a matter of prescriptive right, as in the case, among others, of former proprietors whose lands had been recently incorporated into taluqdari estates, the rent could only be raised by the court or a settlement officer according to fixed principles. Yet no attention was paid to these double tenures in the process of assessment. The enhanced revenue demand was levied in the same way as on ordinary lands, and in many cases brought into force before the maze of claims to subordinate rights had been sorted out and new rentals fixed. The subsettlement holders meanwhile, under no obligation to pay more, refused to do so—and sometimes withheld even their accustomed rents in the hopes of getting better terms—and so drove the superior holders into debt or default. In Faizabad district, where much of the land was subsettled, the overwhelming proportion of the arrears of government revenue during the late 1860s was attributed to this cause. Only in the revision of the 1870s was the government demand moderated, usually by a reduction of about 10 percent in the assumed gross rental of the estate, and the burden on taluqdar and subordinate holder alike mitigated.[26] In like fashion the assessing officers usually made no distinction in the initial settlement between lands held by members

23. Finanl. Commr. to Chief Commr. 5 August 1868, B.R. Pratabgarh File 385, Part II.
24. *Ibid.* This arrangement was sanctioned by the Chief Commissioner in Sec. C.C. to Finanl. Commr. 22 August 1868.
25. Sec. C.C. to Commr. Faizabad 3 August 1859, and Depty. Commr. to Commr. Faizabad 10 September 1859, Faizabad Collectorate Records, Bundle 33. See also Sec. C.C. to all Commrs. 7 October 1861, B.R. Oudh General File 1492.
26. Millett, *Fyzabad S.R.*, pp. 396–403. See also *Oudh Rev. Admin. Report for 1871-72,* pp. 12, 21; and *Oudh Rev. Admin. Report for 1872-73,* pp. 14-15, 18.

of industrious agricultural castes such as the Kurmis and those held at preferential rates by Brahmin and Rajput tenants. At the same time the taluqdar
was told not to raise his rents on such privileged tenants during the course of
the settlement. The result was a further diminution of the funds available to
the taluqdar, and an attempt, when the assessment was revised in the 1870s,
to take more fully into account the rent-paying capacities of the various
castes.[27]

Despite the heavy burden the settlement so often placed on the landholding community, still as time went on payment became less and less difficult.
Never again after 1875 till the last years of the century were revenue balances
so numerous as in the early years of the settlement.[28] In part this was because
the taluqdars and other landlords had learned to live with the higher level of
demand, and became, as we shall see later, increasingly adept at squeezing
ever greater sums out of their tenantry. In part too this "comparative ease"
of payment in the later years of the settlement reflected the rural prosperity,
and the general rise in prices, that the construction of roads and railroads,
and the growth of larger marketing networks, brought with them.[29]

The second regular settlement of Oudh, carried out during the 1890s,
resulted like the first in a substantial enhancement of the land revenue. It
was also contested every inch of the way by the taluqdars, now organized and
politically aware in a way they had not been thirty years before. The reassess-
ment of the 1890s was at the same time made the occasion for an attack from
below by dissatisfied British officers on the basic principles of the "Oudh
Policy." The controversy was from the outset focused upon Pratabgarh district, and especially on the Patti pargana, for the new assessment of this
tract, involving an enhancement of 54 percent, was among the first in the
province to be announced. Even before the release of the Patti figures,
however, the taluqdars through their association put pressure on the government to abandon all use of estimated rentals and to base their assessments
instead solely on the landlords' actual receipts.[30] The British were not prepared to give up their claim to "the full half of the assets" which would be
deduced from a valuation of all lands at the rates paid by ordinary tenants.
But they did so far concede the taluqdars' demands as to permit reductions
from the full assessed valuation of 25 percent in the case of *sir* (home-farm)
land, and 12½ percent where land was held by tenants with occupancy

27. Millett, *Fyzabad S.R.*, pp. 393-94; and Sec. C.C. to all Commrs. 7 October 1861, B.R.
Oudh General File 1492.

28. Whitcombe, *Agrarian Conditions*, pp. 150-54, and Figures 8 and 9, pp. 340-41.

29. See for instance H. R. Nevill, *Fyzabad District Gazetteer* (Allahabad, 1905), p. 117;
Nevill, *Sitapur D.G.*, pp. 102-03; and Nevill, *Bahraich D.G.*, pp. 99-100. A fall in the value of
silver also contributed to the rise in prices. See ch. 6 above for similar developments in the
North-Western Provinces.

30. Memorandum by the Taluqdars on the Rules for the Revision of Land Revenue of 26
May 1892, N.W.P.&O. Rev. Progs. September 1894, No. 307; Notes on Deputation of British
Indian Association to Lt. Gov. 6 September 1892, *ibid.*, No. 312; and Memorial of British
Indian Association to Lt. Gov. of 5 April 1893, *ibid.*, No. 323.

rights. The government further ruled that where underproprietors intercepted a portion of the rental, the revenue demand, no matter what the estimated assets, would not be permitted to exceed 75 percent of the landlord's receipts.[31]

The taluqdars of Pratabgarh district had been treated with comparative leniency in the settlement of the 1860s. They rarely defaulted on the revenue demand, and were believed to be paying much less than half-assets after a few years. As rents had risen sharply since the previous settlement, in some cases up to 50 percent, J. Sanders, the settlement officer, had no hesitation in raising the assessments by a similar amount. Nor did he make any reductions on account of proprietary cultivation on *sir* land, or for land held by high-caste or underproprietary tenants. In Patti, in particular, he applied full standard rates throughout except for the customary rebate on occupancy holdings.[32] Not surprisingly these assessments came at once under attack. The taluqdars of the pargana, led by Ran Bijai Bahadur Singh of Patti Saifabad, bombarded the Lieutenant Governor with petitions demanding reduction of Sanders's "excessive" enhancements, while the taluqdars' association dispatched its assistant secretary, M. Nusrat Ali, to Patti for an on-the-spot investigation. After ten days in the pargana, during which he claimed to have visited all 816 villages, he reported that the new government demand would take "more than half of the net assets" recorded in the rent rolls.[33]

By now thoroughly alarmed, the Lieutenant Governor Sir Charles Crosthwaite himself came to Pratabgarh in January 1894 to meet with a deputation of the district's taluqdars. After listening to their complaints he sent J. R. Reid, Senior Member of the Board of Revenue, on tour to check the Patti assessments at first hand. Reid had already on his own initiative reduced the Patti total by Rs. 20,400 and he now lopped off another Rs. 12,300. As objections still continued to pour in, Sanders was himself sent back to reexamine his own figures, and he reduced the demand by a further Rs. 13,000. Finally the Lieutenant Governor, before finally sanctioning the assessment, cut it back yet again, this time by Rs. 10,000, so that the ultimate enhancement for the pargana was brought down to 38 percent over the previous settlement.[34]

Despite appearances, neither Sanders's original assessments nor the subsequent reductions were based solely upon dispassionate calculations of rental assets. The severity of Sanders's initial assessment was, to be sure, in part a product of his inexperience as a settlement officer, together with a too

31. Sec. Govt. India to Sec. Govt. N.W.P.&O. 21 July 1892, *ibid.*, No. 309; and Sec. Govt. N.W.P.&O. to Pres. B.I.A. 24 September 1894, *ibid.*, No. 334.

32. Sanders, *Pratabgarh S.R.*, pp. 20-21, 98-99, 227; and Nevill, *Partabgarh D.G.*, pp. 123-25.

33. Report on Pratabgarh Settlement by Assist. Sec. B.I.A. of 12 December 1893, N.W.P.&O. Rev. Dept. File No. 707A. See also Ran Bijai Bahadur Singh to Lt. Gov. 23 January 1895, *ibid.*; and Sanders, *Pratabgarh S.R.*, p. 272.

34. Sanders, *Pratabgarh S.R.*, pp. 227, 230, 238-39. For a summary see office note of 12 January 1921, N.W.P.&O. Rev. Dept. File No. 707A.

rigid adherence to the "hard and fast rules" he was given to work with. Like so many of his predecessors he was determined above all else to "secure the interests of the Government." He learned too from his mistakes, so that his later assessments were not so heavy as that of Patti.[35] Yet Sanders was clearly never enamored of taluqdars. While insisting that he was not prejudiced—unless, he added sarcastically, "all that is not panegyric is prejudice"—Sanders in fact throughout his report judged the taluqdars and found them wanting. Time and again he contrasted unfavorably their lack of enthusiasm for agricultural improvement, and their lack of interest in the welfare of their tenants, with their readiness to raise rents at every opportunity without regard to anything other than the tenant's ability to pay.[36] Angrily setting aside as unfounded the objections raised to his assessments, he argued that they came as often as not from the owners of the most highly rented estates, and that few of these landlords, often men who had "ruined themselves by extravagance," had any claim to special consideration at the hands of the government.[37]

Much of the opposition within the government to Sanders's assessments sprang from a concern for the fate of precisely these men. Crosthwaite came away from his meeting with the taluqdars in January 1894 convinced that Sanders had not paid enough attention to "those reasons of flesh and blood" that ought to move a settlement officer. With the old village proprietors "thoroughly dissatisfied" as a result of their supersession by the taluqdars, it was "a matter of moment," he said, to see at least the Oudh landlords contented. Their assessments "must be made lighter."[38] In this Crosthwaite echoed the views of the long powerful "Oudh School" of officials. Of these the most outspoken, on this occasion as on others, were W. C. Benett and Harcourt Butler. Benett, now as Settlement Commissioner in charge of the assessment operations throughout the province, still maintained that the taluqdars were the "acknowledged heads of the agricultural community," and men of great political consequence, important especially "as a bulwark between the fermenting masses of the eastern districts on the one side and the Doab and Rohilkhand on the other." As landlords, he insisted, the taluqdars had been "careful not to endanger their position by inconsiderate treatment of their tenantry," while their load of debt was not a mark of "personal incompetence" but was rather a product of the new conditions of life and the expensive litigation forced upon them since annexation. They thus deserved, if not an especially lenient assessment, at any rate one that should not "err

35. For appraisals of Sanders's work see Note by J. R. Reid, Sr. Member Bd. Rev., n.d., ca. February 1894, N.W.P.&O. Rev. Dept. File No. 707A; Note by J. O. Miller, Chief Sec. Govt. N.W.P.&O., of 14 April 1899, *ibid.*; and Resolution of Rev. Dept. of 17 April 1899, N.W.P.&O. Rev. Progs. April 1899, No. 182.

36. Sanders, *Pratabgarh S.R.*, pp. 60-62, 105, 275-76.

37. *Ibid.*, pp. 90, 272.

38. Note by Crosthwaite of 20 January 1894, N.W.P.&O. Rev. Dept. File 707A.

on the side of exaggeration." He suggested that the government take from them no more than 45 percent of the cash tenant rate.[39]

Butler too saw in the enhancements proposed by men like Sanders a threat to the political stability of Oudh. Indeed he wrote his first pamphlet on "Oudh Policy" in 1896 primarily in order forcibly to put the case for "unusual moderation" in taxing the taluqdars. These men, he argued, upon whose goodwill and support the government was wholly dependent for the maintenance of civil order in the province, had been exasperated, and had their attachment to British rule strained, by "every large political measure since Lord Canning's day," from tenancy legislation to the loss of control over village patwaris and police. To subject them now to the further "common misfortune" of a severe enhancement of their revenue demand would bind together this "powerful aristocracy," and drive them, together with their clansmen and subordinate proprietors, a long way toward opposition. A "sacrifice" of part of the government's dues, by contrast, would secure the taluqdars' cooperation for the unsettled times ahead and so make of Oudh a "solid buffer of loyalty." It was not necessary to go so far as a permanent settlement, though that measure might be kept in reserve, but it was essential, as Butler reiterated in 1898 when criticizing Sanders's settlement from his post as Secretary to the Board of Revenue, to use "special moderation," above all when assessing the lands of those who stood, like the taluqdars of Pratabgarh, at the head of the old Hindu clan system.[40]

Sir Antony MacDonnell, Crosthwaite's successor as Lieutenant Governor, while rejecting Butler's rhetorical hyperbole, agreed that moderation in assessment was wise. He insisted only that the "full measure" of the taluqdars' hardship should be shown, and that the "measure of our abstinence" be made clear to the intended beneficiaries.[41] One such beneficiary, again over Sanders's objections, was Raja Rampal Singh of Kalakankar. No one contested the fairness of Sanders's assessment of the estate, which involved an enhancement of 50 percent, from Rs. 96,142 to Rs. 1,43,360. Rampal Singh himself, though complaining that the new demand was "crushing," asked not to have it reduced but rather that it be introduced in graduated steps over a number of years. He based his claim squarely upon the fact that his was "a very old family of the Bisen clan," and that he had reduced the debt on the estate while at the same time establishing schools, dispensaries, and experimental farms. He thus deserved at least as much consideration in the imposition of the new assessment as Barrow had given his grandfather Hanwant

---

39. Note on Oudh Settlements by W. C. Benett of 5 June 1896, N.W.P.&O. Rev. Dept. File No. 431B.

40. Butler, *Oudh Policy* (1896), pp. 55-64, 68-69. See also his draft Note on the Political Aspect of the Oudh Settlements, N.W.P.&O. Rev. Dept. File No. 158B; and Sec. Bd. Rev. to Chief Sec. Govt. N.W.P.&O. 17 October 1898, published with Sanders, *Pratabgarh S.R.*

41. Note by A. P. MacDonnell of 3 February 1896, N.W.P.&O. Rev. Dept. File No. 158B. See also his marginal comments on Butler's Note, *ibid.*

Raja Amir Hasan Khan
of Mahmudabad.

Singh in 1868.[42] Sanders agreed that some remission was appropriate, but adamantly refused to concede more than Rs. 18,000 a year for the first five years only. This estate, he insisted, "has no better claims than any other in the district for a more favourable assessment in the manner asked for by the taluqdar."[43] Benett, after a detailed examination of the raja's receipts, concluded that the new demand would bring about a diminution of some 40 percent in his cash income. This, he said, was too great a burden to impose suddenly on a man who was a "good landlord," representing a "very old family."[44] The Lieutenant Governor, concurring, postponed Rs. 15,000 of the final demand for five years and Rs. 7,500 for a further period of five years.[45]

Raja Amir Hasan Khan of Mahmudabad lobbied even more energetically to secure a light assessment for his estate. So early as 1892 he had written a 58-page printed *Memo on the Re-Assessment of Land-Revenue in Oudh*, in which, denying that the settlements of the 1860s were moderate, he argued that the occasion of the impending settlement ought to be used to lower the percentage of assets taken from one-half to one-third, and to declare the

42. Rampal Singh to Settle. Commr. 3 September 1895, N.W.P.&O. Rev. Progs. November 1895, No. 8.
43. Report by J. Sanders, Settle. Officer Pratabgarh, of 25 September 1895, *ibid.*, No. 11. See also Sanders, *Pratabgarh S.R.*, pp. 242–43 for his dislike of progressive enhancements.
44. Note by Settle. Commr. of 4 October 1895, N.W.P.&O. Rev. Progs. November 1895, No. 12. See also Benett to J. LaTouche 15 September 1895, N.W.P.&O. Rev. Dept. File No. 707A.
45. Chief Sec. Govt. N.W.P.&O. to Sec. Bd. Rev. 4 November 1895, N.W.P.&O. Rev. Progs. November 1895, No. 14.

resulting jama fixed in perpetuity. Even the two-thirds remaining, he said, would barely suffice to maintain the taluqdar's "family, honor, dignity, and his rights and privileges," as well as to enable him to discharge his duties to the government and his tenantry.[46] Early in the following year the Mahmudabad raja sent the Deputy Commissioner of Sitapur a 26-page printed collection of testimonials to his managerial competence and government service, while in December of the same year he spoke "at length" with Butler, newly appointed settlement officer of the district, about the approaching settlement and the pamphlet he had written. The taluqdars are all, Butler wrote home afterwards, "very anxious. Their assessment is very light and they fear a large enhancement."[47]

In 1896, Amir Hasan twice wrote Benett as Settlement Commissioner pleading for a light assessment, and then in January of 1897, when the new jama was released, he protested its severity in a petition to the Chief Secretary. He rested much of his case upon the supposed unrecognized loyalty of his father during the Mutiny, an argument even Butler, by now the Mahmudabad raja's close personal friend, rejected out of hand as invalid. There remained, however, Amir Hasan's own "special services" to the government, which included acting as the Oudh representative on the Imperial Legislative Council. These, when put together with his "conspicuous" charity, his reputation as "one of the best landlords in Oudh," and his still "very great" political influence, gave him a claim, in the eyes of Benett and Butler alike, to some "special consideration" in the matter of assessment.[48] In the end the government reduced the enhancement of revenue on the Mahmudabad estate from the rise of 37 percent originally proposed to one of 32 percent, and delayed the imposition of the full demand until the eleventh year of the settlement. MacDonnell was, however, at pains to point out that this reduction had been granted solely because the Bara Banki portion of the estate at a full 50 percent of the assets, with an enhancement of 49 percent, had been too heavily assessed, and not because the "personal qualities" of the raja entitled him to an especially favorable rate of assessment. Such a step, he said, would "be difficult to justify except on grounds that would justify a similar concession to many other loyal zamindars."[49]

The taluqdars' association had meanwhile mounted one final campaign to secure low assessments. While not abandoning their effort to have the

46. Raja Muhammad Amir Hasan Khan Bahadur, *Memo on the Re-Assessment of Land-Revenue in Oudh* (Lucknow, 1892), esp. pp. 52–54.
47. Petition of Amir Hasan Khan to Depty. Commr. Sitapur January 1893, N.W.P.&O. Rev. Dept. File No. 158B; and Harcourt Butler to Isabel 19 December 1893, IOL Butler Papers, MSS Eur. F.116/5.
48. Settle. Officer Sitapur to Settle. Commr. 27 May 1896, N.W.P.&O. Rev. Dept. File No. 158B; Settle. Commr. to Sec. Bd. Rev. 13 June 1896, *ibid.*; and Settle. Commr. to Sec. Bd. Rev. 19 April 1897, *ibid.*
49. Notes by H. F. Evans, Chief Sec., of 14 July 1897, and A. P. MacDonnell of 29 September 1897, *ibid.* Under the final arrangements the proportion of assets taken was fixed at 45 percent throughout the estate. See Chief Sec. to Sec. Bd. Rev. 13 October 1897, *ibid.*

revenue demand based upon "the actual amount realized" by the land-holder, the taluqdars now turned their attention to the cesses, or taxes for specific local purposes such as schools and roads. Superimposed upon the land revenue, these had increased, with the imposition after 1889 of special chaukidari and patwari cesses, to 16 percent, rather than the old 2½ percent, of the government demand. As a result, the taluqdars charged, the government now took not its agreed-upon half but almost 60 percent of the gross rental. This added taxation, they argued, when combined with the government's refusal to make any allowance for uncollected arrears of rent, so diminished the landholders' profits that "at no distant time" they would be unable "to maintain their positions" and their estates would fall into the hands of the moneylenders. They suggested instead that these cesses be deducted from the gross rental of the estate before it was divided in half between the government and the landholder.[50] The MacDonnell government wasted little sympathy on this request. The taluqdars, they maintained, had always paid for the upkeep of the patwaris and chaukidars; so the conversion of the old arrangements into a regular cess involved only a change in form, not an increase in the burden on the landholder. Moreover, they went on, the extra charges for cesses had already been offset by the reduction of the government demand on the land under the Saharanpur rules from 66 to 50 percent of the total assets. So, as the new assessments were in any case "moderate," the taluqdars had no cause for complaint.[51]

The final assessments, then, embodied the results of an uneasy compromise between two conflicting goals of British policy: to keep the taluqdars contented, and to bring in the greatest possible revenue for the government. Some few officials, like Sanders, cared little for the political consequences of high assessments, and looked only to the ability of the land to bear the charges placed upon it. A larger and more influential group, led by Butler and Benett, were prepared to make substantial financial sacrifices in order to secure the willing cooperation and support of those whom they regarded as a powerful landed aristocracy. In the end the views of men like MacDonnell usually prevailed. Assessments might be lowered where some real injustice was perceived, as in the case of the taluqdars of Patti, or where, as MacDonnell told the president of the taluqdars' association, the higher level of payment would "seriously affect the deserving proprietor's standard of comfort." Progressive jamas similarly could be granted whenever the rise in demand was steep or payment would be difficult. But there was to be no

50. Memorial of the Taluqdars of Oudh of 21 April 1896, N.W.P.&O. Rev. Progs. September 1896, No. 126. See also Minutes of Conference between Lt. Gov. and Deputation from the B.I.A. Oudh of 16 July 1896, *ibid.*, No. 132. The taluqdars' complaints were echoed by Benett and Butler. See Benett's Note on the Oudh Settlements of 5 June 1896, N.W.P.&O. Rev. Dept. File No. 431B, (para. 8), and Butler, *Oudh Policy* (1896), pp. 65–67.

51. Chief Sec. Govt. N.W.P.&O. to Pres. B.I.A. 25 September 1896, N.W.P.&O. Rev. Progs. September 1896, No. 133. For the position and pay of chaukidars and patwaris see below ch. 10.

wholesale sacrifice of revenue, no indiscriminate "special consideration" for taluqdars. Their estates were everywhere assessed on the average at about the same rates as those of other landholders, that is, at between 45 and 47 percent of the gross assets. The "Oudh Policy," though it remained a loadstone for the British in Oudh, was always in practice tempered by a stern sense of fiscal responsibility.[52]

The question remains as to whether these assessments were at all burdensome. Did they, that is, exact from the taluqdar more than he could fairly be expected to pay? It is, of course, impossible to judge this at all accurately without a detailed scrutiny, estate by estate, of prices, productivity, and rentals. Much, too, depends on what behavior pattern one expects of an Indian landholder. To a large extent a burden is what is felt as a burden. It would seem nevertheless that on balance the second regular settlement placed less of a strain on the resources of the landholders than the first. Certainly the rise in the demand during the 1890s was in most districts markedly less than that of the 1860s (see Table 21). Default also, apart from the famine year of 1896–1897 and the two years immediately following, was a relatively uncommon occurrence. A good many districts indeed paid up their revenue in full throughout the early years of the new settlement. The government liberally conceded remissions and suspensions of the demand during the famine, and in two districts delayed by a year the introduction of the new levies. But with the single exception of Hardoi no permanent downward revision on account of difficulties of payment took place anywhere in the province.[53]

One might argue, then, that while the new assessments were undoubtedly heavy, and the enhancements often substantial, for the bulk of the taluqdars the new revenue demand was not crushing. Far more so than the petty zamindari proprietors, the taluqdars could usually find the funds to meet the government's demands, and did so without any marked fall in the lavish style of living to which they were accustomed. Indebtedness there was in plenty, as we shall see, but there is no evidence that after 1875 this debt was, for the owners of large estates at any rate, caused by the heaviness of the assessment. In the 1900s too, as in the years after 1875, the taluqdars were almost always

52. See Chief Sec. Govt. N.W.P.&O. to Pres. B.I.A. 25 September 1896, *ibid.*, esp. para. 8. For the varying rates of assessment in different districts, which show taluqdars and coparcenary communities treated slightly more favorably than ordinary zamindars, see, e.g., Nevill, *Gonda D.G.*, p. 122; and Nevill, *Fyzabad D.G.*, p. 119. The assessment was set at less than the full 50 percent of the assets in order to make some provision for unrealizable rents, precarious cultivation, extensive subproprietary holdings, or other circumstances that might reduce the landholder's total receipts. The coparcenary communities were given favorable treatment because of the fragmentation of their holdings into small parcels.

53. Discussion of the working of the new assessments can be found in the various district gazetteers. See, e.g., H. R. Nevill, *Sultanpur District Gazetteer* (Allahabad, 1903), p. 116, and Nevill, *Partabgarh D.G.*, p. 127. For the troubles in Hardoi, where the enhancement was reduced by 9 percent, see Nevill, *Hardoi D.G.*, pp. 107–09. The introduction of the higher demand was postponed in Faizabad and Rae Bareli.

able to recoup their losses at settlement by raising rents afterward. Indeed the assessments themselves, so far as they were based upon a rent-paying capacity higher than the actual rents paid on an estate, inevitably drove the landholders in this direction. So certain was the "tendency" of rents to rise, and so moderate the assessments, argued the Director of Agriculture in 1896, that landlords could ordinarily make good their losses "within a few years," thus "leaving a considerable and increasing surplus in excess of double the revenue to them for the remainder of the period of settlement."[54]

By the 1890s, however, the powers of the landlords over their tenants were no longer the same as they had been thirty years before. By the provisions of the Oudh Rent Act of 1886, landlords were prohibited from enhancing the rent of any tenant by more than 6¼ percent in any seven years, or from ejecting a tenant prior to the expiry of the seven-year term. Nor could a new tenant be made to pay more than the old. Such constraints obviously rendered it more difficult for a landowner to recover his position after an increase in the revenue demand. Baillie, the Director of Agriculture, estimated that it would now take an ordinary landlord from fifteen to twenty years to get over the effects of an enhancement of 33 percent.[55] Yet the Rent Act not only could be evaded, such evasion was a frequent occurrence, not least in order to shift the revenue burden onto the backs of the tenants. Just how this was accomplished, and why the government set such "narrow limits" on enhancements of rent when it subjected itself to no restraint in enhancements of revenue, is a subject to which we must now turn.

Occupancy Rights and Tenancy Legislation

As part of the initial taluqdari settlement of Oudh, Lord Canning, together with his Chief Commissioner Sir Charles Wingfield, decided not to make any effort to secure rights of occupancy in the soil for ordinary tenant cultivators. Neither believed that such rights had existed in the days of Nawabi rule, while the doctrinaire Wingfield also argued, in his Record of Rights Circular of 1860, that "to give a right of permanent occupancy at an unvarying rate to the tiller of the soil is an invasion of the rights of property and a clog on enterprise and improvement."[56] This decision reflected as well of course the preoccupation of both men with conciliation of the taluqdars, at whose expense any award of occupancy rights would of necessity have to be made.

54. D. C. Baillie, Director of Land Records and Agriculture, Note on the System of Assessment and Collection of Land Revenue, n.d., N.W.P.&O. Rev. Progs. June 1896, No. 147. On the level of assessment as a force behind the enhancement of rents, see Whitcombe, *Agrarian Conditions*, pp. 153-54.

55. Baillie, Note on Assessment (see n. 54 above). See also Benett, Note on Oudh Settlements of 5 June 1896, N.W.P.&O. Rev. Dept. File No. 431B, (para 5).

56. Sec. C.C. Oudh to Sec. Govt. India 7 September 1860, NAI For. Rev. A, March 1862, No. 7-13. For discussion of the tenant right controversy in Oudh, which was part of a general reconsideration of the position of the tenant throughout northern India, see my *Aftermath of Revolt*, pp. 187-95.

The tenantry were, however, not without defenders in the government. Most prominent among them was Sir John Lawrence, Viceroy from 1864 to 1869. Profoundly dissatisfied with Wingfield's cavalier treatment of their claims, which cut directly across his own experience in the Punjab, as well as the legislative protection accorded twelve-year occupiers in Bengal and the N.W.P. after 1859, Lawrence set out to salvage as much as he could for the cultivators of Oudh. Before his first year of office was out he had initiated an inquiry, under a Punjab officer R. H. Davies, into the question of whether occupancy rights in fact existed in Oudh at the time of annexation. The inquiry revealed that while few raiyats could claim any legal right to hold land against the will of their landlord, most cultivators found in local usage and custom substantial protection against arbitrary enhancement or eviction. Rents often remained stable for long periods of time, Davies reported, and were never set by competition, while cultivators were invariably allowed to retain their holdings so long as they paid their rents. In addition, high-caste cultivators usually paid at preferential rates, about three-quarters those paid by the lower castes.[57] But the Secretary of State, Sir Charles Wood, anxious to avoid upsetting the powerful taluqdars, insisted that the inquiry must be narrowly confined to the question of legal rights.[58] Lawrence thus found himself, despite Davies's findings, unable to extend any measure of protection to the Oudh cultivators. Apart from a few scattered ex-proprietors who were given rights of occupancy at favorable rates on their ancestral fields, the Oudh tenantry were by the "Oudh Compromise" of 1866, and the subsequent Rent Act of 1868, handed over to the tender mercies of their landlords.[59]

The one measure Wingfield took to regulate relations between landlord and tenant was to require the exchange of *pattas* (contracts) at the beginning of the agricultural year. The patta specified the terms, including the rent to be paid, on which the tenant held his lands, and thus afforded him protection against a sudden or arbitrary enhancement in midseason.[60] Despite heavy pressure brought to bear on them by the government, however, neither taluqdar not tenant showed much enthusiasm for these written contracts. The taluqdars, fearful that their revenue demand might be based upon the sums recorded in these documents, wanted to keep concealed their true

57. For a detailed summary of the results of this inquiry see Raj, *The Mutiny and British Policy*, ch. v. For a similar assessment of the position of the cultivator in the N.W.P. see above p. 62.

58. For Wood's views see Dispatch of 10 February 1865, *P.P.* 1865, 40:347–51, and his private letters to Lawrence of 7 January and 16 June 1865, IOL Lawrence Papers, MSS Eur. F. 90.

59. For the detailed negotiations see Raj, *The Mutiny and British Policy*, ch. vi.

60. Sec. C.C. Oudh to all Commrs. 28 April 1860, B.R. Oudh General File 2043; and Sec. C.C. to Commr. Baiswara 9 May 1862, Oudh General File 2037. In Rae Bareli the Depty. Commr. even convened a meeting of taluqdars to point out to them the necessity and advantage of giving out pattas. See Proceedings of Meeting of 18 April 1862, and letter of Depty. Commr. to Commr. Baiswara of same date, Oudh General File 2037.

rental assets, while the tenant, always on the lookout to lower his rent, disliked having "to agree in writing to a sum which under our revenue court practice will be, he knows, held as a minimum for the future and be decreed against him by every Revenue Court."[61] What is more, when forced to reduce their customary rental arrangements to writing the landlords often responded by drawing up the contracts for a "much higher" rent than they had hitherto collected, and so turned the patta into an engine of enhancement. By 1868 it was clear that British insistence upon this kind of contractual landlord-tenant relationship had helped substantially to propel rents upward during the preceding decade.[62]

The taluqdars did not in any case require much encouragement to raise their rents. As the customary barriers to enhancement broke down in the face of British indifference, and land at the same time became increasingly valuable, the Oudh landlords, throwing aside the restraint of the Nawabi days, embarked on a concerted effort to secure for themselves more of the produce of the soil. The rise in rents commenced so early as 1860, but speeded up appreciably after 1868 with the British abandonment of the occupancy cultivators and the simultaneous levy of the new and sharply enhanced revenue assessments. By 1870 suits for ejectment, commonly brought by landlords to compel recalcitrant tenants to accept a higher rent, from 3,400 annually a decade before, had reached a level of 52,000 a year, and touched cultivators in 22 percent of the villages of the province (see Table 23).[63]

Many among the British saw no cause for alarm in this rapid rise in rents, and with it of eviction notices. Wingfield regarded the process complacently in 1863 as "an unmistakeable symptom of the progress which has already been made in developing the agricultural resources of the province," and he insisted that the tenants shared as much as the landlords in its benefits.[64] The Chief Commissioner a decade later, Sir George Couper, after pointing out that upwards of one-third of the ejectment notices had no effect whatever, with the tenant continuing in his old holding at his old rent, argued that the landlords "very rarely" abused their power over the tenantry.[65]

61. Depty. Commr. Pratabgarh to Commr. Rae Bareli 13 January 1868, *ibid.* For the taluqdars' reluctance to issue pattas see Depty. Commr. Faizabad to Commr. Bahraich 17 January 1861, Oudh General File 2043; and Depty. Commr. Sitapur to Commr. Sitapur 8 February 1868, Oudh General File 2037.

62. See, for instance, Depty. Commr. Bahraich to Commr. Faizabad 7 January 1868, and Commr. Faizabad to Finanl. Commr. 1 February 1868, Oudh General File 2037. The Faizabad Commr. urged the government to stop encouraging the issue of pattas, and adopt instead an attitude of strict *laissez-faire* in the matter.

63. For the use of ejectment notices to secure enhancement see *Oudh Rev. Admin. Report for 1868-69*, Part I, p. 23; and P.A. to C.C. to all Commrs. 27 February 1873, Oudh Rev. Progs. February 1873, No. 8, reporting the results of an inquiry into the outcome of the 1872 ejectment notices.

64. *Oudh General Administration Report for 1862-63* (Lucknow, 1864), p. 21.

65. *Oudh Rev. Admin. Report for 1872-73*, Part I, pp. 34-35; and *Oudh Revenue Administration Report for 1874-75* (Lucknow, 1876), pp. 68-71.

Table 23. Notices of Enhancement and
Ejectment[a]

Year	Notices of Enhancement	Notices of Ejectment
1860–1861	3,927	3,486
1861–1862	4,892	5,014
1862–1863	7,117	4,364
—	—	—
1868–1869	*[b]	25,744
1869–1870	*	52,151
1870–1871	*	59,393
1871–1872	*	21,927

[a]Figures for notices of enhancement and ejectment are taken from the annual provincial revenue administration reports.
[b]The recording of notices of enhancement was
discontinued following the enactment of the 1868
Rent Act, for the British courts no longer concerned themselves with the level of rents paid by
ordinary cultivators. See *Oudh Rev. Admin. Report for 1867–68,* Part I, pp. 24–25.

To be sure the tenants had some weapons of their own. Of these the most
effective was to threaten to abandon their holdings, and thus hit the landlord
in his pocket. The tenant, as J. Woodburn observed, "holds relinquishment
in terrorem over his landlord when he desires to enforce, and thinks he can
obtain, a reduction in rent." In Unao district 1,372 tenants resigned their
holdings in 1871, while in Lucknow in the subsequent year 1,749 served
notices of relinquishment on their landlords. Of the latter, one-third were in
villages where notices of ejectment had previously gone out.[66]

Yet such a show of "independent spirit" among the tenantry was rare.
Throughout the later nineteenth century the overwhelming bulk of ordinary
cultivators always acquiesced quietly in enhancements of their rent. One-half
even of those who had protested in Lucknow in 1872 soon took up their holdings anew at the old rates, while a few years later in Pratabgarh, during Raja
Rampal Singh's prolonged absence from the country, his Kalakankar estate
was let out to contractors, who "raised rents in order to recoup themselves for
the high sums that they offered for the villages entrusted to them." The tenants, mostly Ahirs and Kurmis, "well known as good cultivators and rent-
payers," submitted to these new rents, which were not reduced when the

66. *Oudh Rev. Admin. Report for 1870–71,* Part I, p. 25; and P.A. to C.C. to all Commrs.
27 February 1873, Oudh Rev. Progs. February 1873, No. 8.

contracts expired, "with little or no murmur."[67] By and large, lacking leadership and the strong bargaining position a scarcity of numbers could alone secure for them, the Oudh cultivator was in no position to contest the demands of his landlord.[68]

As the years went by, and cash rents and competition extended their hold over the countryside, the scales tipped ever more sharply against the tenant. By the late 1870s the number of ejectment notices (though not of course actual ejectments), from a low point of under 20,000 a year in the middle of the decade, was once again on the rise. In each of the three years following 1879 over 50,000 notices were issued, while in 1882 the number jumped suddenly to 91,000. These notices affected altogether a total of 25 percent of the area held by tenants-at-will, and when combined with several instances of severe rack renting which came to light at the same time finally stirred the Oudh government into action.[69]

In the village of Sadruddinpur on the Jahangirabad estate, for instance, "nearly all" the tenants found their rents enhanced by 10 to 20 percent in one year. "Some submitted to the inevitable and so were not served with notices. Those who stood out were forced to consent by the issue of notices of ejectment." In order to secure these increased rents, the district officer reported, "the landlord turned many of the tenants out of their old farms and obliged them to take others instead, while in the general scramble some lost their position in the village altogether." The landlord's task was, however, much facilitated by a "feud between some of the principal cultivators," a group of whom "to spite their enemies" took leases of their opponents' land at enhanced rents. But "as soon as they had signed the *kabuliats* [rental agreements] they found themselves ejected by notice from their own old holdings, which the other side had then to take, also at enhanced rents." Rents, he concluded, were set not with reference to the quality of the tenant's land, but "to his desire to retain it and his ability to pay."[70]

Far more serious were events on the Sahlamau estate of Lucknow district. There the taluqdar, Muhammad Nasim Khan, had over the course of the preceding ten years raised the rent of four villages from Rs. 16,543, or about twice the government jama, to Rs. 22,658, while levying in addition an "arbitrary cess" of 2 percent on the rental. At the same time he charged

67. Report by J. Sanders, Settle. Officer Pratabgarh, of 25 September 1895, N.W.P.&O. Rev. Progs. November 1895, No. 11.

68. Cultivators did, however, where they could get away with it, sometimes withhold a portion of their rent. See below ch. 9. There were also organized Kurmi tenant protests across the provincial border in Allahabad during the late 1860s. See F. W. Porter, *Allahabad Settlement Report* (Allahabad, 1878), pp. 47–48. Such combinations were perhaps facilitated in the N.W.P. by the existence of occupancy rights, which secured a stronger footing to these prospering "middle peasant" castes.

69. See Note by J. Woodburn of 26 July 1882, on the issue of notices of ejectment in Oudh from 1869 to 1882, in NAI Legislative Dept., Papers Relating to Act XXII of 1886.

70. Offg. Depty. Commr. Bara Banki to Commr. Lucknow 14 February 1882 and 4 April 1882, B.R. Oudh General File 456.

tenants four annas per bucket each day for the use of water from his wells, and made those who wished to cultivate poppy or sugarcane pay a further ten rupees per bigha. Muhammad Nasim Khan was, the Lucknow Commissioner concluded, a "harsh and unimproving" landlord who used "unscrupulously" the powers the law gave him with "little or no regard for the welfare of his tenants."[71] As soon as this report reached his desk Sir George Couper, now in his last days of office as Lieutenant Governor, decided that the time had come to put a stop to such "gross oppression." Alleging that Muhammad Nasim Khan had failed to fulfill the obligations imposed upon him by the sanad under which he held his estate, Couper, in a stunning and unprecedented move, stripped the Sahlamau taluqdar of his property and placed it under government management. At the same time he warned the taluqdari community that anyone else who "flagrantly" transgressed the conditions of his sanad, which required the taluqdars to "promote the agricultural prosperity" of their estates, would meet with the same punishment.[72]

The Government of India, taken completely by surprise, refused, on the advice of Couper's successor Sir Alfred Lyall, to sustain this precipitant act. Lyall, together with the new Lucknow Commissioner, after an examination of rentals in the remaining eight and a half villages of the estate, which showed a rise of only 8 percent in the thirteen years since settlement, argued that, "judged by the average standard" of the Oudh taluqdar, Muhammad Nasim Khan was not such an "exceptionally bad" landlord, nor guilty of such "willful and indefeasible mismanagement," as to justify the infliction of the extreme penalty of dispossession.[73] Ripon, the Viceroy, was a Gladstonian liberal and no landlord enthusiast. He was appalled that the acceptable standard of behavior for an Oudh taluqdar should be so low as to include the "unquestionably harsh, illegal, and oppressive" conduct of the Sahlamau landlord. But he agreed that arbitrary sequestration of the entire estate, without further specific evidence of mismanagement, would be an act of excessive severity. Indeed he doubted that the government could, if challenged, ever prove before a court of law a breach of the vague conditions of the taluqdari sanad, nor did he feel it appropriate to deprive men of their property by executive fiat. Ripon was not, however, prepared to let the matter drop at that point, with the landlord's control over his tenants totally unfettered. Instead he set on foot a search for a remedy both more general and less extreme than that of confiscation.[74]

About the condition of the tenantry there was not much doubt. Although

71. Commr. Lucknow to Sec. Govt. N.W.P.&O. 1 April 1882, Oudh Rev. Dept. Progs. December 1882, No. 1.

72. Sec. Govt. N.W.P.&O. to Commr. Lucknow 10 April 1882, and Sec. Govt. N.W.P.&O. to Pres. B.I.A. 10 April 1882, *ibid.*

73. Offg. Commr. Lucknow to Sec. Govt. N.W.P.&O. 27 May 1882, and Sec. Govt. N.W.P.&O. to Sec. Govt. India 8 July 1882, *ibid.*

74. Sec. Govt. India to Sec. Govt. N.W.P.&O. 2 October 1882, *ibid.*; and Dispatch of 7 June 1884 to Sec. of State, NAI Legislative Dept., Papers Relating to Act XXII of 1886.

the district officers during the course of a special inquiry in 1883 refused to charge the landlords with "wanton and unjustifiable exaction," and indeed many even asserted that the material condition of the tenantry had improved over the preceding twenty years, nevertheless they agreed that rents had been largely and rapidly increased in recent years, that the enhancement often bore "little or no relation to the capabilities of the field or holding upon which it was imposed," and that rents as a result had begun to "press heavily" on the tenants, especially in years of bad or indifferent harvests. However well off the cultivating community might still be, Major G. E. Erskine, the officer in charge of the inquiry, concluded, as "the inevitable multiplication" of their numbers proceeded and the competition for land became "more keen" their condition would unquestionably "deteriorate" unless the government stepped in to protect them.[75]

While anxious to secure the cultivator against rack rent and eviction, the Oudh government was at the same time determined on no account needlessly to antagonize the taluqdars. Indeed Lyall set himself the task from the outset of carrying these powerful landlords along with him in any legislation. He therefore refused even to consider any award of hereditary occupancy rights of the sort enjoyed by the tenants of Bengal and the North-Western Provinces under Act X of 1859. The award of such rights, he asserted, would not only be incompatible with the promises made to the taluqdars at the time of the 1865 inquiries, it would breed a fatal "animosity" between landlord and tenant as each tried to increase his hold over the property. Lyall wished moreover to see all tenants, not simply those who had resided in a given place for an arbitrary length of time, given some protection. So he put forward a scheme that barred a landlord from increasing the rent of any tenant during a statutory period of seven years. At the end of that term the tenant could be evicted, but in no case could the rent, either of the old or the new tenant, be enhanced by more than 6¼ percent. If ejected, the old tenant would receive a year's rent as compensation for disturbance. The heir of a tenant, however, would have no rights, either to compensation or to continued occupancy of the holding. In this way, as Lyall saw it, the rise in rents could be controlled without at the same time conceding any permanent rights in the soil to the tenantry.[76]

75. The results of this inquiry were published as *The Condition of the Tenantry in Oudh* (Allahabad, 1883), 2 vols. The original papers are in B.R. Oudh General File 2236. See, e.g., Memo by Offg. Commr. Lucknow of 29 March 1883, 1:15; Offg. Depty. Commr. Lucknow to Commr. Lucknow 26 March 1883, *ibid.*, p. 17; Depty. Commr. Unao to Commr. Lucknow 27 March 1883, *ibid.*, pp. 30-31; and *passim*. For Erskine's views see his report of 1 June 1883 to Sec. Govt. N.W.P.&O., *ibid.*, 2:276-77. The district officers of Bahraich and Gonda reported that in their as yet backward areas enhancements had not been excessive, nor was rack renting prevalent.

76. Minute by A. C. Lyall of 28 December 1882 on the Revision of the Oudh Rent Law, and Sec. Govt. N.W.P.&O. to Sec. Govt. India 21 December 1883, in NAI Legislative Dept., Papers Relating to Act XXII of 1886.

Ripon, dissatisfied, urged that heirs as well as sitting occupants come under the scope of the act. Otherwise, he said, "every non-occupancy holding in Oudh will fall absolutely into the landlord's hands once in every generation." He wished also to see the power to vary the limit of enhancement, which Lyall had reserved to the government for use in exceptional circumstances, restricted to cases of downward revision below the 6¼ percent limit.[77] The India Office, on the other hand, questioning the need for any legislation whatever, wanted the entire scheme scrapped and replaced by a simple authorization enabling the executive government, whenever it was satisfied that the conditions of the sanad were being violated by taluqdari mismanagement or oppression, to fix rents binding on the owner, or even to take over charge of the estate for a term of years.[78] With the higher authorities so sharply at odds, and Ripon in any case replaced after 1884 by a Viceroy, Lord Dufferin, far less willing to risk antagonizing the taluqdars, Lyall managed easily to have his way. The bill ultimately introduced into the Legislative Council in January 1886 hewed closely to the lines he had originally laid down.[79]

The taluqdars however were yet to be heard from. Despite Lyall's assurances, these men were reconciled to legislation of any sort only with difficulty. Even Sheikh Inayatullah, one of the more enlightened among them, insisted in a long Memorandum in 1883 that landlords never made "capricious" enhancements, or forced their tenants to submit to "unfair" rents, but rather were actuated by "sympathy with" their raiyats. He was prepared only to see the tenants' leases run for a period of three to five years.[80] The local press, sympathetic to the landlords if not actually controlled by them, echoed the same views.[81] By 1886, largely due to the efforts of their leaders, including Inayatullah and their legal adviser Munshi Imtiaz Ali, who pointed out that a "hostile attitude" would not induce the government to abandon its efforts on behalf of the tenantry, the taluqdars had brought themselves to accept legislation along the lines of Lyall's draft.[82] But on one provision, that

77. Sec. Govt. India to Sec. Govt. N.W.P.&O. 12 April 1884, and Note by Ripon of 20 May 1884, *ibid*.

78. Revenue Dispatch (No. 103 of 1884) of 13 November 1884 to G.-G.-in-C., *ibid*. Lord Kimberley was Secretary of State. For Ripon's objections to the India Office proposals see his Minute of 12 December 1884, *ibid*.

79. See G.-G.-in-C. to S. of S. 22 September 1885, *ibid*. London's approval was conveyed in a telegram of 1 December 1885.

80. Memorandum of 2 June 1883 in *Condition of Tenantry in Oudh*, 2:353–73, esp. 357–58, 371.

81. See for instance the "Anwar-ul-Akhbar" of 16 February 1882, in *Selections from Vernacular Newspapers of N.W.P.&O. 1882*, p. 123, (hereafter *S.V.N.*); the "Oudh Punch" (Lucknow) of 2 May 1882, *ibid*., p. 301; the "Mumtaz-ul-Akhbar" (Nawabganj) of 8 and 16 December 1882, *ibid*., pp. 894–95; the "Oudh Punch" of 8 May 1883, *S.V.N. 1883*, p. 411; and the "Mirat-ul-Hind" (Lucknow) for April 1883, *ibid*., p. 464–65.

82. See speeches of Munshi Imtiaz Ali and Sheikh Inayatullah at meeting of British Indian Association of 22 April 1886, enclosure to Vice-Pres. B.I.A. to Sec. Govt. N.W.P.&O. 24 April

of compensation for disturbance, they stood firm. To pay such compensation, Rana Shankar Bakhsh argued before the Legislative Council, would imply the existence of some right in the tenant's hands, for which the payment was an equivalent, and so would infringe upon the landlord's absolute ownership of his property.[83] The government was reluctant to give up this provision, which it regarded as an important check on "capricious eviction," and one carrying with it, in its view, no imputation of tenant occupancy right. But it was equally anxious, with the bill so close to enactment, to secure the assent of the taluqdars. So a compromise was reached under which the landlord, in lieu of paying compensation to the tenant, would pay a stamp duty of half a year's rent, subject to a maximum of Rs. 25, in cases of ejectment.[84] With this amendment the measure came into force as Act XXII of 1886.[85]

It remains to consider how effectively this act, which remained on the statute book until 1921, achieved its stated purposes. From the outset it was apparent that the act could not put a stop to the rise in rents. Landlords soon discovered that they could easily evade the 6¼ percent limit on enhancement by exacting a *nazrana* (gift, present) in a lump sum from their tenantry before reinstating them in their holdings at the expiry of the seven years' term. In this way a much increased rent could be concealed under the cover of a regular enhancement, and the intent of the act nullified. Often too a landlord would eject an old tenant at the end of the seven years and put in his place, as a nominal tenant, a servant or relative paying the legal rate. The actual cultivator would then be readmitted as an unprotected subtenant at a rent increased by 20 to 50 percent.[86] Similar results could sometimes be obtained by forcibly converting cash into grain rents, with the landlord taking a portion of the crop rather than a fixed sum each year. And of course it was easy enough in collusion with the village patwaris to conceal the actual rents paid by entering fictitious sums in the revenue records.[87]

1886, in Papers Relating to Act XXII of 1886. Many of the taluqdars' friends in the government, such as J. Woodburn, also brought pressure on them to accept Lyall's proposals. Nor could all the taluqdars stand the pressure. Raja Amir Hasan of Mahmudabad, slated to be the taluqdars' spokesman before the Legislative Council, went temporarily insane just before the rent bill was introduced and had to be relieved of his assignment.

83. Speech of Rana Shankar Bakhsh of 9 June 1886, *Proceedings of the Governor-General's Legislative Council*, 25:205–06.

84. See speeches of J. Quinton of 9 June 1886, *ibid.*, p. 202; of Dufferin of 9 June 1886, *ibid.*, p. 213; and of Quinton of 30 September 1886, *ibid.*, pp. 326–28. Dufferin even pointed out how he as an Irish landlord always paid compensation for disturbance without this being regarded as conceding occupancy rights to the tenants.

85. During these same years, and under the impetus of the same concern for the well-being of the peasantry, the Bengal Tenancy Act of 1885 was taking shape. For the controversy surrounding its provisions, which at least on paper secured to the tenantry a much greater measure of protection than in Oudh, but which were similarly watered down when Dufferin succeeded Ripon, see Spangenberg, *British Bureaucracy*, pp. 169–98.

86. See, for instance, Sanders, *Pratabgarh S.R.*, p. 183; and Nevill, *Sultanpur D.G.*, p. 117.

87. On the effect of conversion from cash to grain rents see Depty. Commr. Bahraich to Chief Sec. Govt. N.W.P.&O. 20 December 1893 discussing the estate of Nawabganj-Aliabad,

By the early 1890s evasion had already become commonplace. In 1892, 280 cases of enhancement of rent by 25 percent or more were reported from Faizabad alone, while two years later the Board of Revenue, alarmed, called a conference of Oudh officers to consider possible amendment of the Rent Act. With settlement operations in progress the time was not regarded as "opportune" for a formal inquiry, and so the matter was dropped, but MacDonnell, on taking office in 1896, remarked that he too, as he had expected, had "heard everywhere that the law is disregarded."[88] More than simple willfulness drove landlords to illegal enhancement. Deeply in debt, and hard hit by the agricultural depression and drought of the 1890s, many turned to "secret devices to screw money out of their tenants" simply in order to raise some cash. The settlement revision also, with its substantial increase in the government's demand on the landlords, encouraged them, after first holding off raising their rents in anticipation of the new assessments, to pass on their increased burdens to their tenants. Nor was there, with "ejectment practically unlimited and competition for land keen," any real incentive for them to adhere to a low and arbitrary limit on enhancement. Strict enforcement of the law could alone secure compliance, and this, as we shall see, the government was unwilling to insist upon.

Among the most deeply embarrassed of the taluqdars, and the most hard-hit by the provisions of the new rent act, was the Maharaja of Ajodhya, Pratap Narayan Singh. Ever since the early days of British rule the Ajodhya (Mehdona) estate had been in financial difficulties. Man Singh's struggles with the underproprietors, which we shall examine in the next chapter, together with his protracted absences in Lucknow on government business, left the estate burdened with a heavy debt. During the decade and more following his death in 1870, as the heirs struggled in the courts for control of the property, it remained under Court of Wards management, with rents kept relatively low. Soon after Pratap Narayan obtained uncontested charge, in 1885, the new Rent Act, with its severe restrictions on enhancement, came into force. Even then, however, for some years, partly out of fear of the new assessment, and partly, it would seem, out of pure inertia, the maharaja did little to raise his rents. By the late 1890s as a result, rents on the Ajodhya estate were lagging substantially behind those paid elsewhere. The total enhancement secured over the preceding thirty years was estimated at only

---

enclosure in Chief Sec. Govt. N.W.P.&O. to Pres. B.I.A. 3 January 1894, BIA Records. Instances of concealment of true rent are numerous. See, e.g., P. Harrison, Pargana Hisampur (Bahraich) Assessment Report of 9 September 1897 (para. 13), N.W.P.&O. Rev. Progs. October 1897, No. 55; and S. H. Butler, Assessment Report for Parganas Kasta, Aurangabad and Pasgawan (Kheri) of 18 June 1898 (para. 9), N.W.P.&O. Rev. Progs. September 1898, No. 163.

88. Sec. Bd. Rev. to Sec. Govt. N.W.P.&O. 29 July 1895, N.W.P.&O. Rev. Progs. August 1895, No. 32. A. Cadell, Acting Lt. Gov. at the time, was opposed on principle to further tenancy legislation. See his Notes of 14 April and 22 August 1895, N.W.P.&O. Rev. Dept. File No. 329B. MacDonnell's remark was recorded on the margin of Butler's Note on the Political Aspect of the Oudh Settlements, N.W.P.&O. Rev. Dept. File No. 158B.

one-third the provincial average, with a consequent loss to the maharaja of over Rs. 50,000 annually. In 1899, in debt to the extent of thirty-one lakhs of rupees, and in arrears on the government revenue demand, Pratap Narayan finally decided to make up for lost time. Unable to raise his rents directly, he instead requested an exemption from the normal rules under Section 51 of the Rent Act, which allowed the government in exceptional circumstances to vary the rate of enhancement.[89] The Faizabad Commissioner and the Board of Revenue, calculating that the Ajodhya tenantry could well bear a rental enhanced by up to 25 percent, supported the maharaja's petition.[90] The taluqdars, and with them Sir Alfred Lyall, had from the beginning looked upon this section of the act as a valuable "escape clause" should market rates rise rapidly or other special considerations necessitate some change in the legal limit of enhancement.[91] The section had, however, never previously been invoked, and the Lieutenant Governor in 1899, Sir Antony MacDonnell, no more a friend of the taluqdars than Ripon, saw no justification for an exception in this case. Arguing that the act must not be worked "in the landlord's interest alone," he pointed out that for the tenant a 6¼ percent enhancement every seven years was a burden "much more easily borne" than a cumulative enhancement of 25 percent all at once. Simply because the Maharaja of Ajodhya had not "enhanced his rents as he might have done" was, he insisted, no sufficient reason for enabling him now to make good his "neglect" at the expense of the tenants.[92]

Not a man to be so easily stymied, Pratap Narayan got the taluqdars' association, of which he was conveniently Life President, to take up the cudgels on his behalf. In January and again in December 1900, the association petitioned the government to ease the restrictions on enhancement where landholders were suffering "hardship." While willing to let a government revenue officer fix rents in such cases, they insisted that no arbitrary limit on

89. Memorial of Pratap Narayan Singh of 9 June 1899, N.W.P.&O. Rev. Progs. October 1899, No. 17. The low Ajodhya rents were also in part a result of the large number of high-caste, often defiant, tenants who held their lands at favorable rates. See below p. 250. Long periods of rental stability were not uncommon. On Rampal Singh's Kalakankar estate the dramatic rise in rentals of the late 1870s, when its villages were let out to thikadars, was followed by a twelve-year period, up to the revision of settlement in 1895, when rents "remained unchanged." Report by J. Sanders, Settle. Officer Pratabgarh, of 25 September 1895, N.W.P.&O. Rev. Progs. November 1895, No. 11.

90. Commr. Faizabad to Sec. Bd. Rev. 27 June 1899, N.W.P.&O. Rev. Progs. October 1899, No. 16; and Sec. Bd. Rev. to Sec. Govt. N.W.P.&O. 5 August 1899, ibid., No. 15.

91. See for instance speech of Shankar Bakhsh of 30 September 1886, Progs. Legis. Counc., 25:331; and A. C. Lyall to Sir Steuart Bayley 13 May 1884, Papers Relating to Act XXII of 1886.

92. Sec. Govt. N.W.P.&O. to Sec. Bd. Rev. 26 September 1899, N.W.P.&O. Rev. Progs. October 1899, No. 18. See also Note by A. P. MacDonnell of 6 September 1899, N.W.P.&O. Rev. Dept. File No. 758C. One of the few senior ICS officials of the later nineteenth century with a genuine commitment to the peasantry, MacDonnell had played a major role with Ripon in formulating the 1885 Bengal Act and in carrying out a survey and record of rights in Bihar. At the same time, however, he was willing to temporize in the face of strong opposition if necessary to secure his own advancement. See Spangenberg, British Bureaucracy, esp. pp. 219-20, 248-49, 260-61; and C. A. Bayly, The Local Roots of Indian Politics (Oxford, 1975), pp. 150-55.

*Pratap Narayan Singh
as a young man, ca. 1880.*

enhancement should be set in advance, and that no rents should be decreased as a result of such an investigation, nor should action of any sort be taken except on the landlord's initiative.[93] MacDonnell rejected out of hand these "obviously one-sided" proposals, but he was prepared to consider a more general scheme for the fixation by government of nonoccupancy tenant rentals, perhaps at the time of settlement, for a term of years. For this, as MacDonnell had anticipated, the taluqdars had no stomach, and so the idea of amending the Rent Act was dropped.[94]

The Maharaja of Ajodhya was not, however, prepared to let such legal niceties stand in the way of getting what he regarded as his just dues. No sooner had his appeal for exceptional treatment been rejected than he began covertly leasing out his estate to thikadars with instructions to raise rents all around. The work was carried out methodically. The maharaja, Woodburn reported, after looking through the settlement papers of every village, "worked out from these what would be a reasonable enhancement on lightly rented tenants—often 4 and 5 annas in the rupee [25 to 40 percent]—and it was on this revised basis he offered a lease to a thikadar." But, Woodburn went on, as "no absolute limitation was placed on the thikadar," there was nothing to stop him, wherever he saw the way clear, from going on to demand rents at 75 to 100 percent or more above the old figures. Indeed often, where leases were given for sums equal to the recorded rental, there was no other

93. Life Pres. B.I.A. to Sec. Govt. N.W.P.&O. 17 January 1900, N.W.P.&O. Rev. Progs. February 1900, No. 104; and Pres. B.I.A. to Sec. Govt. N.W.P.&O. 15 December 1900, N.W.P.&O. Rev. Progs. January 1901, No. 65.

94. Chief Sec. Govt. N.W.P.&O. to Pres. B.I.A. 26 February 1900, N.W.P.&O. Rev. Progs. February 1900, No. 106; and Notes by A. P. MacDonnell of 1 February 1900 and 8 July 1901, N.W.P.&O. Rev. Dept. File No. 233D.

way for the contractor to recover his investment. By the time the government found out what was going on, in 1902, the process was almost complete, its only visible sign being an increase in the number of ejectment notices on the estate from 132 to 700 in one year.[95]

Confronted with this *fait accompli*, the government decided to condone what it would not allow. Woodburn warned the maharaja in a futile gesture that "he must never do a thing of the kind again," while the new Lieutenant Governor, J. LaTouche, who was in any case prepared to "wink at" excessive enhancements on the low-rented lands of Brahmin and Rajput tenants, lamely concluded that "to accept and record an enhancement of more than 1 anna in the rupee is of course to go outside the provisions of . . . the Act, but the thing has been done and we must deal with the facts as they are." He suggested only that where the new rents were contested they be revised, and then accorded an ex post facto legitimacy under Section 51.[96] In fact however, almost no one protested, and the riots which the district officers had feared in Faizabad and Gonda never materialized. The new rents were paid "without objection or complaint." Partly no doubt this was because, as the maharaja insisted, the tenants acknowledged that the enhancements were "reasonable." But the thikadars, many of them "men of doubtful character or worse," had ways of their own of securing acquiescence. When Porter, the Deputy Commissioner, asked why "one Munna, a professed *lathial* [club-wielding tough], was included in the *thika* [contract] of a village, the reply was that if he wasn't, they couldn't collect a penny of rent."[97]

Not only in Ajodhya but throughout the province the first years of the new century witnessed a vast upsurge in illicit enhancement. With the settlement behind them and a run of good seasons to whet their appetites, the taluqdars began running up their rents so rapidly as to threaten, in W. H. Moreland's view, "in time to reduce the law to a nullity." Yet the government did nothing. Moreland, together with a few like-minded local officers, wished at least to see pressure brought to bear upon the leading taluqdars to obey the law, while Hailey, Deputy Commissioner in Gonda, wanted the right of ejectment limited and the thikadari system abolished as well. Butler, on the other hand, as might be expected, argued that while there was no doubt evasion of the law, "the law had done good as a whole," and that it would in any case be foolhardy, with nationalist agitation rising up on all sides, to tamper with the loyalty of the taluqdars, now "the only breakwater between Bengal and the Punjab." The Lieutenant Governor, J. P. Hewett, convinced that the government had already "gone much further" than it ought to have done in

95. J. Woodburn to J. LaTouche 24 August 1902 (demi-official), N.W.P.&O. Rev. Dept. File No. 758C. Woodburn was at this time Lt. Gov. of Bengal, and had come to Oudh to participate in a ceremony honoring the memory of Raja Man Singh.
96. LaTouche to G. W. Anson (Commr. Faizabad), 1 September 1902 (demi-official), *ibid.* See also his Note of 8 June 1902, *ibid.*
97. Commr. Faizabad to Chief Sec. Govt. N.W.P.&O. 28 May 1902, *ibid.*

restricting the landlord's rights, insisted that there was no evidence that the landowners of Oudh, even though they were enhancing their rents more rapidly than the law permitted, were "tyrannizing over their tenants" to such an extent as to warrant government interference. As matters now stand, he concluded, echoing Butler, "it is far more important to retain the goodwill of the taluqdars than to start an enquiry which may have the effect of putting the whole of Oudh into a blaze." And so the matter was dropped.[98]

In the end, then, the British were unwilling to pay more than lip service to the 1886 Rent Act. They would not, to be sure, amend it to suit the landlords' interests, for they did not want to be seen to be partial. But they did not hesitate to connive at wholesale violation of its most important provision—that regulating enhancement—in order to keep the taluqdars contented. With the rise of revolutionary nationalism at the turn of the century, political considerations mattered more than ever before since the days of the Mutiny. So long as the landlords' support was regarded as essential to "the stability of our rule in India," the British dared not risk offending them. The tenants, inert, could be ignored. But once the tenants showed that they too were a force to be reckoned with, and spoke out on their own behalf, as they did in the *kisan* movement after 1920, then the political balance rapidly shifted in the other direction. The Oudh Rent (Amendment) Act of 1921, which gave every resident cultivator a life tenure, was, though conceding much to the taluqdars as well, a tangible sign of the tenants' newfound political strength.

The Government as Nursemaid: Debt and Entail

British support for the taluqdars was not confined to letting them charge whatever rents they pleased. The government also, from the earliest years of the taluqdari settlement, helped them to preserve their estates from the mounting burden of debt which the taluqdars heaped up upon themselves. While debt had been a persisting feature of rural life for centuries, the coming of British rule brought both the occasion and the incentive for a vast increase in its amount. Hit, particularly under the first regular settlement, with a sharply enhanced revenue demand from which there was no escape by defiance, the taluqdars at the same time often found their resources restricted by the inam and fixed rent tenancies they had given years before to their kinsmen and retainers. Now, though the military assistance of these subordinates was no longer required, the landholders were still reluctant to embark upon the onerous task of separating them from their favored position. Borrowing alone provided a temporary measure of relief. At the same

---

98. Notes by W. H. Moreland of 17 March 1907, S. H. Butler of 6 July 1907, and J. P. Hewett of 3 October 1907, N.W.P.&O. Rev. Dept. File No. 329B. Moreland was at that time Director of Land Records and Agriculture for U.P.; Butler was Deputy Commissioner of Lucknow. For a detailed analysis of the extent of rental enhancement in the first decade of the twentieth century see W. H. Moreland, *Notes on the Agricultural Conditions and Problems of the U.P. and of its Districts* (Allahabad, 1913), pp. 87–91.

time the unrestricted hold over their property Lord Canning's sanads secured to the taluqdars, which much expanded the credit available to them, encouraged them to give vent to their desires for display and conspicuous consumption. Indeed expenditure of this sort, as we shall see in a subsequent chapter, became, in the absence of opportunities for plunder and warfare, the only psychologically satisfying way the taluqdars knew of keeping up their self-esteem and their status in society. Nor was debt wholly without practical use in the running of an estate, for borrowing, in India as elsewhere, financed such remunerative expenditures as the purchase of land and the building up of capital assets. Taluqdari debt, in sum, was of different sorts and contracted for different purposes, which the British, with their wholesale condemnation of its amount, almost never appreciated.

So early as 1865 a number of heavily burdened taluqdars in Faizabad and Gonda petitioned the Divisional Commissioner, F. O. Mayne, asking him to take over the management of their estates in order to clear off the debts and restore them to solvency. The British were reluctant to resort to "special nursing measures" of this sort on behalf of the taluqdars. They did not want after all to give a handle to those critics who insisted that the taluqdari system was too weak to stand upon its own feet. Yet at the same time they were determined not to see these men, whom they had raised up just a few short years before, "wrecked in the shoals and quicksands which surround them." For the new Oudh land system to be successful, Mayne insisted, the estate owners had to be given a "fair start" free of debt. In 1866, therefore, the Chief Commissioner authorized assistance, in the form of loans or temporary management of their estates, to "old hereditary chiefs of clans whom, on political grounds, it may be desirable to preserve from extinction."[99]

Four years later, with taluqdari indebtedness now standing at thirty-seven lakhs of rupees spread over seventy-one estates, and the government besieged by clamorous landholders, Lord Mayo, the Viceroy, reluctantly brought forward a general measure of relief, the Taluqdars' Encumbered Estates Act (XXIV of 1870).[100] Under its provisions a taluqdar could on petition vest the management of his estate in the government for a period not to exceed twenty years. During that time the property would be secure from attachment or sale; all income, beyond the government revenue demand and a fixed maintenance allowance for the taluqdar and his family, would be used to liquidate the debts and liabilities. Upon the discharge of the debts the estate would be restored to its owner. As a measure "avowedly of exceptional character," however, it was to be in effect for one year only. A taluqdar who neglected to apply during that year, or who later fell into debt, would "have no right to

99. Commr. Faizabad to Finanl. Commr. 13 October 1865 and 28 November 1865; Finanl. Commr. to Sec. C.C. 2 January 1866; and Sec. C.C. to Finanl. Commr. 17 January 1866, NAI For. Dept. Rev. A Progs. April 1866, No. 20. See also B.R. Oudh General File 2, Part I.
100. Finanl. Commr. to Sec. C.C. 13 August 1869, For. Rev. A Progs. March 1871, No. 17.

expect that Government would again interfere to save him from the consequences of his own folly."[101]

Some fifty taluqdars with debts of over thirty-three lakhs, attracted not only by the barrier the act erected against their creditors but by the opportunity of freeing their estates from "the incubus of the host of hangers-on whom they have not themselves the moral courage to get rid of," handed their estates over to the government. The latter in turn moved energetically to carry out its self-imposed mission. Debts were consolidated and refinanced at lower rates of interest, ranging from 6 to 9 percent; funds were made available from the government treasury, including a massive loan of three and a quarter lakhs to Mehdona in 1874, to pay off estate creditors; while specially appointed European superintendents, usually junior members of the ICS, let slip no occasion to reduce expenditure and increase the rental income of the estates under their charge. In Mehdona, for instance, the cost of management was cut in one year from Rs. 2,477 a month to Rs. 1,912, and the number of pensioners maintained at estate expense was reduced by 301, with a net monthly saving of over Rs. 3,000.[102] Nor were the taluqdars' own personal allowances exempt from this drive for economy. In 1870, when Rampal Singh's Dharupur estate first came under government management, the payments to his old retainers were halved, and he was obliged to accept a 15 percent reduction in his annual Rs. 13,557 allowance. Two years later, commenting that with the surplus then available it would take "nearly a century" to clear the estate's debts, the Chief Commissioner, over the violent protests of the raja, struck Rs. 6,000 more from his annual stipend.[103] In Mehdona, likewise, the dowager maharani's proposed monthly maintenance allowance of Rs. 6,373 for the young taluqdar and his dependents was slashed by nearly 50 percent, to Rs. 3,609.[104]

The government was equally ruthless in dealing with the taluqdars' privileged tenants. In Faizabad, where the subordinate holders on the Mehdona, Kapradih, and Sihipur estates had for years resisted payment of the enhanced revenue demand, the "most notoriously recusant" of the subproprietors, once the government had taken over the estates, were promptly thrown into jail, with, the Commissioner reported, "every prospect of excellent results

101. See speech of John Strachey of 28 January 1870, *Progs. Legis. Counc.*, 9:40–41; and of 6 September 1870, *ibid.*, p. 392. For Mayo's distaste for the principle of the act see his Note of 31 December 1869, For. Rev. A Progs. March 1871, No. 22.

102. Depty. Commr. Faizabad to Commr. Faizabad 10 November 1870, B.R. Faizabad File 6, Part I. For the government loan see Commr. Faizabad to Sec. C.C. 23 March 1874, *ibid.* Complete budget records for the Mehdona estate while under government management are included in this file.

103. See Minute by Finanl. Commr. of 6 June 1870; Sec. C.C. to Commr. Rae Bareli 7 October 1872; Supt. of Estates to Depty. Commr. Pratabgarh 5 December 1872; and Rampal Singh to Commr. Rae Bareli 15 December 1872, in B.R. Pratabgarh File 16. The Dharupur estate was released from government management on Rampal Singh's application in April 1873.

104. Depty. Commr. Faizabad to Commr. Faizabad 10 November 1870, B.R. Fyzabad File 6, Part I.

in getting in the balances." In the neighboring district of Rae Bareli, the government was at the same time "pressing on the sale of recusant subordinate tenures," though with little immediate success in breaking the "stiff-neckedness" of these privileged holders. By 1882, however, even in Kapradih, where the first four years of government management had only seen the estate debt balloon from Rs. 40,000 to Rs. 49,000, while the revenue payments fell in arrears to the extent of almost Rs. 36,000, the subproprietary tenantry had at last "been settled in a punctual payment of their rents." They all know now, the Deputy Commissioner reported, "that it is useless to resist the payment of the estate's just dues," though he hastened to add that "they also are equally well assured that their rents will not be raised capriciously."[105]

In addition to fixing rents the government endeavored to raise the standard of agriculture on the estates they controlled. Wells were sunk, sometimes 270 in a year; *taqavi* advances were handed out in the amount of some Rs. 20,000 annually to enable the tenantry to dig wells or purchase seed and cattle; while every occasion was used to promote new and improved techniques of cropping. In Bara Banki district in 1884, for instance, the Deputy Commissioner introduced the "useful and pleasant institution" of yearly gatherings of the tenantry. "Small presents" were distributed to tenants who had distinguished themselves by "enterprise in well-building and punctuality with their rents," while "the opportunity was taken of showing some improved ploughs, sugarcane-presses, and cane-juice evaporators, which were kept in constant use throughout the meetings, and are said to have excited the keenest interest among the country-people. Pandit Ajudhia Parshad, well known in Shahjahanpur for his skill and enterprise as a practical agriculturist, attended the first of these gatherings and delivered a very useful address . . . which was listened to with eager attention." Despite all this activity the results were nevertheless rather meagre. The district officers were frequently chastised for their failure to expend even the small sums allotted to them, and for their reluctance to make taqavi loans available freely and easily. Hedged about with red tape, and with repayment rigidly insisted upon, the loans were rarely of much use. Imported agricultural machinery was, of course, so complicated and expensive as to be almost comically inappropriate in a peasant community, yet the spread of more practical improvements such as masonry wells was deterred by the fact that their construction was "followed by an early and remunerative enhancement of rental."[106]

The Oudh government meanwhile, ignoring its threat to leave the taluq-

---

105. Commr. Faizabad to P.A. to C.C. 30 September 1872, B.R. Oudh General File 853; Commr. Rae Bareli to P.A. to C.C. 18 October 1875, Oudh General File 944; and *Review of Management of Estates . . . in Oudh for 1881–82* (Allahabad, 1883), pp. 38–40.

106. *Oudh Court of Wards Report for 1883–84* (Allahabad, 1885), pp. 8, 10–17. For the general ineffectuality of government efforts to improve agriculture see below ch. 11, and Whitcombe, *Agrarian Conditions*, pp. 97–118.

dars to their own devices after the expiry of the 1870 act, continued to assist them. In 1882, for instance, without even taking over the management of the estate, they extended a loan of almost two lakhs of rupees to the taluqdar of Kakrali, who had neglected to take advantage of the Relief Act.[107] The taluqdars too, chafing at the tight government control of their estates, began piling up new debts as fast as the old were paid off. One impatient land-holder, the taluqdar of Azizabad in Rae Bareli district, even borrowed Rs. 11,000 from a local banker in order to pay off the remaining debts and so regain the personal management of his estate. The local authorities, shocked at this evasion of the spirit of the act, at once drafted an amendment which would prohibit an indebted taluqdar not only from mortgaging his immovable property but from incurring fresh debts of any sort. Otherwise, they told the Government of India, it would be impossible to prevent the growth of new encumbrances, and with them the defeat of the purposes of the Relief Act. Lord Ripon, unimpressed, coldly replied that there was no need of further legislation "for the protection of the talukdars against the consequences of their own acts."[108]

By the mid-1890s, with almost no estates still under government manage-ment and the taluqdars as burdened with debt as ever, the question of what, if anything, should be done to "preserve from ruin" these old landlords had become once again a matter of public concern. In 1894 the taluqdars them-selves, through the British Indian Association, asked the government to revive the 1870 Encumbered Estates Act, and at the same time to provide some way by which they could protect their estates, or some part of them, for-ever from "any kind of alienation or transfer." The experience of the thirty-five years since the British had remodeled and reconstituted the taluqdari system, they argued, in a telling commentary on their financial difficulties, showed that without some such measure "the majority of the taluqas will, within a short time, pass out of the families of the present holders."[109] The Lieutenant Governor, Sir Charles Crosthwaite, was, as might be expected, sympathetic, so long only, he said, as these measures did not "have the effect of converting the Taluqdars into mere pensioners divorced from their land"; so too was the Government of India, just embarked upon the extensive inves-tigation of land transfer and indebtedness which was ultimately to end in the famous, and highly restrictive, Punjab Land Alienation Act of 1900.[110]

107. Sec. Govt. N.W.P.&O. to Sec. Govt. India 1 October 1881, Oudh Rev. Progs. October 1881, No. 1; and Sec. Govt. India to Sec. Govt. N.W.P.&O. 2 December 1881, Oudh Rev. Progs. December 1881, No. 4.
108. Sec. Govt. N.W.P.&O. to Sec. Govt. India 15 June 1882, Oudh Rev. Progs. June 1882, No. 1; and Sec. Govt. India to Sec. Govt. N.W.P.&O. 31 July 1882, Oudh Rev. Progs. August 1882, No. 4.
109. Memorial of B.I.A. to Sec. Govt. N.W.P.&O. 6 November 1894, N.W.P.&O. Rev. Progs. April 1898, No. 113; and Pres. B.I.A. to Chief Sec. Govt. N.W.P.&O. 23 June 1895, *ibid.*, No. 115.
110. Sec. Govt. N.W.P.&O. to Pres. B.I.A. 15 November 1894, *ibid.*, No. 114. For the general India-wide discussion see the 1898 *Selection of Papers on Agricultural Indebtedness and the Restriction of the Power to Alienate Interests in Land.*

Despite this agreement on principle, the process of legislation for Oudh was to be long and difficult. Slapped down by the Secretary of State when it tried in 1894 to secure a "perpetual settlement" of property in the hands of hereditary title-holders, the Government of India the following year urged upon the local authorities instead a scheme under which the estates of "spendthrifts" could be taken without their consent and placed in the Court of Wards. It also suggested that the owners of such estates might be debarred, even after their property had been returned to them, from burdening them with any charges valid beyond the term of one life. Both the local government and the taluqdars, who had included a somewhat similar idea in their 1894 memorial, gave a general assent to these proposals.[111] Yet the attempt to incorporate them in legislation met with frustration at every turn. A. Cadell, the Acting Lieutenant Governor in 1895, wanted all estates put together by "landjobbers" in the years since the Mutiny excluded, while the taluqdars, consulted anew by MacDonnell two years later, drew back from their earlier enthusiasm. They saw no way of deciding who as a "spendthrift" should have his estate taken from him which would not stir up dissension and involve the making of too many invidious distinctions. The British Indian Association, in particular, refused to jeopardize the "unanimity and good feeling" of its members by taking any responsibility in this matter. Nor, the taluqdars felt, would the proposed denial of access to long-term credit accomplish anything other than to make it difficult for proprietors to borrow even for legitimate purposes, while at the same time deterring them from placing their estates voluntarily under government management.[112] MacDonnell on his part, reluctant to move without the taluqdars and increasingly convinced of the validity of the practical objections to these measures, finally recommended that all element of compulsion be dropped.[113] As a result, the Court of Wards bill introduced in 1898 provided only that proprietors who wished to do so could place their estates in the government's hands, and put no restrictions on their power to contract debts after the release of their property.[114]

The taluqdars meanwhile had revived their pet scheme of preserving their estates by the enactment of a law of entail. So far back as 1862, in its first year of existence, the taluqdars' association, fearful of the wholly unrestricted

111. Sec. Govt. India to all Local Govts. 10 May 1895, N.W.P.&O. Rev. Progs. July 1895, No. 59; and Sec. Govt. N.W.P.&O. to Sec. Govt. India 19 July 1895, ibid., No. 62.

112. Note by Cadell of 4 July 1895, N.W.P.&O. Rev. Dept. File 169B; and Pres. B.I.A. to Chief Sec. Govt. N.W.P.&O. 29/30 August 1897, N.W.P.&O. Rev. Progs. December 1897, No. 83. A few individual taluqdars favored taking over the estates of "spendthrifts." See, e.g., Seth Raghubar Dyal to Depty. Commr. Sitapur 14 June 1897, ibid., No. 80.

113. Chief Sec. Govt. N.W.P.&O. to Sec. Govt. India 11 December 1897, ibid., No. 102. The Government of India had also by this time lost much of its enthusiasm for these proposals. See Sec. Govt. India to Sec. Govt. N.W.P.&O. 24 April 1897, ibid., No. 51.

114. Sec. Govt. India to Sec. Govt. N.W.P.&O. 30 May 1898, N.W.P.&O. Rev. Progs. July 1898, No. 14; and "Statement of Objects and Reasons" accompanying the draft bill, ibid., No. 17. The measure was enacted as N.W.P.&O. Act III of 1899.

power of bequest and sale conveyed to them by Lord Canning's sanads, had sought some way to "tie down" the hands of heirs.[115] Provision was made at that time for succession by primogeniture for those taluqdars who desired it, an arrangement formalized by Act I of 1869. But this, of course, provided no protection against sale or transfer during the owner's lifetime. So when the other schemes put forward by the government fell apart in the late 1890s, the taluqdars eagerly turned once again to the idea of placing some restriction on the alienation of land. A general ban on sale or transfer by decree of court, or along the lines of the Punjab Act of 1900, was briefly considered, but rejected in large part because, as the district officers all pointed out, any such legislation would abrogate the legitimate rights of creditors and unduly depreciate the value of land.[116] In any case the taluqdars sought no such general legislation, but only a way to "put it out of the power of careless and extravagant landlords to ruin the fortunes of an old and dignified family." MacDonnell, fully supporting this objective, in 1898 in close consultation with the taluqdars drafted a bill that would enable a taluqdar to declare the whole or a part of his property inalienable, either for a period of time or in perpetuity. Such property, to be called a "settled estate," could not be sold or transferred either by the owner or by court decree. The bill ultimately reached the statute book as N.W.P.&O. Act II of 1900.[117]

This long series of "nursing" measures was finally completed a few years later when, over the strenuous objections of the urban members of the Legislative Council, most notably Motilal Nehru, provision was made for the disqualification of "spendthrift" proprietors from the management of their estates. The knotty question of deciding who should be so disqualified was resolved by providing that no estate should be taken over until the aggregate annual interest on the debt exceeded one-third of the estate's gross annual profits. This however made it impossible for the Court of Wards to interfere at an "early stage in the downhill career of an indebted estate," and so rendered the provision of relatively little use.[118]

By the first decade of the twentieth century, then, the structure of agrarian

115. Memorandum by Maharaja Man Singh approved by B.I.A. 10 March 1862, NAI For. Dept. General B Progs. March 1863, No. 262. See also Chhail Bihari Lal, *Taluqdari Law*, pp. 115–16. Some British officers also favored the adoption of a law of entail. See Commr. Khairabad to Finanl. Commr. 12 February 1866, B.R. Oudh General File 2, Part I.

116. Sec. Govt. N.W.P.&O. to Sec. Govt. India 26 May 1896, *Papers on Agricultural Indebtedness*, 3:1–120, esp. 4, 11. See also Sec. Govt. N.W.P.&O. to Sec. Govt.India 1 October 1897, N.W.P.&O. Rev. Progs. October 1897, No. 33; and the reports of the district officers, *ibid.*, No. 12–25.

117. Sec. Govt. N.W.P.&O. to Sec. Govt. India 27 April 1898, N.W.P.&O. Rev. Progs. April 1898, No. 119; G.-G.-in-C. to S. of S. 27 October 1898, N.W.P.&O. Rev. Progs. May 1899, No. 102; and "Statement of Objects and Reasons" by Chief Sec. N.W.P.&O. of 19 September 1899, N.W.P.&O. Rev. Progs. February 1900, No. 152.

118. For a summary of these developments see Sec. Bd. Rev. to Sec. Govt. U.P. 6 August 1919, U.P. Rev. Dept. Confidential File No. 578/1918. This legislation was proposed by Nawab Sir Faiyaz Ali Khan of Pahasu in the Council meeting of 7 April 1908 and enacted the following year. See N.W.P.&O. Rev. Dept. File No. 169B.

law for Oudh was complete. Overwhelmingly its beneficiaries were the taluqdars, who had won nearly all the boons they had sought from the government which had restored them, defeated, to their estates fifty years before. They had an assessment as lenient as the demands of the Exchequer could make it, and tenancy legislation enacted with their consent which they were then tacitly permitted to ignore. Yet the taluqdars' position was not so strong as it sometimes appeared. Despite the passivity of the ordinary tenantry, they had, as we shall see, by no means bent all the elements of rural society to their will. Their heavy and growing burden of debt indeed was in some measure a mark of the incompleteness of their control over the countryside. Nor were they, again in large part because of their indebtedness, free of a continued unseemly dependence on the government, of which the 1870 Relief Act was but the first, and most visible, sign. Yet the problem was not easily resolvable. In 1902, moved by a deep concern for their well-being, Sir John Woodburn, one of the taluqdars' oldest friends, warned them above all else to "beware of debts." For you, he said, "it is the direst and most terrible of dangers."[119] But debt was inextricably tied to the taluqdars' position in society, and the way they managed their estates. Nor did borrowing carry for them the stigma awarded it by the British, who looked with distaste on the style of life it supported. Any assessment of the taluqdars' situation must begin by examining their goals, and activities, as estate managers.

119. Speech of Sir John Woodburn of 13 August 1902, B.I.A. Records, File No. 19.

Nine | Taluqdars as Estate Managers

N 1865 THE Faizabad Deputy Commissioner said of the district's taluq-dars that they all "live as a rule much below their position, and have actually nothing to show for what they undoubtedly receive from their estates."[1] That same year the Mehdona estate of Maharaja Man Singh reported a net surplus of receipts over expenditures of Rs. 1,451 in a total budget of two and a half lakhs of rupees. Two years later, with receipts totaling Rs. 4,60,000, the surplus was still only Rs. 3,678. Yet in 1867, after two lakhs had been put aside for the government revenue, one lakh for the repayment of debts, and Rs. 60,000 for management charges, there still remained a further full lakh of rupees. Of this some Rs. 46,000 were given over to the personal expenditure of the maharaja and his retainers; Rs. 19,500 went for the costs of lawsuits; Rs. 15,000 for the feeding of cattle; and Rs. 5,400 for the marriage of the taluqdar's grandson. The personal expenditure included such items as Rs. 10,000 spent on camels, horses, and elephants; Rs. 2,500 for the support of nine pandits in Ajodhya, Benares, and elsewhere; and nearly Rs. 8,000 for

1. Depty. Commr. Faizabad to Commr. Faizabad 19 October 1865, B.R. Oudh General File 2, Part I.

the upkeep of some 92 armed retainers and 67 domestic servants.[2] At the end of the century, after a protracted and expensive succession contest following the death of Man Singh, the new maharaja Pratap Narayan Singh, despite the persistence of a heavy burden of debt, embarked on an extensive building program which dotted the ancient town of Ajodhya with new palaces, bungalows, ceremonial gateways, and temples.[3] Where, we must ask, did the money come from to finance these expenditures, and how was it collected? To what extent can it truly be said of the taluqdars that their annual receipts from their estates left them financially hard-pressed?

The Struggle with the Underproprietors

When the taluqdars were restored to their estates after the Mutiny they found themselves at once face to face over much of their land with the village zamindars, beneficiaries of the short-lived 1856 settlement, but now pushed aside to make room for their former masters. In order effectively, and profitably, to manage their estates the taluqdars had first of all to come to terms with these subordinate holders. This was not to be a task quickly or easily accomplished.

During the course of the Mutiny, as we have seen, the village zamindars, trooping in with their followers to form local militia forces, joined the taluqdars in revolt. This military subordination to the taluqdar did not, however, necessarily imply, as the British assumed at the time, any desire to see him set up anew as a superior landholder over them. Indeed, to the contrary, the village communities seem most often to have thrown in their lot with the taluqdar for the want of any real alternative. As the "raja," or traditionally acknowledged leader of the locality, and often the chief of the local Rajput lineage as well, the taluqdar was a man of power and position whose authority it would be foolhardy to defy. A mere year of British rule, despite the 1856 settlement, had deprived him of almost none of the levers by which he commanded the allegiance of those beneath him. A good many villagers were no doubt also drawn into the rebellion for other reasons, above all perhaps a sense of fellowship with the mutinous sepoys, many of them kinsmen and compatriots from Oudh. Some too may have shared in the widespread loyalty to and compassion for the deposed dynasty of Wajid Ali Shah, or simply wished to prosecute old feuds with their neighbors, and so fell in with the rebellious taluqdars only as a matter of mutual convenience. In any case the villagers' conduct, as Sir Charles Wood cogently observed in 1860, "proved that they hated and feared the British power under the circumstances of the

2. Depty. Commr. Faizabad to Commr. Faizabad 15 September 1870, with three appendices showing receipts and expenditure of Mehdona estate for 1865 to 1868, B.R. Faizabad File 6. For a detailed listing of items see below Appendix 3.
3. Kunwar Durga Prasad, *Tarikh-i-Ajodhya* (Urdu) (Lucknow, 1902), pp. 175–76.

time more than they disliked the talookdar, but not that they preferred his rule to their own independence.''[4]

As the fighting died down, toward the end of 1858, and it became apparent that the British intended restoring the taluqdars to power, the villagers put up a stubborn opposition to the new arrangements. An officer in Hardoi reported in December that the 1856 settlement had "so thoroughly broken up the talooks that the mokuddums [village leaders] who then got settlement now get up their backs at the talookdars," while Barrow himself acknowledged, in his final report on the settlement the following June, that the subordinate holders had again "come forward" to claim their independence, "and now watch the slightest signs of our relenting in their favor once more to resume the contest warmer than ever.''[5] The resistance took the form for some, among them Hardeo Bakhsh's tenants, of "running about the country" to petition the Viceroy, but most simply vented their indignation on the taluqdar by refusing to pay him their rent, or giving him no more than the government revenue demand plus a malikana allowance of 10 percent. To put a stop to this agitation, which continued throughout 1859 and into 1860, Wingfield, the Chief Commissioner, instructed his officers to impress upon the villagers the absolute finality of the new arrangements.[6] Indeed the decision to issue sanads to the taluqdars was in large part prompted by a desire to show the discontented villagers that the new settlement could not be overturned.[7]

No doubt the disarmament of the taluqdars, and their consequent loss of political power, emboldened the subordinate zamindars to challenge them. At the same time the taluqdars were determined to cut these upstarts down to size, in part perhaps as a way to "revenge themselves" for the zamindars' "short lived prosperity" after 1856. Hence the conclusion of the settlement did not lead to any reconciliation. The villagers simply shifted their ground, and fought to preserve for themselves the largest possible amount of independence as privileged tenants or underproprietors, while the taluqdars, picking up to some extent where they had left off at annexation, set out to reduce these men so far as possible to "mere cultivators at will.''[8]

4. Dispatch (No. 33) of 24 April 1860, *P.P.* 1861, 46:439. For the government's view of the villagers' behavior during the revolt see above ch. 7.
5. From [illegible] to Sec. C.C. 1 December 1858, B.R. Oudh General File 396; and Spec. Commr. Rev. to Sec. C.C. 24 June 1859, *Papers Relating to Land Tenure in Oude*, p. 47.
6. Offg. Depty. Commr. Faizabad to Commr. Faizabad 6 December 1858, B.R. Faizabad File 115; Wingfield to Canning 24 December 1859, Canning Papers; and Sec. C.C. to Commr. Faizabad 22 August 1860, B.R. Oudh General File 2057. The villagers were also told that they must pay rent at the old customary rates. See, e.g., Note by L. Barrow of 9 December 1858, B.R. Faizabad File 115.
7. For the motives behind the award of sanads see Sec. C.C. Oudh to Sec. Govt. India 4 June 1859, NAI F.C. 30 December 1859 (Supplement), No. 493. See also Metcalf, *Aftermath of Revolt*, pp. 148-50.
8. Depty. Commr. Pratabgarh to Spec. Commr. Rev. 30 April 1859, B.R. Pratabgarh File

In the face of this agrarian strife the government set itself the task of holding the balance even between the contenders, and more particularly of securing the subordinate holders against any further fall in status. Hence, while awarding sanads to the taluqdars, the Viceroy Lord Canning at the same time ordered that the rights of all inferior holders were to be preserved as they had existed before annexation, and that the rental demand of the taluqdar against such persons was to be limited to a sum fixed for the duration of each thirty-year settlement.[9] Underproprietary right encompassed a variety of privileged tenures, ranging downward from the right to hold an entire village in subsettlement through the holding of *sir* land at favorable rates to various petty privileged grants originating in awards to encourage reclamation of waste or to reward religious or military service. Of these tenures, by far the most consequential, and the most hotly contested, was that of subsettlement, known as a *pakka* or *pukhtadari* tenure, awarded to the holders of formerly independent villages incorporated in taluqas, and entitling them to management of the village on payment of a fixed rent proportioned to the government revenue demand.[10] Eventually in 1864, after considerable controversy and extended negotiations with the taluqdars, it was agreed that underproprietary rights were to be protected if they had been enjoyed at any time during the twelve years preceding annexation. This decision was given legal form, and the rules relating to underproprietary right defined, in the Oudh Sub-Settlement Act (XXVI of 1866).

This effort at legal protection, however, by no means put a stop to the antagonism between taluqdar and village zamindar. Partly this was because the most influential officials in Oudh continued throughout to give support to the taluqdars. Barrow put the matter forthrightly when he argued that the government "must support one side." The "*sure* success" of the new land system, he said, could be secured only by "our making the talookdars *sole* proprietors" vested with the "*full* profits" of their estates.[11] In pursuit of this objective Wingfield as Chief Commissioner sought first to have annulled all underproprietary rights in lands conferred on new grantees as a result of the rebellion of their former owners. When rebuffed in this endeavor he then

389. See also Settle. Offr. Pratabgarh to Settle. Commr. 2 June 1863, *P.P.* 1865, 40:207; and Report of Settle. Offr. Lucknow of 28 May 1864, *Papers Relating to Underproprietary Rights and Rights of Cultivators in Oude* (Calcutta, 1865), p. 177. For the subjugation of the subordinate holders in the Nawabi period see above ch. 2.

9. Sec. Govt. India to Sec. C.C. Oudh 19 October 1859, *P.P.* 1861, 46:429. This letter is reprinted in Chhail Bihari Lal, *Taluqdari Law*, pp. 393–95.

10. For discussion of these various tenures see I. F. MacAndrew, *On Some Revenue Matters Chiefly in the Province of Oudh* (Calcutta, 1876), pp. 24–39; and B. H. Baden-Powell, *Land Systems of British India* (Oxford, 1892), 2:229–31 and 235–43. The pukhtadari tenure, with its fixed rent based on the government demand, was a British innovation, "established as the nearest thing which would combine the certainty of a tenure under English rule with the status of a former proprietor leasing a village under a talukdar" (MacAndrew, p. 26).

11. L. Barrow to Wingfield (demi-official), n.d., ca. November 1859, B.R. Oudh General File 66, Part I (italics in the original).

tried to confine the award of underproprietary rights within the narrow limits of those enjoyed in the single year 1855. Rights that had lapsed before that date, even during the course of the previous year, were, he told his district staff in the Record of Rights Circular of 1861, not to be recognized. Again Wingfield was rebuffed by the Governor-General, and the twelve-years rule instituted for the determination of claims. Yet even then the subsettlement rules placed subordinate holders at a severe disadvantage in making good their claims. The burden of proof, for instance, was thrown upon their shoulders, and they were required in order to obtain a subsettlement of their village to show continuous possession recognized by a lease from the taluqdar over the entire area.[12]

The taluqdars did not, however, require much encouragement to press home their attack upon the subordinate holders. Indeed the universal disarmament that accompanied the restoration of British rule, by doing away with the need for the stout arms of these men in the taluqdars' conflicts with government revenue collectors or rival landholders, had removed whatever incentive remained to treat liberally with them. The taluqdar's interest now lay almost wholly in the amount of rent he could obtain from his property. The British worked hard, and with some success, to encourage "a spirit of conciliation" among the taluqdars and to bring about compromise settlements of underproprietary claims.[13] Often too the taluqdars conceded freely *sir* and *nankar*, together with other petty underproprietary rights, and sometimes they would even give the subordinate holders a short-term lease of the village. But almost invariably they contested "to the last" claims to subsettlement, which by taking villages out of their control would hit them "not only in pocket but in pride." In this, helped by the "strict rules" of the 1866 act, they achieved a very solid success. Of 22,000 claims to underproprietary rights of all kinds settled by the end of 1868 just under two-thirds were decided in favor of the taluqdar. But while the villagers won 50 percent of the suits for petty rights, they gained only 28 percent, or barely one in four, of their claims to subsettlement.[14] As R. M. King, settlement officer in Pratabgarh, put it so early as 1863, "The talookdar is in the saddle, and

12. For discussion of the controversy over underproprietary rights see Raj, *The Mutiny and British Policy*, ch. iii; and Chhail Bihari Lal, *Taluqdari Law*, pp. 122-213. (The latter is a reprint of ch. iii of J. G. W. Sykes, *Compendium of the Law Specially Relating to the Taluqdars of Oudh* [Calcutta, 1886].) For the subsettlement rules see Lal, *Taluqdari Law*, pp. 517-43. Baden-Powell called the law "in practice unfavourable to the existence of a proprietary body between the Taluqdar and the village cultivators" (*Land Systems*, 2:230).

13. Annual Settlement Report of Faizabad by P. Carnegy, 7 May 1864, B.R. Faizabad File 11, Part I; Settle. Offr. Faizabad to Commr. Faizabad 22 December 1864, B.R. Oudh General File 2235, Part II; and Sec. C.C. to Settle. Commr. 18 July 1864, *P.P.* 1865, 40:316. Some 2,800 cases, or nearly one-quarter of the total number brought forward up to 1869, were settled by compromise in the Faizabad Division. *Oudh Rev. Admin. Report for 1868-69*, Part II, pp. 15-16.

14. *Oudh Rev. Admin. Report for 1867-68*, Part II, pp. 14-16. See also Settle. Offr. Rae Bareli to Settle. Commr. 31 May 1864, *Papers Relating to Underproprietary Rights*, p. 179.

the underproprietor has to unhorse him; this he can seldom do, and he loses all in the encounter."[15]

The course of this struggle can perhaps best be appreciated by looking closely at two or three districts. Faizabad, thickly peopled with "the highest caste and boldest" Rajput clans, was hit harder than any other district in the province by the shifts in land policy between 1856 and 1859. More of its villages were taken from taluqdars at the first settlement, and more small zamindars deprived of independent management at the second.[16] The largest estate in the district, that of Mehdona, as a "mushroom" growth put together by the two Brahmin brothers Bakhtawar and Darshan Singh, contained many Rajput brotherhoods only recently subjected to taluqdari overlordship. Despite repeated attempts by Darshan, and his successor Raja Man Singh, to break these former village holders, the Mehdona family had never completely obliterated their rights. The estate was too vast and scattered, and had grown too rapidly, to enable sufficient pressure to be brought to bear at any one point, while the taluqdars were continually distracted by their official duties as nazims for the Oudh government. As a result the old village zamindars usually held their land on "easy" terms, with rents set 25 percent or more below those of ordinary cultivators.[17] So strong were their claims that at the 1856 settlement the holders of all but six of the estate's villages were given revenue engagements for their lands. Hence it is not surprising that the decision after the revolt to restore Raja (later Maharaja) Man Singh touched off an exceptionally fierce struggle. Restive, at times even moved to violence during 1859, the village zamindars for years after, when they did not withhold their rent altogether, paid no more than they were "absolutely compelled to." The taluqdar on his part refused to issue the new written pattas until the leaseholders acquiesced in an enhancement of their rent.[18]

The conflict flared up in a particularly acute form during 1867 and 1868, just after the passage of the Sub-Settlement Act. The storm center was the Amsin pargana, located along the southern bank of the river Ghagra. The bulk of the pargana was in the possession of a "powerful and pugnacious" clan of Barwar Rajputs, who had once owned 159 villages, but who during

15. Settle. Offr. Pratabgarh to Settle. Commr. 2 June 1863, *P.P.* 1865, 40:207.

16. For the district figures see above Table 17, and *Papers Relating to Land Tenures . . . in Oude*, Appendix "E," p. 79.

17. Millett, *Fyzabad S.R.*, pp. 449–51. Among the Rajput-held lands taken over by the Mehdona family were those of the Bais of Ruru and Raipur; the Surajbansis of Haveli Oudh and Amsin; the Gargbansis of Pachhimrath; the Bisens of Mangalsi; and the Barwars of Amsin. Some Brahmins, including the holders of forty villages in Pachhimrath, also lost their lands to the Mehdona taluqdars. See Nevill, *Fyzabad D.G.*, pp. 75–76, 195–96, 227–28, et al.

18. Millett, *Fyzabad S.R.*, p. 452; and Depty. Commr. Faizabad to Commr. Faizabad 18 November 1859, B.R. Faizabad File 6. Wingfield was prepared to let the maharaja hold the entire estate *kachcha* (directly with the cultivators) if the village muqaddams refused to take leases "on fair terms." Sec. C.C. to Commr. Faizabad 24 April 1860, *ibid.*

the years just before annexation had lost all of them, mostly to the growing Mehdona estate. In 1867, while their claims to subsettlement were being adjudicated, the revised government revenue demand, involving an enhancement of 55 percent, was levied upon the pargana. To protect those claiming underproprietary rights, the settlement officer proposed that so long as their suits remained undecided those men should pay no more than the new government demand plus 5 or 10 percent. Instead, the maharaja used the occasion to issue notices of enhancement indiscriminately to all his tenants, underproprietary claimants and ordinary cultivators alike, demanding that they pay rent henceforth at double the new revenue demand plus 8 percent.[19] At this the Barwars dug in their heels. Never very regular in their rent payments they now withheld everything, even the money they had already collected. John Woodburn, sent into the pargana to induce them to pay at least their old rent, after alternately threatening and remonstrating with them, reported despairingly that they were "obstructive from spite" and deserved no sympathy. Despite Woodburn's exasperation this defiance had little to do with the government. It was a measure rather of the "deep-rooted" enmity between the Barwars and the maharaja, and reflected above all the state of desperation to which they had been driven by the maharaja's persistent attack on their privileged position.[20]

In the end, confined by the strict rules of the 1866 act, and perhaps made more desperate because they foresaw the outcome, the Barwars lost their suits for subsettlement. But in the process they exacted a heavy toll from the maharaja. Throughout the proceedings they invoked every legal stratagem to delay a decision on their subsettlement cases, often absenting themselves for months on end and then appearing in court just in time to avoid a decree against them. In so doing they also forced a delay in the decision of the suits for arrears of rent brought against them by the maharaja, for the district courts were clogged with subsettlement cases. During this period—and the subsettlement cases were not finally decided until February 1869—the maharaja was called upon to pay a sharply enhanced revenue demand, while he was not permitted to oust the leaseholders or to collect directly from the cultivators, and the underproprietors on their part continued to withhold payment of even the old rent. Furthermore, even after all the suits in court had been decided, the maharaja had little hope of collecting the large arrears

19. See Memorandum of P. Carnegy, Settle. Offr. Faizabad, of 5 November 1867, B.R. Faizabad File 6; and Millett, *Fyzabad S.R.*, p. 464. For the history of the Barwars see Carnegy, *Fyzabad Tehsil*, Part II, pp. 71–72.

20. J. Woodburn, Assistant Settle. Offr., to W. E. Forbes, Depty. Commr. Faizabad, 28 October 1867, B.R. Faizabad File 6. One of the Woodburn's threats was that "if I had to tell the Lord Sahib [Governor-General] that the pookhtadars were backward in their payments of the Government revenue, there would simply be an order to have not a pookhtadar in the province." See also Forbes to J. Reid, Commr. Faizabad, 29 October 1867, and Reid to R. H. Davies, Finanl. Commr., 1 November 1867, forwarding Woodburn's letter, *ibid*.

of rent to which he was entitled, for the defaulters had disappeared with their valuables and he could find next to no property to proceed against.[21] As a result, the Mehdona estate was driven ever more deeply into debt. By the time of his death in 1870 Maharaja Man Singh's total debt, principal and accumulated interest taken together, amounted to over three lakhs of rupees.[22]

The stubborn resistance of the Amsin underproprietors was widely duplicated elsewhere in the district. The subordinate holders on the Pirpur estate, for instance, not only withheld their rent for years, but forced the taluqdar to employ police guards in support of his authority; on Malik Hidayat Husain's Samanpur estate the tenants, pakka holders and ordinary cultivators together, protested "exorbitant" enhancements of their rents by a refusal to plough and by setting on fire huge heaps of grass and leaves; in Meopur-Dhaurua the withholding of rent reached such proportions that the government sanctioned the sale of the lands held by the "specially insubordinate" underproprietors of Bhudui as an "example" to the others. On each of these estates, as in Mehdona, this defiance drove the taluqdar into arrears on the government revenue and into the hands of the moneylender.[23] Perhaps most dramatic of all was the situation on the Birhar and Kapradih estates. On both, the subordinate holders, many of them clansmen and near relatives of the taluqdar, kept the bulk of the profits in their own hands. Unlike Mehdona, where the absence of any tie between the Brahmin taluqdar and his Rajput subjects helped breed antagonism, here the "excessive closeness" of the tie produced much the same result. The Gargbansis of Kapradih, and the proud Palwars of Birhar, "turbulent and independent," though acknowledging the taluqdar as the chief of their brotherhood, regarded themselves as in no way inferior to him. He was, in their view, simply "a leader of their own body selected by themselves from among themselves," and they adamantly refused to hand over to him anything more than the bare revenue demand.[24] Nor could even the government easily emancipate these taluqdars from their

21. Capt. G. Erskine, Offg. Settle. Offr. Faizabad, to Commr. Faizabad 25 February 1870, and Petition of Maharaja Man Singh of 14 January 1870, *ibid*. In his petition Man Singh asked to have the estate exempted from payment of the revised assessment for one year and to have the demand permanently lowered. Both requests were denied.

22. For a list of Man Singh's debts see Depty. Commr. Faizabad to Commr. Faizabad 26 August 1870, and 15 September 1870, *ibid*. The loans were taken from a variety of banks and moneylenders at interest rates up to 15 percent.

23. G. Elphinstone, Settle. Offr. Faizabad, to Commr. Faizabad 20 April 1870, B.R. Faizabad File 11; *Oudh Rev. Admin. Report for 1866-67*, Part II, p. 17; Commr. Faizabad to Finanl. Commr. 28 October 1868, and Depty. Commr. to Commr. Faizabad 6 December 1868, B.R. Faizabad File 438; and Depty. Commr. to Commr. Faizabad 12 August 1868, C.O.F. Bundle 15, File 74.

24. Depty. Commr. Faizabad to Spec. Commr. Revenue 13 April 1859, B.R. Faizabad File 11; Depty. Commr. to Commr. Faizabad 20 January 1860, and Note by Commr. of 6 December 1860, Faizabad Collectorate Records, Bundle 33; Commr. Faizabad to Sec. C.C. 26 November 1877, Oudh Rev. Progs. July 1878, No. 12; and Millett, *Fyzabad S.R.*, pp. 402, 437-39.

"thraldom to mere leaseholders." So late as 1876, after ten years of government management, underproprietary rental arrears in Kapradih amounted to Rs. 67,000, and the British officials sent to collect the revenue, despite the quartering of police in the villages and the filling of the jails with these subordinate holders, often returned empty-handed.[25]

With the old proprietary bodies so tenacious and widespread it is not surprising that the subsettled area in Faizabad district reached sizable proportions. Some two-thirds of Birhar, for instance, and one-third of Mehdona, were held under pukhtadari tenure, while over the district as a whole some 860 villages encompassing one-fourth of the total area and upwards of one-third of the taluqdari holdings were decreed in subsettlement to some 10,000 underproprietary shareholders.[26]

Where the taluqdar's authority was less vigorously contested, the number of subsettlements was correspondingly fewer. The most striking instances of unchallenged taluqdari power are to be found in the Gonda and Bahraich districts. Cut off by the river Ghagra from the seat of government at Lucknow, these two districts contained in their northern reaches vast areas of jungle-clad land bypassed by the flow of settlement in medieval times. The Mughal Emperors, and later the Oudh Nawabs, anxious to see these lands on the revenue rolls, had made over large tracts to enterprising courtiers and soldiers with instructions to bring them under cultivation. The rajas of Nanpara and Charda got their start in this way, as did Himmat Singh of Pyagpur, given a "clearing lease" in the late eighteenth century of an area later to contain 1,712 villages. On such estates the cultivators, placed in their holdings by the original grantee or his descendants, enjoyed no rights apart from the favor of the taluqdar, and so put forward no claims to subsettlement.

Even where independent village bodies did exist, the relative freedom from outside intereference that the taluqdars of these northern marches enjoyed emboldened them almost from the outset to claim lordship over the soil. On the Ikauna estate of Bahraich, for instance, though the original grantee, a Rajput *risaldar* in the service of the Delhi Sultan Firoz Shah, had been put in only to restore order and collect taxes on behalf of the government, his successors refused to acknowledge any subordinate rights not of their own creation. Even after the Mutiny, when the estate was conferred on the Sikh raja

25. Memo by A. Harington, Supt. Encumbered Estates Faizabad, of 29 July 1875, B.R. Oudh General File 944; Depty. Commr. Sultanpur to H. W. Gibson, Assist. Commr., 10 December 1877, B.R. Faizabad File 23, Part I; and Depty. Commr. Sultanpur to Commr. Rae Bareli 6 August 1879, *ibid*. For Birhar see Millett, *Fyzabad S.R.*, pp. 439–42. For the eventual British success in breaking this defiance see above pp. 231–32.

26. *Oudh Rev. Admin. Report for 1870-71*, Part II, p. 6; and Millett, *Fyzabad S.R.*, Appendix IV, p. 17A. Smaller holdings involving a further 847 taluqdari villages were also held in subsettlement. Rajputs held 53 percent of the subsettled area, Brahmins 26 percent, Muslims 11 percent, and Kayasthas and others 10 percent. Nevill, *Fyzabad D.G.*, p. 102.

of Kapurthala, the subordinate holders were deterred from putting claims forward by the threatening attitude adopted by the raja's agents, who made it clear to intending claimants that their only hope of obtaining any concessions was to look to the taluqdar and not to the courts. As a result no underproprietary rights of any sort were recorded on this estate.[27] The raja of Balrampur likewise, living in almost regal splendor, had by annexation become so powerful that none of the subordinate holders, much as they might resent his power, dared defy him. The clan feeling, the Commissioner of Faizabad wrote in 1873, "is opposed to anyone bringing a suit in court against the Maharaja. It is known that though a kind landlord on the whole, he would unhesitatingly do all in his power to crush anyone who asserted a right against him, and it is thought that his personal interest with all the hakims [officials] of the district and with the authorities at Head Quarters is great. So that the man claiming a subordinate interest in the land will long hesitate before he brings a suit to be judicially tried, and perhaps dismissed, when he feels that he would be at the mercy of a powerful landlord now converted into a foe."[28]

In southern Gonda, toward Faizabad, awards of subsettlement were more common. Yet even there the subproprietors' rights for the most part originated with the taluqdars themselves. Most usual was the so-called *bai birt*, under which impecunious rajas sold the rights of zamindari management of villages over which their hold was weak or ill-defined. The other common grant was that of *birt jangal tarashi*, under which an award of wasteland carried with it an understanding that the grantee should hold the land reclaimed on favorable terms. While powerful families like the Pandes ultimately suppressed these privileged tenancies, on the Mankapur and Babhnipair estates where the *birtias* were numerous and strong they successfully secured revenue rights in 1856, and at the revised settlement an underproprietary title.[29] In southeastern Oudh too, where the land was often held by compact clan groups, subordinate rights owed much to the voluntary act of the taluqdar, and extended well beyond the normal forms of subsettlement. Of Rampal Singh's 200 villages, for instance, in addition to the 34 held by old village zamindars as underproprietors, 48 were awarded by the

27. For the growth of an unfettered taluqdari power in Bahraich see *Oudh Gazetteer*, 1:177–78, 191–93; and *Oudh Rev. Admin. Report for 1866–67*, Part II, pp. 18–20. Only 2 percent, or 31,885 acres, of Bahraich was held in subsettlement. *Oudh Rev. Admin. Report for 1870–71*, Part II, pp. 7–8; and Nevill, *Bahraich D.G.*, p. 88.

28. Commr. Faizabad to C.C. 23 December 1873, B.R. Faizabad File 11, Part II. Of the over 700 Balrampur villages in Gonda district only 26 were awarded in subsettlement.

29. Nevill, *Gonda D.G.*, pp. 108–09. In Bahraich too *birt* grants for reclamation were common during the early days of settlement, but they were almost all reabsorbed into the estate of the original grantee. *Oudh Gazetteer*, 1:181–83. In Gonda district as a whole 17 percent of the land was held in subsettlement (*Gonda D.G.*, p. 76). Overall, throughout all twelve Oudh districts taken together, about 10 percent of the land was held in subsettlement. No comprehensive figures exist, but see *Report on the Administration of the N.W.P. and Oudh for 1882–83* (Allahabad, 1883), pp. 38–39.

taluqdar on perpetual leases to clansmen unable fully to prove their under-proprietary right, and a further 10 were alloted on the similar *guzara* tenure for the maintenance of the younger branches of various families.[30] Though often involving heavy rental payments, in the case of Rampal Singh's perpetual leases sometimes double the government revenue, these grants by reinforcing clan ties no doubt help account for the relative absence of agrarian strife in this area.

Subsettlement was not by itself an effective bar against erosion of the underproprietor's position. Above all, these men were hit hard by the intro-duction of the revised assessment. Despite the efforts of some early settlement officers, fearful of underproprietary discontent, to "humbug" the subordinate holders into believing that they would be maintained in their old position under the new arrangements, in fact the proportion of the govern-ment revenue that the underproprietor had to pay was alone fixed. He com-mitted himself, that is, to pay the government revenue demand plus a fixed additional percentage. Hence the entire burden of a sharply enhanced assess-ment, together with a further percentage now also grown much larger in absolute terms, fell upon his unsuspecting shoulders. The result, not surprisingly, was massive underproprietary default, and renewed animosity between superior and subordinate holder.[31]

As they watched their own income fall, the taluqdars, ever critical of the dilatory procedures of the courts, clamored for a more certain and summary means of realizing underproprietary arrears, preferably by distraint and sale. In this they won considerable support among the British, who saw their revenue imperiled as well by widespread default. In 1876 the taluqdars ob-tained a summary process similar to that the government itself possessed for the collection of revenue arrears.[32] Yet many of the taluqdars' troubles with the courts were of their own making. Maharaja Man Singh, for instance, on one occasion accumulated 374 rent decrees before pouring all of them into the court for execution within two days. On another, a full thirty years later, one of the Ajodhya (Mehdona) *mukhtars* (attorneys)

30. Assessment Report of Behar, Manikpur, and Rampur by J. Sanders, 5 February 1895, N.W.P.&O. Rev. Progs. July 1895, No. 67. On the Qila Pratabgarh estate 24 mahals were held on perpetual leases and 20 on guzara. See Nevill, *Partabgarh D.G.*, pp. 113-14; and *Sultanpur D.G.*, pp. 105-06.

31. C. Currie, Settle. Commr., to J. Reid (demi-official) 5 March 1863, B.R. Oudh General File 2235, Part I; Commr. Faizabad to P.A. to C.C. 23 December 1873, B.R. Faizabad File 11, Part II; Settle. Offr. Faizabad to Commr. Faizabad 19 September 1876, Oudh Rev. Progs. December 1876, No. 3; and Sec. Govt. India to Sec. Govt. N.W.P.&O. 11 August 1882, com-menting on the Faizabad Settlement Report, B.R. Faizabad File 11, Part III.

32. See Taluqdars' Memorandum on the Rent Bill (1868), and P. Carnegy's Memo of 29 February 1868, B.R. Oudh General File 2236; Offg. Commr. Rae Bareli to Sec. C.C. 5 Septem-ber 1871, and enclosed Report of Committee on Underproprietary Balances (of three taluqdars and three government officers, with J. Woodburn, Offg. Settle. Offr. Faizabad, as President), Oudh General File 2077; and Commr. Faizabad to Sec. C.C. 4 October 1871, *ibid.* See also MacAndrew, *Some Revenue Matters*, pp. 122-23. The special powers were conveyed under section 158 of the Oudh Revenue Act (XVII of 1876).

filed an application for recovery of arrears amounting to Rs. 66-3-3 from Talwand Singh. His deposition was duly recorded and the amount ordered to be realized. On the 7th August [one month later] the same Mukhtar filed an application for recovery of Rs. 57-6-3 against Chandi Singh and Talwand Singh. Both cases were sent to the tahsil and then after enquiry it was found that the second case was for the same demand from the same person for the same year. In other cases . . . credit is not given for sums collected, or the fixed pukhtadari rent is shown wrong, or the application is made for the recovery of arrears of two mahals at one time, the application being so drawn as to make it appear that there is only one mahal.[33]

The Ajodhya tenantry too, despite the maharaja's enhanced powers, remained stubborn and defiant. In 1899 the estate's agent complained that not only would the pukhtadars not pay "but they succeed in making the ordinary tenants discard their obligations," and the Maharaja Pratap Narayan, desperately in debt and in arrears, appealed to the government to take over responsibility for the collection of these rents, paying him as taluqdar a cash malikana instead.[34] The following year, moved by the same sense of frustration, and in part perhaps at the behest of their Life President, the taluqdars' association formally asked the government to relieve landlords of the necessity of collecting underproprietary rental arrears. The delays in the courts, and the expense of bringing these men to heel, they asserted, had become so great that they simply could no longer be borne. For the government, shocked, this was going too far. To allow the taluqdars to divest themselves of their responsibilities in this fashion, Antony MacDonnell, the Lieutenant Governor argued, would be "tantamount to modifying a principal condition of their sanads," and so would cut at "the very root" of the Oudh land system. Even Harcourt Butler protested that this scheme, by converting an estate owner's rent into revenue paid to the government, involved an "altogether untenable" alteration of the taluqdari settlement. The threat of sale would, he argued, be sufficient to bring these "most recusant and unreasonable of men" to pay their dues to their superiors.[35]

33. Depty. Commr. to Commr. Faizabad 14 December 1868, B.R. Oudh General File 118; and Depty. Commr. to Commr. Faizabad 18/21 November 1899, N.W.P.&O. Rev. Dept. File 823C.

34. Major Johnston, Agent Ajodhya, to Commr. Faizabad 21 July 1899, and Commr. Faizabad to Sec. Bd. Rev. 25 July 1899, N.W.P.&O. Rev. Dept. File 823C. For the maharaja's simultaneous attempt to secure an extraordinary enhancement of rent on ordinary tenant lands see above pp. 226–27.

35. Life Pres. B.I.A. to Sec. Govt. N.W.P.&O. 17 January 1900, N.W.P.&O. Rev. Progs. June 1900, No. 5; Settle. Offr. Kheri to Commr. Lucknow 6 March 1900, ibid., No. 12; and Chief Sec. Govt. N.W.P.&O. to Pres. B.I.A. 16 May 1900 ibid., No. 14. Those officials who were opposed in principle to taluqdari settlement, such as H. C. Irwin, as well as those faced as superintendents of encumbered estates with the onerous task of collecting rent from underproprietors, had long recommended the severance wherever possible of the tie between taluqdar and subsettlement holder, and direct collection by government of the latter's dues as revenue. See Irwin, Garden of India, p. 306; Annual Report for 1871–72 by A. H. Harington, Supt. Encum. Estates Faizabad, 28 February 1873, and Note of 30 November 1873, Oudh General File 2236; and Report on Oudh Encumbered and Court of Wards Estates for 1873–74 (Lucknow, 1875), pp. 22–23.

The outcome, then, of almost half a century of struggle between taluqdar and underproprietor was to give neither side a clear-cut victory. The taluqdars, not unsurprisingly, had the upper hand. Building upon the strength they had amassed during the later years of Nawabi rule, the taluqdars after 1859 turned to good advantage the support the new government, and its officers in Oudh, so readily extended to them. The strict rules of the 1866 act, together with the decision to tie the underproprietors' rents to a severely enhanced revenue demand, and to saddle them all too often with the "enormously heavy call" of an additional 50 percent, reduced many of these once independent communities to virtual impoverishment. So early as 1880 the Amsin Barwars were described as "very badly off," and their chiefs as "comparatively speaking poverty stricken gentlemen."[36] By the 1890s the settlement officers frequently observed that the subordinate proprietors' lot "is a hard one often," and they sometimes lowered the assessment so that it might press less heavily on them. In Pargana Dhingwas, for instance, in 1894 the underproprietors were reported to be living "like their own tenants and have no greater expenses than tenants of their own class. Many eke out their resources by cultivating as tenants in other villages . . . [while] in each under-proprietary family one or two members is in service in the Native Army or Police or elsewhere, and send remittances home whereby they have a surplus for luxuries."[37] Nor did the taluqdars relent in the pressure they brought to bear upon these men. When the holding of a defaulting underproprietor was brought to sale his superior almost always stepped forward as purchaser, and so extinguished the tenure.[38]

Yet the underproprietors were not wholly at the mercy of the taluqdar. As they were hard hit by an enhanced revenue demand, so too could they benefit from the growth of cash cropping, and the profits that brought with it. Indeed it might be argued that the existence of these profits spurred on the taluqdars in their challenge to underproprietary rights, and that the 1890s were a period of exceptional difficulty for these subordinate holders precisely because an enhancement of their revenue payments coincided with a temporary setback, exacerbated by drought and famine, in rural prosperity. The underproprietary communities too, where they were powerful and well

36. Millett, *Fyzabad S.R.*, pp. 280–81.

37. Pargana Dhingwas (Pratabgarh) Assessment Report by J. Sanders, 25 January 1894, N.W.P.&O. Rev. Progs. March 1895, No. 10(b) (para. 21). See also Pargana Aldemau (Sultanpur) Assessment Report by F. W. Brownrigg, 21 February 1895, N.W.P.&O. Rev. Progs. May 1895, No. 63 (para. 65); Pargana Rudauli (Bara Banki) Assessment Report by J. A. Norrie, 5 August 1896, N.W.P.&O. Rev. Progs. June 1897, No. 47 (para. 28); Pargana Rae Bareli Assessment Report by D. C. Baillie, n.d., N.W.P.&O. Rev. Progs. October 1897, No. 65 (para. 12); and Settle. Commr. to Sec. Bd. Rev. 23 October 1897, commenting on the Haveli Awadh (Faizabad) Assessment Report, N.W.P.&O. Rev. Progs. May 1898, No. 20 (para. 4).

38. See, e.g., Assessment Report of Pargana Baraunsa (Sultanpur) by F. W. Brownrigg, 7 August 1896, N.W.P.&O. Rev. Progs. June 1897, No. 42 (para. 49); MacAndrew, *Some Revenue Matters*, p. 29; and Nevill, *Rae Bareli D.G.*, p. 103.

organized, sometimes gave teeth to their defiance by threatening physical violence against those who sought to displace them. In Faizabad, though heavily indebted, the subsettlement holders were not, so H. F. House reported in 1899, more frequently "extruded" from control of their lands because "from their number and their lawless spirit, they would be apt to render a purchaser's life a burden to him, and the possession of their inheritance a loss to him rather than a gain."[39] The underproprietors' position, even where they had not gained a full subsettlement, was further strengthened by their high-caste status. As the Settlement Commissioner wrote of the Ajodhya lands in Mangalsi, "High caste tenants hold considerably more than half the cash rented area; and numbers of them, as representing the former proprietors, possess *sir* and other underproprietary tenures in addition to their ordinary holdings. This gives them an exceptionally strong position; and it would be difficult for the taluqdar to raise their rents materially even if the provisions of the Oudh Rent Act were not in force."[40]

The old village holders, even under taluqdari overlordship, thus remained into the twentieth century a force to be reckoned with in rural Oudh. Their role was not however that of peasant leaders. Though they sometimes rallied the ordinary tenantry to their side, they fought for their own interests—above all for the preservation of their privileged status—not for any general amelioration of the condition of the rural masses. Ajodhya estate was the focus of so much of the protest not because the tenantry there were exceptionally badly treated, but because the manner of its creation, in the years just before annexation, had kept alive in its cohesive Rajput proprietary bodies the memory of the years when they had held their lands directly from the government. A truly peasant-based protest had to await the crisis of the 1920s, and the appearance of such outside leaders as Baba Ramchandra.[41] The effect of the underproprietary struggle was neither to mobilize the peasantry, nor to shake the taluqdari system, for even hard-pressed Ajodhya survived as a flourishing enterprise, but rather to mark out limits to the taluqdars' control of the resources of the countryside. Rural Oudh was not theirs alone.

39. H. F. House, *Final Report on the Settlement of Fyzabad District, 31 December 1899* (Allahabad, 1900), p. 3. See also Millett, *Fyzabad S.R.*, p. 401. A half-century later, in 1942, apart from Khandasa where shares were fractional and the holders hardly distinguishable from ordinary tenants, Faizabad subsettlement holdings averaged five acres, or about the same size as those of the district's smaller zamindars. S. M. Abbas Zaidi, *Final Settlement Report of Fyzabad* (Allahabad, 1942), p. 4.

40. Note by Settle. Commr. of 8 April 1897, N.W.P.&O. Rev. Progs. July 1897, No. 25. No doubt the existence of these low-rented holdings gave added impetus to the estate's efforts after 1900 to raise rental income. It is not clear how far they were caught up in that undertaking. Favorable rents, from 15 to 30 percent below those paid by ordinary cultivators, were common throughout the province on the lands of high-caste Brahmin and Rajput tenants.

41. See M. A. Siddiqi, "The Peasant Movement in Pratapgarh, 1920," *IESHR* 9 (1972): 305-26 for an account of Ramchandra and evidence of antagonism between the underproprietors and the Kurmi-based *kisan* movement. Further study might however reveal links between these old proprietary bodies, as natural village leaders, and the rural protest of the 1920s.

The Management of the Estate: Structure and Personnel

In order to collect their rents the taluqdars, like estate owners everywhere, had to rely upon a staff of agents and servants. These men, sometimes known collectively as *karindas*, were responsible for the day-to-day operation of the estate, not only collecting rent but meting out justice and helping to maintain law and order, and so played a critical role as intermediaries between the taluqdar and his tenantry. Yet they have so far remained almost wholly invisible in the vast literature on rural India.[42]

The size and geographical contiguity (or lack of it) of an estate determined much of its administration. The smaller the estate, and the more compact, the more informally it could be run. The larger properties by contrast developed bureaucratic structures rivaling in complexity, and often duplicating in detail, those of the British Indian government. At its most rudimentary, on tiny properties of half a dozen villages, the landlord would employ only a few servants, with whose assistance he personally collected the rents due him. On slightly larger estates the villages would be grouped into two or three circles, each placed under the charge of a *ziladar* responsible for collecting the rents from his villages. The Isanpur taluqa, for instance, with fifteen villages in Pratabgarh district, employed two ziladars, each assisted by two sepoys, and one *sarbarakhar* or overseer. At the taluqdar's headquarters (*sadr*) were a mukhtar and a clerk-cashier.[43] On middling-sized taluqas of 40 to 100 or so villages a manager would be placed above the sarbarakhar, a second sarbarakhar might be taken on if the estate were scattered, and the numbers of ziladars and headquarters staff would be correspondingly increased. The Khajurhat estate in Faizabad, for instance, divided its 50 villages into five ziladari circles, while nearby Hanswar, with about the same revenue assessment but spread over some 42 whole and 200 portions of villages throughout Birhar pargana, employed twelve ziladars, each with a clerk and six sepoys, grouped under an eastern and a western circle officer.[44] The largest estates—those of over 100 villages—added an assistant manager, further ziladars and supervisory sarbarakhars, together with a highly specialized headquarters staff. The Tiloi estate, with 130 villages assessed at a lakh and a half of rupees, had twenty-two ziladars, each with three sepoys, under four sarbarakhars, and at the center two *peshkars*

42. Two recent short accounts are P. J. Musgrave, "Landlords and Lords of the Land: Estate Management and Social Control in Uttar Pradesh, 1860-1920," *Modern Asian Studies* 6 (1972):257-75; and T. Raychaudhuri, "Permanent Settlement in Operation: Bakarganj District, East Bengal," in R. E. Frykenberg, ed., *Land Control and Social Structure*, pp. 163-74. The former is however based entirely upon British sources, and uses no estate or family records, while the latter is largely a product of the author's personal recollections.

43. Interview with Thakur Rameshwar Prasad Singh, taluqdar of Isanpur, Pratabgarh, 16 December 1969.

44. Interviews with Audhesh Pratap Singh, taluqdar of Khajurhat, Faizabad, 5 December 1969; and Nripendra Bahadur Singh, taluqdar of Hanswar, Faizabad, 6 December 1969. For the peculiar history of Hanswar, and its twin Makrahi, with which it shared many villages, see Nevill, *Fyzabad D.G.*, pp. 90-91.

(assistants), one each for the manager and the taluqdar, an accountant, several treasury officers, various mukhtars, and a recordkeeper.[45] At the very top of the estate hierarchy, on such behemoths as Balrampur, where the problems of administration were complex and demanding, the taluqdars sometimes abandoned the ziladari system altogether in favor of leasing villages in blocks to thikadars, or rent-farmers, who in return for handing over a sum of money fixed in advance were given free rein in the management of their holdings. The headquarters staff, of course, remained large and diverse.[46]

At the same time, the administrative structure on all but the smallest estates, not unlike bureaucracies elsewhere, tended to grow in size and complexity. In part no doubt this reflected the influence of British Indian models of government, with their elaborate hierarchies and division of responsibility. It may sometimes too have been tied to the landholder's desire to increase the income from his estate by tightening the administrative net over it, or even simply to find jobs for the clamorous retainers who hung about him. The raja of Mahmudabad, for instance, over the last quarter of the nineteenth century, abandoned the Court of Wards instituted contracting system, under which the estate's villages were let out in blocks to *dafadars* as a device to lower the cost of management, and introduced in its place direct administration through tahsildars. By the 1930s the number of tahsils had mushroomed from an initial eight to some forty-four, while the supervisory post of *munsarim*, equivalent to that of sarbarakhar, and originally instituted to provide more effective control over the isolated Kasta tract, had spread to encompass the entire estate.[47] The initial change to the tahsil system at least was clearly a product of the raja's anxiety to keep his retainers employed and yet a good distance away from his own residence.[48]

Central to the operation of the estate were the ziladars (or tahsildars). These men, at the bottom of the administrative ladder, and comparable in the small world of the estate to the British district Collector, carried on its day-to-day affairs in the countryside. With their attendant sepoys they moved continuously through the villages of their circle. In each they collected rents as they fell due from the individual villagers, relying on the sepoys to produce recalcitrant tenants, and then deposited the proceeds in the estate treasury; they nominated candidates for vacant tenancies; and they acted as an

45. Interview with P.N.S. Singh, raja of Tiloi, Lucknow, 12 March 1970.
46. For Balrampur see below ch. 10.
47. Interviews with Amir Haidar Khan, Maharajkumar Mahmudabad, Lucknow, 30 October 1969; and Ali Bahadur Habibullah, Manager Mahmudabad estate 1931–38, Lucknow, 9 March 1970. For the introduction of the dafadar system see Depty. Commr. Sitapur to Commr. Khairabad 15 October 1862, B.R. Sitapur File 209; and Ali Hasan, "Tarikh-i-Mahmudabad" (Urdu) (n.d.), 2:2:105. Under this system the management charges were reduced from Rs. 1,800 to 1,050 per month. For a description of the system in existence before 1862, which the author erroneously implies remained in effect throughout, see P. J. Musgrave, "Landlords and Lords of the Land," pp. 267–68.
48. Ali Hasan, "Tarikh-i-Mahmudabad," 2:2:106.

informal court of first resort in disputes between tenants. The latter were mostly civil cases—disputes over boundaries, groves, and water rights—but included petty fights and affrays as well where both parties were tenants of the estate. The sarbarakhar, who was usually supplied with a horse for touring, checked the ziladars' accounts, listened to appeals by dissatisfied tenants, and in general acted as a sort of estate version of the British Divisional Commissioner. The manager toured as well, during the winter, usually on elephant, spending a few days in each circle to inspect the crops, hear complaints, on larger estates as the final court of appeal, and to ensure that the subordinate staff were up to the mark. His was the deciding voice too in the placement of new tenants in their holdings.

The bulk of the manager's work, however, lay at estate headquarters, where he directed the work of the various mukhtars and other specialized staff. He kept the taluqdar informed by regular oral or written reports, and handled as well the estate's relations with the British, often conveying himself the revenue payments in cash to the district treasury. Far more than the taluqdar he was likely to know English as well as Urdu, and so helped prepare the suits and petitions that were to go to the courts or government officials.[49] The taluqdar's own involvement in estate affairs, as we shall see, varied widely from individual to individual, depending in large part on taste and temperament. Some, usually on smaller estates where the bureaucracy was less formidable, were active and readily accessible to their tenants; most intervened occasionally, often forcefully but sometimes arbitrarily; while others were remote grandees, concerned with little but their own pleasure. For almost all taluqdars tours of their estates were a by-product of *shikar* (shooting) expeditions.

What kind of men staffed these various posts, and how were they recruited? The Mahmudabad estate, upon the death of the old raja Nawab Ali Khan during the last days of the revolt, fell to his minor son Amir Hasan Khan. The Court of Wards at once took charge of the property, and a few months later brought in a manager of its own, a Punjabi, Ram Datta Mal, formerly Agent of the raja of Mandi and *mir munshi* (superintendent) in the Chief Commissioner's office. "Capable and honest," Ram Datta not unnaturally soon fell out with the dowager rani, who proceeded to flood the district offices with petitions demanding his removal. The harried Sitapur district Collector on one occasion threw one of the rani's partisans out of his office, while the Chief Commissioner threatened to have the lot of them run off the estate. In the end, however, the government bowed before the storm, and replaced Ram Datta Mal, first with another official, Babu Har Prasad Bhargava, and then, when he was promoted to Deputy Collector, with Maulvi Mazhar Ali, a petty landholder who owed his position as taluqdar to

49. Interview with L.P.S. Singh, Manager Mankapur Estate 1944-1952, Mankapur, 9 January 1970; S. N. Saksena, Manager Kasmanda Estate 1939-1952, Lucknow, 12 March 1970; and the interviews cited in the preceding notes.

Chart 4. Mahmudabad Estate

Manager		Assistant Manager	
?-1859	Munshi Nisar Ali	1862-1867	Munshi Ahmad Husain (*naib sarbarakhar*)[a]
1859-1862	Munshi Ram Datta Mal	1862-1890	Lala Sita Ram (*peshkar*)[a]
1862-?	Babu Har Prasad Bhargava	1890-1891	Lala Bachu Lal (*diwan*)
?-1867	Maulvi Mazhar Ali	1892-1904	Munshi Wajid Ali Khan (*diwan*)
1867-1869	Qasim Ali Khan		
1869-1890	Nawab Ali Husain Khan	1905-1916	Sheikh Ashiq Ali
1890-1891	Lala Sita Ram	1916-1919	Chaudhuri Asghar Ali
1891-1905	Sheikh Inayatullah	1919-	Maulvi Ahmad Hasan
1905-1931	Sheikh Muhammad Habibullah		

[a]These two posts were created by the Court of Wards to provide effective supervision of the *dafadars*, or lessees, who collected the estate's rents. The first lapsed on the release of the estate, while the *peshkar* remained as de facto assistant to the manager.

his loyalty in 1857, and who had worked as Har Prasad's assistant.[50] (See Chart 4.)

In March 1867 the eighteen-year-old Raja Amir Hasan Khan took over the management of the estate. He promptly dismissed the court's manager and assistant, replacing them with two of his own uncles, both of whom, he said, had "always taken a lively interest in the estate." The Deputy Commissioner, who thought well especially of Ali Husain, who took sole charge of the estate after two years, gave his blessing to the scheme, while Amir Hasan on his side agreed to retain the whole of the remaining staff employed by the Court of Wards.[51] Seniormost among these were a group of Kayasthas (the scribe or writer caste), headed by Munshi Sita Ram, who lived together in a separate quarter of Mahmudabad town. After serving the Nawabs, Sita Ram had worked for the British as *wasilbaqi-navis* in Bari tahsil of Sitapur before being brought as peshkar to Mahmudabad, where he stayed for the rest of his life. Under him were the estate *wasilbaqi-navis* and *siyaha-navis* (accountants), Lalta Parshad and Kalka Parshad, as well as two Kayastha brothers who held the posts of *bakhshi* (pay clerk) and *muhafiz-daftar* (record keeper), all of whom owed their initial appointments to the Court of Wards.[52] There were in addition a number of senior Muslim employees—the estate physician, the office superintendent, and the manager's private secretary among

50. Ali Hasan, "Tarikh-i-Mahmudabad," 2:1:27-32; and Sec. C.C. to Commr. Khairabad 28 May 1860, Depty. Commr. Sitapur to Commr. Khairabad 21 August 1861, and *passim*, B.R. Sitapur File 209. Nisar Ali, first manager under the Court of Wards, had been manager for Nawab Ali Khan before his death.

51. Amir Hasan to Depty. Commr. Sitapur 8 March 1867, and Depty. Commr. Sitapur to Commr. Khairabad 11 March 1867, B.R. Sitapur File 409. See also Ali Hasan, "Tarikh-i-Mahmudabad," 2:1:78-82.

52. *Ibid.*, 2:1:83, and 2:1:93-97. A third brother was assistant record keeper. Their father had been bakhshi to the nazim of Khairabad under the Nawabi.

them—who came from a family of respected *sufi pirs* of Fatehpur and had long been associated with the estate. Amir Hasan also took on a few new men, largely to look after newly purchased or distant tracts. Sayyid Tajammul Husain, a *rais* (noble) of Bara Banki, who had besought the raja for employment even while the estate was under the Court of Wards, was, for instance, appointed as the estate's attorney for settlement cases in Kheri district.[53]

A learned Sheikh, schooled in Persian and Arabic, and familiar with British administrative practice from a long residence in Bareilly, Ali Husain Khan served with distinction as the estate's manager until his death in 1890. Indeed he left the estate richer by four lakhs of rupees, squirreled away in the treasury. For a successor the raja turned to Ali Husain's long-time deputy, Sita Ram. Unfortunately, despite Sita Ram's detailed knowledge of the affairs of the estate, this appointment turned out to be a mistake. So long habituated to the style and manner of a *lala* (subordinate clerk), Sita Ram could not overnight, so the Mahmudabad historian informs us, take on the "dignity of an officer," or talk comfortably with the European district authorities. Dismissed after a year and a half, he was replaced by Sheikh Inayatullah, taluqdar of Saidanpur in Bara Banki district.[54]

The Saidanpur taluqdars had long had close ties of friendship with their neighbors of Mahmudabad. Inayatullah's father Sheikh Wajahatullah had been counsellor to Nawab Ali Khan, receiving in return an allowance, ostensibly for kitchen expenses, of Rs. 100 a month. The sons continued the same relationship, Inayatullah even looking after the Mahmudabad estate's legal and other interests in Lucknow, where he maintained his residence. The then manager, Ali Husain, resented Inayatullah's privileged access to the raja, and so contrived to have him sent off as munsarim of the estate's isolated Kasta property in Kheri district. Even then Inayatullah retained his Lucknow residence, and his position of confidential adviser to the raja, discharging his duties in Kasta during a brief two- or three-month stay each year.[55] His appointment to the charge of the estate in 1891 was thus in some measure only a formal recognition of this long-standing intimacy. Yet at the same time it inaugurated a new relationship between the Mahmudabad and Saidanpur families, one that was to endure for over fifty years and three generations.

As manager, Inayatullah soon gained a reputation for astute dealing. Harcourt Butler called him in 1897 "the shrewdest native in these parts," and remarked in wonderment that "I never know now, after four years intimate acquaintance, when he is genuine and when he is not." Still, he concluded,

53. *Ibid.*, 2:1:84, and 2:1:98.
54. For Ali Husain see *ibid.*, 2:1:102–03, 203–05, and 2:2:61–62. For Sita Ram, *ibid.*, 2:1:206, 236, and 2:2:63–66.
55. For the early connection between the Mahmudabad and Saidanpur families see *ibid.*, 2:2:67–74.

Sheikh Inayatullah.

"It is impossible not to like him, he is so entertaining."[56] Perhaps the most conspicuous feature of Inayatullah's years as manager of the Mahmudabad estate was his unremitting attempt to curb the lavish expenditure to which the raja and his son Ali Muhammad were addicted. On taking office he consolidated the estate's various debts into one massive loan from the Delhi-London Bank, which he secured by a mortgage of the entire property. A decade later, with the debt at last cleared by a rigorous campaign of economy and rental enhancement, the latter undertaken with scant regard for the provisions of the Rent Act, the headstrong Ali Muhammad, not yet even on the *gaddi*, plunged the estate into debt once again, over Inayatullah's strenuous objections, in order to take up a mortgage of the bankrupt Isanagar property.[57]

For the most part, however, throughout the years that Inayatullah, and after him his son Sheikh Muhammad Habibullah, had charge of the Mahmudabad estate theirs was the decisive voice in its administration. Under Habibullah, especially, no appeal could be carried from the manager to the raja. In all except intimate personal matters, such as Ali Muhammad's taking of a second wife, which Habibullah protested unavailingly, he simply acted as he saw fit, and the raja acquiesced. An anecdote, perhaps apocryphal, has it that when Ali Muhammad, now maharaja, promised Motilal Nehru three lakhs as a contribution to the Congress, but Habibullah refused

56. Butler to his family 12 January 1897, Butler Papers IOL MSS. Eur. F.116/5.
57. Ali Hasan, "Tarikh-i-Mahmudabad," 2:2:75–78. The mortgage was ultimately redeemed when Kapurthala stood surety for the Isanagar debts. For the life style, and expenditures, of the Mahmudabad rajas see below ch. 12.

to disburse the funds, he simply threw up his hands and said, "The world says that I am maharaja, but I say Habibullah is maharaja." Perhaps because of this, and partly also to secure his independence, so that he might freely criticize the raja, Habibullah took a salary from the estate of only Rs. 300 per month, known as *kharch-i-pandan* (money for *pan*).[58]

This extraordinary delegation of authority was no doubt in part a product of Ali Muhammad's waning interest, after his initial youthful burst of enthusiasm, in the problems of estate administration, as compared with the more attractive pursuits of politics and the arts. Yet it was possible only because of the relationship of reciprocated trust and confidence between the two families which had been built up over time and was cemented anew in each generation. Ali Muhammad and Habibullah, separated in age by only a few years, and playmates from childhood, grew up almost as brothers, with Habibullah, as the elder, given, perhaps on that account, an even greater measure of deference. Sheikh Habibullah was, moreover, exceptionally well qualified for his wide-ranging responsibilities. Educated in English from his youth, he was the first taluqdar to obtain a university degree, and the first to be appointed a Deputy Collector, in which position he served for several years before taking up his estate duties and again near the end of his term in the 1920s. He thus easily commanded respect both within the government and without.[59] Habibullah's son Ali Bahadur, on his return in 1928 from his education in Europe, was similarly taken into Mahmudabad service as a matter of course, and treated by the maharaja as his own son. For both Habibullahs, their Saidanpur properties, which they hardly ever visited, always took second place to their work for Mahmudabad, and their involvement in taluqdari politics in Lucknow. Precisely why this should be so remains a puzzling question. No doubt their estate was small, and the opportunities for power and profit were greater across the district border in Mahmudabad. Nor were they the only taluqdars who worked for larger neighbors. Yet the Saidanpur taluqdars enjoyed a uniquely privileged intimacy with their masters, which surely helped sustain the relationship.[60]

Most of the top administrative personnel on the Mahmudabad estate were recruited from amongst the friends and relatives of the taluqdar or manager.

58. Interviews with Ali Bahadur Habibullah (see n. 47 above); and I. Habibullah, Karachi, 26 May 1974. Both were sons of Muhammad Habibullah. As manager M. Habibullah also criticized, and himself rewrote, a will Ali Muhammad had drawn up gifting portions of the estate and a fixed maintenance allowance to the second wife and her family. The one area of the estate's operations Habibullah stayed clear of was the kitchen, so that no one could blame any poisoning attempts, or the raja's illnesses, on him.

59. Ali Hasan, "Tarikh-i-Mahmudabad," 2:2:79, 3:1:137, and 3:2:120-24. Throughout his estate service Habibullah retained his substantive appointment, and salary, as a Deputy Collector. This, together with his Saidanpur rentals, provided the bulk of his income.

60. Interviews with Ali Bahadur Habibullah (see n. 47 above), and I. Habibullah (see n. 58 above). The Habibullah family always maintained its primary residence in Lucknow. In part this was to enable the children to escape the confining "feudal" atmosphere of the countryside, and to facilitate the maintenance of their distinctive anglicized style of life. See below p. 367.

Wajid Ali Khan, diwan under Inayatullah, was first brought into estate service by his neighbor from Bareilly, Nawab Ali Husain Khan, while the latter was manager. Initially hired as an *amin* at Rs. 15 a month, Wajid Ali rose under the Nawab's patronage to supervisor of building construction, and then, after catching the raja's eye, to charge of Mahmudabad tahsil before his appointment as Inayatullah's deputy. Successive munsarims of Kasta, an important post because of the relative isolation of that portion of the estate in Kheri district, where it received little supervision from the manager, were Nawab Ali Khan, the raja's maternal uncle, jointly with Sheikh Ikram Ali, Inayatullah's cousin, Sheikh Ali Husain Fatehpuri, a nephew of a former manager of the estate for Raja Nawab Ali Khan, and Munshi Hadi Hasan, a Bara Banki zamindar befriended by Nawab Ali Khan who served Amir Hasan as the estate's agent in Lucknow until his appointment as munsarim of Kasta.[61]

Yet men from outside, wholly unconnected with the estate, were from time to time brought into its service. Such men most frequently came from government, where they commanded skills the estate also required. Sheikh Ashiq Ali, Wajid Ali's successor as assistant manager, had previously been a sarbarakhar under the Court of Wards, while another sarbarakhar of the Court of Wards at one time held the post of munsarim of Kasta, and Court of Wards ziladars were sometimes brought over as estate tahsildars. Sheikh Habibullah himself hired as accountants for the estate a retired *sadr qanungo* of Lakhimpur and a treasury clerk whom he had met during his own years of government service.[62]

Once a family had succeeded in gaining a footing in estate service, it quickly put down roots. The Kayastha brothers who had come to Mahmudabad under the Court of Wards, for instance, kept the estate record office under their family's control for several generations. When the eldest brother Kalka Parshad died in 1881, his younger brother Lalta Parshad, who had been his assistant, took charge of the office. Upon his death in 1906 his nephew Sita Ram was in his turn appointed record keeper. Meanwhile Govind Parshad, Lalta Parshad's son, who had initially planned to go into government, and had been appointed booking clerk in Benares Cantonment—for the traffic between government and estate service did not flow only in one direction—joined the estate instead and rose ultimately to the post of wasilbaqi-navis. But a modicum of competence was essential. When the third brother Shiv Dayal, who had been estate bakhshi, died, his son Lala Chedi Lal succeeded to the post. But as "his abilities were not equal to the demands of the position," he was soon demoted and ultimately retired on pension.[63]

61. Ali Hasan, "Tarikh-i-Mahmudabad," 2:2:83–93. In Habibullah's time as well "many" of his relatives and friends were in estate service. Among them was Chaudhuri Asghar Ali, Habibullah's son-in-law, assistant manager 1916–19. *Ibid.*, 3:2:125, 128.

62. *Ibid.*, 3:2:126–28, 134–35. Ashiq Ali was however "distantly related" both to the raja and Habibullah.

63. Ali Hasan, "Tarikh-i-Mahmudabad," 2:2:96–97; and 3:2:136–37.

Similar patterns of recruitment and promotion can be found elsewhere. The Taroul, later Qila Pratabgarh estate, when it was awarded to Ajit Singh for his loyalty during the Mutiny, comprised some ninety villages assessed at Rs. 14,699. Ajit was given in addition a revenue-free *jagir* yielding Rs. 10,000 annually. Initially this comprised 34 of the villages taken from the raja of Bhinga as a punishment for his attempt to conceal cannon. In fact however this property, the Deotaha estate, though included in the Bhinga raja's sanad, was not held by him in full proprietorship. So the government in 1876 made over to the Taroul raja instead five villages in Unao, sixteen in Hardoi, and twenty-four in Kheri, assessed at Rs. 16,227.[64]

By the 1890s, under Raja Pratab Bahadur Singh, the administrative machinery of the estate was headed by a diwan, or manager, from 1892 to 1894 Swami Sewak Singh and then Munshi Harprasad Singh. Under him were four senior administrative officers, the *naib* (deputy) diwan, and the heads of the revenue, judicial, and treasury departments. Together these men, subject only to the raja, ran the day-to-day affairs of the estate and controlled its personnel. Altogether separate was the raja's private secretariat. Its top officials—the *peshdast* and the *mutamad-i-khanagi*—were accorded a status only slightly lower than that of the five chief administrators. The peshdast handled the raja's official correspondence, sending out letters and orders in his name, inspected and reported on the working of the various estate departments, and in general acted as the raja's right-hand man for all estate business. The mutamad-i-khanagi supervised the raja's kitchen and domestic arrangements. He was in charge of the palace and its staff, and the entertainment of guests. For a brief two and one-half year period, from 1896 to 1898, Pratab Bahadur experimented with the notion of bringing all his top administrative personnel together in an executive committee. During these years the diwanship was formally abolished, and the committee members shared responsibility for all decision-making. For the most part, however, such collaboration being too cumbrous, each officer held charge of his own separate post, with the powers allotted to each laid down in elaborate detail in the estate *Dastur-ul-amal*, or management manual.[65] (See Chart 5.)

As on the Mahmudabad estate, the top officers were recruited either from government employ, or from the families of those already working for the estate. The two seniormost officials in the later 1890s, Munshi Harprasad Singh and Maulvi Saadat Husain, both old and trusted friends of Pratab

---

64. Commr. Faizabad to Finanl. Commr. 17 July 1867, and Sec. C.C. Oudh to Sec. Govt. India 4 March 1872, 1 September 1873, and 14 February 1876, B.R. Pratabgarh File 62. For a list of the estate's holdings, and a summary of the Deotaha controversy, see B. N. Tholal, *Sombansi Raj*, pp. 75, 101-03. By 1893 the original Taroul taluqa had grown by purchase to include 135 villages assessed at Rs. 65,579. Ajit Singh also purchased the Shahabpur estate in the adjacent district of Allahabad, and scattered villages elsewhere.

65. *Dastur-ul-amal-i-riyasat-i-qila pratabgarh* (Urdu) (Pratabgarh, 1900), esp. chs. i, ii, and vi. The volume is 328 pages in length. For the 1896 arrangements see the 1897 edition of this *dastur*.

Chart 5. Senior Employees, Qila Pratabgarh Estate, 1899[a]

1. *Diwan-i-riyasat* (manager)   Munshi Harprasad Singh
2. *Afsar sigha-i-adalat* (chief judicial officer)   Maulvi Saadat Husain
3. *Afsar sigha-i-mal* (chief revenue officer)   Munshi Mahendar Singh
4. *Afsar sigha-i-khazana* (chief treasury officer)   Munshi Satnarayan Singh
5. *Peshdast*   Munshi Surajpal Singh (acting)
6. *Munshi-i-peshi* (English clerk)   Munshi Prabunath
7. *Mutamad-i-khanagi* (personal assistant)   Raghubir Saran Singh
8. *Naib mutamad-i-khanagi* (deputy personal assistant)   Pandit Shiv Prasad
9. *Assistant afsar sigha-i-mal*   Lal Singh
10. *Assistant afsar sigha-i-mal*   Naresh Bahadur Singh
11. *Mukhtar* (pleader)   Munshi Durga Prasad
12. *Mukhtar*   Sheikh Mufarrih-ud-din

[a]For a list of the top 33 employees of the estate see Pratab Bahadur's Urdu manuscript diary, entry for 27 March 1899. The post of *naib diwan* was then vacant.

Bahadur from the days before he took charge of the estate, came over at his request from government service. The latter, whose initial contact with the estate had been that of arranging the lighting at festivals, gave up the head-mastership of the Pratabgarh Government High School in 1890 for the post of mutamad-i-khanagi. After a stint as the estate's chief mukhtar he was in 1898 given charge of the judicial department. Pratab Bahadur likewise hired for the estate his old Persian tutor, Mir Bande Ali, a man for whom he had "great respect," and who had been employed as *sarishtadar* in the honorary magistrate's office, paid partly by the estate and partly by the government. Appointed *sar-i-daftar* (head clerk) in 1890, Bande Ali later served as *girda-war* (officer on circuit), acting peshdast, and second ranking member of the executive committee, before resigning from service on grounds of ill health in 1898.

Harprasad Singh's predecessor as diwan, Swami Sewak Singh, and Munshi Mahendar Singh, chief revenue officer from 1898, were by contrast from families long connected with the estate. Both owed their rise under Pratab Bahadur to the fact that leading members of their families, above all Basheshar Singh, Mahendar's father, who had been a powerful karinda in the early 1880s, had fallen out with Raja Ajit Singh, and so turned to the heir apparent. This alliance, given depth by the youthful friendship of Pratab Bahadur with Basheshar's nephew Shiv Saran Singh, grew over the years until by the time Ajit Singh died in 1889 Pratab Bahadur considered trust-worthy only the members of this family. As he recollected some years later, after he had shaken loose their dominance, "the reason I used to trust Basheshar Singh and Sewak Singh was that when I was living in the fort they used to complain about Raja Ajit Singh in front of me and gave me the impression that they were very obedient and loyal servants of mine."[66]

The top estate employees were paid partly in cash and partly by the award of *dawami pattas* (permament leases) of estate villages. When Harprasad Singh was appointed permanent diwan in 1896, his salary was fixed at two hundred silver rupees a month, while Shyam Bihari Lal, peshdast in 1890, got one hundred. Far more lucrative, and more coveted, were the dawami pattas. Ajit Singh gave such grants to Basheshar Singh and to a number of other employees and servants, including even his litter bearer. Pratab Bahadur in his turn gave dawami pattas to his two successive diwans, Swami Sewak Singh and Harprasad Singh, as well as to his cousin Samar Bahadur Singh, to a subpostmaster and a *darogha* (steward), among others. Together these grants involved some 25 villages of the estate and cost it by 1899 Rs. 4,500 a year. But such permanent leases by no means always secured the loyal service of the recipient. While the dawami patta tied its holder to the estate, at the same time it encouraged him to flaunt his independence of the raja. Swami Sewak Singh, or so Pratab Bahadur complained, neglected his duties as diwan once he had obtained his dawami patta, and even insolently refused to receive the raja when the latter visited his village during the course of an estate tour. "This clearly shows," the raja recorded later, "the effect a dawami patta has on a person." Sewak Singh was fired, but Pratab Bahadur nevertheless continued to give out these leases.[67]

The employees of the estate were transferred frequently from post to post—at least seven men paraded through the office of peshdast between 1890 and 1899—and they seem rarely, despite the elaborate bureaucratization of estate service which had taken place since the early days of Ajit Singh, when all orders were given verbally, to have been encouraged to develop much specialized expertise. Competence in Urdu was required for most top officeholders; among Pratab Bahadur's complaints against Sewak Singh was that he knew only Hindi. The peshdast, or more usually the *peshi* clerk, was expected to know English, for someone was needed in the raja's private secretariat who could draft English letters and read out the English newspapers for him. There were in addition two senior officers appointed solely for their technical skills. These men—the legal adviser and the head pandit—were exempt from the normal rules of subordination, and were not transferred. The legal adviser, appointed from among the lawyers at the district bar, helped in the preparation of legal documents and argued important cases for

66. See Pratab Bahadur's "Memoirs," covering the years through 1898, written in Urdu in his own hand, December 1898, esp. Part I (through 1892), pp. 65–66, 90–92, 97, and *passim*. Basheshar Singh finally resigned from estate service in 1896.

67. Pratab Bahadur, "Memoirs," Part I, pp. 96–98; and Part II (1893–1895), pp. 10–12. See Sanders, *Pratabgarh S.R.*, Appendix X, pp. 88ff. for a list of the estate's subsettled, permanently leased, and *guzara* (maintenance grant) villages. Though stripped of the diwanship, Sewak Singh remained in estate employ as a member of the Executive Committee until 1898.

the estate in the British courts. Kishan Lal, who succeeded Sheikh Ataullah in this post in 1892, was a trusted friend of Pratab Bahadur, and served the estate, like many such lawyers elsewhere, in areas far removed from his formal charge. He arranged, for instance, the purchase of the key village of Nagra in Kheri district, winning in the process a Rs. 4,000 commission, and he served on the local district board, to which he was elected in 1896 after an energetic lobbying campaign on his behalf by the raja.[68] Apart from these few exceptional posts, however, all senior estate staff were available for service wherever the raja chose to employ them. In this, of course, the estate was not so very different from the British Indian government, whose officers themselves proudly proclaimed an ideal of omnicompetence.

One further qualification for senior estate service, though perhaps an implicit one, was high-caste status. Almost all the top Hindu employees of the estate were, so far as one can judge from the names, either Brahmin, Rajput, or Kayastha. Among the top twenty officers in 1899 only one, the *khazanchi* (treasurer), Ram Autar a *lohar* (ironsmith), was of low caste, and he had held the same post for ten years. Even more clear-cut evidence of discrimination was Pratab Bahadur's decision in 1890, following Ajit Singh's lavish award of dawami pattas, to reduce the number of villages held by low-caste *pattidars*, but not others, to one each. Religious affiliation seems by contrast to have been of relatively little consequence. Pratab Bahadur was fully aware of which of his employees were Hindu and which Muslim, but such distinctions were not matters of serious import. Once when one of his employees, Bihari Lal, in 1891 gave his name to the census taker as "Qudratullah," Pratab Bahadur, although himself a devout Hindu, enjoyed the joke with the rest. As raja, Pratab Bahadur hired and promoted Muslims with unselfconscious frequency. Among his closest associates, as we have seen, were Maulvi Saadat Husain and Mir Bande Ali. On one occasion in 1891 the diwan, Munshi Ahmad Ali Shauq, the peshdast, and the mutamad-i-khanagi were all Muslims. Indeed it was a Muslim, the legal adviser Sheikh Ataullah, who encouraged Pratab Bahadur to cut down the size of low-caste dawami pattas.[69] A traditionally educated elite, with skills much in demand, Muslims were as likely to be overrepresented in estate administration as they were in government service itself.

The Muslim Mahmudabad estate, reflecting perhaps the devoutly religious character of its rulers, was more self-consciously communal than others in its employment practices. Yet even there, although the Hindu staff was confined for the most part to Kayastha clerks and accountants, promo-

68. For the duties of the legal adviser and head pandit see the 1900 *Dastur*, pp. 59–66. For Kishan Lal see Pratab Bahadur, "Memoirs," Part I, pp. 92, 100, 110; and Part III (1896), p. 3. For the appointment of a head pandit see *ibid.*, Part I, p. 107.

69. Pratab Bahadur, "Memoirs," Part I, pp. 91, 100, 101, 103, 105. The 1899 list of estate employees is taken from the raja's diary entry for 27 March 1899. The Muslim peshdast in 1891 was Maulvi Muhammed Rafi, and the mutamad-i-khanagi Hakim Qamar Ali.

tion to more responsible positions was not altogether unknown. Munshi Lalji, the son-in-law of the wasilbaqi-navis Lalta Parshad, after serving himself as wasilbaqi-navis, worked for over ten years as assistant to the manager, and then saw duty as tahsildar of Seota. In 1891, while the top Pratabgarh posts were filled by Muslims, both the manager and assistant manager of Mahmudabad were Hindu.[70]

As time went on the taluqdar's preference for literate, and hence high-caste, employees may well have increased. By the twentieth century even the ziladars on the Khajurhat estate were required to be literate, with the result that Kayasthas were employed exclusively in that lowly position.[71] Behind these changed hiring practices almost certainly lay the growing bureaucratization of estate management. On the estate as in government more formal procedures, with an increased load of paperwork, inevitably made literacy a more important qualification for employment than personal ties of dependency or kinship. Most marked on the largest estates, but not confined to them, this new managerial style owed much to government. Not only did it set a model in its own organization, but such agencies as the Court of Wards, by recruiting outside personnel into estate service and separating old hangers-on from estate payrolls, did much during their occasional bouts of management to push forward the process.[72] As estate administration grew more rule-bound, with the old deferential ties of patron and client eroded away, the stage was set for the harsh encounters of the nationalist years.

Surveillance, Control, and Power

By themselves books of rules and the arrangement of posts signified nothing. What mattered was how, and how well, the various estate officials performed their duties. On this all else hinged. At the top, instances of senior secretariat officials found taking bribes, or embezzling estate funds, and dismissed, are not uncommon. Among them are Qasim Ali Khan, removed from the charge of the Mahmudabad estate in 1869 because of his "diseased love of *nazrs* [gifts]," and Lakshmi Narayan, peshdast at Pratabgarh, dismissed for embezzlement in 1898.[73] Other men were dismissed for simple incompetence, like Lal Bachhu Lal, removed from the post of diwan of Mahmudabad after a few month's service, or the siyaha-navis Babu Beni Prasad,

70. Ali Hasan, "Tarikh-i-Mahmudabad," 2:2:93–94. Of a list of 135 employees who swore loyalty to the raja in 1893 a total of 30, headed by Sita Ram, were Hindus. Mahmudabad Estate Records (loose papers).

71. Interview with Audhesh Pratap Singh of Khajurhat (see n. 44 above). As literacy widened in the countryside other castes apart from the old Persianized elite may have been drawn into estate employ. Twentieth-century estate employment practices require, however, a great deal more study.

72. For further discussion of the work of the Court of Wards, with special reference to Balrampur, see below ch. 10.

73. Ali Hasan, "Tarikh-i-Mahmudabad," 2:1:81–82; and Pratab Bahadur, "Memoirs," Part IV (1897–98), p. 17.

fired for habitual drunkenness in court. Some too, despite their personal failings, managed to hold on to responsible positions for years together or even to gain reinstatement at the hands of a compliant raja.[74]

The opportunities for fraud were, however, substantially greater for the officials in the countryside, far removed from any continuing scrutiny by the center. The Pratabgarh raja systematically toured the villages of his estate, usually for a few days each month in the winter, and he set aside a specified time each day while he was in residence in the fort to hear cultivators' complaints. But such measures amounted to very little in practice. On his tours Pratab Bahadur traveled in lavish style, on elephant back, with a large retinue of staff and servants, sometimes including even his sitar teacher. In January 1899, for instance, for a week's tour of the estate's villages in Patti tahsil, he took with him 117 men, five elephants, eleven horses, three camels, six bullocks, and a cow. On such tours he would often race through half a dozen villages before breakfast, and then spend the rest of the day shooting and transacting routine business. As a result few villages were inspected at all thoroughly, and a good many, especially those outside Pratabgarh district, never saw the raja for years on end.[75] Nor were many aggrieved *asamis* (cultivators) likely to trek long distances to the fort to confront the raja in the presence of all his senior officials.

It was no doubt at least partly with such considerations in mind that the raja in 1896 appointed his sometime physician and personal secretary Hakim Qamar Ali, now so desperate that he had written Pratab Bahadur begging for employment even without salary, as officer on special duty [girdawar] for the districts of Unao, Kheri, and Hardoi. Given a salary of Rs. 80 a month, and membership of the executive committee, Qamar Ali set off in February 1896, after a brief stay in Unao, to inspect the estate's most distant villages—those in Hardoi and Kheri. The private letters and reports he sent back to the raja during the subsequent eight months have all been preserved, and provide us with an extraordinary insight into the actual operation of an estate at the village level.[76]

The estate's holdings in both Kheri and Hardoi districts, reflecting no doubt their origin as a hastily put together reward grant, were exceptionally

74. Ali Hasan, "Tarikh-i-Mahmudabad," 2:2:82, 95. Beni Prasad's successor as siyahanavis, though unequaled in "doctoring accounts and accepting bribes," retained his post until he "went home on leave never to return." Balwant Singh in Pratabgarh, dismissed for taking a bribe, was later reinstated by Ajit Singh over the protests of Pratab Bahadur, who had conducted the initial investigation. "Memoirs," Part I, pp. 68, 91.

75. Pratab Bahadur, "Diary," entries for 19 to 24 January 1899 and *passim*. The raja toured the Shahabpur *ilaqa* in Allahabad, for instance, in 1895, but on no other occasion (so far as the records indicate) during that entire decade. "Memoirs," Part II, p. 9. The Mahmudabad raja never went on tour, while Habibullah as manager toured only in the winter, remaining the rest of the year at his residence in Lucknow. Interview with Ali Bahadur Habibullah (see n. 47 above).

76. Qamar Ali's letter requesting employment, of 13 December 1895, and his orders of appointment of 1 February 1896, are in the Qila Pratabgarh Estate Archives, "File of Letters from the Employees" (Urdu). For the full text of one of Qamar Ali's inspection reports see Appendix 2.

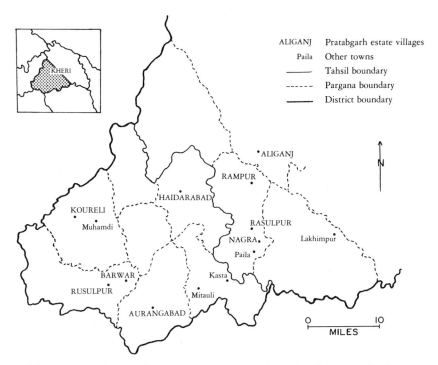

Map 5. A Portion of Kheri District Illustrating Pratabgarh Estate Holdings.

widely scattered. The raja's sixteen Hardoi villages, known as the Harouni-Qutbnagar estate, were spread across four parganas, while the larger Kheri holding, comprising by the mid-1890s not only the twenty-four reward villages but a further eight purchased from European grantees, lay stretched across six parganas in the south and west of the district. In only one pargana, moreover, that of Paila, with nineteen villages clustered about the estate's district headquarters at Nagra, did the Pratabgarh raja own a substantial block of territory. No other pargana held more than five villages, and most had but one or two. To complicate matters further the largest and most prosperous villages were the most isolated. Aurangabad, for instance, was a thriving town of 3,500 people, with a market, post office, and school, but it was the Pratabgarh estate's only property in the entire pargana. Much the same was true of Aliganj and Haidarabad, and of Akbarpur-Binaika in Hardoi. None of the estate's villages in pargana Paila by contrast could boast of so much as a post office, or even a separate listing in the district gazetteer.[77]

Qamar Ali was from the start anxious to consolidate and rationalize this jumble. He pressed upon the raja a scheme by which the estate would sell off, even though they were its "top" villages in the district, Aurangabad, Aliganj,

77. Nevill, *Kheri D.G.*, pp. 91–92, 160, 164, 186, 236, and *passim*; and Nevill, *Hardoi D.G.*, pp. 83, 235, 248, 270.

and Haidarabad, because the costs of administration were disproportionately high. The proceeds would then be used to extend the estate's holdings in the area around Nagra, where previous purchases had created the nucleus of a compact *halqa* (circle). The sale of Aurangabad, Qamar Ali admitted, posed a difficult problem, for much of the town was subsettled with Tasadduq Husain, a descendant of its original Sayyid founders, and a man with whom the Pratabgarh estate had never got on well. Were the town put up for sale it would therefore be assumed that the harrassed Pratabgarh raja was on the run, and the price he could get would be correspondingly reduced. To put people off, Qamar Ali argued, it would be best to proceed by way of a ruse. He suggested that some estate official might appear to conspire with Tasadduq Husain, offering in return for a surreptitious payment to have him made owner of the village at a specially favorable price. At the same time the smaller outlying villages might be sold off first, with the announced intention of adding property around Aurangabad, and then Aurangabad could be sold last, after the estate's motives for the sale had become apparent.[78]

The raja unfortunately had no interest in selling any property in Kheri, nor for that matter in buying any. He refused to put even Aurangabad up for sale despite Qamar Ali's repeated pleas that it "at any rate" should be sold, and he turned a deaf ear to Qamar Ali's glowing descriptions of the cheap prices, and assured profits, of the villages in the Nagra area. Throughout the entire period from 1896 to 1908 no changes took place in the estate's holdings in Kheri district.[79] One can only surmise as to the raja's motives. He was certainly not averse to buying property, for he expanded his holdings in Pratabgarh and elsewhere considerably during these years. Perhaps he just mistrusted Qamar Ali as an agent in such dealings, or was reluctant to part with such choice, if unremunerative, properties as Aurangabad. There is no evidence that the raja consciously sought a dispersed estate.[80]

Qamar Ali devoted a good deal of time, especially during the first few months of his tour, to watching over the government officials engaged in preliminary measurement of the land for the forthcoming regular settlement. Eager to win the favor of these men, in March, explaining that it was customary on the estate, he got the assistant surveyor fresh from England to let him tie a protective amulet ("Imam Zamin") on his wrist. At the same time he distributed the material for a feast—ghee, flour, pulses, sugar, and firewood—to the entire official party, including the local bania. This feast, he proudly told the raja, had not only gained the estate a more favorable treatment at the hands of the survey party, but it was "in the opinion of the people

78. Q.A. to Raja 11 April 1896, 20 June 1896, 14 August 1896, and 8 September 1896, Qila Pratabgarh Estate Archives, "File of Letters from the Employees."
79. Q.A. to Raja 20 April 1896, 8 September 1896, and *passim*. For the estate's holdings see B.I.A. Records, File 41, "Papers Relating to Lists of Talukdars."
80. For a discussion of estate dispersal, and an argument that the taluqdars preferred such scattered holdings, see P. J. Musgrave, "Landlords and Lords of the Land," *Modern Asian Studies* 6(1972):262–66.

of this area better than the one arranged by Raja Amir Hasan Khan [of Mahmudabad]."[81] He was not always so successful, however, for a few months later he reported in some alarm that a new assistant surveyor had arrived, who with his whole staff had been entertained for five days by Tasadduq Husain, the estate's arch-rival, at his house in Aurangabad. Certain that the local officials, all Shias and friends of Tasadduq, would not "go against him on my behalf," Qamar Ali decided against distributing any food or money in the Aurangabad area.[82] Clearly, in the wooing of junior British officers, much depended on who got to them first.

In the surveyors' wake came the amins and munsarims who compiled the village-by-village record of landholding, and who were also fed by the estate while on duty. For Qamar this was a heavy burden. He complained bitterly that with some sixteen men at work in one village "the real motive of the Government is the training of patwaris, and we have become the scapegoats." And on several occasions he endeavored to stop the supply of food to these men.[83] Much greater cause for concern, however, was to be found in the behavior of these petty revenue officials. Fearful that they might defraud the estate or make erroneous entries in the village records, Qamar Ali during his travels stayed close upon their heels, and he instructed his subordinate Mata Parshad never to leave their side. But even this arrangement was not infallible, for Mata Parshad, as Qamar Ali soon discovered, was not above conniving with them for his own personal enrichment.[84]

Qamar Ali was anxious as well to increase the estate's productive assets. He urged the raja to have repopulated several deserted village sites, and he himself set about building bazaars in the two large villages of Nagra and Haidarabad. A bazaar in Nagra, Qamar Ali reported enthusiastically in April, "will rapidly develop and be patronized," for the estate owned ample property in the area and could provide every assistance. If left untaxed at the outset it could easily bring in a profit of Rs. 40 or 50 per year thereafter. He had initially thought to conciliate the Kurmi taluqdar of Paila, Rai Ram Din Bahadur, who owned nine villages in the vicinity, by asking him to perform the inauguration ceremony of the Nagra bazaar. In the end, however, "as it was an auspicious time," the local tahsildar opened the bazaar, and Qamar Ali, after he had attended two marketing days, told the raja that the place gave the appearance of having been "established for a long time."[85]

Far more important, and time-consuming, was the humdrum task of securing for the estate all the income to which it was already entitled. In each

81. Q.A. to Raja 26 March 1896.
82. Q.A. to Raja 28 May and 12 August 1896.
83. Q.A. to Raja 28 March and 19 April 1896.
84. Q.A. to Raja 18 April, 21 April, 27 April, 9 September 1896, and *passim*.
85. Q.A. to Raja 19 April, 20 April, 20 and 28 May 1896. The Paila taluqdar was not invited because Qamar Ali himself could not be present at the opening. The bazaar in Haidarabad, Qamar Ali admitted, was a more uncertain proposition, as the estate owned no property in the neighborhood.

village Qamar Ali examined the rent receipts, and endeavored to collect arrears due to the estate. On one occasion he even abused, and then slapped, a recalcitrant cultivator, only to find the entire village, including the women, swarming round with sticks, ready for a fight.[86] In outlying villages, where direct collection was unremunerative and sale prohibited, he sought out contractors who would pay a fixed fee to the estate in return for the right to collect the rents. Nor was income always the sole consideration. For Burahi Bhader, Qamar Ali preferred Nand Lal, a moneylender and tenant of the estate who had before been thikadar and was known for fair dealing, to a man who had bid Rs. 5 more but was of another village and came of a family with whom the estate's sepoys had quarreled.[87] And where a contractor or lessee, or a mortgagee of estate property, had defaulted Qamar Ali did his best to recover what he regarded as the estate's just dues, even instituting suits in court.[88]

Arrears were as often as not, however, a product of the slipshod work habits and underhanded dealings of the estate's own subordinate staff. Judging from the amount of space devoted to it in his letters, Qamar Ali clearly saw as his primary task that of ensuring that the estate's servants did what they were supposed to do, and of rooting out those who were inefficient or corrupt. The chaotic state of the records first demanded his attention. For a full two weeks in early June he labored over the Aurangabad accounts, unable to determine who was in arrears or what funds had in fact been collected. The bulk of responsibility for the confusion he lay at the door of Thakur Shamsher Singh, the estate ziladar at Aurangabad, whom he accused of adopting methods of "loot and robbery." Shamsher Singh, Qamar Ali charged, had lent estate money to people from whom there was no hope of its recovery, and even worse had conveniently forgotten to enter into the *siaha* (account book) sums that he had collected from the tenantry. "He received Rs. 10 from someone but gave a receipt for eight only, so that Rs. 2 are missing. One maund of corn, though received in 1302F.[1895], is entered as being only now received. When the corn came into his custody he fixed the rate according to his own wishes. At the end of the season he sold it, keeping the profit and entering the remaining sum in the siaha." Even when entries were made in the siaha, moreover, the actual cash was often "nowhere to be found." Insisting that there was "no one more untrustworthy" in the estate's service, Qamar Ali recommended that Shamsher Singh be brought before the raja for trial, and he took the responsibility himself of suspending him from duty as of September 1, 1896.[89]

86. Q.A. to Raja 5 May 1896. This is the only instance in the correspondence of physical maltreatment of a tenant. More commonly Qamar Ali evidenced a kind of distant sympathy for the cultivators. See below p. 307.

87. Q.A. to Raja 12 August 1896. Nand Lal's bid was Rs. 50. A bid of Rs. 60 came in later from the mukhtar of a small zamindar of the district. Q.A. to Raja 21 August 1896.

88. See, for instance, the case of Bahudhar Kurmi who refused to pay the sum due on his thika and was threatened with court action. Q.A. to Raja 4 October 1896.

89. Q.A. to Raja 9 June, 12 June, 27 July, 16 August, and 18 September 1896.

Shamsher Singh protested vehemently, charging in a letter to the raja written out for him in English that these accusations had been manufactured by Tasadduq Husain out of enmity towards the estate. The raja too was skeptical of the methods Qamar Ali had used in his inquiry, which consisted largely of asking cultivators whether they had paid any money to Shamsher Singh without getting receipts in return.[90] But Qamar Ali, undeterred, pressed on with his investigations. In July he brought similar charges against Lachman Singh, ziladar at Birwa, who, he claimed, had taken large sums of money, some of it destined for the government revenue, from the cultivators without either entering it in the siaha or issuing receipts. While prepared to overlook the money taken as "gratification," Qamar Ali insisted that if he did not deposit the estate funds in the treasury he should be suspended, or at the very least reduced to "a place among the sepoys at the gate of the fort." Lachman, like Shamsher, steadfastly denied any wrongdoing, and instead turned the tables on Qamar Ali by accusing him of having taken and pocketed the missing sums. The raja, while unconvinced by these counter-accusations, evidenced no enthusiasm for suspending Lachman, or anyone else. He evidently regarded Qamar Ali as overly zealous, perhaps even a bit self-righteous in his willingness to find fault with others, and he forced him on one occasion to admit that he had no real "proof" of anything. Qamar Ali nevertheless stuck by his charges, and in October, at the end of his stay in Kheri, warned the raja against too generous a forgiveness of those who willfully caused loss to the estate.[91]

It is of course impossible to assess the accuracy of Qamar Ali's charges. Closer to the scene than the raja, yet with no particular local ties, he no doubt saw, and was prepared to report, a good deal that others would have chosen to ignore. Nor did Qamar Ali invariably recommend severe punishment for all transgressions. Though he considered Thakur Daulat Singh an "ordinary man," who "did not do his duty in my presence," he was willing to see him continued in estate service with only a reprimand.[92] Qamar Ali too went along, if reluctantly, with such illicit practices as the concealment of assets and the acceptance of *nazrana*. The latter he justified on the ground that as it was common practice on all estates it would be a "deviation" from custom for him not to take it.[93] Qamar Ali nevertheless clearly wished to see the estate, at least in Kheri and Hardoi, run more tightly, and its servants kept up to a higher standard of efficiency, than did the raja. Perhaps because of this divergence of views Qamar Ali was once again dismissed from estate service in 1897.[94]

90. Shamsher Singh, ziladar Aurangabad, to Maharaja Pratab Bahadur Singh 4 September 1896; and Q.A. to Raja 14 July 1896.

91. Q.A. to Raja 19 July, 1 August, 3 September, and 4 October 1896. As the raja's letters to Qamar Ali have been lost we can only infer his views from Qamar Ali's responses to them.

92. Q.A. to Raja 19 July and 3 September 1896.

93. Q.A. to Raja 28 March, 9 April, 29 April, and 27 July 1896. In July he acknowledged receipts of Rs. 18 in nazrana during the preceding three months.

94. For Qamar Ali's dismissal see Pratab Bahadur, "Memoirs," Part IV (1897–98), p. 9. No

Yet tours by specially appointed girdawars such as Qamar Ali, who admitted that he was "as a flood that comes and passes away," could in any case be only marginally more effective in controlling the estate's subordinate staff than tours by the raja himself. Were these subordinate servants, then, the effective masters of the estate, able to go their own way essentially unchecked? It has recently become fashionable to see the superior powerholders in Indian society as little more than puppets in the hands of their underlings, fed funds and information only as it suited the interests of those below.[95] With Musgrave one might argue that "the landlord, rather like the Collector, was hardly the 'Lord of the Land,' but rather the head of a complex and arcane system of government, which seems to have been effective at all levels in concealing information." Yet one cannot jump straightaway to the conclusion that the landlord had no way of enforcing his will upon the subordinate estate staff. An enterprising landlord in fact had open to him at all times a number of ways of asserting his mastery over the estate. The mere threat of surveillance by such a man as Qamar Ali, together with a landlord's ability to reach through the levels of the estate bureaucracy and discipline even the lowliest peon, served to restrain too flagrant a resort to extortion or embezzlement. Some landlords employed inconspicuous members of low-caste groups, such as *dhobis* or *harijans*, as spies to report confidentially upon happenings in their localities.[96] Most also played upon, if they did not encourage, caste and factional antagonisms among their employees. Throughout the last quarter of the nineteenth century, for instance, the Mahmudabad estate staff was split into two rival factions: one, supported by Sheikh Inayatullah, led by the disgruntled wife of the former manager Qasim Ali Khan; the other headed by Nawab Ali Husain Khan, the then manager, and including Sheikh Ikram Ali, Munshi Hadi Hasan, the estate's agent in Lucknow, and others. As each sought to discredit the other, the raja's task was substantially eased.[97]

Landlords sought ways especially of preventing fraudulent combinations among those posted in the countryside. The ziladars, and the sepoys who assisted them, as the men responsible for the collection of the estate's rentals at the village level, had above all to be kept honest. These men were customarily recruited from among the residents of the estate, and secured their posts by simple hereditary succession. Though no one had a vested right to

reason is given. The raja did however have the charges of embezzlement against Shamsher Singh investigated afresh by Munshi Harprasad Singh during 1897. The outcome is not recorded. *Ibid.*, p. 10.

95. For a classic statement of this position see R. E. Frykenberg, *Guntur District* (Oxford, 1965). For its application to the estate see P. J. Musgrave, "Landlords and Lords of the Land," *Modern Asian Studies* 6 (1972):269–72.

96. In Mahmudabad the tahsil office dhobi was used as a spy upon the estate tahsildar. Interview with Maharajkumar Amir Haidar Khan, (see n. 47 above). For the harijan as informer within the village see interview with Nripendra Bahadur Singh of Hanswar (see n. 44 above).

97. Ali Hasan, "Tarikh-i-Mahmudabad," 2:2:61–62, 73. In 1880 Nawab Ali Husain was accused of embezzling nearly a lakh of rupees, but was cleared after an investigation by the raja.

his father's post, nevertheless custom and convenience gave him at the very least a preferential claim and usually a certain hold upon it.[98] As a result strong local ties grew up, capable of deflecting a ziladar's loyalties from his employer to his neighbors and kinfolk. By insisting that they be residents of the estate the taluqdar gained some hold over these men should they embezzle or abscond with estate funds, for he could then take action against their family and property. At the same time they were normally employed only outside their home villages. Qamar Ali, for instance, strongly urged that sepoys "should be appointed from the *sadr* [Pratabgarh] and from within the Thakur caste." Though the cost in salaries, he admitted, would be greater, such an arrangement was cheaper in the long run, for "sepoys of the village show favor to the cultivators of the village." One Ram Narain at Aurangabad, he pointed out, "if he gets four annas from an *asami* will readily let land worth ten or fifteen rupees go free of rent." Where local sepoys were employed, he insisted, they should be required to furnish cash securities for their behavior on penalty of dismissal. But the raja, as with the financially compromised ziladars, was in no hurry to move, so that finally the exasperated Qamar Ali, who had himself suspended Ram Narain from duty, offered to arrange for a replacement from his own village.[99]

Yet the problem of discipline in such remote areas (for the Pratabgarh estate) as Kheri and Hardoi was not so simple as Qamar Ali imagined. A locally recruited staff might cost an estate income to which its rent rolls entitled it, but at the same time, as Qamar Ali's own tour indicated, effective supervision in a remote area was bound to be a haphazard, and occasional, affair. Better, the raja no doubt reasoned, to lose some revenue than to risk the animosity of men whose local connections, arrayed against the estate rather than on its side, could deny it even more. Pratab Bahadur too was clearly partial toward those who had "eaten his salt" for so long. The drive for a more bureaucratic managerial style, among some landholders at least, was still very much tempered by a personal sense of reciprocal obligation or responsibility which kept alive, especially at the lower levels of the estate hierarchy, older ways of handling men.

The award of villages on *thika* (contract) served much the same purpose: that of securing a steady income for the estate without committing scarce, perhaps unreliable, managerial resources. Even more than the ziladars, thikadars were likely to be local people, who played a critical hinge role between the estate bureaucracy and the cultivators. Men of moderate means but usually prospering, of various castes, Ahir and Kurmi among them, they combined contracting with other occupations—moneylending, pleading in

98. Interviews with Nripendra Bahadur Singh (see n. 44 above); P.N.S. Singh, raja of Tiloi (see n. 45 above); S. N. Saksena, Manager Kasmanda (see n. 49 above); Audhesh Pratap Singh of Khajurhat (see n. 44 above); and L.P.S. Singh, Manager Mankapur (see n. 49 above). L.P.S. Singh noted that "ziladars of three generations' service were common."
99. Q.A. to Raja 17 June, 25 July, and 12 September 1896. See also his Hardoi inspection report of 28 May 1896 (para. 14), Appendix 2.

the courts, even cultivation—which gave them the funds to make good their contracts. The terms of the contracts are nowhere specified, but they clearly involved a percentage, most likely 10 to 25 percent, of the rentals, and perhaps some rent-free land as well. At times thikadars may even have supplied cultivators credit for seed or cattle, and so played a role in agricultural production itself.[100]

For the estate owner, thikadars had a number of advantages. They could be played off against the ziladars to the landholder's benefit as villages were shifted from one form of management to the other. They were useful, as Ajodhya discovered at the turn of the century, when a taluqdar sought a rapid rise in rents. A landowner might also turn to them to free himself of the burden of management at a time when he could not give it adequate attention. Such surely was Rampal Singh's motive in letting out his villages to the highest bidder before his departure for Europe in 1874. But thikadars most frequently found employment on remote or isolated tracts where supervision by the regular estate bureaucracy was costly and difficult. One estate alone, that of Balrampur, whose immense size obviously posed exceptional problems of management, consistently let out the bulk of its lands to rent contractors.[101]

No landholder, then, certainly no one who owned more than a few villages, could altogether escape sharing control over the resources of the countryside with entrenched local interests. Even the ordinary cultivators could not be taken wholly for granted. Although most rentals, as Sanders reported of Rampal Singh's in 1895, were "usually collected in full within the year for which they are due," arrears were not unknown. Even on Court of Wards estates, where the government itself supervised the collection, the shortfall was often greater than the 7 percent Benett calculated as the overall Kalakankar average, while in remote areas, or where underproprietors gave a lead, arrears might be substantial.[102] Qamar Ali, for instance, in 1896

100. The Qamar Ali correspondence indicates the caste and occupation of a few of the Pratabgarh estate's thikadars, but neither these letters nor the British revenue records provide more than a glimpse into the working of the system. A fuller account must await further research into estate archives. For Bihar see the forthcoming work of Anand Yang.

101. For a view of the contracting system in Balrampur see Gertrude Emerson, *Voiceless India* (New York, 1930), pp. 158-60. Although Balrampur contractors who were negligent in meeting their contracts, or who "behaved crookedly," might be coerced by the dispatch of sepoys or by suits in court, these men appear to have been but little disturbed, with their contracts regularly renewed and even handed down to heirs. For a list by tahsil of delinquent thikadars see the Annual Report for 1888-89, Balrampur Estate Records 1889-90, Dept. No. 54, File No. 3. On other estates, where villages were frequently shifted from one form of management to another, short-term contracts, often with competitive bidding, appear to have been most common.

102. Report by J. Sanders, Settle. Offr. Pratabgarh, of 25 September 1895, N.W.P.&O. Rev. Progs. November 1895, No. 11; and Note by Settle. Commr. of 4 October 1895, *ibid.*, No. 12. Sanders and Benett both insisted that Rampal Singh's rent rolls were "transparently honest" and could be relied upon for accurate information. Very little data are available for actual rental collections. It is however unlikely that, with the possible exception of Ajodhya, arrears anywhere in Oudh ever approached the 40 to 50 percent recorded on wards' estates in Bengal. See Rajat

reported the amount due the Pratabgarh estate from its sixteen Hardoi villages at Rs. 3,640, some of it outstanding for five years or more, and he laid the blame on the local ziladars, who, he alleged, had made no effort to check the state of the crop before it was harvested, nor to intercept it after the harvest, with the result that "the cultivators consumed whatever they got from the crop and it was not possible to get anything from them."[103] Despite his criticism of the ziladars' inactivity it was clear that many of these arrears never were to be, and never could be, realized. The limits to the taluqdar's control of the resources of the countryside, as indeed that of the government itself, were real and palpable, and must not be forgotten when engaged in the easy task of labeling these men oppressors of the peasantry.

Too much indulgence of local connection, however, could be very costly. The Murarmau estate of Unao, reported W. H. Moreland in 1894, was "practically in the hands of numerous low-paid ziladars, who, so far as I can learn, rarely submit any accounts and still more rarely remit any money." On the Samanpur estate in Faizabad under the lax supervision of Malik Hidayat Husain the agents entrusted with the task of letting some thirty villages "took the opportunity of putting themselves down as lessees at absurdly low rates," and so deprived the taluqdar of some Rs. 3,000 to 4,000 per year. On the Panwansi estate of Pratabgarh during the 1870s, and in Tiloi a decade later, while they were under the control of *parda nashin* (secluded) women, "the karindas did as they liked, and no doubt, while ostensibly satisfying their mistresses' desire to act benevolently toward their tenants, by not showing increased rents in the rent-rolls, really made money at the expense of the latter." But the ordinary tenants did sometimes benefit as well, for "unscrupulous and dishonest" agents, though invariably exacting heavy nazrana, readily let land at nominal or very low rents. Nor did they have any incentive to collect rents in full. Indeed as Moreland wrote of Murarmau, they kept rents low "to maintain the solidarity of interest between themselves and the tenants of the estate, and so secure the continuance of their private net profits."[104]

To bend the subordinate estate staff to the will of the landlord was never to be an easy task. But it was not on that account a wholly impossible undertaking. It was indeed essential if the estate, and with it the taluqdari system of landholding, were to prosper. Some income had no doubt always to be

---

and Ratna Ray, "Zamindars and Jotedars: A Study of Rural Politics in Bengal," *Modern Asian Studies* 9 (1975):99–100.

103. Inspection Report of Hardoi (paras. 8–12). See Appendix 2 below.

104. Assessment Report on the Seven Baiswara Parganas, Unao, of 19 September 1894, N.W.P.&O. Rev. Progs. August 1895, No. 21; Depty. Commr. Faizabad to Commr. Faizabad 6 December 1868, B.R. Faizabad File 438; J. Sanders, Pargana Dhingwas Assessment Report of 25 January 1894, N.W.P.&O. Rev. Progs. March 1895, No. 10(b); and Assessment Report of Pargana Ateha of 19 February 1895, N.W.P.&O. Rev. Progs. July 1895, No. 70(a). See also the account of Nuruddinpur in Rae Bareli, where a "rascally mukhtar colluded with underproprietors in certain villages to obtain decrees for them in all the best land" (S. H. Fremantle, Tahsil Salone Assessment Report, N.W.P.&O. Rev. Progs. August 1896, No. 72).

sacrificed, but a steady flow of cash into the estate treasury could be, and usually was, secured. In this endeavor everything depended on the balance of forces within the estate, and above all on the vigilance and ability of the taluqdar. Success was most likely when the estate owner, regularly resident on his property, was master of the factional alignments and individual shortcomings of his employees, assisted by an able manager, and not faced in his villages by a large body of truculent underproprietors. A prolonged period of absentee management, on the other hand, or a preoccupation with other concerns, inevitably posed difficulties, as did minorities, which might produce years of vigorous Court of Wards administration or the ineffectuality of dowager ranis attempting to govern from behind the screen.

Investment, Sales, and Prosperity

Perhaps the clearest mark of the taluqdars' success as estate managers was the purchase of additional land. The taluqdars chose of course to spend their money in various ways, above all, as we shall see, to sustain a lavish style of life. But as a landed aristocracy proud of their position on the land, and often judged by the size of their estates, they commonly turned prosperity to advantage in the land market. Sale, by contrast, was a sign of incapacity if not of impoverishment.

As a group the taluqdars held their own, and in many districts substantially added to their holdings, during the half-century after the Mutiny. The professional moneylender, who had purchased so much land in the North-Western Provinces at the expense of the smaller Rajput and Muslim proprietors, was "comparatively little heard of" in Oudh. Most of the land that comes onto the market, the Lucknow Commissioner reported in 1896, "is bought up either by great taluqdars for the purpose of increasing their estates, or by their relatives, or by Government servants who had acquired a competence in the public service, and who wish to have the status of landowners."[105] Land circulated, that is, mainly within the landed community, rather than being transferred from Rajputs and Muslims to Banias and Khatris.[106]

The most conspicuous of the purchasers of land was the Balrampur estate. During the first two decades after the Mutiny, Maharaja Digvijai Singh purchased, among other properties, the Bichla estate in Bahraich for Rs.

105. Commr. Lucknow to Sec. Bd. Rev. 9 January 1896, in *Papers on Agricultural Indebtedness*, 3:67–68.

106. For a summary account of changes in landholding by caste see Francis Robinson, "Municipal Government and Muslim Separatism," in J. Gallagher, G. Johnson, and A. Seal, eds., *Locality, Province, and Nation: Essays on Indian Politics, 1870–1940* (Cambridge, 1973), pp. 81–84. Near Lucknow city, though the taluqdars were expanding their holdings, the lesser Rajput and Muslim proprietors were losing land to commercial castes. See Nevill, *Lucknow D.G.*, pp. 88–90. One notable nontaluqdari purchaser was the Kayastha publisher of Lucknow, Munshi Newal Kishore, whose son Prayag Narain gained honorary membership of the B.I.A.

40,000; some 7,972 acres of government grant land, either at auction or from the original purchaser, for a total of Rs. 58,077; five scattered villages in Gonda and Lucknow for Rs. 71,900, together with eight villages in Basti at prices that are not recorded.[107] During the later years of the century the Balrampur estate acquired, as they came on the market, some 135 villages comprising 80,000 acres of the Singha Chanda and Ramnagar estates of Gonda, and 27 villages worth two and a quarter lakhs of rupees from the Patti Saifabad taluqa in Pratabgarh, while as mortgagee it took possession in 1900 of half the Birwa estate of 80 villages.[108]

In this as in so many other respects Balrampur was exceptionally well situated. The estate was so large, and so much of its land was permanently settled at low rates, that ample funds were always available for the purchase of property. The estate regularly reported a surplus of receipts over expenditures of between two and four lakhs of rupees a year.[109] When Balrampur did not use its funds to buy up other estates it often lent them money. In 1925, for instance, it had outstanding loans of twenty lakhs advanced to such prominent estates as those of Ajodhya, Bilehra, and Qila Pratabgarh; and during the course of that year, while under Court of Wards management, it advanced a further nine and a half lakhs to Kakrali and Dalippur.[110] Size, together with its favorable treatment by government, especially during two prolonged minorities, gave Balrampur always a decisive advantage.

Mahmudabad, like Balrampur, expanded its holdings considerably in the years after the Mutiny. Its first, and largest, purchase it owed to the Court of Wards. By 1862, after only three years of government management, the estate had accumulated cash reserves of almost four lakhs of rupees. Two lakhs were put aside to meet the estate's debts, and the remainder invested in government securities.[111] Two years later, when the Kheri estates of Mitauli and Kasta, awarded after the Mutiny to European grantees, came on the market, the Khairabad Commissioner urged that they be purchased for Mahmudabad. "There can be no doubt" he wrote, "that judicious investments in land pay better than Government securities, while they are more to the taste of the family concerned, and prevent that very serious evil to a young man coming of age—the command of large sums of ready money."

107. Baldeo Singh, "Life of Digvijai Singh," pp. 301–02.
108. Nevill, *Gonda D.G.*, pp. 82, 86–87; and Nevill, *Partabgarh D.G.*, p. 105.
109. In 1882 the surplus was Rs. 2,75,285; in 1889, Rs. 4,21,899; in 1890, Rs. 3,21,673; and in 1902, Rs. 1,97,828. See Balrampur Sadr Annual Report for 1889–90, by Mumtaz Ali Khan; and Balrampur Estate Annual Report for 1901–02, Balrampur Estate records. Figures for other years are not available. The largest surpluses were amassed during the prolonged period of government management from 1886 to 1901.
110. Bilehra owed Rs. 7,61,271, Qila Pratabgarh Rs. 4,07,000, and Ajodhya Rs. 3,82,000. Balrampur Estate Annual Report for 1925–1926 by Kunwar Jasbir Singh, Spec. Manager Ct. of Wards, Estate Records. In 1901–1902, with no debt of its own, the estate had loans outstanding to the amount of almost seventeen lakhs. Annual Report for 1901–1902.
111. Commr. Khairabad to Sec. C.C. 20 October 1862, B.R. Sitapur File 209. See also Depty. Commr. Sitapur to Commr. Khairabad 2 January 1864, *ibid.*

After some hesitation the government sanctioned the purchase in 1865 of Mitauli for Rs. 2,30,000, and of Kasta the following year.[112]

Once Amir Hasan took charge of the estate, the pace of expansion slowed, for the raja's lavish style of living continually undercut the efforts of his managers Ali Husain and Sheikh Inayatullah to put aside funds. Indeed the two major land transactions that the estate entered into at the end of the century, the mortgages first of Jarwal and then of Isanagar, involved risky speculations, and were undertaken only because of the insistence of the taluqdar. The Jarwal mortgage, for instance, fixed no regular rate of interest, but gave the Mahmudabad estate the right only to the profits of the individual villages included in the deed, while the Isanagar deal, as we have seen, carried out over Inayatullah's strenuous objections, involved Mahmudabad itself in debt.[113]

For estates less well endowed than Mahmudabad or Balrampur, expansion depended almost wholly on the enterprise and enthusiasm of the ruler. Two successive rajas of Pratabgarh—Ajit Singh and Pratab Bahadur Singh—over the years invested substantial sums of money in the purchase of landed property. They made no single large purchases, but rather picked up a few villages almost every year. By his death in 1889 Ajit Singh had spent over thirteen lakhs, not only in Pratabgarh district, where he bought a good many villages from the tottering Bahlolpur estate, but in Benares, Allahabad, and Jaunpur as well. During his first eleven years as raja, Pratab Bahadur put a further five lakhs into expanding the estate's holdings both in these districts and in western Oudh.[114] By the time of his death in 1921 he had got hold of the remainder of the Bahlolpur estate, some sixty-four villages assessed at a government revenue of almost Rs. 36,000.[115] Clearly, despite Qamar Ali's worried reports, the estate was at no time short of cash. Nor was it all that badly managed, for the expansion could not have taken place had not both Ajit Singh and Pratab Bahadur exercised a close and continuing scrutiny over its affairs. Indeed one revenue officer complained in 1919 that Pratab Bahadur could never keep a manager for long because he continually interfered in his work.[116]

112. Commr. Khairabad to Sec. C.C. 23/25 August 1864, Finanl. Commr. to Sec. C.C. 19 December 1864, and Finanl. Commr. to Commr. Khairabad 4 April 1866, *ibid*. See also Ali Hasan, "Tarikh-i-Mahmudabad," 2:1:76. The Kasta property cost three lakhs. Together these two purchases gave the estate holdings in Kheri of 56 villages comprising 46,900 acres of land. *Oudh Gazetteer*, 2:220.

113. Ali Hasan, "Tarikh-i-Mahmudabad," 2:1:208–12, 2:2:77–78, and 3:1:81–86. The Jarwal speculation was ultimately successful, so that by 1897 Mahmudabad "practically owned" that estate. Pargana Hisampur Assessment Report of 9 September 1897, by P. Harrison, N.W.P.&O. Rev. Progs. October 1897, No. 55 (para. 7). For the outcome of the Isanagar transaction see above n. 57.

114. Pratab Bahadur, "Memoirs," Part I, pp. 94–95; and Appendix, "Details of Ilaqa. . . ." See also Sanders, *Pratabgarh S.R.*, pp. 23, 85; and n. 64 above.

115. Abul Hasan, *Rent Rate Report of Pargana Pratabgarh* (Allahabad, 1928), para. 10.

116. Depty. Commr. Pratabgarh in "Report on the Condition of Landowners (1919)," U.P. Rev. Dept. Confidential File No. 578/1918.

Small taluqdars who substantially enlarged their holdings usually did so at the price of a reputation for tight-fistedness. Thakur Jawahir Singh of Kasmanda, in Sitapur district, a man "proverbially fond of improving and enlarging his estates," managed between 1857 and the turn of the century to more than quadruple the amount of land in his possession.[117] But the methods by which he brought this about were not too attractive. "He advances money to needy landlords, treats them with the utmost indulgence until the right time to pounce comes and then their property is absorbed. It is legal but harsh management. To the tenants he is equally hard and he looks into every detail of his estate. . . . There is no waste with him . . . his activity is marvellous."[118] His successor Suraj Bakhsh Singh was likewise characterized as a "hard landlord," who "never pays a penny interest without an eye to its manifold return."[119]

Some landlords raised funds for their purchases by lending money to their tenants. The Khatri Seth Raghubar Dyal of Muizuddinpur, who added an estate assessed at Rs. 12,452 to an ancestral holding paying Rs. 19,104, was perhaps the most renowned of taluqdari bankers. He even set up on his estate an agricultural bank, with a capital of Rs. 25,000, which lent funds to the tenants at moderate interest for the purchase of seed and the payment of their rents.[120] Raja Rampal Singh of Kurri Sidauli in Rae Bareli, the head of an ancient Rajput lineage, with an estate paying Rs. 34,610, received an income of nearly Rs. 50,000 a year from moneylending, together with an additional Rs. 2,500 from bank accounts.[121] In similar fashion Babu Udresh Singh of Meopur-Dhaurua, the settlement officer reported in 1895, "has made large profits out of indigo in recent years, got out of debt, taken to lending money himself, and buying property. He is a strict, hard landlord."[122] Nor were strictly commercial pursuits unheard of. The taluqdar of Gopalkhera in Unao in the 1880s "engaged in a considerable mercantile business, moneylending, cloth, copper, brass and spices," while his uncle, the estate's manager, "had embarked on the part of the estate in a grain trade."[123]

Urban investments too were commonplace, and brought in a good income for many taluqdars. A list compiled in about 1910 showed eighty-five as owners of shops and houses, apart from their own residences, in Lucknow

117. "Heliodorus," *A Taluqdar of the Old School* (Allahabad, 1912?), pp. 72-73. In the mid-1870s Jawahir Singh held 47 villages assessed at Rs. 38,000; in 1905 the estate comprised 146 villages and 133 *pattis* (shares), assessed at almost one lakh of rupees, in fourteen parganas of the district. Nevill, *Sitapur D.G.*, p. 75.

118. Harcourt Butler to his family 4 December 1894, Butler Papers IOL MSS. Eur. F. 116/5.

119. Depty. Commr. Sitapur in "Report on the Condition of Landowners (1919)," U.P. Rev. Dept. Confidential File No. 578/1918.

120. Kunj Behari Seth, *The Seths of Biswan*, pp. 19, 21.

121. Depty. Commr. Rae Bareli in "Report on the Condition of Landowners (1919)," U. P. Rev. Dept. Confidential File No. 578/1918.

122. Pargana Aldemau Assessment Report by F. W. Brownrigg, 21 February 1895, N.W.P.&O. Rev. Progs. May 1895, No. 63 (para. 109).

123. Sec. Govt. N.W.P.&O. to Commr. Lucknow 20 May 1882, Oudh Rev. Dept. Progs. May 1882, No. 4.

city. Most prominent were Balrampur, who owned property in some half-a-dozen different areas of the city, and the raja of Jahangirabad, perhaps the major private property holder in the fashionable Hazratganj area. He not only collected rents from four houses on Neill Road, together with the Jahangirabad Terrace and the Jahangirabad Mansion, the latter comprising "thirteen big double storey shops," but he owned as well the houses occupied by the five most senior British civil servants in the city.[124] Taluqdars were also among the major shareholders in, and supplied much of the original capital for, Lucknow's major industrial enterprise, the Upper India Paper Mill. Founded in 1878, the mill by the turn of the century was producing annually over 2,500 tons of paper with a value of some seven lakhs of rupees.[125]

As the purchase of land denoted prosperity, so too was sale a mark of financial difficulty. Over the short run, of course, the sale of land signified nothing, for taluqdars, like landowners everywhere, sold property for a host of reasons, among them to gain funds to purchase better lands, or make more remunerative investments, elsewhere. But sales of ancestral property sustained over a long period of time were invariably a sign of decline, for the possession of an estate alone gave the taluqdar his distinctive status. During the half-century after the Mutiny a number of taluqdars, three or four in each district on average, suffered substantial losses of property, while a few saw their entire estates disappear, though sometimes, as in the case of Patti Saifabad when it came on the market, a small portion might be saved "in order to maintain the ancient name."[126]

Most common among the causes that led to sale was simple inattention to estate affairs on the part of the owner. The Bahlolpur estate of Pratabgarh from the outset teetered on the brink of bankruptcy. So early as 1858 the Deputy Commissioner had despaired of the young raja, Bijai Bahadur, who, he said, was already "in the hands of bad karindas."[127] Nine years later the government took over the property and brought Bijai Bahadur to trial as a lunatic. The court, however, ruled in favor of the raja, arguing that mismanagement of an estate was not evidence of "unsoundness of mind"; and so the Bahlolpur estate was handed back to its owner.[128] But matters did not

124. "List of Taluqdars who own houses and shops in Lucknow City," n.d., File No. 48, B.I.A. Records. In 1902 Balrampur's rental income from shops and houses, in Balrampur and Tulsipur towns as well as Lucknow, was Rs. 21,000. Annual Report for 1901–02, Balrampur Estate Records. Most taluqdars also obtained income from dues levied on the operation of bazaars on their estates.

125. Nevill, *Lucknow D.G.*, p. 50; and *Oudh Gazette* (Urdu), 4 April 1881, pp. 1107–08 and *passim*. Taluqdars invested heavily as well in government paper. In 1902 Balrampur held government promissory notes worth Rs. 15,14,100 which gave the estate, together with its paper mill shares, an annual income from securities of Rs. 45,000. Annual Report for 1901–02.

126. Nevill, *Partabgarh D.G.*, p. 105.

127. Depty. Commr. Salone to Spec. Commr. Rev. 19 November 1858, B.R. Pratabgarh File 618.

128. Civil Court Judgement in the case of Depty. Commr. Pratabgarh vs. Bijai Bahadur Singh, 6 November 1871, B.R. Pratabgarh File 20. For the raja's ignorance of estate affairs see Settle. Commr. to Sec. C.C. 29 April 1864, B.R. Pratabgarh File 21.

improve. In 1898 the Pratabgarh settlement officer reported that the Bahlol-pur taluqdar was "perhaps the most inefficient landlord in the district. He is a man of weak character, almost illiterate, and quite unfit to manage a large estate. He leaves everything to poorly paid karindas and other underlings, goes about in shabby clothes, and is habitually in arrears of revenue, to recover which his estate is periodically attached."[129] A few years later the estate was gone. The Isanagar taluqa likewise had a long history of misman-agement behind it. Already in 1868, a full thirty years before it passed out of its owner's hands, it was encumbered with debt to the extent of a lakh of rupees, while the taluqdar, the Deputy Commissioner reported, "trusts entirely to his karindas and looks after nothing but his pooja himself."[130]

Litigation too, especially when it was associated with the partition of pro-perties, brought a good many taluqdars to the brink of ruin. The Barai taluqa, "by far the finest property" in the Rudauli pargana of Bara Banki, comprising some forty-eight villages, was, so the settlement officer noted in 1896, "gradually being split up as the family increases." A few years before, Khalil-ur-Rahman, the holder of one-fourth of the estate, had "commenced expensive litigation against his brother's widows, who hold another one-fourth share, unseparated from his own; and both branches of the family have contracted heavy liabilities." The other half of the property was divided among the eight sons of one Ghulam Farid, all of whom were in debt, with gross liabilities amounting to some Rs. 1,70,000. "The share of one of the eight brothers, equivalent to one-sixteenth of the taluka, is now gradually being sold, and the other seven are litigating with the money-lenders over it."[131]

In Faizabad district the debilitating effects of litigation were exacerbated by the recalcitrance of the entrenched underproprietary bodies. The exten-sive, and heavily subsettled, Birhar taluqa, was for instance, divided into four shares—Hanswar, Makrahi, Lakhanpur, and Sultanpur—with the latter two further split among a total of eight individual shareholders. The members of this family, the settlement officer commented in 1895, "have indulged in senseless litigation—notably the talukdars of Haswar and Makrahi, whose feuds, if ever at rest, cease from troubling the civil courts only when the criminal courts' attention is engaged by them." The *pukhta-dars* meanwhile were "doing very well. As a class they are very strong, espe-cially in the east of the pargana, where the talukdars' hold has always been weak." Hence it was not surprising that the Birhar taluqdars were all "more

129. Sanders, *Pratabgarh S.R.*, p. 85. Sanders noted especially that the Bahlolpur raja did not give written receipts for rent payments, "perhaps the first principle of efficient management."
130. Depty. Commr. Kheri to Commr. Sitapur 19 March 1868, B.R. Oudh General File 2, Part I.
131. Assessment Report of Pargana Rudauli by J. A. Norrie, 5 August 1896, N.W.P.&O. Rev. Progs. June 1897, No. 47 (para. 27, 31); and Nevill, *Bara Banki D.G.*, pp. 108–09. See also the accounts of Singha Chanda and Ramnagar in Nevill, *Gonda D.G.*, pp. 101–02.

or less in debt," while the property of one of them, Babu Bhairon Bakhsh Singh of Sultanpur, "overburdened with debts," was in the process of being sold.[132] Overall, the taluqdars of Faizabad lost some 8,870 acres of land between 1870 and 1900.[133]

Yet the picture was rarely so bleak as it appeared. Taluqdari indebtedness, though heavy, was not usually overwhelming, and sometimes reflected the cash requirements of prospering landholders. Nor did the sales, even in debt-ridden Faizabad, involve more than a small percentage of the taluqdars' lands. By and large these men retained land enough, and secured income enough, to keep their heads well above water. Nor were their investment decisions wholly irrational. While perhaps not ideal "profit maximizers" by economic theory, they nevertheless held properties that brought them a reasonable return on their capital, and gave them, what they sought above all else, a secure position as the premier landlords of Oudh.

132. Tahsil Tanda Assessment Report by H. F. House, 18 December 1895, N.W.P.&O. Rev. Progs. August 1896, No. 29 (para. 85); and House, *Fyzabad S.R.*, p. 19.
133. House, *Fyzabad S.R.*, p. 4. The largest single sale was that of the Baragaon taluqa of some 21 villages. See Nevill, *Fyzabad D.G.*, pp. 74, 80. The 8,800 acres were 1 percent of the total taluqdari landholdings in the district.

Ten | *Landlords and Local Government*

NEVER MERE collectors of rent, the taluqdars always played a major role in the governance of rural society. To be sure, under the British, they no longer enforced their will by armed might, or meted out justice with only a cursory nod toward Lucknow. Yet British rule still offered the rural magnate substantial scope for the exercise of governmental authority. Indeed the British were anxious to turn to their own advantage the "authority the taluqdars had always exercised over their tenants and which it would have been impolitic, if not impossible, wholly to have deprived them of."[1] And where official sanction was not forthcoming their sheer weight in the countryside by itself secured for the taluqdars a voice in local government. The result was a mixing of taluqdari and British jurisdiction, of officially recognized and informal authority, in which responsibility often remained diffused and ambiguous.

The Estate as Government: Balrampur

One estate, that of Balrampur, took over virtually all the functions of government. By far the largest property in Oudh, comprising some 1,000 villages

1. Sec. C.C. Oudh to Sec. Govt. India 28 March 1861, *P.P.* 1861, 46:468. See also Sec. Govt. India to Sec. C.C. Oudh, 2 November 1859, *ibid.*, p. 432.

281

spread across almost a million acres of land, Balrampur saw little of government officers. Initially, in the first years after annexation, the two parganas
of Balrampur and Tulsipur, both after 1859 wholly owned by the Balrampur
maharaja, constituted together a government tahsil under the charge of a
tahsildar. In the 1870s, however, upon the conclusion of the first regular
settlement, this tahsil was abolished, and its territories included in the
adjacent tahsil of Utraula, which thus came to comprehend seven parganas,
and at 1,500 square miles was the largest tahsil in the entire province. (See
Map 6.) By the end of the century the total government presence in the two
parganas of the old tahsil consisted of four police thanas and seven post
offices. The closest civil court was that of the *munsif* of Utraula.[2]

This retrenchment was not primarily dictated by fiscal considerations. It
reflected rather a decision to leave to the Balrampur estate, and to its chief
the maharaja, who was vested with the powers of an honorary magistrate,
much of the business of government. In some measure this award, like the
permanent settlement of the land revenue conceded at the same time for the
bulk of his estate, was a further mark of the British government's appreciation for Digvijai Singh's conspicuous loyalty during 1857. But it was appropriate as well, for the estate, so large and compact, with no intervening
"foreign" villages to break up its jurisdiction, and relatively isolated in
northern Oudh, had long possessed a considerable measure of independence.
The administrative and judicial work of the Utraula tahsil, wrote Nevill in
the Gonda *Gazetteer*, "is lighter than elsewhere in the district, partly
because the inhabitants are less civilized and therefore do not so readily have
recourse to the courts, but in the main because the executive machinery of
the Balrampur estate is largely self-contained."[3]

Nor was the estate's administrative structure in the countryside at all extensive. Balrampur employed no supervisory sarbarakhars, only two assistants to the manager, one each for the Bahraich and Gonda territories; and
the estate was divided into but sixteen tahsils. Such a reduced staff was sufficient because the work of rent collection had been handed over to the estate's
thikadars. These men, retained on long-term contracts, made their own
arrangements with the tenantry, with whom they shared the grain heap at
harvest. The estate tahsildar simply saw to it that the agreed-upon sums were
paid into the estate treasury.[4]

The working of the estate administration can perhaps best be appreciated
by looking at one relatively well-documented tahsil, that of Pachperwa, a
tract some twenty miles long and eight to ten miles wide under the mountains
in northeastern Gonda. A portion of the confiscated Tulsipur estate, Pachperwa had come under the Balrampur raj in 1859, and the estate tahsil had

2. Nevill, *Gonda D.G.*, pp. 115–16, 271–72.
3. *Ibid.*, p. 272. For Balrampur's quasi-independent position under the Nawabs see above
ch. 2.
4. *Ibid.*, p. 180. For a list of Balrampur estate staff in 1881 see Baldeo Singh, "Life of
Digvijai Singh," pp. 311–14. For the contracting system see above ch. 9, n. 101.

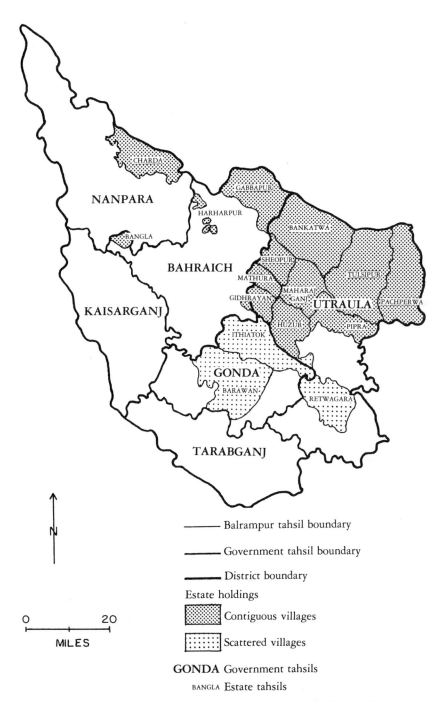

CHARDA

GABBAPUR

NANPARA

HARHARPUR

BANKATWA

BANGLA

SHEOPUR

BAHRAICH

TULSIPUR

MATHURA

MAHARAJ
GANJ

GIDHRAYAN

PACHPERWA

UTRAULA

KAISARGANJ

HUZUR

PIPRA

ITHIATOK

GONDA

BARAWAN

RETWAGARA

TARABGANJ

N

———— Balrampur tahsil boundary

———— Government tahsil boundary

———— District boundary

Estate holdings

Contiguous villages

Scattered villages

GONDA Government tahsils

BANGLA Estate tahsils

O   20

MILES

Map 6. Bahraich and Gonda Districts to Show Balrampur Estate Holdings.

been established there ever since. The estate owned three buildings in the town—the tahsil headquarters, a pakka storehouse, and a thatched residence—and they housed a staff, headed by the estate tahsildar and peshkar, which in 1888 comprised some twenty-seven people.[5] (See Chart 6.)

The tahsildar devoted some time to supervising the work of the tahsil's thikadars, in 1888 some 216 in number, of whom 44 were alleged to be dilatory in their rent payments. He also auctioned off himself various contracts given out by the estate on a yearly basis for such commodities as mangoes, wild grass, and hides. By far the greater portion of the tahsildar's time was, however, given over to the settlement of disputes. Some were handed over to the peshkar, but the bulk, brought to his office by the complainants, were investigated and decided by the tahsildar himself. These ran the gamut from disputes over the building of houses and the location of boundaries to assaults, affrays, and thefts, and even such intimate family matters as divorces and dowries. In addition, the tahsildar heard charges of extortion brought by the tenants, and of poaching, refusal of service, or infringement of estate rules brought by disgruntled thikadars. Appeals could be carried to the estate headquarters at Balrampur or to the government tahsil at Utraula—twenty-two miles away over a rough road impassable during the monsoon—but this seems rarely to have occurred. For the most part the Pachperwa tahsildar, with his staff of sepoys under the command of the jamadar, enforced his own decrees. In practice, as Gertrude Emerson concluded after her lengthy stay in the 1920s, "the tahsildar is supreme within the limits of the territory assigned to him."[6]

Though it also supported a post office and an upper primary school, the government was represented in the Pachperwa tahsil above all by a police outpost, or thana, under a *thanadar* (subinspector) with ten constables. The police thana, established in 1880 and responsible for an area substantially larger than that of the estate tahsil, operated quite independently of the estate. When the thanadar received news, usually from a village watchman, that a serious, so-called cognizable, crime had been committed, such as murder, dacoity, burglary, or theft, he at once on his own initiative conducted an investigation and arrested suspects, to be remanded to the district jail in Gonda. Such crimes were, however, comparatively few in number. For the rest the thanadar, who usually remained at the police

5. Tahsil Bhamber Annual Report for 1888-89, compiled by Munshi Bishan Singh, Assistant Manager, Balrampur Estate Records 1889-90, Dept. No. 54, File No. 3. The number and character of the tahsil staff had not changed much by the 1920s. Nor had the pay scales, for the tahsildar then received about Rs. 80 and the peshkar Rs. 30. These sums were of course supplemented by the exaction of *nazrana* from the thikadars and tenants. See Emerson, *Voiceless India*, pp. 161-62 and *passim*.

6. *Ibid.*, p. 158. For discussion of the various types of cases handled by the tahsildar and peshkar see pp. 161-72. Unlike ziladars elsewhere, who had to go from village to village collecting rent, the Balrampur tahsildar left his office only occasionally, to examine disputed building sites or boundaries on the spot.

Chart 6. Estate Establishment, Pachperwa, 1888

Staff	*Salaries (Rupees per month)*
Jai Govind Ram, *tahsildar*	100
Ram Narain Pande, *peshkar*	10
Ishwari Prasad, *mutasaddi* (Hindi)	10
Ram Lal, *mutasaddi* (Urdu)	10
Jagannath, *khazanchi*	8-5-3
Bhagwan Das, *mukhtar*	13
Samarnath Singh, *jamadar*	7
16 sepoys @ Rs. 2 to Rs. 3 per month	37
2 gardeners @ Rs. 2-8-0 per month	5
1 cartman	2-8-0
1 sweeper	0-8-0
Total monthly salaries	203-5-3

station in Pachperwa town, dealt with the petty assaults and quarrels of the villagers, which came under police scrutiny whenever they involved a breach of the peace. These disputes were also of course taken to the estate tahsildar. Yet there is no evidence of any serious clash of jurisdiction. Although the thanadar might insist upon his right to investigate such cases, often simply for the bribes that he could extort, he possessed no independent power of arrest for these lesser, or noncognizable, crimes; and the villagers often seem to have been able to choose whether to approach the government policeman or the estate tahsildar. One might argue that they sought out the tahsildar when they wanted an amicable resolution of a dispute, the thanadar when they wanted to extend or create a quarrel.[7]

Apart from the adjudication of village disputes the Balrampur estate performed a number of other quasi-governmental functions. It maintained a large forest establishment, with a permanent staff of some ninety persons, headed by two forest officers, to look after the estate's extensive jungle-clad holdings in the Himalayan foothills. Discipline of the forest staff, and the meting out of punishments for trespass, illicit grazing, and theft of wood, were handled almost wholly within the estate.[8] The estate took responsibility also for the decennial census operations. In 1891, for instance, the assistant agent, Mumtaz Ali Khan, put in "direct charge" of the census in the Balrampur and Tulsipur parganas, appointed the enumerators, mostly village *patwaris* (accountants), and, together with the estate tahsildars, supervised

7. *Ibid.*, ch. ix, esp. pp. 207–08, 222–23.
8. Balrampur Estate Annual Report for 1901–02, Estate Records 1902–03, Dept. No. 54, File 2. Of twenty-six cases brought during that year in the Forest Department only two, one a theft, were sent to the courts for settlement.

the collection and compilation of the returns. The only government employees involved were four qanungos, who directed the day-to-day work of the enumerators.[9]

Balrampur was clearly exceptional in the degree to which the estate had taken over the functions of government. Nowhere else in Oudh were such vast tracts of land under the charge of so few government officers. Of nowhere else could it be said so late as 1926, after the severe shock of the noncooperation movement, and the agrarian agitation which ensued, that the tenants, though they often petitioned the assistant managers to resolve their disputes, "seldom if at all resort to the law courts."[10] Indeed so marked was the estate's autonomy that Maharaja Digvijai Singh had at one time even entertained the notion of being raised to the status of a ruling prince, and so excluding British officers altogether. But no such elevation took place. The Balrampur rajas remained taluqdars and British subjects. As the Pachperwa police thanadar stood as symbol of the ultimate authority of the British Raj in the village, so too was the maharaja himself liable to the jurisdiction of the district courts in Gonda. Oudh was never Jaipur, nor even Northern Nigeria.

If the estate might take on some of the functions of government, so too did the government from time to time take on those of estate manager. Though most estates came under the Court of Wards occasionally, Balrampur was again exceptional in that it experienced two prolonged periods of government management. The effects of this upon the estate are not easy to assess. The objectives the government set for itself were not always clear, nor were they even mutually consistent. The British wished invariably to improve the efficiency of the administration and, where possible, to reduce expenses, and yet at the same time to avoid undue disturbance of the traditional arrangements by which the estate was governed. The first two almost always took precedence. As G. W. Anson, Agent throughout the first period of government management in Balrampur, commented in 1890, "I trust year by year the administration will be placed on a better footing and though there is no necessity for its funds being expended or the accounts kept in exact imitation of Government funds, still the broad principles of Government that efficiency and good management cannot co-exist with extravagance or heedless waste of money must always be kept in mind." Already by that time, after only three years of government management, the net estate income had been increased by over a lakh of rupees, the accounts had been overhauled, three

9. Memo by G. W. Anson, Agent Balrampur Estate, of 3 July 1890, and Agent Balrampur Estate to Depty. Commr. Gonda 11 March 1891, Balrampur Estate Records 1891–92 (loose papers). In none but these two parganas of the district were the supervisory qanungos placed under the charge of anyone other than a government Deputy Collector or tahsildar. See Depty. Commr. Gonda Memo of 24 June 1890, *ibid*.

10. Balrampur Estate Annual Report for 1925–26 by Kunwar Jasbir Singh, Special Manager Court of Wards, Estate Records 1926–27, Dept. 65, File 1. Throughout these years the tenants were engaged in a concerted effort to break the hold of the thikadars and to secure the substitution of cash for grain rents.

Chart 7. Balrampur Estate

Ownership and Administration

1836–1882	Maharaja Digvijai Singh (d. 1882)
1882–1886	Maharani Indar Kunwar (d. 1893)
1886–1893	Board of Revenue for the maharani
1893–1900	Court of Wards for minor Maharaja Bhagwati Parshad Singh (b. 1879)
1900–1921	Bhagwati Parshad
1921–1936	Court of Wards for minor Maharaja Pateshwari Prasad Singh (b. 1914)

Managers

?–1865	Lala Ram Shankar Lal
1865–1866	Bhaiya Jang Bahadur Singh (maharaja's illegitimate son; dismissed for incompetency)
1866–1882	Lala Ram Shankar Lal (d. 1882)
1882–1883	Bhaiya Har Rattan Singh (taluqdar of Majhgawan; dismissed)
1883–1884	Mir Muhammad Hasan (assistant manager since 1860s)
1884–1886	Munshi Shams-ud-din
1886–1901	Colonel G. W. Anson, Agent
1901–1910	Munshi Barakat Ali
1910–1912	Babu Madan Lal (formerly Deputy Collector, Gonda)
1912–1918 (?)	Rai Pitambar Das

new offices created, and a variety of public works, ranging from a memorial statue of the late maharaja to the repair of roads and buildings, had been taken in hand. Indeed, the Assistant Agent Mumtaz Ali Khan complacently reported, "The present epoch in the annals of the Balrampur Estate will be ever held as a period of prosperity, and it would not be too much to say that the improvements now left untouched will never be carried out."[11]

There can be no doubt that the thrust of government management was toward bureaucratization. In particular the rules laid down in the Court of Wards Manual provided a kind of Procrustean bed to which all else was made to conform. When Balrampur went back under the Court of Wards in the 1920s, first among the rules laid down for the guidance of the Special Manager was that, "except where otherwise provided" in a fifty-page pamphlet of *Special Rules*, he should act in accordance with the rules "from time to time in force for the management of Court of Wards estates." Nor did the *Special Rules* make much of a concession to customary ways. The Special

11. Balrampur Sadr Annual Report for 1888–89 by Mumtaz Ali Khan, and marginal notes by G. W. Anson of 6 January 1890, Balrampur Estate Records 1889–90, Dept. No. 54, File 3. The only area still left untouched was the rationalization of pay scales and retrenchment in staff. Anson cautioned Mumtaz Ali against moving too rapidly in this direction. *Ibid.*

Manager was empowered under them to "grant wood for fuel and thatching purposes according to the old practice obtaining in the estate at his free discretion." But, beyond that, he and his assistants were as tightly bound as any government officers by a meticulous detailing of their duties. Each was told how much expenditure he could authorize, how far he could discipline his subordinates, and even how he was to travel while on tour. The Special Manager, for instance, was entitled to two elephants and an army guard of a *naik* and four sepoys, while the assistant managers had to content themselves with the camp equipage of a Deputy Collector.[12]

How far did the importation of the ways of government into the estate benefit it? The Court of Wards staff clearly profited a good deal. Of Colonel Anson, who as Agent in Balrampur pulled down a salary of nearly Rs. 2,000 a month, Butler remarked enviously that his was "a nice berth for a man who is interested in estate management and is fond of shooting and outdoor life. He has a splendid house, like a one-storied English Park House." The other Europeans, "all excellently housed and paid," were a tutor to the young raja, at Rs. 800 a month, and an English couple, man and wife, who looked after the stables, gardens, and dispensary.[13] Nor did the Indians brought over by the Court of Wards fare badly either. Mumtaz Ali Khan, formerly a government tahsildar in Lucknow, employed in 1887 as Anson's assistant on a salary of Rs. 300 per month, four years later was making Rs. 500, or more than three times the pay of Digvijai Singh's assistant manager. Because the money did not come from its own funds, the government could afford to be generous. When the estate was handed over to Bhagwati Parshad, the post of Agent was promptly abolished, with a "large saving" in management costs.[14]

No doubt a landlord's employees supplemented their meagre salaries by extortion and bribery, but there is no certainty that Court of Wards' functionaries "fleeced the cultivators" any the less. Indeed, a recurrent theme of late nineteenth-century writings on rural society was the "unsatisfactory" character of Court of Wards' management. Between the appointment of managers unacquainted with zamindari affairs, the corrupt behavior of petty officials with no ties to the estate where they worked, and the rigidities of a rule book that took no account of the traditional bonds between landlord and tenant, there was, so Sheikh Inayatullah concluded, "no perceptible difference between the condition of the tenants under the landlord and those under the Court of Wards." He even urged the court to let out its villages on *thika* so as to check the rapacity of the subordinate ziladars.[15] The government

12. *Special Rules for the Balrampur Court of Wards Estate* (Lucknow, n.d. [ca. 1928]), pp. 1, 8, *passim*.

13. Harcourt Butler to his father 9 July 1893, Butler Papers IOL MSS Eur. F. 116/5. Ram Shankar Lal, manager under the maharaja, received a salary of Rs. 500 per month, plus various concessions of unspecified amount. Baldeo Singh, "Life of Digvijai Singh," p. 311.

14. Balrampur Estate Annual Report for 1901–02, Estate Records 1902–03, Dept. No. 54, File 2. In 1912 Pitambar Das as manager received a salary of Rs. 700 per month.

15. Memo by Sheikh Inayatullah sent to Sec. Govt. U.P. 19 July 1908, N.W.P.&O. Rev. Dept. File 169B. See also "Azad" (Lucknow) of 15 December 1884, *S.V.N. 1885*, p. 907; and "Hindustan" (Kalakankar) of 7 August 1897, *S.V.N. 1897*, p. 520.

clearly ventured at some risk, and with uncertain results, into an area so far removed from its central concerns as estate management.

Taluqdars as Magistrates

The Balrampur estate was not alone in exercising judicial powers over its tenantry. Elsewhere throughout Oudh, estate officials, and taluqdars with them, acted informally to settle a wide variety of disputes. Qamar Ali, while on tour as the raja of Pratabgarh's agent, disposed of a number of criminal cases, including even cognizable offenses. Once, where grain had been stolen, he made the thieves pay the price of the grain to its owner, and then exacted as a fine Rs. 5 from them and Rs. 2 from the person in whose house they had stayed; Rs. 2 he gave as a reward to the village *chaukidar* (watchman) who had helped in the settlement of the case.[16] Qamar Ali sought further to keep the police out of the estate's affairs, on one occasion instructing a ziladar to pay them not to interfere, and on another penalizing a vegetable seller who had testified before a police subinspector about a riot in which the estate's sepoys were involved.[17]

It is impossible to assess at all precisely the extent of such informal mediation or adjudication of disputes. It surely occurred on every estate, and encompassed the bulk of petty quarrels and conflicts among the tenantry, which as a result never reached the British courts. The mechanism for this dispute settlement, however, never took on an institutionalized form. There were no set procedures, no special judicial officers or courts, while the taluqdar himself could always overturn the decision of any subordinate. The settlement of disputes was, to use Weberian terminology, simply an incident of the taluqdar's patrimonial position as ruler of his estate. Not content with such informal arrangements, the British from the outset sought to tie these landholders directly into the machinery of local government. Their power "regulated" and "legitimized," these men could, so argued such men as Sir Charles Wingfield, play a central role under the new regime in the governance of the countryside. Most prominent among the schemes to bring this about was the formal award of magisterial powers to the leading taluqdars. Indeed in Wingfield's view this measure promised nothing less than the "dawn of a new era for the landed gentry of India."[18]

Initially, in October 1859, six taluqdars were invested with the power to adjudicate revenue and criminal suits within the limits of their estates. In the role of Assistant Collector the taluqdar decided suits for arrears of rent brought by his agents or by thikadars and *pukhtadars* (underproprietors) against recalcitrant tenants. Tenants on their part could bring claims of

16. Q.A. to Raja 20 April 1896. In January in Unao he heard the testimony of a witness to a burglary and took the burglar to the district jail. Q.A. to Raja 7 February 1896.

17. Q.A. to Raja 24 June and 18 August 1896. The sepoys were permitted not to pay a sum of Rs. 22 owed by them for food they had purchased.

18. Sec. C.C. Oudh to all Commrs. 28 November 1859, B.R. Oudh General File 2093. For discussion of the motives behind this policy see Metcalf, *Aftermath of Revolt*, pp. 154-56. Various other notables were at the same time given powers as honorary magistrates in the towns.

290 LAND, LANDLORDS, AND THE BRITISH RAJ

exaction or ejectment into the taluqdar's court. As deputy magistrate the taluqdar could try offenders brought before him by the police for a number of petty crimes. By 1862 the number of taluqdar-magistrates had grown to forty-eight, with jurisdiction now extended to include civil as well as criminal and revenue suits, and often encompassing the pargana of their residence in addition to their estates.[19]

From the start this scheme was subjected to severe criticism. The Governor-General Lord Canning, although wholly in sympathy with its basic objectives, warned Wingfield not to let the taluqdars abuse their powers for personal advantage. The Secretary of State, Sir Charles Wood, even more skeptical, suggested that the taluqdars' revenue jurisdiction ought not to extend to cases in which they were personally interested, but that such cases should be reserved for the decision of European officers.[20] In this he was supported by the Oudh Judicial Commissioner, George Campbell, and two of the four divisional Commissioners.[21] Whether the taluqdars in fact abused their magisterial powers is by no means clear. Campbell in 1862 charged that of nineteen persons punished by Maharaja Man Singh in one month, eleven were convicted for opposition to his processes in the revenue department, four of them illegally for simply resisting the maharaja's servants.[22] Wingfield had himself earlier noticed that taluqdars sometimes used their official magistrate's seal on *dastaks* (warrants) issued in their private capacity for the collection of rental arrears. The taluqdar's *karinda* (agent), he said, should instead issue the dastak. "When he complains for arrears the usual legal process will issue, of course under the official seal."[23] The Chief Commissioner further agreed with his critics that "the more liberal and considerate the landlord, the fewer revenue cases will there be on his estate." But he refused to withdraw this authority altogether from their hands. As these men would, he argued, inevitably continue to exercise such power, it was best to recognize it and bring it under the check of official review.[24]

More common than outright abuse of their powers were dilatory and haphazard methods of dealing with the work. Of Raja Madho Pratab Singh of Kurwar the local Commissioner wrote, "His proceedings consist of little more than plaint, reply, and statement of putwaree, and decisions seem always

19. Sec. C.C. Oudh to Sec. Govt. India 24 October 1859, *P.P.* 1861, 46:468; and Oudh Administration Report for 1861–62, *P.P.* 1865, 40:151.

20. Sec. Govt. India to Sec. C.C. Oudh 30 March 1860, *P.P.* 1861, 46:450; and Political Dispatch No. 105 of 17 August 1861, *ibid.*, p. 543.

21. Annual Judicial Report for 1860, of 3 May 1861, *P.P.* 1865, 40:157; Faizabad Division Administration Report for 1861–62, *ibid.*, p. 149; and Baiswara Division Administration Report for 1861–62, *ibid.*, p. 150.

22. Annual Judicial Report for 1861, of 28 April 1862, *ibid.*, p. 158. Wingfield defended Man Singh in the Oudh Administration Report for 1862–63, *ibid.*, p. 165.

23. Sec. C.C. to Commr. Bahraich 22 May 1861, C.O.F. Bundle No. 134, File 41.

24. Oudh Administration Report for 1861–62, *P.P.* 1865, 40:152; and Oudh Admin. Report for 1862–63, *ibid.*, pp. 164–65. In 1864 Wingfield authorized a tenant to institute a revenue suit in the district rather than in his landlord's court, and to remove to the former any suit brought against him in the latter.

founded on the latter."[25] Even Wingfield admitted that honorary magistrates handed down extremely light punishments in civil and criminal cases, and that they often allowed undecided cases to accumulate while they were on tour or caught up in other activities.[26] The influential *Oudh Akhbar* newspaper suggested that fledgling taluqdar-magistrates should undertake the study of law, employ competent clerks, and attend some court for a fixed period of time, at the end of which they would take an examination.[27]

Such advice fell on deaf ears, however, for the overwhelming majority of the taluqdar-magistrates had no interest at all in the powers conferred upon them with such *éclat*. From the outset a very few taluqdars did the bulk of the work. In 1864-1865 four men—Maharaja Man Singh, Chaudhuri Gopal Singh, Rana Shankar Bakhsh of Khajurgaon, and Muhammad Ashraf—between them decided 535 out of a total of 792 revenue cases. Nor were matters much different on the criminal side, where Muhammad Ashraf and Chaudhuri Gopal Singh alone dealt with almost one-third of the 1,284 cases decided in 1862-1863.[28] Man Singh's dominant position in the lists can be attributed in part at least to the large size of his estate, its hopelessly chaotic management, and the recalcitrant character of its tenantry, which made necessary the frequent recovery of rent by suits for arrears. In addition Wingfield in 1860 took Man Singh "in charge, in camp, for ten days or more; taught him the business; chose some of his *amlah* [staff] for him; and launched him."[29] But such arguments cannot account for the activity of such men as Chaudhuri Gopal Singh, who was given no special encouragement and whose estate in Unao district yielded a rental of under Rs. 10,000 a year. He was simply attracted by a kind of work that interested almost no one else.

Nor were revenue cases, despite the fear that the taluqdars would seek personal advantage by their abuse, eagerly sought after. Indeed by 1867 they had sunk to less than one-fifth the number decided four years before. (See Table 24.) Civil cases had never proved very attractive. As one taluqdar told Campbell so far back as 1861, "What is the good of deciding shopkeeper's civil suits; that will be very great trouble and no good." The decision of criminal cases, the same taluqdar continued, increases "our power and authority," and so remained relatively popular. But on the revenue side the taluqdars soon discovered that the mere possession of jurisdiction was sufficient for their purposes. It was not necessary to exercise it. "Our tenants, knowing that we have revenue powers, pay up."[30] The Commissioner of Khairabad, in more elegant language, ascribed the falling off of revenue

25. *Oudh Rev. Admin. Report for 1866-67*, Part I, p. 29.
26. Oudh Admin. Report for 1862-63, *P.P.* 1865, 40:164.
27. "Oudh Ahkbar" of 28 December 1878, *S.V.N.* 1878, p. 1067.
28. "Statement of Cases Tried by Honorary Assistant Commissioners," *P.P.* 1865, 40:151, 173-74; and *Oudh Rev. Admin. Report for 1865-66*, Part I, Appendix 14.
29. Canning to Wingfield 22 November 1860 and Wingfield to Canning 4 December 1860, Canning Papers. See also Memorandum by Wingfield of 4 December 1860 enclosed in above.
30. Annual Judicial Report for 1860, of 3 May 1861, *P.P.* 1865, 40:157.

Table 24. Cases Decided by Taluqdar-Magistrates, 1860–1867

Year	Number of Taluqdars with Powers	Number of Cases Decided[a]			
		Revenue	Civil	Criminal	Total
1860–1861	32	1,320	—		1,714
1861–1862	43	1,415	253		2,480
1862–1863	48	1,655	357	1,287	3,299
1863–1864	48	1,284		1,984	3,268
1864–1865	47	792		2,010	2,802
1865–1866	47	836	—	—	—
1866 (five months)	47	241	—	—	—
1866–1867	47	242	—	—	—

[a] Civil and criminal case totals are not available for 1865–66, 1866, and 1866–67.

cases to the same cause. "My impression is that Talookdars generally are able to settle these cases out of court and no doubt the fact of their having such powers induces would-be suitors to adjust their differences without coming into Court."[31] So long as it was clear to all that the taluqdar retained his dominance in society, the use of formal or official methods of procedure served no particular purpose.

Despite these disappointments the scheme of taluqdar-magistrates was not abandoned. Some few enthusiasts continued to decide cases, primarily on the criminal side, transferred to them by the local authorities, and so kept the total numbers up to respectable levels. In 1893, for instance, twenty-nine taluqdars disposed of 1,607 criminal cases. Of these, however, over half were decided by only five men, who took on some 200 cases each.[32] Nor had taluqdari adherence to official procedure improved much in the intervening quarter century. The raja of Pratabgarh, Pratab Bahadur Singh, a devoted honorary magistrate, who set aside time almost every day to hear such cases, complained on one occasion in 1896 that he had not been sent enough cases for decision by the police. Yet twice within that same year he was admonished by the Deputy Commissioner: once for ignoring Clause 560 of the Penal Code which imposed payment of damages on the plaintiff when a defendant was acquitted; and again for failure to remand accused suspects and sentenced convicts daily to the district jail before 5:30 P.M., the hour fixed in the Jail Manual.[33]

31. Khairabad Division Administration Report cited in *Oudh Administration Report for 1863-64*, p. 93. See also Khairabad Division Administration Report for 1862-63, *P.P.* 1865, 40:172.

32. "Lucknow Divisional Statement of Taluqdar-Magistrates," N.W.P.&O. Rev. Progs. December 1894, No. 11; and "Fyzabad Divisional Statement," *ibid.*, No. 9. The five were Rai Narain Singh (Bara Banki), Lala Durga Prasad (Hardoi), Raja Jagmohan Singh of Atra Chandapur (Rae Bareli), Raja Pratab Bahadur Singh of Qila Pratabgarh, and Raja Rampal Singh of Kalakankar (Pratabgarh).

33. Notification issued by Raja Pratab Bahadur Singh of 7 August 1896 to Deputy Commissioner and Tahsildar of Pratabgarh; Memorandum by Depty. Commr. of 12 October 1896 with

Throughout, the aspects of their position as magistrates that most exercised the taluqdars were those that affected their standing in society. In March 1894 Raja Amir Hasan Khan of Mahmudabad, while readily acknowledging the superiority of the European civil officer, protested vigorously against the exercise of judicial powers within the bounds of a taluqdari estate by any Indian other than the taluqdar himself. To submit to the jurisdiction of men of such humble origin as those who filled the posts of Deputy Collector and tahsildar was humiliating, he said, while to allow the tenants of one taluqdar to go to the court of another "makes a dispute between the two taluqdars and causes mischief." The judicial powers granted by government were "a sign of proprietorship," and as such ought to extend to every tenant on the holder's estate.[34]

The government refused to grant the taluqdars or their tenants favored access to European officials over the head of the subordinate native magistrates. Similarly they refused to revive the revenue and civil jurisdiction of the taluqdars, which, they claimed, had become obsolete through disuse. But the government recognized the force of Mahmudabad's argument that the taluqdars should not be treated in the same way as ordinary honorary magistrates, and they agreed that the most effective way of emphasizing their position as taluqdars would be to make their jurisdiction coterminous with their estates in the districts in which they resided.[35]

This decision—carried into force by a government order of March 9, 1898—was not, however, free from difficulties of its own. The scope of taluqdari jurisdiction, as it had grown up over the years, was very much of a patchwork quilt. Some taluqdars had powers granted in one *thana* (police circle) while the bulk of their estates lay elsewhere; others, probably the majority, gazetted to power in several adjacent thanas, exercised jurisdiction over most of their estate, though not always every village, and sometimes a great deal else besides; while a few men, most notably the rajas of Pratabgarh and Dera (Sultanpur), had powers extending over an entire district, of which their estates of course comprised only a very small portion. The process of placing taluqdari jurisdiction on a "special basis" therefore substantially curtailed the area over which many of the most prominent taluqdars could exercise authority, and added very little to that of most others. The raja of Mahmudabad, the original complainant, gained jurisdiction in only one additional thana. He was not given criminal power over the remaining thanas in which his property lay because they were regarded as too far from the town of

reference to Criminal Case No. 218 of 22 August tried in the court of Raja Pratab Bahadur Singh; and Memorandum of Depty. Commr. of 18 July 1896. Pratabgarh Estate Records.

34. Raja Amir-ud-daula to Lieutenant Governor 24 March 1894, N.W.P.&O. Rev. Dept. File No. 205B. Two years later he protested strongly against the appointment of an Indian, Kunwar Jwala Parshad, as District Judge of Sitapur. Memo of 1 May 1896 and letter of same date to Depty. Commr. Sitapur, *ibid*.

35. Sec. Govt. N.W.P.&O. to Commrs. of Faizabad and Lucknow 8 December 1894, N.W.P.&O. Rev. Progs. December 1894, No. 15. See also Note by H. W. Pike of 30 June 1895, N.W.P.&O. Judl. Dept. File No. 560C, K.W. Notes and Orders.

Mahmudabad, where he held his court. The raja of Pratabgarh by contrast lost not only the extensive powers he had formerly enjoyed outside his estate, but was denied jurisdiction as well over his own outlying villages and those in which he only held shares jointly with others.[36]

No sooner had the new regulations been brought into force than the work of the taluqdar-magistrates began to suffer. By 1902, from an annual average of 1,350 in the mid-1890s the total number of cases decided had fallen to 760. For some individuals the decline was even more precipitous. The raja of Jahangirabad, who had decided 94 cases in 1896, disposed of only 4 in 1903. Pratab Bahadur's case load went down from over 200 a year in the mid-1890s to a mere 7 in 1902, while Raja Rampal Singh of Kurri Sidauli told the government two years later that the new arrangement made the taluqdar-magistrate "practically useless in the administration of justice."[37]

The government therefore reversed itself, and in 1904 awarded powers as before by thana. But this arrangement too was not without its difficulties, for feuding taluqdars often lived in hostile proximity to each other with their villages hopelessly intermixed. The reversion to thanawide powers thus at once produced a clash of jurisdiction, and with it a new source of friction. In Sitapur district, for instance, the raja of Mahmudabad and Seth Raghubar Dyal, "who are not on good terms," both owned villages in the three thanas of Biswan, Sidhauli, and Muhammadabad. The Seth was initially slated for jurisdiction in thana Biswan, while Mahmudabad was to have powers in all three. Before the new rules could take effect, however, Harcourt Butler, who as settlement officer a decade before knew the area well, protested against the arrangement, and suggested that in Biswan, Raghubar Dyal's home, Mahmudabad "should stick to his own villages and Raghubar Dyal should have the rest." Although duly approved by the government, this alteration did not settle the matter, for Raghubar Dyal at once protested that while he was now deprived of jurisdiction in the villages of thana Biswan belonging to the Mahmudabad raja, the latter still retained jurisdiction in the villages of thanas Sidhauli and Muhammadabad which belonged to him. Ultimately the dispute was put to an end by a complex formula under which each taluqdar retained jurisdiction over all his own villages, while Raghubar Dyal had in addition the remainder of Biswan thana, and Mahmudabad the remainder of thanas Sidhauli and Muhammadabad.[38]

36. See Notes by T. Stoker of 14 November 1895 and H.R.C. Hailey of 12 April 1898, *ibid.* For the raja of Pratabgarh see Depty. Commr. Pratabgarh to Commr. Faizabad 15 September 1898, N.W.P.&O. Rev. Progs. January 1899, No. 56; and Sec. Govt. N.W.P.&O. to Commr. Faizabad 7 December 1898, *ibid.*, No. 57. From the outset the government had on practical grounds opposed the exercise of jurisdiction over areas located a great distance from a taluqdar's residence.

37. "Statement of work done by Taluqdar Honorary Magistrates (1895–1903)," U.P. Judl.-Crim. Progs. May 1904, No. 5; and letter of Raja Rampal Singh of 12 July 1904, U.P. Judl.-Crim. Progs. September 1904, No. 42.

38. Notes by S. H. Butler of 10 June 1904 and 15 July 1904, U.P. Judl.-Crim. Dept. File No. 560C/1; Depty. Commr. Sitapur to Commr. Lucknow 8 December 1905, U.P. Judl.-Crim.

Despite all this wrangling neither of these two taluqdars ever did much work as honorary magistrate. Indeed in 1905 the Deputy Commissioner of Sitapur suggested that the jurisdiction of the bench magistrates of Sitapur town be extended to these thanas in order to take up the slack.[39] What then was the dispute about? The answer is to be found in the taluqdar's persisting quest for status and prestige. Most taluqdars, perhaps despite his disclaimers even Mahmudabad, saw in the extent of their jurisdiction a mark of their standing with the British authorities. When omitted from the original notification of March 1898, for instance, Seth Raghubar Dyal, despite the fact that he was already a bench magistrate in Sitapur town, pleaded with the government to add his name to the list of honorary magistrates sitting separately on their estates. LaTouche, then Chief Secretary, opposed the move on the ground that the Seth usually lived in the town and had "large money-dealing by way of loans with the tenants," but the government nevertheless soon capitulated.[40] The family biographer lists the possession of these powers prominently among Raghubar Dyal's achievements.[41]

The dramatic falling off of taluqdari interest in magisterial work once their powers had been confined to their estates reflects again this same concern. Within their estates the taluqdars simply had no need to exercise formal magisterial powers. There, as Wingfield, and after him Harcourt Butler, had cogently observed, they still continued "the old Oudh practice" of settling petty disputes out of court. Under such circumstances it was clearly hopeless to expect them, with no particular incentive, to subject themselves to the restraints and forms of official procedure. Only outside the estate did work as honorary magistrate bring any rewards in power and authority, and so the loss of such jurisdiction was both highly visible and looked upon as a severe deprivation. Yet even then the return in prestige from the mere possession of these powers was for most taluqdars entirely sufficient. They saw little to be gained from expending their energy on the adjudication of such suits. The endeavor to make over the Oudh taluqdar into a public-spirited country magistrate on the model of the English J.P. was, from the start, doomed to failure.

The Landlord and the Police

The exercise of the powers of honorary magistrate was but a small part of the landholder's responsibilities in the field of criminal justice. He was also

---

Progs. February 1906, No. 6; and Notification of 16 May 1907, U.P. Judl.-Crim. Dept. File No. 560C/1.

39. Depty. Commr. Sitapur to Commr. Lucknow 26 August 1905, U.P. Judl.-Crim. Progs. October 1905, No. 15.

40. Petition of Seth Raghubar Dyal of 9 July 1898, N.W.P.&O. Judl.-Crim. Progs. January 1899, No. 20; Note by J.J.D. LaTouche of 2 August 1898, N.W.P.&O. Judl.-Crim. Dept. File No. 560C; and Notification of 15 October 1898, N.W.P.&O. Judl.-Crim. Progs. January 1899, No. 46.

41. Kunj Behari Seth, *The Seths of Biswan*, p. 20.

expected to aid the police in the apprehension of criminals, and generally to maintain order within the bounds of his estate. This was not a new task imposed upon him by the British. Landholders had always exercised substantial police powers, above all by controlling the resident chaukidars on their estates. Their armed bands of retainers too gave them a force they could use to ensure tranquillity among those beneath them. The British, however, sought above all an "efficient" police administration, and so continually narrowed the landlord's police powers until hardly anything remained.

The first step, an inevitable accompaniment of British rule, was the establishment of a regular paid police force, under a superintendent of police, in each district, together with the disbandment of private militia. The landholders, of course, retained a force of sorts in the sepoys who assisted the ziladars in the collection of rents, and who with sticks alone could usually cow individual peasants. But the universal disarmament dramatically reduced the amount of coercive force at the landholder's disposal.

The British next turned their attention to the village chaukidars. These men customarily received their pay either by a small plot of rent-free land or, like many other craftsmen and village servants, as a fixed percentage of the crop at harvest, and they took their orders from the owner of the village, who met the cost from his share. The British did not at first interfere openly with these arrangements. Both payment and the power of appointment remained in the landlord's hands. But so early as 1859 the Chief Commissioner, Robert Montgomery, concerned about inequities in payment, while urging that the "characteristics of the system in each village community" be preserved, recommended that additional cash payments be made where necessary to "secure the condition of the village policeman from starvation." At the same time he ordered the chaukidars placed under the superintendence of the district police, who while avoiding drill or military discipline were to bring the work of these men up to "some degree of efficiency."[42] Ten years later the government withdrew from the landlord the power of summarily dismissing recalcitrant chaukidars. He had now to secure the permission of the Deputy Commissioner, and that was not easily forthcoming.[43]

Deprived of so much of their former control over him, the landlords soon let the chaukidar's pay fall into arrears. As the Faizabad superintendent of police complained in 1868, after he had processed 769 petitions in one year, "even when arrears are proved, if the order is merely a decree in favour of the chokidar . . . the confusion will in no way be removed, . . . for the landholders have been given the chance to pay if they would, and shown that they *won't*."[44] Bitterly disillusioned, some officials urged that the chaukidars be paid in cash out of the proceeds of a special chaukidari cess, and that land-

42. "A General Report on the Administration of the Province of Oudh" (1859), NAI Foreign Miscellaneous File No. 382, pp. 106–07.
43. Chief Commissioner's Circular No. 28 of 5 May 1868, cited in *Oudh Police Administration Report for 1868* (Lucknow, 1869), p. 90.
44. "Remarks by District Superintendent Police Fyzabad," *ibid.*, p. 89. See also remarks by Dist. Supt. Police Kheri (pp. 91–92), and Lucknow (pp. 93–94).

holders be severed from all connection with these watchmen. The police, in particular, anxious to bring the chaukidars completely under their control, saw no other alternative. As the Inspector General put it in 1872, "The introduction of law and regulation have so altered relations between the landholder and the chaukidar, and made village responsibility as it is so called, so entirely nominal, that ere long the chaukidar must become the paid Government servant. . . . "[45]

The government, still convinced that landholders could "give valuable assistance to the police," were not yet ready to go that far. They did, however, authorize the payment of chaukidari salaries in cash, by the imposition of a punitive 6 percent cess, whenever a landlord did not provide adequate compensation. But the basic principle of shared responsibility was not abandoned, with the result that the working of the chaukidari system remained highly unsatisfactory.[46] Ultimately, in 1894, the government took control of the village police wholly into its own hands, and levied for the purpose a special cess of 3 percent on the value of each estate. The taluqdars protested vehemently against the imposition upon them of this additional tax, but showed no reluctance to be rid of the maintenance of the village watchmen.[47]

The landlords displayed no greater enthusiasm for their more general police responsibilities, of which the most important were the prevention of crime and the detection and apprehension of criminals on their estates. Montgomery in 1859 enunciated the basic principle that "the Government looks to the landholder" in such matters, and would not allow the police or chaukidars to be made scapegoats for their negligence.[48] But there was considerable uncertainty as to just what was expected of the landlord. So in the late 1860s, under prompting from the police authorities, the government set out to "revise and consolidate" the existing law on the subject. The initial draft, submitted by the Inspector General of the N.W.P. police, was rejected by the Lieutenant Governor as "too stringent." It would be unfair, he pointed out, to burden the landholder with duties that properly belonged to the police, or to hold him responsible for all thefts and robberies committed on his property regardless of whether he knew of them in advance or could have done anything to prevent them.[49] The taluqdars through the British

45. *Oudh Police Administration Report for 1872* (Lucknow, 1873), pp. 78-79.
46. Sec. C.C. to I.G. Police 17 July 1873, *ibid.*, p. 6; Sec. C.C. to I.G. Police 18 July 1877, *Oudh Police Administration Report for 1876* (Lucknow, 1877), p. 3; and Commr. Faizabad's Review of Divisional Police Administration Report for 1877, of 2 March 1878, N.W.P.&O. Police Progs. July 1878, No. 16.
47. Memorial of Oudh Taluqdars of 21 April 1896, N.W.P.&O. Rev. Progs. September 1896, No. 126; and Chief Sec. Govt. N.W.P.&O. to Pres. B.I.A. 25 September 1896, *ibid.*, No. 133. For the taluqdar's response to Act V of 1894 see the various memoranda and correspondence in unnumbered file relating to "Chowkidari Pay (1894)," B.I.A. Records.
48. "General Report on the Administration of Oudh" (1859), NAI For. Mis. File No. 382, p. 107.
49. Sec. Govt. N.W.P. to I.G. Police 30 January 1868, N.W.P. Police Progs. 1 July 1871, No. 1. The Oudh Chief Commissioner agreed that the laws should not be worked in "too vigorous a manner." Sec. C.C. to Sec. Govt. N.W.P. 20 February 1869, *ibid.*, No. 15.

Indian Association protested even more vigorously against any proposal that made them responsible for acts they had not the power to forestall. "As he [the landholder] does not possess Police powers no care and vigilance on his part, and no precautions that he may take, can prevent the commission of these crimes [theft and robbery] on his estate. We submit that as a Police, with which he has no connection whatsoever, has been organized the landholders have been absolved from any responsibility they might have had before."[50]

The act as finally brought into force in 1871 carefully restricted the landholder's responsibility to those offenses committed with his knowledge or ascribable to his "want of care or vigilance." Beyond this the landholder was charged simply with giving "early and punctual" information to the police regarding offenses committed on his property or fugitives who took shelter there. He was also required to cooperate with them in putting down riots or affrays, and in apprehending persons charged with crimes.[51] This more precise definition of their responsibilities did not, however, put a stop to the landholders' neglect of police duties. Even the taluqdars, reported the Faizabad Commissioner sadly, "from whom, considering their position and the favours they have received from Government, we should at any rate expect some assistance, stand aloof and do not help the police in the slightest degree."[52]

Sometimes indeed landholders even connived at criminal activity for their own private advantage. On occasion they took dacoit bands into their pay, or gave them protection. One of the most notorious "bad characters" of the Sitapur district, so the British discovered in 1876 when he was convicted of murder, had received a monthly stipend and the rank of *dafadar* from the raja of Mahmudabad on the understanding that he would prevent the thieves of the area from committing depredations.[53] At times, too, landholders encouraged, or permitted, their own *lathials* to indulge in acts of extortion, or even physical violence, against rivals or insubordinate underlings. As evidence of such behavior was obviously scanty, there was little the government could do. At best they had recourse to such expedients as sending letters of commendation to those who rendered conspicuous service to the police, while persistent malfeasance was met by quartering extra police at a landholder's expense in his villages.[54]

50. "Opinion on the Draft Act. . . ." by the B.I.A. 16 April 1868, *ibid.*, No. 17.
51. "Police Responsibilities of Landholders Act," *ibid.*, No. 14.
52. Commr. Faizabad's Review of Divisional Police Administration Report for 1877, N.W.P.&O. Police Progs. July 1878, No. 16. See also Remarks of Depty. Commr. Sitapur in *Oudh Police Administration Report for 1875* (Lucknow, 1876), p. 16.
53. Remarks of District Superintendent Police Sitapur cited in C.C. Oudh to I.G. Police 18 July 1877, *Oudh Police Admin. Report for 1876*, p. 3.
54. For a letter sent to the raja of Nanpara when he captured two dacoits, see N.W.P.&O. Police "B" Progs. November 1898, No. 66. On the difficulty of proof and the quartering of police see Commr. Faizabad's Review of Divisional Police Administration Report for 1877, N.W.P.&O. Police Progs. July 1878, No. 16; and Sec. Govt. N.W.P.&O. to I.G. Police 18 April

The ineffectuality of the landlord as policeman was not accidental. It was an integral part of the Oudh settlement, as certain as the imperfect conversion of the taluqdar to a public-spirited magistrate. In each case new ideals of administrative efficiency and rationality were yoked in uneasy harness with politic notions of conciliation and vague ideas of aristocratic *noblesse*. The creation of a disciplined police force, and the subordination of the chaukidar to police supervision, quickly drained the old landlord-based policing system of most of its vitality. Yet the British were reluctant simply to convert the Oudh chaukidar into a salaried government servant as they had done in the North-Western Provinces. Tied by their own notions of how Indian rural society ought to operate, and the role landowners ought to play in it, they long argued, with the Deputy Commissioner of Kheri, that "it is not the policy of the Government to uproot old institutions, or cause the interests of the paid village servant to clash with those of the landlord in a way to lead to discontent. . . . " Similar motives led the Chief Commissioner in 1878 to urge "great caution" in imposing the punitive 6 percent cess.[55] Nothing was to be done that might antagonize those powerful magnates who, in their view, could do so much to help maintain order and stability in rural India.

But the British could not have it both ways. They could not take over the bulk of responsibility for the police, and expect others to throw themselves wholeheartedly into the small portion that remained in their charge. They could not impose new and more exacting standards of accountability, and expect an immediate or indeed any effective response from men moved by wholly different traditions. For the taluqdar, an estate was an area to control, not to police, while his objective was to maximize the number of people dependent upon him, not to minimize the number of crimes committed. Disinterested police work formed no part of his conception of his role as landholder. So the British had in the end no option but to jettison their social theories, and take full charge of the police.

The Landlord and the Patwari

As important as the watchman to the well-being of the villager was the accountant, or patwari, who kept the books in which were recorded the details of the holdings and rent payments of each cultivator. In the days of the Nawabi this powerful servant of the village was, like the chaukidar, largely under the control of the landholder, who paid and appointed him. Some degree of independence was secured by the usually hereditary nature of the post, and the fact that the patwari himself collected the dues set aside for his remuneration.[56]

1878, *ibid.*, No. 18. No punitive action was taken in the Mahmudabad case on the ground that the raja had acted "in perfect good faith."

55. Remarks by Depty. Commr. Kheri in *Oudh Police Admin. Report for 1868*, p. 92; and Sec. Govt. N.W.P.&O. to I.G. Police 18 April 1878, N.W.P.&O. Police Progs. July 1878, No. 18.

56. For the status of the patwari at the time Oudh came under British rule see the reports of

When the British took over the government of Oudh they made no attempt to interfere with the working of this system. Rather the coming of the new regime helped tighten the control of the landholder over the patwari, and of the latter over the village. The Oudh Land Revenue Act (XVII of 1876) formally secured to taluqdars the powers of appointment, dismissal, punishment, and remuneration of the patwaris on their estates and required them only to maintain accurate papers for production to the government on demand. Nontaluqdari landlords were authorized to submit nominations for vacant patwariships to the Deputy Commissioner of the district, who was then supposed to satisfy himself as to the candidate's competence before confirming him in the post. At the same time the introduction of a court system which relied almost exclusively upon written records inevitably, if inadvertently, enhanced the position of the patwari. As one officer commented in 1876, "Rent-suits are decided on the *ipse dixit* of the patwari for the most part, as there is no other evidence forthcoming in nine cases out of ten; for pattas and kabuliats are rare, and there is nothing else but the patwari's papers."[57]

In 1882, by a stunning *volte-face*, the government took into its own hands control over the appointment and payment of patwaris. The ostensible motive behind this act was a desire to find some way of affording relief from taxation to the cultivating as well as the landowning classes. Despite the fact that the patwari was paid by the landlord, the Lieutenant Governor asserted, it was customary for him to levy a special cess of one half anna in the rupee on the tenant as his contribution to the maintenance of the patwari. "When it became known that the patwari was paid by Government, this contribution could hardly be demanded"; and so the cultivator, who paid nothing directly in taxation to the government, would gain a measure of relief. The remission was estimated at seven and a half lakhs of rupees. But there was another motive as well. The only method of getting a full and accurate return of rentals, the Lieutenant Governor argued, "is to make the patwari entirely independent of the landowner." This required that the powers of appointment and dismissal be vested in the district officer, who must then also furnish his pay so that "the zamindar would have no grounds for demanding a voice in the election."[58] As with the chaukidar, so too with the patwari, administrative efficiency required government control.

The taluqdars were not, however, at all prepared to acquiesce in the loss of what they regarded as one of their "ancient rights and privileges." In May 1882 through the British Indian Association they protested strongly against

the district officers submitted to government during May and June 1860 in B.R. Oudh General File 747.

57. MacAndrew, *Some Revenue Matters*, pp. 82–83.

58. Sec. Govt. N.W.P.&O. to Sec. Govt. India 7 February 1882, Oudh Rev. Progs. May 1883, No. 4. A further Rs. 24,10,000 was remitted in the North-Western Provinces. MacAndrew had also urged that the patwari be put on the government payroll and kept "perfectly independent of all parties in the village" (*Some Revenue Matters*, p. 84).

this "precipitant" abandonment, without consulting or even informing those most affected by its provisions, of legislation enacted a mere six years before. The inevitable result of the new arrangements, they insisted, far from promoting agricultural prosperity, would be "disorder and confusion," in which the taluqdar "will experience great difficulty in collecting rents," while the patwaris, instead of helping the landlords will "as Government officers pretend to sit in judgment over them and their tenants." The taluqdars further denied that they had ever forced tenants to pay any part of the patwari's wages, and they promised if this new legislation were repealed "to publicly renounce any right they might otherwise lay claim to" of demanding contributions on this account. "The cultivators would thus . . . have all the benefits the Government is desirous of bestowing on them."[59]

Lala Ram Shankar Lal, the manager of the Balrampur estate, on behalf of the maharaja and several other prominent taluqdars, in a separate memorandum candidly admitted that taluqdars did usually levy "patwari charges" from the tenants, and that even if they remitted these charges in accordance with the government resolution, they could afterwards increase the rent, or "collect a similar amount under some other pretence." Hence it was foolish to try to benefit the tenant through the landlord. Ram Shankar suggested cogently that the government, if it really wished to do good to the tenants, should advance *taqavi* loans without interest directly to the needy cultivator.[60]

Under this barrage of criticism the government hurriedly retreated. The new Lieutenant Governor, Sir Alfred Lyall, denied—despite his predecessor's clear statement to the contrary not six months before—that the measure had been undertaken with the aim of improving the accuracy of the rent rolls, and he admitted that the discussions preceding the 1876 act had given the taluqdars some ground for anticipating that the system of private patwaris was a permanent arrangement which would not be altered without their consent. As it had been so recently enacted, Lyall refused to recommend repeal of the new law. But he resolved, when issuing rules to give effect to its provisions, to avoid "unnecessary umbrage" to the landowners or undue disturbance of the existing relations between landlord and patwari.[61]

Hence the new act brought about almost no substantive changes. The taluqdars kept in their hands the nomination and "immediate control" of the patwaris of their villages. Patwari salaries, though now borne by the government, were disbursed through the landlord, who received a remission from the land revenue demand equivalent to the salary. The landlords in return promised to make good their pledges not to collect patwari dues from the tenants, and to ensure that the patwaris prepared full and accurate village

59. Offg. Pres. B.I.A. to Sec. Govt. N.W.P.&O. 22 May 1882, Oudh Rev. Progs. May 1883, No. 4.

60. Lala Ram Shankar Lal to Sec. Govt. N.W.P.&O. 22 May 1882, *ibid*.

61. Sec. Govt. N.W.P.&O. to Sec. Govt. India 23 June 1882, *ibid*. Lyall's arrangements were approved in Sec. Govt. India to Sec. Govt. N.W.P.&O. 16 October 1882, *ibid*.

accounts. Only "persistent default" in the payment of a patwari's salary, or "habitual" error or delay in the preparation of village papers, would cause a patwari to be brought onto the register as a "State servant" and paid directly at the tahsil office. Dismissal of a patwari was to be made in consultation with the landlord, or if initiated by the landlord with the sanction of the Deputy Commissioner. The net result of all this was, as Lyall himself noted, to place the Oudh patwari on a basis not so different from that of "that other important class of village servants, the chaukidars."[62]

In 1889, pressed for funds, the government revoked the special tax concession. Instead it imposed itself a patwari rate of 1½ percent on the annual value (*nikasi*) of all estates in Oudh, and authorized the landlord to recover from the tenant on this account a sum equivalent to one and a half pies in the rupee on his rental. The patwari was ordered to collect his monthly salary in cash from the proceeds of this fund at the government tahsil office. To mollify the landlords the act gave explicit recognition to their right of nomination and overall supervision, and left intact their right to be consulted before the dismissal or suspension of any patwari on their estates.[63] The taluqdars at once realized that the motives behind the act were not entirely fiscal. Pointing out that control over the disbursement of patwari salaries had been secured to them even when the government bore the cost, they insisted that it was essential to their interests as landlords to prevent the growth, which government payment would encourage, of "an overweening sense of independence in the patwaris."[64] In his reply the Lieutenant Governor tried to minimize the extent of the change by pointing to the landlord's continued influence over appointment and dismissal, but he concluded with the flat admission that since the passage of the 1886 Rent Act "the patwari is called on to register and record the important rights secured to tenants, and the taluqdars' claim for exclusive control, based on a former law and other conditions, is no longer acceptable."[65]

A few years later a concerted attempt was made to take the last step to exclusive government control. In 1895 a committee appointed to revise the revenue law of the province recommended that the landlord's right of nomination be abolished and the Collector take into his own hands all authority over appointments. The slow transformation of the patwari into a government servant, whose circle might comprise parts of several estates, had, they said, undermined all incentive on the part of the landholder to keep the patwari up to the mark. Yet with assessment now based on his records, rather than on an independent survey, "they have assumed far

62. Sec. Govt. N.W.P.&O. to all Commrs. and Depty. Commrs. in Oudh 2 April 1883, *ibid*.
63. Resolution of Oudh Revenue Dept. of 29 May 1889, Oudh Rev. Progs. August 1889, No. 7.
64. Pres. B.I.A. to Sec. Govt. N.W.P.&O. 12 March 1890, Oudh Rev. Progs. April 1890, No. 3-4. The taluqdars also wanted tenants holding any statutory rights to be charged the full amount of the cess.
65. Sec. Govt. N.W.P.&O. to Pres. B.I.A. 2 April 1890, *ibid*., No. 6.

greater importance than they formerly possessed, and the interests of Government are more closely connected with their correctness." At the same time the increasing competition for land had made these records far more important to the peasantry than in the days when cultivators were fewer and land less in demand. "Honesty, efficiency, and independence" could now only be secured by empowering the Collector to appoint to the post of patwari the most suitable man he could find.[66]

Although this proposal won the support of the Lieutenant Governor, and of most revenue officials in the province, it was ultimately vetoed by the Government of India. They coldly pointed out that the Collector could already refuse to approve an unqualified nominee. Nor would a change in the law necessarily act to "counterbalance the influence of a powerful and unscrupulous zamindar." Indeed so far as the scheme were successful in bypassing the zamindar it might well only inflict on the villager a rapacious underling of the Collector's office bent on making money out of his charge. They suggested that the principle of hereditary succession should be legally recognized as the appropriate way of filling vacant patwariships. In the absence of an heir the proprietor should be allowed to nominate, and if he recommended an unqualified person the Collector should himself appoint.[67]

The patwari thus entered the twentieth century still a servant of two masters—the government and his landlord. From the point of view of the government, which paid him, he was expected solely to maintain the records of rent and revenue, ownership and occupancy, which were required by the Revenue Department, and in general to expedite the work of government in the area of his circle. But the villager did not see it that way, nor did the landlord. So late as 1911 W. H. Moreland reported that "the patwari is still looked on as the servant of the landholders, is expected to help in rent-collecting and in the general management of the land, and in particular to side with the landholders against the revenue officers of Government."[68]

Before the changes of the 1880s this blurring of the patwari's responsibilities had of course been even more pronounced. Indeed one of the taluqdars' motives for opposing the 1889 act, which gave the government control of patwari salaries, was the fear that they would lose "the added benefit" of having these men work in their estates as their *mutasaddis* (accountants).[69] Government patwaris and estate mutasaddis were, moreover, at all times drawn from the same caste, the Kayasthas, and frequently in a given locality came from the same family. "It often happens," remarked the Sitapur Deputy Commissioner in 1860, "that a man whose proper functions are those of a

66. Secretary Revenue Act Committee to Sec. Govt. N.W.P.&O. 23 April 1895, N.W.P.&O. Rev. Progs. July 1895, No. 12.

67. Sec. Govt. India to Sec. Govt. N.W.P.&O. 15 June 1898, N.W.P.&O. Rev. Progs. May 1899, No. 125. Only minor modifications were accordingly made in Act IX of 1889.

68. Moreland, *Revenue Administration of the United Provinces*, p. 76.

69. Memorandum of Athar Ali, Legal Adviser to the B.I.A., on the 1889 Patwari Bill, of 25 February 1889, B.I.A. Records.

putwary is exalted to the position of a personal servant of the talookdar, some other member of his family performing the proper village duties." Thirty-five years later, in 1896, Qamar Ali protested against the suspension of one Musaddi from Pratabgarh estate service on the ground that "he is the brother of the patwari of Aurangabad and many matters are settled because of him. . . . If he is suspended without due cause it means that the patwari will go against us."[70]

The landlord, then, clearly guarded his control over the patwari far more jealously than he did with the chaukidar. Both men to be sure increased the number of his dependents, and his power in the locality. But control of the village accountant brought the landlord immediate and tangible benefits in his central role of rent receiver. Hence while the landholders of Oudh, so long as they were not saddled with extra charges, willingly abandoned their police responsibilities, they fought stubbornly to keep the patwari subordinated to them, and salvaged more of their predominance in the contest. But the drift toward increased government control could still not be stopped. The decision first in 1886 to award statutory rights in the soil to the cultivators, and a few years later to use recorded rentals in place of detailed surveys as the basis of assessment, gave a powerful impetus to this movement; for without accurate land records, and impartial revenue agents, neither measure could hope to succeed. A gauge of its incompleteness can be found in the ineffectuality of the 1886 Rent Act in practice.

The structure of local governance in Oudh thus brought together the informal and personal style of the landholder with the rationalizing bureaucratic spirit of the British Raj. Nor was this curious amalgam wholly a product of conscious choice, dictated by the policy of conciliating traditionally powerful groups in society. In part, too, surely it was a confession of administrative weakness. The British, that is, though far more powerful than any previous imperial regime, had still not the resources to penetrate deeply into the village, and so of necessity left much responsibility in the hands of those who had exercised it before. The taluqdars' continued exercise of quasi-judicial powers on their estates, in particular, owed nothing to their conquerors' beneficence. In the North-Western Provinces, where conciliation was less of an issue, the British went further in subordinating such men as the village patwari and chaukidar to their authority. But even there the influence of the local landholder was by no means wholly brought to an end.[71]

Nevertheless as time went on the landlord came to play an ever less important role in the machinery of local governance. A few, above all the Balrampur rajas, remained effective rulers of their localities, and some participated, as we shall see, in the new district boards the British created at the end of the

70. Depty. Commr. Sitapur to Commr. Khairabad 25 June 1860, B.R. Oudh General File 747; and Qamar Ali to Raja Pratabgarh 27 July 1896, Pratabgarh Estate Records.
71. For the N.W.P. see Whitcombe, *Agrarian Conditions*, pp. 246–51, 258–60.

century. But by and large as they lost control over the petty agents of government, and at the same time found the authority delegated to them too confining or too awkward to exercise, the landholders' interest dwindled, and their concerns shifted elsewhere. They remained of course powerful figures in the countryside, and impinged always on government from the outside, so that men pledged to new masters were often bent to serve the old. But they now increasingly sought other means to secure their predominance.

Eleven

Taluqdars and the Modern World:

Agriculture, Education, Politics

T HE COLLECTION of rents, and the settlement of disputes, were not ends in themselves. Rather they were the base on which was raised a distinctive taluqdari style of life. A part of this was derived from the ideals and expectations of their British rulers, who saw in this group of landholders a force for the development of Oudh agriculture, and the reinvigoration of the province's social and political life. Yet the taluqdars only partially cast themselves in such a role. For the most part their values and attitudes, and the opportunities open to them, drove them in a wholly different direction. This chapter investigates the extent and character of the taluqdars' participation in the new world the British were opening up before them. The next examines the distinctive features, and indigenous roots, of their now vanished style of life.

The Taluqdars and Agriculture

Above all of course the taluqdars were landlords. So one must begin by asking how far these men were involved in the agricultural process, and what they sought to accomplish with their lands. To what extent, that is, did they as landlords devote themselves to the expansion and improvement of cultivation, and direct the production and marketing of the produce, with the aim of maximizing their returns from the soil? Can it be said that the estate was an economic unit organized for some central purpose, or was it a collection of autonomous cultivators tied together only by an extractive mechanism?

The basic structural fact of the land system in Oudh, as throughout India, was the universality of peasant agriculture. *Sir* (home farm) land cultivated by hired labor existed almost everywhere, but it was only a tiny proportion of any estate, and seems rarely to have attracted much of its owner's attention until the twentieth century, when its freedom from the statutory tenancies created by the 1886, and even more the 1921, rent acts encouraged the landlord to try to preserve and enlarge it.[1] For the most part therefore the taluqdars had to work through or with their settled tenants to accomplish whatever they might wish to do. This at once ruled out as impracticable much that might otherwise have transformed agriculture in Oudh. Above all it made almost hopeless any effective response to the ideal of the "improving landlord" held out by the British. Though deeply engrained in British agricultural practice and popularized from the eighteenth century onward by such men as "Turnip" Townsend and William Cobbett, "improvement" was dependent on enclosure, which brought the old medieval strips of land together in large tracts, and relied for its success upon a capitalist farmer who controlled under the landlord the actual elements of production. No such transformation, which in effect would have made a landlord's entire estate a *sir* holding, was possible on the thickly settled peasant-held lands of northern India. Nor, with so much cheap labor in the countryside, was mechanization an economic proposition. The Indian landlord was tightly hedged in as to what he could do, or could be expected to do, a fact that must always be kept in view when assessing the taluqdars' activities, and their presumed shortcomings, as agricultural entrepreneurs.

There is no evidence to show that the taluqdars made concerted efforts to exploit their tenantry, nor indeed, as we have seen, would their limited administrative machinery normally have permitted them to do so. For the most part they sought little more than a steady rental income, and they viewed those on the land with a distant aloofness moderated on occasion by a paternalism that might move them to grant special favors or remissions of rent. To a very large extent they looked upon the misfortunes of their tenants as acts of God for which they were in no way responsible. During the 1896 famine, for instance, Qamar Ali did his best to arouse the raja to the seriousness of the situation. "Nowadays, Your Honor must realize," he wrote, "thousands of men die of hunger. No one gets bread. Big money-lenders live upon *sakho* [jungle tree] fruits." But even he admitted that after a time one became "stone hearted," and concluded only "may God show his mercy."[2]

1. In Faizabad, e.g., 39,600 out of an assessed area of 700,000 acres in the 1870s were held in *sir* or other forms of proprietary cultivation on estates of all sorts. Millett, *Fyzabad S.R.*, p. 509. For one taluqdar's productive use of his *sir* land see Nevill, *Fyzabad D.G.*, p. 23.

2. Qamar Ali to Raja Pratab Bahadur 14 August, 8 September, and 22 September 1896, Pratabgarh Estate Records.

Yet Pratab Bahadur, unlike many other taluqdars, did exert himself to relieve suffering at the time of the famine. He opened a poorhouse, sunk some thirty *pakka* (masonry) wells and gave tenants aid to build another forty, and distributed cash for the purchase of grain, though, as Qamar Ali noted, with only Rs. 50 daily for the entire Shahabad tahsil no one "gets anything other than a handful of grain." In 1897 after the famine had subsided, the estate built a storehouse where foodgrains, purchased on the market, could be kept until needed.[3] Pratab Bahadur also contributed to the district relief funds, and joined with other taluqdars in managing the government relief works. For the latter, the initiative came from the government, anxious for both fiscal and political reasons to "associate" the taluqdars and other "men of local influence" with its relief effort. Given responsibility, following a precedent set down in the Rae Bareli scarcity of 1878, for the supervision of such works as the building of tanks and embankments, the landholders of the province expended in all during 1896 and 1897 nearly five lakhs of rupees of government money, some of it in the form of interest-free loans repayable over two years.[4]

But participation in the relief effort, often undertaken in large part to gain the approbation of government, did not appreciably affect the taluqdar's attitude to his tenants. The maharaja of Balrampur, whose estate contributed over Rs. 40,000 for famine relief in 1896, was in this respect perhaps not an untypical figure. Frequently during the course of shooting tours of his estate Maharaja Digvijai Singh would stop in villages that he passed and lecture the villagers on the need for agricultural improvement. In the village of Varichorya, for instance, where he found almost 6,000 *bighas* of land lying fallow, he spoke at great length, and in great detail, on crop rotation, the proper seeds to use in different soils, and the techniques of manuring, ploughing, and irrigation. But when he went away, the maharaja's involvement in the agricultural practices of the village came to an end.[5] Digvijai's successor in the 1920s, the young Pateshwari Prasad, when chided by Gertrude Emerson for permitting dirty fly-ridden villages to exist in his estate, replied—tersely and simply—"Yes, the villagers are very naughty. They should keep their village clean."[6]

3. Pratab Bahadur, "Memoirs," Part III, pp. 4–6; Part IV, pp. 1–2. His efforts won Pratab Bahadur a commendation from the Lt. Gov. Sir A. MacDonnell. Minute by A. P. MacDonnell of 15 December 1897, N.W.P.&O. Rev. Progs. (Scarcity Dept.) March 1898, No. 167. Sanders also praised the raja for advancing money and seed to his tenants when heavy rains destroyed the *rabi* crops in 1894. Sanders, *Pratabgarh S.R.*, pp. 62, 85.

4. *Resolution on the Administration of Famine Relief in the North Western Provinces and Oudh During 1896 and 1897* (Allahabad, 1897), pp. 107–08. A total of 1,147 tanks and 247 embankments were constructed. See also Memorandum of a Meeting of the B.I.A. with the Lt. Gov. of 2 November 1896, *ibid.*, appendix, p. 152. For the Rae Bareli scarcity see Commr. Rae Bareli to Sec. Govt. N.W.P.&O. 19 February 1878, N.W.P.&O. Rev. Progs. July 1878, No. 18.

5. Hasan Rizvi, *Ahsan-ut-Tawarikh*, 2:415ff. Balrampur did, in the 1870s, introduce Punjabi wheat into some of its villages, with what results we are not informed.

6. Emerson, *Voiceless India*, pp. 155–56.

There were several ways in which taluqdars might—despite the constraints of peasant agriculture—increase the outturn or improve the standard of cultivation on their estates. The simplest, and one of the most profitable, was expansion of the cultivated area. This of course was not always possible. The Ajodhya properties in Faizabad had been "highly cultivated" since the later days of the Nawabi; hence there was little room for extension. During the revised settlement, between 1865 and 1895, the cropped area (excluding that held by underproprietors) grew by only 1,275 acres, from 92,278 to 93,552.[7] Some grantees, with capitalist entrepreneurs who had purchased waste tracts, eagerly set to work, like Dakhinaranjan Mukherjee, settling new villages, and even "stubbing the roots" of the jungle, in order to increase the value of their holdings.[8] By far the greatest opportunities for the extension of cultivation, however, lay in the thinly peopled sub-Himalayan districts of Bahraich and Gonda, further laid waste by Raghubar Dyal during his years as *nazim* just before annexation. In Bahraich the total cultivated area, some 35 percent of the district's surface in 1858, had risen to 50 percent in 1870, and to 65 percent by 1901. During the thirty years of the revised settlement some 60,000 acres of land in one pargana alone were brought under cultivation, much of it by the pargana's premier landlord, the raja of Pyagpur, a frugal "man of business," who by 1898 had secured the "almost complete recovery" of his estate from the devastation of half a century before. The spur, of course, was the hope of "largely increasing his rent roll," for such lands retained their old low assessments until the end of the existing settlement.[9]

Sometimes the extent of improvement was a matter of dispute. During his fifteen-year tenure of the Deotaha estate in Gonda Ajit Singh claimed to have spent Rs. 48,800 in clearing jungle, constructing wells and houses, and bringing in settlers of his own and "other superior and low castes" from as far away as Pratabgarh, and so increased the cultivated area from 6,841 to 10,487 acres.[10] The Gonda settlement officer, on going through the property, could find evidence of expenditures of only Rs. 972 on houses and wells, and "no trace" of any large jungle clearings. The increase in cultivation he attributed to the settled tenants extending their holdings and to "old residents who had absconded, trooping back to their villages," while the increase in the

7. Commr. Faizabad to Finanl. Commr. 22 September 1868, B.R. Faizabad File 41, Part I; and Memorial of Pratap Narayan Singh to Commr. Faizabad 9 June 1899, N.W.P.&O. Rev. Progs. October 1899, No. 17 (Statement B). Over the district as a whole the cultivated area grew by 62,000 acres, or 10 percent, over the same period. House, *Fyzabad S.R.*, p. 6.

8. Depty. Commr. Rae Bareli to Commr. Baiswara 17 August 1860, C.O.F. Bundle 148, File 54; and George Smith, *Life of Alexander Duff* (London, 1879), 2:354-55. See also Nevill, *Partabgarh D.G.*, pp. 25-26; *Sitapur D.G.*, p. 23; and N.B. Bonarjee, *Under Two Masters* (Calcutta, 1970), pp. 10-12.

9. Nevill, *Bahraich D.G.*, pp. 33-34, 82; and P. Harrison, Assessment Report of Pargana Bahraich of 13 February 1898, N.W.P.&O. Rev. Progs. April 1898, No. 20.

10. Ajit Singh Petitions of 6 November 1871 and 28 March 1872 to Chief Commissioner, B.R. Pratabgarh File 62.

value of the land, assessed at Rs. 6,232 in 1859 and Rs. 15,885 at the revised settlement, "arose from communications having been opened up and the rise in value of all agricultural produce. Over both of these causes the grantee [Ajit Singh] exercised no influence whatever."[11]

Perhaps most heated of all was the controversy that raged about the construction of *pakka* wells. Sanders, settlement officer in Pratabgarh, insisted that landlords rarely ever built wells for the use of their tenants, and indeed more often than not opposed tenants' building them themselves. Before 1886, he acknowledged, some landlords encouraged their tenants to build wells so that they might profit from the enhanced value of the land; a few, among them Ajit Singh, constructed wells for their tenants as a way of inducing them in the face of high rents to stay on the land. Even then tenants were required to obtain the landlord's permission before starting construction, and often as well to execute a *bazdawa*, or written deed, giving up all claim to compensation if the holding were later vacated. With the enactment of the Rent Act, he argued, the taluqdars, fearful that cultivators might use the existence of wells as a "fresh weapon of tenant right," almost invariably refused permission, so that there was no incentive at all for well-building.[12] Benett, reviewing the settlement reports, hotly contested this assertion. The mere fact that so many wells had been built, some 9,000 in Pratabgarh district, two-thirds of them by tenants, since the last settlement was, he insisted, ample proof that landlord opposition, if it existed, was "wholly ineffectual." To the contrary, he said, landlords commonly encouraged well-building by granting to the tenant desirous of making a well a few acres of land on which to plant a grove. This "very valuable property" represented his contribution to the enterprise.[13]

Nor did an expenditure on improvements, even when unquestioned, necessarily produce a useful result. Of the lakh and a half of rupees spent by the Nawab of Aliabad on his estate in Bahraich, the settlement officer reported, "a large part" had been wasted, with nothing to show for it. Despite heavy expenditures in the villages of Forest Circle No. II, he said, "the cultivated area of those villages at survey was actually lower than at the last settlement. Again, an irrigation pump was set up in one of the villages of the estate on

11. Settle. Offr. Gonda to Commr. Faizabad 30 September 1872, *ibid*.
12. Sanders, *Pratabgarh S.R.*,p p. 58-60, 275-76. Tenants who went ahead on their own faced ejectment, and were sometimes denied compensation in court. See J. A. Norrie, Assessment Report of Pargana Subeha (Bara Banki) of July 1896, N.W.P.&O. Rev. Progs. April 1897, No. 17 (para. 106).
13. Note by Settle. Commr. of 3 May 1895, on Assessment Report of Parganas Behar, Manikpur, and Rampur (Pratabgarh), N.W.P.&O. Rev. Progs. July 1895, No. 68; and Settle. Commr. to Sec. Bd. Rev. 20 August 1896, N.W.P.&O. Rev. Progs. April 1897, No. 18. Sanders denied that landlords in Pratabgarh ever made over land for groves, or supplied more than timber for the construction of new wells. H. F. House in Faizabad described the landlord's part in well-building as "giving him [the tenant] a stick or two, smiling approval and raising his rent" (Settle. Offr. Faizabad to Settle. Commr. 10 January 1896, N.W.P.&O. Rev. Progs. May 1898, No. 29, para. 10). See also W. H. Moreland, Assessment Report on 7 Baiswara Parganas (Unao) of 19 September 1894, N.W.P.&O. Rev. Progs. August 1895, No. 21 (para. 39).

the River Bakla, by the late Nawab. The expenses in connection with this pump are set down as being Rs. 20,000; it broke down after six years' use . . . and was sold for Rs. 800."[14]

One successful taluqdari enterprise, until the market collapsed in the years after 1900, was the growing of indigo. So early as 1868 2,500 acres were under indigo in Pratabgarh; at its peak in the 1890s the crop extended over some 4,000 acres in Pratabgarh and nearly 6,000 in Faizabad, the two major producing districts of the province.[15] Rarely taken up by ordinary cultivators because of the heavy outlay involved, indigo cultivation found favor among a number of the more well-to-do taluqdars, who were prepared even to build wells to encourage the crop. Most prominent among them was Raja Rampal Singh of Kalakankar, who derived a "considerable profit" from the produce of the twelve factories he put up and supplied with indigo grown on his estate.[16] Rampal Singh also, more perhaps than any other taluqdar, made a sustained effort to introduce European "improvements" into Oudh. In large part no doubt as a result of ten years' residence in England as a youth, and the anglicized style of life he brought back from it, he opened schools and dispensaries for his tenants, conducted experiments in cattle breeding, and initiated silk manufacture in the district. Benett, who disliked his advanced political opinions, nevertheless hailed Rampal Singh as "one of the most enlightened and useful members of Oudh society."[17]

Apart from indigo almost no other crops benefitted from active taluqdari encouragement. Qamar Ali told the Pratabgarh raja of his intention to take a graft of one variety of mango which he found particularly tasty, but there is otherwise no reference throughout the whole of that correspondence to the improvement of agriculture.[18] The two most remunerative and widely grown commercial crops, sugarcane and opium poppy, were wholly the product of

14. A. T. Holme, Pargana Charda Assessment Report of 6 May 1899, N.W.P.&O. Rev. Progs. November 1899, No. 171 (para. 29). The only productive expenditure was some Rs. 22,000 spent on wells, houses, and unrecoverable advances for seed. For similarly useless expenditure on the Tiloi estate see D. C. Baillie, Assessment Report on Parganas Inhauna & Mohanganj, of 25 May 1895, N.W.P.&O. Rev. Progs. July 1895, No. 86. One "well-conceived" improvement was the drainage canal built by Rana Shankar Bakhsh of Khajurgaon in the adjacent Rae Bareli pargana. Rae Bareli Assessment Report, n.d., N.W.P.&O. Rev. Progs. October 1897, No. 65 (para. 7).

15. Nevill, *Partabgarh D.G.*, pp. 51–52; and Nevill, *Fyzabad D.G.*, p. 25. For districtwise crop figures for 1868–69 see J. G. Forbes, *Report on the Sardah Canal Project* (Lucknow, 1871), Appendix J.

16. J. Sanders, Assessment Report of Parganas Behar, Manikpur, and Rampur (Pratabgarh) of 5 February 1895, N.W.P.&O. Rev. Progs. July 1895, No. 67; and Bhajan Lal, *Handbook of Pargana Rampur* (Lucknow, n.d. [ca. 1898]), p. 3. By 1923 only 227 acres were still planted to indigo in Pratabgarh district.

17. Rampal Singh to Settle. Commr. 3 September 1895, N.W.P.&O. Rev. Progs. November 1895, No. 8; and Note by Settle. Commr. of 4 October 1895, *ibid.*, No. 12. Rampal Singh's two silk factories, opened in 1896, were closed fifteen years later, after his death in 1909. See Nevill, *Partabgarh D.G.*, pp. 52–53; and H. N. Sapru, *Report on Industrial Survey of Partabgarh District* (Allahabad, 1923), pp. 8, 23. For Rampal Singh's educational and political activities see below pp. 328.

18. Q.A. to Raja 8 July 1896, Pratabgarh Estate Records.

Raja Rampal Singh
of Kalakankar.

tenant initiative. Indeed for the most part they were grown in order to obtain cash to pay the landlord's rent. Poppy was especially attractive because the Opium Department gave out advances at times when the cultivators most needed cash.[19] By and large, then, the tenants were the ones who responded to the incentives of the market, and made the decisions about what to grow and when. Nor did the British, even though it undercut much of their justification for the taluqdari system, object to this state of affairs. As Benett complacently commented, "It is not to be regretted that the landlords do not attempt to dictate to their tenantry, who are quite competent judges of their own interests in the matter, and who have already brought about the productive garden cultivation of every fertile inch of land, what crops they ought to grow."[20] Except insofar as it compelled tenants to grow cash crops, the estate was essentially a unit of management, not of production.

The government's own efforts on behalf of agriculture were directed to the running of demonstration farms, the importation of machinery, and, above all, the holding of agricultural exhibitions. Almost all of this was an exercise in futility. In one single year, for instance, attempts were made to introduce into Oudh American cotton, Carolina paddy, Muscat dates, and bulls of "a larger and stronger breed." The results were total failure. The bulls, the government regretfully reported, "have not been appreciated by the people.

19. See, e.g., Nevill, *Rae Bareli D.G.*, p. 33; and Nevill, *Sitapur D.G.*, pp. 30–31. In Faizabad district in the 1890s about 10,000 acres were usually laid down to poppy and 40,000 to sugar. House, *Fyzabad S.R.*, pp. 7–8.
20. Note by Settle. Commr. of 3 May 1895 on Assessment Report of Parganas Behar, Manikpur, and Rampur, N.W.P.&O. Rev. Progs. July 1895, No. 68 (para. 33).

They consider them too leggy and heavy for the little native cow of the country, and the Government bull lives fat but neglected. The truth seems to be that the Oudh peasant finds the small but inexpensive breed of his own country is amply strong enough to plough the light and friable soil. . . . "[21] Imported agricultural machinery was of course even more ludicrously inappropriate. Even though the Balrampur raja conceived the idea of using one of his 120 elephants to pull the large European plough, such equipment was purchased only as a novelty, or to please the government, and was then left to rust unused. The carefully controlled and lavishly funded experiments on the government farms likewise evoked no response from a hard-nosed agricultural community. These farms in the end devoted themselves almost wholly to the domestication of European fruits and vegetables for sale to the Anglo-Indian gardener.[22]

Fairs and exhibitions, designed to "arouse an interest in agricultural improvement amongst the landed proprietors" of the province, did strike a response—though hardly that intended. So early as January 1864, when an Agricultural Exhibition was held in Calcutta, the government "urged" the taluqdars to participate. Though most declined the invitation, and sent in for exhibition such items as, so the district officer described the raja of Tiloi's contribution, "a pot of dirty looking ghee of average quality and a bundle of bad tobacco," still the maharaja of Balrampur led a delegation of twenty-eight taluqdars, and brought home himself Rs. 2,345 in prize money for his draught cattle.[23] In December of the same year the first Oudh exhibition was held in Lucknow. Committees in each district, presided over by the local officials, rounded up exhibits from the taluqdars; these were then judged by the provincial Fair Committee, and prizes awarded on the final day of the fair by the Chief Commissioner, Sir Charles Wingfield. As a spectacle and entertainment the fair was a great success. English bands played, regiments marched in parade, public durbars were held, and people flocked to the grounds; but they came to be "amazed," or as the taluqdars put it in their letter of appreciation to the government, to "amuse ourselves by seeing strange English contrivances."[24]

An even grander exhibition was held in 1881. Convinced that if only the aid of the large landholders could be secured then "their influence and resources" would spread "far and wide" the principles of improved agriculture, the Lieutenant Governor Sir George Couper "induced" the taluqdars to form an organizing committee, with a British officer as secretary, and to throw open the Kaiserbagh, transformed for three days into an "attractive

21. *Oudh Rev. Admin. Report for 1872-73*, Part I, p. 53.
22. For an account of these activities see Whitcombe, *Agrarian Conditions*, pp. 97-110. For a scathing note on the Oudh Agri-Horticultural Society see McMinn, "Introduction to the Oudh Gazetteer," p. 369.
23. Sec. C.C. to all Commrs. 13 October 1863, et seq., B.R. Oudh General File 1068; and Baldeo Singh, "Life of Digvijai Singh," p. 251.
24. Hasan Rizvi, *Ahsan-ut-Tawarikh*, 4:530-40.

and colorful garden," to house displays of agricultural stock, produce, and implements, together with an array of local handicrafts. Wrestling contests, a flower show and fireworks provided diversion for the casual visitor, while the taluqdars met to discuss irrigation, cattle breeding, and improved ploughs. This conference, the central feature of the exhibition, provided a forum for much well-intentioned rhetoric, and drew from the taluqdars a commitment to hold such exhibitions annually, in the districts as well as at Lucknow.[25]

The Urdu *Oudh Akhbar*, full of praise for the taluqdars' efforts in organizing the exhibition, described it as "a successful beginning of the great task of developing the country."[26] Yet this initial burst of enthusiasm led nowhere. The first district exhibition, held in Bahraich two months later on the occasion of the annual fair at the shrine of the saint Sayyid Salar, elicited contributions of a mere Rs. 100 each from the four major taluqdars of the district, and did nothing to alter the "purely religious" character of that hugely attended event. Nor did the maharaja of Balrampur's offer of Rs. 300 for cattle prizes at the Debi Patan fair in Gonda leave any mark on that fair, which remained, as it had always been, a mart for the sale of hill produce.[27] The skeptical correspondent of the *Pioneer*, writing during the Lucknow exhibition, acknowledged that it was "in appearance at any rate" wholly the work of the taluqdars, but he went on to ask whether "these gentlemen, who love to swagger about in gold embroidered hats and coats, with postillions, outriders, *chobdars*, and all the tag-rag of oriental finery, really mean business, or do they merely dance like marionettes at the pull of the official wire?" The answer was never in doubt.[28]

Yet the taluqdars' indifference to schemes of agricultural development was not without its benefits, often no doubt unintended, for the province. In 1870 Capt. J. G. Forbes of the Irrigation Department put forward a scheme for the irrigation of all of Oudh north and west of Lucknow, at a total cost of 301 lakhs of rupees, from the waters of the Sarda River, which flows out of the

25. See *Papers and Proceedings of the Talukdars' Agricultural Meeting and Exhibition* (Lucknow, 1881) for the full text of all reports and speeches connected with the conference. In their role as patrons of arts and manufactures the taluqdars awarded prizes to exhibits set up in a host of different categories.

26. *Oudh Akhbar, passim*, esp. 14 March 1881, p. 871; 15 March 1881, p. 882; and 19 March 1881, p. 927. The local government also expressed considerable optimism.

27. For the Bahraich fair see *Oudh Akhbar*, 18 April 1881, pp. 1271–72; and Nevill, *Bahraich D.G.*, p. 55. The four taluqdars were Bhinga, Nanpara, Kapurthala, and Aliabad. The raja of Bhinga also offered Rs. 200 for the "best practical treatise, in Hindi or Urdu, on Improvement in Agriculture in Oudh." For Balrampur, and further schemes to use local fairs for the holding of cattle shows, see Maj. C. S. Noble, Secretary Talukdars' Agricultural Meeting, to Dir. Agri. & Commerce N.W.P.&O. 22 March 1881, *Papers and Proceedings of the Talukdars' Agricultural Meeting*, p. 4.

28. The *Pioneer*, 14 March 1881, p. 3; and 19 March 1881, p. 2. The taluqdars were still being exhorted to introduce improved methods and implements, and form agricultural associations, thirty years later. *Proceedings of the Agricultural Conference* (Allahabad, 1911), pp. 21 and *passim*.

A telling commentary on the taluqdars' indifference to schemes for agricultural improvement, this cartoon depicts the Lieutenant Governor Sir George Couper addressing in broken Urdu the Balrampur maharaja, president of the taluqdars' association. Of the ox, which represents the association, Couper says: "I knows it has great power. Every year surely it can pull the cart of the fair" [i.e., organize the exhibition].

The maharaja replies simply: "Whatever Your Honor says" (from the Oudh Punch *of April 15, 1881, reproduced by courtesy of the Director of the India Office Library and Records).*

Himalayas into Kheri district. Preliminary work had begun, with 100 miles of line surveyed and six bungalows built, when suddenly in September 1872 work was brought to an abrupt halt. The cause was the adamant hostility of the taluqdars. Such a canal was, in their view, wholly unnecessary, for Oudh possessed abundant supplies of water in its rivers and lakes, and had as well an ample rainfall. Canal water by contrast was "positively injurious" both to the soil and to human health. Mixed as it was with sand and gravel, such water, when spread over the land, would gradually "destroy its productive powers" and so leave the fields "perfectly barren." At the same time the "increased humidity" the canal brought with it would "contaminate the surrounding air," giving rise to "diseases hitherto unknown here, and epidemics peculiar to damp climates."[29] The taluqdars knew little about salinization and the spread of malaria, though a few had seen the depradations canals had wrought in the nearby Ganges-Jumna Doab. Their perceptions, though acute, were thus not couched in scientific terminology, and did not convince the skeptical British. What moved the government was rather the taluqdars' political weight, or as the Chief Commissioner, himself no enthusiast for the project, put it, the absence of "such a local call" as would make construction "the duty" of the Government of India.[30] The *Pioneer*, an ardent supporter of the scheme, remained convinced that the Sarda canal, "like a Thakoor's daughter," had been "smothered in the dark."[31]

But enthusiasm for the Sarda project would not be stilled. In 1879, after two years of poor harvests throughout India, the central government, at the urging of the Famine Commission, pressed upon Lucknow a revised proposal of Captain, now Major, Forbes, for the irrigation of the Ghagra-Gumti Doab. The Chief Commissioner, Sir George Couper, gave a reluctant assent on the understanding that the work was to be purely a protective measure against famine. Taluqdari opposition remained as intense as before, while the Government of India, anxious to avoid undue expenditure, ultimately refused, after the initial famine crisis had passed, to sanction the scheme except as a "productive" work with the local government as guarantor of the loan. So the matter was dropped.[32] The Irrigation Department, ever reluc-

29. See "Proceedings of a Meeting of the Committee of the B.I. Association Oudh of 29 May 1872," and B.I.A. Memorial of 12 August 1872 to C.C., B.I.A. Records, File 1. Among the speakers were Sheikh Inayatullah, Diwan Banna Mal, Amir Hasan Khan of Mahmudabad, and Dakhinaranjan Mukherjee.

30. Offg. P.A. to C.C. to Sec. Govt. India 5 September 1872, B.R. Oudh General File 2068, Part I. By 1881 the taluqdars were alluding to the "impregnation" of the soil with *reh* and "other alkaline substances" as one of the deleterious effects of canal irrigation. See Amir Hasan Khan to Maj. C. S. Noble 2 March 1881, *Papers and Proceedings of the Talukdars' Agricultural Meeting*, Appendix "B." For a full discussion of the salinization problem see Whitcombe, *Agrarian Conditions*, pp. 76–82, 285–89.

31. The *Pioneer*, 2 April 1873, p. 1. The paper reiterated its support of the canal in 1881 (12 March 1881, p. 2), though by 1904 it appeared to have changed its mind (9 September 1904, p. 2).

32. See "Memoranda on the Project for the Sarda Canal," by F. V. Corbett, Chief Engineer,

tant to abandon this "magnificent public undertaking," promoted the project once again in 1896. The taluqdars, their views solicited afresh, remained adamantly hostile, and they found a powerful ally in W. C. Benett, the Settlement Commissioner. Benett, citing figures that showed nearly one-fourth of the cultivated area of some districts already irrigated by wells, and much of the remainder by tanks, argued that the introduction of a canal would involve the needless supersession of one form of irrigation by another. Moreover, he contended, a canal could not be made to pay, for rents in Oudh were so high that it would be impossible to collect any additional charge for water. The Lieutenant Governor, Antony MacDonnell, concerned about the already high water table in the proposed canal tract, agreed with Benett; and so the Sarda canal was again laid to rest.[33] But not for long. Only a few years later, in 1903, a scheme was put forward to irrigate, from the waters of the Sarda River, the Ganges-Gumti Doab, especially the districts of Hardoi, Lucknow, and Unao, badly hit by the famine of 1896–1897. Initially conceived of as a mere inundation channel, which would run only in dry seasons to fill exhausted reservoirs, the project, once handed over to the Public Works Department's engineers, soon blossomed out into a fully developed "scientific" canal. The taluqdars reiterated their previous objections, while the government was not convinced that the canal would not add to the already substantial water-logging in Hardoi. So nothing was done.[34]

A decade later, in 1913, the taluqdars suddenly reversed themselves, and abandoned their forty-year opposition to the Sarda project. What moved them above all, apart from an apparently greater faith in the ability of British engineering to remove the obstacles of siltation and water-logging, was a proposal to divert the waters of the Sarda River to the Ganges Canal, and thence out of the province to Delhi and the Punjab. "One thing is certain," Sheikh Shahid Husain argued before his brother taluqdars, "that if we do not take early measures the water of the Sarda river may be lost to us forever. Now or never seems to me the question we have to settle." The increased frequency and severity of famine, together with the drying up of wells and the appearance of malaria even in dry seasons, had caused the taluqdars as well to question their long-settled conviction that Oudh, the "garden of India," was immune from drought and disease. In a canal, with its assured water

of 27 August 1896, N.W.P.&O. Rev. Dept. File 449B. For the taluqdars' views see Pres. B.I.A. to Sec. Govt. N.W.P.&O. 21 March 1881, Oudh Rev. Dept. Progs. March 1881, No. 8; and B.I.A. Records , File 1, *passim*.

33. Note by W. C. Benett of 17 September 1896, N.W.P.&O. Rev. Dept. File 449B; and Sec. Govt. N.W.P.&O. to Sec. Govt. India (P.W.D.) 9 May 1899, N.W.P.&O. Rev. Progs. May 1899, No. 202. To induce the taluqdars to support the canal, Corbett was prepared to let them raise rents on canal irrigated tracts beyond the limits set in the 1886 act. Corbett to Evans, Chief Sec. Govt., 20 October 1896, N.W.P.&O. Rev. Dept. File 449B.

34. Note by H. Marsh, Chief Engineer Irrigation, of 10 October 1903; and B.I.A. Memorial of 10 May 1904 to Lt. Gov., in B.I.A. Records, File 1. See also "Memo on Sarda Canal History" by Shahid Husain of 19 January 1912, *ibid.*

318 LAND, LANDLORDS, AND THE BRITISH RAJ

supply, they now saw the only guarantee of continued prosperity. Hence on August 16, 1913 a delegation of twenty taluqdars met with the Lieutenant Governor to urge upon him the construction of a full-fledged Sarda Canal in Oudh.[35] Not perhaps wholly by coincidence, the work was taken in hand almost at once, and fifteen years later the canal was in operation. Its benefits, however, remain to this day ambiguous and uncertain, so the province may well have cause to be grateful to those who for so long delayed its construction.

The Taluqdars and Education

The taluqdars' involvement in education, like their support for agricultural innovation, was fitful, sporadic, and often conspicuous, designed to show the British that they were an enlightened aristocracy. They put the bulk of their money where it would bring the most immediate returns in prestige. The tenants of course saw little of schools. The maharaja of Balrampur, playing the role of munificent grandee, during the 1860s opened ten schools in remote areas of his estate, such as Bankatwa, and from time to time when his shooting tours took him nearby he would lecture the villagers, especially those of the higher castes, on the need to educate their children. Yet these lectures accomplished little more than those on crop rotation. The combined enrollment in these poorly funded and rather "disorganized" schools never exceeded 250, and by the mid-1870s all were closed. Mirza Abbas Baig during the same years sponsored a vernacular school, to which he contributed Rs. 15 a month, on his Baragaon estate in Sitapur. But it too was closed after a short while when the taluqdar discovered that most of its former students had "forgotten what they had learnt a few years after leaving."[36]

Somewhat greater success attended the Anglo-Vernacular schools, aided for the most part by the government and located under the taluqdar's eye near his place of residence. Sometimes these were funded rather lavishly: Raja Udai Pratap Singh endowed his school at Bhinga with a sum of Rs. 16,500 on top of an initial expenditure of some Rs. 9,000, while Balrampur in the 1860s put Rs. 2,000 annually into a school for 150 pupils. But these schools were very few in number. In 1884 the Inspector of Schools counted only five with any prospect of lasting survival.[37] By the end of the century

35. Notes by Shahid Husain of 19 January 1912, 13 April 1913, and 5 September 1913; and extract from speech of 29 March 1912, *ibid*. Shahid Husain was Joint Secretary of the B.I.A. The scheme was framed in 1914, sanctioned in 1921, and put into service in 1928.

36. Hasan Rizvi, *Ahsan-ut-Tawarikh*, 4:481, 524-27, 569-72; *Oudh Education Report for 1868-69* (Lucknow, 1869), p. 51; *Oudh Education Report for 1874-75* (Lucknow, 1875), p. 30; and Evidence of J. C. Nesfield, Inspector of Schools Oudh, before Education Commission, *Report by the North-Western Provinces and Oudh Provincial Committee* (Calcutta, 1884), p. 256. The Balrampur maharaja's total expenditure on these schools at its height was Rs. 700 per year.

37. *Oudh Education Report for 1868-69*, pp. 5, 49-50; Note on Bhinga endowment in N.W.P.&O. Education Dept. Abstract B Progs. of 13 August 1881; and Evidence of J. C. Nesfield before Education Commission, *Report by N.W.P.&O. Provincial Committee*, p. 267. The five schools were those of Balrampur, Bhinga, Kapurthala (2), and Mahmudabad.

taluqdari expenditure on such schools had risen considerably. The Balrampur school had blossomed out into the Lyall Collegiate School, maintained by the estate at a cost of Rs. 6,000 a year; the rajas of Pratabgarh and Kalakankar, and the Bhadri estate, had founded schools which gave Pratabgarh district as many private as government high schools; the rajas of Jahangirabad and Nanpara, with Seth Raghubar Dyal and Sheikh Shahid Husain, among others, had endowed scholarships for the study of Persian or Sanskrit; while the raja of Mahmudabad, in addition to supporting the Colvin Anglo-Vernacular School in Mahmudabad town, which provided a hundred boys a day with a free education, gave generous annual grants to the fledgling Aligarh college and other Muslim schools.[38]

Even then those who founded schools still comprised but a small number of taluqdars, nor were they interested simply in disseminating learning as widely as possible. Schools were, for instance, always set up at the taluqdar's headquarters, even though this might involve inconvenient locations such as Kalakankar, a village on the banks of the Ganges twenty miles from the nearest paved road or railway; and concessions were often offered to members of the taluqdar's caste or clan. The prestige of English language instruction counted for a great deal as well. Two-thirds of Balrampur's educational expenditure was devoted to the Lyall School, while the Bhinga endowment was from the start made conditional on the continuance of English teaching in the school. For the most part the founding of schools was but a part, and not a very prominent part, of the taluqdar's assertion of his view of himself as a beneficent aristocrat. Results mattered hardly at all.[39]

Much the same motives lay behind the taluqdars' major corporate educational enterprise—the Canning College, Lucknow. Upon the death in 1862 of the former Viceroy Lord Canning, Maharaja Man Singh proposed to the assembled taluqdars, gathered in mourning, that they establish a memorial in his honor, to take the shape of a college, the first of its kind in the new province. As Man Singh grandly declared, such a college would "not only perpetuate the memory of our great benefactor, but so educate our children as to enable them to develop the material resources of our country, to eradicate the baneful effects of error, to excel in political wisdom and learning, and to . . . walk in the paths of virtue." The taluqdars further agreed to pay an annual levy of eight annas on every hundred rupees of land revenue as a

38. See Balrampur Annual Report for 1901–02, Estate Records 1902–03, Dept. 54, File 2; Nevill, *Partabgarh D.G.*, pp. 139–40; N.W.P.&O. Education Dept. Abstract B. Progs. October 1887, No. 3, and March 1898, No. 1; and S. K. Bhatnagar, *History of the M.A.O. College Aligarh* (Bombay, 1969), pp. 67, 125, 180, 205, and *passim*. Raja Amir Hasan Khan gave Aligarh Rs. 600 annually from 1879 onward. See below ch. 12 for further discussion of taluqdari patronage of education.

39. For some perceptive comments on the taluqdars' attitude to education see the evidence given before the Education Commission by J. C. Nesfield, *Report by the N.W.P.&O. Provincial Committee*, pp. 256, 267; Munshi Durga Prasad, Assistant Inspector of Schools, *ibid.*, p. 186; Sayyid Ikbal Ali, Offg. Subordinate Judge Gonda, *ibid.*, pp. 222–23; and Raja Udai Pratap Singh of Bhinga, *ibid.*, pp. 346–48.

perpetual endowment for the maintenance of the school. The college opened as a high school in temporary quarters in 1864. Two years later a European headmaster, M. J. White, was employed, and college instruction commenced. By the end of the decade, enrollment had grown to 700, mostly in the school department; a few years later, in 1877, after lengthy wrangling over the proper site, the college's own building was constructed in Kaiser-bagh, near the taluqdars' town residences.[40]

This enterprise, which cost the taluqdars some Rs. 25,000 a year in the late 1860s and over Rs. 40,000 twenty years later, offered the exciting prospect of a truly educated aristocracy in Oudh, masters of English language and learning, working together for the good of the province. Yet this vision was not to be. From the outset, after their initial surge of enthusiasm, the taluqdars took little interest in the college they had founded. So early as 1865, after only one year of operation, the government had to step in to collect arrears of subscriptions due to the college, a practice soon regularized by the conversion of the college subscription into an additional educational cess. Twenty years later, J. C. Nesfield insisted, taluqdari zeal had so far slackened that were the payment of the college tax made purely optional, "the Canning College would in a few years cease to exist."[41] Nor were the sons of taluqdars at all prominent on the rolls. Amir Hasan Khan of Mahmudabad, while a minor under the Court of Wards, was among the first students of the school, but few followed him. In 1869 only 24 taluqdars had sons in attendance, compared with 49 zamindars and other petty landholders, 380 government and private servants, 119 *hakims* and professional men, together with smaller numbers of traders, artisans, and pensioners.[42] In 1884 one taluqdar's son alone was studying for the B.A., the other students being overwhelmingly of Brahmin and Kayastha service and professional families.[43]

The taluqdars nevertheless refused to give up their control over the college, exercised through an independent governing committee, presided over by the Commissioner of Lucknow Division, and containing equal numbers of

40. Speeches by Man Singh of 18 August 1862 and 27 February 1864, *Proceedings of the Meetings of the British Indian Association of Oudh, 1861–1865* (Calcutta, 1865), pp. 61, 161, (hereafter *Progs. B.I.A. 1861–65*); and Khan Bahadur Sheikh Siddiq Ahmad, *Tarikh-i-Anjuman-Hind-Avadh* (Lucknow, 1935), 1:121–29. The government matched the taluqdars' contribution each year.

41. Evidence of J. C. Nesfield before Education Commission, *Report by the N.W.P.&O. Provincial Committee*, p. 265. For correspondence regarding the government collection of college subscriptions see B.R. Oudh General File 86, Part I. A good many taluqdars protested this enforced payment.

42. "Report of the Fourth Annual Examination of the Canning College" (Lucknow, 1869), UPSA C.O.F. Bundle No. 50, File 64. See also *Oudh Education Report for 1867–68* (Lucknow, 1868), p. 25.

43. *Report by the N.W.P.&O. Provincial Committee* (of the Education Commission), p. 95. Of the parents, 72 were in government or private service, 7 were pleaders, 7 priests, 6 shopkeepers, 2 bankers, and 15 zamindars and other petty landholders. For an account of life at the college in its early days see Brajendranath De, "Reminiscences of an Indian Member of the Indian Civil Service," *Calcutta Review* 129 (1953):155–69.

taluqdars and government officers. On several occasions the Education Department, concerned over the pension and promotion prospects of its staff, and the availability of funds to finance expansion, sought to bring the college under its wing. But they were as often rebuffed. Indeed in 1909, when new college buildings were under construction across the Gumti, where they formed the nucleus of the later University of Lucknow, the taluqdars agreed to raise their annual subscription by 50 percent, to twelve annas in the rupee of land revenue, rather than see the government take over the college.[44] Similarly they long resisted government efforts to lop off the lower school and the Oriental Department. The latter, which taught Sanskrit, Arabic, and Persian "on the native method," they especially cherished, and the Education Department as much disliked. Power and patronage were of course at stake here. So too was the taluqdars' conception of themselves as a munificent aristocracy. While they might not attend the college, it provided a conspicuous philanthropic enterprise which catered admirably to their self-esteem. Support of the college, the secretary of their association wrote in 1870, gives the taluqdars "the feeling that they are both benefiting the cause of education and keeping up, as a permanent mark of their gratitude to a Governor General to whom they owe much, an institution which bears his name."[45]

The taluqdars themselves meanwhile remained for the most part without formal schooling. In 1868–1869 only some 70 taluqdari pupils were enrolled in schools of any sort, while no more than a handful at any time during the later nineteenth century were well versed in English. Indeed among the major taluqdars the number of English educated hardly extended beyond the successive rajas of Mahmudabad, Raja Udai Pratap Singh of Bhinga, and Rampal Singh of Kalakankar. A special Wards' Institution set up in conjunction with the Canning College did little to overcome this lack of interest. The institution was "so excellently managed," lamented W. Handford, the Director of Public Instruction, "that only some extreme reluctance to part with their boys or a sad indifference to education" could account for the taluqdars "as a body not gladly taking advantage of it." Handford, with Barrow, lay much of the blame on the "weakness" of taluqdars unwilling to face *zanana* opposition. One might more appropriately fault the cultural attitudes of the kshatriya class, whose warrior ethos, though it no longer found an outlet in battle, still gave but little place to

44. *Oudh Education Report for 1870–71* (Lucknow, 1871), Appendix "D"; *Oudh Education Report for 1871–72* (Lucknow, 1872), p. 136; and Siddiq Ahmad, *Tarikh-i-Anjuman*, 1:131–38. See also the unnumbered file "Papers Relating to Canning College 1878-1919," B.I.A. Records. The maharaja of Balrampur donated a special three lakhs, and the taluqdars in 1912 came up with a further reluctant Rs. 50,000, to meet the construction costs of the new buildings.

45. Siddiq Ahmad, *Tarikh-i-Anjuman*, 1:129–31; *Oudh Education Report for 1875–76* (Lucknow, 1876), p. 70; and Sec. B.I.A. to Pres. Cann. Coll. Comm. 31 October 1870, in *Oudh Education Report for 1870–71*, Appendix "D," p. vi. See also *Report by N.W.P.&O. Provincial Committee* (of Education Commission), p. 48. The school departments were closed in stages between 1884 and 1891 as space became scarce in the college building.

bookish learning.[46] In any case by the mid-1870s, with no one in attendance except nine pupils sent by the Court of Wards, the government, despairing, closed down the Wards' Institution, and sent the remaining students home.[47]

Nevertheless the cause of taluqdari education was not dead. In 1884 the educated raja of Bhinga put forward a scheme for a special school to prepare the "sons of the upper class" for the discharge of the duties expected of them. Neither the government colleges, which turned out "dabblers" in newspapers and "noisy agitators," nor the discredited wards' institutions, which only opened the way to debauchery, were, he argued, at all appropriate for the education of taluqdars. They must be taught English, he insisted, but they must also be given "religious, moral, aesthetic, and physical" training, including elocution, drawing, and etiquette. For this they required a school of their own.[48] Four years later, in 1888, at the urging of Sir Auckland Colvin, the Lieutenant Governor, the taluqdars set up a committee to raise funds for a school. In 1890 Colvin laid the foundation stone of the building, on a plot donated by the government, where the school still stands opposite the Lucknow University, and classes commenced in 1892. Despite the apparent ease with which the Colvin School, named in honor of the Lieutenant Governor, was started, the project by no means commanded universal support among the taluqdars. Only the enthusiastic raja of Bhinga put a sizable sum of money—Rs. 20,000, twice that of Balrampur—into the school, while the other major taluqdars contributed no more than Rs. 2,000 to 4,000 apiece. In the end sufficient funds were raised only by the sale of Rs. 40,000 worth of promissory notes issued by the taluqdars' association, coupled with a donation of Rs. 20,000 from the Canning College Committee.[49]

Even more difficult was the task of securing students for the new school. Before its opening, the government had made up lists of those who ought to attend, and they put pressure on recalcitrant taluqdars to send their sons. The results were not promising. The Commissioner of Faizabad in 1891 submitted the names of sixty-seven eligible boys, but, he said, the parents of only seventeen were willing to see their sons enrolled. The rest were either wholly uninterested in the scheme, or else, cowed by "zanana influence," gave in to the wishes of ranis who did not want to part with their sons. Some too claimed that their sons knew too little Urdu to succeed in the school, or

46. *Oudh Education Report for 1868-69*, p. 8; and address by Colonel Barrow, in "Report of the Fourth Annual Examination of the Canning College," C.O.F. Bundle No. 50, File 64. Many taluqdars were however tutored privately. See below ch. 12.

47. Siddiq Ahmad, *Tarikh-i-Anjuman*, 2:651-53. See also the file of "Papers Relating to Canning College," B.I.A. Records.

48. Memorandum on the Education of the Sons of Landlords, by Udai Pratap Singh, raja of Bhinga, for Education Commission, *Report of the N.W.P.&O. Provincial Committee*, pp. 351-52. He was prepared to make attendance compulsory if the taluqdars did not willingly send their children.

49. Siddiq Ahmad, *Tarikh-i-Anjuman*, 2:653-57. In return for their donation the Canning College Committee won the right to sit as managing committee of the new institution.

were being satisfactorily educated at home. Even the raja of Bhinga, with two school-age sons, refused to send them, arguing that with a European tutor and Sanskrit pandit employed to teach them they were already learning as much as they would at the school![50] Exceptional pressure was brought to bear on the influential raja of Mahmudabad, Amir Hasan Khan, from whom the Lieutenant Governor himself extracted a "solemn promise" to send his two teen-age sons. Yet only fifteen boys actually appeared on the opening day of school. As an exasperated Commissioner of Lucknow, President of the School Committee, wrote, "Of course we ought to have opened with 30. But the excuses and shifts of the evasive talukdar-baccha [children] are endless. Some are being married, others are engaged in family ceremonies, and one went so far as to have epileptic fits. I have had endless personal correspondence. Raja Amir Hasan Khan still promises to send his eldest son in July, but he is so cracked that one cannot trust him. . . . I think one boy will come in the end. The trouble will be to keep him. The two Oel boys came for a day and then without leave went home: partly, I fear, owing to Raja Amir Hasan's bad example, for they asked me why the Mahmudabad boy had not come." When later questioned, the boys said they had left because "the Rani had sent two telegrams recalling them."[51]

Before the year was out the government had abandoned the attempt to coerce the taluqdars into sending their children to the school. Benett from the outset had questioned the advantage of government interference in such matters, and Colvin himself ultimately admitted that the school must "be left to time to prove its usefulness. If it works well boys will gradually come and its popularity will increase. . . . But if they are forced to join, we shall make it hated and feared by the taluqdar families."[52] But this did not stop district officers, or successive Lieutenant Governors, from lecturing the taluqdars on the need to educate their sons. Colvin himself had set the tone, while opening the school, when he warned the taluqdars that they would be "supplanted" as the political leaders of the province if they continued to neglect English education. Sir John Woodburn in 1902 reiterated that "in these modern times" success in any walk of life was impossible without education.[53] Yet the

50. Commr. Faizabad to Sec. Govt. N.W.P.&O. 2 October 1891, N.W.P.&O. Educ. Progs. March 1893, No. 103–105; and Commr. Faizabad to Sec. Govt. N.W.P.&O. 16 September 1892, *ibid.*, No. 153. See also Statement of Taluqdar Sons or Relatives in Lucknow Division, in Commr. Lucknow to Sec. Govt. N.W.P.&O. 28 October 1891, *ibid.*, No. 110. The Bhinga children did ultimately attend the school.

51. H. D. O'Moule to J. LaTouche 16 May 1892 (demi-official), N.W.P.&O. Educ. Dept. File 410; and Commr. Lucknow to Sec. Govt. N.W.P.&O. 25 May 1892, N.W.P.&O. Educ. Progs. March 1893, No. 143.

52. W. C. Benett Note of 8 October 1891, and A. Colvin Note of 23 September 1892, N.W.P.&O. Educ. Dept. File 410. See also Sec. Govt. N.W.P.&O. to Commr. Faizabad 27 September 1892, N.W.P.&O. Educ. Progs. March 1893, No. 155.

53. For discussion of Colvin's speech see "Oudh Punch" of 5 May 1892, *S. V.N. 1892*, p. 165; and "Hindustan" (Kalakankar) and "Hindustani" (Lucknow) of March 1892, *ibid.*, p. 106. Woodburn, at the time Lt. Gov. of Bengal, spoke on the occasion of the unveiling of a statue of Maharaja Man Singh, 13 August 1902. B.I.A. Records, File 19.

taluqdari response to these exhortations was never more than halfhearted. Apart from 1892 itself an average of no more than seven new boys a year joined the Colvin School throughout its first two decades, and total enrollment rarely rose much above thirty. So late as 1918 Sir Harcourt Butler was still urging the taluqdars to "fortify your position" by "educating your children."[54]

In the organization and running of the school only a few subjects aroused much interest among the taluqdars. Perhaps most empassioned was the controversy that raged about the status-laden question of servants. The government had initially proposed that each boy be allowed to keep with him at school no more than three personal servants, only one of whom was to be allowed to reside in the building. The taluqdars at once sought to raise the number to five. Colvin, exasperated by the "excessive importance" the taluq-dars attached to this question, determined to hold fast at three. His successor, Crosthwaite, gave way and let each boy have four, to live wherever they wished. But he was not happy with the decision. "If no servants were allowed," he wrote confidentially, and corporal punishment was permitted, "there might be some hope for the boys."[55]

The principal, H. G. Siddons, an Oxford graduate and former principal of the M.A.O. College, Aligarh, nevertheless did his best to run the school along the lines of an English public school. He was instructed by the rules to "strive to train the boys to habits of order and industry, to inculcate good manners and moral conduct [and] . . . more especially seek to cultivate in them manliness and self-respect." One "old boy" remembers Siddons as a "very strict disciplinarian" who took his own school, Harrow, as his model.[56] Sports were of course emphasized from the start. Each boy was expected to keep a riding horse, a Games Club was formed, and school teams competed in various sports, though, as one writer lamented in the school journal, "We are greatly handicapped by our small numbers, the result of which is that the same few boys represent the school in almost every branch of sport." The high point of the school year was the annual Old Boys' Day, presided over by the Governor of the province. On this occasion tournaments and competi-tions, sometimes pitting old boys against scholars, were held in an array of

54. The *Colvinian* (Lucknow, 1912), pp. 21-23, gives a complete list of the school's "Old Boys." By the 1920s, enrollment, though fluctuating between 45 and 60, averaged 50 boys annually. For Butler's speech of 10 April 1918 see File of "Addresses to Viceroys and Lt.-Govs.," B.I.A. Records. In a speech of 15 February 1915 Butler reminded the taluqdars of Woodburn's 1902 advice. The *Colvinian* (1915), p. 2.
55. Sec. B.I.A. to Commr. Lucknow 23 March 1892, enclosing suggested amendments to the proposed rules for Colvin School, N.W.P.&O. Educ. Progs. March 1893, No. 131; Sec. Govt. N.W.P.&O. to Commr. Lucknow 23 April 1892, *ibid.*, No. 138; Note by A. Colvin of 10 November 1892, *ibid.*, No. 159; and Rules for the Colvin School enclosed in Commr. Lucknow to Sec. Govt. N.W.P.&O. 8 March 1893, *ibid.*, No. 170. For Crosthwaite see his Note of 5 January 1893, N.W.P.&O. Educ. Dept. File 410.
56. Interview with Raja Jagannath Bakhsh Singh of Rehwan (Rae Bareli), Lucknow, 13 March 1970. The principal was required to be a European educated in Europe, a restriction that remained in force until 1947.

sports, from tennis and hockey to chess and billiards, with an entire afternoon given over to riding sports, drill, tent-pegging, and the like. The social
elite of Oudh, taluqdars and officials together, formed the audience. At the
conclusion of the festivities the Governor distributed prizes, many of them
cups donated by taluqdari patrons, to boys who had excelled in sports and
studies.[57]

Yet Colvin was still in no way an English school. Not only were servants
allowed, and corporal punishment prohibited, but the physical setup itself
reflected the distinctive Indian environment. Each boy, for instance, had his
own separate set of rooms, and was responsible for his own meals. There was
no common messing. Hindu and Muslim, furthermore, lived apart. Though
the school was praised for imparting religious instruction equally to all, with
"the *Pandit* sitting side by side with the *Maulvi*," each community jealously
guarded its own autonomy. Indeed Udai Pratap Singh of Bhinga, fearful that
the Hindu taluqdars might be outdistanced in the race for English education,
wanted guarantees that the wing of the building set aside for Hindu boys
would never "be made use of for the accommodation of the Muhammadan
students." Otherwise, he said, "the Colvin Institute may in course of time be
converted into another Aligarh College." Although the predominantly
Muslim taluqdars of the districts around Lucknow did take disproportionate
advantage of the school—during the decade 1901–1910 some 55 percent of
the students came from Lucknow, Bara Banki, and Sitapur—the Colvin
School remained always wholly nonsectarian, and had a substantial Hindu
element.[58]

The instruction at the school conformed closely to the normal Indian pattern, with its end point the entrance examination of the Allahabad University. Major emphasis was placed upon gaining facility in the use of English.
The teaching so far as possible was carried out in that language, and the boys
were encouraged to converse in it. Some elements of traditional culture were
included in the curriculum as well. Instructors were hired for Persian,
Arabic, and Sanskrit, while the principal was specially directed to see that
boys so far as possible did not abandon their national dress. The taluqdars
insisted too that three religious teachers, a Hindu pandit and Sunni and Shia
maulvis, be appointed to "enforce the performance of their religious duties"
upon the boys. When turned aside by the government in their request for
funds they agreed to pay the salaries of these men out of their own pockets.[59]

Practical education, designed to fit the taluqdars for their special position
in life, was another matter. While the school was being organized, M. J.

57. The *Colvinian* (1911), p. 10; (1913), p. 7; and *passim*. This annual function was still
being held so late as 1969, when I was resident in Lucknow. By this time, though the Governor
still presided, it had been compressed from two days into an afternoon.

58. The *Colvinian* (1912), p. 12; and Memorandum by Udai Pratap Singh of 4 April 1892,
N.W.P.&O. Educ. Progs. March 1893, No. 137. In 1918 all but one of the masters were Hindu.

59. Sec. Govt. N.W.P.&O. to Commr. Lucknow 23 April 1892, N.W.P.&O. Educ. Progs.
March 1893, No. 138; and Rules for Colvin School, *ibid.*, No. 170.

White, principal of Canning College, had proposed that in such subjects as arithmetic and grammar "technicalities" be eschewed in favor of, for instance, quick and accurate calculations of interest rates. He further urged that the Colvin boys not sit for the middle school examination, which would require them to learn "a great deal that is of no use to them," but rather undertake studies "specially adapted to their circumstances." The taluqdars would have none of it, and insisted that the boys take the usual examination.[60] In 1893, as plans were taking shape to found a government agricultural school at Kanpur the taluqdars asked that the school be located instead in Lucknow. In that way, they said, the Colvin students, for whom such "useful instruction" would be of great value, could have the opportunity of attending the lectures. The Agricultural School remained in Kanpur near the government experimental farm, but its principal urged, three years later, that an agricultural instructor, and a small demonstration farm, be attached to the taluqdars' school. Despite the taluqdars' presumed interest nothing was done.[61]

In 1904 Ali Muhammad Khan, the young raja of Mahmudabad, in an elaborate and lengthy note raised once again the question of a "special course of study" designed to meet the taluqdars' "peculiar wants." First and foremost among these, he argued, was instruction in agricultural science. With every taluqdar "head of an agricultural community," his continued ignorance of this subject was "inexcusable." Beyond this taluqdars were capitalists and employers of labor, and so needed to know something of political economy, while many of them aided in the administration of justice, and so required some knowledge of law. These subjects, he suggested, together with Oudh history and revenue policy, should form a two years' course to be taken at Colvin School after the passing of the matriculation exam, to be followed by a further year of "practical training" on some Court of Wards estate. As few taluqdars went to university in any case, the new course would not curtail their general studies, but give an "impetus" to their further education.[62]

The press, often critical of the exclusive Colvin School, applauded Mahmudabad's scheme.[63] Yet nothing came of it until finally, in 1912, classes in agriculture, and belatedly in science as well, were started. An agricultural instructor was hired, some equipment purchased, and a plot of land put under cultivation. Boys were taken once or twice a week to the field to observe the agricultural work, and they did occasional laboratory exercises

60. Memorandum by M. J. White of 22 November 1889, *ibid.*, No. 92; and Note of 27 June 1891, *ibid.*, No. 93. The taluqdars claimed that the stimulus of a public examination would make the boys work harder.

61. Pratap Narayan Singh to Commr. Lucknow 4 February 1893, *ibid.*, No. 76; Sec. Govt. N.W.P.&O. to Commr. Lucknow 6 March 1893, *ibid.*, No. 77; and Note on Agricultural Education by P. V. Subbiah, Principal, Kanpur Agricultural School, of 1 March 1896, N.W.P.&O. Rev. Progs. June 1896, No. 150.

62. Ali Mahomed Khan, *Note on the Education and Training of Taluqdars of Oudh* (Lucknow, 1904), pp. 1, 4-5, 8, 11-12, and *passim*.

63. For extracts of press comment see *ibid.*, pp. 15-24.

with seeds and the like. The objective was not to turn out "Scientific Agriculturists" but simply to give the students "as much [knowledge] as is possible of agricultural matters and what is more important . . . such an interest in them as will add to the attractions of a country life." Much of what took place in these classes, however, if not wholly bookish, was hardly relevant, such as using the school's pump to irrigate the hockey field. Nor did the school evidence much enthusiasm for these classes. They left the government to pay the salary of the agricultural instructor, and in 1917, when the government proposed the creation of a proper two-year course, somewhat along the lines of the Mahmudabad proposal, the school committee, insisting that agriculture was an "extra" subject to which only limited time could be devoted, rejected it.[64]

The Colvin School clearly did little to advance the cause of agricultural improvement in Oudh. Its successes were most marked in English language instruction. By the later years of British rule almost all the major taluqdars, and many of the lesser as well, could converse easily in that tongue, and had at least a general familiarity with the culture that lay behind it. But their understanding of Western ways was never very deep. Their image remained always, as it had been in 1904, that of "fashionable gentlemen only, playing hockey, smoking cigars, riding bikes, and aping European customs and manners."[65]

Politics and Social Reform

The taluqdars took part in the political life of the province both as individuals and through a common organization, the British Indian Association of Oudh, founded in 1861, to which they all belonged.

With the introduction from the mid-1880s onward of representative institutions at the local level the taluqdars individually, each in his own home area, participated in them. The district boards set up under the Ripon reforms they dominated until well into the twentieth century. Raja Rampal Singh of Kurri Sidauli reported in 1908 that he had been a member of the Rae Bareli district board, with only a three-year break, continuously for twelve years. Raja Pratab Bahadur Singh joined the Pratabgarh district board in 1884, soon after it was established, and a few years later was elected vice-president. When not himself a member he secured representation of his interests by the nomination of such men as the estate's legal adviser.[66] As few taluqdars resided in towns they played a less conspicuous role in municipal affairs. Even so, Pratab Bahadur from time to time sat on the municipal board of nearby Bela, four miles from his residence, while the Ajodhya

64. The *Colvinian* (1912), pp. 1, 8–9; and (1914), pp. 8–10; and Meeting of School Committee of 20 August 1917, Proceedings 1917–1927, Colvin School Records.
65. "The Advocate" (Lucknow) of 18 August 1904, cited in Ali Mahomed, *Note*, pp. 20–21.
66. Raja Rampal Singh evidence before decentralization commission, *P.P.*, 1908, 45:726; and Pratab Bahadur, "Memoirs," Part I, pp. 74–75; Part II, p. 2; Part III, p. 3. See also p. 262 above.

Maharaja Pratap Narayan Singh, in collaboration with a Khatri mercantile family, controlled the affairs of the large city of Faizabad, with which Ajodhya was itself incorporated, up to 1905.[67] A logical and natural extension of the taluqdars' local predominance, such political activity was encouraged both by the smallness of the electorate, which made manipulation easy, and by the active support of the British, who frequently nominated taluqdar members when they were not elected.

From local boards the taluqdars moved easily into the provincial legislative council, especially after its enlargement under the 1892 Councils Act. Some few, the maharaja of Balrampur and Amir Hasan Khan of Mahmudabad among them, appointed by the Viceroy, had sat briefly on the Imperial Legislative Council in the 1870s and 1880s. But it was the Allahabad Council, which usually had two or three sitting taluqdari members, that offered the greatest prospects for political activity. Though most taluqdars served by the nomination of the provincial government, a few secured entrance by election, from constituencies composed of municipal and district board members.[68]

The most outspoken of taluqdari politicians was the maverick raja of Kalakankar, Rampal Singh. Victorious in the first election, that of 1893, and after 1896 a nominated member, Rampal Singh made the legislative council for almost a decade a sounding board for the advanced political opinions he had brought back from England. He was at the same time a member of the Indian National Congress, which he joined in 1886, a year after its founding. In 1888, when the Congress met at Allahabad, he served as secretary of the Reception Committee; and he attended the annual sessions regularly until almost 1900. On the platform, as in the columns of his Hindi newspaper, the *Hindustan*, published from Kalakankar, he spoke out on behalf of the Congress program of the time, including simultaneous ICS examinations in India, Council reform, and the "drain" of money to England. Nor did he forget the interests of the privileged group of which he was a member. He argued for instance in favor of breaking the Aligarh hold on the Muslim council seat by awarding it to a Muslim taluqdar such as the raja of Jahangirabad. He was at pains as well to deny the imputation that the "Congressists" were disloyal. They fully appreciated, he insisted, the "blessings of British rule," but simply asked for "their rights and privileges."[69]

67. Harold A. Gould, "Local Government Roots of Contemporary Indian Politics," *Economic & Political Weekly* 6 (1971):459-60.

68. Three of the six elected members were usually men with large landed interests. For a list see F.C.R. Robinson, "Consultation and Control: The United Provinces' Government and Its Allies, 1860-1906," *Modern Asian Studies* 5 (1971):334, n. 66.

69. "Hindustan" of 17-22 January 1888, *S.V.N. 1888*, p. 52; 12 April 1888, *ibid.*, p. 261; 1 May 1894, *S.V.N. 1894*, p. 191; 8 June 1898, *S.V.N. 1898*, p. 315; and 28-29 September 1898, *ibid.*, p. 533. Rampal Singh actively canvassed other taluqdars in his losing 1896 election bid. See his letter of 14 September 1895 to Pratab Bahadur requesting his support, in Pratabgarh Estate Records. For a sketch of Rampal Singh's career see B.D. and B.P. Majumdar, *Congress and Congressmen in the Pre-Gandhian Era* (Calcutta, 1967), pp. 104-05, 367-77; and Bayly, *Local Roots of Indian Politics*, pp. 71-72, 147.

Rampal Singh however stood alone as both taluqdar and Congressman. Udai Pratap Singh of Bhinga voiced the sentiments of the overwhelming majority of Oudh landlords when in a series of pamphlets and newspaper articles he denounced the Congress as a collection of "lawyers without briefs" and "authors without readers." These men, he said, echoing the views of the taluqdars' British patrons, levelers and innovators, represented no one in the countryside, neither the peasantry nor their "natural leaders," the landed gentry and aristocracy. To give in to their demands would be tantamount to handing the country over to an irresponsible clique of Bengalis.[70] This landlord antagonism to the Congress, an inevitable product of their conflicting interests, hardened as the nationalist movement grew more populist. By 1901 even Rampal Singh had become disillusioned. In subsequent years, though the Balrampur estate lent tents to the Congress for its 1916 Lucknow session, and later Kalakankar rajas, close to the Nehrus, revived the family's dissident tradition, the taluqdars remained almost wholly walled off from nationalist politics.

The taluqdars' political activity as individuals was supplemented, and rendered far more effective, by the work of the British Indian Association. Through this organization, which contained as members all Oudh taluqdars and no one else, the taluqdars dealt with the government, acted together on behalf of their joint educational and social reform activities, and pursued their common interests as a privileged group of landholders. Above all the association dedicated itself to the defense of the taluqdari land settlement. Unquestionably the basic motivating force behind its founding, in 1861, was the taluqdars' fear of losing their newly won position on the land. In subsequent years on scores of occasions, and on subjects ranging from the appointment of patwaris to the constitution of the Court of Wards, the association fought to secure recognition of the taluqdars' "special rights and privileges." Proposed enactments relating to land revenue and tenancy, in particular, were subjected to a detailed clause-by-clause scrutiny. Similarly the association never let slip an opportunity to press for lower assessments. It doggedly fought the enhancements of the 1890s; thirty years later, in 1927, it was still asking the Viceroy for a permanent settlement on the Cornwallis model.[71]

With the widening of the political arena after the mid-1880s the association worked as well to secure taluqdari representation on the new councils. In 1896 when the provincial legislative council, though it contained three taluqdari members, had none recommended by the B.I.A., the association demanded the right, as "the representative institution of the landed classes of Oudh," of nominating a member of its own. MacDonnell refused this request, but the government, as we have seen, saw to it that the taluqdars

70. See, e.g., "The Growth of Radicalism in India and Its Dangers," *Calcutta Review* 167 (1887):1–7; and his pamphlet *Democracy Not Suited to India* (Allahabad, 1888).
71. Address to Lord Irwin of 22 February 1927, File of "Addresses Presented to Viceroys," B.I.A. Records. For the 1890s settlement see above ch. 8.

were always well represented. In 1918, with the coming of the Montague-Chelmsford reforms, their patron Harcourt Butler won for the association at last the right to select four members of the province's enlarged legislative council.[72] In its political views the B.I.A. reflected always the unremitting hostility to nationalism, and the Congress, of the bulk of its members. Although a divided executive committee in 1893 voted support for simultaneous ICS examinations in India (in part, some alleged, to secure Congress votes for the election of the Ajodhya maharaja to the Imperial Legislative Council), the association had already in 1888 voiced its strong disapproval of the Congress and all its works. This opposition it never altered or abated.[73]

The government solicited the association's views on almost all legislation affecting the province, and a good many more general questions besides, from the revision of the criminal procedure code to the regulation of the Hajj pilgrimage. On some of these matters the taluqdars held strong convictions. They strenuously opposed, for instance, regulations requiring mukhtars to be certified and to know English.[74] Above all, however, they were determined to see Oudh's separate identity as a province retained. They fought the 1877 amalgamation with the North-Western Provinces, and the 1902 change of name to the United Provinces. They argued for the maintenance of an appellate court at Lucknow outside the jurisdiction of the Allahabad High Court. When the government proposed consolidating the revenue laws of Oudh and the N.W.P., the taluqdars pleaded that the laws of Oudh, like its land tenures and local customs, were "special" and "peculiar," and so should be kept separate.[75]

The taluqdars did of course have an interest in Oudh's continued existence as a separate province, where they could wield a greater influence. But amalgamation in fact made little difference to the working of the Oudh administration, nor did it appreciably diminish the taluqdars' political weight. Throughout, the B.I.A. remained a focal point of the consultative political

72. Memorial of 20 April 1896, enclosed in Pres. B.I.A. to Sec. Govt. N.W.P.&O. 21 April 1896, N.W.P.&O. Rev. Progs. September 1896, No. 127; and Sec. Govt. N.W.P.&O. to Pres. B.I.A. 25 September 1896, *ibid.*, No. 133. For the 1918 controversy over landlord representation see P. D. Reeves, "Landlord Associations in U.P. and Their Role in Landlord Politics, 1920–1937," (Australian National University seminar paper, 1961).

73. For the anti-Congress stance of the B.I.A. and of various taluqdars, including Jahangirabad, Mahmudabad, Khajurgaon, and Sheikh Inayatullah, see "Najmu-l-Akhbar" (Etawah) of 12 April 1888, *S. V.N. 1888*, p. 261; "Azad" (Lucknow) of 4 May 1888 et seq., *ibid.*, pp. 307, 514–15, 532, 552, 575, 637; and "Anjuman-i-Hind" (Lucknow) of 28 July 1888, *ibid.*, p. 496. For the 1893 vote see Udai Pratap Singh, "The Cow Agitation, or the Mutiny-Plasm in India," *Nineteenth Century* 35 (1894):670.

74. *Anjuman Report for 1871–72* (Urdu), pp. 11, 14, and Supplement No. 7. The regulations affected the taluqdars by restricting whom they could hire to plead their cases in court.

75. Memorial of Taluqdars of 20 April 1896, enclosed in Pres. B.I.A. to Sec. Govt. N.W.P.&O. 21 April 1896, N.W.P.&O. Rev. Progs. September 1896, No. 127; Memorandum by Sec. B.I.A., *ibid.*, No. 130; and Minutes of Conference of B.I.A. Deputation with Lt. Gov. of 16 July 1896, *ibid.*, No. 132.

system the British had set up in India after the Mutiny. To be sure the association was sometimes ignored, or treated peremptorily—the taluqdars were
told, for instance, to submit their views on the 1889 patwari bill within three
days of its receipt, while they found out about the proposed reform of the
chaukidari system in 1894 only from newspaper reports of the Legislative
Council debates.[76] They disliked too having to seek out the officers of government in Allahabad or far-off Naini Tal, for few taluqdars cared to travel. But
for the most part the taluqdars were not only listened to, but were remarkably successful in getting their views incorporated into legislation. In large
measure of course this was because the "Oudh Policy" was built upon the
taluqdars, who could therefore not be pushed too far. But the leaders among
them, above all such men as Maharaja Man Singh, were themselves skilled
political lobbyists. They always couched their requests in respectful terms,
and won over the British by persistent persuasion, coupled with the cultivation of high officials. One of the taluqdars' few maladroit moves was sending
the unbalanced raja of Mahmudabad, Amir Hasan Khan, as their spokesman to the Legislative Council debates on the 1886 tenancy act. Yet even
then they secured by their steadfast determination the amendments they
wanted.[77]

The taluqdars' association did not confine itself exclusively to politics. It
proclaimed as well its dedication to rooting out the "moral and social evils"
of the province. First among these was the practice of female infanticide,
long prevalent among the Rajputs of Upper India, who commonly did away
with half or more of their infant daughters. In November 1861, at its first
regular meeting, the association vowed to enlist its members' support in a
campaign against this custom. Each taluqdar agreed to take the lead in sup-
pressing infanticide on his estate, to keep records of female births and
deaths, and to hand over for punishment all those suspected of conniving at
the crime.[78] Behind infanticide lay the high cost of marriage. Ever conscious
of their status, Rajputs refused to see their daughters married into clans
lower ranked than their own, with the result that the higher, such as the
Chauhans, could demand large sums in return for their daughters; while
lavish expenditure at the time of marriage was universally regarded as a
mark of social standing, and so added to the burden. Man Singh had spoken

76. See Chief Sec. Govt. N.W.P.&O. to Pres. B.I.A. 21 February 1889, File regarding
Patwari Act, B.I.A. Records; and B.I.A. Resolution of 2 April 1894, File regarding Chowkidari
Pay, B.I.A. Records. When its president protested, the government relented and gave the B.I.A.
a month to submit its objections to the Patwari bill.
77. For Mahmudabad's mental breakdown on this occasion see Ali Hasan, "Tarikh-i-
Mahmudabad," 2:1:152–60; and ch. 8, n. 82 above. For a general account of the consultative
political system in the province see Robinson, "Consultation and Control," *Modern Asian
Studies* 5 (1971):313–36.
78. Speeches by the maharaja of Balrampur and Dakhinaranjan Mukherjee of 30 October
1861, and Man Singh of 1 November 1861, *Progs. B.I.A. 1861–65*, pp. 1–8. For the records the
taluqdars were to keep, see pp. 9–10.

out against the payment of heavy dowries in the 1861 debates on infanticide, but it was left to the government, ever hostile to the conspicuous social consumption the Indian wedding represented, to push for action. In 1863, appalled by the "unprecedentedly lavish" expenditure at the wedding of the raja of Dera's niece, when 35,000 people were fed for six days, they urged the association to find a remedy for this "evil" before the landed families of Oudh, already in debt, were ruined by its demands.[79] The taluqdars duly took the matter under consideration, and a year later, in February 1864, adopted a series of five resolutions. These rules were by no means excessively stringent. Although payment of dowry was restricted to defraying the expenses of the *barat* (groom's wedding party), a taluqdar was still permitted to spend up to half his annual income on the festivities. The rules were, moreover, directed to one caste only, the Rajputs, and sought not a widening of the circle of potential marriage partners but rather, to check hypergamy, forbade the giving of a Rajput girl to anyone not of equal rank.[80]

The effect of the regulations was vitiated not only by straightforward noncompliance—so late as 1892 the association was still considering proposals to curtail "extravagant" marriage expenditures—but by the fact the Rajput taluqdars commonly intermarried with landlords across the border in the North-Western Provinces, to which the writ of the British Indian Association did not run. To get over this problem, the N.W.P. Board of Revenue sent copies of the Oudh Resolutions to all "Heads of Chuttree Families" in that province, and the Commissioner of Gorakhpur division, where many such marriages took place, even convened a meeting of leading Rajputs to point out to them the evils of lavish expenditure and the advantages of reduction.[81] Clearly the taluqdars' association, though it took the lead on this occasion, was not a useful vehicle for the reform of caste practices. Only those directly affected by such practices, and able to wield effective sanctions, could hope to achieve success.

Nor was the taluqdars' commitment to the "cause of reform" all that deep in any case. Although some of its members were unquestionably outraged by it, much of what the association did even in regard to infanticide was done with an eye to winning the approbation of the British. It is surely no coincidence that the campaign against infanticide was launched only a few days before the taluqdars were to meet the Chief Commissioner in durbar, where they presented an address to the Viceroy on the subject. But the taluqdars

79. Sec. C.C. Oudh to Sec. B.I.A. 25 March 1863, *P.P.*, 1865, 40:171. See also extract from Oudh Admin. Report for 1862-63, *ibid.*, p. 163.
80. Resolution of 25 February 1864, *Progs. B.I.A. 1861-65*, p. 141.
81. Sec. Bd. Rev. to Chuttree Families 6 September 1864, N.W.P. General Progs. September 1864, No. 109; and Commr. Gorakhpur to Sec. Govt. N.W.P. 31 October 1864, N.W.P. General Progs. November 1864, No. 66. The Gorakhpur meeting suggested reducing the allowable limit of expenditure to one-fifth of a landholder's annual income, to which the B.I.A. agreed provided both parties would abide by its terms. *Progs. B.I.A. 1861-65*, p. 191. For the 1892 discussions see memos by Rana Shankar Bakhsh and Tasadduq Rasul Khan, File 44, B.I.A. Records. For taluqdar marriage patterns see below ch. 12.

were not prepared always to bow to British standards of morality. In the great controversy over the Age of Consent Bill of 1892, which raised the age of marriage to twelve, they took their stand in opposition to the measure behind the traditional religion and customs of the land.[82] Two years later, when the Lieutenant Governor Sir Charles Crosthwaite proposed to establish a girls' school in Lucknow, the taluqdars, led by Amir Hasan Khan of Mahmudabad, vigorously opposed it, with the result that the Crosthwaite School was ultimately set up in Allahabad.[83] As reformers, as in so much else, the taluqdars were at best fitful and half-hearted.

In its structure and working the association closely reflected the taluqdars' hierarchical view of the world, and their preoccupation with status and prestige. Though in form a model voluntary society, with elected officers, annual meetings, and voting by show of hands, the association was in fact run as a close body by the most powerful taluqdars. The holder of the largest estate with an adult male head was invariably made president, and held the post for life. The ordinary members rarely challenged in open meeting decisions taken by the executive committee or forced contentious matters to a vote. Indeed few attended even the annual general meeting. During the first years of its existence, when the association was still a novelty and the fate of the taluqdari settlement uncertain, as many as 200 of the 270 taluqdars sometimes flocked to its meetings. But this enthusiasm did not last long. In January 1865 the taluqdars voluntarily abdicated their responsibilities to a special committee empowered to "accomplish all the purposes for which the society was established." Though set up as an extraordinary measure to meet the crisis of John Lawrence's tenant right campaign, the committee remained in existence, and no general meetings took place, for nearly a decade.[84]

Those who controlled the association were not just the most powerful but the ablest among the taluqdars. Mere size alone, while it might secure respect and even office, was no guarantee of leadership. Digvijai Singh of Balrampur, for instance, though unanimously placed in office as the association's first president, was little more than a ceremonial figurehead. His ineffectuality met with criticism even in the public press at the time of his death.[85] Lesser taluqdars by contrast, when they were educated or well-connected, could often find a place on the executive committee or as secretary,

82. Memo enclosed in Sec. B.I.A. to Sec. Govt. N.W.P.&O. 18 February 1891, File 44, B.I.A. Records. For the durbar, and address on infanticide, see *Progs. B.I.A. 1861-65*, pp. 13-14.

83. Ali Hasan, "Tarikh-i-Mahmudabad," 2:1:244. The B.I.A. did however make a politic annual contribution to the school. Even those taluqdars less vehemently opposed to female education than Mahmudabad had, with rare exceptions, no desire to encourage it, even among their own wives.

84. Meeting of 1 January 1865, *Progs. B.I.A. 1861-65*, p. 189. The committee was initially appointed for six years, and extended for a further three years in 1871. *Anjuman Report for 1871-72*, p. 5.

85. "Anwar-al-Akhbar" (Lucknow) of January 1882, and "Akhbar-i-Hind" (Lucknow) of 8 June 1882, *S.V.N. 1882*, pp. 45, 355. See also report of a speech by Sheikh Wajid Husain in the "Akhbar-i-Tamanni" (Lucknow) of 1 May 1882, *ibid.*, p. 284.

Chart 8. Officers of the British Indian Association

President

Digvijai Singh	Maharaja of Balrampur	1861–1882
Amir Hasan Khan	Raja of Mahmudabad	1882–1890
Pratap Narayan Singh	Maharaja of Ajodhya	1890–1906
Bhagwati Parshad Singh	Maharaja of Balrampur	1906–1917; 1920–1921

Vice-President

Man Singh	Maharaja of Mehdona	1861–1870
Amir Hasan Khan	Raja of Mahmudabad	1871–1877; 1897–1900
Shankar Bakhsh	Rana of Khajurgaon (acting president during illness of Mahmudabad 1887–1890)	1877–1897
Tasadduq Rasul Khan	Raja of Jahangirabad	1900–1911
Pratab Bahadur Singh	Raja of Qila Pratabgarh	1911–1918

Secretary

Dakhinaranjan Mukherjee	Raja of Shankarpur	1861–1866
Sharfuddin Husain Khan		1866–1869
Mirza Abbas Baig	Taluqdar of Baragaon	1869–1871
Diwan Banna Mal	Manager of Kapurthala estates	1871–1873
Chaudhuri Muhammad Nemat Khan	Secretary of Maharaja Kapurthala	1873–1874
Diwan Achrumal (acting)	Son of Banna Mal	1874
Diwan Mathura Das	Manager of Kapurthala estates	1874–1878
Chaudhuri Khaslat Husain	Taluqdar of Kakrali	1878–1882
Harnam Singh Ahluwalia		1882–1930

Source: Siddiq Ahmad, *Tarikh-i-Anjuman* (Lucknow, 1935) 3:456–63.

and so wield disproportionate influence. The most exceptional perhaps was the association's first secretary, Dakhinaranjan Mukherjee. A Bengali, awarded a small confiscated estate in Oudh by Lord Canning, Mukherjee brought with him to Lucknow the political skills, and commitment to modern ways, he had gained while a student of Alexander Duff, and member of the Calcutta British Indian Association, at the time the most advanced political body in India. Mukherjee was largely responsible for the founding of the taluqdari society and for shaping it in the image of the earlier organization; his too was the driving force behind its early social reform activities.[86] It

86. For Mukherjee's career see Smith, *Life of Alexander Duff*, 2:354–55; and *Oudh Admin. Report for 1862–63*, p. 38. For an appreciation of his services see speeches of Man Singh and Balrampur 12 November 1862, *Progs. B.I.A. 1861–65*, pp. 98–100.

was indeed precisely in order to prod his "less instructed fellow landholders" along the road to modernity that Dakhinaranjan had been brought to Oudh. Yet he remained always a controversial figure. He was opposed by a faction in the association which chafed under the "tutelage" of an outsider, and John Strachey, who knew him well, described him in 1871, when his name was put forward for the award of a title, as "very clever, very intriguing, and very slippery."[87]

Mukherjee's work was complemented, and his influence in part offset, by that of Man Singh, vice-president until his death in 1870. Though entitled to the office as holder of the second largest taluqa, Man Singh threw himself wholeheartedly into the association. For the four years following Mukherjee's resignation in 1866, he ran its affairs almost single-handedly (though the treasury was given over to the Kapurthala maharaja), and at all times he financed many of its activities out of his own pocket. Chief among them was the English language newspaper the *Oudh Gazette* (later *Lucknow Times*), whose publication he subsidized to the extent of a lakh of rupees.[88] As W. Capper, the Faizabad Commissioner, wrote in 1874, "He was the leading talukdar of Oudh, and after the Mutiny was looked to as the channel of communication between the Government officials at Lucknow and the talukdars, and was the lever by which that somewhat inert and obstructive body were moved. . . . He worked with body and soul in the political field of the day and has left his mark heavily on the legislative and administrative policy of this province." He was largely responsible in particular, as we have seen, for drawing up the final list of taluqdars which was incorporated into Act I of 1869.[89] Indeed much of the reason for the disorganization and indebtedness of his estate can be found in the extraordinary amount of time and money he devoted to public affairs.

On the death of Man Singh the Mahmudabad Raja Amir Hasan Khan, backed by a petition signed by 100 taluqdars, was named as his successor. An appropriate choice for the post by virtue of his huge estate, the third largest among the taluqdars, Amir Hasan was at the same time highly educated in Persian and English and also, like his successors in the twentieth century, able, energetic, and outspoken. His years at the association's helm, which lasted with interruptions for nearly a quarter of a century, were punctuated by a number of stormy episodes. At the very outset he fought with the secretary Mirza Abbas Baig, who resigned in protest, while a few years later, in 1877, after a quarrel with the Chief Commissioner Sir George Couper over

87. Brajendranath De, "Reminiscences of an Indian Member of the I.C.S." *Calcutta Review* 129 (1953):161-62; Sec. C.C. Oudh to Sec. Govt. India 2 February 1871, and Note by J. Strachey of 22 February 1871, NAI For. Pol. A Progs. May 1871, No. 83. Dakhinaranjan was awarded the life title of raja.

88. See the *dastur-ul-amal* of 5 April 1866, and report of committee meeting of 31 May 1866, *Majmui Report Anjuman* (for 1865-70) (Urdu) (Lucknow, 1873), pp. 5-11, (hereafter *Progs. B.I.A. 1865-70*); and Siddiq Ahmad, *Tarikh-i-Anjuman*, 1:82, 357-64.

89. Commr. Faizabad to Sec. C.C. Oudh 23 March 1874, B.R. Faizabad File 6. See above p. 189.

Oudh's amalgamation with the North-Western Provinces, he himself resigned, and remained outside the association until called back in 1882 on the death of Balrampur.[90] Yet for the most part these were quiet years for the association. The resolution of the most important settlement questions, together with the completion of the revenue assessment, left it in the eyes of most members with little to do. Only in the 1890s, under the spur of renewed settlement operations, and the flurry of legislative activity that marked MacDonnell's tenure as Lieutenant Governor, did the association shake off its lethargy. Between 1894 and 1901 a steady parade of taluqdari deputations, often with as many as twenty-five or thirty members, waited upon the officials of government, petitions in hand.[91]

The association was handicapped throughout by an incredible mismanagement of its own affairs. Most serious perhaps was the chaotic state of the secretariat, and the lackadaisical business habits of its officers. So early as 1864 the president, Digvijai Singh, chastised the members of the executive committee for their dilatory ways. When a meeting was set for a particular date, he said, "a few members come four days ahead of time and a few others come four days late." Whenever the members did get together, he continued, then "instead of discussing important matters, they waste their time in gossip and in telling stories of the past." Nor were there any proper seating arrangements or restrictions on who might attend the meetings.[92] But matters did not improve. The death of Maharaja Man Singh, who had taken charge of so much, left the association's affairs in great disarray, its papers scattered from Lucknow to Faizabad, its accounts mixed in with those of the Mehdona estate. An attempt was finally made in 1873 to organize the office, by assigning particular duties to each employee; a special finance committee was appointed; and publication of the society's proceedings resumed after a six-year lapse.[93]

Inattention to duty, and disregard of established procedures and forms, nevertheless continued to plague the association's working. The members of the special finance committee did not show up for work, so the secretary was authorized to draw funds up to Rs. 500 on his own account. The secretary sometimes issued circulars without authorization, or left Lucknow without leave. In 1889, when revision of the patwari act was under consideration the president, Rana Shankar Bakhsh, arrived in Allahabad for talks with the government to find present none of the other members of the delegation,

90. *Progs. B.I.A. 1871–72*, pp. 3, 5, and Supplement No. 2, pp. 1–3; and Ali Hasan, "Tarikh-i-Mahmudabad," 2:1:127–28 and *passim*.

91. See, for instance, the list of 26 taluqdars, headed by Pratap Narayan and Rana Shankar Bakhsh, who met with the Lt. Gov. on 16 July 1896 to discuss the Oudh legal and judicial system, N.W.P.&O. Rev. Progs. September 1896, No. 132–33.

92. Hasan Rizvi, *Ahsan-ut-Tawarikh*, 4:509–12. Significantly this meeting was not included in the society's own published account of its proceedings.

93. See *Progs. B.I.A. 1865–70*, pp. 1–2; *Progs. B.I.A. 1871–72*, pp. 6–7, 17, 28, and *passim*; and *Progs. B.I.A. 1873*, pp. 4–7.

which included the association's legal adviser and secretary.[94] A few years later, in 1898, the association's officers came under attack for "caprice" and "irregularity" in revising the taluqdars' deeds of endowment without consulting the membership as the rules required. When the secretary did belatedly solicit approval, by a letter requiring a response within two weeks, the raja of Nanpara reported that his letter, though dated May 1, did not arrive until the sixteenth, two days after the expiry of the grace period. "So the expression of opinion invited by the Secretary was simply a farce; but this is not all. The Life President took upon himself on the 11th of May (that is, four days before the term of grace expired) to notify to the Government . . . the final acquiescence of the British Indian Association in the proposals. . . . "[95]

This mismanagement affected the society's finances as well. The government was supposed to audit the accounts, but they had no settled procedure for disallowing expenses, nor any person especially charged with seeing that the job was done. As a result the association's books grew ever more chaotic. An outside auditor, called in to examine the accounts in 1922, threw up his hands in despair. Without proper ledgers of receipts and expenditures, not even a record of the balances due from each individual member, nor any rules defining the power over expenditure of the various officers of the association, it was, he said, impossible to do more than "grope in the dark." There was no hope of an effective audit.[96] But the more serious problem was the taluqdars' unwillingness to pay their dues to the association, even though they had agreed by covenant to pay annually one-half percent of their land revenue demand. By 1869, with only a few of the larger taluqdars paid up, the despairing secretary was imploring the government to collect the association's dues as a compulsory levy along with the land revenue and the Canning College subscription. The Chief Commissioner, W. H. Davies, had little stomach for such a deal, but repeated appeals by the association, supported by the taluqdars' old patron Colonel Barrow, who argued that the association's funds were largely devoted to public and charitable objects, ultimately had their effect. In 1878 the district officers were instructed to collect B.I.A. subscriptions in the same manner as those for Canning College.[97]

94. Memo by Rana Shankar Bakhsh of 5 March 1889, B.I.A. Records. The extensive file of correspondence on this subject, which includes subsequent solicitation of taluqdars' views by telegram, and a sparsely attended meeting in Lucknow, provides a fascinating insight into the actual working of the association. Most common among excuses for non-attendance were illness and wedding celebrations.

95. Raja Nanpara to Depty. Commr. Bahraich 29 August 1898, N.W.P.&O. Rev. Progs. April 1899, No. 144. The Lt. Gov. publicly chastised the B.I.A. Exec. Committee for its arbitrary behavior on this occasion. Notes of Conference of 23 March 1899, *ibid.*, No. 154.

96. J.K. Balkrishna, pleader and auditor, to Pres. B.I.A. 24 October 1922, File No. 10, B.I.A. Records. For the confusion within the government over who was to audit the accounts and how, see B.R. Oudh General File 838.

97. Finanl. Commr. to Sec. C.C. 10 August 1869, 29 April 1870, and 18 November 1870, Sec. C.C. Oudh to Sec. Govt. India 25 September 1869, and *passim*, B.R. Oudh General File 86, Part II. See also Siddiq Ahmad, *Tarikh-i-Anjuman*, 1:139–43.

Once the government had come to its rescue the association was rarely short of funds. In 1884 they had an unexpended surplus of Rs. 16,100 out of total receipts of Rs. 45,000. Fifteen years later when an increase in costs compelled them to base the charges for Canning College and the Colvin School on the newly enhanced land revenue demand, they kept the subscription to the association at its old level.[98] Rarely too, despite Barrow, was the association's expenditure, though avowedly public, of much real use to the province. Above all they spent money on the entertainment of British officials. In 1884 Rs. 5,500 went to entertain the Lieutenant Governor and a further Rs. 1,100 for a reception for the Duke of Connaught. The following year they entertained the Viceroy Lord Dufferin at a cost of Rs. 16,000. A detailed list of the funds expended on one such ceremonial gathering, the unveiling of a statue of Maharaja Man Singh in 1902, included such items as Rs. 50 on pâté de foie gras and caviar sandwiches, Rs. 113 on hock and claret, and Rs. 1,200 on a jeweled belt and medal. The association also supported the Lucknow race meetings, giving Rs. 1,000 in 1863, Rs. 250 in 1864, and Rs. 500 in 1871. Charitable contributions by contrast were limited in extent. The association maintained a *dharmsala*, or travelers' rest house, the Wingfield Manzil, built at a cost of two lakhs of rupees, to which they gave annually some Rs. 380 for upkeep. They also supported the Lucknow Poor House, at Rs. 3,600 a year, and a branch school at Rs. 1,000. Sometimes too they gave small donations to various Hindu pandits and holy men.[99]

Yet government aid did not put an end to all the association's financial troubles. Some few taluqdars stubbornly withheld funds the association claimed as its due, while others, heavily embarrassed, sought—unsuccessfully—to resign, on the grounds that they had never signed the deed of endowment.[100] Perhaps the most serious of these encounters were those with the Balrampur estate and Raja Rampal Singh of Kalakankar. From Balrampur, the association demanded payment of arrears totaling Rs. 16,933 by 1889, which it alleged had been left unpaid by Maharaja Digvijai Singh. Anson, the Court of Wards administrator, adamantly refused to pay more

98. Minutes of Conference with Lt. Gov. of 16 March 1898, N.W.P.&O. Rev. Progs. June 1898, No. 17; Notes of Conference of 23 March 1899, N.W.P.&O. Rev. Progs. April 1899, No. 154; and Siddiq Ahmad, *Tarikh-i-Anjuman*, 1:143–52.

99. "Translation of B.I.A. Annual Report for 1883–84," B.R. Oudh General File 838; "Hindustani" (Lucknow) of 11 December 1885, *S.V.N. 1885*, p. 883; "Refreshments Supplied to B.I.A. 13 August 1902," B.I.A. Records File 19. See also "Expenses Incurred on Occasion of Unveiling of Woodburn Statue 4 December 1906," *ibid*. The contribution to Canning College was of course a separate levy of one-half percent of their revenue assessment. The association's own administrative costs, including salaries, ran to Rs. 12,000 to 15,000 a year. The branch school was abolished in 1888. During the 1890s, besides contributing to the Crosthwaite Girls' School, the B.I.A. awarded several fellowships annually to needy students.

100. For the attempted resignation of the taluqdar of Antu see B.R. Pratabgarh File 476; for Birhar, Sihipur, and Kapradih see B.R. Faizabad File 23, Part I; for Nanpara, Oudh Rev. Dept. Abstract B Progs. June 1886, No. 36–38. Government pressure helped secure the withdrawal of these resignations, especially that of Nanpara, ever at odds with the association's management.

than Rs. 1,000. The association, he said, recounting his negotiations with it, "spring on us different accounts at different times each account differing from the others"; had denied an estate official access to its records to reconcile the accounts; and refused to credit the estate with sums remitted on account of scarcity or expended by the maharaja as its president on association business. Ultimately in 1900, the account still unpaid, the association reported the estate to the Lieutenant Governor as a defaulter.[101]

With Rampal Singh on the other hand the dispute was, at least in appearances, a matter of principle. As an outspoken nationalist the Kalakankar raja regarded the enforced collection of association dues by the district officer as an unseemly admission of dependence upon the government. He therefore demanded, and received, permission to pay his own subscription directly. The government at the same time assured the association, agitated by the precedent this might set, that if Rampal Singh's payments fell into arrears, he would be denied the "social privileges of a Taluqdar."[102] Despite his assurances Rampal Singh nevertheless soon found excuses not to pay his full dues to a society of whose politics he disapproved. From 1891 to 1897, alleging "bad weather" and "crop failure" he paid nothing at all. By 1903, despite occasional remittances over the preceding few years, he was in arrears to the extent of Rs. 4,414. At this point at the association's urging, the government stepped in. After being given one last chance to pay up, Rampal Singh was summarily struck from the durbar list, and so placed "outside the incorporated taluqdars' community of Oudh."[103]

Rampal Singh's objections were no doubt exceptional. Yet many taluqdars shared his distaste for the British Indian Association. Except in periods of crisis few paid their dues other than reluctantly, or cared much about the modern-style political activity it embodied. Nor was this at all surprising, even though the society had as its major purpose the defense of the taluqdars' preeminence in Oudh. Amply secured by the Canning settlement, this preeminence was never seriously threatened before 1920, so that an active political role carried with it no sense of urgency. The society owed its effectiveness in the quiet years of the later nineteenth century almost wholly to its able leaders and to the government's willingness to accord it a central place in the province's consultative political system.

For most taluqdars the British Indian Association occupied much the same place in their self-perception as did the improvement of agriculture and

101. Sec. B.I.A. to Agent Balrampur 26 September 1889, G.W. Anson to Harnam Singh 1 June 1890, Memo by Mumtaz Ali, Assistant Agent, of 15 March 1900, and *passim*, Balrampur Estate Records 1889–90, Dept. No. 8, File 3.

102. P.A. to Lt. Gov. to all Commrs. 30 April 1878, Depty. Commr. Pratabgarh to Commr. Rae Bareli 1 November 1888, Pres. B.I.A. to Commr. Lucknow 11 May 1889, Rampal Singh to Sec. Govt. N.W.P.&O. 11 July 1889, and *passim*, N.W.P.&O. Rev. Dept. File No. 326B.

103. Report of Assist. Sec. enclosed in Pres. B.I.A. to Commr. Lucknow 29 August 1903, and L. Porter to Rampal Singh 7 November 1903, *ibid*. In February 1904, without abandoning his objection to payment, Rampal Singh petitioned the Viceroy for reinstatement.

the acquisition of western learning. They appreciated the abstract utility of all these enterprises, and were careful, in large part because it won them the approbation of government, to make a show of patronizing them. Some taluqdars may conceivably have realized that a more active involvement in politics, together with the building of schools and the holding of agricultural exhibitions, was essential to their survival as a landed elite in the modern world fast growing up around them. Yet in fact these activities were for the most part irrelevant to their lives as they led them. What really mattered were other things altogether.

Twelve	*The Taluqdari Style of Life:*
	A Leisured Aristocracy

Tʜᴇ Oᴜᴅʜ taluqdars, with other wealthy Indian landholders, devoted much of their time and energy to the prosecution of lawsuits, the patronage of poets and pandits, the pursuit of personal honors and titles, and an ostentatious display in adornment and amusement. None of this won them any praise from their British rulers. Yet these various activities defined for the taluqdars a coherent way of life, and one well adapted to making good the position in the world they felt to be theirs. In this chapter we will endeavor to comprehend this life style, and the values it enshrined, which set these men apart from their Nawabi predecessors and their English landed contemporaries alike.

Status, Titles, and Precedence

A central feature of taluqdari life was the quest for marks of British favor. These included even such seemingly inconsequential matters as the seating arrangements, and order of presentation, at audiences with the Lieutenant Governor or Viceroy, scrutinized by the taluqdars for clues as to their standing with the authorities. Far more consuming was the general fray which focused about the special honors the government had to bestow. These

341

ranged from the jeweled robe and sword, or *khillat*, through a hierarchy of Indian titles topped by the prestigious hereditary title of raja, to the rare distinction of the newly created European-style awards of the Star of India and order of the Indian Empire.

The lowliest of these awards, no less than the greater, were subjects of contention, and of heart-burning. When the seals of office for the newly appointed taluqdar-magistrates were inadvertently sent out to some taluqdars with the word "bahadur" inscribed after the recipient's name, the Chief Commissioner decided that not only could the error not be rectified but the same inscription must be placed on all the seals. This may seem a small matter, he wrote in justification of his decision, "but it is of importance in a province where personal dignity is so much thought of."[1] When the Viceroy in 1873 sought to drop the award of khillats at his durbar, the taluqdars, and the vernacular press, raised a storm of protest. Twenty-five years later, when Curzon in 1899 inquired whether the taluqdars wished him to hold a durbar on his forthcoming visit to Lucknow, they responded with enthusiasm, and urged him to distribute khillats as well. The taluqdars, wrote the B.I.A. president, "attach much importance to Darbars in which nazars [cash gifts] are accepted by the Representative of their Sovereign and khillats are bestowed in return. They feel proud of receiving a khillat and consider it to be a especial mark of imperial favour."[2]

Confronted with this clamor, the British Indian government, like the Mughals and Nawabs before it, reserved to itself the sole prerogative of deciding who was to get what honors. Unlike their predecessors, however, the British were determined to introduce some order into the process. In 1862 the district officers were directed to prepare lists of "those gentlemen generally supposed to have some sort of claim" to the title of raja. "Having prepared this list they should send for each person on it, hear what he has to say on the subject, examine such evidence documentary or oral as he may produce, and then record their opinion pro or con. . . . "[3] Even so they were not always fully informed. The raja of Utraula, denied a hereditary title by Wingfield in 1860 because of the poverty of the family, eventually made good his claim in 1879, with the publication of the *Oudh Gazetteer*, which showed, as the local government lamely admitted, that "the title of Raja has been enjoyed by the family for over two hundred years, and by some twelve generations."[4]

Sometimes too their passion for orderliness led the British astray. In 1871, when the Oudh government sent up the names of two Muslim taluqdars for the award of the title of raja, the foreign secretary C.U. Aitchison protested

1. Sec. C.C. Oudh to Sec. Govt. India 4 September 1860, B.R. Oudh General File 2093.
2. *S.V.N. 1873*, p. 600; Private Sec. Viceroy to Pres. B.I.A. 26 August 1899, Pres. B.I.A. to Chief Sec. Govt. N.W.P.&O., n.d., and *passim*, B.I.A. Records, File "1899 Lucknow Durbar."
3. Assist. Sec. C.C. to Commr. Baiswara 24 November 1862, C.O.F. Bundle No. 110, File 77. At the same time "red books" of family history were compiled for each district.
4. Sec. Govt. N.W.P.&O. to Sec. Govt. India 26 February 1879, NAI For. Pol. B Progs. April 1879, Nos. 11-12.

that it was "incongruous" to award Hindu titles, among which he included rao, raja, and maharaja, to "Mahomedan gentlemen," who should properly be styled khan, khan bahadur, or nawab. The Chief Commissioner replied that such was nevertheless a "very common custom" in Oudh. "If the British Government give *Native* titles," he argued, "it hardly seems . . . incongruous to bestow such titles according to native established custom. It does appear a strange practice certainly, but there is little doubt that the Talookdars themselves prefer the title of Raja to that of Nawab. . . . " And so the awards were sanctioned. The communal lines could not always be drawn as tightly as the British would have liked.[5]

The government still measured out its awards very carefully. Even such a petty matter as giving the additional title "bahadur" to the hereditary raja of Tiloi was the subject of a lengthy secretariat debate over whether the title should be simply "recognized" by an "Erratum Notification" or be "distinctly conferred" by the Viceroy.[6] For the award of major titles, where prior usage did not force its hand, the government insisted upon outspoken loyalty, substantial public service, and an influential position in society. The chief officers of the British Indian Association were almost invariably rewarded, as were the holders of the largest estates, not from any love of mere size, but because such men were assumed to be more influential and so worth conciliating. Recommending Amir Hasan Khan of Mahmudabad for a special style of address, the local government laid emphasis not only on his English education and recent election as vice-president of the taluqdars' association but on his "considerable" influence with "his fellow talookdars, particularly Mahomedans," an influence, moreover, which they said "has on more than one occasion been exerted in a way which has met the approval of the Chief Commissioner." Of Tajammul Husain Khan, recommended for the life title of raja, they reported that his family "was an influential one in the late King's time," and that his "considerable" influence had always been used "for good."[7]

Ordinary taluqdars had to work hard to get the titles they coveted. Behavior was continually scrutinized to see whether it met the standards, always of course implicit, set for the award of a title. Even Tasadduq Rasul Khan of Jahangirabad, "the most influential nobleman" in Bara Banki district, who had applied for the title of raja in 1881 on his accession to the estate, had to wait twelve years before his wish was granted. The cause of the delay may have been in part his notorious rack renting in the early 1880s. As the Divisional Commissioner commented at the time, "it is clear that a landlord who

5. Note by C.U.A. of 16 March 1871, Sec. Govt. India to C.C. Oudh 31 March 1871, Sec. C.C. Oudh to Sec. Govt. India 6 April 1871, and Sec. Govt. India to C.C. Oudh 5 May 1871, For. Pol. A Progs. May 1871, No. 84–92 (italics in original).

6. See notes in For. B. Pol. G. Progs. February 1883, No. 32–33. In the end the title was "recognized" by a special viceregal notification.

7. Sec. C.C. Oudh to Sec. Govt. India 2 February 1871, For. Pol. A Progs. May 1871, No. 83.

could so abuse the power which the law gives him over defenceless tenants is not a fit subject on whom to bestow honors or titles."[8]

The Qila Pratabgarh family similarly put in almost a quarter-century of effort to have the life title of raja, awarded to Ajit Singh at the 1877 Delhi durbar, made hereditary. From the outset Ajit Singh, far from being pleased, had chafed under this uncertain distinction. By 1887 he had gained the support of the district Collector in petitioning for an hereditary award, but the government then simply extended the title for a second life, that of his heir Pratab Bahadur Singh. Infuriated, Ajit Singh denounced this "novel arrangement" to the Lieutenant Governor's face.[9] Pratab Bahadur kept up the pressure. In 1897 the Divisional Commissioner went to bat on his behalf, and finally on New Year's Day of the next year, the long campaign was at last crowned with success.

What prompted the government to concede the title was almost unquestionably Pratab Bahadur's active participation in measures for the relief of the 1896 famine. During 1897, for instance, he met with the Lieutenant Governor four times to discuss the famine relief effort, and was publicly commended for his work. How far Pratab Bahadur threw himself into famine relief designedly as a way of amassing credits with a reluctant government can never be known. Twenty years later, in 1918, when Pratab Bahadur "stood out above everyone else in the district" in his efforts on behalf of war recruiting, he won in return a khillat of robe and sword of honor. On this occasion the district Collector said of him simply that "the Raja Sahib of Pratabgarh has a great sense of public duty, and can always be relied on to do his best for the State, whatever the cost."[10] There can be no doubt that the British held out the award of honors, and with considerable success, as a way of securing taluqdari support for those activities they wished to see encouraged.

One title the taluqdars coveted, that of "His Highness," the government adamantly refused to concede. It was reserved for ruling princes, hence inappropriate for British subjects however powerful. Some taluqdars nevertheless sought the prestige of this title. Digvijai Singh of Balrampur, rumored at one time to be a candidate for the award of princely power, was always privately designated as "His Highness," and even, according to his biographer, had the words engraved upon his visiting cards.[11] The feisty Raja Rampal Singh of Kalakankar, while in England, adopted the title "highness," and even attempted to get himself presented at court under it.

8. Commr. Lucknow to Sec. Govt. N.W.P.&O. 27 February 1882, B.R. Oudh General File 456. For the rack renting see above ch. 8. Tasadduq Rasul was ultimately also awarded a C.S.I. and served on the provincial legislative council. Nevill, *Bara Banki D.G.*, p. 102.

9. Depty. Commr. Pratabgarh to Commr. Rae Bareli 6 May 1887, B.R. Pratabgarh File 127; and Pratab Bahadur, "Memoirs," Part I, pp. 61, 81–83.

10. "Condition of Landowners," U.P. Rev. Dept. Conf. File 578/1918. See also Pratab Bahadur, "Memoirs," Part III, p. 5; Part IV, pp. 1–3, 7–11; and p. 000 above.

11. Baldeo Singh, "Life of Digvijai Singh," p. 281.

When the India Office challenged him, insisting that "your proper style is 'Raja of Kalakankar,'" Rampal Singh retorted somewhat ingenuously that "Highness" was "the nearest approach to the Indian equivalent to what I am entitled, and as such I adopted it." In the end, refusing either "raja" or "sir," he settled for "janab" (although this was a Persian term of generalized respect, not a title at all) as an appropriate form of address.[12]

There were other marks of distinction to be had as well as titles. The maharaja of Balrampur secured, for instance, on Wingfield's initiative, an armorial ensign and crest from the College of Arms in England, and he also kept up seven cannon for purposes of salute. The possession of arms cut close to the taluqdar's sense of self-esteem. Deprived after the Mutiny of those armed bands that had formerly sustained them, the taluqdars cherished all the more those symbolic marks of military status that remained to them. The Balrampur maharaja, as a special favor, was allowed 500 armed retainers, together with the seven cannon. But even he could not do with them as he wished. When in 1879 he attempted to outfit his retainers with Enfield rifles, he was obliged to purchase smooth-bore muskets instead. The government was taking no chances.[13] Other taluqdars had to make do with a good deal less. The raja of Ramnagar in Bara Banki, after dacoits had stolen several guns from his house, was allowed to retain only five muzzle-loading rifles, two pistols, and five swords, a number judged sufficient for his personal use.[14]

Much prized also was exemption from the licensing provisions of the Arms Act. Conceded in 1879 to all "titled native gentlemen," this boon was extended only "with a certain sparingness" to lesser taluqdars. This restriction in its scope was not a product of chance, nor even of a desire to regulate taluqdari armament, for those exempted, following the raja of Ramnagar incident, were held in any case to "reasonable" quantities of arms and ammunition. Rather the government wished to make the exemption a "mark of special distinction." In this they succeeded.[15]

The award of honors, then, of whatever sort, was a carefully calculated business, and one on which substantial effort was expended. The British at the same time set up the arenas in which competition was to take place, laid down the rules, and awarded the prizes. When a taluqdar's behavior was adjudged unsatisfactory, they had no hesitation in stripping him for a time

12. Rampal Singh to S. of S. 29 May 1883, Under S. of S. to Rampal Singh 13 June 1883, and Rampal to S. of S. 20 June 1883, NAI For. Sec. I, September 1883, No. 1-6. See also For. A Pol. I March 1883, No. 92-96.

13. Baldeo Singh, "Life of Digvijai Singh," pp. 266, 274; and Jr. Sec. Govt. N.W.P.&O. to Maharaja 16 June 1879, Estate Records 1878-79, File 122.

14. Depty. Commr. Bara Banki to Commr. Faizabad 12 October 1897, Sec. Govt. N.W.P.&O. to Sec. Govt. India 1 December 1897, and Sec. Govt. N.W.P.&O. to Commr. Faizabad 26 August 1898, N.W.P.&O. Judl.-Crim. Progs. September 1898, No. 2-8.

15. Sec. Govt. N.W.P.&O. to all Commrs. 13 August 1879, N.W.P.&O. Judl.-Crim. Progs. November 1880, No. 2. The *Oudh Akhbar* commended the government for limiting the number of exemptions. *S.V.N. 1879*, pp. 85-86.

even of the "special social privileges" of taluqdari status, as they did with Raja Rampal Singh in 1903 after his refusal to pay B.I.A. dues. The awards themselves served not only to reward loyalty, and to bend taluqdari enterprise toward the goals the British saw as most appropriate, but to keep these men dependent. So long as they remained jealous and divided, competing for honors against each other, they were little likely to combine against the government.

The taluqdars did nevertheless share one substantial grievance. They disliked the way they were treated by the officers of government. While willing to let the British dispense titles and honors, even those of Indian origin, no doubt because they accepted this as the unquestioned prerogative of the ruling authority, they hotly resented the snubs and rebuffs to which they were often subjected in their day-to-day encounters with the British. Raja Rampal Singh of Kurri Sidauli, for instance, complained to a Royal Commission in 1908 that, when calling on European officials, taluqdars were "kept outside the compound [in their carriages] and we have to wait in the sun for an hour or more or sit in the verandah, and so on, and we have to conciliate the chaprasis before we can get to see the officials, and unless we give tips to the chaprasis we cannot get chairs." W. S. Blunt reported of Amir Hasan Khan that "he does not go into English society because he dislikes being disrespectfully treated."[16] The vernacular press too was full of accounts of taluqdars searched for weapons at the door of Government House, cold-shouldered by district officers who refused to shake their hands, and snubbed by high officials who unceremoniously walked out of entertainments given in their honor.[17] Even Pratab Bahadur, who makes no mention of such snubs in his "Memoirs," had still to pocket insults to his religion and his home district from officials who lectured him on the benefits of Christianity and the "hell" that Pratabgarh was as a place to live.[18]

Treatment of this sort, whenever it was encountered, rankled deeply in the hearts of men sensitive to gradations of rank and accustomed to courtesy, even deference. But there was nothing they could do about it. It was part and parcel of the colonial situation, which the raja shared with the raiyat. For too many Englishmen all Indians, whatever their rank or title, were an inferior breed, and hence entitled to little more than condescending notice. As the Englishwoman in *A Passage to India* put it, "Don't forget that you're superior to everyone in India except one or two of the Ranis, and they're on an equality."[19]

16. Evidence of Rampal Singh before Royal Commission on Decentralization 12 February 1908, *P.P.* 1908, 45:726–27; Wilfred Scawen Blunt, *India Under Ripon* (London, 1909), pp. 151–52.

17. "Mashiri Kaiser" (Lucknow) 6 November 1883, *S.V.N. 1883*, pp. 920–21; "Hindustani" (Lucknow) 9 December 1885, *S.V.N. 1885*, p. 885; "Hindustani" 20 December 1893, *S.V.N. 1893*, p. 571; "Azad" (Lucknow) 6 April 1894, *S.V.N. 1894*, p. 152.

18. Pratab Bahadur, "Diary" for 18 May and 19 September 1899.

19. E.M. Forster, *A Passage to India* (New York, 1924), pp. 41–42.

Disputes, Debts, and the Courts

Much of the taluqdars' time, and money, was consumed in protracted legal tussles over land and property. Indeed the taluqdars were often charged with an extravagant, and senseless, litigiousness. Yet these legal battles were not purposeless encounters. They too, despite their cost, played a role in securing for the taluqdar the esteem he sought.

The example was set at the very top. Following the deaths of Maharaja Man Singh in 1870, and of Maharaja Digvijai Singh twelve years later, both estates, Mehdona and Balrampur, the two largest in Oudh, were torn apart by litigation among the deceased's relatives. In each case the initial resort to the courts took place because the taluqdar had died without clearly designating an heir. In both too the combatants were the women of the taluqdar's family. Digvijai Singh in his will had given his widow the right, in the absence of a natural born son, to adopt an heir to the property. He had however two wives, and when the elder, with the encouragement of local officials, adopted as heir Bhagwati Parshad Singh, a distant relative of the deceased, the junior maharani promptly brought suit, claiming an equal share in the property. The district Judge, in October 1884, dismissed the suit, and ordered the elder maharani simply to pay the younger an annual allowance of Rs. 25,000. The aggrieved junior maharani appealed to the Judicial Commissioner's court, where she won a reversal of the lower court's finding. But matters did not stop there. The senior, unwilling to abate her claim to the whole of the property, took the suit to the Privy Council in London, the highest court of the British Empire. There, in November 1887, she gained final confirmation of her title, and that of her adopted heir.[20]

The Mehdona succession dispute was far more tangled and embittered, and was not finally resolved until almost fifteen years after Man Singh's death. In 1864, long before he died, the maharaja had executed a will in which, like the Balrampur maharaja, he gave his wife control over the property after his death, and empowered her to nominate a successor. This she did in 1872 in favor of Triloki Nath, a minor son of one of the deceased taluqdar's brothers. At once, however, a daughter of Man Singh, Brij Raj Kunwar, brought suit against Triloki Nath on behalf of her minor son Pratap Narayan Singh, whom she claimed Man Singh had treated as his own son and had intended to nominate as his heir. It was an uphill fight, for not only were the provisions of the will clear, but in Hindu law an heir in the male line took precedence over a daughter's son. Both the district court, and the Judicial Commissioner, decided in the maharani's, and Triloki Nath's, favor. During the trial, the stubborn Pratap Narayan disdained an offer of a lease of the estate's Gonda properties put forward as a gesture of conciliation. Two

<hr>

20. Thakur Raj Indar Bahadur Singh, *Tarikh-i-Raj-i-Balrampur* (Urdu) (Lucknow, 1909), pp. 138–39. The senior maharani was ordered to pay her younger rival an allowance from the day of the taluqdar's death. In 1889 Rs. 33,000 were disbursed on this account.

years later, disheartened, he accused the maharani of cutting off his stipend, and set out in search of support. He first journeyed to the holy places of Kashmir, where he implored the aid of the gods, and then visited several of his neighbors, above all Maharaja Jang Bahadur of Nepal, who received him graciously.[21]

In July 1877 Pratap Narayan's persistence was rewarded with a favorable Privy Council decision. Their Lordships decided that Man Singh had in fact from 1867 onward treated Pratap Narayan as his son by such acts as overseeing his investiture with the sacred thread and describing him as his heir while arranging his marriage. They further ruled that he had endeavored to retract the will, and that he would have done so had it not been for the forgetfulness of the Faizabad Commissioner, who neglected to return it to him.[22] The disgruntled Triloki Nath determined to fight back. He is alleged to have run at Pratap Narayan with a sword during the latter's first Dussehra durbar, while two years later, in 1879, he brought suit in the district court for possession of the estate. He insisted that as he had already been recognized as Man Singh's successor, and been received as such by the Viceroy, he could not now be dispossessed. Judgment went against him, but, as tenacious as Pratap Narayan before, he appealed to the Judicial Commissioner, from whom he won a favorable decision. Again the aggrieved Pratap Narayan undertook a religious pilgrimage. Again he appealed to the Privy Council. Finally, in 1884, he obtained a second, and now conclusive, award from that tribunal. On December 2 he took charge of the estate for good.[23]

The cost to the Mehdona estate of this protracted litigation, from lax supervision of its affairs as well as actual cash outlay, was enormous. To the legal battles of these years can be attributed many of the financial difficulties that plagued the estate to the 1890s and beyond. Yet the stakes were high. The estate was after all the second largest in Oudh. So it is not surprising that Man Singh's heirs fought so bitterly over it. Even Triloki Nath's last despairing suit, which he could hardly have expected to sustain in the Privy Council, was no more than a due recognition of the size and importance of the property, and of the position he had expected to inherit.

Even when succession was not at issue, family feuds remained fruitful sources of litigation. These usually centered around such matters as the partition, or sharing of rights over property, and the payment of stipendiary allowances. Even a generally agreed upon principle for the sharing of assets by no means put an end to court fights. The Palwars of Birhar in Faizabad, for instance, divided their lands equitably among the members of each

21. Durga Prasad, *Tarikh-i-Ajodhya*, pp. 161–66; Petition of Brij Raj Kunwar of 28 July 1875, B.R. Faizabad File 6, Part II.

22. Muhammed Rafique, St. George H.S. Jackson, and Brijnath Sharga, eds., *The Oudh Privy Council Decisions* [from 1864 to 1913] (Lucknow, 1913), pp. 276–87.

23. Durga Prasad, *Tarikh-i-Ajodhya*, pp. 168–70; Plaint of Trilokinath Singh in Court of Depty. Commr. Faizabad, n.d. (c. 1879), B.R. Faizabad File 6, Part II.

succeeding generation. The division was carried out, however, not "by the separation of entire villages to each son, but by the partition of each village and each portion of a village between every descendent. There are now eight estates and . . . many villages in which each of the eight has a share." The result was a continual series of quarrels. Indeed, so the Deputy Commissioner reported, in no part of the district were there "so many complaints in the criminal courts," while the disputes "to which this intermixture of tenure has habitually led, have occasioned such an embitterment of feeling between the Talukdars, that, related though they are, they are to each other, the most resolute enemies."[24]

To put a stop to this bickering the British tried, without success, to get the Palwars to adopt the "Rajpoot rule" of the younger brothers having a claim only to support. Yet litigation over the size and payment of allowances was itself not infrequent. Sometimes attempts were made, usually at British initiative, to resolve such conflicts by inducing the parties to accept outside arbitration. Perhaps the most significant such effort, though one hardly productive of family amity, was undertaken in the dispute between the two Kalakankar rajas, Hanwant and Rampal Singh. In 1859 Hanwant Singh gifted the Kalakankar property on a life tenure to his grandson Rampal Singh, retaining, however, control over the estate as manager. Rampal Singh was to receive a fixed annual stipend out of the profits of the estate. But the two soon fell to squabbling over the size and payment of the allowance, as well as over the management of the property. Finally in 1867 both rajas handed over their dispute to the binding arbitration of a panchayat of taluqdars, headed by Maharaja Man Singh, together with Ajit Singh of Taroul and three Muslim landlords. The arbitrators awarded Rampal Singh an annual pension of Rs. 13,557, to be met out of the proceeds of thirty-three villages of the Dharupur portion of the estate. But this did not still the quarrel. Rampal Singh complained bitterly of arrears in the payment of his allowance, while Hanwant Singh's dislike of his grandson grew ever more intense with the latter's conversion to the Brahmo Samaj faith and subsequent adoption of an anglicized style of life. In an endeavor to set things right Barrow treated Hanwant Singh to a mixture of threats and exhortation. "Do not," he wrote about 1869, "act on your present hostile feeling to Rampal. You know I wish to do the best I can in your affairs, but you must not go on like this or I shall no longer befriend you." Finally in 1871, the dispute found its way into the government court, which ordered the interests of the two men separated. Rampal was put in full charge of the Dharupur property, and Hanwant of the Kalakankar portion of the estate.[25]

24. Depty. Commr. Faizabad to Commr. Faizabad 7 April 1880, B.R. Faizabad File 226.
25. Panchayet Namah of 6 October 1867; Depty. Commr. Pratabgarh to Commr. Rae Bareli 23 June 1868, 11 May 1871, and 1 March 1872; Barrow to Hanwant Singh, n.d.; Kavanaugh to Woodburn 5 April 1872, and *passim*, B.R. Pratabgarh File 385. By the terms of the 1859 deed, Rampal succeeded to the entire property on Hanwant's death.

Mediation was undertaken in other kinds of disputes as well. Under the prodding of the Deputy Commissioner, P. Carnegy, who gathered the district's principal taluqdars together in his tent in January 1863, the Faizabad landholders agreed to exchange villages erroneously entered in each other's sanads during the haste of the 1859 settlement. More importantly, where two or more taluqdars held lands in one village, or had lands that were "greatly interspersed," they agreed to "such an exchange of fields as would place each man's holding in a ring fence." If the parties could not come to a mutually satisfactory arrangement, then panchayat committees, comprising in each case two neighboring taluqdars with Man Singh as *sarpanch* (head), would carry out the redistribution of villages or fields.[26] A few years later, in 1866, the British Indian Association appointed its own set of mediators to "settle disputes and remove misconceptions." The government for some years deferred to these men in such matters as the claims of relatives to maintenance. The government also sometimes sought advice from special *ad hoc* committees. In 1871, for instance, the Commissioner of Rae Bareli assembled a committee of taluqdars to inquire into the difficulties landholders encountered in collecting rents from underproprietary tenants. Not surprisingly the committee recommended the adoption of "sterner measures," including the forced sale of tenures, to put a stop to default.[27]

A striking feature of the entire mediation effort was the prominent part played, until his death, by Maharaja Man Singh, who headed so many of the panchayats. A mark of the exceptional regard in which he was held by taluqdars and Englishmen alike, this mediating role antedated even the annexation of the province. In 1855, when communal rioting broke out over the alleged existence of a mosque within the sacred precincts of the Ajodhya Hanuman temple, the Nawab Wajid Ali Shah, at the urging of the Resident Sir James Outram, appointed a committee of inquiry composed of the local *nazim* Agha Ali Khan, Captain A. Orr of the Oudh Frontier Police, and Man Singh. As Outram told the Governor-General, a "mixed commission" possessing "an equal Mahomedan and Hindoo element, with a Christian umpire," would be most likely to inspire confidence in its impartiality. At their first meeting, however, the committee empowered Raja Man Singh, despite the fact that his followers had participated in the battle for the temple, to open private negotiations on their behalf with the temple *mahants*. He returned bearing written permission for the committee to dig up any one spot the Muslims pointed to as the likely site of their mosque. No mosque was

26. Proceedings of a Meeting of Talookdars of 31 January 1863, Memos by P. Carnegy of 2 February 1863 and 28 February 1863, and Settle. Commr. to Sec. C.C. 12 February 1863, B.R. Oudh General File 2235, Part I. The process of transfer had however hardly begun when it was brought to a halt by a government order to deal first with claims to underproprietary rights in these lands. Sec. C.C. to Settle. Commr. 12 March 1863, *ibid.*

27. *Progs. B.I.A. 1865–70*, p. 10; Finanl. Commr. to all Commrs. 20 March 1869, B.R. Oudh General File 699; and Report of Committee on Subproprietary Balances in Commr. Rae Bareli to Sec. C.C. 5 September 1871, Oudh General File 2077.

discovered, and the British were full of praise for Man Singh's effective diplomacy.[28]

Mediation settled few disputes, however. For the most part quarrels were fought out in court, and cost the litigants substantial sums of money. The Mehdona estate, even before the death of Man Singh and the subsequent succession struggle, spent Rs. 15,000 or more annually on legal expenses. In 1870 they paid out Rs. 5,640 in salaries alone to pleaders and mukhtars employed in various government courts. Balrampur too, despite the resolution of the succession dispute, in the 1890s still expended between Rs. 15,000 and Rs. 25,000 a year on legal charges.[29] Even seemingly minor disputes were made the subject of protracted, and expensive, court fights. In 1891, for instance, when one Shiv Raj brought suit before the local judge, Deputy Muhammad Wasi, claiming a single Pratabgarh village, Raja Pratab Bahadur called in barristers from Allahabad and Lucknow; and when the decision went against him, in Pratab Bahadur's view because Muhammad Wasi had joined a party hostile to him, he at once challenged Shiv Raj with a fresh suit in another court.[30] The only real beneficiaries of such litigation were the urban lawyers, men such as Motilal Nehru, with whom the Pratab-garh raja formed a close friendship.

That such conspicuous litigation drove landholders into debt, and occasionally forced them to sell their property, is well known, and was the subject of frequent unfavorable comment by the British. Indeed these intense quarrels sometimes even brought agricultural progress to a halt. None of the Palwar taluqdars, the district officer reported in 1880, "can build a well, for he has rarely an area compact enough to utilize all its water, and he will do nothing to better his cousins' field. The roads that were made ten years ago have developed no traffic. Pack-buffaloes still as before pass up or down but not a cart has begun to ply."[31] Why did taluqdars persist in behavior so apparently unproductive? Part of the answer lies in their attachment to their land. The taluqdar's status and position in society, as well as the bulk of his income, was tied to, if not derived from his role as landed proprietor. Any challenge to his control of the land, whether from a neighbor, a tenant, or a family member, would therefore be fiercely resisted. The taluqdar saw only too clearly that without his land he was nobody.

No doubt on occasion the cost of a fight in court might be greater than that of acquiescence or conciliation. But more was at stake than money alone.

28. Resident Lucknow to Sec. Govt. India 4 August 1855, Notes on a Conference of 1 August 1855 between the King and Resident, and Captain A. Orr to G. R. Weston Supt. Oudh Frontier Police 29 July 1855, 13 August 1855, and 15 August 1855, NAI F.C. 28 December 1855, No. 339, 342, and 351-58.

29. Account of Receipts and Charges of Mehdona Estate in Depty. Commr. to Commr. Faizabad 15 September 1870, B.R. Faizabad File 6; and Balrampur Annual Reports 1888-89 and 1901-02, Estate Records.

30. Pratab Bahadur, "Memoirs," Part I, pp. 106, 108, 111-12.

31. Depty. Commr. to Commr. Faizabad 7 April 1880, B.R. Faizabad File 226.

With armed combat prohibited, a victorious encounter in the courts provided one of the most effective ways by which a landholder could visibly affirm to the world his power and position in society. His enemies broken, the successful litigant emerged from the courtroom a man of consequence, better able to rally his followers and perhaps even enlarge his circle of dependents. What he lost financially was amply compensated by the enhanced influence and prestige he commanded. Nor was the taluqdar alone in his frequent recourse to the courts. The reputation of the judicial system as a lottery in which anyone could hope to succeed encouraged the disgruntled, or ambitious, of all sorts to try their hand before the law. The taluqdars were distinguished not so much by any greater propensity for litigation as by the greater opportunities that came their way. They had more to spend—and more to lose—than anyone else in the province.

Religion, Culture, and the Arts

The law court was not the only arena in which the taluqdar could assert his status in society. Equally effective was the building and patronage of temples, hospitals, and other works of charitable purpose. We have already noticed the taluqdars' role as patrons, at times perhaps reluctant, of Western education. Support of Hindu (or Muslim) religious institutions was almost certainly a more congenial, because more traditionally acceptable, enterprise. Indeed the endowment of a temple had long been the accustomed way an aspirant landholder laid claim to a higher status.[32]

British rule, with its greater wealth and security of property, accelerated this philanthropic competition. The maharajas of Ajodhya, from Man Singh's time onward, in part no doubt because of the location of their residence in its center, contributed heavily to the support of the temples, and the pilgrim visitors, in the sacred Hindu town of Ajodhya. They thus earned a reputation for religiosity which has lasted to the present day.[33] The Pratabgarh raja during the 1890s fed pilgrims at the Allahabad Magh Mela; awarded a regular stipend to a wandering holyman Baba Avtar Das, who traveled with an entourage of fifty pandits, singers, and musicians; and gave *muafi* lands and furnished houses to several local pandits. At the same time he built and endowed a new temple within the Pratabgarh fort.[34] Sometimes taluqdars managed to combine religious and pecuniary advantage. Thakur

32. See, e.g., Raja Madho Singh of Amethi, the growth of whose estate in Sultanpur during the 1840s was followed by the building of a temple in Benares, which when it burnt to the ground shortly after its completion was at once rebuilt in 1854 at a cost of a lakh of rupees. Property yielding Rs. 6,000 a year was set aside for its upkeep and the feeding of Brahmins. Pandit Kanhya Lal Ashiq, *Tarikh-i-Raj-i-Riyasat-i-Garh Amethi* (Urdu) (Lucknow, 1882), p. 47; and *Sultanpur D.G.*, pp. 96–97.

33. Durga Prasad, *Tarikh-i-Ajodhya*, pp. 175–78. Estate land with an income of Rs. 60,000 was set aside for the maintenance of temples. It is problematic whether the Ajodhya taluqdars' Brahmin caste position, or relatively recent rise to prominence under the Nawabs, affected their continuing philanthropic activity in subsequent years.

34. Pratab Bahadur, "Memoirs," Part II, p. 8; Part III, pp. 8–9; and Part IV, pp. 15–17.

Jawahar Singh built at Kamalpur "a temple dedicated to Shri Radhakrishna and another dedicated to Shiva. The *Ganj* [market] at Kamalpur, built by him round these temples, has a flourishing market, and through his exertions Kamalpur has now become one of the first class grain markets on the Rohilkhand and Kumaon Railway line."[35]

Taluqdars supported simultaneously traditional and modern style charity. Balrampur, for instance, financed both the Lyall Collegiate School on the estate and a Sanskrit Pathshala in Puri. Raghubar Dyal Seth in 1884 gave away a thousand cows to the local Brahmins, but soon followed up this gift with a clock for the Sitapur Town Hall, and then in 1891 a sum of Rs. 4,500 for the building of a Female Hospital in the town. His brother Jai Dyal Seth during the same four years built a marble temple in the sacred town of Nimkhar, gave away an elephant in charity as *gajdan*, and established an Anglo-Vernacular school at Biswan. Sometimes objects of traditional religious merit could be combined with those attractive to the British, so that the taluqdar might reap a double benefit. Raghubar Dyal's "Jubilee Scholarship" for the study of Sanskrit at Canning College no doubt reflects such calculations, as did his Diamond Jubilee Anglo-Sanskrit School in Sitapur.[36]

In lists of taluqdars' charities benefactions of the modern sort, often sponsored by government, invariably predominate. All of Balrampur's other contributions pale in comparison with the seven lakhs of rupees given over in the 1870s to the building of the Balrampur Hospital, Lucknow, or the three lakhs spent thirty years later on the Prince of Wales Medical College.[37] Sometimes the government even tried to increase the level of contribution by evoking a spirit of competitive rivalry. As the provincial secretary wrote to the Balrampur manager in 1894, "Sir Charles Crosthwaite is keen on getting a hospital for natives in the bazaar of Naini Tal and looks to Balrampur . . . for a handsome contribution. Rampur has given 2000 and he hopes Balrampur will give the same amount which I think he may. . . . "[38] Often too, as we have seen, the government used the award of honors as a device to get the taluqdars to increase their support of government sponsored or approved charities. Yet despite these pressures unrecorded donations of cash and grain, and of cows and elephants as well, continued to be made in the old way, and were often dispensed informally by the taluqdar himself.[39]

35. "Heliodorus," *A Taluqdar of the Old School*, p. 76.

36. Kunj Behari Seth, *The Seths of Biswan*, pp. 16–17, 23.

37. "Akhbar-i-Alam" 26 September 1872, *S. V.N. 1872*, p. 601; Annual Report for 1901–02, Balrampur Estate Records; Indar Bahadur Singh, *Tarikh-i-Raj-i-Balrampur*, p. 152. In 1922 three gifts of one lakh of rupees each—to the Balrampur Hospital, the new Lucknow University, and the Lucknow Zoo—consumed almost two-thirds of the estate's total charity. A further Rs. 50,000 was given for a statue of Harcourt Butler. Annual Report for 1921–22.

38. G. Adams to G. Anson 6 July 1894, Estate Records 1893–94, Dept. No. 64, File 14. Balrampur gave its Rs. 2,000.

39. On the Lorpur estate in Faizabad the grain from the *sir* land was kept in a special storehouse for the raja's personal use, and was dispensed as he saw fit without consulting anyone. Interview with Saiyid Badshah Husain, raja of Lorpur, 19 November 1969, Lucknow. See also

It is clear from the pattern of their charity that the taluqdars participated in the movement of Hindu revival that swept across northern India during the latter decades of the nineteenth century. For the most part they supported only its more conservative manifestations, contributing to Sanatan Dharm rather than Arya Samaj activities, and they carefully disassociated themselves from the cow protection agitation of 1893. Much as they may have sympathized with its objectives, they had no wish, once the movement had turned violent, to imperil their good relations with the government.[40] But the taluqdars did, over time, come increasingly to identify with their religious community. To be sure the communal lines were not always tightly drawn. The Muslim raja of Nanpara helped support a *goshala* (cow shelter) in Bahraich, while the Hindu raja of Dera gave his Muslim tenants Rs. 1,500 to build a mosque.[41] Yet the earlier Hindu contributors to the Aligarh college, such as the raja of Bhinga, slowly dropped away, while the Muslim raja of Jahangirabad, who had endowed two scholarships in honor of the Queen's 1887 Jubilee, one for the study of Sanskrit and one for Arabic or Persian, a decade later rewrote the endowment deed to require that one scholarship go to a Hindu and one to a Muslim and that they be used only for the study of Persian.[42]

Perhaps the clearest evidence of the taluqdars' new communal orientation were the sums devoted to sectarian education. In 1901 the maharaja of Balrampur put Rs. 25,000, and the much less wealthy Raghubar Dyal Rs. 1,000, into Pandit Madan Mohan Malaviya's scheme for a Hindu boardinghouse at the Allahabad University. Hindu taluqdars, several of whom put up a lakh of rupees each, a few years later were among the major contributors to Malaviya's projected Hindu university at Benares.[43] The major Muslim taluqdars, above all Mahmudabad and Jahangirabad, at the same time took the lead in the campaign to convert the Aligarh college into a properly endowed Muslim university.[44] All of this could be justified to the British as a

---

Kunj Behari Seth, *Seths of Biswan*, p. 13; Siddiq Ahmad, *Tarikh-i-Anjuman*, 3:474; and "Anjuman-i-Hind" (Lucknow) 30 January 1892, *S.V.N. 1892*, p. 37.

40. See for instance, Raja Udai Pratap Singh, "The Cow Agitation, or the Mutiny-Plasm in India," *Nineteenth Century* 35 (1894):667–68, where he attempted to blame Congress for the agitation. For the cow movement and its ties to Hindu revivalism and the Congress see Bayly, *Local Roots of Indian Politics*, pp. 111–15.

41. "Azad" (Lucknow) 11 November 1887, *S.V.N. 1887*, p. 718; and "Hindustani" 27 September 1893, *S.V.N. 1893*, p. 409. Taluqdars commonly contributed to the upkeep of all religious buildings on their estates.

42. Bhatnagar, *History of the M.A.O. College*, p. 67; Depty. Commr. Bara Banki to Sec. Govt. N.W.P.&O. 27 May 1897, and Notification of 3 February 1898, N.W.P.&O. Educ. Progs. March 1898, No. 1–6.

43. Annual Report for 1901–02, Balrampur Estate Records; Kunj Behari Seth, *Seths of Biswan*, p. 18; and interview with Raja Jagannath Bakhsh Singh of Rehwan, 13 March 1970, Lucknow. Raghubar Dyal had already contributed Rs. 500 to the Central Hindu College, Benares, in 1899. Among the contributors to the B.H.U. were the rajas of Tiloi, Kasmanda, and Kurri Siddauli.

44. Ali Hasan, "Tarikh-i-Mahmudabad," 3:1:244–47. Mahmudabad and Jahangirabad each contributed one lakh and Pirpur, Rs. 50,000. Mahmudabad also supported various Shia political and educational movements in the 1910s and 1920s.

way "to promote the laudable cause of higher education." Yet it served communal ends as well.

With this enhanced communal identity went a new emphasis upon caste solidarity and advancement. Much Rajput philanthropy from the 1890s onward was channeled into the schooling of caste fellows. Raja Udai Pratap of Bhinga in 1891 funded thirteen scholarships for Kshatriya students at a cost of Rs. 32,000; a few years later he toyed with the idea of building a Kshatriya boardinghouse at the Muir Central College, Allahabad; and subsequently he donated Rs. 50,000 toward the establishment of the Hewett Kshatriya College.[45] Raja Pratab Bahadur in 1898 set up a school, named the Ajit Sombansi School in memory of his predecessor Ajit Singh, which he supported from a special Charitable Endowment with an annual rental income of Rs. 45,000. The school, in which the raja took a keen interest, was specially directed to the education of the members of his own Sombansi clan.[46] Even the anglicized Raja Rampal Singh, anxious to rehabilitate himself in the eyes of his caste fellows, took up the cause of Rajput education, and was made chairman and permanent vice-president of the Rajput Mahasabha of Agra in 1899 for his work in its behalf.[47] Though in part simply a paternal solicitude, akin to that for one's less well-off relations, this interest in schooling reflected also a fear, widespread among Rajputs at the time, as they observed the growth of the Congress and of agitational politics, that despite their high ritual status they would be distanced in the race for preferment by other more highly educated castes. At no time, of course, did the taluqdars abandon their support of the nonsectarian Canning College, nor did they but rarely send their sons anywhere other than to the Colvin School. Nevertheless, as the twentieth century progressed, ties of caste and community loomed increasingly large alongside those of class and interest which brought the taluqdars together as a landed elite.

Communal consciousness is not, of course, the same as individual piety. For this we must look elsewhere. The British were often surprised by the intensity of the taluqdars' religious convictions. As Harcourt Butler wrote in 1897, "It is not possible to detach the Hindus from Brahmanism. . . . The leading taluqdars are strongly orthodox and very much under the influence of Brahmanism. Rana Shankar Baksh KCIE not long ago announced his intention of retiring from the world to end his days in meditation at Benares. The Raja of Bhinga has already done the same, although he was in his public

45. "Bharat Jiwan" (Benares) 28 September 1891, *S.V.N. 1891*, p. 677; N.W.P.&O. Educ. B Progs., December 1900, No. 3; and Udayapratapa Sinh, *History of the Bhinga Raj*, pp. 50–51. In the 1900s the raja increased the scholarship endowment fund to Rs. 80,000.
46. Pratab Bahadur, "Memoirs," Part IV, pp. 17–19; Nevill, *Partabgarh D.G.*, pp. 139–41; and "Report on the Condition of Landowners," U.P. Rev. Dept. Confidential File 578/1918. Sombansi children received free schooling, together with meals and a stipend. Ajit Singh had himself earlier given scholarships to Sombansi students. Tholal, *Sombansi Raj*, p. 55.
47. "Hindustan" (Kalakankar) 11 May 1899, *S.V.N. 1899*, pp. 240–41; and "Al Bashir" (Etawah) 15 May 1899, *ibid.*, p. 255. His Kalakankar school was intended primarily for the education of Rajputs. See above p. 319.

views thoroughly westernized. . . . " The Bhinga family had a tradition of such renunciation. Raja Krishna Datta Singh, who died in 1862, a Sanskrit scholar and patron of poets, "for days together used to live on milk only, and to practice other austerities." His successor Udai Pratap had long intended to retire from public life, so that the death of his eldest son in 1895 only "hastened his retirement to Benares and his adoption of an ascetic life."[48] Thakur Jawahir Singh of Kasmanda, "a most orthodox Hindu" with a "touching and unbounded faith in its ritualism," in 1883 took along with him on a pilgrimage to Gaya 400 of his tenants, "for like a true adherent of the Hindu *Shastras* he believed that he would be a sharer in the *punya* [fruits of good acts] of them all." In 1891 he journeyed to the remote Himalayan shrine of Badrinath with another 100 tenants, and then followed it up with a systematic seven-month tour of all the major shrines of southern and western India.[49]

Those less driven to austerity or pilgrimage still remained devout. The most conscientious in their religious observances were often the women of the taluqdar's household, for whom such activities consumed a large amount of time. The *bari rani* (eldest wife) of Raja Pratab Bahadur, for instance, had a temple built in her *kothi* (residence) at the Pratabgarh fort. An idol of Ram was installed, a priest appointed to conduct daily services, and wandering *sadhus* and Brahmins fed. Outside the temple was a small house where lived a special cow venerated by the rani.[50] The raja too was very regular in his prayers. Every morning without fail he did his *puja* (worship), and most evenings as well. In addition he attended a regular worship of Shiva, and frequently visited the rani's temple for *darshan* (receiving the blessing) of its deity. When his travels took him nearby he invariably stopped for worship in the temples at the holy cities of Benares and Ajodhya. Often he would visit three or four of these temples in succession, and pay his respects to the priests and holymen affiliated with them. Sometimes, too, on particularly auspicious or important occasions, he would make a special trip to one or another of these shrines.[51]

The successive rajas of Mahmudabad, exceptionally devout Shias, from the 1860s right up till the time of zamindari abolition, devoted much time and huge sums of money to religious observances, and prided themselves as well on their religious learning. Raja Amir Hasan for forty years supported a

48. Butler to his father 6 March 1897, IOL MSS. Eur. F. 116/5; and Udayapratapa Sinh, *History of the Bhinga Raj*, pp. 46, 50. Udai Pratap endowed the Kshatriya School in Benares as a memorial to his son. Interview with Chandramani Kant Singh, raja of Bhinga, 10 December 1969, Lucknow.

49. *A Taluqdar of the Old School*, pp. 74–75. See also Munshi Kalka Parshad, *Jawahar Nama* (Urdu) (Allahabad, 1911), Part II, pp. 165–73.

50. Pratab Bahadur, "Memoirs," Part II, p. 12; Part III, p. 3; Part IV, pp. 15–16; and his "An Account of Pratabgarh Fort," *passim*, Pratabgarh Estate Records.

51. Pratab Bahadur, "Memoirs," Part III, pp. 1, 4; Part IV, pp. 3–4, 7, 10; and "Diary," 20, 21, 22 August 1899, and *passim*.

The Imambara, Mahmudabad.

learned family of *ulama* in Lucknow, first father and then son, who were given a stipend of Rs. 75 a month, together with clothes, fruit, and ceremonial delicacies. In return the raja looked up to these men as his religious guides, and entrusted them with the management of the Islamic College he founded in Lucknow in 1888. In Mahmudabad itself Amir Hasan employed a distinguished Lucknawi *maulvi*, at a salary of Rs. 50 a month, to lead the prayers five times a day in the family mosque, and two *qaris*, who recited the Quran and Shia *marsias* (elegiac poems). Every Thursday the maulvi was given from Rs. 100 to Rs. 500 to distribute among the faithful.[52]

As a Shia Amir Hasan was drawn especially toward the shrine of Karbala in Iraq, site of the martyrdom of Hasan and Husain, to which he journeyed on pilgrimage with a large entourage in December 1888. Welcomed by the Ottoman government as an honored guest, he remained a full year, lavishing money upon the Shia shrines, and the needy of the land.[53] Most distinctive of the Mahmudabad family's religious observances was their celebration of Muharram, commemorating the death of Hasan and Husain. On this occasion all the Shia employees of the estate, no matter where they normally

52. Ali Hasan, "Tarikh-i-Mahmudabad," 2:1:170–80, and 2:2:110–21. An entire village was given to the Lucknow ulama family, and 300 bighas of rent-free land to the Mahmudabad maulana, on the occasion of the heir apparent's circumcision (1891).

53. Siddiq Ahmad, *Tarikh-i-Anjuman*, 3:486.

resided, were required to be present in Mahmudabad and to take part in the mourning observances. The residents of the town as well, even the Hindus, participated by bringing out *tazias*, which the estate encouraged by giving them cash contributions ranging from a few annas to a hundred rupees or more each. The raja himself led the *majlis* (mourning assemblies) in the estate Imambara, often reciting elegies of his own composition. Various estate employees, and specially hired dirge-singers, also took part in these twice-daily services. Not content with the usual Muharram celebration—which extended over ten days, with a subsequent *chahlum* ceremony forty days later—the Mahmudabad family in a most extraordinary fashion slowly lengthened the period of its observance. First, in the later nineteenth century, the women of the family kept up the ritual mourning for the forty days between the tenth of Muharram and the chahlum. By the early twentieth century the men had begun participating as well, and the period of observance extended a further sixteen days.[54]

As a group then, the taluqdars, despite their changing social role under the British, and their rulers' expectation that they would become as secular as their counterparts in England, remained always devout Hindus or Muslims. Indeed in this the taluqdars in no way differed from the urban merchants, and later the industrialists of twentieth-century India, who did not let a new occupational status, or participation in the modern economy, undermine their religious devotion.[55]

Nor were the Hindu religious convictions of the bulk of the taluqdars at all incompatible with the persistence in these men of a markedly Islamicized style of life. The taluqdars indeed by the later nineteenth century had become the residuary legatees, as it were, of the old Mughal culture. Kept alive in Lucknow by the Nawabs of Oudh until 1856, this culture found shelter, after the deposition of the Nawab and the subsequent spoliation of Lucknow during the Mutiny, in the Oudh countryside, in the petty courts and palaces of the taluqdars. Of course it was a culture much attenuated—a "husk culture" it has been called—but it nonetheless remained a vital force in the lives of the taluqdars, Hindu and Muslim alike, in the years up to the First World War.[56] No doubt its appeal derived in large part from its symbolic connection to the old political order. Though the taluqdars had participated hardly at all in this court culture during the years of Nawabi rule, they found in it now a footing in the past, a traditional legitimacy, which fed not only their self-esteem but their regal pretensions.

54. Ali Hasan, "Tarikh-i-Mahmudabad," 2:2:148, 197–210. This lengthened observance continues within the family to the present day.
55. For a discussion of Madras industrialists' religious observances see Milton Singer, *When a Great Tradition Modernizes* (New York, 1972), pp. 315–50; for Allahabad bankers, see C. A. Bayly, "Patrons and Politics in Northern India," in Gallagher, Johnson, and Seal, eds., *Locality, Province, and Nation*, pp. 42–48 and *passim*.
56. For the concept of "husk culture" see D. A. Low, ed., *Soundings in Modern South Asian History* (Berkeley, 1968), pp. 8–9.

The most visible manifestation of this culture in the later nineteenth century was the widespread use, and patronage, of Urdu, and of Persian as well, as languages of literature and cultivated discourse. Urdu was in addition the language of estate administration and the basic medium of school instruction. Even such petty taluqdars as Thakur Ragunath Singh, the owner of fifteen villages in Pratabgarh, Narendra Bahadur Singh of Hanswar in remote eastern Faizabad, and the Khatri Seth Jai Dyal prided themselves on their knowledge of Persian.[57] Pratab Bahadur began his schooling at age seven with Nagri in the Mullupur village school, but within five years had shifted to the Pratabgarh school and the study of Persian. He took up Sanskrit with a pandit at the age of eighteen, and he toyed with learning English. But he did not persevere with either, in the case of English largely because Ajit Singh "did not want me to become like Raja Rampal Singh." As raja, Pratab Bahadur conducted his correspondence and estate business in Urdu. He had the English newspapers, and the Sanskrit classics, read out to him.[58] Rampal Singh too, despite his later anglicization, first learned Nagri, and then moved on at age twelve to Persian, which he mastered while in England by conversing with officials of the Iranian Embassy there.[59]

Taluqdars usually learned their Persian from a maulvi who came to their home for the purpose. Pratab Bahadur read the poetical works of Saadi with his tutor, while Suraj Bakhsh Singh of Kasmanda studied first Arabic and Persian grammar, then calligraphy and Urdu poetic composition, with various Muslim divines.[60] Successive maharajas of Balrampur were likewise tutored in Persian, together with Hindi and later English. Digvijai Singh as a youth in the days before the British studied Persian under one Mirza Zulfiqar Baig, a faith healer, who taught him stick fighting as well, while so late as 1922 the Court of Wards arranged for the minor Maharaja Pateshwari Prasad a tutor in Urdu, Persian, and "Hindustani manners."[61]

Some few taluqdars remained always aloof from this Islamicized culture. Most prominent among them was the Ajodhya family. Immersed in the Hindu culture of holy Ajodhya, Maharaja Pratap Narayan Singh seems not

57. Interviews with Thakur Rameshwar Prasad Singh, taluqdar of Isanpur, Pratabgarh, 16 December 1969, and Nripendra Bahadur Singh, taluqdar of Hanswar, Faizabad, 5 December 1969; Kunj Behari Seth, *Seths of Biswan*, p. 22.

58. Pratab Bahadur, "Memoirs," Part I, pp. 54, 64, 65, 72, 103, 107. The raja's bari rani studied English with a European lady tutor, and became quite proficient in the language. She also knew Sanskrit and wrote Hindi poetry. In this respect she was almost unique among taluqdars' wives, who for the most part remained wholly uneducated.

59. Munshi Kishan Lal, *Manual of Titles of Oudh* (Lucknow, 1899), Part V, p. 60.

60. Pratab Bahadur, "Memoirs," Part I, pp. 65, 68; and Kalka Parshad, *Jawahar Nama*, Part I, pp. 72-73. Suraj Bakhsh also studied Sanskrit with a pandit, and English both at home and in the Sitapur District School. The raja of Hasanpur similarly employed a European tutor and a maulvi for his son at their Sultanpur residence. Enclosure in Commr. Faizabad to Sec. Govt. N.W.P.&O. 16 September 1892, N.W.P.&O. Educ. Progs. March 1893, No. 153.

61. Hasan Rizvi, *Ahsan-ut-Tawarikh*, 1:87-91; and Annual Report for 1925-26, Estate Records 1926-27, Dept. 65, File 1. Pateshwari Prasad's tutor was not a maulvi but the estate historian Hasan Rizvi's son, a trained teacher.

to have studied Persian or even Urdu. He wrote in the local Hindi Bhasha dialect, and was a leader of the deputation to Antony MacDonnell that sought, and finally secured, recognition of Devanagari as a court language in 1900.[62] Indeed by the end of the nineteenth century this Islamicized culture was beginning generally to come under attack from a resurgent Hindu communalism. Raja Rampal Singh was criticized by a Benares newspaper so early as 1883 for naming his new journal the "Hindustan" rather than the more Sanskritic "Bharat Varsh" or "Arya Varta," and he was urged to "make its Hindi more idiomatic." A few years later another Benares journal applauded the raja of Sisaindi for introducing the Nagri character in place of Persian in his estate offices. By 1918 even the raja of Pratabgarh was writing his diary in Hindi.[63]

The composite character of the taluqdars' culture naturally inclined them, whether Hindu or Muslim, toward a tolerant view of religious affiliation. Even after they had begun to identify more closely with their own religious communities, they still participated in the other's festivals and refrained from censorious judgments. The pious Muslim rajas of Mahmudabad celebrated Dussehra with pomp equal to that of any Hindu, even calling in pandits to solemnize the occasion, while the raja of Pratabgarh, himself resisting the call of the "famous Mahatma" Baba Avtar Das, looked on with amused disdain as his Muslim private secretary fell under his spell. "Saadat Husain would ask for Babuji's blessings in everything," Pratab Bahadur wrote, "and would stay awake late at night with him and as a result used to sleep in the office during the day."[64] In similar fashion the taluqdars greeted wandering European missionaries hospitably, sometimes even offering them baskets of fruit, but, to the missionaries' intense dismay, invariably refused conversion. Even Raja Rampal Singh, whose anglicized style of life excited much missionary interest, was, wrote one, "altogether too careless for his soul's interest [for me] to urge him much to receive baptism."[65]

Despite their studies few taluqdars were very learned. Not wholly uncommon was the situation of Digvijai Singh of Balrampur, of whom Hasan Rizvi, his Urdu biographer, said that he "could write Persian a little," and that when given drafts of the history "he made comments with his own pen 'How

62. Durga Prasad, *Tarikh-i-Ajodhya*, pp. 179–80.
63. "Kavi Vachan Sudha" (Benares) 15 October 1883, *S.V.N. 1883*, p. 872; "Bharat Jiwan" (Benares) 20 June 1887, *S.V.N. 1887*, p. 390. In 1970 there was only one man in the employ of the Pratabgarh raja still capable of reading the earlier Urdu volumes.
64. Ali Hasan, "Tarikh-i-Mahmudabad," 2:2:213–16; and Pratab Bahadur, "Memoirs," Part III, p. 9. For discussion of the Dussehra festival see below p. 365. This tolerant attitude began to change in the 1930s as the taluqdars abandoned landlord for communal politics. See P. D. Reeves, "Landlords and Party Politics in the United Provinces 1934-37," in D. A. Low, *Soundings*, pp. 272–74.
65. Annual Report of C. G. Daeuble, Lucknow C.M.S. Mission, of 29 December 1873. See also, for an account of a missionary visit to Hanswar, A. W. Newboult, ed., *Padri Elliott of Faizabad* (London, 1906), pp. 156–62. For a German missionary attempt to convert the Balrampur maharaja see *S.V.N. 1865*, p. 439.

nice this story is, what a nice passage this is, and so forth.'"[66] Several taluqdars, among them the cultured Suraj Bakhsh Singh of Kasmanda and the
successive Mahmudabad rajas, tried their hand at Urdu or Hindi poetry.
Raja Amir Hasan even kept one poet on the estate payroll, employed first as
munshi then as tahsildar, solely to act as his *ustad* (mentor) and to correct his
poetic compositions. But, drawn away by estate management and other
interests, the taluqdari poets did not persevere very long, nor did they win
applause outside the circle of their dependents and admirers.[67]

The taluqdars' literary role was rather that of patron. The best educated
among them knew Urdu and Persian well enough to appreciate Mir and
Dabir, and the *ghazals* (verse) of their contemporaries. Amir Hasan himself
supported a number of Lucknawi poets. Among them were such men as
Ghulam Husnain "Qadr," teacher of Persian at Canning College, whose
qasidas (odes) in praise of the raja brought him, so it is said, a better income
than estate employment; Saiyid Hidayatullah, who received a regular allowance of Rs. 15 a month; and Sheikh Fida Ali "Aish," who accompanied
Amir Hasan on his Karbala pilgrimage. When the raja was in Lucknow at his
Kaiserbagh residence, these and other poets would visit him almost daily.
Gathered around the *huqqa*, they would swap jokes, abuse each other in
elaborate language, and recite poetry, sometimes couplets of their own composed for the occasion, at others the verse of the masters. Whenever any of
these poets came to Mahmudabad, they would be received with great courtesy, especially by the young Ali Muhammad, who invited them all to recite
their compositions at his durbar.[68]

The taluqdars were not of course the only props of the old Lucknawi culture. Some urban Hindu professional families supported it, Kayasthas
steeped in the Islamicized ways of the past, and above all Munshi Newal
Kishore, publisher of the influential *Oudh Akhbar* and an array of Urdu and
Persian books. Its truest representatives were undoubtedly the "Jolly
Nawabs," the descendants of the former Oudh royal family, all given the
courtesy title Nawab. Among these men the Urdu language, and poetic
appreciation, reached their greatest refinement. They kept alive too an ele-
gance of dress and many of the old aristocratic pastimes. During the day they
indulged in the flying of pigeons and kites. "In the evening after dusk, in
their white angarkha [Mughal-style long coat], tight pyjamas and fine white
caps, with their mouths full of betelnut and their dress wafting a bewitching

66. Testimony of 24 September 1885 in Civil Suit No. 83 of 1883 cited in Baldeo Singh, "Life
of Digvijai Singh," p. ii. The *Ahsan-ut-Tawarikh* itself was of course fullsome in its praise of the
majaraja's literary ability. Forty years later the Court of Wards special manager, and the visiting
Gertrude Emerson, both spoke of Maharaja Pateshwari Prasad as "unusually simple," and
"undoubtedly slow on the up-take." Annual Report for 1925–26, Estate Records; and Gertrude
Emerson, *Voiceless India*, p. 157.
67. Kalka Parshad, *Jawahar Nama*, Part I, pp. 73, 78; and Ali Hasan, "Tarikh-i-Mahmudabad," 2:2:21–30 and 101–02. See also Durga Prasad, *Tarikh-i-Ajodhya*, p. 179.
68. Ali Hasan, "Tarikh-i-Mahmudabad," 2:2:129–52; and 3:1:41–42.

odour of oriental perfume they walked towards the Chowk, where most of them had dancing girls in their pay. . . . "[69] These Nawabs, men such as Nawab Sardar Sahib and Nawab Mehdi Ali Khan, held *mushairas* (poetic assemblies) in their homes and encouraged, much like the taluqdars, the fledgling poets of Lucknow. But the Nawabs were for the most part not men of wealth. They subsisted on *wasiqas*, the interest on debts owed the old Oudh government by the British, and money which as the years went on had to be divided among more and more people. The taluqdars by contrast had large purses. As they took away, when they wanted them, the Nawabs' dancing girls, so too did they draw the poets to their courts. Though the Nawabs might be the more cultivated, it was taluqdari patronage that sustained, inside the city as well as out, the distinctive culture of Lucknow. Without this support that culture would have, as it ultimately did, withered and died.

Family, Friends, and Dependents: The Circle of Society

Taluqdari social life, like that of most Indians, was largely regulated by rules of status and dependency. Marriages were arranged in accordance with the appropriate strictures of endogamy and avoidance, and had as their objective the production of a male heir. Rajput taluqdars also observed hypergamy, taking wives from lower ranked clans, but giving daughters only to those above them. The marriage networks that resulted were often widely extended. Raja Udai Pratap of Bhinga, a Bisen Rajput, married the daughter of a Chandel raja of Mirzapur, found wives for his two sons in Gorakhpur and in Jaipur, and gave his daughters, one to a nobleman of Udaipur, the other to a nephew of the Jodhpur maharaja.[70] The social as well as geographic distance between bride and groom could be quite extensive. Pratab Bahadur as a youth of nine was married to the daughter of the Isanpur taluqdar, the holder of a mere fifteen villages in nearby Patti tahsil. Pratab Bahadur's father supervised the wedding arrangements, and Raja Ajit Singh footed the bill. A few years later, after the death of his first wife, Pratab Bahadur married again, the daughter of the taluqdar of Antu, who owned but five villages. Suraj Bakhsh Singh of Kasmanda by contrast, though he himself married a taluqdar's daughter from nearby Kheri district, arranged his own daughter's marriage with the maharaja of Vizianagram, a Benares resident but one of the wealthiest zamindars of the Madras Presidency.[71] These marriages, which cemented lasting ties between the families involved, were, for the most part, relationships of dependence, entered into

69. Chaudhri Khaliquzzaman, *Pathway to Pakistan* (Lahore, 1961), pp. 6–8. For the term "Jolly Nawab" see Syed Abdul Ali to Ali Muhammad 5 February 1902, Mahmudabad Family Papers.
70. Udayapratapa Sinh, *History of the Bhinga Raj*, pp. 12, 46–47.
71. Pratab Bahadur, "Memoirs," Part I, pp. 54–55; and Kalka Parshad, *Jawahar Nama*, Part I, p. 76.

in order to enhance the superior family's status by enlarging its circle of followers. Thakur Ragunath Singh of Isanpur, for instance, even after his sister's death, was a constant visitor to the Pratabgarh fort and the raja's indefatigable traveling companion. Pratab Bahadur in return over the years advanced him large sums of money, recommended him for appointment as an honorary magistrate, and secured him a place on the taluqdari delegation to London for the 1902 coronation of Edward VII.[72]

Much the most contentious aspect of taluqdari family life was the continued favor given to polygamy. When Pratab Bahadur, not content simply to remarry after his first wife's death, took first a third, and then a fourth and a fifth wife, he did so in the face of fierce household opposition. His first polygamous match, with his wife's younger sister from Antu, was, he later insisted, forced upon him by Raja Ajit Singh and he always "loved the Bari Rani [the elder surviving wife] more." But the bari rani, full of sorrow and anger, at once moved out of the old fort where she had lived with Pratab Bahadur since their marriage, and established herself in a recently constructed bungalow which she remodeled as her own residence. Pratab Bahadur's next marriage, to the daughter of the Dhingwas taluqdar three years later, was undertaken wholly on his own initiative, and over the combined resistance of both his existing wives. His motive was no doubt to use the match as a way of extending his influence further in the district. It was as a result a lavish affair with some 6,000 people joining the raja in the *barat* procession at a cost of several thousand rupees. His last marriage, with a cousin of his first two wives, a daughter of the Antu taluqdar's brother, appears to have been dictated by family considerations, and involved only a "simple" ceremony. Looking back years later, Pratab Bahadur noted sadly that "ever since my second marriage my private life has become unpleasant."[73]

Pratab Bahadur's relations with the members of his own family were also difficult—though for different reasons. Above all his two elder brothers, who had for years basked in Raja Ajit Singh's favor, looked with jealous hostility on Pratab Bahadur's designation as heir apparent. This decision Pratab Bahadur attributed to Ajit Singh's disgust with the brothers' excessive religiosity, at one time so great that "they would take a bath even if a housefly landed on them." The bitterly disappointed Sukhdeo Singh nevertheless brought suit in court to stop the succession; frustrated, he then snubbed his upstart brother on the latter's occasional visits to his home village. Pratab

72. Pratab Bahadur, "Memoirs," Part I, p. 68; Part IV, pp. 3–4, 18; "Diary" 19 January, 6 October, 17 December 1899 and *passim*. Pratab Bahadur's relations with Surajpal Singh of Antu were much the same.
73. Pratab Bahadur, "Memoirs," Part I, pp. 85, 93, 100, 109; and "Account of Pratabgarh Fort," *passim*. When the Mahmudabad Raja Ali Muhammad took a second wife late in life even his normally discreet manager Muhammad Habibullah protested. See above p. 256. Sometimes a taluqdar took a second wife because the first could not produce a male heir.

Bahadur's parents too, partisans of Sukhdeo, refused to eat with him after he had been named heir apparent, while the other brother Jagdeo, suspicious, sought from Pratab Bahadur not just a subsistence allowance but independent control of a portion of the estate. The family rift was only mended on Sukhdeo Singh's deathbed when the dying man presented Pratab Bahadur with a horse and rifle as a gesture of reconciliation.[74]

To escape these confining relationships and at the same time to widen still further their circle of followers or dependents, taluqdars sought out the company of *musahiban*, or boon companions. Thakur Ragunath Singh was for Pratab Bahadur such a person, with whom he could feel at ease and uninhibited. Maharaja Ali Muhammad too developed close ties of intimacy with several smaller landholders. Besides Muhammad Habibullah, his trusted manager, these included Kunwar Bam Bahadur Shah, of a Nepali Rajput family settled in Kheri, whom he met through Habibullah, Chaudhuri Mushtaba Husain, and two Colvin School classmates, Mirza Faiz Husain Baig and Raja Prithipal Singh. Other musahiban, less distinguished, were estate employees, expected to attend the raja on request and subject to the discipline of his private secretary. These men, two of whom in Pratabgarh were appointed "just to serve the *pan*," like their Mahmudabad counterparts, Shia of aristocratic lineage selected for their skills in pigeon flying and card-playing, were little more than courtiers. Their presence served to enhance the taluqdar's prestige, and helped keep alive his image as a petty potentate, or ruler of men.[75]

Beyond the immediate circle of family and friends lay, at least for Rajput taluqdars, the members of their clan, the descendants of those who had settled or conquered the land in times past. No doubt these kin ties were often highly attenuated. Yet where the clan members, whether as underproprietors or independent landholders, still lived in a compact area, as in Pratabgarh where clan and pargana boundaries nearly coincided, this relationship could easily take a visible form and one mutually beneficial to taluqdar and ordinary clansmen alike. The raja of Pratabgarh, for instance, by virtue of his position as the leading Sombansi landholder, acted as the head of the clan from the later nineteenth century. He encouraged education among the Sombansis, in part by special grants for schools and scholarships from the Pratab Bahadur Charitable Trust. He gave the poorer clan members grants of money on the occasion of marriage, bereavement, or disaster. He sometimes, too, arbitrated clan disputes, on one occasion even having the satisfaction of seeing his decision in a case of affray involving a number of Sombansis, appealed to the British courts, upheld by the Judicial

---

74. Pratab Bahadur, "Memoirs," Part I, pp. 54–58, 70, 72, 79, 96; and Part II, pp. 1, 8–11.

75. *Dastur-ul-amal-i-riyasat-i-qila pratabgarh* (1897), pp. 63–67, and (1900), pp. 166–74; Pratab Bahadur, "Memoirs," Part III, p. 6 and *passim*; Ali Hasan, "Tarikh-i-Mahmudabad," 2:2:153–59, and 3:1:51–52. For lists of the Mahmudabad raja's companions on his travels, and those in attendance at court ceremonies see *ibid.*, 3:1:88, 100, 127 and *passim*. The Pratabgarh raja's "Diary" entries contain similar lists.

Commissioner.[76] The Pratabgarh Sombansis in return as a gesture of solidarity would gather at the raja's fort at times of birth, marriage, or death in his family. So late as 1970, twenty years after zamindari abolition, over one thousand Sombansis from throughout Pratabgarh pargana joined the raja in mourning the death anniversary of his mother, and were fed by him. A year before a similar congregation had participated in the funeral rites themselves, and submitted to the shaving of their heads by the officiating Brahmins. The giving of *nazrs* (cash gifts) to the raja as a tangible mark of subordination had been abandoned. But the essence of the relationship remained undisturbed.[77]

Perhaps the most important such ceremony, uniting the taluqdar symbolically not only with his clansmen but with all his tenants as well, was the annual Dussehra durbar. The high point of the estate year, when accounts were settled and the new year begun, Dussehra was always celebrated with great pomp and ceremony. On most estates the observance began with a grand parade. Its approach would be announced by drumbeaters, together with whatever show of military force the estate could muster, from armed *sowars* (horsemen), spearmen, and lancers to simple lathi-bearing sepoys each dressed in full uniform. The taluqdar, outfitted in all his jewels and finery, rode out resplendent on an elephant decorated with an ornate silvered howdah. Behind him came the members of his family and senior estate officials, also on elephant-back. Then followed the estate's horses and camels with their riders, and lastly the subordinate staff—*dafadars, khidmatgars* (servants), peons—marching along on foot. The route of march was marked by the roar of guns and the explosion of firecrackers, and sometimes too by a scramble for coins the raja tossed from his elephant. At times the procession simply wended its way from the taluqdar's residence to the local bazaar and back again. More often it halted at the town common (*maidan*) where the effigies of Ravana and his consort stood ready for burning, and returned only after these evil deities had been reduced to ashes.

In the evening the taluqdar, seated on the *masnad* (throne) under an embroidered canopy, held his durbar. This took place either in the open courtyard of the palace, or for wealthier taluqdars in a special durbar hall, adorned with chandeliers and mirrors, and ringed with trays of sweets and flowers. All the estate's employees, most of its contractors and underproprietors, and a concourse of respectable village folk gathered round, together with the members of the taluqdar's family and clan. Each was carefully

76. Pratab Bahadur, "Memoirs," Part II, p. 8; and interview with Ajit Pratap Singh, raja of Pratabgarh, Lucknow, 28 November 1969. Pratab Bahadur also had written, by a schoolmaster of Kanpur long associated with the estate, Bishambar Nath Tholal, an English history of the Sombansi clan and the taluqdars which emerged from it. See Tholal, *Sombansi Raj*. Pratab Bahadur turned down, however, the author's suggestion that he write an Urdu version of the work.

77. Interview with Rajkumar Abhay Pratap Singh, Pratabgarh, 30 July 1970. For similar feasts following the deaths in the 1880s of Ajit Singh and Bijai Bahadur Singh of Bahlolpur, see Pratab Bahadur, "Memoirs," Part I, pp. 83, 89.

seated according to his position and rank, and came forward in order, beginning with the heir apparent, to present a nazr as token of subservience. The amounts ranged from several gold mohurs down to a few annas from the lesser tenantry. The taluqdar then distributed khillats, cash awards, or *inam* (rent-free) lands to deserving employees of the estate. Everyone present got pan, cardamom, and sweets, and occasionally a gift of a new turban or suit of clothes as well. After the formal ceremony the taluqdar might retire to his own quarters for private worship and feasting, to the accompaniment of *qawwali* singers and dancing girls, while other musicians entertained the assembled crowd outside. The festivities often continued late into the night. In addition taluqdars sometimes sponsored special musical concerts and wrestling matches as part of the Dussehra celebration. The raja of Tiloi, for instance, was reputed to spend up to a lakh of rupees bringing together the best wrestlers from the entire region.[78]

Taluqdars held durbars on other occasions as well. Mahmudabad celebrated the Persian *nauroz* (New Year) and the two Muslim Ids. The estate's Muharram celebration too, with its enforced attendance of Shia employees and participation by Hindu townspeople, served much the same purpose, of social control as well as religious solidarity. On Hindu estates large crowds congregated at Holi to throw colors at the raja and to watch the dancing girls and musicians who performed at this festive time. The accession of a new taluqdar, or the award of a title such as that of raja, was marked also by a solemn durbar, and the distribution of rewards to servants and employees.[79] Yet none of these ceremonies were so lavishly staged, or so fraught with meaning, as the Dussehra durbar, which brought together the taluqdar and his subjects in an annual reenactment of the ties that united them.

Habits and Customs: A Distinctive Style of Life

The taluqdars were renowned for their eccentricities. Once a well-known doctor of Lucknow, so Chaudhuri Khaliquzzaman recounts the story, when asked how many kinds of insanity there were quickly replied, "as many as the Taluqdars of Oudh." N. B. Bonarjee too says of the taluqdars that "more than one might have stepped straight out of the pages of Havelock Ellis or

78. Ali Hasan, "Tarikh-i-Mahmudabad," 2:2:213–18; Hasan Rizvi, *Ahsan-ut-Tawarikh*, 4:364–66, 510–23, 695–97; *Dastur-ul-amal* of Pratabgarh (1900), p. 61; Pratab Bahadur, "Diary" for 14 October 1899; and interviews with Nripendra Bahadur Singh, Faizabad, 6 December 1969; L.S.P. Singh, Mankapur, 9 January 1970; P.N.S. Singh, raja of Tiloi, Lucknow, 12 March 1970; and Jagannath Bakhsh Singh of Rehwan, Lucknow, 13 March 1970. There were of course variations in observance from estate to estate. In Mahmudabad, for instance, the durbar was held in the afternoon before the parade, and the raja, not wishing to participate in the Hindu Ram Lila, marched to an open field where a blue jay was released as an omen of good fortune in the coming year. On some smaller estates tenants paid in a portion of their rent to the taluqdar at the durbar.

79. For the Pratabgarh *raj gaddi* (sitting on the throne as raja) ceremony see Pratab Bahadur "Memoirs," Part IV, pp. 16–17. For the estate's celebration of Holi see *ibid.*, Part I, pp. 75, 103, and "Diary" for 27 March 1899, which includes a list of those who presented nazrs on the occasion.

von Kraft-Ebbing." This eccentricity took varied forms—from miserliness to profligacy, sensual indulgence to obsessive religiosity, lethargic seclusion to a punctilious concern with the winding of clocks. Raja Amir Hasan Khan, for instance, when in Lucknow came out for his drive "with the Treasurer with a big purse sitting in front of him in the buggy, throwing cash on both sides, followed by *shohdas* [gangs of beggars] quarrelling and cursing each other to benefit from the loot." His son Ali Muhammad was fascinated with scents and perfumes. At first he simply purchased perfume, with no regard for the cost or quantity, from the established dealers of Lucknow, who flocked to Mahmudabad to show him their wares. Then, determined to create a long-lasting scent, he began distilling his own, with his attendants set to work boiling vats of essence, until finally the palace storehouse overflowed with bottles of perfume and the smell permeated the entire building.[80]

The taluqdars' dress was also marked by extravagance. Amir Hasan appeared at a Sitapur reception for the Lieutenant Governor, as Butler described his costume, "in a magnificent heavy gold coat—i.e. gold on velvet. He had shoes worked with silver and pearls. A sword with a chaced silver scabbard and a highly jewelled hilt. He had also magnificent rows of pearls hanging round his neck and down to his waist. And to crown all was a splendid tiara about a foot high and eight inches broad of brilliants and emeralds."[81] No doubt this costume was intended, as it did, to impress the British, perhaps even the other assembled taluqdars, with the wearer's wealth and position. But even the taluqdars' everyday wear of embroidered cotton *angarkha* and cap, with *kurta* and pajama, "cost the sight of many workmen, and more than the dowry of their wives and daughters."[82] A few taluqdars adopted the European style of dress. Sheikh Muhammad Habibullah consistently wore European clothes, spoke English even at home, kept his bearers in uniform and his house tidy, and so gained the distinction of being known as a "sahib." Raja Rampal Singh of Kalakankar, too, usually dressed in European clothes, and appeared for a formal portrait in a morning suit complete with wing collar and gold watch chain. But he still "wore his hair in the Hindustani fashion, down to his neck," and he sometimes came dressed "as a Taluqdar, resplendent in cloth of gold."[83]

Occasionally, even for those less anglicized than Rampal Singh, showy

80. Khaliquzzaman, *Pathway to Pakistan*, pp. 5–6; Bonarjee, *Under Two Masters*, p. 19; and Ali Hasan, "Tarikh-i-Mahmudabad," 3:1:43–49.

81. Butler to Isabel 19 December 1893, Butler Papers IOL MSS Eur. F. 116/5. For the taluqdars' varied and colorful attire see the collection of photographs in Darogha Haji Abbas Ali, *An Illustrated Historical Album of the Rajas and Taluqdars of Oudh* (Allahabad, 1880).

82. Attia Hosein, *Sunlight on a Broken Column* (London, 1961), p. 33. For a description of Ali Muhammad's dress, of *angarkha* in summer and *sherwani* in winter, see Ali Hasan, "Tarikh-i-Mahmudabad," 3:2:288.

83. Interview with Ali Bahadur Habibullah, Lucknow, 9 March 1970; and Nagendranath Gupta, *Reflections and Reminiscences* (Bombay, 1947), p. 155. Rampal Singh is the only taluqdar pictured in European dress in the *Illustrated Album*. (See Photo 6.) Ali Muhammad wore English suits in European company and while employed on official business.

expenditure took a European form. Suraj Bakhsh Singh's nephew, Sripal Singh, a racing enthusiast, kept a stable of horses which he entered in the top race meetings throughout India, and once even won the Civil Service Cup. Ali Muhammad in the late 1890s had electricity, powered by a generator, installed in the Mahmudabad Imambara, which thus became, when the generator was in working order, one of the first electrically illuminated buildings in the entire province. He went on to decorate it, and the bungalow he had built for his own use, with furniture of the latest fashion ordered from the catalogs of Bombay and Calcutta dealers. A few years later, in 1905, he purchased from Bombay an automobile, which he garaged in the stable, along with his fifty horses and dozen or more carriages.[84]

The construction of buildings, above all of palatial residences, was a popular, and costly, taluqdari pastime. In this both European and Nawabi models provided inspiration. As the wealthiest estate, Balrampur consistently led the way in magnificence. The principal private building in Balrampur town, the *Gazetteer* recorded in 1877, "is, of course, the Maharaja's house, an imposing pile in the Indo-Palladian style of architecture, enclosing a large court, on one side of which are ranged the dwelling-houses, and offices, on the other the stables and outhouses for the accommodation of its master's hundred elephants." On the death of Digvijai Singh the estate spent a lakh and a half of rupees on a "beautiful carved statue hall" containing a bronze likeness, designed and cast in England, of the late maharaja. During subsequent years the estate built up, on the edge of town near a large maidan used for polo and cavalry parades, a country house, the Nilbagh Palace, increasingly frequented by the later maharajas, and an ornate European Guest House, elaborately furnished with tapestries and overstuffed settees. Most whimsical perhaps of Balrampur's building projects was its zoo, holding some fifty animals, lions, tigers, leopards, bears, even porcupines and kangaroos. They were kept no doubt not only to entertain the taluqdar and his courtiers but to impress the estate's credulous villagers.[85]

Less pretentious, but still suitably grand, was the Pratabgarh fort, residence of the rajas of Pratabgarh. Initially a tight cluster of buildings, some dating back to the eighteenth century, the fort was dramatically expanded in size, and made more European in character, by Ajit Singh and Pratab Bahadur. By 1900 it comprised some 1,300 acres and a number of impressive new structures. These included not only the bari rani's bungalow, painted and fitted with electricity under the supervision of the district survey, but a

84. Kalka Parshad, *Jawahar Nama*, Part I, p. 77; and Ali Hasan, "Tarikh-i-Mahmudabad," 3:1:31, 42–43, 178–79. For an account of the estate's transport animals and carriages see *ibid.*, 2:2:190–92.

85. *Oudh Gazetteer*, 1:211; Indar Bahadur Singh, *Tarikh-i-Raj-i-Balrampur*, pp. 141–43; Baldeo Singh, "Life of Digvijai Singh," pp. 276, 281–82; Annual Report for 1925–26, Estate Records. During visits to Balrampur in 1965 and 1970 I stayed in the European Guest House, now wholly deserted and choked with dust, but with its furnishings still intact. Digvijai Singh also entirely rebuilt the bazaar of Balrampur town.

Entrance Gateway, and a portion of the palace of the rajas of Mahmudabad.

round reception room furnished "with great care" by Pratab Bahadur himself in the European style, a large ceremonial gateway in the middle of the fort, built in 1890 at a cost of Rs. 10,000, and two carefully tended gardens, one adjacent to the rani's residence containing a pavilion set in the center of a tank, the other the Pratab Bahadur Park. In this park, laid out by Pratab Bahadur himself in 1893, a *pakka* road wide enough for carriages wound under sheltering banyan trees and through groves of mangoes, oranges, guavas, and bananas, all irrigated by raised brick channels radiating out from a massive well. Here every year Pratab Bahadur entertained the local British officials, including sometimes even the provincial Lieutenant Governor, at festive garden parties.[86]

Imposing ceremonial gateways in the Mughal, or rather Nawabi, style were a common feature of the residences of all taluqdars who could afford them. So too were the grouping of offices and living quarters around a central courtyard, and the strict separation of the quasi-public or formal areas, including guest rooms and often an apartment for the taluqdar himself, from the private family quarters. With parda almost universal among taluqdari families the women's apartments were always tightly guarded against even the glance of an outsider. As European-style wings, or buildings, were added

86. Pratab Bahadur, "Memoirs," Part II, pp. 2–3, and "Account of Pratabgarh Fort"; and "Diary" entries for 3, 6, 7 June and 6 December 1899.

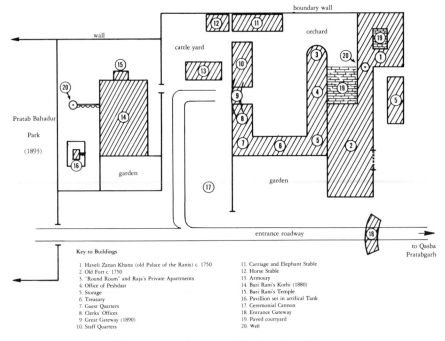

A sketch of the layout of the Pratabgarh fort.

on in the later nineteenth century, both for the entertainment of European visitors and to accommodate the taluqdars' increasingly Europeanized life style, the older sections usually remained the domain of the women and of family life. On the rare occasions when the women took over a new building, as in the case of the bari rani's bungalow at Pratabgarh, it was at once closed off from the remainder of the compound by a high blank wall.[87]

The taluqdars were devoted too to outdoor sport, *shikar* (shooting) above all else. No doubt this was partly a mark of their gentry style, which they shared with those equally enthusiastic *shikaris*, the resident British. But shooting was as well an inheritance from their more martial forebears, perhaps even a way of recapturing some of the spirit of those challenging days. Taluqdars usually took their guns along on tours of their estates, and found, or made, opportunity for sport in the intervals of inspecting villages. Where no forests were nearby, they shot birds in the ponds and marshes

87. This paragraph is based on observation and photographing of taluqdari residences, principally in Balrampur, Ajodhya, Mankapur, Mahmudabad, Jahangirabad, and Pratabgarh. Residences of lesser taluqdars usually omitted gateways and separate European-style wings but retained the focus around a central courtyard. For a description of the residence of the Hanswar taluqdar in Faizabad, who over the years slowly converted his rambling "half-brick half-mud palace" to all brick, see Newboult, *Padri Elliott*, pp. 154-57.

along the line of march.[88] Those whose estates extended into the Terai jungles, where big game was to be found, were of course exceptionally keen, often mounting tiger-hunting expeditions each year until the sport was finally prohibited in 1970.

Most lavish in their shikar arrangements were the maharajas of Balrampur, whose estate encompassed over a hundred square miles of jungle and abutted an equally large area of government reserved forest. During the later nineteenth century the estate built up an extensive network of forest rest houses, including a spacious mansion at Bankatwa in the heart of the jungle, and it maintained an armory, so Butler reported in 1893, "chock full of English sporting rifles and guns of every description by the best makers." The successive maharajas, from the time of Digvijai Singh onward, undertook elaborate and lengthy shooting tours, often several months in duration. Frequently they were accompanied by senior British officials, including the provincial governor, for whose comfort indeed the Bankatwa rest house had been "expressly constructed."[89] Even when the maharaja was a minor, in the 1880s, the Lieutenant Governor, local divisional and district commissioners, as well as stray "European gentlemen from the Punjab" and elsewhere, sought out the game in the Balrampur jungles. Such distinguished visitors no doubt brought honor, perhaps influence, upon the Balrampur estate, but it was not without cost. One estate official complained in 1889 that "in supplying their camps with *rasad* [supplies] and in making arrangements for the beating of the forest for the shikaris, the tahsil *amlas* [staff] from the tahsildars down to the sepahis, have to work very hard." A decade later the estate reported expenses of Rs. 2,500 on shikar charges, Rs. 3,900 for rasad, and Rs. 1,050 for upkeep of the armory.[90]

Almost alone among taluqdars Balrampur also sponsored *kheda*, the roundup of wild jungle elephants, which were then added to the estate stable. Begun in 1866, these kheda were held every three or four years, even during the years of British administration, at a cost of some Rs. 50,000 each. The continued patronage of this expensive sport brought down upon Anson, the estate's manager, the criticism of the vernacular press, but it remained ever popular with the Balrampur maharajas. Even as a minor, accompanied by his tutor, Bhagwati Parshad joined in the kheda of 1897, which brought back some 500 elephants, and so recovered a good part of its cost.[91]

88. See, e.g., Pratab Bahadur, "Memoirs," Part III, p. 1; and "Diary" entries for 23 January and 4 February 1899, and *passim*.

89. Hasan Rizvi, *Ahsan-ut-Tawarikh*, 4:524, 581–603, 699–722; and Butler to his father 9 July 1893, Butler Papers IOL MSS Eur. F. 116/5. Wingfield inaugurated the Bankatwa rest house with a month-long stay in 1865.

90. Annual Reports for 1888–89 of estate tahsils Gabbapur and Bankatwa, Balrampur Estate Records 1889–90, Dept. 54, File 3; and Balrampur Estate Annual Report for 1901–02, Estate Records. In 1889 the estate's agent, G. W. Anson, made Bankatwa his headquarters for a full two months.

91. Indar Bahadur Singh, *Tarikh-i-Raj-i-Balrampur*, pp. 147, 154; Baldeo Singh, "Life of

Lavish expenditure on rituals and ceremonies was as much a part of a taluqdar's life as shikar. In this, of course, he differed little from the ordinary Indian other than in having a much greater amount of money to spend. The government itself, after consulting with neighboring taluqdars, authorized Rs. 4,000 in 1868 for the head-shaving ceremony of the eleven-year-old taluqdar of Patti Saifabad, a not particularly large estate in Pratab-garh. Purses of Rs. 1,000 each, altogether apart from actual expenses, were given in 1904 to the officiating maulvis at the marriage of the Mahmudabad raja Ali Muhammad, while two years before the Balrampur maharaja spent Rs. 3,600 on the birth ceremonies of the heir apparent. When Bhagwati Parshad himself died, in 1921, the estate feasted 125 Brahmins once a month for a year at a total cost of Rs. 7,000. Exceptional occasions such as the 1902 coronation durbar called forth even greater expenditure. Balrampur paid out then some Rs. 15,600, of which half went for the rent of a house in Delhi and 4,000 for an ornate casket containing an address to the King-Emperor. Far more striking, however, was the high level of continuing day-to-day personal expenditure. The Balrampur maharaja in that same year (1902) ran up charges on his own account of over a lakh of rupees. These included such items as Rs. 19,000 on clothes, Rs. 15,000 for "pocket and pen money," Rs. 10,000 on ornaments, Rs. 4,000 for living costs in Naini Tal, and Rs. 2,000 for a billiard table.[92]

Expenditure, and income, of this sort sustained a distinctive style of daily life among the taluqdars, one built upon leisure. It had, of course, its disagreeable aspects, not least the continual badgering for money or employment to which they were subjected. During 1896, for instance, Pratab Bahadur received requests for aid not only from destitute former employees and the promoters of such projects as a Women's Hospital in Bareilly, but even from the respectable Gadia family of Bara Banki, with whom the Pratabgarh raja had no ties of either kin or community. Twice within three months Shahid Husain wrote imploring Pratab Bahadur for a loan of Rs. 20,000 to help pay off his debts, and when ignored affected a tone of desperation. "My difficulties are increasing day by day and I have no one to offer me advice or counsel. . . . I am waiting for the hour when God will deliver me from my plight." His younger brother Ashhad, a student at Colvin School, at the same time asked Pratab Bahadur for a watch—"Please get me the same type of watch as you have bought for Sajid Bhai and also exactly the same

Digvijai Singh," pp. 261, 266, 274; and "Azad" (Lucknow) of 6 September 1889, *S.V.N. 1889*, p. 552. The assistant agent in 1889 estimated the sale price of the elephants captured that year at Rs. 40,000. Balrampur Sadr Annual Report for 1888–89 (para. 6), Estate Records. Earlier kheda were less successful. Only 14 elephants were taken in 1872, and 27 in 1878.

92. Depty. Commr. Pratabgarh to Commr. Rae Bareli 8 February 1869, B.R. Pratabgarh File 30; Ali Hasan, "Tarikh-i-Mahmudabad," 3:1:173; Ct. Wards Manager Balrampur to Depty. Commr. Gonda 3 July 1921, Estate Records Dept. 38-1, File 88 of 1920–21; and Annual Report for 1901–02, Balrampur Estate Records.

type of chain"—together with Rs. 100 for clothes and a monthly allowance of Rs. 60, allegedly promised the last time they had met.[93]

Leisure nevertheless made possible a daily routine determined almost wholly by inclination. Some few taluqdars, punctilious in their habits, regulated their lives as much by the clock as any working man. Pratab Bahadur indeed himself checked the accuracy of the clocks in Pratabgarh fort every Sunday morning, while his diary contains a meticulous hour-by-hour record of his doings. Some taluqdars too led abstemious and disciplined lives. Jawahir Singh of Kasmanda, a teetotaler and in his later years a vegetarian as well, commonly rose before dawn, took only cold baths, and drank a rigidly limited amount of water. His successor Suraj Bakhsh Singh was also a man of "orderly habits," who rose early, took morning and evening exercise, and maintained a fixed daily routine, with time set aside to hear tenants' complaints and to supervise the office staff. The taluqdars of this sort were generally also those who administered their estates vigorously and expanded them by purchase.[94]

The taluqdar's day usually began with a bath and morning puja, followed by meetings with officials or a brief inspection of the stable or grounds. Once, carrying out a surprise early inspection after several days away, Pratab Bahadur found several estate officials asleep and garbage lying about in heaps. "The officials were instructed not to sleep late and keep their tents clean." Lunch, the first meal of the day, was taken about eleven o'clock, and was followed by several hours of rest. At Balrampur the entire palace staff had to remain quiet during this period, whose end was announced by the firing of a cannon. From about three to five the taluqdar sat in his *kachcheri* (office), together with his senior officials, to transact estate business. He then performed his evening puja, followed by a walk in the garden or perhaps a ride. Pratab Bahadur often went into the nearby district town of Bela to visit friends. In free intervals during the day, and then again at night, before a late dinner at ten or eleven o'clock, taluqdars amused themselves with sport and card games. Ajit Singh, like Digvijai Singh of Balrampur, used to watch specially staged fights of bulbuls or cocks, while Pratab Bahadur, with many other taluqdars, was fond of chess and cards, especially the Indian game of "ganjifa," which he often played with the bari rani. The successive Balrampur maharajas spent many afternoons playing football, cricket, and tennis, and perfecting their skills as horsemen. Nights were frequently given over to

93. Shahid Husain to Pratab Bahadur 15 April and 2 July and Ashhad Husain to P.B. 25 July 1896, Family Papers. Bound in the same volume are the other requests for financial assistance of that year. The Mahmudabad rajas were similarly beseiged. See, e.g., letter of 7 January 1903 from a Kathiawar taluqdar to Ali Muhammad thanking him for his assistance in a dispute with Junagadh state.

94. Pratab Bahadur, "Diary" for 8 January 1899 and *passim*; *A Taluqdar of the Old School*, pp. 78–80; Kalka Parshad, *Jawahar Nama*, p. 74; and interview with S. N. Saksena, manager of Kasmanda estate, Lucknow, 12 March 1970.

music, both vocal and instrumental. Pratab Bahadur even took up the sitar himself, and practiced faithfully, while Digvijai Singh kept professional musicians, as well as a snake charmer and a chess player, on the estate payroll.[95]

More indolent, or less conscientious, taluqdars usually rose later in the morning and devoted more of their time to amusement. Ali Muhammad, when he was not involved in public affairs, to which he never stinted of his time and energy, would sometimes rise as late as noon, tend to estate matters for an hour or two after lunch and then spend the afternoon playing chess or other indoor games. In the evening he would go for a drive and then gather his friends about him to discuss poetry and politics until late at night.[96]

Whether easygoing or disciplined in their daily habits, the taluqdars were united by what one perceptive observer has called "a strange arrogance and a will to exercise power—always to be in a position which forced men to reach up to them; and if they ever stepped down themselves it was an act of grace."[97] This spirit manifested itself in petty matters as well as great. Pratab Bahadur, for instance, insisted that his clothes be washed apart from those of other people, and that his barber keep three sets of utensils, one for himself, another for distinguished guests, and the third for ordinary people. Even such mundane events as the payment of the government revenue were often invested with ceremony. From Mankapur a grand procession, including an armed guard, mounted sowars and elephants, once each year bore the estate's dues, collected in silver rupees, to the district treasury at Gonda, where the money was weighed and deposited.[98]

The taluqdars sought also, and cherished, whatever marks of favor they could wring from the British government. Pratab Bahadur was in no way unique when he took pride in even so small a distinction as being seated next to the Deputy Commissioner at a district meeting of taluqdars, with his speech singled out for praise.[99] The taluqdars too endeavored to ingratiate themselves with the British by doing small personal favors for them. They would often lend the local memsahib a car and driver for shopping, while they responded with alacrity to requests such as that Mahmudabad received from the Sitapur police superintendent to borrow "the four wheeler bullock cart I had last year."[100] No doubt there was a tension, and one that taluqdars

95. Pratab Bahadur, "Diary" 24 March, 6 September, 2 November 1899, and *passim*; Hasan Rizvi, *Ahsan-ut-Tawarikh*, 1:27–38; Indar Bahadur Singh, *Tarikh-i-Raj-i-Balrampur*, pp. 149–50; Gertrude Emerson, *Voiceless India*, pp. 156–57; *A Taluqdar of the Old School*, pp. 62–63. The particular routine varied of course with the individual and from day to day.

96. Ali Hasan, "Tarikh-i-Mahmudabad," 3:2:289–90.

97. Attia Hosein, *Sunlight on a Broken Column*, p. 34.

98. *Dastur-ul-amal* of Pratabgarh (1900), pp. 157–59; and interview with L.S.P. Singh, Manager Mankapur, 9 January 1970.

99. Pratab Bahadur, "Diary" for 29 October 1899. See also his pleasure at receiving the "special treatment" of a personal introduction to Lord Curzon at his Lucknow durbar, *ibid.*, 12 December 1899.

100. Letter of E. H. Sabine-Pasley to Raja Mahmudabad 19 December 1899, Mahmudabad Family Papers. Mahmudabad and Balrampur both maintained large stables in Lucknow, and

must surely have felt, between these two divergent ways of enhancing their status in society: the one involving a lordly splendor, the other an obsequious sycophancy. Yet the taluqdars had no choice but to pursue both paths, and both helped them secure the position they regarded as rightfully their own.

The quest for status is not of course an ignoble one, nor was it, in the Oudh of the later nineteenth century, at all a novelty. But it came in those years increasingly to dominate the taluqdars' lives, while at the same time the channels for its expression became very much restricted. No longer was the martial style of the young Digvijai Singh, or Ajit Singh, who "received the education of a soldier and was a bold and skillful rider," at all possible. The British conquest, together with the Mutiny, had put an end to that. Yet the taluqdars remained too deeply embedded in their own society, and in the cultural values of that society, to take up the ways of the English landed gentry. To work for agricultural improvement, to speak out for social reform, these won little applause. Nor indeed did they serve any real purpose, for the taluqdars' supremacy had already been secured by the British revenue settlement, backed by the armed might of the Raj.

So, then, almost of necessity the taluqdars turned to self-indulgence and refinement of taste, in poetry as in perfume. These—interior pleasures—brought satisfaction and self-esteem. So too did flamboyance in dress and extravagance in expenditure. More importantly, such display provided an arena in which the taluqdars could compete, each against the other, for status and prestige. Even such seemingly eccentric behavior as Amir Hasan's throwing cash to the beggars from his buggy may have had a calculated motive: to impress the people of Lucknow with his wealth and piety, and so enhance his reputation. Much too that the taluqdars did was designed to pull around them the symbols of past rulership. Mughal-style gateways, elaborate Dussehra durbars, the fawning of courtiers, though but a pale reflection of a world lost, still kept alive a sense of awe and deference which fed taluqdari pride, and power. With this went a manipulation for their own advantage of the new symbols and institutions the British made available. In the court of law, as in the viceregal durbar, taluqdars could affirm for all the world to see their standing and position in society. Much as the British may have wished to change it, the behavior of these men was neither perverse nor wrongheaded. It was rather an appropriate response to the situation in which they found themselves, as an aristocratic elite within a colonial society.

lent coaches with horses to British officials at the time of the annual race meeting and for ceremonial processions on the occasion of viceregal visits. Ali Hasan, "Tarikh-i-Mahmudabad," 2:2:191-92.

Conclusion

I N 1850 THE Nawab Wajid Ali Shah, at a cost of eighty lakhs of rupees, built a palace for his concubines in the center of Lucknow. This square of ornately decorated buildings, the Kaiserbagh, the last, and in British eyes the most debased, of the architectural monuments of Oudh, sheltered the ladies of the court for but a few years. After the annexation, and the Mutiny, the Kaiserbagh was confiscated by the British government, and turned over to the taluqdars for use as town residences. Split up into separate apartments, it provided the Nawab's erstwhile antagonists, now themselves become politicians and patrons of the arts, with an urban base. The Kaiserbagh in its fate thus mirrored the shifting fortunes of the province in whose capital it stood: once dominated by a royal court, now by a band of wealthy landlords. But as courtiers the taluqdars were courtiers without a court. The hollow square of the Kaiserbagh enclosed, to be sure, the white-pillared *baradari*. In it the taluqdars gathered for the annual meetings of the British Indian Association. But most of the year the baradari was empty. Power resided elsewhere, in the British Government House, whose inhabitants and their viceregal visitors provided the guests at the taluqdars' Kaiserbagh garden parties.

376

Entrance gateway of the Kaiserbagh, Lucknow. (Reproduced by the courtesy of the Director of the India Office Library and Records.)

Yet, despite the disappearance of the royal court, regal symbolism, a royal style even, continued to flourish in Oudh. In the Indian political tradition whoever was powerful enough to make good a claim to control over sizable human and material resources could act like a king, and be accorded the deference due a king. Such clearly was the case with the various regional states that sprung up in the waning years of the Mughal Empire. So too did something of a royal aura cling to the taluqdars of Oudh. Even after 1858, with their power much attenuated, these men, some of whom after all held the title of raja, conceived of their own role in terms of the kingly tradition. They appropriated as many of the symbols of regality as they could, and they patterned their behavior so far as possible in accordance with its demands. Much of what they did indeed had the specific aim of making credible their claims to kingly status. The king in Indian tradition was charged, for instance, with the duty of redistributing wealth. He took money from the people and returned it to them by the support of temples and public works, and even by the disbursement of cash in his durbar and elsewhere. No doubt this redistribution was largely symbolic, involving very small sums of money compared with what was taken in, but it was nevertheless important in validating the ruler's authority. The taluqdar's charity thus served not simply to bring him as an individual religious merit but sustained his image as a benevolent ruler, one who acted as a proper Indian raja ought to act.[1]

A king too was expected to live magnificently. Such lavish display not only helped evoke a sense of awe in his subjects but tightened the bonds between them. This it did by giving them a sense of vicarious participation in kingly grandeur. The more splendidly their overlord was attired, the more ornate his mansion, the more their own self-esteem was enhanced. To see their taluqdar in gilt and jewels was for his dependents in some measure to be so clothed themselves. Similarly his triumphs over his rivals—in the law courts or in the magnificence of his style of life—were at one level their triumphs as well, and so reaffirmed his position as a true raja, deserving of their support and able in turn to nourish and sustain them. In short by living and acting as befitted a king the Oudh taluqdars at once put forward, and in some measure made good, a claim to regal status.

Throughout the nineteenth century, then, along with the persisting Islamic veneer of its "husk culture," a basic and more Hindu structure of attitudes and values continued in north Indian society. At its heart lay a hierarchical view of society, with status roles, each carrying reciprocal duties and obligations, defined and accepted by all. Of these the kingly role as protector and sustainer of the social fabric had perhaps the highest sanction. But similar hierarchies, charged with similar qualities of deference and dependence, could be found elsewhere—in the family, where the husband reigned supreme, and, for Hindus, even among the pantheon of the gods, where the lesser paid court to the greater. Indeed religious and political symbolism were often intermixed. One aspect of regality, at least in the popular mind, was a near-divinity, in which the king was approached with reverence, and even a glimpse of him worked wonders for the beholder; religious leaders by contrast were sometimes called *maharaj*, sat on the gaddi and held durbars. Such notions obviously made a substantial difference to the position of the taluqdar. With the people habituated to subordination, and to the idea of diffused kingship, the concept of the taluqdar as raja, all-benevolent and all-protective, found ready acceptance. No one insisted that the relationship between the taluqdar and those beneath him be changed to reflect the new realities of power that British rule brought with it.

Yet the changes were far-reaching, and cut into the very basis of the old order. In the North-Western Provinces the reordering of power in the countryside was exceptionally profound. In this process the two decades from 1835 to 1857 stand out as critical. Though the British during their first thirty years of rule, following the cession in 1801, made good their hegemony over the substantial local powerholders, they did little to shake the fabric of

1. I am endebted to Pamela Price, Robert Goldman and the other members of the Berkeley South Asia Research Discussion Group for helping me develop the ideas presented in this and the subsequent two paragraphs.

society. Much that they did then, tentative and illconsidered, was soon undone, while of the rest a very large part existed only on paper. The introduction from 1835 of the "revised" settlement dramatically altered this state of affairs. No landholder could escape the new ideology of agrarian reform, nor the more precise definition of property rights the settlement brought with it. The hard-hit taluqdars, despite their tenacious rearguard action in the courts, found themselves within little more than a decade stripped of the bulk of their land. Even the village zamindars, the intended beneficiaries of the settlement, pressed by heavy assessments and their novel responsibilities as revenue managers, all too often ended up on the brink of bankruptcy, if not as tenants at the mercy of creditors who had purchased their property in the courts.

This process of leveling down, and of dispossession, did not of course wholly disrupt rural life, nor can the entire upheaval be attributed to the workings of British land policy. Many of the landholders' difficulties, the product of years of drought and depression, owed little to the new settlement, while the old structures of power often proved more resilient than the British had anticipated. Even those who lost their land in the courts were rarely physically dispossessed. Sometimes indeed, where the local lineage was determined and tightly knit, they could thwart, or at least delay the transfer of their land to outsiders. The taluqdars too remained almost always, by comparison with those around them, wealthy individuals. Where they controlled large blocks of productive land, or the allegiance of compact groups of clansmen and former tenants, they could blunt much of the effect of the new settlement. Few villagers willingly tangled with their erstwhile overlord in court, and none dared go against him in the crisis of 1857. Nevertheless the position of the old rural chieftains, and of the village zamindars with them, became slowly but irrevocably transformed. Those whose ties in the countryside were weakest, or whom commercial agriculture bypassed, suffered most severely. But no one escaped unscathed. The resources at the command of the British were too great, the reorientation of policy too profound. As the years went by new men, and new property relations, based upon more individualistic and exclusive concepts of ownership, came increasingly to dominate rural society. Bird and Thomason had left their mark.

The Mutiny was a last convulsive protest against these cumulative and unsettling changes. It might appropriately be called, to use the African terminology, a "post-pacification" revolt, in which the disruptive and differential impact of colonialism, for long hardly noticed by the bulk of the people, finally fuels a violent, disorganized, and invariably unsuccessful outburst of mass discontent.[2] Yet the revolt cannot be explained as easily or straightforwardly as one might wish. People joined the uprising, we now know, for many different reasons, some of which had nothing to do with British rule at

2. J. Iliffe, "The Organization of the Maji Maji Rebellion," *Journal of African History* 8 (1967):496–512.

all. At the same time others, aggrieved, with every incentive to throw in their lot with the rebels, stayed staunchly loyal. One might even go further and argue that the terms "loyalty" and "rebellion" had meaning primarily for the British. The rural populace, given the virtual disappearance of British rule over most of northern India during the summer of 1857, simply looked to their own interests, and endeavored as best they could to preserve, or extend, their wealth and power. This sometimes involved them in acts the British labeled rebellious, but it sometimes also led to an alignment of their interests with those of the colonial overlord.[3] In the end too, despite its dramatic character, the Mutiny in the North-Western Provinces brought about little change in the institutional framework of the Raj. Nor did it leave a visible mark on the structure of landholding. During the years that followed, agrarian change, propelled now by demographic and economic forces, moved slowly along the paths laid down in the decisive, and turbulent, two decades which preceded the uprising of 1857.

In Oudh, annexed only a year before, the revolt, involving as it did the old royal court and the bulk of the taluqdars together with a goodly number of villagers, was clearly more popular, and contained a greater leaven of anti-British sentiment. It was followed too by a reversal of British land policy in which, bulwarked by a traditionalist ideology, the taluqdars were proclaimed an "ancient, indigenous, and cherished" aristocracy. Oudh was thus spared the upheavals which marked the early years of British rule across the Ganges. Yet the continuity with the past was more apparent than real. Although the same men remained on the land, the structuring of power in rural society had been radically transformed. Numbered and labeled, the community of taluqdars were now frozen in time, while their relations both with the government and with those beneath them on their estates took on an increasingly novel shape. In the end little remained but the name to tie the taluqdars to their Nawabi past.

The greatest change was in the taluqdar's position on the land. Stripped of their armaments and retainers, with their jurisdiction confined as honorary magistrates to a few petty cases, these men retained but a fragment of their old quasi-kingly authority. Even over the village servants—the lowly patwari and chaukidar—they had to share control with the new government. Informally, of course, the taluqdars still exercised a good deal of coercive power over those beneath them, and they still settled disputes the villagers, or their own estate staff, brought them. Their regal style too, as we have seen, together with their role as clan chieftains, substantially enhanced the taluqdars' standing in society, and hence their ability to move men. But none of this could disguise the fact that under the British the taluqdar had been fitted for a new role in society—that of landlord.

As landlords the taluqdars commanded considerable power and influence.

3. See, for instance, E. I. Brodkin, "The Struggle for Succession: Rebels and Loyalists in the Indian Mutiny of 1857," *Modern Asian Studies* 6 (1972):277-290.

They remained still the central figures in the countryside, intermediaries whose estates linked the villager as rent payer to the government as revenue collector. From Canning's award of taluqdari sanads in 1859 onward they held their estates in full proprietorship, subject only to a revenue demand that was but rarely burdensome. Until 1886 too they were absolutely unfettered in their dealings with their tenantry. Even the legislation then passed, which limited enhancement to 6¼ percent every seven years, made surprisingly little difference to the course of rents. By evasion, and even outright defiance of the law, the landlords continued to have their way. During the first decade of the twentieth century rent-rates in Oudh rose an average of 1 percent a year, or more than the maximum permissible limit.[4]

This landlord pre-eminence was not wholly a product of the colonial ruler's tenurial arrangements, nor was the persisting pressure upon the tenantry simply the result of avarice. Both owed much as well to the growth in the later nineteenth century of a commercial economy. Investments in urban real estate, and in such industrial ventures as the Upper India Paper Mill, brought the taluqdars new kinds of income, while on the land the cultivation of new and more valuable crops, with the growth of the area under tillage and the extension of railways and markets, substantially increased the landholder's wealth and influence. The growth of population too, as uncultivated land grew scarcer, brought with it a competition for tenancies, and so further tilted the balance in favor of the owners of land. At the same time the creation of new arenas for the exercise of power—law courts, district boards, and the like—which the taluqdars were quick to turn to their own advantage, helped reinforce their position on the land. To some extent their ability to manipulate these institutions may have helped compensate the taluqdars for their loss of control over the subordinate government servants.

The taluqdar's power, even as landlord, was not without its limits. The British, to be sure, fearful of antagonizing these influential magnates, did little to restrain them. But those beneath them on their estates were not wholly at the taluqdars' mercy. The underproprietors above all, resentful of their enforced subordination, fought stubbornly against it, usually by withholding rent. Success did not always attend this defiance, nor were the underproprietors able but rarely to induce the ordinary cultivators, inert and poverty-stricken, to join them. Still their disaffection reduced the resources available to the landlord, and kept alive independent sources of power and influence in the countryside. In similar fashion the subordinate estate staff, though theoretically simple agents of the taluqdar's will, had in fact interests and ambitions of their own. Knowledgeable and close to the scene, they skillfully diverted the estate's dues, whenever they were not closely supervised, to their own pockets and those of their friends. In the process they built up patronage networks which established them as petty centers of power in their

4. W. H. Moreland, *Notes on the Agricultural Conditions and Problems of the United Provinces*, p. 89.

own right. It is not surprising that when nationalist activity came to the U.P. countryside after 1920 sons of estate servants, men of influence, often educated yet not bound to the old agrarian order, provided a good deal of its leadership.[5]

Yet even before the nationalist challenge the taluqdar's position on the land had begun to erode. During the First World War especially, as the value of produce rose dramatically, the landlords, unable directly to raise their rents, found themselves increasingly under financial pressure. To keep ahead they turned to a more intensive exploitation of their *sir* land, unencumbered by settled tenants, and to enhancement of their manorial tolls and dues. These latter involved a host of petty payments by an estate's cultivators and the tradesmen in its bazaars. Some, such as the provision of fodder for the landlord's elephants or the supply of a fixed portion of the sugarcane and other valuable crops, were effectively rental surcharges; others, known as *begar*, involved free labor, usually in the ploughing and weeding of the landlord's fields; while still others, largely symbolic marks of subservience, included such items as offerings of food on the occasion of a death or marriage in the landlord's family and the presentation of *nazrs* to a taluqdar on tour or at the time of a durbar. Taken together these manorial dues might amount to 8 to 10 percent of a tenant's rental.[6] In 1901 they brought the Balrampur estate Rs. 67,484, and the following year, with increased income from bazaar dues, a sum of Rs. 78,328.[7] The British had never cared for these *ad hoc* payments, and sought always to regulate if not to suppress them. Nevertheless they remained in existence, tokens of the days when the taluqdar was lord of the people as well as the land. Hence an increase in the number and extent of these exactions offered a way out of the landlord's twentieth century financial squeeze. The novel payments exacted for the purchase of motorcars and elephants, and to secure reinstatement of a tenant in his holding, had by the 1920s entered Indian folklore as evidence of the evils of landlordism, and helped fuel the fires of peasant discontent.

As disruptive as the tenurial innovations of the colonial regime were the novel values and expectations the British brought to rural India. The taluqdars were not only made over into landlords, they were expected as well to take an interest in improving agriculture, in social reform and education, and to act as responsible advisers to the government on district boards and legislative councils, and through their own British Indian Association. They were, that is, now to model their behavior on that of the English landed gentry. At the same time men such as W. C. Benett and Harcourt Butler elaborated a vision of an idealized "traditional" India in which the taluq-

5. There is little research yet done on this subject. However both R. S. Sharma, from his knowledge of Bihar, and C. A. Bayly, on the basis of his research in Allahabad, confirm this view.

6. See D. M. Stewart, *Report on Inquiry Regarding Cesses in Oudh 1922* (Allahabad, 1923), passim, esp. pp. 50–52.

7. Balrampur Estate Annual Report for 1901–02, Estate Records.

dars, given reverence by a contented peasantry, presided over a society unchanged from time immemorial. The British adamantly refused, however, to acknowledge any incompatibility between these two views, nor did they take effective measures to bring either into existence. Indeed they could do little, for these were British, not Indian, models of behavior, and evoked little response from those for whom they were intended.

The taluqdars did of course make occasional gestures toward education and modern political organization; and, anxious to be regarded as an enlightened aristocracy, they continually paraded their philanthropic enterprises before the British. They were flattered too, and to some extent taken in, by the vision of themselves as "traditional" chieftains at the head of a deferential and harmonious rural order. Much of their political rhetoric was little more than a rehash of Butler's views, which they had adopted as their own. But for the most part they conceived of themselves, and their role in society, in ways markedly different from those employed by the British. Above all they continued to define their position in terms derived from the Indian kingly tradition, and they cast the British in the role of their old royal superiors, whom they sought to impress by display and magnificence. Their objective was, as it had always been, to win honors from their overlord as they dispensed honors to those beneath them. Indeed as their political and military power waned under the new regime, they redoubled their efforts to obtain marks of approbation from their governors. But they did not, by and large, change their methods. Rather the taluqdars used the increased income their new landlord status gave them to live ever more grandly, even extravagantly. They endeavored, that is, to offset the loss of effective regal power by manipulating the symbols of regality. Where they could no longer command they would overawe.

The colonial system in northern India was thus shot through with inconsistency. The British neither sustained the traditional order, much as they sometimes thought they were doing so, nor did they transform society so as to encourage capitalist enterprise, as the early reformers had anticipated. By and large, apart from the years of the Thomason settlement in the North-Western Provinces, the old elites were kept in place, with their old view of themselves largely unchanged. Beneath them the old structures of production, and of relationships within the village, remained largely intact. Yet at the same time the tenurial system was restructured on the basis of individual property rights, while the old patrimonial system of government gave way to a colonial bureaucratic one which, if it did not penetrate fully into the village, still caught up almost all government servants in its disciplined network. Even on the estate the attraction of the British model was so compelling as to bring about by the turn of the century a bureaucratization of the landlord's relations with his own subordinate staff.

Nor were institutional forces alone at work in reshaping the character of rural society. As the countryside became integrated into ever larger trading networks, tied to the fluctuating prices of grain and indigo, yet still at the mercy of famine and drought, a complex and far-reaching set of social consequences was set in motion. At times, as we have seen, the landlords were the beneficiaries, at others the settled tenantry, of these economic and demographic changes. In any case by 1900 rural U.P. was no longer a custombound society organized around traditional styles of governance. Despite the continued presence of its old taluqdari chieftains, northern India was in no sense a region of "indirect rule," with responsibility divided between colonial and indigenous authorities. Unlike Uganda or Northern Nigeria, where traditional chiefs continued to exercise governmental authority, and even gained new responsibilities as the colonial ruler's agents, their north Indian counterparts paid rather than collected taxes, and were subject, along with their tenants, to the jurisdiction of British Indian courts and magistrates.[8]

As time went on the rural gentry of the U.P. became increasingly isolated from the society around them. The creation of district boards and provincial councils in the later nineteenth century gave them a new political footing, but, not fitted to participate effectively in party and constituency politics, they failed to press home their advantage. For many years, sustained by wealth from tenant rentals and the persistence of a deferential respect among the villagers, together with the political support of the British, they carried on unchanged their old style of life. Yet, as nationalism spread through the countryside after 1920, the landlords' ties with those beneath them on their estates grew ever more attenuated. Even their kingly style, drained of substance in the effort to increase their income, ceased to command respect, while the coercive mechanism of the estate administration broke against the force of a tenantry organized from outside. During the cow protection agitation of 1893 the landlords, at a word from the British, had put an end to riotous behavior on their estates. Forty years later, in the 1937 elections, despite a flurry of last minute canvassing, they could not secure for themselves the votes of their tenants.[9]

By the later 1930s, then, under the twin hammer blows of severe economic dislocation and a greatly expanded franchise landlord hegemony was fast crumbling. Some landlords, drawn by the communal politics of the time, sought to avert the inevitable by participation in the Muslim League or Hindu Mahasabha. Others, more politically adept, above all those in the neighboring Punjab, took advantage of enduring rural-urban and Hindu-Muslim antagonisms; and, bulwarked by strong clan loyalties, retained their

8. See, e.g., D. A. Low, *Lion Rampant* (London, 1973), esp. pp. 95–105; and Lloyd Fallers, "The Predicament of the Modern African Chief: An Instance from Uganda," *American Anthropologist 57* (1955):290–305, esp. 298–99. The situation was of course different in the Indian princely states, which suffered if anything from an excess of indirect rule.
9. See P. D. Reeves, "Landlords and Party Politics in the United Provinces, 1934–37," in D. A. Low, ed., *Soundings in Modern South Asian History*, pp. 261–93. For an account of the ways these landlords coped with the loss of their estates see my "Landlords without Land: The U.P. Zamindars Today," *Pacific Affairs* 40 (1967):5–18.

dominance in the legislature as in the countryside until the eve of independence. But throughout most of northern India the great landlord had become as anomalous a figure as the British district officer. The results of the 1937 election, when Congress swept the polls, prefigured the fate that was to befall both together a decade later.

Appendices

Appendix One
Taluqdari Land Holdings in Oudh by Caste,
Community, and District

Note: The data in the following tables are taken from the "Lists of Taluqdars" attached to the district articles in the *Oudh Gazetteer* (1877), and as appendices to the Oudh volumes of the series of *District Gazetteers of the United Provinces* (1903-1905). The figures in parentheses at the head of each column represent the number of taluqdari estates in each district at the time. They do not however provide an accurate total of the number of taluqdars, for some estates were shared among several holders, while some taluqdars held estates, counted separately, located in two or more districts.

The percentage figures for the various castes indicate the percentage of the total taluqdari-held villages in each district owned by members of that caste. The inset totals for Rajput and Muslim are summations of the individual clans' holdings.

The district totals are not supplied with the taluqdar lists, but are taken from other sections of the Gazetteer volumes. As these figures were sometimes compiled by different criteria for other purposes they cannot be wholly relied upon as guides to the taluqdars' overall position within the district. Some of the discrepancies encountered are noted on the individual tables.

The two sets of figures, for 1877 and 1903-1905, are not precisely comparable, for the revenue assessments of most estates, and sometimes the definition of a village, underwent alteration during that period. Hence they should be used with caution as guides to changes in landholding patterns over the intervening thirty years.

Appendix Table 1. Lucknow

Caste	Clan	1877 (25)[a]			1903 (34)[a]		
		Villages	Percentage Taluqdari	Jama (Rupees)	Villages	Percentage Taluqdari	Jama (Rupees)
Rajput	Panwar	75	27	49,500	76	27	55,200
	Bais	25	9	14,600	24	9	19,800
	other	6	2	4,100	14	5	19,900
Rajput total		106	38	68,200	114	41	94,900
Brahmin		37	13	40,400	30	11	41,300
Kayastha and Khatri		29	10	16,400	29	10	34,700
Nanakshahi Faqir		4	1	2,400	4	1	2,700
Muslim	Saiyid	35	13	35,800	31	11	44,200
	Pathan	33	12	34,300	26	9	39,400
	Sheikh	22	8	16,100	35	12	27,400
	Mughal	14	5	10,700	12	4	13,300
Muslim total		104	38	96,900	104	37	1,24,300
Total Taluqdari		280	100	2,24,300	281	100	2,97,900
Total District		956	29	8,02,700	938	30	9,86,600

a. Number of taluqdari estates at the time.

Appendix Table 2. Unao

Caste	Clan	1877 (21)			1903 (37)		
		Villages	Percentage Taluqdari	Jama (Rupees)	Villages	Percentage Taluqdari	Jama (Rupees)
Rajput	Bais	50	16	29,600	68	24	81,800
	Batam	22	7	14,600	19	6	15,300
	Sengar	21	7	16,400	8	3	11,100
	Dikhit	15	5	14,500	9	3	8,000
	other	20½	7	39,900	24	8	52,100
Rajput total		128½	42	1,15,000	128	44	1,68,300
Khatri		115	38	1,09,600	52	18	1,18,100
Nanakshahi		42	14	33,000	23	8	20,300
Brahmin		2	1	4,200	34	12	37,900
Kayastha					3	1	3,700
Muslim	Saiyid	9	3	11,900	15	5	21,400
	Sheikh	7	2	5,900	34	12	40,100
Muslim total		16	5	17,800	49	17	61,500
Total Taluqdari		303½ᵃ	100	2,79,600	289	100	4,09,800
Total District		1195	25ᵃ	12,87,300	1633	18ᵇ	15,45,300

a. A different set of figures in the same volume (*Oudh Gaz.*, 3: 534) gives a taluqdari total of 267, or 21 percent. The two calculations cannot be reconciled.
b. Taluqdari holdings are elsewhere (*DG*, p. 63) recorded as 21 percent of the district.

Appendix Table 3. Rae Bareli

Caste	Clan	1877 (35)			1904 (62)		
		Villages	Percentage Taluqdari	Jama (Rupees)	Villages	Percentage Taluqdari	Jama (Rupees)
Rajput	Bais	547	57	3,93,900	539	48	4,46,600
	Kanhpuria	197	20	1,73,000	241	22	2,54,800
	Amethia	29	3	25,700	80	7	73,600
	Janwar	22	2	17,000	25	2	22,900
	other	8	1	4,700	21	2	15,000
Rajput total		803	83	6,14,300	906	81	8,12,900
Brahmin		16	2	7,500	23	2	18,600
Khatri					23	2	22,600
Kayastha		9	1	9,400	2	0	4,400
Kurmi					3	0	5,300
Muslim	Pathan	40	4	21,100	43	4	23,600
	Sheikh	19	2	7,000	31	3	14,500
	Saiyid	10	1	5,400	16	1	7,500
	Chauhan	11	1	8,300	11	1	13,400
Muslim total		80	8	41,800	101	9	59,000
Sikh		47	5	37,700	58	5	51,600
European		12	1	20,200			
Total Taluqdari		967	100	7,30,900	1116	100	9,74,400
Total District		1735	56	12,39,200	1767	63	16,07,600

392

Appendix Table 4. Bara Banki

Caste	Clan	1877 (52)			1903 (61)		
		Villages	Percentage Taluqdari	Jama (Rupees)	Villages	Percentage Taluqdari	Jama (Rupees)
Rajput	Raikwar	203	21	4,31,900[a]	199	21	1,82,400
	Bais	65	7	63,000	69	7	80,900
	Surajbansi	60	6	61,300	60	6	74,400
	Amethia	34	4	35,700	26	3	34,400
	other	19	2	18,400	14	2	18,700
Rajput total		381	40	6,10,300	368	40	3,90,800
Kayastha		43	5	37,100	46	5	47,300
Brahmin		33	3	24,300	32	3	32,300
Khatri		1	0	400	1	0	400
Muslim	Sheikh	340	35	3,13,000	343	37	4,43,300
	Saiyid	83	9	80,600	79	9	96,400
	Rajput	22	2	16,700	4	0	6,200
	other	5	1	12,700	6	1	22,900
Muslim total		450	47	4,23,000	432	47	5,68,800
Sikh		46	5	10,600	49	5	15,000
Total Taluqdari		954	100	11,05,700	928	100	10,54,600
Total District		2038	47	15,84,500	2057	45	20,76,900

a. This figure, though correctly taken from the Oudh Gaz., probably contains a typographical error, and should be read as 1,31,900 to be made comparable to the other data supplied.

393

Appendix Table 5. Faizabad

		1877 (29)			1904 (26)		
Caste	*Clan*	*Villages*	*Percentage Taluqdari*	*Jama (Rupees)*	*Villages*	*Percentage Taluqdari*	*Jama (Rupees)*
Brahmin		405	19	2,48,900	360	26	2,51,500
Rajput	Rajkumar	576	28	1,16,700	154	11	1,78,500
	Palwar	360	17	1,70,600	245	18	2,05,200
	Bachgoti	194	9	95,100	155	11	1,16,900
	Gargbansi	169	8	75,800	140	10	67,700
Rajput total		1299	62	4,58,200	694	50	5,68,300
Muslim	Saiyid	191	9	93,000	138	10	1,35,400
	Sheikh	182	9	90,700	169	12	1,10,700
	Rajput	10	0	6,900	19	1	17,500
Muslim total		383	18	1,90,600	326	23	2,63,600
Kayastha and Other		13	1	19,000	9	1	2,500
Total Taluqdari		2094	100	9,16,700	1389	100	10,85,900
Total District		2568	82	11,68,500	n.a.[a]	75[a]	14,61,900

a. Village totals for the entire district, comparable to those in the taluqdar list, are not available. However 75 percent of the total acreage of the district was in taluqdari hands. *DG*, p. 73.

Appendix Table 6. Sultanpur

Caste	Clan	1877 (25)			1902 (34)		
		Villages	*Percentage Taluqdari*	*Jama (Rupees)*	*Villages*	*Percentage Taluqdari*	*Jama (Rupees)*
Rajput	Bandhalgoti	338	34	2,01,000	334	28	2,38,600
	Rajkumar	207	21	1,25,200	278	23	2,04,200
	Bachgoti	86	9	53,300	90	8	59,700
	Kanhpuria	65	6	46,600	68	6	60,100
	Rajwar	45	4	24,800	44	4	29,300
	Durgbansi	31	3	8,400	39	3	17,300
	other				65	5	35,000
Rajput total		772	77	4,59,300	918	77	6,44,200
Brahmin					43	4	25,200
Muslim	Bachgoti	193	19	94,400	192	16	1,15,300
	Bhale Sultan	32	3	27,700	37	3	48,300
	Saiyid				2	0	1,400
Muslim total		225	23	1,22,100	231	19	1,65,000
Total Taluqdari		997	100	5,81,400	1192	100	8,34,400
Total District		1967	51	12,37,700	2428	49	14,86,400

Appendix Table 7. Pratabgarh

		1877 (28)			1904 (33)		
Caste	*Clan*	*Villages*	*Percentage Taluqdari*	*Jama (Rupees)*	*Villages*	*Percentage Taluqdari*	*Jama (Rupees)*
Rajput	Bachgoti	660	41	2,58,000	532	36	3,41,900
	Bisen	523	33	2,78,700	493	33	3,84,900
	Sombansi	296	19	1,61,800	333	22	1,93,100
	Kanhpuria	72	5	54,000	74	5	66,500
	other	46	3	20,600	59	4	37,000
Total Taluqdari		1597	100	7,73,100	1491	100	10,15,500
Total District		2215	72	9,85,600	2171	69	13,46,500

Appendix Table 8. Gonda

Caste	Clan	1877 (23)			1905 (24)		
		Villages	Percentage Taluqdari	Jama (Rupees)	Villages	Percentage Taluqdari	Jama (Rupees)
Brahmin		758	33	5,31,800	369	22	3,32,400
Rajput	Janwar	661	29	4,22,000	782	46	5,20,700
	Kalhans	343	15	1,75,500	168	10	1,46,200
	Bisen	342	15	1,16,000	298	17	1,09,700
	other				1	0	4,000
Rajput total		1346	59	7,13,500	1249	73	7,80,600
Nanakshahi Faqir		32	1	19,800	22	1	19,400
Muslim	Pathan	85	4	34,600	73	4	44,900
Sikh		3	0	300	3	0	1,200
Unidentified		46	2	18,900			
Total Taluqdari		2270	100	13,18,900	1716	100	11,78,500
Total District		3145	71	16,99,300	2835	61	17,70,200

397

Appendix Table 9. Bahraich

Caste	Clan	1877 (23)			1903 (24)		
		Villages	Percentage Taluqdari	Jama (Rupees)	Villages	Percentage Taluqdari	Jama (Rupees)
Sikh		497	30	2,02,200	479	32	2,64,900
Rajput	Janwar	369	22	2,32,700	371	24	2,98,400
	Bisen	93	6	68,500	90	6	92,100
	Raikwar	88	5	59,600	72	5	60,500
	other	75	5	49,700	44	3	42,300
Rajput total		625	38	4,10,500	577	38	4,93,300
Nanakshahi Faqir		57	3	21,100	2	0	3,700
Muslim	Pathan	325	20	1,86,300	333	22	2,48,600
	Sheikh	57	3	23,100	50	3	31,800
	Afghan	53	3	28,700	51	3	41,400
	Saiyid	45	3	18,900	26	2	23,600
Muslim total		480	29	2,57,000	460	30	3,45,400
Total Taluqdari		1659	100	8,90,800	1518	100	11,07,300
Total District		2011	82	10,91,700	1898	80	11,29,600

Appendix Table 10. Kheri

Caste	Clan	1877 (30)			1904 (25)		
		Villages	Percentage Taluqdari	Jama (Rupees)	Villages	Percentage Taluqdari	Jama (Rupees)
Rajput	Chauhan	315	28	2,07,400	326	33	2,49,800
	Jangre	168	15	1,36,600	161	16	1,54,700
	Surajbansi	107	10	87,200	110	11	72,000
	Raikwar	56	5	48,000	51	5	32,800
	Sombansi	23	2	5,500	33	3	14,400
	other	19	2	10,900	4	0	2,200
Rajput total		688	62	4,95,600	685	69	5,25,900
Kayastha and Khatri		33	3	15,800	21	2	15,400
Kurmi		15	1	10,900	14	1	11,200
Nanakshahi Faqir		15	1	7,400	15	2	8,300
Muslim	Ahbans	100	9	45,200	53	5	26,900
	Saiyid	104	9	51,100	59	6	31,100
	Sheikh	56	5	34,700	68	7	46,600
Muslim total		260	23	1,31,000	180	18	1,04,600
Sikh		45	4	27,600	38	4	28,200
European		62	6	26,600	40	4	14,400
Total Taluqdari		1118	100	7,14,700	993	100	7,08,000
Total District		1774	63	11,88,700	1749	57	10,28,500

Appendix Table 11. Hardoi

Caste	Clan	1877 (17)			1904 (20)		
		Villages	Percentage Taluqdari	Jama (Rupees)	Villages	Percentage Taluqdari	Jama (Rupees)
Rajput	Nikumbh	59	14	60,600	51	12	75,400
	Katyar	47	11	44,000	66	16	86,300
	Bais	40	9	32,200	37	9	34,000
	Gaur	24	6	23,200	19	5	20,500
	Sombansi	23	5	13,200	38	9	19,400
Rajput total		193	45	1,73,200	211	51	2,35,600
Kayastha		65	15	49,400	46	11	50,600
Nanakshahi Faqir					1	0	1,500
Muslim	Sheikh	80	19	67,300	67	16	70,900
	Saiyid	65	15	48,800	52	12	48,100
	Pathan	29	7	21,600	31	8	24,900
	Mughal				4	1	1,400
Muslim total		174	40	1,37,700	154	37	1,45,300
Total Taluqdari		432	100	3,60,300	412	100	4,33,000
Total District		1961	22	13,30,100	2072	20	15,53,000

Appendix Table 12. Sitapur

Caste	Clan	1877 (24)			1904 (32)		
		Villages	Percentage Taluqdari	Jama (Rupees)	Villages	Percentage Taluqdari	Jama (Rupees)
Rajput	Gaur	124	14	1,17,000	118	11	1,20,100
	Bais	89	10	60,400	203	19	1,41,300
	Raikwar	52	6	33,000	94	9	69,100
	Panwar	49	6	36,800	48	5	53,600
	Janwar	15	2	13,600	15	1	19,600
	other				14	1	9,600
Rajput total		329	38	2,60,800	492	46	4,13,200
Khatri		47	5	36,800	79	7	57,100
Kayastha		40	4	17,600	30	3	26,500
Muslim	Sheikh	268	31	1,74,000	308	30	2,68,800
	Mughal	140	16	94,700	113	11	1,04,900
	Gaur	39	5	26,300	36	3	30,800
	Saiyid	1	0	100	5	0	2,000
Muslim total		448	52	2,95,100	462	44	4,06,500
Total Taluqdari		864ª	100	6,10,300	1063	100	9,03,300
Total District		2498	35	13,03,700	2366	45	16,15,800

a. A different set of figures in the same vol. (*Oudh Gaz.*, 3: 374) gives a taluqdari total of 937, and a district total of 2,572, or 36 percent. The two calculations cannot be reconciled.

Appendix Table 13. Oudh Totals

Caste	Clan	1877			1902-1905		
		Villages	Percentage Taluqdari	Jama (Rupees)	Villages	Percentage Taluqdari	Jama (Rupees)
Rajput	Amethia	63	0.57	61,400	106	0.85	1,08,000
	Bachgoti	940	6.89	4,06,400	777	6.22	5,18,500
	Bais	816	5.99	5,93,700	940	7.53	8,04,400
	Bandhalgoti	338	2.48	2,01,000	334	2.67	2,38,600
	Batam	22	0.16	14,600	19	0.15	15,300
	Bisen	958	7.03	4,63,200	881	7.06	5,86,700
	Chauhan	315	2.31	2,07,400	326	2.61	2,49,800
	Dikhit	15	0.11	14,500	9	0.07	8,000
	Durgbansi	31	0.23	8,400	39	0.31	17,300
	Gargbansi	169	1.24	75,800	140	1.12	67,700
	Gaur	148	1.09	1,40,200	139	1.11	1,40,600
	Jangre	168	1.23	1,36,600	161	1.29	1,54,700
	Janwar	1,067	7.83	6,85,300	1,193	9.55	8,61,600
	Kalhans	343	2.52	1,75,500	168	1.35	1,46,200
	Kanhpuria	334	2.45	2,73,600	383	3.07	3,81,400
	Katyar	47	0.34	44,000	66	0.53	86,300
	Nikumbh	59	0.43	60,600	51	0.41	75,400
	Palwar	360	2.64	1,70,600	245	1.96	2,05,200
	Panwar	124	0.91	86,300	124	0.99	1,08,800
	Raikwar	399	2.93	5,72,500	416	3.33	3,44,800
	Rajkumar	783	5.74	2,41,900	432	3.46	3,82,700
	Rajwar	45	0.33	24,800	44	0.35	29,300
	Sengar	21	0.15	16,400	8	0.06	11,100

	Number	%	Area	Number	%	Area
Sombansi	342	2.51	1,80,500	404	3.24	2,26,900
Surajbansi	167	1.22	1,48,500	170	1.36	1,46,400
other	193.5	1.42	1,48,300	260	2.08	2,35,800
Rajput total	8,267.5	60.6	51,52,000	7,835	62.8	61,51,500
Brahmin	1,251	9.18	8,57,100	891	7.14	7,39,200
Kayastha	196	1.44	1,31,800	162	1.43	1,55,100
Khatri	186	1.36	1,60,600	179	1.43	2,28,200
Kurmi	15	0.11	10,900	17	0.14	16,500
Nanakshahi Faqir	150	1.10	83,700	67	0.54	55,900
Muslim Rajput	368	2.70	1,99,200	316	2.53	2,27,600
Afghan	53	0.39	28,700	51	0.41	41,400
Gaur	39	0.27	26,300	36	0.29	30,800
Pathan	604	4.43	3,52,900	593	4.75	4,53,600
Mughal	154	1.13	1,05,400	129	1.03	1,19,600
Saiyid	543	3.98	3,45,600	423	3.39	4,11,100
Sheikh	1,031	7.56	7,31,800	1,105	8.85	10,54,100
other	5	0.04	12,700	6	0.05	22,900
Muslim total	2,797	20.5	18,02,600	2,659	21.3	23,61,100
Sikh	638	4.68	2,78,400	627	5.02	3,60,900
European	74	0.54	46,800	40	0.32	14,400
Unidentified	59	0.43	37,900	9	0.07	2,500
Total Taluqdari	13,633.5	100	85,61,800	12,486	100	1,00,85,300
Total Province	24,063	57	1,49,19,000	n.a.[a]		1,76,08,300

a. Due to discrepancies in the sources consulted this total cannot be calculated.

Appendix Table 14. Taluqdari Estates[a] By Size and Distribution

District	Total	Revenue Assessment (1905)				
		Above 1 lakh	*50,000 to 1,00,000*	*(Rupees) 10,000 to 50,000*	*5,000 to 10,000*	*under 5,000*
Lucknow	34	0	0	7	9	18
Unao	37	0	0	18	7	12
Rae Bareli	62	2	2	22	9	27
Bara Banki	61	2	3	20	12	24
Faizabad	26	3	3	10	6	4
Sultanpur	34	1	3	17	7	6
Pratabgarh	33	1	7	12	9	4
Gonda	24	2	2	12	1	7
Bahraich	24	4	1	9	6	4
Kheri	25	1	3	12	3	6
Hardoi	20	0	4	8	3	5
Sitapur	32	3	0	16	4	9
Total	412	19	28	163	76	126

a. These figures are taken from the District Gazetteer volumes, and show the number of separately owned estates in each district. Where an individual taluqdar holds an estate extending over more than one district, it is entered once for each district. The total number of estates is therefore somewhat inflated.

Appendix Two
Inspection Report of Pratabgarh Estate Villages in Hardoi, 1896

Report of inspection of ziladars and tahsildars by Qamar Ali, dated May 28, 1896.*

Report of the inspection of the circle in district Hardoi under the charge of Thakur Raghunath Singh tahsildar, and Thakur Parmeshari Din Singh ziladar, of the ilaqa of Maharaja Pratab Bahadur Singh:

1. The rabi harvest has been good. According to some people it is better than those of the previous two or three years. But many lands were left fallow. Because of the scanty rain and unavailability of means many cultivators could not sow their seeds. The cultivators who did till fields had a very good yield.

2. The mango crop is moderate.

3. Tahsildar Thakur Raghunath Singh is a very intelligent and able person and has much ability, but it is unfortunate that his subordinates are free beyond proper limits. From this one can conclude either that the tahsildar is too lenient, and hence doesn't take any notice of their activities, or that he is so much under the sway of his subordinates that he forgives them for fear of their revealing his secrets. Thus the tahsildar should be careful in future.

4. Although I am opposed to the transfer of sipahis, ziladars, and tahsildars since their transfer results in loss to the estate, still there are four young persons of a free nature who happen to be together in the halqa of Thakur Raghunath Singh so that there is a possibility of the incident pertaining to Shankar Singh being repeated. Therefore for the sake of the administration in my opinion all these four people should be transferred to different places and four new persons sent from the fort [Pratabgarh] in their place:

    1. Shiv Saran Singh

*Translated from the Urdu original in the Pratabgarh estate records.

2. Balak Singh, sipahi
3. Ujagar Lal, sipahi
4. Jalpa Lal, sipahi

5. The celebration of Holi in the style of last year and the taking of subscriptions from the cultivators is not objectionable to me. This is common practice among many landholders. But the participation of prostitutes [lit., "randi"] and their stay overnight in the district [lit., at the door of the police station] is definitely objectionable. I agree that these things might have happened in the absence of the tahsildar, but it is unthinkable that the tahsildar did not know about them. The tahsildar should be cautious in future, and should not let such activities be repeated. Though obviously the people who engaged in these activities wasted their own money and the estate has nothing to do with it, still, in my opinion, ultimately such occurrences may result in loss to the estate because when these people fall into the habit of squandering money their pay will not suffice and finally they will embezzle estate money to meet their expenses.

6. In my opinion a circular should be sent from headquarters to all the districts saying that married people should keep their wives with them. Though the estate does not prohibit this, there is a general misunderstanding among the employees that it is against the maharaja's will for them to keep their wives with them. They ascribe the constant transfer of Badri Parshad to this. I think that if the employees keep their wives with them, they will be able to do their official work more peacefully and with more concentration.

7. The arrears for 99 F. [1892] in mauza Alipur which are shown due from Usman Khan in the papers of the estate are really due from Shankar Singh deceased as that land was jointly under his cultivation. The suit which was filed against Kunma Chamar in the mauza of Akbarpur for Rs. 1/8/- was dismissed because the witnesses said in court that Rs. 1/8/- were received by Shankar Singh. In this way Rs. 3/8/- became due from Shankar Singh in addition to court expenses. A cow has been purchased by Balak Singh, sipahi, from Shankar Singh's estate, and the price of the cow has not yet been paid. I suggest that the money should be deducted from the pay of Balak Singh and the remainder claimed from the person who inherits the property of Shankar Singh. It is a matter of dispute whether Balak Singh purchased that cow for Rs. 4 or Rs. 2. In any case Balak Singh agrees to pay Rs. 2. The tahsildar should be instructed to realize from the persons concerned whatever they owe.

8. By inspection of the papers it was revealed that up to 1302 F. [1895] the amount of Rs. 529/8/11¼ was due from the circle of Thakur Raghunath Singh. Though from the entries in the papers the amount is shown as realized, these cannot be trusted, because the current year's income has been shown as arrears. Unless this year's papers are prepared and arrears shown properly, it cannot be ascertained whether the circle owes more. If the arrears of the present year are of the same size, it is not praiseworthy. Rather it will be deemed that the collection exists on paper but in fact the funds were not realized.

9. This year the tahsildar of village Nagla Bhag, known as Nagarya, has cleared all the amounts due [i.e., no arrears remain]. For fifteen or twenty days he stayed there, checked the property of each person, and realized the amount. Arrears in this village had continued since 1297; now all has been realized. If such an effort were made in other villages, then the whole circle would have been free of further payment. So far as my experience goes, nowhere has such an effort been made except in this village, nor has any village cleared its account like this. Maybe I am wrong in my opinion. The same kind of effort might have been made in other villages. If the papers of the current year are ready and other villages besides Nagla Bhag are shown as clear then they [the estate staff] are worthy of praise and deserve compensation for their efforts.

10. The arrears in the circle of Thakur Parmeshwari Parshad amount to Rs. 3,109/3/1 up to 1302 F. His circle brings in an income of Rs. 7,742/9/7. So much arrear in such a circle is too great. I may also remark that apart from village Todhakpur the arrears of the other villages stand unrealized. I think no effort has been made in realizing the arrears; that is, no method was adopted for checking the crop, so that whatever the peasants intercepted, they carried away stealthily. If practical steps were taken, much would have been realized. The reason for my opinion is that I have toured the area as a flood that comes and passes away. I stayed only three or four hours, and no more, in each village. Even then Rs. 25/7/6½ were realized for 1297 to 1302 F. and entered in the siaha of the estate. So I think that the ziladar who resides there permanently might have realized all the arrears.

11. With regard to those cultivators who have standing arrears against them for a long time, I think the fault is that of the ziladars, who do not check or intercept the crop at harvest time. If there is an excuse given of bad crops the question is whether the crop failed for five or six years. To me it is not at all difficult to realize arrears from a cultivator. Of course it is difficult to collect from a cultivator who has left cultivation. The ziladars have been orally instructed that the siaha should not be filled up without realizing the arrears. Similarly such arrears as are time-barred should be struck off.

12. Innumerable complaints are lodged in the courts for arrears and I think many of them are unnecessary. The reason for these complaints is that at the time of harvest no check was made, with the result that the cultivators consumed whatever they got from the crop and it was not possible to get anything from them. Only to save themselves from blame do they [the estate's officials] lodge complaints against them. Tahsildars and ziladars should look into the matter so that they might lessen the number of complaints. As far as possible they should get arrears cleared by attachment of the cultivator's property.

13. Regarding Thakur Parmeshari Din Singh, I have always framed this charge against him: that he did not try to collect the rent, that he did not realize it on time, and that he did not check the state of the crop. But if the committee members consider the case justly, these charges would not be sustained. There are only five sipahis in his halqa. One of them is named Moti, a Chamar by caste. Except for bringing grass for the ziladar's horse and feeding the estate she-buffalo, he is incapable of doing any other work. Another sipahi, named Yar Muhammad, is appointed at Alipur. Now three remain. One should always be present at the district headquarters. How is it possible that two sipahis will be able to collect the rent of seven villages? Even to keep watch and demand the rent is impossible.

14. In my opinion Moti Chamar should be dismissed and another sipahi sent in his place from headquarters. Two more new sipahis should be appointed here. Only then will things become normal. Otherwise no ziladar can collect the full amount. The order that people of this place alone should be selected and employed is not advisable. The new appointments which are made should be made from headquarters. I think the chief characteristics found in those sipahis are absent in these. I might have requested the dismissal of a sipahi in Thikri, for he is unworthy to be counted as a sipahi. As his appointment has found favor, I excuse him.

15. It will be reasonable to examine the papers of the preceding four years before the appointment of Parmeshari Din Singh. That will give some idea of how many sipahis there were and how much arrear was outstanding. If the number of sipahis was the same before his appointment and there were no arrears, then Parmeshari Singh is at fault and my recommendation for the appointment of two more sipahis should not be favored. Otherwise orders for the appointment of two more sipahis should immediately be issued.

16. It is in my opinion advisable to give on contract all the villages which are widely separated because the whole estate is scattered in this district. It would have been better had Alipur been given on contract.

17. Mangal and Lalita Ahir have applied for the contract of villages Gohniya and Ghorahai. As far as I know these people are well-to-do and are inhabitants of Gohniya. The tahsildar should be asked to furnish information about them. If he too verifies this, then it will be appropriate to give them the contract.

18. Qutb-ud-din's contract has expired this year. I have learned that there was fluctuation in the tax on irrigation water from the Ganges in his thika. It will be advisable that the tahsildar be asked to settle the accounts first and then renew the contract. I recommend that the water tax not be included in the new contract.

19. The village Ghorahai is uninhabited. If populated it may bring more income. The land is good and has much potential. Now is the proper time to have it peopled. A village has come into existence near it. During the flood in the river the whole village was covered with sand. The peasants of this village are in difficulty. If a little attention is given it will be populated. I think that an order for its population must be given to the tahsildar.

Appendix Three
Accounts of Receipts and Disbursements, Mehdona Estate, Faizabad, 1865 and 1866

Accounts of Receipts and Disbursements, Mehdona Estate, Faizabad, 1865
(Rupees)

Receipts		Disbursements	
Collections from Mehdona	1,34,091	Government revenue with sub-scriptions	1,63,570
Collections from Tulsipur	37,441	Pay of establishment	10,702
Collections from Daryabad	1,862	Expenditure of toshakhana	
Borrowed from Lalta Parshad	31,000	[maharaja's private expenses]	19,784
Value of trees sold	5	Amount of decree passed against	
Decrees of courts	46	*Oudh Gazette* paid by	
Salary savings on establishment		maharaja	10,675
costs	25	Debts paid to Bank of Bengal	26,347
Deposits to be credited in sub-sequent year's account	41,771	Amount paid to Lalta Parshad	3,740
Balance in hands of tahsildars	1,541	Amount paid to Sahu Harak Chand	500
Grand total	2,47,782	Interest paid to Delhi Bank	137
		Maintenance of relatives	3,482
		Court expenses	1,882
		Feeding of cattle, etc.	3,795
		Stationery charges	138
		Hire of dak garis [mail carts]	127
		Amount paid to Dwarka Nath	10

Accounts of Receipts and Disbursements, Mehdona Estate, Faizabad, 1865
(Rupees) *cont.*

	Disbursements
Diet money	8
Cloth for bastas [parcels]	30
Repairs of furniture	252
Telegraph charges	17
Receipt stamps	3
Repairs to carts, etc.	48
Rewards to chaprassis, etc.	91
Pay of police constables at Gopalpur	372
Charges for cleaning Darshan-nagar Bazar	250
Pay of patwaris	26
Costs for presents made	13
Taqavi advance	5
Rent of house	5
Repairs to house	40
Cost of food given to faqirs at Hanuman Ghari	125
Miscellaneous charges	59
Grand total	2,46,233

Accounts of Receipts and Disbursements, Mehdona Estate, Faizabad, 1866
(Rupees)

Receipts		*Disbursements*	
Balance in hand from previous year	1,451	Government revenue of Mehdona Estate, etc.	1,76,309
Collection of revenue for past years	12,124	Pay of establishment including patwaris and chaukidars	56,649
Collection for current year	3,87,333	Paid to Mohan Ram for toshakhana charges	29,814
Miscellaneous receipts	103	Paid to Shandhur for toshakhana charges	21,013
Surplus collection for coming year	211	Money paid in liquidation of debts	1,38,456
Collection on a/c market dues	2,063	Charges for feeding cattle	6,375
Collection on saltpeter	18	Purchase of necessary articles	3,015
Collection on zamindari right	16	Charges for feasts given to officers	1,877
Collection on mango garden	51	Contributions	855
Collection on taqavi advance	70	Amount paid for charitable and religious purposes	1,022
Collection on fisheries	8	Rewards	562
Collection on value of trees	20	Telegraph charges	40
Savings from pay of establishment	18		
Fines, etc.	4		
Presents	182		

Receipts		*Disbursements*	
Decree money	840	Newspaper subscriptions	422
Receipts on a/c of refunds	1,723	Charges for "Janooye" ceremony	
Remittance from Gonda	5,000	for taluqdar's grandson	7,267
Remittance from maharaja	16,610	Same for grandson of Bhaya	
Loans contracted	80,952	Deonath	196
Amount received for repairs to		Small shopkeepers' bills	796
Dilkhusha	400	Amount sent to Agha Ali Khan	140
Same for B.I.A.	51	Rent of houses	79
Value of a mare paid by Pandit		Coolie hire	37
Dwarka Nath	62	Charges for cutting Kasari	96
Surplus receipts to be credited		Dak gari expenses	442
in next year's account	2,108	Wages of bearers	56
		Money given as loans	585
Grand total	5,11,418	Remittance charges	70
		Stationery charges	412
		Repairs to tahsil houses	159
		Amount paid for satisfaction of	
		decrees	1,642
		Charges for B.I.A.	51
		Revenue talabana for collection	
		of revised rents	379
		Paid to bankers	518
		Wages of chaukidars	1,811
		Paid to Harbhujua Singh for	
		cost of decrees	135
		Sundry charges	159
		Court expenses and settlement	
		charges	12,053
		Charges in tahsil Tulsipur	2,049
		Charges in tahsil Kundarkha	117
		Charges in tahsil Mehdona	241
		Charges in tahsil Bhartipur	219
		Charges in tahsil Darshannagar	1,343
		Charges in tahsil Salipur	344
		Charges in tahsil Tandauli	73
		Charges in tahsil Daryabad	71
		Tahsil contingencies	6
		Refund of surplus receipts	
		deposited in past year	41,771
		Grand total	5,09,726

Appendix Four
Senior Officials of Balrampur Estate, 1881–1882*

It will be interesting to the reader to know the names of the responsible officers and notable officials of the time of the Honourable Maharaja Sir Digvijai Singh Bahadur K.C.S.I. The following is a list of selected estate employees with the scale of their salaries [in rupees], extracted from the Bakhshigiri Lists for the years 1288 and 1289 Fasli [1881 and 1882]:

1. General Ram Shankar Lal, Prime Minister (Plus concessions of Khurak, etc.) — 500/-
2. Mir Muhammad Hasan, Assistant Pargana Balrampur — 150/-
3. Pandit Daya Shankar, Assistant Pargana Tulshipur — 87/-
4. Munshi Madho Dayal, Mir Munshi [office superintendent] — 150/-
5. Munshi Jawahir Singh, Musahib [companion] — 101/-
6. Munshi Tara Chand, Head Clerk — 80/-
7. Babu Mahadeo Singh, Private Secretary — 80/-
8. Mirza Ali Hasan, Translator — 80/-
9. Babu Ram Lal Chakravarti, Doctor — 100/-
10. Mr. Johns, miscellaneous work — 85/-
11. Mr. Marsh, Superintendent stables — 130/-
12. Pandit Bishwa Nath, Head Master — 130/-
13. Sayyid Aqa Hasan alias Miran Sahib, Bakhshigiri officer [paymaster] — 101/-
14. Lala Sarju Prasad, Treasurer — 45/-
15. Munshi Bhola Nath, Jama kharch [daily disbursement] officer — 40/-

*From Thakur Baldeo Singh, "Life of Sir Digvijai Singh," pp. 311–314.

16. Munshi Sheo Nath Singh, Sarishtadar to the Prime
    Minister   30/-
17. Munshi Nand Prasad, Clerk of the office of the Prime
    Minister   45/-
18. Munshi Kali Prasad, Mutafarriqat Officer   25/-
19. Babu Durga Prasad, Engineer   50/-
20. Munshi Ajodhya Prasad, Nazir   43/-
21. Munshi Chhabi Lal, Muhafiz-daftar [record keeper]   25/-
22. Lala Kakka Mal, Vakil   70/-
23. Bhaya Jagat Singh, Officer of the Akhbar Navisan   30/-
24. Munshi Ilahi Bakhsh, Mistri   50/-
25. Captain Sheo Datt Singh, Forest Officer Tulshipur   ?
26. Babu Har Dayal Singh, Forest Officer Kuwana   30/-
27. Lala Sitla Sahai, Mal Officer   30/-
28. Bhaya Harhar Datt Singh, Agent Lucknow   50/-
29. Pandit Jaigovind Tewari, Tahsildar Bhanbher   100/-
30. Bhaya Sarup Singh, Tahsildar Bijaipur (Tulshipur)   50/-
31. Munshi Jai Narain Lal, Tahsildar Dond Garawar
    (Bankatwa)   30/-
32. Bawa Bishan Singh, Tahsildar Chaowrahia (Gabbapur)   60/-
33. Bhaya Atiwant Singh (Gaurahwa), Tahsildar Bhinga
    (Hariharpur)   35/-
34. Bakhshi Debi Prasad, Tahsildar Charda   70/-
35. Lala Gur Prasad, Tahsildar Bangla   27/-
36. Pandit Guptar Tewari, Tahsildar Mathura   40/-
37. Bhaya Sanwal Singh, Tahsildar Sheopur   35/-
38. Pandit Jagannath, Tahsildar Mahrajganj   (mujraidar)
39. Pandit Gaya Datt Pande, Tahsildar Pipra   25/-
40. Bhaya Debi Singh (Gentheha), Tahsildar Kharsari   15/-
41. Bhaya Adhar Singh, Tahsildar Huzur Tahsil   30/-
42. Pandit Jai Ram Pathak, Tahsildar Gidhraiyan   25/-
43. Pandit Khushi Nand Dube, Tahsildar Barawan   20/-
44. Bhaya Kishan Datt Singh, Brigadier General   250/-
45. Bhaya Lachman Datt Singh, Captain Infantry   47/-
46. Bhaya Ratan Singh, Captain Artillery   17/-
47. Pandit Hardwar Upadiya, Lieutenant Cavalry   18/-
48. Mr. Bell (?), Band Master   200/-
49. Sayyid Mahndi Hasan, Binbaz [musician]   87/8
50. Munshi Gokal Prasad, Hindi poet   22/-
51. Munshi Abdul Hakim, Shatranj-baz [chess player]   30/-
52. Pandit Sital Prasad, Watchmaker   33/-
53. Munshi Piriya Lal, Press Officer   32/-

In the Bakhshigiri list the names of Major Jas Karan Singh and Bhaya Asman
Singh are not found. They were constant companions of the Maharaja Bahadur. It is
possible some other important names might have been left out by oversight or some
other cause.

Appendix Five
Account of Income and Expenditures, Balrampur Estate, 1901–1902

(Rupees)

Income		Expenses	
Rents:	18,78,732	Government revenue	6,52,898
cash	18,71,476	Local cesses	64,057
kind	7,256	Patwari rate	31,024
Sayer	57,116	Chaukidar cess	44,860
Rent (houses)	21,142	Income tax	7,104
Manorial dues	78,328	Ground rents	818
Patwari rate	19,003	Manuscript tax	3,786
Chaukidari	35,320	Forest and grazing	1,316
Interest on securities	45,240	Law charges	14,670
Miscellaneous income:	6,589	Taqavi	1,500
talabana	2,466	Deposit to agricultural bank	
fees amin	358	(Tahsil Pipra)	7,359
interest on rent due	12	Cost of management	1,40,788
fines	288	Improvements	1,71,026
rasad	3,465	Travel expenses:	12,516
Grand total	25,18,793	raja's tour	10,118
		sadr officials	2,110
		tahsil officials	288
		Personal expenses:	1,17,759
		establishment	7,241
		ornaments	10,618
		clothing	18,984
		furniture	12,170
		charity (daily and	
		ordinary)	7,679

The discrepancy between the total given and the sum of the various items is due to a probable failure to include all sources of Balrampur income.

(Rupees)

	Expenses	
charity (extraordinary)	163	
puja path (ordinary)	1,216	
puja path (extraordinary)	2,839	
medical expenses	8,787	
jrenar [sic]	18,736	
uniforms	1,417	
riayat [gifts] and reward	1,425	
traveling expenses	427	
pocket and pen money	15,314	
pankha and tatti [fans]	729	
billiard table, etc.	2,094	
expenses for birth of Maharaj Kumari	3,674	
Anna Prasan [sic] ceremony	246	
Mahadeo for nawa [sic]	5	
mango crop protection	51	
Naini Tal expenses thro' Pt. Kannahiya Lal	1,922	
Pt. Lokenath	2,022	
Allowance to junior maharani		25,000
Majraidars [allowance holders]		88,342
Guests		8,361
Military and band		35,293
Garden		13,360
Stable and grounds:		1,97,216
pay of establishments	44,156	
food for animals, etc.	86,327	
shikar charges	2,490	
rasad	3,833	
purchase of motor car, bicycles, horses, etc.	60,410	
Armory		1,052
Support for hospitals		13,590
Schools:		8,923
contribution to L.C. School	6,000	
sweets	43	
cricket	180	
scholarships	1,400	
Jagannath Puri	1,300	

(Rupees)

Expenses		
Balrampur poor house		14,043
Bahraich poor house		120
Orphanage		1,054
Vaccination, Gonda		200
Rajsee charity:		3,410
Dehra Dun	180	
pandits	1,985	
sadhus	126	
prasads	98	
dachina saradh	242	
miscellaneous	362	
Tahsil charity	417	
Puja path:		14,253
puja Bhagwati	12,241	
puja Thakurji	146	
puja Hanumanji	82	
puja Mahadeoji	220	
pay of pujaris	224	
puja at tahsils	789	
miscellaneous	551	
Press		2,835
Pensions and gratuities		15,564
Fairs:		510
police, Debi Patan	146	
medicine	11	
sanitation, Debi Patan	353	
Repayment of loans		4,93,332
Subscriptions:		51,999
B.I.A.	3,241	
Canning College	3,240	
Newspapers[a]	392	
Indian Bradshaw	10	
Ramlila Lucknow and Gonda	80	
Anjuman and Company Bagh Gonda	180	
Rifle Association	100	
Rifah-i-Am Gonda	100	
Mission school, Balrampur	55	
fire policy (Naini Tal houses)	60	
inter high school tournament	100	
flower show, Balrampur	30	
fine arts exhibition, Naini Tal	522	
Hindu boarding house, Allahabad	25,000	
MacDonnell statue	5,000	
Crosthwaite hospital,		

(Rupees)

	Expenses	
	Naini Tal	1,100
	Bahraich clubhouse	2,000
	renovation of Bal-rampur Hospital, Lucknow	10,000
	Naini Tal volunteer rifle	100
	gymkhana, Naini Tal	100
	Indian Law Reports	23
	Railway Guide	4
	mission, Gonda thro Pt. K.S., Pt. L.N. and dys. [sic]	552
Total law costs:		24,708
	suits (costs of)	10,776
	establishment	10,135
	stationery	202
	contingencies	35
	miscellaneous	3,560
Miscellaneous:		29,667
	hangota [gifts to visitors to estate]	750
	neota and rukhsatana [gifts on coming and leave taking; severance pay]	5,885
	riayat [gifts given at will]	1,047
	installation charges	981
	Ma Kandar's estab-lishment	1,443
	miscellaneous raji establishments	2,557
	coronation charges[b]	15,603
	Hakim Baed establish-ment	1,296
	other miscellaneous	105
Grand total		23,83,965

a. Newspapers subscribed to are: The *Pioneer, Gazette of India, U.P. Gazette*, London papers, Civil and Army lists, *The Asian*, Society of Arts London, *Indian Daily Telegraph, Oudh Akhbar, Samachar, The Colonel.*
b. Coronation charges are given as:

rent of Delhi kothi	8,000
casket for address	4,000
coronation addresses	2,179
travel of officials	236
subscription to corona-tion jalsa	170
darbar uniforms for orderlies	532
preparation of howdah	486

Glossary

Diacritics used to indicate words in this glossary are the same as those in Platts, *Dictionary of Urdu, Classical Hindi, and English*, with the exception here of "ch" in place of "ć," "sh" in place of "ś," and "gh" in place of "g."

amani (amānī)—Held in trust or deposit; revenue remitted when amount is based on actual collection without any previously stipulated terms.

amil (ʿāmil)—Officer of the government, especially a collector of revenue or a farmer of the revenue; contractor for revenue invested with supreme authority both civil and military.

amin (amīn)—Surveyor, auditor, subordinate revenue officer.

asami (asāmī)—Cultivator, tenant, one who tills the soil.

badhni (badhnī)—Loan for meeting revenue payments made on the security of the crop.

bakhshi (bakhshī)—Paymaster.

bania (baniyā)—Moneylender, banker.

barat (barāt)—Wedding procession.

basta (basta)—Bundle; file of papers tied together.

bhaiacharya (bhā'ī chārā)—Tenure in which lands of a village held jointly by co-sharers are apportioned among holders on an equal basis.

bigha (bīghā)—Measure of land, in upper India usually standardized at 3,025 square yards.

birt (birt)—Maintenance grant awarded by a landholder.

birtia (birtiyā)—Holder of a *birt*.

biswadar (biswādār)—Holder of a share or shares in a coparcenary village, especially under a superior *taʿluqdār*.

chakladar (chaklādār)—Superintendent or collector of the revenue of a *chaklā*, i.e., a large division of country comprehending a number of *parganas*.

chaprassi (chaprāsī)—Messenger, orderly, especially in a government office.

419

chaudhari (chaudharī)—Headman, usually of a village.
chaukidar (chaukīdār)—Watchman.
dacoit (dacoit)—Robber.
dafadar (dafᶜdār)—Commandant of a body of horse, head of a party of police.
darogha (dārogha)—Steward, head of a department, manager.
darshan (darshan)—Appearance, sight of an image of a god, visiting a sacred shrine.
dastak (dastak)—Passport, permit; warrant, especially served for revenue default.
dastur-ul-amal (dastūr-ul-ᶜamal)—Rules, regulations; manual of management.
diwan (dīwān)—Chief officer of state, especially head financial minister charged with the collection of the revenue.
durbar (darbār)—Court, hall of royal audience; the holding of a court.
gaddi (gaddī)—Cushion, seat; throne.
gajdan (gajdān)—Charitable gift of an elephant.
ghazal (ghazal)—Verse, love poem.
girdawar (gird āwar)—Patrol, watch; an officer who goes on circuit to supervise the work of subordinate officials.
goshala (goshālā)—Cow shelter.
guzara (guzāra)—Living, subsisting; tenure for providing an individual's subsistence.
hakim (ḥakīm)—Doctor.
halqa (ḥalqa)—Circle; group of villages.
haq (ḥaqq)—A right.
huzur tahsil (ḥuzūr taḥsīl)—System of revenue collection in which head of village proprietary body pays revenue directly to government treasury.
ijara (ijāra)—Price, profit, especially to denote the farming or lease of revenue of an area on a contract basis.
ilaqa (ᶜilāqa)—Area of land; estate; division of territory.
inam (inᶜām)—Gift from a superior to an inferior; land free of either rent or revenue.
izzat (ᶜizzat)—Honor, credit, reputation.
jagir (jāgīr)—Land of which the revenue was made over to an individual, usually as payment for service.
jama (jamᶜ)—Sum, total; total rent or revenue payable by cultivators to a landholder; total government revenue assessed on land.
jamadar (jamᶜdar)—Head of any body of men; officer of police.
kachcha (kachchā)—Unripe, crude; built of unbaked bricks; below standard; uncertain; incomplete.
kachcheri (kachahrī)—Court, office; place of public or legal business.
karinda (kārinda)—Manager, agent or officer.
kayastha (kāyasth)—Caste with the occupation of writer or accountant.
khalisa (khālisa)—Lands not given out as inᶜām or jāgīr or held by an intermediary; land for which government dues are paid directly to the revenue ministry.
kham (khām)—Raw, unripe; settlement made with cultivators without the intervention of a zamīndār, hence an estate managed directly by officers of the government.
kharif (kharīf)—Autumn; the fall harvest, fall crops.
khazanchi (khazānchī)—Treasurer, cash keeper.
kheda (khedā)—Enclosure for the capture of wild elephants; expedition for capturing wild elephants.
khidmatgar (khidmatgār)—Servant.
khillat (khilᶜat)—Robe of honor.
khudkasht (khudkāsht)—Resident, as contrasted with nonresident (paikāsht); settled, permanent.
kisan (kisān)—Cultivator.
kothi (koṭhī)—Residence, house.

kshatriya varna—Warrior or kingly division of the four classical Hindu divisions of society: brahman, kshatriya, vaishya, shudra.
lakh (lākh)—One hundred thousand (1,00,000) by Indian system of counting; so five *lākhs* are 500,000, and ten *lākhs* one million. One hundred *lākhs*, or ten million, equal one *crore*, written 1,00,00,000.
lakhiraj (lākhirāj)—Land free from revenue payment.
lakhirajdar (lākhirājdar)—Holder of *lākhirāj* land.
lathi (lāthī)—Club, long stick used as weapon.
lathial (lāthiyāl); also lathiwalla (lāthī wālā)—Man armed with a *lāthī*.
mahajan (mahājan)—Merchant, banker, money dealer.
mahal (mahall)—Revenue paying unit; palace.
mahant (mahant)—Head of a Hindu religious order.
maidan (maidān)—Field, square, parade ground.
majlis (majlis)—Assembly; mourning assembly during Muharram.
malguzar (mālguzār)—One who pays revenue; landholder.
malik (mālik)—Landholder; owner.
malikana (mālikāna)—Allowance, usually a percentage of government revenue paid to a *zamīndār* or *mālguzār*. Under the British awarded also to those excluded from settlement in recognition of a former title.
marsia (marsiya)—Lamentation for the dead, especially the one sung during Muharram in commemoration of Imām Husain.
masnad (masnad)—Seat; throne.
maulvi (maulwī)—Islamic religious teacher; priest.
mir munshi (mīr munshī)—Chief secretary; office superintendent.
muafi (muʿāfī)—Land held free of rent or revenue.
muafidar (muʿāfīdār)—Holder of *muʿāfī* land.
muhafiz-daftar (muhāfiz-i-daftar)—Record keeper.
mukhtar (mukhtār)—Agent, representative, attorney; but not empowered to plead in court. *See* vakil (wakīl) below.
munsarim (munsarim)—Manager.
munshi (munshī)—Writer, secretary.
munsif (munsif)—Arbitrator, judge; Indian civil judge of lowest rank.
muqaddam (muqaddam)—Chief, leader; headman of a village or caste.
musahiban (musāhibān)—Companions.
mushaira (mushāʿira)—Gathering for the recital of poetry.
mustajir (mustājir)—One who holds lands under a proprietor at a stipulated rent; revenue farmer, collecting on behalf of a *zamīndār* on payment of a fixed sum.
mutamad-i-khanagi (muʿtamad-i-khānagī)—Personal assistant, private secretary.
mutasaddi (mutasaddi)—Writer, clerk.
naib (nāʾib)—Deputy.
nankar (nānkār)—Allowance or payment in land or money, usually in return for service to the government.
nazim (nāzim)—Administrator, governor; superior officer of a province in charge of police and criminal law.
nazr (nazr)—Gift or offering from an inferior to a superior.
nazrana (nazrāna)—Tribute, present, gift.
nikasi (nikāsī)—Total net proceeds or income; assessed valuation.
nizamat (nizāmat)—Office of *nāzim*; government, administration.
nuzul (nuzūl)—Property that falls to state as escheat on failure of heirs; crown or government land.
pakka (pakkā)—Ripe, mature; of baked brick, solid, permanent; land held at a fixed rent.

pan (pān)—Betelnut wrapped in a leaf for chewing.

panchayat (panchāyat)—Council of elders, traditionally five in number, to settle disputes.

parda (parda)—Veil, screen, curtain.

parda nashin (parda nashīn)—Female observance of seclusion.

pargana (pargana)—Revenue subdivision of a district; group of villages of which several go to make a *chaklā* or a *tahsīl*.

patta (paṭṭā)—Deed of lease.

patti (paṭṭī)—Part or portion of a village; division of land; in N.W.P., a share in a coparcenary village or estate.

pattidar (paṭṭīdār)—Holder of a *paṭṭī* (share).

patwari (paṭwārī)—One who keeps the revenue accounts for one or more villages; village accountant.

peshdast (peshdast)—Manager.

peshi (peshī)—Clerk.

peshkar (peshkār)—Assistant; manager; deputy, agent; one exercising delegated authority in revenue and customs affairs.

puja (pūjā)—Worship, honor, veneration.

pukhtadar (pukhtadār)—Holder of land on a fixed rental; underproprietor.

qabuliyat (qabūliyat)—Written agreement, especially signifying assent or acceptance.

qabz (qabẓ)—System of payment in which soldiers procure their own pay from a given area; seizure, confiscation.

qanungo (qānūngo)—Pargana accountant or registrar.

qari (qārī)—Reader, especially of the Qur'ān.

qasba (qaṣba)—Small town, large village, market town.

qasida (qaṣīda)—Poem, similar to but shorter than the *ghazal*.

qawwali (qawwālī)—Music associated with Islamic mysticism.

qazi (qāẓī)—Judge.

qist (qisṭ)—Portion, installment, usually of revenue.

qistbandi (qisṭ bandī)—Settlement or payment by installment.

rabi (rabīᶜ)—Spring; spring harvest, spring crops.

rais (ra'īs)—Head, chief; respectable person.

raiyat (raᶜīyat)—Agriculturalist, subject, especially a cultivator.

raiyatwari (raᶜīyatwārī)—Settlement directly with the cultivator for revenue payment.

raj (rāj)—The government.

rasad (rasad)—Store of grain for the army or for hunting expeditions.

risaldar (risāldār)—Commander of a troop of horse.

sadhu (sādhū)—Hindu holyman, mendicant.

sadr (ṣadr)—As a noun: headquarters, seat of government.
　　　　As an adjective: main, chief, principal.

sahukar (sāhūkār)—Banker, moneylender.

sanad (sanad)—Grant, diploma; charter, patent; document conveying to an individual a title, privileges or rights to revenue.

sarbarakhar (sar ba rāh kār)—Manager, agent.

sar-i-daftar (sar-i-daftar)—Head clerk.

sarishtadar (sarishtadār)—Record keeper, especially head Indian officer of a court of justice or of a Collector's office.

sarkar (sarkār)—The government; a district.

sarpanch (sarpanch)—Chairman, president; head of a *panchāyat*.

shahna (shaḥna)—Lien.

shankalapdar (sankalpadār)—Holder of a charitable land grant (sankalpa); holder of rent-free land.

shikar (shikār)—Hunting; the chase; game, prey.

shroff (ṣarrāf)—Banker, money changer.

siaha (siyāh)—Account book.

sipahi (sipāhī)—Soldier.

sir (sīr)—Lands cultivated by a landholder or village *zamīndār* directly or with hired labor; home farm.

siyaha navis (siyāh nawīs)—Accountant, keeper of daily accounts.

sowar (sawār)—Mounted soldier; rider, horseman.

suba (ṣūba)—Province of a state or kingdom.

subadar (ṣūbadār)—Governor of a province.

tahsil (taḥṣīl)—Subdivision of a district, or an estate, under the charge of a *taḥṣīldār*. In British administration intermediate in size between district and *pargana*.

tahsildar (taḥṣīldār)—Officer in charge of a *taḥṣīl*; collector of revenue or rent from a *taḥṣīl*.

taluqa (taʿluqa)—Dependence upon, or connection with a superior; a collection of villages formed into an estate.

taluqdar (taʿluqdār)—Holder of an estate, or *taʿluqa*; in Oudh after 1858 only those so designated by the British.

tappa (ṭappā)—Tract of land smaller in size than a *pargana*; in N.W.P., a tract containing a small town or large village (*qaṣba*).

taqavi (taqāwi)—Advance of money to cultivators at sowing time, in bad season, or for capital investment.

tazia (taʿziya)—Model of the tombs of Imam Ḥasan and Imam Ḥusain carried in procession during Muḥarram.

thakur (ṭhākur)—Lord; *rājpūt* title of respect.

thana (thāna)—Subordinate police outpost; area under the charge of such a police station.

thanadar (thānedār)—Police officer in charge of a *thāna*.

thika (ṭheka)—Contract, usually entitling the holder in return for the payment of a specified sum to collect rents or other produce on an estate.

thikadar (ṭhekedār)—Holder of a *ṭheka*; contractor.

tilak (ṭilak)—Spot of paint or color placed on the forehead of an incoming raja.

ulama (ʿulamā', plural of ʿālim)—Islamic scholars.

ustad (ustād)—Teacher.

vakil (wakīl)—Representative; authorized public pleader.

wakalatnama (wakālat nāma)—Plenipotentiary commission, full powers; power of attorney.

wasilbaqi-navis (wāṣilbāqī nawīs)—Account keeper for collections and payments.

wasiqa (waṣīqa)—Endowment; promissory note.

zamindar (zamīndār)—Landholder; one who controls land and is responsible for the payment of the assessed revenue to the government; under the British a landowner.

zanana (zanāna)—Women's section of the house, female apartments.

zila (ẓilaʿ)—District; tract under jurisdiction of a British Collector or Deputy Commissioner.

ziladar (ẓilaʿdār)—District superintendent; collector of rent for an estate.

Bibliographic Note

GOVERNMENT RECORDS

Government of Uttar Pradesh

The bulk of the research for this work was carried out in the Uttar Pradesh State Archives, Allahabad (UPSA); and in the Lucknow Secretariat Record Room, whose old records have since been transferred to the U.P. State Archives, Mahanagar, Lucknow. The series of records that proved most useful were:

1. The Proceedings of the Board of Revenue, North-Western Provinces (B.R. Progs.). These are preserved in full in bound manuscript volumes for the period up to 1855; and in abstracts, of much less value, for later years. They constitute the main source for the revenue history of the N.W.P. before the Mutiny.

2. The Board of Revenue district records for Aligarh, Mainpuri, and the Oudh districts of Faizabad, Pratabgarh, Sitapur, and Rae Bareli. The Oudh district files are indexed in individual printed volumes.

3. The Board of Revenue Oudh General series, bound together by subject, for the period 1858-1900. This is the most comprehensive set of documents for the development of revenue policy in Oudh.

4. The Proceedings of the Government of the North-Western Provinces and Oudh, 1860-1900. The Revenue proceedings, printed, bound, and indexed annually, are a necessary supplement to the Board of Revenue records for this period, and are particularly full for the Oudh settlement revision of the 1890s. I also consulted the proceedings of the General, Education, and Judicial departments on particular subjects, together with the various departmental files, organized topically, containing the original notes and letters, where available. Many of the printed proceedings volumes are also found in the India Office Records, London.

5. The Commissioner's records for Agra Division (C.O.A.), and for Faizabad (C.O.F.). Voluminous but poorly indexed, these files duplicate much available elsewhere.

Government of India, National Archives, New Delhi (NAI)

The Foreign and Secret Consultations (F.C., S.C.) contain the fullest accounts of British relations with the Nawabs of Oudh, the annexation of that province, and the course of the 1857 revolt. I consulted the files for the years 1840-1858. The Foreign Miscellaneous series contains as well a set of six volumes of Lucknow Residency correspondence for 1824 to 1826 and 1830 to 1832.

I also examined scattered proceedings of the Home and Foreign departments, relating mainly to revenue policy and the award of titles and honors.

India Office Library and Records, London (IOL)

I found most useful the Library's unrivaled collection of official government publications and printed books, cited individually in the footnotes. I also consulted a few N.W.P. government proceedings volumes not available in India and several European manuscript collections, most notably the Harcourt Butler papers.

PRIVATE MANUSCRIPT HOLDINGS

The British Indian Association of Oudh (B.I.A.)

This extensive archive, in the possession of the Nehru Memorial Museum and Library, New Delhi, and not fully catalogued when I consulted it, provides a detailed account of the working of the taluqdars' association, and its dealings with the government. These papers shed little light however on the informal distribution of power within the association or on the activities of individual taluqdars.

Taluqdari Estate Archives

Few taluqdari archives remain intact, or are organized so that particular items can be readily identified and located. By and large, where an archive exists at all, cloth-bound *bastas* of documents are simply heaped up in a jumble in the record room. Lacking time to put such archives in order myself, I was unable on most estates to examine more than a few stray items. Often however these were of great value. The Balrampur annual reports, for instance, (see Appendix 5) were dug out of that estate's chaotic record room. The most coherent collection I consulted was that of the Qila Pratabgarh estate, which comprised among others the following items:

1. Printed *Dastur-ul-amal* (management manuals) for 1896 and 1900.
2. The manuscript memoirs (to 1898), and diary (in annual volumes from 1899) of Raja Pratab Bahadur Singh.
3. Pratab Bahadur's correspondence regarding his work as honorary magistrate and with the British Indian Association of Oudh.
4. Several bound volumes of letters to Pratab Bahadur from estate employees, mostly of 1896, and including Qamar Ali's reports from Hardoi and Kheri.
5. Over a dozen bound volumes of the raja's personal correspondence, mostly of the years 1896 to 1909. These include letters from other taluqdars, from British district officers and lieutenant governors, and from local political figures, among them Motilal Nehru and M. M. Malaviya, together with bills from merchants and English letters written to the bari rani.

PRINTED BOOKS

The most useful published sources for this project were the periodical district settlement reports (*S.R.*) and the various series of provincial and district gazetteers (*D.G.*).

They alone provide detailed yet comprehensive accounts of the changing patterns of land holding, together with much general information on local life and customs. The annual departmental administrative reports, with the published selections from the records, provided a broader context in which to assess government policy, while the translated selections from the vernacular press offered a glimpse into a world otherwise inaccessible (apart from a short run of the *Oudh Akhbar* at the British Museum).

For the taluqdars' cultural and political activities, the Urdu history and annual proceedings of the British Indian Association are indispensable. Of equal importance are the various accounts of individual families. Although these family histories, written for the families themselves, usually contain exaggerated praise of their subjects, they still provide insights available nowhere else. I found exceptionally helpful the lengthy manuscript history of the Mahmudabad family "Tarikh-i-Mahmudabad" by Ali Hasan.

All printed books are cited in full in the footnotes at the time of their first appearance.

Index

Allahabad district, 47, 56–57, 98, 103, 114; land sales and transfer, 115, 126; land confiscated and awarded, 159
Amethi estate, 182, 352n
Amir Hasan Khan (Mahmudabad): assessment of estate, 212–13; political activity of, 224n, 328, 331; management of estate, 253–54, 276; as honorary magistrate, 293–95; protected criminal, 298; support of education, 319; education of, 320; education of sons, 323; against girls' school, 333; and BIA, 334, 335; special style of address for, 343; disrespectfully treated, 346; religious observances of, 356–58; patron of poets, 361; daily life and behavior, 367
Azamgarh district: agriculture, commercialization of, 114, 116; land sales, 115, 124, 125; land confiscated and awarded, 159

Bachgoti Rajputs, 5, 9; empowered to invest rajas with tilak, 14; landholding, 389–403
Bahlolpur estate, 24, 365n; Pratabgarh purchase of, 276; management of, 278, 279
Bahraich district, 6, 17, 31, 41, 43, 314; landholding in, 171, 398; taluqdars and Revolt in, 175, 182; unchallenged taluqdari power on estates, 245; assessments, 202–203, 204, 206; Balrampur estate management in, 282, 283; taluqdari estates in, 404
Bais Rajputs: consolidation of power of, 8, 14, 15; settled with, 82; on both sides during Revolt, 178; landholding, 389–403
Bakhtawar Singh, 27–28, 35, 38
Balrampur estate, xiii, 6, 14, 18, 27, 43, 304; Revolt behavior of raja, 175–76; awards after Revolt, 182, 184–85; and underproprietors, 246; estate bureaucracy, 252, 272, 287, 412–13; estate expansion, 274–75; expenditures and income, 278, 351, 372, 414–17; estate management, 281–89; patwaris, memorandum on, 301; and agricultural improvement, 308, 313, 314, 315; patronage of education, 318–19, 321n, 322, 353, 354; political activities of, 328–29; and BIA, 333, 334, 336, 338; kept cannon and retainers, 345; title of "His Highness", 344–45; succession dispute, 347; education of rajas, 359, 360; and residences, 368; and sport, 371; daily life and behavior of raja, 373; and manorial dues, 382
Banda district: land sale, 115, 125; and Revolt, 157, 159
Bara Banki district, 8, 184–85, 393, 404
Baragaon estate, 318, 334
Bareilly district, 47, 54, 115, 125
Barrow, Major L., 170, 179, 180, 181, 186, 189, 190, 201, 206, 239, 337–38, 349

Basaidih estate, 184–85. See also Kasmanda estate
Baundi estate, 175, 184–85
Benares city, 50, 114
Benares district, commercialization of agriculture, 49, 135; land sales, 115, 125; retention of power by landholders, 128–29; land confiscated and awarded, 159
Benett, W. C., 310, 311, 312, 383; as spokesman for "Oudh Policy", 191–94, 197; need to conciliate taluqdars, 210, 214; on assessment of Kalakankar, 212; on rental arrears, 272; and Sarda Project, 317; and education of taluqdars, 323
Bentinck, Lord William, 60–67
Bhagwant Singh (Mursan), 51–52, 53, 54
Bhagwati Parshad (Balrampur), 287, 288, 334; succession disputes, 347; and sport, 371; estate expenditure and income, 372, 414–17
Bhaiacharya. See Zamindar
Bhawani Singh (Mainpuri): and Revolt, 139–40, 143, 149, 177; awards after Revolt, 141; succession dispute, 145–48
Bhinga estate: and Revolt, 175; confiscation after Revolt, 186; fair, 314n; patronage of education, 318, 322, 354, 355; education of rajas, 321, 322, 323; political activities of raja, 329; religious patronage and observance, 354, 355–56; marriage arrangements, 362
Bhitauli estate, 176, 184–85
Bijnour district, 115, 125
Birhar estate, 244, 245, 279
Bird, Robert M., 57; and raiyat rentals, 61–62; and settlement revision, 64–74, 93
Bisen Rajputs, 211; settlement of, 7, 8, 9; treatment of clansmen by raja, 34; marriage arrangements, 362; landholding, 389–404
Bishambarpur estate, 24, 34, 184
Biswadar. See Zamindar
Bohras, 110, 128
Boulderson, H. S., 85, 120, 122
Brahmins: landholding, 8, 29, 129, 163, 390–95, 397, 403; settled with in Mainpuri, 82; and rent rates, 112, 208, 228; and "Oudh Policy", 192; and estate management, 262; and Canning College, 320
British Indian Association, 315, 376; and assessments, 209, 213–14, 329; representations to government on legislation, 226, 233, 234, 235, 248, 300–301, 329–31, 383; and Colvin School, 322; organization of, 327, 329, 333–39; political activities of, 329–31; and social reform, 331–33; and award of honors, 342, 343; role of in mediating disputes, 350
Budaun district, 115, 125, 159

Designer: Al Burkhardt
Compositor: Freedmen's Organization
Printer: Thomson-Shore, Inc.
Binder: Thomson-Shore, Inc.
Text: Compugraphic Times Roman
Display: Compugraphic Times Roman
Cloth: Holliston Roxite B 53565
Paper: 55 lb. P&S Offset Regular